Iran

a travel survival kit

David St Vincent

ایران

Iran – a travel survival kit

1st edition

Published by
    Lonely Planet Publications
    Head Office: PO Box 617, Hawthorn, Victoria 3122, Australia
    Branches: PO Box 2001A, Berkeley, CA 94702, USA and London, UK

Printed by
    Colorcraft Ltd, Hong Kong

Photographs by
    Richard Everist (RE)
    David St Vincent (DStV)
    Robert van Dreisum (RVD)
    Phil Weymouth (PW)
    Front cover: Minaret of Masjed-é Emām, Esfahān (DStV)
    Back cover: Arg-é Bam, Bam (DStV)

Published
    August 1992

Although the author and publisher have tried to make the information as accurate as possible, they accept no responsibility for any loss, injury or inconvenience sustained by any person using this book.

National Library of Australia Cataloguing in Publication Data

St Vincent, David -
    Iran: a travel survival kit.

    1st ed.
    Includes index.
    ISBN 0 86442 136 2.

    1. Iran – Description and travel – 1979 – Guidebooks. I Title

915.50454

David St Vincent

Born in the late '60s and brought up in the south of England, David took a year off after leaving school and travelled to Australia via the (then) USSR, Eastern Europe, the Middle East and Central Asia. He has made four lengthy visits to Iran, during which he has been brought before a revolutionary court on the imaginative charge of plotting to import Salman Rushdie's *Satanic Verses*, and deported in retaliation for the expulsion of some Iranians from the UK. He is currently taking an extended break from a degree course in Oriental studies at Oxford University, and co-writing LP's new edition of *Pakistan – a travel survival kit*.

From the Author

This book was produced entirely without the help of the Iranian central tourism authorities, so I owe a very large debt of gratitude to all those Iranians who were prepared to involve themselves in this project, quite a few at risk to themselves. I shall never forget the kindness and assistance extended to me by private Iranians throughout my travels, always making up for any frustrations I suffered through the vagaries of politics. It would be incautious for me to name many of them here, and the following list includes only a few of those who helped me. First I would like to thank those farsighted Iranian officials who saw their way to granting me a visa, despite my incriminating British passport. Inside Iran I am grateful to the various tourist officers in the provinces who provided useful information or practical help, particularly those in Ahvāz, Kermān, Shīrāz and Mashhad. I also owe something to the managing director and public relations officer of KIDO in Tehrān for arranging an otherwise unobtainable ticket to Jazīré-yé Kīsh, and to Mortezā of KIDO for looking after me on the island itself.

Major Mais Hussainov and other galant members of the Azerbaijan militia, and Oskar Nagiyev of Julfa deserve my gratitude for their overwhelming hospitality during an unexpected stay on their side of the border.

I would also like to thank Rolf Viktor and Dūzī Hāshemī of the then British Interests Section in Tehrān for so effectively using their powers of diplomacy on my behalf.

In London, I would like to thank Ali Pakpour for his financial wizardry. My thanks also to the staff at Lonely Planet for their patience and encouragement during the production of this book, especially James Lyon, Tamsin Wilson, Richard Everist, Tony Wheeler and Michelle de Kretser.

Most of all I want to thank the extended Sa'īdī family of Tehrān, among whom I number all my oldest and best friends in Iran, for showing me the meaning of Iranian hospitality throughout the best and the worst of times. Agdas, Alī, Āmé Zībā, Hajībābā, Hamīd, Mahlā, Mohammad, Sa'īdé and Soheilā Sa'īdī, Sayyed Mohammad Hosain and Sayyed Sepand Vafā'ī, and all their cousins, aunts, uncles and other relatives who looked after me in Tehrān, thank you. In particular I would like to thank Alī Sa'īdī whose loyalty and friendship since 1987 defeat my powers of expression.

Note Writing a book on contemporary Iran so soon after the revolution presents many special difficulties. Doing so without incurring the wrath of the Iranian authorities on the one hand, or being accused of whitewashing the facts on the other, is all but impossible. Since the primary purpose of this book is to provide a practical guide for travellers inside Iran, I have chosen the path of prudence rather than risk the book being banned in that country. Those who want a more critical appraisal of recent Iranian history – to read before going and leave at home – will not be short of literature.

Dedication

I dedicate this book to Alī and Mahlā Sa'īdī, who in their own ways provided me with the inspiration to return to Iran despite the most difficult of circumstances, and the motivation to write this book.

From the Publisher

This book was edited by James Lyon and David Meagher. Tamsin Wilson drew the maps, with help from Paul Clifton, and also did the layout, illustrations and cover design. Thanks also to Dan Levin for his computer expertise, Sharon Wertheim for indexing, and Michelle Coxall and Stephanie Bunbury for proofing.

Warning & Request

The golden rule of travel in Iran is 'expect the unexpected'. Things change, prices go up, timetables are revised, good places go bad and bad ones go bankrupt; nothing stays the same. So if you find things better or worse, recently opened or long since closed, please write and tell us and make the next edition better.

Your letters will be used to help update future editions and, where possible, important changes will also be included as a Stop Press section in reprints.

All information is greatly appreciated, and the best letters will receive a free copy of the next edition, or any other Lonely Planet book of your choice.

Contents

Map Legend

BOUNDARIES

— · — · — · —	........International Boundary
▬ · · ▬ · · ▬	...............Internal Boundary
++++++++++++	....National Park or Reserve
------------	.........................The Equator
....	.........................The Tropics

SYMBOLS

◉ NEW DELHI	.........................National Capital
● BOMBAY	.........Provincial or State Capital
● Pune	.................................Major Town
◆ Barsi	.................................Minor Town
■	.........................Places to Stay
▼	.............................Places to Eat
▲	.................................Post Office
✈	......................................Airport
i	......................Tourist Information
⊖	.............Bus Station or Terminal
66	............Highway Route Number
ᛞ ✝ ✝	......Mosque, Church, Cathedral
∴	.........................Temple or Ruin
✚	.....................................Hospital
☀	.....................................Lookout
⚑	.........................Camping Area
⋒	...............................Picnic Area
⌂	...........................Hut or Chalet
▲	.......................Mountain or Hill
	.........................Railway Station
	...............................Road Bridge
	...............................Railway Bridge
	...............................Road Tunnel
	...............................Railway Tunnel
	....................Escarpment or Cliff
	....Pass
	............Ancient or Historic Wall

ROUTES

————————	.......Major Road or Highway
------------	.........Unsealed Major Road
————————	........................Sealed Road
------------	.....Unsealed Road or Track
════════	.................................City Street
+++++++++	...................................Railway
———◉———	...................................Subway
....	.......................Walking Track
------------	.........................Ferry Route
+++++++++++	........Cable Car or Chair Lift

HYDROGRAPHIC FEATURES

	....................River or Creek
	.............Intermittent Stream
	........Lake, Intermittent Lake
	...........................Coast Line
	.....................................Spring
	...............................Waterfall
	.....................................Swamp
	...............Salt Lake or Reef
	.....................................Glacier

OTHER FEATURES

	Park, Garden or National Park
	........................Built Up Area
	...Market or Pedestrian Mall
	.........Plaza or Town Square
	...................................Cemetery

Note: not all symbols displayed above appear in this book

Introduction

Iran is a strange sort of country. The Iranian authorities make little effort to attract foreign tourists, and for the most part Western holidaymakers respond with equal scorn to the idea of spending even a day in the Islamic Republic. Yet even in the worst days of the Iran-Iraq War the country managed to attract a steady stream of Western visitors, and many of them returned with stories of almost overwhelming hospitality from private Iranians, and of a magnificent cultural legacy entirely unspoilt by tourism. In those days you could visit Persepolis, one of the world's most inspiring archaeological sites, for a whole day and have the place virtually to yourself. And at almost no time were individual Western travellers in any great danger, despite the impression created by international press reports and the fact that Iran's record on human rights can most charitably be described as inconsistent with Western values.

In the early 1990s, after a decade as probably the world's leading pariah state, feared or at least shunned by most Western travellers, the country's new leadership announced that it was now ready to open its doors to foreign tourists. Iran being Iran, the authorities failed to inform its consulates of this new policy, and for many nationalities just obtaining a visa is considerably more than a formality.

Iran is changing, and changing more than many of its leaders would like to admit. Slowly and subtly it is becoming something like a normal country again. New tourist developments are being built, old facilities brought into the '90s and a handful of Western travel agencies have started to send tour groups to Iran for the first time since the revolution.

For the individual traveller, now is a good time to visit Iran. The country has quietened down considerably since the excesses of the revolution and the disastrous war against Iraq that followed it, yet foreign visitors are

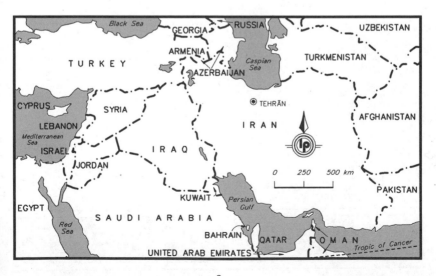

still a novelty and you can still have many of the country's sites virtually to yourself.

Iran has a vast amount to offer the traveller and, at least with the help of this book, most of it can be easily explored by the individual visitor. For its size, Iran boasts a remarkably high number of archaeological, historical and cultural monuments, most of them completely or almost completely neglected by foreigners. A long succession of native and invading dynasties has, since ancient times, founded and embellished a wealth of great cities and monuments, patronised architecture, literature and learning, and nurtured one of the greatest civilisations in the world. For some visitors even Iran's political oddities will be an attraction.

At the same time, the Islamic Republic of Iran does not actively encourage Western tourists to visit. It does not need them and by and large is not fully equipped to entertain them. It is not the purpose of this book to encourage people to visit Iran – anyone who is still undecided after reading the introductory chapters should probably consider another destination.

Iran will appeal to the genuine traveller, rich or poor, who is prepared to respect the local people and their traditions, to be open-minded and to adapt to unfamiliar circumstances. For such people, postrevolutionary Iran is one of the most exciting, interesting, welcoming and rewarding countries yet to be discovered by tourists.

Facts about the Country

HISTORY

Iranian history is a catalogue of disasters and short-lived triumphs, of occasional brilliant rulers succeeded by incompetents who failed to secure their inheritance.

During the 6th century BC Cyrus the Great appeared as the first notable Persian ruler. The Achaemenian Empire which he founded lasted from 558 to 330 BC, and his successors, Darius I and Xerxes, expanded all the way to India in the east and the Aegean Sea in the west. Even Egypt came under Persian rule and the magnificent complex of Persepolis became the hub of the empire. It is from the date of the founding of this dynasty that the last Shāh, Mohammad Rezā Pahlavī, celebrated the 2500th anniversary of the Persian Empire in 1971.

Xerxes' defeat by the Greeks at Marathon in 490 BC marked the end of the Achaemenians and this great period of Persian history. In the 4th century BC Alexander the Great invaded Persia and 'accidentally' burned down Persepolis. After Alexander's death the Greek influence rapidly diminished, first with the breakaway region of north-east Iran ruled by the Parthians.

The Sassanians controlled Persia from 224 to 638 AD, but through these centuries Persian history was a story of continuing conflict with the Roman Empire and later the Byzantine Empire. Weakened by this scrapping, the Persians, who followed the Zoroastrian religion, fell easily to the spread of Islam and the Arabs. It was at this time that the not wholly suitable Semitic alphabet was moulded into the Persian script. Between 637 and 642, all Persia was taken by the Arabs and, except for Yazd and Kermān, the country almost entirely forsook Zoroaster for Mohammad. Muslim rule in Persia was confused by the great split between the Sunnis and the Shi'ites. Even today Iran is unique in the Muslim world for following the breakaway Shi'ite sect.

Arab control over Persia continued for nearly 600 years, but towards the end of that period they were gradually supplanted by the Turkish Seljuq dynasty. At that time the Turks were still gradually absorbing the tattered remnants of the Byzantine Empire. The History;ISeljuqsSeljuqs heralded a new era of Persian art, literature and science, marked by people such as the mathematician-poet Omar Kayyām. Then in 1220 the Seljuq period abruptly collapsed when Genghis Khan swept in and commenced a cold-blooded devastation that was to last for two centuries.

Another invasion by Tamerlane (Teimūr-é Lang in Persian) in 1380 did not help matters, but in 1502 the Safavid era commenced, bringing a Persian renaissance. Under Shāh Abbās I (1587-1629) foreign influences were again purged from the country, and he went on to perform his architectural miracles in Esfahān and leave a permanent reminder of this period.

The decline of the Safavids was hastened by an invasion from Afghanistan, but in 1736 Nāder Shāh overthrew the now impotent Safavids and proceeded to chuck out Afghans, Russians and Turks in all directions. For an encore he rushed off to do a little conquering himself, returning from India loaded with goodies, but virtually exhausting the country with his warring. It was a relief to all, both within Iran and without, when he was finally assassinated.

The following Zand and Ghajar periods were not notable except for a brief period of glory under Karīm Khān-é Zand at Shīrāz. In 1926 the father of the last Shāh founded the Pahlavī dynasty. Foreign influence (and oil) then became an important element in Iran's story.

After WW II

In WW II Iran was officially neutral, although it suffered from being a strategic buffer zone between Nazi Turkey and the Allied USSR. In 1941 Rezā Khān was forced

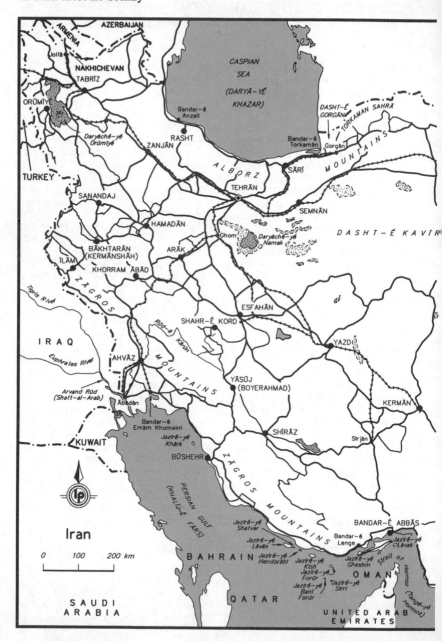

into exile, to South Africa, because he was felt to be too friendly with the Axis powers. His 22-year-old son, Mohammad Rezā Shāh, succeeded him. After the war, the invading Russian forces were persuaded to depart (with difficulty and with American connivance), the Shāh assumed absolute power and Iran was firmly aligned with the West. At one time there were more than 50 British diplomatic missions throughout Persia.

The Shāh's government was repressive, but forward-looking, and Iran was rapidly modernised – at least in some ways and in some places. Illiteracy was reduced, women emancipated, land holdings redistributed, health services improved and a major programme of industrialisation embarked upon, but the country experienced problems of rapid modernisation.

The 1974 oil price revolution turned out to be the Shāh's undoing. He allowed US arms merchants to persuade him to squander Iran's vast new wealth on huge arsenals of useless weapons. Fortunes were wasted on inappropriate development schemes. Sycophants and courtiers grew rich beyond their wildest dreams. In the end, the flood of petro-dollars ended up lining the pockets of a select few while galloping inflation made the vast majority of the country worse off than before. Moves to ban the wearing of the *chādor* (the tent-like dress worn by Muslim women to cover them from head to foot) aroused great resentment and proved counterproductive when devout women preferred to stay indoors rather than appear in public dressed immodestly. At the same time he changed the name of the country in English from Persia to Iran, which had always been the native word. (I have used both names when talking about the country up to that date, and it's not necessarily wrong to call the country Persia even now. A Persian carpet will always be Persian.)

Since the beginning of the Pahlavī dynasty there had been a smouldering resistance that occasionally flared into violence. Students wanted faster reform, devout Muslims wanted reforms rolled back, and everyone attacked the Pahlavīs' conspicuous consumption. As the economy went from bad to worse under the Shāh's post oil boom mismanagement, the growing opposition made its presence felt with sabotage and massive street demonstrations. The Shāh responded with all the power and brutality available to the absolute ruler of an oil-rich country backed by major Western powers, and his security force, Savak, earned a horrific reputation.

In the late '70s the Shāh's attempts to save his régime became increasingly desperate and brutal, and the previously total US support began to falter. In November 1978 he imposed martial law and hundreds of demonstrators were killed in street battles in Tehrān. He finally fled the country on 16 January 1979 (now a national holiday). In exile he was harried from country to country, and died in Egypt in 1980.

Āyatollāh Khomeinī

His Holiness Grand Āyatollāh Hajjī Sayyed Rūhollāh Mūsavī Khomeinī, the leading Shi'ite cleric, had been acknowledged as the leader of the Shāh's opponents – a group covering every political shade from fundamentalist Muslims to Soviet-backed leftists. Many saw him as a figurehead, who, once the Shāh was ousted, would retire to a position akin to that of a constitutional monarch. They were very wrong. A charismatic figure commanding absolute loyalty in his followers, he is very little understood in the West. His impassivity contrasted strongly with the emotion he aroused in his people – when he returned to Iran in triumph after his long exile to be greeted by unprecedented scenes at Tehrān airport he was asked the classic interview question, 'What do you feel?', and he responded without emotion 'Nothing'.

Born into a small village in central Iran, Khomeinī followed in the family tradition by studying theology, philosophy and law in the holy city of Ghom. In the 1920s he earned the title of *āyatollāh* (the highest rank of Shi'ite cleric) and settled down to teach and write. He first came to public attention in 1962 when he opposed the Shāh's plans to reduce the clergy's property rights and emancipate women. In 1964 he was exiled to Turkey, then pushed on to Iraq where he remained until 1978 when he was shunted on to France. Here he found the eyes of the international press turned on him, and it is ironic that his cause was boosted by Western media organisations, the BBC in particular, at a time when he was little known even in his home country.

Āyatollāh Khomeinī returned to Iran in triumph on 1 February 1979, to be greeted by adoring millions. His fiery brand of nationalism and Muslim fundamentalism had been at the forefront of the revolt, but few realised how much deep-rooted support he had and how totally he reflected the beliefs, dreams and needs of millions of his people.

Once in control the Āyatollāh, soon to be known officially as Emām (the leader), was to prove the adage that 'after the revolution comes the revolution'. His intention was to

Āyatollāh Khomeinī

set up a clergy-dominated Islamic republic – the first true Islamic state since the time of the caliphs – and he went about achieving this with brutal efficiency.

Much of the credit for undermining the Shāh lay with groups like the People's Fedā'īyin and the Islamic People's Mojāhedīn, as well as the communists, but once the Shāh was gone they were swept bloodily aside. People disappeared from the streets, executions took place after brief and meaningless trials and minor officials took the law totally into their own hands. It looked as if the country might topple into civil war.

Postrevolutionary Iran

Almost immediately, the Islamic Republic of Iran found itself in a struggle against the rest of the world. As the only custodian of 'true Islam', the republic has followed policies that are confrontationist and un- ashamedly designed to promote similar Islamic revolutions.

The main opponent is the 'Great Satan', the USA, although the USSR was included as a Great Satan for good measure. It is important to see this struggle from the Iranian point of view. Aside from its godless culture, the USA had supported the hated Pahlavīs, and later Iraq (until Saddam Hussein went out of style). It was even guilty in 1988 of shooting down an unarmed Iran Air plane over the Persian Gulf. There is also the memory of the period when Iran was carved into spheres of influence by the Great Powers without consultation with the Iranians, and a long succession of inept and even self-defeating moves by the West in the Middle East.

On the other side, the first nightmare for Americans was the embassy hostage crisis in October 1979, when so-called students seized the US Embassy in Tehrān, along with 52 hostages. The hostages (called spies by the Iranians, not entirely without justification) were held for 444 days and the crisis effectively destroyed Jimmy Carter's presidency. Since then various Iranian-backed groups, most notably Hezbollāh, have been held responsible for taking hostages in Lebanon, killing 241 US marines in a truck-bombing in Beirut, and numerous other actions. At the time of writing there was still an Iranian Revolutionary Guard camp in the Bekaa Valley, and the Iranian government is strongly suspected of complicity in the assassination of the former Iranian prime minister, Shāhpūr Bakhteyār, at Paris in September 1991.

Iran-Iraq War

All this pales into insignificance, however, by comparison to the ghastly Iran-Iraq War that consumed hundreds of thousands of lives. In 1980, Iraq's President Saddam Hussein made an opportunistic land grab in Khūzestān, taking advantage of Iran's domestic chaos, on the doubtful pretext that the oil-rich province was historically part of Iraq. It was a tragic miscalculation. He presented the shaky Iranian revolution with an outside enemy and an opportunity to spread the revolution by force of arms. Although the much smaller Iraq was better equipped, Iran drew on a larger population and a fanaticism fanned by the mullahs. For the first time since WWI the world witnessed the hideous reality of trench warfare and poison gas. The West and the USSR supported Iraq in the war, in the belief that it was the lesser of two evils, and weapons were sold to Iran only at vastly inflated black market prices. A ceasefire was finally negotiated in mid-1988, with neither side having achieved its objectives.

Note that this conflict was often referred to as the 'Gulf War', but that term is now widely used to describe the more recent conflict between Iraq and much of the rest of the world over Kuwait. To avoid confusion, I have used the terms 'Iran-Iraq War' and 'Kuwait War'.

After Khomeinī

On 4 June 1989 Āyatollāh Khomeinī died, leaving an uncertain legacy to the country he had dominated for a decade. At his funeral an estimated crowd of 10 million, unprecedented in world history, came to pay their last respects, and the throng was so great that the car carrying the corpse had to be abandoned for a helicopter. It is difficult to unravel the complicated power structures within the country. When the Emām was alive, with his divine authority, the factions had no choice but to follow his dictates. After his death the Muslim clergy and the Revolutionary Guards established their own, sometimes competing, spheres of influence and private bureaucracies, and the parliament was also factionalised.

In August 1989 the leader of the parliament, Hojjat-ol-Eslām Rafsanjānī, was elected president, a post which had previously been largely ceremonial, and he gradually consolidated that position. A canny politician who was behind the ceasefire in the Iran-Iraq War, he will have to use all his skills to stay on top. In recent times he has tried to normalise relations with the outside world, but certain major obstacles on both sides have largely thwarted these aims.

The hostage issue in Lebanon and Israel, evidence of continuing Iranian involvement in international terrorism, apathy or outright opposition to his policies at home, and a failure to get to grips with the disastrous economy are all factors.

In an astonishing piece of timing, Iran restored diplomatic relations with Iraq just after the start of the Kuwait War, Rafsanjānī calling Saddam 'our brother' on one occasion. During the conflict a number of Iranian mullahs called on the nation to fight on behalf of its Muslim brothers against the Great Satan, prompting the question of whether Iran's martyrs in the earlier war against Iraq had been killed in vain.

The Kuwait War came as a piece of good fortune to Iran at a time when Rafsanjānī was intent on bringing about the country's rehabilitation in the eyes of the Western world. Iran's strictly observed neutrality throughout the war gave Iran a great deal of credit in the West, and it remains to be seen whether the country is able to consolidate this position. The one thing Rafsanjānī wants for his country is the very thing most feared by his opponents, and that is normality.

GEOGRAPHY

The Islamic Republic of Iran (Jomhūrī-yé Eslāmī-yé Īrān) is bordered to the north by the states of Armenia, Azerbaijan and Turkmenistan (formerly of the USSR) and the Caspian Sea, to the east by Afghanistan and Pakistan, to the south by the Sea of Oman and the Persian Gulf, and to the west by Iraq and Turkey. With an area of some 1,680,000 sq km, just under half the size of India, Iran is the fifth largest country in Asia.

Iran can be described as a vast upland plateau bounded by mountain ranges on three sides – the Alborz to the north and the Zāgros to the south and west – and by scattered mountains to the east. Most of the rivers in the country drain into lakes, marshes and inland seas or else evaporate before achieving very much. The Caspian Sea (Daryā-yé Khazar) to the north is the world's largest lake, with an area of some 370,000 sq km. It is a salt lake with about a

Hojjat-ol-Eslām Rafsanjānī

third of the salt content of average world seawater, and its surface is on average about 30 metres below world sea level. The whole of Iran is in an earthquake zone, and there have been several major tremors this century.

The central Iranian plateau is mostly desert of either sand or compacted silt and rock, and – except at its fringes where the tableland merges into the Zāgros and the Alborz – most of its mountains are unconnected and of low altitude. Salty marshes occur in many of the lowest basins. The settled areas are almost entirely confined to the foothills of mountains. The two great Iranian deserts, the Dasht-é Kavīr (also Kavīr-é Bozorg) and the Dasht-é Lūt, occupy a large part of the north-east and east of the central plain.

The Ghanāt

Many parts of Iran, but especially the almost rainless settlements of the central plateau, are heavily dependent for irrigation on artificial watercourses. The traditional Iranian method of water supply – first seen in the central plateau at least 2000 years ago and still very much in use – is the *ghanāt* or underground water channel. To build a ghanāt – which is a highly skilled, dangerous and well-paid job in Iran – you need first to bore a well down to an underground water source, which may be over 100 metres deep, but must be at a higher level than the point at which the water is to be collected. Then you dig a tunnel, just wide and tall enough to crawl along, to carry the water at a very low gradient to that point. Narrow wells are dug down to the tunnel at regular intervals for ventilation and to dispose of the excavated soil or rubble.

Because of the hazards and expense involved in constructing a ghanāt, complex laws govern every aspect of its use and maintenance. There are reckoned to be over 50,000 ghanāts in Iran, the longest of which measure over 40 km. Although modern irrigation projects such as the hydroelectric dam at Karaj have been a priority since the 1960s, ghanāts and other traditional methods of water supply are still of great importance, and the ghanāt builders of Yazd (which is where they traditionally come from) are not yet redundant.

CLIMATE

Patly because of its altitude, Iran experiences great extremes of climate. Winters can be unpleasantly cold in most parts of the country, while in July temperatures as high as 40°C are nothing out of the ordinary. Regular rainfall is more or less restricted to the far north and west – generally also the coldest parts of Iran. Spring and autumn are the ideal times to tour Iran, but summer or winter can be OK, so long as you do a little planning and take a few precautions.

The north-west of Iran is generally the coldest and among the rainiest parts of the country. The winters in Āzarbāyjān and Kordestān can be severe: temperatures well below zero are very much the rule between December and February and sometimes fall as low as -20°C. Snow frequently remains until early spring, or even later in the mountains. Summers are relatively mild, and spring and autumn are pleasant, although a cardigan won't go amiss at night. Rainfall is heavy by Iranian standards: up to about 2000 mm annually. Further south (in Bakhtarān, Īlām and Lorestān provinces) the winter is less severe, although hardly mild, spring and autumn are pleasant, and summer is hot but rarely scorching.

The region around the Caspian Sea and north of the Alborz range is also fairly well-provided with rain, with an annual average of around 1300 mm. The all-year cloud cover helps to keep summer temperatures a little more manageable than in places a short distance to the south, although humidity can be high. Winter is milder here than elsewhere in the north of Iran. Spring and autumn are the best times to visit, although rainstorms can put a damper on sunbathing between September and November. The Caspian Sea is a popular destination with Iranians in the summer.

In the north-east of Iran winters are cold, with temperatures hovering around or below zero, thanks to some icy air currents straight from Siberia. Summers are hot and dry. April to May and late September to early November are generally the most pleasant times to visit. Rainfall is about 250 mm a year, highest around March and virtually non-existent between June and September.

The Dasht-é Kavīr, south-east of the capital, is harsh, inhospitable and very, very hot in summer. Winters are not much better, and at night the temperature can fall well below zero. If any time of year can be called pleasant in this salty wasteland, it would have to be between October and December. The Dasht-é Lūt to the south is, if anything, even worse; almost completely devoid of water from any direction and the last word in extreme aridity.

In Tehrān, in the central plateau, the climate can vary considerably from one end to the other. Central and southern Tehrān in summer are hot, dry and stuffy, but you only have to take a short bus ride up to the foothills of Kūh-é Damāvand to cool down by several degrees. But it's not humid, and the evenings are cool and refreshing. Winters in the capital can be very chilly, extremely so at night (frequently as low as -15°C), although any snow usually disappears by early March. Showers are frequent between November and mid-May, but rare in summer – annual rainfall is about 240 mm. May and autumn are generally the best times to visit.

Central Iran is very hot in summer, and it gets hotter the further south you go, although there is some relief at higher altitudes. Humidity is generally manageable. Winters are cold but not as severe as in the far west and north. Frost is common from late autumn until early spring, and snow not unusual at higher altitudes. Rainfall is erratic and varies from place to place, although it rarely averages much more than 250 mm a year; some places like Yazd have hardly any rain at all. Spring and autumn are generally very pleasant throughout central Iran, sunny but not oppressive in the day and cool at night.

Further south, anywhere within about 200 km of the Gulf is going to be frying-pan hot in summer (regularly up to 45°C or even 50°C), with very oppressive humidity; and there's little relief after dusk either. This part of Iran is to be avoided between late May and early September if at all possible, but the winters are warm and highly agreeable: between late November and early March Khūzestān and the Persian Gulf are probably the most pleasant parts of Iran to visit. Rainfall is only about 150 mm annually – mostly falling in winter.

In the far south-east of Iran, away from the Gulf proper, temperatures are a little lower. Summers are hot and dry, winters mild and dry. Up in Sīstān conditions are harsh: the hot season lasts from April to November with an average temperature of 50°C; winter is equally unpleasant with extreme cold until March. Down in the south of Balūchestān, along the coast of the Sea of Oman, the climate is similar to that of the Persian Gulf region, or even hotter, with strong winds during summer. There is very little rain throughout south-east Iran and frost would be a great novelty. March to April and October to November are the best times to visit.

FLORA & FAUNA
Fauna
Red, roe, fallow and Mesopotamian deer, wolves, jackals, cheetahs, wild cats, Persian squirrels, foxes, wild boars, hyenas, browń bears, mongooses, Persian gazelles, wild goats, lynx, porcupines, badgers, wild asses, rabbits, ibex, hares and wild sheep – all these are to be found in the plains, forests, deserts or mountains of Iran. Most of the larger species are most common in the unexplored depths of the *jangal* (forest) of Māzandarān Province. You quite possibly won't see any of Iran's wild animals, but they are there if you look in the right places. One prize specimen of fauna that you are almost guaranteed not to find is the Persian lion, once the proud symbol of imperial Iran but generally believed to be extinct until a recent alleged sighting by a peasant in the Māzandarān forest. You might still however, with great patience or luck, manage to track down a leopard in south-east Iran, or even perhaps a tiger in the plains or forests of the Caspian provinces. There are camels, mostly belonging to nomadic or seminomadic communities, in the provinces of Kermān, Sīstān va Balūchestān and Khorāsān.

Look up and you'll be able to enjoy a wide variety of birds, either indigenous to Iran or migrant visitors. Permanent residents include swans, geese and the occasional eagle in the Caspian provinces, pelicans and flamingoes along the Persian Gulf, and owls, partridges, kestrels, falcons, snipe, pheasant and grouse throughout most parts of the country.

The Persian Gulf has a wide range of tropical fish, including sharks and swordfish, as well as porpoises; unfortunately scuba-diving has yet to catch on. The Caspian Sea has large shoals of sturgeon, salmon-trout and other fish, as well as a species of seal unique to the lake. Some of the commonest river fish are trout, chub and carp.

Flora

The northern slopes of the Alborz Mountains, up to a height of about 2500 metres, are densely covered with a forest of broad-leaved deciduous trees which forms the largest area of vegetation in Iran. In total contrast, the southern face is almost bare save for some scattered juniper trees. There are smaller, less dense forests of oak and juniper on the higher slopes of the central and north-west Zāgros and south Khorāsān.

Palm trees grow in the southern coastal lowland – especially around the Strait of Hormoz – and in the Makrān.

Most of the central plateau is extremely sparsely vegetated, with little more than the odd tree, shrub or clump of herbs, although there are a few green areas in the oases, around the few lakes and on the sides of valleys. The Makrān is even more barren, with hardly anything growing but prickly shrubs of the kind favoured by hungry camels.

GOVERNMENT

Iranian politics are a complete mystery.

ECONOMY

The Iranian economy has looked decidedly shaky ever since the revolution, and oil production has only recently reached anything like pre-1980 levels. Trade embargoes, a fall in petroleum output, a slump in world prices, the punitive cost of an eight-year war, and official indifference to the state of the

economy have all left a heavy mark. Many observers believe it was the spectre of imminent bankruptcy, more than anything else, that forced Iran into accepting a ceasefire with Iraq. Even so, petroleum was the lifeblood of the Iranian economy, and without its flow the country would have had little more than revolutionary fervour to fuel its war effort.

Oil was first produced in Iran at Masjed-é Soleimān in 1908, and first exploited on a large scale after WWI by the then Anglo-Iranian Oil Company. Ābādān proved early on to be the most prolific site, and it wasn't long before it became a virtual colony of the international oil companies. There are several other major oil wells in the far south-west of Iran, and the government must be thankful that there's no independence movement to contend with in Khūzestān, the richest province of all Iran. Current estimates suggest there's enough of the black stuff left to tide Iran over for the next 100 years.

The last Shāh had launched what he called his White Revolution with the aim, among other things, of diversifying the Iranian economy away from petroleum dependency. While he did succeed in making Iran one of West Asia's leading car producers, and in bringing about a much-needed land reform programme, Iran never really developed any further than being a Third World country with a bonanza in oil wells. Iran actually had to import petrochemicals for lack of refining facilities at home. And although far more Iranians worked on the land than in industry, rural income never amounted to more than a fraction of urban income; while a good many people in Tehrān were doing very nicely thank you, the flow of petrodollars was a mere trickle by the time it reached the rural masses. As the money poured into Iran it was all too easy to import even the most basic commodities rather than go to the effort of modernising domestic industry and agriculture.

While his White Revolution was not without its successes, the Shāh's legacy was an economy almost totally dependent on petroleum and self-sufficient in hardly anything.

During the Iran-Iraq War there was precious little cash to spare from the front, and even the factories which had been built before the revolution were largely neglected. In some cities as many as three out of four industrial installations were out of use by the end of the war.

Caviar is the second most lucrative export (not hard to believe if you consider what it sells for in the West), closely followed by carpets. Other exports include pistachios, dried fruits, spices, various ores and minerals, cotton and silk, but all these put together are a trifle compared with oil which nets about 80% of government revenues and 95% of foreign currency earnings.

Less than half the country is considered cultivable, and only a small proportion of that actually goes under the hoe or the goat's hoof at any one time. Agriculture is hampered by extremes of temperature, lack of rain, soil salinity, plant diseases and the combination of inefficiency, poor infrastructure and lack of technology. Wheat, rice and barley are the most important cereal crops, while all manner of fruits are grown in the less arid parts of the country, including apricots, peaches, pomegranates, figs, dates, melons, grapes, apples, lemons and strawberries. Other important crops include sugar-beet, potatoes, nuts, tea, tobacco, saffron and henna, most of which are exported no further than the nearest bazaar. There is a small fishing industry on both the Persian Gulf and the Caspian Sea. Opium used to be a great money-spinner, but international pressure had become too intense, and the last legal poppy was processed back in 1955.

One foreign currency earner which didn't do too well out of the Khomeinī era was tourism. In the mid-'70s there were as many as 500,000 foreign visitors a year, and hotel development was a priority of the Shāh's fifth five-year plan (1973 to 1978). In 1987 (the latest year for which statistics are available) official foreign tourist receipts measured only US$25 million.

The war wreaked havoc on the Iranian economy. Power cuts are still an almost daily occurrence nearly everywhere in Iran, housing projects half-finished in 1979 remain half-finished over a decade on, and it takes five to 10 years for most Iranians to have a new telephone installed by the state company. While prices on many goods have increased as much as tenfold since the revolution, wages have hardly risen at all until very recently. The latest inflation rate is unofficially something like 70% per annum. The government has had to retain rationing for most staple goods, as Iran is nowhere near self-sufficient in food. Rice imports alone have made a sizeable dent in foreign currency reserves. Even with the high level of state imports, it's a rare Iranian who makes do without recourse to the black market, which has over the last few years drifted into almost complete legality. Iranians are always telling visitors how different things were in the old days, how the rial was actually worth something and how foreigners even found Iran expensive.

And yet it's a remarkable testament to Iranian private enterprise just how many Western goodies find their way into the country's thriving parallel economy – from the Marlboro cigarettes for sale at every street corner to the latest fashions from Paris at the smarter boutiques of Tehrān's Kheyābūn-é Gāndī.

Now that Khomeinī has gone and the war is over, more and more people, even ardent supporters of the revolution, are openly expressing their dissatisfaction at the crumbling economy, and it is clear that getting the country going again is going to be one of the biggest tests for the present leadership. Unlike its wartime adversary, the Islamic Republic did not borrow from abroad to keep the tanks rolling. As oil production returns to normal, and with no foreign debts to pay off, Iran is going to have a lot more money on its hands over the next few years. With a more pragmatic line in foreign policy likely in the post-Khomeinī era, few doubt that Iran will open up to the outside world in economic matters if in nothing else. Certainly there is no shortage of potential trading partners willing to cash in on the reconstruction

programme: the first postwar Tehrān Trade Fair was so heavily over-subscribed that many foreign companies had to be turned away. Iran clearly has the potential to be no less of a major economic power than it was in the '70s, only this time more money should stay inside the country.

POPULATION

The latest census, in 1986, put Iran's population at 50 million, with 27 million in towns, 22.6 million in rural areas, and a nomadic population of 250,000. In 1956 the population was only 19 million, and with an annual growth rate of 4.2% Iran has one of the world's fastest-growing populations. There is a very high proportion of young people: over 50% of the population are under 17 years old. All population figures in this book are based on the results of the 1986 census.

There has also over recent years been a dramatic demographic shift from the country to urban areas, worsened by the upheavals caused by the Iran-Iraq War, when millions of internal refugees headed for the large towns and stayed put. Many Iranian towns have at least doubled in population since the revolution, without any corresponding increase in housing or other facilities. There is a very high proportion of young people: some 46% of Iranians are under 14 years old.

Since the late '70s there has been an exodus of several million Iranians to Turkey and the West, and an influx of a similar number of refugees from Afghanistan and Iraq. Most recently Iran has had to cope with a flood of Kurds escaping from the murderous Iraqi regime of Saddam Hussein. There used to be a large number of Westerners living in Iran, but nowadays there are very few. There are, however, quite large Pakistani, Indian and Bangladeshi communities in Iran, not all of them in the country legally.

PEOPLE

Iran is by no means a homogeneous nation. Its location at the crossroads of Arabia, Turkey and Central Asia, and the changing frontiers of the Persian Empire have helped to ensure that a multitude of peoples make

Provinces & Provincial Capitals

their home within Iranian borders. The sheer diversity of the Iranian population, combined with centuries of mixing and migration, have made it difficult to draw even the vaguest of boundaries for the various ethnic groups inhabiting present-day Iran.

Just over half of the inhabitants of Iran can be called Persians, or Fārsīs, the descendants of the Aryan races who first set up camp in the central plateau back in the 2nd millennium BC and gave Iran its name. Āzarīs, the Turkic-speaking inhabitants of Āzarbāyjān, form the largest minority in Iran with

perhaps 25% of the population. There is a sizeable minority of Kurds, estimated at about three million, and there are also smaller numbers of Lors, Arabs, Turkomans, Bakhteyārīs, Baluchis, Ghashghā'īs, Armenians, Jews and others. Although the tribal element is still evident in many parts of Iran, most of the traditional nomads have become at least partially settled over the last few decades.

The Kurds are spread across a large area of the Middle East, including a good part of eastern Turkey and north-east Iraq, small pockets of Syria, some states of the former

USSR, and much of western Iran. Although they have been around longer than any other people in the region, at least since the 2nd millennium BC, the Kurds have never enjoyed the status of nationhood.

The Lors, or Lurs as they are sometimes known in English, are thought to be part Persian, part Arab in origin. They inhabit the province of Lorestān as well as a wider, mountainous region of western Iran.

The Iranian Arabs live mostly in the region of Khūzestān Province and in many of the smaller Iranian islands of the Persian Gulf, where they still speak a dialect of Arabic. They are also found along the rest of the southern coast of Iran, where they have become at least partly Persianised and are often known as Bandarīs, from the Persian word for 'port'.

The Turkomans are, as you might expect, of Turkic origin. Their home is the Torkaman Sahrā, the plain occupying much of the east of Māzandarān Province and the north of Khorāsān Province, just over the border from the former Soviet state of Turkmenistan. Traditionally nomadic horse-riders and warriors, the Turkomans are now largely settled as farmers and horse-dealers.

Another of the nomadic tribes of Iran, the Bākhtarīs (Bactrians) are native to remoter parts of the provinces of Chahārmahāl va Bakhteyārī and Khūzestān, although many of them have now adopted a more sedentary way of life in the villages and towns.

The Baluchis (Persian Balūch), whose name literally means 'the Wanderers', are one of the few peoples who largely retain a seminomadic way of life, perhaps because the extremely arid and barren area which they roam is hardly suited to the settled life. They occupy the very sparsely populated desert region covering the far south-east of Iran and the far west of Pakistan. Very able riders, they are famous for their camel races. In recent times, many of the Baluchis who moved to the towns have proved their nomadic roots by going overseas to work every now and then, picking up very good English in the process.

The Ghashghā'īs of south-west Iran, espe-

cially Fārs Province, are traditionally wandering herders, although many have now settled in Shīrāz and other towns. Like so many of the minority peoples of Iran, the Ghashghā'īs are of Turkic stock.

The Armenians and Jews, as much religious as ethnic minorities, are scattered throughout Iran, mostly in the cities. Armenians are particularly prominent in Tehrān and Esfahān. A few Jews remain in Tehrān, Shīrāz and Esfahān. Both communities are renowned in Iran, as elsewhere, as merchants and traders.

On the whole, ethnic strife isn't too much of a problem in Iran, the government being a lot more tolerant of minorities than many in the region. What little racial animosity the Persian majority may have is largely reserved for the dwindling number of Afghan refugees, who are privately blamed for almost every unresolved murder case or suspicious going-on from Khorāsān to Khūzestān. There are a few problems between the government and Kurdish separatists in Kordestān Province, but even there I haven't heard of examples of the discrimination for which Turkey and Iraq are infamous. By and large the racial minorities of Iran are free to enjoy their own culture, religion and language.

EDUCATION

Schooling is compulsory and free of charge for all Iranians from the age of seven to the end of secondary education. Great publicity has been given to the so-called Literacy Movement, which aims to teach reading and writing, as well as 'the revolutionary culture of Islam and religious matters'. At the level of higher education, demand far outstrips supply and only the cleverest and most favoured students can hope to get a place at one of the state universities. There are a few private universities, but a large number of Iranians who can afford to study abroad attend courses in Europe (especially Eastern Europe) and Turkey. Iran leads the world in facilities for Islamic theological students.

At the age of 16 all male Iranians are eligible for conscription to a unit of their choice, unless exempted for health reasons or because a brother has been killed in military service since the revolution. Those who are entering a university can choose whether to do their military service before or after their course. Medical graduates are sent to work as doctors in less developed regions of the country.

According to 1986 statistics, 62% of Iranians aged six or over are literate, 71% of males, and 51% of females; 73% of the urban population and 48% of the rural population. These are all much higher than the 1976 figures.

ARTS

In Iran, as in all Islamic societies, art favours the non-representational, the derivative and the stylised rather than the figurative, the innovative and the true-to-life. Accurate representation of the human form has never been a part of traditional Islamic art, and although portraiture is not forbidden by Shi'ite Islam, it never really caught on in Iran until the introduction of the camera. Portraits of Allāh or the face of Mohammad have always been taboo.

Many Iranian art forms predate the Arab conquest, but since nearly all of them reached their peak within the Islamic era, religious influences are rarely completely absent. Favourite motifs in Iranian art are geometrical shapes and patterns such as lozenges, medallions and meanders; grapevines and other floral patterns, often very complex; and highly stylised real or imaginary creatures such as lions, elephants, peacocks, phoenixes and griffins. Human figures do turn up, but they tend to be very formalised. Calligraphy is highly prized in Iran and often merges into pictorial art, although modern examples usually stand in their own right.

Fine Arts

Calligraphy became important soon after the Arab conquest. Not only was the Qoran faithfully reproduced as a whole, but verses from it, and holy names such as Allāh and Mohammad, were used as decorations on religious buildings and elsewhere, as they are to this day. The formal, upright Kufic style of calligraphy was imported from the Arabian Peninsula, but several distinctly Persian calligraphic styles also emerged, some of them so elaborate as to verge on the illegible.

Persian miniature paintings are deservedly famous throughout the world. Although few are miniature portraits in the Western sense of the word, the best examples do display great intricacy and attention to detail. Favourite themes include courting couples in traditional dress, polo matches and hunting scenes. Some of the best modern miniatures come from Esfahān.

Applied Arts

Pottery is one of the oldest Persian art forms, examples of which have been unearthed

Qoranic Calligraphy

16th-century Cat-shaped Persian Bottle

around. Glassware is also something to look out for.

Carpets

Carpets are the best known of all Iranian cultural exports. Because of the lack of furniture in most Iranian houses, carpets are far more than just floor-coverings. It is still partly true to say that Iranians display their wealth on the floor and – because the most valuable carpets are certainly not for walking over – on the wall.

The earliest Persian carpets were probably made of rushes. By the 7th century Persian carpets of wool or silk had become famous in court circles throughout the region for their quality and subtlety of design, and were exported to places as far away as China, although for many centuries they must have remained a great luxury in their country of production, with the finest pieces being the preserve of royalty. The patterns were usually symmetrical with geometric and floral motifs designed to evoke the beauty of the classical Persian garden. Towards the end of the pre-Islamic period, stylised animal and human figures (especially royalty) began to turn up on some carpets.

After the Arab Conquest, Qoranic verses were incorporated into some carpet designs, and prayer-rugs began to be produced on a grand scale; secular carpets too became a major industry and were highly prized in European courts. Very few examples remain from before the 16th century, however, and little is known of early methods of weaving and knotting, or of differences in regional styles; classification of existing pieces is often arbitrary.

During the 16th and 17th centuries, carpet making was given a high level of royal patronage and a favoured designer or weaver could expect great privileges at court. Sheep were specifically bred to grow the finest possible wool for weaving, and vegetable plantations were tended with scientific precision to provide permanent dyes of just the right shade. The more lavish carpets, even the largest of which often used gold thread in the design, were fantastically expensive

from burial mounds (*tappé*s) dating from the 5th millennium BC. Originally pottery was painted unglazed, but from the start of the third millennium it began in some places to be glazed. From the earliest days ceramics were painted with the simple geometric, floral and animal motifs that developed into the characteristic Persian style. Some of these early finds can be seen at Tehrān's Mūzé-yé Īrān-é Bāstān. Chinese influences became very strong after the Mongol Conquest and remained so until the mid-18th century. The classic period for Iranian ceramics is generally considered to have lasted from the 12th to the 14th century.

There are many very fine examples of metalwork, especially copper and bronze, to be found in Iran. Trays, dishes, bowls, tea-services and jewellery are some of the most common objects. Gold and silver have traditionally been an indulgence of royalty and the very rich, and some beautiful works are and the last thing anyone would do was walk on them. The reign of Shāh Abbās I marks the peak of Persian carpet production, when the quality of the raw materials and all aspects of the design and weaving were brought to a level never seen before or since, perhaps anywhere.

Towards the end of the 17th century, as demand for Persian carpets grew, so standards of production began to fall and designs tended to lack inspiration. A long period of stagnation followed, but the fall in standards has to be seen in perspective, for the finest Persian carpets of the 18th century and later still often led the world in quality and design. The reputation of modern Persian carpets has still not entirely recovered from the almost sacrilegious introduction of artificial fibres and aniline dyes earlier this century.

ARCHITECTURE

Persian architecture has a very long and complex history, and it is often regarded as the field in which Persia made its greatest contribution to the world's culture. Arthur Upham Pope's *An Introduction to Iranian Architecture*, a very compact yet comprehensive and lavishly illustrated paperback, is strongly recommended to anyone interested in the subject.

Although Persian styles differ sharply from any other Islamic architectural tradition, they have strongly influenced architecture throughout much of the Islamic world, especially to the north and east. Some of the best examples of particular Persian styles or periods are outside present-day Iran. Many political and natural disasters have taken a heavy toll on structures throughout the ages – earthquakes in particular have all but destroyed many towns.

The two important religious influences are Zoroastrianism before the Arab Conquest and Islam afterwards. Most of the greatest buildings were built with a religious purpose, and even in secular buildings religious influences are rarely entirely absent – even Persian churches often incorporate Islamic features. Patronage, especially royal patronage, has always been very important.

The greatest periods of architectural expression coincide more or less with periods of relative stability and prosperity. Persian architecture follows evolution rather than revolution, with a continual refinement of existing styles and major innovations being relatively few and far between.

Persian architecture shows a refined sense of scale and a monumental simplicity, combined with lavish use of surface ornamentation and colour. Since the depiction of religious figures is not part of the Islamic artistic tradition, decorations are geometric, floral or calligraphic. Often they are so closely moulded into the design that they appear to be an intrinsic part of the structure. The colours need to be bright and bold because the sunlight is often extremely harsh. Blank surfaces and recesses were filled with increasingly complex stalactites, mosaics and frescoes, and decorated with arabesques, geometric patterns and calligraphy. Mosaics forming the single word 'Allāh', repeated hundreds of times in a highly stylised script, may alone make up the decoration of a wall.

Structural elements include domes, high vaults, arcades, rectangular porticoes and *eivāns* (rectangular, barrel-vaulted halls opening onto a courtyard). The development of the dome is one of the greatest achievements of Persian architects. In Sassanian times they were the first to discover a satisfactory way of building a dome on top of a square chamber by using two intermediate

Dome of Malik Shahr, Masjed-é Jame', Esfahān

levels, the lower octagonal and the higher 16-sided, on which the dome could rest. This device, known as a squinch, is one of the most characteristic features of Persian architecture. It developed over the centuries from a purely mechanical structure, supported by simple corner arches, to a graceful work of art entirely masking its structural importance. Domes are usually semicircular rather than onion- shaped, and progressively larger ones were constructed over the centuries.

The typical Persian mosque design evolved from a standard model based on the design of the Prophet Mohammad's house at Medina. It comprises an entrance eivān which leads into a large courtyard surrounded by arched cloisters. Behind these are inner eivāns, one of them featuring a *mehrāb*, a decorated niche indicating the direction of Mecca, which is the focal point of the interior of the mosque. The main exterior feature is the minaret, a tower from which the faithful are called to prayer.

Before 7th Century BC
The only substantial remains are those of the remarkable Elamite ziggurat at Choghā Zambīl. The earliest building material was sun-dried mud brick. Baked brick was used for outer surfaces by the 12th century BC.

The ancient inhabitants of Persia imbued the mountains with great religious symbolism, and structures were built in imitation of mountains, giving rise to the characteristic pyramidal temples called ziggurats.

The Persian Empire to the Arab Conquest
The surviving sites from the Achaemenian era (558 to 330 BC) include the magnificent ceremonial palace complexes and royal tombs at Pasargadae, Susa, Persepolis and Naghsh-é Rostam. They are decorated with bas-relief figures of kings, soldiers, suppliants, animals and the winged figure of the Zoroastrian deity Ahura Mazda. The architecture was designed to glorify the king rather than to serve the purposes of a political seat of government.

Remains from the Achaemenian dynasty show links with the earlier ziggurat in both shape and decoration. The Achaemenian style incorporated features based on Egyptian or Greek models. Colossal halls were supported by stone and wooden columns with typically Persian bull's-head capitals. Materials were imported from throughout the Persian Empire and beyond, but the usual building materials were sun-dried brick and stone.

Alexander the Great's conquest (about 330 BC) brought a virtual end to the Achaemenian style in Persia. The following relatively dormant period under the Seleucids marked the introduction of Hellenism to Persia. No great examples remain today, although the Temple of Artemis (Ma'bad-é Ānāhītā) at Kangāvar, with Greek capitals and built to a Greek goddess, is the best preserved.

Under the Parthians (about 250 BC to 224 AD), Hellenism and indigenous styles merged, along with some Roman and Byzantine influences, and several characteristically Persian features arose, including the eivān.

In the Sassanian period (224 to 642), buildings became larger, heavier and more complex. The four-eivān plan with domed square chambers became increasingly common. Decoration became more adventurous and more use was made of colour, especially in frescoes and mosaics. The Sassanians built fire-temples throughout their empire, and the simple plan of the earliest examples was retained throughout the pre-Islamic era, even in the design of churches. The most important pilgrimage site of the pre-Islamic Persian Empire, Takht-é Soleimān, was established in the Sassanian era.

The Islamic Period
The Arab Conquest in the 7th century AD did not supplant the well-developed Sassanian style, but it did introduce the Islamic element which had such a pervasive impact on most Persian art forms. Not only did it shape the nature and basic architectural plan of religious buildings but it also defined the type of decoration – no human representa-

tion, however stylised, was permitted, and ceremonial tombs or monuments to individuals were also out of favour. Instead of grand palace complexes built as symbols of royal majesty, there came mosques designed as focal points for the social life of ordinary people.

9th to 11th Century As Sassanian and Arab ingredients merged, a distinctly Persian style of Islamic architecture evolved. From about the mid-9th century, under the patronage of a succession of enlightened rulers, there was a resurgence of Persian nationalism and Persian values which had laid dormant since the Arab Conquest. Architectural innovations included the high pointed arch, stalactites (rib-like mouldings used to decorate recesses) and an emphasis on balance and scale, though the perfection of the Persian Islamic style took many centuries to achieve. Calligraphy became a principle form of architectural decoration, which sometimes consisted wholly of inscriptions. Little remains of the architecture of these dynasties, or of the Ghaznavids who succeeded them, but one good example is the Masjed-é Jāme' at Nā'īn.

The period also marks the emergence of a series of remarkable tomb towers, usually more secular than religious in purpose, which in different forms lasted until the late 15th century. Built of brick and usually round, they show a development of ornamentation progressing from the simple to the lavish, starting with little more than a single garter of calligraphy and graduating to elaborate basket-weave brickwork designed to deflect the harsh sunlight. The most famous and earliest example is the extraordinary Gombad-é Kāvūs, but there are many others in Māzandarān and Semnān Province.

Seljuq Era to the Mongol Conquest The Seljuq era (mid-11th to early 13th century) saw a succession of enlightened rulers who took a great personal interest in their patronage of the arts. Architectural developments included the double dome, designed to achieve the best visual impact from both interior and exterior, a widening of vaults, improvement of the squinch and refinement of glazed tilework, especially in mehrābs. A meticulous unity of structure and decoration was attempted for the first time, based on rigorous mathematical principles. Stucco, incorporating arabesques and Persian styles of calligraphy, was increasingly used to enhance brick surfaces. Minarets became tall, tapering spires of decorative as much as practical value. The best example of the period is the original part of the Masjed-é Jāme' in Esfahān.

Mongol Era Although traditionally seen by Iranians as a dark age in their history, the Mongol era (early 13th to mid-14th century) did add much to the development of Persian architecture. The conquest of Persia by Genghis Khan was at first purely destructive, and many Persian architects fled the country. By the early 14th century the Il-Khanid Mongol dynasty, now used to relative peace, embarked on a massive programme of civic building that not only glorified the rulers but created whole new towns, especially in Āzarbāyjān and the north-west.

The Mongol style, designed to overawe the viewer, was marked by towering entrance portals, colossal domes, and vaults reaching into the skies. It also saw a refinement of tiling, often based on geometric and floral lines, and calligraphy, often in the formal angular Kufic script imported from Arabia. Increasing attention was paid to the interior decoration of domes, which were more closely moulded into the whole design. The most magnificent surviving example is the Gombad-é Soltān Oljeitū Khodābandé at Soltānīyé.

Timurid Era The Timurid period (late 14th century to 1502), which followed the accession of Tamerlane, marks a refinement of Seljuq and Mongol styles. The period features an exuberance of colour and a greater harmony of structure and decoration. Even in buildings of colossal scale, the monotony of large empty surfaces was avoided by the use of translucent tiling. Arcaded cloisters around inner courtyards, open galleries, and arches within arches were notable developments. The best surviving examples inside Iran are the remarkable Masjed-é Azīm-é Gōhar Shād in Mashhad, and the Masjed-é Kabūd in Tabrīz.

Safavid Era The period from 1491 to 1722 was one of comparative stability and prosperity, and a succession of enlightened and cultivated rulers, most notably Shāh Abbās I, saw the final refinement of styles which marks the culmination of the Persian Islamic style of architecture. Its greatest expression is Shāh Abbās I's royal capital of Esfahān, a supreme example of town planning, with one of the most magnificent collections of buildings from one period anywhere in the Islamic world. At its centre is the vast Meidūn-é Shāh (now Emām), still one of the world's largest squares, with the superb Masjed-é Shāh (now Emām) as its focal point.

There are other fine examples of Safavid architecture at Ghazvīn, the earlier capital, while the Holy Shrine of Emām Rezā at Mashhad gained much of its present magnificence in Safavid times.

The death of Shāh Abbās I in 1629 marks the beginning of the end for the golden age of Persian architecture. The Madrasé-yé Mādar-é Shāh (now Chahār Bāgh) of Esfahān, completed in 1714, is an outstanding architectural work for its period, but it and other buildings of the late Safavid period are really little more than a swan song.

After the Safavids Little of architectural greatness followed the fall of the Safavid dynasty, except for a brief interlude during the reign of Karīm Khān-é Zand, who built a fine bazaar and some other worthwhile buildings at his capital of Shīrāz.

The Ghajar period is widely regarded as tasteless and flimsy, although a few examples such as the Kākh-é Eram in Shīrāz and the Masjed-é Soltānī (now Emām Khomeinī) at Semnān do show a certain informal charm.

The 20th Century From the late 19th century, as Persia opened up to the outside world, the importation of European building techniques hastened the decline of traditional styles. Modern Iranian architecture is a sad and very disappointing showpiece of all the worst mistakes made in the West in the 20th century. Many of the excesses of modern architecture were introduced to an Iran hungry for progress during the boom years of the '60s and '70s.

The present regime is making a concerted effort to restore historic buildings, especially Islamic religious ones, and is constructing great numbers of new mosques, many of them reasonably attractive. The ravages of the war economy that followed the Islamic Revolution put a stop to the breakneck housing, commercial and industrial developments that have scarred the face of present-day Tehrān, but a distinctive modern style of Persian architecture has yet to emerge. One of the most ambitious architectural undertakings in modern Iran is the Ārāmgāh-é Emām Khomeinī outside Tehrān, still under construction.

Gardens

In a country where the shortage of water has always been a predominant factor in people's lives, the deep Iranian love of gardens and all things green is hardly surprising. Sometimes Iranians will rave to a foreigner about a park or garden which would hardly warrant a second glance in a less arid country. Nevertheless there are many classical gardens of unquestionable beauty, perhaps the most notable of which is the Bāgh-é Fīn on the edge of Kāshān.

CULTURE

If you observe the same simple courtesies as you would in Western societies, and keep within Iranian law, you will be doing more than many modern-day foreign travellers in Islamic countries, and you will be respected by the vast majority of Iranians with whom you come into contact. At the same time, there are inevitably different ways of doing things in a country with such an ancient civilisation as Iran's. Iranian etiquette is complex and Iranians are usually very forgiving of innocent gaffes by foreigners, but the rewards for learning the rules will more than repay the initial investment in time and effort.

Iranians are, on the whole, extremely hospitable to foreigners – almost embarrassingly so sometimes – but you do have to do your bit. The theory is that anyone for whom you do a favour has a duty to do another for you at some later date. Of course in practical terms there is no way that foreigners can repay in kind all the Iranians who give them a meal, hospitality or accommodation, but the principle remains. One simple way of showing gratitude is to respect the Iranian social code in your dealings with Iranians.

The following is only a short selection of tips based on my own personal experiences, some of them learned the hard way. It covers many of the potential pitfalls that foreigners are likely to confront.

Always be punctual for appointments, but don't expect Iranians always to turn up on time. In this matter the rules are different for foreigners and Iranians. Adjust yourself to the Iranian sense of time and expect delays: build them into your itinerary.

Never get straight to the point when dealing with Iranians. Accept or offer up to three cups of tea before getting down to serious business of any kind. Expect any preliminary conversation to be confined to enquiries after each other's health and other small talk.

It is the Iranian custom for friends to exchange presents when arriving or leaving. If you have no suitable present to offer, a dinner invitation won't cost you much but will mean a lot to your hosts.

Never accept a present or service of any kind without first politely refusing twice. The same applies in reverse if you are offering something to an Iranian.

Be extremely wary of making comments to strangers that may incriminate yourself or another person, even if innocuously intended or made in a joking way. Never underestimate the ruthlessness or strength of the Komîté and its network of informers. Don't be the first to discuss politics with a stranger. Remember that your views may appear just as extreme to some Iranians as theirs do to you.

If you are male, don't invite a female Iranian out without expecting there to be at least one male chaperon at all times, and even then conduct yourself with extreme caution. The rules are relaxed somewhat for non-Muslim women, but if you're travelling with a companion of the opposite sex who is not your spouse or a close relative, don't expect to be able to share a room together.

Remember that tourism is still very much in its infancy in postrevolutionary Iran. To a certain extent, every foreign visitor has some impact on the success or failure of Iran's tourist industry. Any criticisms should be constructive and directed to the right quarters, especially those officials responsible for tourism.

Sitting cross-legged on the floor is the usual custom in most Iranian households. Try to practise before going to Iran.

Never sit next to a member of the opposite sex who is not your spouse or a close relative unless specifically invited to do so, even if there is no other spare seat.

Respect the Iranian dress code rigorously at all times.

Always remove your shoes when visiting a mosque or other Islamic religious building, or on entering a private house, unless you're specifically invited to keep them on. You may be offered indoor slippers.

Most private houses have a pair of sandals by the entrance to the lavatory, which should be exchanged for any indoor slippers on entering and leaving and not taken into the rest of the house.

If you find the prospect of going to the lavatory without toilet paper unappealing, take a roll with you.

Never turn your back on anyone, point the sole of your shoe or foot at anyone, or walk in front of someone praying to Mecca. If you do so inadvertently or unavoidably, excuse yourself by saying *bebakhshîd*.

Rather than say 'no' outright and risk causing offence, Iranians will use any number of circumlocutions and diplomatic half-promises. These can easily be misunderstood by a foreigner. Frankness and conciseness are not attributes very highly regarded by most Iranians.

Don't shake hands or make any physical contact in public with a member of the opposite sex. Kissing or holding hands in public are only acceptable between members of the same sex, and are not signs of homosexuality.

Don't expect your hosts, Iranian or expatriate, to provide alcohol for you. Even if it is offered there is no obligation to accept and it is always safer to refuse.

When making a personal compliment to or about someone, eg when telling a mother how handsome her child is, always say *māshallāh* ('God has willed it') for fear of invoking divine nemesis. The idea is that all beauty and goodness are the gifts of God and can be taken away by Him at any time.

Don't expect to be told when you have broken one of the many unwritten laws of Iranian etiquette. It is worth explaining to friends that you are a novice in Iranian ways and would appreciate guidance.

Don't be afraid to accept invitations from Iranians. Iranians have always entertained predominantly at home and you will never understand Iran if you don't make an effort to meet Iranians on their own terms.

There are some taboo subjects for conversation: crusading attempts on behalf of feminism, atheism, Zionism or free love are unlikely to prove fruitful. It is an offence to criticise any of the āyatollāhs, or especially to defame any of the prophets of Islam. In Iran you have to be more careful than in most countries about what you say and in whose company you say it. On the other hand, money, politics, religion and even sex are all favourite subjects at the dinner table and elsewhere. In Iran it is not generally considered rude to ask questions about a person's salary, standard of living or marital status. 'Are you married?' and 'How many children do you have?' are standard icebreakers.

Dress

Visitors to Iran of either sex are officially 'requested' to wear 'decent' clothing, and 'ladies should observe the Islamic outfit'.

The Iranian dress code is not only inspired by Qoranic commands and reinforced by social custom, but also rigidly reinforced by law, so flouting the rules is more than just bad manners. Revolutionary Guards have been known to go around on motorcycles during Ramazān toting cans of paint to spray on the bare arms of anyone rash enough to be caught wearing a T-shirt in public. In May

1990 it was announced that computer records would be kept of those caught breaking the dress code – a fine example of 20th-century technology serving 6th-century purposes.

It is not necessary for foreign women, or even Iranian women, to wear the *chādor*, the one-piece cloak traditionally associated with the country. It is however essential for them to cover all parts of the body except the hands, feet and face (from hairline to neckline), and to ensure that the outer layer of clothing gives no hint of the shape of the body. Standard dress for Western women in Iran tends to be a full-length skirt, or a long-sleeved shirt and trousers (jeans are OK), worn underneath a loose-fitting, below-the-knees, black or dark blue coat. A large, plain, dark headscarf should cover the hair and neck (a hat will not do) and thick socks should cover any visible parts of the legs. Apart from plain rings, jewellery and make-up should be discreet to the point of invisibility.

The chādor or outer layer of clothing does not have to be black or dark blue, but it usually is in most parts of Iran. Girls are expected to wear the *hejāb* from the age of about seven. If you want to wear a chādor, you can have one made up quite cheaply and

quickly at any dressmaker's shop, but it is rather unusual for Western women to go this far.

Men must wear full trousers, not shorts, and must keep their arms covered. In most urban areas you can usually get away with shirt-sleeves rolled up below the elbow (except during Ramazān), but it is better to have them done up at the wrist. T-shirts are perfectly acceptable if worn underneath a jacket.

Iran must have one of the highest proportions of men with beards or moustaches of any country in the world, although it is often difficult to distinguish between an attempt at a full beard and what is merely a bad shave. Beards are the height of respectability in Iran, and President Rafsanjānī is even often mocked for not having one.

For reasons beyond my logic, ties have been officially condemned as an unwelcome and un-Islamic symbol of Western cultural imperialism, whereas jeans are almost universally acceptable. Clothes loosely based on Western fashions are the rule for Iranian males, except among the mullocracy and some of the tribal or ethnic minorities. They are also surprisingly common on younger Iranian women, albeit hidden under the *hejāb*. Many of the clothes sold in Iran boutiques today are cheap and nasty imitations of outdated Western models.

The laws on dress are particularly strictly enforced during Ramazān when Iranians, never the most colourful of dressers, avoid reds and any other bright colours. Colours are also subdued during Moharram, the month of mourning.

Visiting Mosques & Churches

If you are a Muslim, you should have no problems, and you will know how to answer any questions about your religion. On no occasion when I asked for permission to enter a mosque was I refused entry, and only once did anyone inside comment disparagingly about an infidel's presence. It is strictly forbidden for non-Muslims to enter the Holy Shrine at Mashhad or any part of the sacred precincts of the shrine of Fātemé

at Ghom, but otherwise most mosques will let non-believers in. However the non-Muslim will often feel a sense of guilt or embarrassment and it is often better to take a Muslim friend as a companion.

Always take your shoes off at the doorstep of a mosque (make sure your feet or socks are clean). There is usually an attendant or someone who looks after the shoes of visitors, and you could ask him for permission to enter, making it clear that you are not a Muslim. Avoid visiting mosques during services. Some historic mosques and other Islamic buildings no longer ordinarily function as such, but have been made into museums or simply abandoned; at a very few there is even a nominal entrance fee.

At one church I was told that I would need permission in writing from the Ministry of Culture & Islamic Guidance to enter, since the same rule applies for any visitor. It is rare for Muslims to enter churches; they can get in trouble with the authorities, and the church authorities do not usually like them to enter either. When I entered a church with an Iranian Muslim friend (who would not otherwise have been allowed in) he was certain that he would have to remove his shoes as on entering a mosque.

SPORT & GAMES

The ancient sports of archery, wrestling and swimming in which the Qoran exhorts Muslims to train their children are also strongly encouraged by the Iranian authorities. Iran has sent wrestlers and weightlifters to the Olympics, and various sorts of traditional Iranian wrestling tournaments and displays can be watched at the *zūrkhūné* (literally 'house of strength'). Although public facilities leave a lot to be desired, football, volleyball and basketball are popular, and Iran has had some limited success in all three at a regional level. There are public swimming pools for both sexes (but not at the same time) in the cities, and less crowded ones (sometimes open only to men) in a few hotels. Skiing is enjoyed at some mountain resorts, and trekking at many

A	B
C	D
E	F

DStV, DStV,
PW, DStV,
PW, DStV

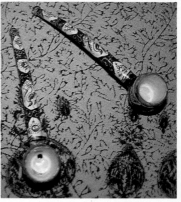

A	B
C	D
E	F

DStV, DStV, DStV, RVD, PW, DStV

Crafts and Markets

more. There is a small water-skiing club which uses the Karaj Dam.

Polo is probably a Persian invention, and was certainly played here in the reign of Darius the Great. Some two thousand years later, Shāh Abbās was famous for enjoying watching his courtiers play the odd chukka in the Meidūn-é Shāh of Esfahān. However the game seems to have died out completely in Iran since the revolution. Camel-racing, which has always been a way of life among the Baluchis, now enjoys a wider audience than ever, thanks to Iranian state television.

Chess, although it has been widely played in Iran for at least 1500 years, and some scholars have even claimed it was a Persian invention, suddenly became illegal shortly after the revolution on the grounds that it encourages the *harām* (forbidden by Muslim law) practice of betting. Chess sets were traded on the black market until early 1989, when the game became legal again by a final goodwill edict of Āyatollāh Khomeinī. Possession of playing-cards, banned for the same reason, is still however a criminal offence.

RELIGION

The Islamic Republic of Iran is, of course, overwhelmingly Muslim, and Islam is the state religion. Iran follows the Shi'ite sect of Islam rather than the more common Sunni sect. According to official 1986 statistics, 99.38% of the population follow Islam, 0.02% are Zoroastrians, 0.05% are Jews, 0.3% are Christians and 0.17% are Hindus, Sikhs and others. The figures for the minorities are probably underestimates as many call themselves Muslims in official documents. No-one admits to being an atheist in Iran today.

The non-Muslim minorities pose little threat to the government. In return for their acquiescence they are granted certain concessions, and in matters of moral laws they are allowed to be tried by their own religious leaders, who have absolute discretion over any decision. For example, if a Muslim girl is caught in bed with a man who is not her husband, whatever his religion, both are liable to very severe punishment under Islamic laws. But if both partners are non-Muslims, or the girl alone is a non-Muslim, then the matter is referred to their respective religious leaders and, in the case of Christians, they will probably be let off with a warning or told to get married or else desist.

Although non-Muslims are a very small minority in Iran, they are worth mentioning because they tend to gravitate towards foreigners. There are churches in almost every large Iranian town, but they are often rather difficult to find. They usually aren't marked on maps, even in Persian, and many of them are hidden behind high walls and are almost unidentifiable from the street. As a general rule, Muslims do not visit non-Islamic religious buildings and their knowledge of other religions is as scant as most Westerners' knowledge of Islam.

Islam

The religion's founder, the Prophet Mohammad (as he is known in Persian; the Arabic is Muhammad), was born in 570 AD in Mecca. He had his first revelation from Allāh in 610; this and later visions were compiled into the Muslim holy book, the Qoran (Ghorān in Persian). As his purpose in life was revealed to him, Mohammad began to preach against the idolatry for which Mecca was then the centre. Eventually, in 622, his attacks on this local business led to Mohammad and his followers being being run out of town. They fled to Medina, city of the Prophet, and by 630 were strong enough to march back into Mecca and take over. Mohammad died in 632, but within two decades most of Arabia was converted to Islam.

The Muslim faith called on its followers to spread the word – if necessary by the sword. It was just the rallying call the Arabs needed, and in succeeding centuries Islam was spread over three continents. Since the Arabs who first propagated the faith had a reputation as ruthless fighters but reasonable masters, people often found it advisable to surrender to them. In this way the Arab Muslims swept aside the crumbling Byzantine Empire, whose people felt no desire to support their distant Christian emperor. Islam spread westward for 100 years, before being pushed back at Poitier in France in 732, but it spread eastward for centuries. The Muslim influence regenerated the Persian Empire and led to the great period of Persian art and literature. From Ghazni, in Afghanistan, Mahmud of Ghazni repeatedly drove into India in the 11th century, and by the 13th century all of the Ganges plain was in Muslim hands, and the Mogul Empire eventually controlled most of the subcontinent. From there, Arab and Indian traders spread the faith on to South-East Asia, where it is strong today in Malaysia and most of Indonesia.

At an early stage Islam suffered a fundamental split that remains to this day. In 656, the third Caliph, successor to Mohammad, was murdered and followed by Alī, the Prophet's son-in-law. Alī was assassinated in 661 by the Governor of Syria who set himself up as Caliph in preference to the descendants of Alī. Today some 90% of Muslims are Sunni, followers of the succession from the Caliph, while the remainder are Shi'ites who follow the descendants of Alī. Only in Iran do Shi'ites form a majority, but there are Shi'ite minorities in other countries, notably Iraq and Bahrain.

Christianity

Christianity thrived in this country long before the introduction of Islam, and some of its first saints were martyred in Persia. The majority of Christians in Iran are Armenians, who first settled at Jolfā on Iran's northern border, then were moved on to 'New Jolfā' in Esfahān by Shāh Abbās I. They are respected for their business skills and powers of organisation, and in more recent times they have controlled the black market in alcohol. There are also smaller communities of Protestants, Roman Catholics, Chaldeans (Catholic Rite), Orthodox, Adventists, Nestorians and others. The Episcopal Church of Iran (part of the Anglican Communion) has churches in Tehrān, Esfahān, Shīrāz and Kermān (the addresses are given

in the text), all of which welcome Westerners. The greatest Christian communities are in Orūmīyé, Tabrīz, Tehrān (especially around Kheyābūn-é Nejātollāhī), Esfahān (especially in the suburb of Jolfā), Shīrāz and throughout Āzarbāyjān.

Zoroastrianism

Zoroastrianism is an ancient religion which was once the state creed, but faded away after the Arab conquest. At one stage Zoroastrianism stretched all the way to the Mediterranean, only to be pushed back by Christianity from the west and Buddhism from the east, before the Muslims flooded all three. Today, Zoroastrians are found mainly in Yazd (their traditional centre), Shīrāz, Kermān, Tehrān and Esfahān, and in parts of India and Pakistan. The Zoroastrians are also known as Mazdaites or, outside Iran, Parsees.

The Zoroastrians are followers of Zoroaster (Zartosht), who was probably born about 550 BC at Mazar-é Sharif in what is now Afghanistan (although several places in present-day Iran also claim the honour). Zoroastrianism was one of the first religions to postulate an omnipotent, invisible god. They worship fire as a symbol of God, and keep 'eternally' burning flames at their temples – one in Yazd has been burning for 1400 years. Since they believe in the purity of the elements, they will not bury their dead (it pollutes the earth) or cremate them (it pollutes the atmosphere). Instead the dead are exposed on 'towers of silence', where they are soon cleaned off by the vultures.

Today the religion is going through a period of updating and readjustment as strict regulations on marriage have resulted in a great decline in the religion's numbers. Even the vultures seem to have lost interest, and in Iran the exposing of corpses ended around 50 years ago, so the towers of silence are no longer in use.

Though Zoroastrians are now very few in number in their place of origin, some of their customs and beliefs are firmly entrenched in Iranian life. Their symbolism is an important part of Iranian art, and many aspects of their faith have a certain appeal to Iranian Muslims. Many of the most famous pre-Islamic monuments in Iran have clear Zoroastrian symbols. Zoroastrian women wear brightly embroidered layers of clothing rather than the chādor, and Zoroastrian elders wear white and are clean-shaven. Many have emigrated in recent years, especially to the West.

Judaism

The Jewish population has fallen sharply since the Islamic Revolution, although there are still significant communities in Hamadān, Tehrān, Shīrāz and Esfahān, where they are active in the bazaar and the jewellery trade.

Other Religions

The vast majority of others are Hindus and Sikhs, who have been settled in Iran for several generations but retain their religion and dress. They are spread throughout Iran but the largest numbers are in Tehrān and Zāhedān. They are almost entirely engaged in business, and a few own Indian restaurants.

LANGUAGE

The national language is Persian, also called Farsi, which is an Indo-European language. The chapter on language at the end of the book provides a basic introduction to Persian, and provides many useful words and phrases. Although no-one will expect you to speak Persian like a native, Iranians very much appreciate foreigners making an effort to learn some of the language. There are, however, a few occasions when it is best for the foreigner not to admit to a knowledge of Persian. When they might be overheard, Iranians may be much more expansive talking in English than in Persian.

The Arabic script was adapted to Persian after the introduction of Islam, but there is no standard method of transliterating Persian so English speakers can pronounce it. The transliteration system used in this book is explained in the language chapter, and is designed to give a good indication of how colloquial Persian is pronounced. Classical Persian, which an Iranian would use for reading a speech or writing a book, is not the language of everyday speech.

Persian script is given in the language chapter, so you can learn to recognise some words on a sign or a menu. Persian script has also been used in the text to help the reader recognise signs. Those who have difficulty with pronunciation can point out the relevant word or expression when asking for directions or assistance.

Translations of many Persian words and phrases are given throughout the text, and also in the glossary. Persian terms are used for many geographical and urban features, and these are also explained in the glossary. For international-standard hotels, travel agencies, transport companies, banks and other organisations which commonly deal with foreigners, I have used the English name as the main reference. For other establishments, where there are signs in Persian and in English, I have given a transliteration of the Persian name as the main reference, and added the English version afterwards in brackets. If there is no English equivalent given, the establishment is signposted only in Persian.

Facts for the Visitor

VISAS & EMBASSIES

Visas can be tricky. For those not in the privileged position of holding an official invitation, Iran runs a sort of self-selection process for visa applicants. Those who want to go badly enough can usually manage to get a visa eventually, while casual telephone enquirers often get the knockback. Regulations can change with little or no notice, and are in any case applied inconsistently from consulate to consulate. It is impossible to give definitive advice, because there are no definitive rules.

Japanese and Turks can enter Iran for up to three months without a visa, and diplomats of certain countries also have arrangements with Iran. Everyone else has to apply for a visa of some kind, which is rarely granted automatically.

How ready the Iranians are to let you into their country depends very much on the state of their relations with your government at the time. Citizens of small inoffensive countries like Ireland, New Zealand and San Marino are the greatest beneficiaries of this policy; Americans, Israelis and South Africans the greatest losers. US citizens have recently been allowed in much more easily than before, but only those with a very cogent reason for visiting. The situation for Britons has improved with the restoration of diplomatic relations, but not very much yet. Australians and New Zealanders have been in relative favour with the Iranian authorities for some time, as have the Irish. Canadians are seen as tainted by US imperialism, however unfairly, but their passports are not necessarily a bar to entry. West Europeans have been coming to Iran in fairly large numbers for several years, but they don't necessarily get the visa in their home country. Whoever you are, the situation is bound to change within the life of this book, and the best source of information is still going to be other travellers.

Wherever you apply, you'll have to fill in two, three or four forms adorned with two or three photos. The visa fee varies according to nationality, type of visa and place of application – from nothing for Australians anywhere they apply, up to US$50 for Britons applying in Budapest.

A transit visa is valid for a stay of up to two weeks (sometimes even less), and a tourist visa for no more than a month. Both tourist and transit visas can be used for entry within a maximum of three months from the date of issue, but you may have to ask specifically for this. Double or multiple entry visas are not normally issued, and it is not possible to apply for a second visa on the same passport while a previous one is still valid. You don't have to be a tourist to get a tourist visa, and business people and others often get one. There are also entry visas, pilgrimage visas, diplomatic visas and press visas.

Technically, everyone who applies for a tourist visa has to wait for the forms to be sent to the Ministry of Foreign Affairs in Tehrān for approval, which can mean a wait of some two or three months, or sometimes the kiss of death. But Iranians are not great lovers of rules, and some consulates either don't appear to know about this requirement, or don't always implement it.

Papers that are sometimes asked for include: tickets in and out (not very often – say that you're going by bus if you haven't got any); letters from employers (rarely); letters of recommendation from embassies or foreign offices (a diplomatic nonsense); proof of funds (very unlikely); and student or press cards. You may also have the visa marked with intended points or means of entry and exit, car registration numbers if applicable and the names of any travelling companions in Iran. At some consulates tourist visas are also inscribed 'Bearer intends to carry X dollars with him/her'.

Some consulates only issue transit visas to ordinary travellers, a few are happy to give one-month tourist visas, and others try very hard to put you off the idea of applying in the first place. Sometimes it is next to impossible to get a visa in your home country, while the Iranian consulate in another country will issue you a full tourist visa in 48 hours. In general I have found that consulates in countries that attract few applicants are the most likely to oblige with visas.

If you can't get a visa in time, or at all, in your home country, don't give up. Either telephone the Iranian consulate in a neighbouring country (see the list below) or make a point of dropping in at every Iranian mission on your way. Going to the consulate in person can make a tremendous difference. If all they'll give you is a transit visa, don't worry – getting an extension inside the country is far easier in most cases than obtaining the visa in the first place.

In Pakistan, foreigners can currently only apply for visas in Islamabad or Karachi, not at the consulates in Quetta or Peshawar. The latest news is that there's no short cut to a transit visa in Pakistan; you'll just have to wait weeks and weeks for a reply from Tehrān. However the situation here, as everywhere else, is very changeable.

In Turkey, latest reports suggest that the Iranian Embassy staff in Ankara are not well disposed to travellers. They take exception to issuing visas in under three months, and then only to bearers of a 'letter of recommendation' from their own embassy. A slightly better place to apply is the consulate in Istanbul. There are also consulates in Erzurum and Trabzon, but neither is in the habit of issuing visas to travellers. Athens is no longer such a good place to apply, but recent reports indicate Damascus and Beirut may be worth trying.

In theory, any evidence in a passport of a visit or intended visit to South Africa or Israel is an automatic disqualification for entry into Iran, although the rule is not always observed. If you have any incriminating visa or entry stamp, it is safer to get a new passport before applying for a visa to Iran.

It's important, if you have previously held Iranian nationality, to take consular advice before travelling to Iran.

Women should wear a veil or chādor for the photos they submit with their application, and when visiting the consulate. This show of good intent is most important, and easily overlooked. Going to the consulate with a male chaperon may help.

One thing to note is that Iranian diplomats and consular staff have rather a bad reputation for giving misleading information to travellers, especially over the telephone. For example, in London the Iranian visa officer currently maintains that British nationals can easily get transit visas in a few days, but that they first need to get a 'routinely issued' letter of recommendation from the British Foreign Office. Of course, when you telephone the Foreign Office, they say that they don't give such a letter to anyone, and you are back where you started. Similar problems are likely to be experienced at other Iranian consulates. Another example is from a Dutch traveller who writes:

In the summer of 1989 I joined the new hordes and tried to get overland from Europe to Asia; on my way I found the route was considerably blocked by Iranian reluctance... Before I left I tried to apply for an Iranian visa at home, but they told me it would take at least two months to obtain such visa in Holland, whereas in Turkey it would probably take a great deal less... I arrived in Istanbul and asked at the Consulate of Iran where I could best apply for Iranian visa in Turkey; they answered that Erzurum (not Ankara) ... was the only place in Turkey to obtain Iranian visa, and it would take 'a couple of days' over there.

In Erzurum they told me an Iranian visa took at least two months to apply for, but in Ankara it would only take 'a couple of days'...I protested, told them I was explicitly sent to Erzurum by the Iranian Consulate in Istanbul, said that they assured me it would take only a couple of days in Erzurum...

At the Tourist Information they told me they received a couple of travellers a day being sent on this ridiculous merry-go-round through Turkey...Going back to Ankara was the only thing I could do... I had to turn back at the very border of Iran and travel 1000 kilometres in the opposite direction. Before I left I phoned the Iranian Embassy in Ankara, and they assured me it would only take 'one day'...at the Embassy itself they refused to let me in, because it would take 'two months' anyway.

Anna

Press Visas

Journalists, photographers, travel writers and the like can apply for press visas by fax to the Press & Mass Media Department of the Ministry of Foreign Affairs on Tehrān 313149. Don't hold your breath; you probably won't even get an acknowledgement unless your presence in Iran fits in with the authorities' own propagandist purposes. All applications have to be approved by the hardliners in the Ministry of Culture & Islamic Guidance. Holders of press visas are not normally allowed to travel freely around Iran, and they will usually be accompanied by a ministry spook and have to apply for permission to visit anywhere outside Tehrān. It is not normally possible to change the category of visa inside Iran, and it is dangerous to enter Iran as a journalist on a tourist visa.

Warning

A copy of every visa application is sent to the Ministry of Foreign Affairs in Tehrān, and it may be used as evidence against you at a later date; so be very careful about what you say. It is risky not to declare any previous visits or rejected applications.

Iranian Embassies & Consulates

Afghanistan
    Shahr-é Nō, Kabul (☎ 26755)
    Consulate: Kheyābūn-é Velāyat, Herat (☎ 2820)
Australia
    14 Torres St, Red Hill, Manuka, Canberra (☎ (06) 295 2544)
Austria
    Jauresgasse 3, 1030 Vienna (☎ 722650)
Azerbaijan
    Bouniat Sardarov ulitsa No 4, Baku 370001 (☎ 926177) Note: this was a consulate in the former USSR, and is now a full embassy.
Bangladesh
    CWN(A)-12 Kamal Atatürk Ave, Gulshan Model Town, Dhaka 12 (☎ 601432)
Belgium
    415 avenue de Tervueren, 1150 Brussels (☎ 7623745)
Canada
    4th Floor, 411 Roosevelt Ave, Ottawa K2A 3X9 (☎ 7290902)

China
    Dong Liu Ji, San Li Tun Embassy Compound, Peking (☎ 5322040)
Denmark
    Grønningen 5, 1270 Copenhagen K (☎ 371480)
Finland
    Bertel Jungintie 4, 00570 Helsinki (☎ 687133)
France
    4 avenue d'Iena, Paris 75116 (☎ 47236122)
    Vice-Consulate: 16 Rue Fresnal, Paris (☎ 47203080)
Germany
    Godesberger Allee 133-7, 5300 Bonn 2 (☎ 8100521)
    Consulates: Peter Lenne Strasse 26, Berlin (☎ 8324061);
    Abtei Strasse 25, Hamburg (☎ 410375);
    Mauerkircherstrasse 59, Munich (☎ 984322)
Greece
    Odos Kalari 16, Palaio Psykhiko, Athens (☎ 6471436)
Hungary
    Délibáb u 29, Budapest VI (☎ 225038)
India
    5 Barakhamba Rd, New Delhi 110001 (☎ 385491)
    Consulates: Galdota Bhavan 117, Maharishi Karve Rd, Bombay (☎ 293303);
    8-2-502/1, Road No 7, Banjara Hills, Hyderabad (☎ 35722)
Irish Republic
    72 Mount Merrion Ave, Blackrock, Dublin (☎ 880252)
Italy
    Via della Tamilluccia 651, 001351 Rome (☎ 3280965)
    Consulate: Piazza Diaz 6, Milan (☎ 8052615)
Japan
    10-32 Minami Azabu 3-chome, Minato-ku, Tokyo 106 (☎ 4468011)
Netherlands
    Javastraat 54, 2585 AR The Hague (☎ 469353)
New Zealand
    PO Box 10249, The Terrace, Wellington
Norway
    Drammensveien 88E, Oslo 2 (☎ 558408)
Pakistan
    3-5 Street 17, Shalimar 6/2, Islamabad
    Consulates: 81 Shahrah-i-Iran, Clifton Beach, Karachi (☎ 530638);
    82-E-1, Gulberg III, Lahore (☎ 870274);
    3 Sir Syed Rd, Peshawar Cantonment, Peshawar (☎ 74643);
    2/33 Hali Rd, Quetta (☎ 75054)
Russia
    Pokrovskiy bulvar 7, Moscow (☎ 2978440)
    Note: Iran is setting up embassies in other former Soviet republics.

Saudi Arabia
 PO Box 94394, Riyadh 11693 (☎ 4826111)
Serbian Republic
 Proleterskiy brigada 9, 11000 Belgrade
 (☎ 338782) Note: this was formerly the embassy
 to Yugoslavia.
South Korea
 726-126 Hannam-Dong, Yongsan-ku, Seoul
 (☎ 7937751)
Spain
 Jerez 5, Villa El Altozano, Chamartin, 28016
 Madrid
Sweden
 PO Box 6031, 18106 Lidingö, Stockholm
 (☎ 7670740)
Switzerland
 Thunstrasse 68, 3006 Berne (☎ 430801)
 Consulate: 25 avenue de Champel, Geneva
 (☎ 474171)
Syria
 Mezzeh Autostrade, near Al-Razi Hospital,
 Damascus
Turkey
 Tahran Caddesi 10, Ankara (☎ 1274320)
 Consulates: Cumhuriyet Caddesi, Kuskay Sitesi
 23/25 (☎ 13876), Erzurum;
 Ankara Caddesi 1-2, Cagaloglu, Istanbul
 (☎ 5138230);
 Uzum Kum, Trabzon (☎ 11129)
UAE
 Shari'ah Hamdan, PO Box 4080, Abu Dhabi
 (☎ 343257)
 Consulate: Bar Dubai, near Kuwaiti Hospital,
 Almulla's Building, PO Box 2832, Dubai
 (☎ 431150)
UK
 27 Prince's Gate, London SW7 1PX (☎ 071-584
 8101)
 Consulate: 50 Kensington Court, London W8
 5DD (☎ 071-937 5225)
USA
 Interests Section: 2209 Wisconsin Ave NW,
 Washington, DC 20007 (☎ 9654990)

Visa Extensions

The general rule with transit and tourist visas
is that you can get two extensions of up to
two weeks each – and sometimes up to a
month – without any problem, and occasionally three times or even more. You can only
apply for an extension a few days before the
visa is due to expire.

For the first extension you have to go to
the visa office in any provincial capital
(usually inside the police headquarters or
shahrdārī), fill in the form in duplicate, pro-

vide one photo and wait, sometimes a few
hours, but more likely for one or two
working days. The fee is a standard 1000
rials. Very occasionally you will have to go
for an interview (in English) before being
given an extension, but this is not likely to
be a great ordeal. Shīrāz is as good a place
as any to apply, and Esfahān is probably the
worst. Tehrān is much better than it used to
be, so long as you are very polite and the
captain likes the look of you.

For a second extension, you may be able
to apply anywhere, but you will save time if
you do it in Tehrān or at the place where you
had your first extension – you may not be
able to get an extension at all anywhere else.
Anything beyond a second extension is a
bonus, and you may only be given a few
extra days to give you time to leave the
country. There's no harm in asking for a
month each time, but you are unlikely to get
it more than once at the most.

Unless you are one of those fortunate
people who can visit Iran for three months
without a visa, it is very unlikely that you
will be allowed to stay in Iran for longer than
that period, and 2½ months is usually about
the maximum allowed for any one visit.
Re-entry visas are not issued for Iran, and
you will probably have difficulty in obtaining another tourist visa for another six
months or so, unless perhaps you apply on
another passport.

Residence & Work Permits

Residence permits and work permits are
issued separately, and are normally arranged
inside Iran by the prospective employer, who
also pays any relevant fees. Note that if you
apply for either while you are actually in
Iran, you will have to leave the country and
pick up the permits at a specified Iranian
consulate. It is common for prospective employees to enter Iran on ordinary tourist
visas, and then to fly to Dubai to collect their
permits, returning to Iran a few days later. It
is not permitted to take up any form of
employment in Iran on a tourist visa. The
only likely circumstance where you can
apply for a residence permit without a work

permit is if you get married to an Iranian citizen, and even then it is very difficult. See also the section on Work, later in this chapter.

Foreign Embassies & Consulates in Iran

Most countries with which you are likely to have any business have embassies in Tehrān, except for the USA. There are also a few consulates in Bandar-é Abbās, Mashhad, Orūmīyé, Shīrāz, Tabrīz and Zāhedān. See the relevant city sections for addresses and telephone numbers.

DOCUMENTS

Apart from a passport with several spare pages for visa extensions and immigration stamps, it is a good idea to take some other convincing identity document with you to Iran. You will quite often have to leave your passport at hotels, visa offices or elsewhere, and you may have some problems in travelling around if you don't have any other identification to show to curious officials. Always carry in your luggage a photocopy of the vital front few pages of your passport, as it may save a lot of time in case of loss or theft of the original. Bring plenty of passport photos of yourself. Not only does Iranian officialdom, with its wads of forms in duplicate or triplicate, require a fair number but it is common for Iranians to swap mugshots with their friends.

Student cards are not particularly useful in Iran, as about all you can do with them as a foreigner is get a small discount on the already desperately cheap train fares. Youth hostel cards have no obvious use in Iran. Visiting cards may impress some people, as will letters of introduction on official-looking letterheads.

A few places, mainly well off the main tourist routes, may require permits or letters of introduction to visit. See under the relevant towns for further information.

Details on health certificates are given in the relevant section below. For information on the documents you need to drive your own vehicle to Iran, see the Getting There & Away chapter.

CUSTOMS

You can bring in, free of duty, a 'reasonable amount of used personal belongings and travel necessities' not intended for sale, with the following additions and exceptions:

Permitted for Import

Used articles and foodstuffs up to the value of 50,000 rials, for non-commercial purposes only, once a year; 200 cigarettes or 50 cigars or 250 grams of tobacco.

The following items must be declared and registered in your passport on entry and exported on departure: a 'reasonable' amount of personal jewellery; one portable still camera and five rolls of film ; one video camera and two rolls of film; one pair of binoculars; one portable musical instrument; one portable tape-recorder; one record-player and 10 records; one portable typewriter; one tent and other camping equipment; one fishing kit, one bicycle, one canoe or kayak not more than 5½ metres in length, one pair of skis, two tennis-rackets and 'other objects of the same kind'.

Forbidden for Import

Alcoholic beverages; narcotics; guns or ammunition without an import licence; aerial survey cameras; radio transceivers; 'vulgar' films; 'unpleasant' records, cassettes, video-tapes and books with 'indecent' pictures; any kind of 'fashion' magazine from any country (worth a fortune on the black market); anything else to which the customs officer takes particular exception.

On exit from Iran you may take out anything you legally imported together with anything you legally obtained in the country, including Iranian handicrafts up to the value of 50,000 rials, with the following exceptions: any kind of carpet, and many kinds of rug; 'antiques'; items of gold or silver (except for one ring and one watch); precious stones; coins; 'old' manuscripts and 'original' paintings; foodstuffs (rarely enforced); 'drugs'.

Customs checks of arriving and departing passengers are much more lax than they used to be, and nowadays foreigners are rarely treated with anything but courtesy. Even Iranians I travelled with recently had few complaints. Many of the duty-free restrictions listed above are regularly waived or completely ignored, such as the limit of five rolls of camera film. However, the prohibitions list is still strictly observed and something which seems perfectly innocent to you may well be considered indecent, offensive or directed against the Islamic Republic in the eyes of a customs officer. Once I had a three-week-old copy of a highly respected London newspaper, without one 'indecent' picture or a single mention of Iran, confiscated without any explanation. I hate to think what would happen to anyone who tried to bring anything seriously pornographic or propagandist into Iran.

Although not specifically listed in the customs regulations, it can safely be assumed that pork or anything porcine is best not taken into Iran. Any of the works of Salman Rushdie are in the same category.

All foreigners, including diplomats, are required to make out a currency declaration on entering Iran: see the Money section for details.

MONEY

Almost any hard currency is acceptable at banks; on the free market the US dollar is king, but pounds sterling and Deutschmarks are also widely traded. Any major travellers' cheques can be changed: American Express, Visa and Thomas Cook are all fine. Now that the exchange laws have been liberalised, the best way to change money is in cash at the bank. Leave your credit cards at home.

Currency

The official unit of currency is the rial (reyāl), although in conversation Iranians usually refer to the tōmān, a unit of 10 rials. In writing, prices are mostly expressed in rials. Since the unit is often omitted, you have to make absolutely sure whether you are talking about rials or tōmāns before settling on a price. To confuse matters, Iranians often give prices in rials when talking to foreigners, and thousands (or millions) are often left to be understood when talking about large sums. Rials are sometimes written in English as Rls or IR, but neither is a standard abbreviation. Since nouns in Persian do not take the plural when preceded by a number, 10 rials is dah reyāl, never dah reyālhā.

There are coins for 50, 20, 10, five and two rials in circulation, although you don't often see the two-rial coin nowadays. One-rial coins, which are no longer minted, are considered lucky despite being otherwise almost worthless, and you practically never see them in circulation. There are notes for 10,000, 5000, 2000, 1000, 500, 200 and 100 rials. Notes for 5000 rials are in short supply and 10,000-rial notes even more so. Banknotes are printed on one side in Persian and on the other in English. The new series have 'Islamic Republic of Iran – Bank Markazi Iran' on the English side, and the old series, which are still valid, just have 'Bank Markazi Iran'. Anything with the Shāh's face on is definitely not OK. Coins are only marked with Persian script and numerals.

Exchange Rates

'Free market' bank rates (see below for explanation) in April 1992 were as follows:

US$1	=	1435 rials
£1	=	2459 rials
DM1	=	856 rials
Y100	=	1070 rials
A$1	=	1084 rials
C$1	=	1200 rials
NZ$1	=	771 rials

Until 21 January 1991 there were several parallel exchange rates in use in Iran according to the type of transaction. The only two that were of much relevance to foreigners were the highly artificial official rate, which had been kept at between 65 and 70 rials to the US dollar since before the revolution, despite spiralling levels of inflation and an unquenchable demand for foreign currency; and the illegal and possibly dangerous (at least for foreigners) 'free market' rate which has risen to around 1500 rials to the US dollar.

On 21 January 1991 a new law required every Iranian bank to offer Iranians and foreigners alike a floating exchange rate equivalent to 'free market' levels. It took some time for news of this change to reach

the banks concerned, but by the time you read this you should be able to go to any foreign exchange branch of any bank in Iran and change any convertible foreign currency at a rate almost as high as the 'free market' rate. However the old official rate of around 65 rials to the US dollar is still in use for certain transactions, such as the sale of international air tickets to foreigners, and you should always check the rate beforehand. Surplus rials can be changed back into foreign currency, if you show the original exchange receipt and your currency declaration.

A list of current exchange rates is sometimes given in *Tehran Times*.

There is a small trade in Iranian currency in most of the neighbouring countries, but especially in Istanbul. Outside the immediate region, even in Western cities with large Iranian communities, it is very difficult to buy or sell rials in cash. Anyone is allowed to bring 20,000 rials in cash into Iran at any border, and to take out 5000 rials.

Banks

Although hours do vary from place to place, Iranian banks are generally open from 9 am to 4 or 4.30 pm, Saturday to Wednesday, and between 8.30 am and noon or 12.30 pm on Thursdays. Banks along the southern coastline usually close for the afternoon and reopen in the early evening, all year round. Branches inside hotels keep their own hours, and airports have a bank open whenever international flights arrive or depart. Banks at land borders should be open 24 hours a day, or at least whenever the crossing is open.

All banks are marked in both Persian and English. Banks offering foreign exchange facilities nearly always have the sign 'Exchange' or 'Foreign Exchange' displayed at the entrance or somewhere else visible from the street. At all such banks there should be at least one person who speaks competent English. You will need to take your passport with you when changing money. Most of the top hotels have a small bank inside, although not necessarily one offering a foreign exchange service.

Changing cash and travellers' cheques in any major convertible currency is fairly straightforward in Tehrān. In the provincial capitals, outside Tehrān, changing cash should be quite straightforward by the time you read this – in most cases you will have to go to the central branch of Bank Melli Iran. Outside the provincial capitals very few banks deal in foreign currency at all. Changing travellers' cheques is likely to be fraught with difficulty, except in a few of the major towns like Shīrāz and Esfahān. Even in Bandar-é Abbās, Iran's major international sea port, the only bank willing to touch my travellers' cheques said it would take a whole month to cash them as they would first have to be sent to Tehrān for authorisation. Travellers' cheques can be cashed in foreign currency, although it is easier to take rials. Commission charges on either cash or cheques are purely nominal. All major travellers' cheques are acceptable, including American Express.

Apart from banks there are also a number of private bureaux de change – nearly always marked in English in some way and with a display of foreign banknotes in the window – offering the 'free market' rate. However it is not entirely clear whether it is now legal for foreigners to use them, and in any case the receipts they issue may not be valid for repurchasing foreign currency. There may also be a temptation for them to give a lower rate to foreigners, since they don't usually display a list of rates.

It is possible for foreigners, whether residents or not, to operate private accounts with Iranian banks, although you will need references and will face lots of problems opening anything but a foreign currency deposit account. The Iranian banking system is not the world's most advanced, and in general money can only be withdrawn from an account at the branch where it is held. Rial cheques do exist, but few people or businesses are willing to accept them because of the hassle involved in cashing them. Rial travellers' cheques are much more useful and can be cashed without commission at any main branch of the issuing bank, or even used to settle hotel and other bills. Many private shopkeepers will cash them for a small commission. If you are carrying a large amount of Iranian currency, it is worth changing at least part of it into travellers' cheques.

A few foreign banks do have representative offices in Tehrān, but they are only there to cater to government and business customers and have no services for private travellers, even if you have an account at home with the bank concerned.

Credit cards are accepted at some of the foreign airline offices, but are otherwise almost completely useless.

Transferring Money

It is possible to have money from abroad transferred to a bank in Iran, and to collect it in foreign or Iranian currency. In theory the process takes three days to a week by telex, but I don't know any foreigner who has tried it. Some of the Iranian banks have branches in the UK, France and Germany among other places. If possible, have the money sent through one of these; otherwise you could discuss the options with a friendly bank manager in Tehrān. All sorts of arrangements are possible with private money-changers. From London I had a £250 cheque transferred to Iran over the weekend, and delivered to friends in used notes at a rate better than I would have been able to get anywhere in Iran; no papers were signed, no receipts issued and no commission was charged.

The Black Market

The black market or 'free market' (bāzār-é āzād in Persian) took quite a shock when the government liberalised the exchange laws, but continues to change US dollars, sterling and Deutschmarks at up to 5% above the bank rate. The current rate is 1370 rials for the US dollar. Other currencies are traded, but only on a small scale now that the banks also buy and sell at floating exchange rates. Along the Gulf there is a thriving business in UAE dirhams, and in the north there is a small trade in roubles, which are not available at the bank. Turkish lira are treated with utmost scorn everywhere except in small places close to the Turkish border. Afghan and Pakistani currencies are bought and sold near the respective borders.

In recent years the black market for currency has become very open, and it is common to see traders flashing wads of banknotes at passing traffic and pedestrians in certain streets of many towns. Although this is now entirely legal for Iranians, it is not clear whether foreigners can also play the game. In the past some foreigners who had been caught selling dollars on the street were forced to exchange US$1000 into rials at the official exchange rate. On the whole, the uncertainty about the legality of changing money privately, the very small advantage over the bank rate, the lack of any official receipt, and the slight risk of being cheated, make it more sensible to go to the bank.

One traveller wrote that he was asked for US dollar travellers' cheques to change on the black market in Shīrāz, at a rate only 5% lower than the cash rate.

Currency Declaration

All foreign visitors to Iran, including diplomats, are currently required to make out a currency declaration at customs on entry. Even if you aren't given a form, you are legally obliged to ask for one. One copy is kept at customs, usually after a check on your cash and travellers' cheques, and the other is for you to hold on to and show to customs when you leave Iran. You are allowed to bring in an unlimited amount of foreign currency in any form, but what you take out is meant to match, or at least not exceed, the amount you declared less the amount that you changed (with official receipts) or otherwise legally used in Iran. If you have foreign currency sent to you in Iran, the amount should be entered in your passport.

Currency checks on foreigners used to be quite strictly enforced, but nowadays nobody seems to care very much. On my last visit, the customs officers at Jolfā were very surprised that I should actually volunteer to make a currency declaration and certainly wouldn't have asked me otherwise; when I left at Bāzargān the old man in a cubicle who was responsible for checking my declaration had no interest at all in the currency, travellers' cheques and bank account book which I was trying to show him, and only wanted the form to add to his collection.

Now that the currency laws have been more or less liberalised, there seems to be little point in bothering with currency declarations, and they may gradually fade out of use in the typical Iranian way. In the meantime, make sure you don't lose the form, as you may still have some problems in taking all your money out without one.

Costs

For most travel necessities, and even luxuries, Iran is inexpensive by international standards, so long as you remember that you aren't always comparing like with like. A bare daily minimum budget, including land transport, would be around 10,000 rials, but it is safer to reckon on around 15,000 rials. If you intend to stay at good hotels, eat at the top restaurants, hire private taxis regularly and travel inside the country by air, you could do so fairly easily on around 30,000 rials a day. The only case where Iran does not offer good value for money is the hotels which require hard currency. At the time of writing there were only a few of these, but recent reports suggest that the practice has become almost universal.

Costs for most things are higher in Tehrān, but the most expensive place in Iran is Jazīré-yé Kīsh (Kīsh Island), a luxury free port and holiday centre in the Persian Gulf. Even here most prices are reasonable by regional standards. One of the cheapest towns in Iran is Zāhedān, a notorious haunt of smugglers and wheeler-dealers.

Some sample costs include:

City bus ticket	10 to 20 rials
Postcard	25 to 100 rials
One litre of regular grade petrol	70 rials
Small bottle of orangeade	70 to 120 rials
Packet of TIR Iranian cigarettes	600 to 800 rials
Packet of Marlboro cigarettes	1000 to 1300 rials
Meal of chelō kabāb-é barg, dūgh, yoghurt and bread	1200 to 1800 rials
One kg of pistachios	2500 to 6000 rials
50 grams of good quality Iranian caviar	5000 rials

Inflation Bear in mind that inflation is currently up to 70% on most things, although some state-controlled prices increase at only about 10% per annum, the 'official' inflation rate. Taxi fares in Tehrān have increased alarmingly of late and are considerably higher than in the rest of Iran. In general, state-controlled prices (such as transport fares and hotel rates) go up on or soon after the Iranian New Year (usually 21 March). Privately imported goods fluctuate in price according to the free market exchange rate against the dollar. Some goods, such as medicines and certain publications, are imported at the official exchange rate (about 65 rials to the US dollar) or one of several other artificial rates.

Stop Press The cost of travelling in Iran has increased substantially since this book was researched. Prices in rials have increased dramatically but the exchange rate has not shifted to compensate for this. Food prices in restaurants and shops have at least doubled, and domestic airfares were tripled from 21 March 1992. Fares for land transport were also increased. Virtually all hotels and *mosāferkhūnés* (cheap lodging houses) now charge foreigners in hard currency, so the price for basic accommodation is now at least US$5.

Tipping

In most cases concerning the short-term foreign visitor, tipping is no more and no less than it should be – an optional reward for good service. Although there are many circumstances where a small tip is expected, you are extremely unlikely to have a waiter hovering expectantly near your table after delivering the bill. For the time being at least, you need never feel that tipping is obligatory, but the situation may change depending on how future foreign visitors behave. If too many foreigners allow themselves to be overcharged and tip excessively, then they will make life difficult for others. On the other hand, it is worth remembering that many Iranians in a service capacity do make a special effort to help foreigners, and probably deserve some extra appreciation.

As a general rule, taxi-drivers are not tipped, waiters and hotel staff sometimes are, and hairdressers always are. Taxi fares are meant to be either fixed or prearranged and include any service charge; the only case where you might pay a tip is if you have

chartered a taxi and the driver has been particularly helpful.

In restaurants the rule is that if the waiter brings the bill to your table, you pay a tip of up to 10% if warranted, or up to 15% in more expensive places, but if you pay the bill to someone sitting at a desk, there is no need to tip.

At the hairdresser, you tip everyone who attends to you, although the largest tip goes to the person who actually cuts your hair. The total amount of tips should be about 25% over the bill, but you can give more if you want.

Hotel bills usually include a service charge, and it is not necessary to pay any extra, although it is normal to round it up. Hotel domestics are very poorly paid and appreciate a small tip in money or kind, but rarely expect one automatically. It is correct to tip hotel receptionists if they have gone out of their way to help, perhaps by making available an otherwise unavailable room (generous contribution appreciated) or by doing something else beyond their normal duty.

Porters at hotels, airports, train stations and bus stations generally expect between 100 and 200 rials for each piece of luggage, more if the bags are heavy or the distance covered is long. If more than one porter is involved, pay each separately.

It is usually correct to offer a small amount of money or a small present to anyone who acts as a guide for you or opens a building which is normally closed, but this may be refused, even if you insist twice, as custom demands.

In cases where what you are paying is more of a bribe than a regular service charge (eg to a receptionist who claims that the hotel is full but may be persuaded to relent) discretion is called for.

Bargaining

It is not true that there is no such thing as a fixed price in Iran. As a rough guide, you can tell whether the price of an item is negotiable by the presence or absence of a price label. In the bazaar virtually all prices are negotiable, whereas in state shops bargaining is probably going to be a complete waste of time. Even where there is no listed price, you may find that everywhere in town charges almost exactly the same for an identical article. If you always assume that you are being cheated, you will offend people who would never try to take advantage of a foreigner, and if you always accept the first price you are offered you will surely be taken for a ride more than once. It is impossible to give any hard-and-fast rules about bargaining; in one place the first price you are offered may be 50% above the going rate, in another 500%, and in a third it may be exactly the same as the locals pay.

At least in theory, taxi fares are fixed by the hour, or by distance for shared taxis, but you may find it impossible to get a taxi at the correct price, or even to find out what the local rate is supposed to be. Sometimes you will be quoted an outrageously high price simply because you are a foreigner, and at other times you will be offered the same price as everyone else.

Rates in all hotels and mosāferkhūnés – whether state-owned or privately operated – are fixed by the government and are almost never negotiable. With Iran's accommodation shortage, at most times of the year most hotels have few problems in filling rooms at the set price. The exception might be if you were planning to stay as a long-term resident, or if you're staying at a hotel in the Gulf region in summer, when some hotels are almost empty.

When it comes to charging for things for which the price is negotiable, there are at least four categories of customer: locals, Iranians from out of town, foreigners speaking Persian and foreigners not speaking Persian. The foreigner who doesn't speak Persian is easy prey, but not only foreigners are overcharged; I was told the story of a Tehrānī who went to Mashhad and took a ride in a local minibus, and before getting off asked what the fare was. The driver said it would be 1000 rials. The correct fare was about 30 rials.

Once you have agreed on a price, you can't change it later. If you don't fix a price at the outset (eg for taxi hire), it is too late to complain about it later. The only sure way to avoid being cheated is to know the correct price, and for this knowledge you have to spend a long time in Iran or rely on the advice of local friends. And even then, the correct price can vary significantly from place to place. The prices I have given in this book are only intended as a guide; you may be able to get a better price than I did, or you may not.

WHEN TO GO

Whatever the time of year, there is always some part of Iran which is at its best for visiting. Although spring and autumn are the ideal times to tour Iran, you needn't worry too much if you can only make it in summer or winter, so long as you do a little planning and take a few precautions.

If you are making an extensive tour of Iran generally the best times to visit are late March to early June and late September to early November, when the climate in most parts of Iran is mild and pleasant. However the most agreeable time to visit the southern coast is in winter, and the north-west and north-east are at their best between late spring and early summer and between late summer and early autumn. The Gulf is horrible in summer. For more specific information, see the Climate section of the Facts about the Country chapter, and the entries on specific places.

Many people prefer not to visit Iran or other Islamic countries during Ramazān, the Muslim month of fasting. Moharram, the month of mourning, can also be a difficult time to travel.

For the whole of the second half of March, transport and accommodation become very difficult as Iranians return to their home towns and villages for the Persian New Year celebrations (usually 21 to 24 March). It is better to avoid travelling around Iran at all at this period.

WHAT TO BRING

The backpack has bad connotations in Iran, and is likely to be associated with the hippy ethos, which has never fitted in very well with the Islamic Revolutionary ideal. I have never seen an Iranian wearing a backpack. Some hotels have been known to refuse to take foreigners possessing such an item. If at all possible, take a shoulder-bag or suitcase instead.

There are willing porters at all airports, ports, train and bus stations, nearly all hotels and even quite a few mosāferkhūnés. Taxi drivers are always ready to lend a hand with bags. You could travel almost anywhere in Iran without having to carry a single piece of luggage yourself. Although it is standard and sensible advice to carry as little as possible, if you are travelling heavy you will have fewer problems in Iran than in most countries. Hotels are usually happy to hold luggage for guests, even for several weeks, and surplus gear can be posted out of Iran at very low cost.

A very good book to read before packing your bags is *The Tropical Traveller* by John Hatt (Pan Books, London, 1985, £2.95). My own selective list of things to consider taking runs as follows:

a universal sink plug (Islamic customs favour washing in running water, and in most places you won't have the choice); any favourite cosmetic or personal items (available locally but imported brands are mostly expensive, although basic things like soap and toothpaste are cheap and easy to find); a complete shaving kit with spare blades and shaving soap; a camera with all the film and equipment you will need (only a limited range is available), with a robust carrying case including a bag of silica gel to protect the camera from changes in temperature and humidity; a pair of binoculars; tubes of detergent and a scrubbing-brush, together with a length of cord or string for a makeshift washing-line; a large number of B&W or colour passport photos; at least one photocopy of the first few pages of your passport (keep another copy at home); the address and telephone number of your embassy in Tehrān or the embassy representing your country's interests (memorise the telephone number); an address book; a notebook; a good short-wave radio; a Swiss Army knife; a compass; spare batteries (Iranian brands are next to useless, and imported ones are expensive); toilet paper, if you can't adjust to local customs (not necessary if you are staying only in the better hotels); a torch, longlife candles and matches or a lighter for those all-too-frequent power cuts; a water-flask; small pres-

ents from home for Iranian friends, chosen more for their novelty than monetary value; a money belt or equivalent; a small sewing kit with spare shoelaces and buttons; a medical kit (see the Health section) with an adequate supply of any special medications and a doctor's note to show at customs or elsewhere; receipts for any travellers' cheques, kept separately from the cheques themselves; a shopping bag or a small supply of plastic bags (very few shops in Iran have them); a small library of reading material as an alternative to the less than frenzied Iranian nightlife; any of those small luxury items without which life isn't worth living.

Clothing
The following is only a rough guide; read the Climate section before considering what clothes to bring. For absolutely essential advice on what is considered acceptable dress for visitors to Iran, refer to the Culture section of the Facts about the Country chapter before packing.

In summer take lightweight and easily washed clothes of natural fabrics, a cardigan or pullover for the cooler nights, a pair of sunglasses and – only if you are male – a hat which will protect your face from the sun. Clothes of synthetic materials will melt next to the skin in a fire and can encourage fungal infections. In winter take mostly warm clothing, including a coat, scarf and hat (men only), and two or three thin sweaters rather than one thick one and, if you're likely to need them, boots or shoes equipped to cope with heavy snow and slippery pavements. In spring and autumn take a sensible compromise, according to the conditions in the places you are going to visit. For men, a suit will only be necessary if you are travelling on business or planning to mix in the higher reaches of Iranian society; a smart jacket is useful but rarely essential. An umbrella may be useful in the Caspian provinces in the rainy season.

Informally Iranians of both sexes often wear sandals or flip-flops (thongs), but these are not generally considered acceptable in formal or business contexts.

TOURIST OFFICES
Local Tourist Offices
There are state tourist offices in all the pro-.

vincial centres as well as Ghazvīn and Ghom. Coming under the control of the rather ominous-sounding Ministry of Culture & Islamic Guidance, each 'Tourism & Exploration Office' is responsible for 'cultural affairs, propaganda, literature and arts, audio-visual production, archaeology, preservation of the cultural heritage, tourism, press and libraries'. Although the officers do often try to be helpful, giving tourist information to foreigners is only a very small part of their job, and you shouldn't expect lots of glossy handouts or even necessarily anything at all in English.

Most, but not all, have useful free maps of the relevant city or province. Anything in the way of hard information usually has to be prised out of the staff, although there are a few honourable exceptions. English may or may not be spoken. Apart from the dismally unhelpful national office in Tehrān, each branch is only responsible for affairs in its own province. Tourist offices are open from 8 am to 2 pm, Saturday to Wednesday, and on Thursday between 8 am and about noon.

In Tehrān, go to the Department of Tourism & Pilgrimage. There are also small branch offices at Tehrān railway station and in the international terminal of Tehrān airport. See the Tehrān section for more details. Outside Tehrān there are tourist offices in Ahvāz, Arāk, Bākhtarān, Bandar-é Abbās, Būshehr, Esfahān, Ghazvīn, Ghom, Hamadān, Īlām, Kermān, Khorram Ābād, Mashhad, Orūmīyé, Rasht, Sanandaj, Sārī, Semnān, Shahr-é Kord, Shīrāz, Tabrīz, Yāsūj, Yazd, Zāhedān and Zanjān. For addresses and phone numbers, see the relevant city sections.

Tourist Offices Outside Iran
There are none. Optimists could try contacting the Press & Information Officer at any Iranian embassy.

USEFUL ORGANISATIONS
There are no budget travel agencies, hostel organisations, or information centres for disabled travellers. Some useful addresses are listed in the Tehrān chapter.

CALENDAR
Three calendars are in common use in Iran. The Persian solar calendar is the one in official and everyday use, the Muslim lunar calendar is used in Islamic religious matters and the Western (Gregorian) calendar is used in dealings with foreigners and in some history books (ie not very much). The Zoroastrians also have their own calendar. Traditionally both the Persian and Muslim days are reckoned as starting at sunset, but nowadays midnight is, for most practical purposes, regarded as the start of the Persian day. There is no easy way of converting a date from one system to another except by referring to an Iranian diary or calendar.

Persian Calendar
The modern Persian solar calendar, a direct descendant of the ancient Zoroastrian calendar, is calculated from the first day of spring in the year of the Hegira (*hejrat*) – the flight of the Prophet Mohammad from Mecca to Medina in 622 AD. It has 365 days (366 every leap-year), with its New Year (*Nō Rūz*) usually falling on 21 March by the Western calendar. For example, 30 March 1989 AD was 10 Farvardīn 1368 by the Persian calendar. Dates given by the Persian calendar sometimes have AHS added after the year, when written in English. The names of the Persian months are as follows:

	Persian Month	Approximate Equivalent
SPRING (Bahār)	Farvardīn	21 Mar-20 Apr
	Ordībehesht	21 Apr-21 May
	Khordād	22 May-21 Jun
SUMMER (Tābestān)	Tīr	22 Jun-22 Jul
	Mordād	23 Jul-22 Aug
	Shahrīvar	23 Aug-22 Sep
AUTUMN (Pā'īz)	Mehr	23 Sep-22 Oct
	Ābān	23 Oct-21 Nov
	Āzar	22 Nov-21 Dec
WINTER (Zamestān)	Dei	22 Dec-20 Jan
	Bahman	21 Jan-19 Feb
	Esfand	20 Feb-20 Mar

Muslim Calendar

The Muslim calendar – in official or unofficial use in all Islamic countries – starts from the month before the Hegira but, since it is based on the lunar year of 354 or 355 days, it is currently out of step with the Persian solar calendar by some 40 years. The Persian names of the 12 months of the Muslim calendar are, in order: Moharram, Safar, Rabī'-ol-Avval, Rabī'-ol-Osānī (or Rabī'-ol-Ākhar), Jamādī-l-Ūlā, Jamādī-l-Okhrā, Rajab, Sha'bān, Ramazān, Shavvāl, Zū-l-Gha'dé and Zū-l-Hejjé.

Western Calendar

The months of the Western (Gregorian) calendar have entered Persian by way of French and are pronounced as follows: Zhānveyé, Fevreyé, Mārs, Āvrīl, Mé, Zhū'an, Zhūyé, Ūt, Septāmbr, Oktober, Novāmbr and Desāmbr.

Zoroastrian Calendar

The Zoroastrian calendar has a solar year of 12 months of 30 days each, and five additional days. The week has no place in this system, and each of the 30 days of the month is named after and presided over by its own angel or archangel. The 1st, 8th, 15th and 23rd of each month are holy days. As in the Persian calendar, the Zoroastrian year begins in March at the vernal equinox. The months of the Zoroastrian calendar (most of which have the same names as in the Persian calendar) run as follows:

SPRING (Bahār)	Farvardīn
	Ordībehesht
	Khordād
SUMMER (Tābestān)	Tīr
	Amordād
	Shahrīvar
AUTUMN (Pā'īz)	Mehr
	Ābān
	Āzar
WINTER (Zāmestān)	Dei
	Bahman
	andarmaz

BUSINESS HOURS & HOLIDAYS

Business Hours

The vast majority of businesses and offices close completely on Friday, the Muslim day of rest, and have a half-day on Thursday. Most shops and markets are open all day on Thursday but closed on Friday. Shops are generally open until about 8 pm, and markets until just before sunset. Bus company offices at the terminals in larger cities open daily from early morning until the evening, more or less without a break. Bus company offices in towns keep shorter, less regular hours, and may or may not be open on Friday and public holidays. In smaller places bus company offices can keep very irregular hours and are sometimes only active just before a bus is due to leave, and perhaps an extra hour or two a day. With very few exceptions (eg the head office in Tehrān and the office on Jazīré-yé Kīsh) Iran Air offices are closed on Thursday afternoons and Fridays but open on public holidays. The working hours of Iran Asseman are a complete mystery, but in general they appear to close after about noon and open on some mornings.

Foreign embassies, consulates and businesses follow the Iranian working week, closing on Friday and often on one other day of the week, usually Saturday or Sunday, as well as on their own national holidays. Some embassies and consulates keep very undemanding hours, and it is sensible to telephone first before visiting.

In the southern islands and along the Persian Gulf and the Sea of Oman, most activity comes to a halt for the afternoon because of the heat, and offices reopen for a few hours in the early evening. The siesta is almost absolute in the islands of the Gulf, although public transport, where it exists, does not stop completely in the afternoon.

Government offices are generally open from 8 am to 2 pm, Saturday to Wednesday. Some offices, especially ministries in Tehrān, are closed completely on Thursday and others open only from 8 to 11.30 am or noon. In general Thursday is not a good day for conducting official business. If in doubt telephone first, or get a Persian-speaker to telephone for you. Because of the relaxed Iranian working life, the person you want or need to see may only turn up at certain times of the week, and there is little point in turning up without checking first.

Most museums are closed on Monday but open on Friday, although some are open every day. Hours are at least from 10 am to 4 pm, sometimes with a break for lunch. Unless you are a Muslim, it is better not to visit mosques on a Friday or on religious holidays. Churches usually have their main service of the week on Sunday, when they are not open for sightseeing.

Religious Holidays

The following holidays follow the Muslim lunar calendar. The dates given here are those announced for 1992. Each subsequent year they will fall roughly 11 days earlier against the Western calendar, but the exact dates depend on various astrological observations by the religious authorities closer to the event. Quite often they are extended by government decree for a day or more if they fall near the Iranian weekend. There are many other religious festivals, including quite a few mourning days, but only the following are listed as public holidays in 1992. The dates given in brackets are those according to the Muslim lunar calendar.

4 to 6 April(1 to 3 Shavvāl)
Eid-é Fetr (Festival of the Breaking of the Fast) – the festival marking the end of Ramazān, the month of fasting. After sunset on the last day of Ramazān Muslims spill out onto the streets, drivers honk their horns in celebration and virtually everyone indulges in some serious overeating. Little business is transacted at this time except in the catering trade.

10 July(10 Moharram)
Āshūrā-yé Hoseinī – anniversary of the martyrdom of Hosein, the third emām of the Shi'ites, in battle at Kerbala in October 680 AD. This is celebrated by religious dramas and also by sombre parades of devout Shi'ite men in blood-splattered black shirts scourging themselves to the near hypnotic chant of Yā Hosein! Yā Hosein! Yā Hosein! ('O Hosein!' etc). Resist the temptation to take a snapshot.

9 September(17 Rabī'-ol-Avval)
Mīlād-é Hazrat-é Mohammad – Birthday of the Prophet Mohammad

Ramazān Muslims don't see Ramazān merely as an unpleasant ordeal to be put up with (although some do), but as a chance of performing a sort of ritual cleansing of body and mind. Many medical experts have come out in support of the benefits of fasting at Ramazān. Many Iranians, especially in the urban areas, don't fully observe the fast, but most people will fast for at least part of it. Ramazān is imposed on everyone in Iran, including foreigners and non-Muslims, although anyone can eat, drink and smoke behind closed doors. Some people are exempted from the fast (including pregnant women, travellers, the old, and those who are sick and do not feel that they are able to keep to the fast) but they are expected not to eat or drink in front of others who are fasting. So Iran Air still serves food to passengers in the daytime in Ramazān, and roadside cafés still serve bus passengers (and anyone else, for that matter).

This can be a trying period for the non-Muslim, and it is traditionally a favourite time of year for expatriates based in the Middle East to take their annual leave. When Ramazān coincides with a spell of hot weather, it can be very difficult indeed to resist the temptation to drink out of doors. When it coincides with public holidays or other festivities, then they are celebrated in a much more sober manner than in other years. It is considered a very great sin to drink alcohol during Ramazān, and the penalties are much stiffer than at other times of year. The Komīté (the Islamic Revolutionary Committee of the Revolutionary Guards) is at its most active in this month, and until very recently it used to make some new widely resented crackdown at the start of every Ramazān. In 1991, for the first time, the Komīté largely retreated from the streets of Tehrān and many other cities during Ramazān.

Many hotels in all categories keep their restaurants open in the daytime during

Ramazān, or at least allow guests to order food in their rooms, since guests can consider themselves to be travelling and hence free from the obligation to fast. Other restaurants either close altogether or else only open for dinner after dark. Many food shops remain open throughout Ramazān, and you can buy food to take away and eat in your room. You shouldn't have great problems in larger cities, but you may not find any source of food at all during the daytime in rural areas and small towns. For this reason, Ramazān is probably not the best time of year to travel adventurously. Offices keep odd hours, tempers can flare and very little serious business gets done.

National Holidays

The following holidays follow the Persian solar calendar and usually fall on the same day each year by the Western calendar. They may be be extended by government decree for a day or more if they fall near the Iranian weekend, and extra holidays are sometimes declared at short notice. Since they can easily disrupt your travel plans, it's worth enquiring about forthcoming public holidays when you arrive in Iran. *Tehran Times* usually gives warning a few days in advance.

The dates given in brackets are those according to the Persian solar calendar.

11 February(22 Bahman)
   Pīrūzī-yé Shokūhmand-é Enghelāb-é Eslāmī-yé Īrān ('Magnificent Victory of the Islamic Revolution of Iran') – anniversary of Khomeinī's coming to power in 1979
20 March(29 Esfand)
   Rūz-é Mellī Shodan-é San'at-é Naft (Oil Industry Nationalisation Day) – anniversary of the nationalisation of the Iranian oil industry in 1951, previously dominated by the Anglo-Iranian Oil Company
21 to 24 March(1 to 4 Farvardīn)
   Eid-é Nō Rūz – Iranian New Year (see below under Nō Rūz)
1 April(12 Farvardīn)
   Rūz-é Jomhūrī-yé Eslāmī (Islamic Republic Day) – the Iranian national day, marking the anniversary of the establishment of the Islamic Republic of Iran in 1979

2 April(13 Farvardīn)
   Sīzdah Bedar (13th Day of the Iranian New Year) – ancient holiday on which Iranians traditionally leave their houses for the day (see below under Nō Rūz)
4 June(14 Khordād)
   Rehlat-é Jāngodāz-é Rahbar-é Kabīr-é Jomhūrī-yé Eslāmī-yé Īrān ('Heart-Rending Departure of the Great Leader of the Islamic Republic of Iran') – anniversary of the death of Emām Khomeinī in 1989
5 June(15 Khordād)
   Sālrūz-é Gheyām-é Ommat-é Mosalmān-é Īrān ('Anniversary of the Iranian Popular Uprising') – anniversary of the arrest of Emām Khomeinī in 1963, following his speech urging the Muslims of the world to rise up against the superpowers, which inspired a number of demonstrations against the Shāh

CULTURAL EVENTS

The holidays listed above are not celebrated as much as might be expected; the religious holidays are times to go to the mosque, and offer few public celebrations of great interest to the non-Muslim, except perhaps for some of the mourning days. Moharram, the month of mourning, and especially Ramazān, the month of fasting, can be rather trying periods for the non-Muslim visitor. Notes on these and the other movable religious festivals are given above under Religious Holidays.

For most Iranians, the main non-religious cultural event of the year is the extended period of celebrations marking the Persian New Year or *Nō Rūz*. Other than this, there are few great cultural events of particular touristic appeal, except perhaps for market day in the provinces, and it is difficult to find information about them except locally.

Nō Rūz

Even before the Achaemenian era, the coming of spring was celebrated on a large scale throughout Persia. Later on, the start of the Zoroastrian year was fixed at the vernal equinox. Nowadays the festivities are largely private, and Iranians traditionally return to their home villages and towns to celebrate the New Year with their friends and relatives, much as people in the West do for Christmas. Apart from the inevitable feasting and entertaining, many ancient rituals still form part of Nō Rūz (literally 'New Day'), some of them to ward off evil spirits and some of them essentially Zoroastrian in origin. This is not an Islamic holiday, and the Khomeinī regime tried, largely in vain, to discourage undue emphasis on the festival with its pre-Islamic associations.

Chahārshambé-yé Sūrī (the last Wednesday of the Persian year) is an important event in the celebrations leading up to Nō Rūz. On its eve it is the age-old custom for Iranians to light small bonfires in the street over which all the assembled guests, young or old, must jump to secure their good luck in the coming year. It is said that the flames purge the body of any evil spirits. Of course, the symbolism of this ritual is purely Zoroastrian in origin, and its observance, while not actually forbidden, is hardly encouraged by the Islamic authorities.

On *Sīzdah Bedar*, the 13th day of the Persian New Year, it is traditional for people to leave their homes for the day, and urban Iranians often go for picnics in the country with their friends and relatives. It would be a perfect day for house-breakers, because whole streets are emptied, but perhaps even criminals think it's bad luck to stay behind.

It is exceptionally difficult to find hotel accommodation throughout the New Year period (roughly for the whole of the second half of March) and most public transport is also booked up very heavily. Although Nō Rūz is an excellent occasion for staying with Iranian friends, it is not very sensible to make any travel plans at this time.

POST & TELECOMMUNICATIONS
Post
The Iranian international postal service is reliable and reasonably swift, the domestic one reliable but paralytically slow. In fact sending a letter from Iran to the other side of the world often takes no longer than getting it from one part of Iran to another. For airmail *(post-é havā'ī)* between Tehrān and Europe count on a minimum delivery time of one week, or two weeks for Canada, USA and Australasia; add up to a week for places outside Tehrān. I don't think it's necessarily

true that letters or aerogrammes are processed any more quickly than postcards.

In 1992, the airmail charge for a letter of minimum weight (50 grams) was around 300 rials, or 250 rials for a postcard, according to destination. There is little point in bothering with an uncertain surface mail when airmail rates are so low. Registered *(sefāresh)* and express *(ekspres)* services are available at a small extra charge, but without advice of delivery. Registered post is always the first to grab the censor's attention, and it may be less risky to send anything sensitive by ordinary mail. It is not safe to send cash through the post.

Iranian decorative stamps are very colourful and you may want to leave space on your envelope or postcard for as many as possible. Post office clerks are usually happy to let foreigners rummage through the latest issues, or else you can buy some of the collectors' items, at upwards of twice face value, from some cigarette vendors or outside a few of the bigger post offices.

Postboxes are few and far between except outside post offices. They are mostly painted yellow.

Parcel Post Sending parcels out of Iran is a major exercise in form shuffling, guaranteed to take at least twice as long as you would ever have thought possible. You have to take

your package – unwrapped – to the parcel post counter *(daftar-é amānāt-é postī)* of the head post office *(postkhūné-yé markazī)* in town, and there have it checked, packaged and signed for in triplicate. You may need to show your passport. Regulations about what may be posted out of Iran were always up to the individual interpretation of the customs officer on duty at every head post office, but they loosened up early in 1991. It is now possible to mail home a reasonable quantity of the usual souvenirs without much difficulty. Airmail parcel rates are very low, and delivery times little more than for letter post.

Courier Services DHL Worldwide Express operates into and out of Iran: see the Tehrān section for its address in the capital. It is also possible to have packages air freighted on most Iran Air international services: enquire locally.

Poste Restante You can have mail, including parcels, sent to you care of the local head post office anywhere in Iran, although the service is very little used, even in Tehrān. Instruct all correspondents to write your name very clearly and to underline your surname. Since most people fronting up at the poste restante counter *(daftar-é post restānt)* are foreigners, mail is filed according to the Latin alphabet. Always ask for a check on every conceivable initial of your first name, surname or title; I once had a letter for me filed under E for Esq. Bearers of multi-barrelled surnames are in for fun. Poste restante mail appears to be held almost indefinitely, even in spite of requests for it to be forwarded. There is a purely nominal collection fee.

Take your passport with you. Have mail addressed very clearly as follows:

Title Name <u>SURNAME</u>
Poste Restante
Head Post Office
Name of Town
ISLAMIC REPUBLIC of IRAN

Telephones
Chaotic is one of many words I could use to describe the Iranian telephone system. I have never even seen an Iranian telephone directory. It is rare to find a public telephone which works properly every time, even for local calls. Trunk calls are often very problematic, and international calls to or from anywhere outside Tehrān are fraught with difficulty.

Local Calls Most of the yellow public telephone boxes you'll find in Iran are only good – if good is the right word – for local calls. They take two-rial coins (which are no longer in common circulation), or five-rial coins, 10-rial coins, or any combination of the three, depending on the age of the cashbox. With some, one coin is enough for any length of call and with others you have to feed the box every few minutes when you hear the rapid bleeping tone. If you cannot find a public telephone that works, you can make a local call from many shops, where the standard charge for every few minutes is 20 rials. You can also make local calls, free of charge, from your hotel room or the lobby. You dial an initial code, usually 9, or go through the switchboard. Airports and main bus stations usually have one public telephone from which local calls can be made without charge.

Trunk Calls Trunk calls can be made from certain telephones at airports and main bus stations, or in ranks outside some post or telegraph offices. Ask *Telefon-é rāh-é dūr kojāst?* ('Where's there a long-distance telephone?'). Instructions are written in English and the telephones take 10, 20 and 50-rial coins. Although charges are very low, a large pocketful of change is called for if you're talking for more than a short time. It is also possible to book trunk calls at any telegraph office *(telegrāfkhūné)* with a wait of perhaps an hour, or at most hotels with a wait of perhaps 15 minutes and a commission charge. It's usually fairly easy to telephone out of Tehrān, but from all other cities it is often difficult to get through even to Tehrān.

From smaller places it is often all but impossible to make a trunk call anywhere at busy times. Lines tend to go down in bad weather. Dialling codes for most places are given under Information or Post & Telecommunications.

International Calls Most hotels, and even mosāferkhūnés with their own lines, have the capacity to make direct-dial international calls, but they are under strict instructions to book foreign calls only through the operator. Even so, hotels are by far the easiest public places from which to make international calls, and the commission they charge is not unreasonable. International calls are relatively easy to make in Tehrān, where they can sometimes be booked less than half an hour ahead, but very frustrating elsewhere in Iran, even in major cities like Esfahān or Bandar-é Abbās. If possible, save up all international calls for Tehrān; if not go to any head telephone or telegraph office (*markaz-é telefon* or *edāré-yé koll-é mokhābarāt*) and expect to be given a booking several hours, if not a day, ahead and even then to have to wait up to a couple of hours for a connection. It's better to get your hotel to book the call for you: you'll still have to wait, but at least you can do so in your own room.

Charges to most Western countries are around 1000 rials a minute; from hotels add a commission of up to 100%. There is a minimum charging period of three minutes; person-to-person calls are charged at the rate for one extra minute. If there is no connection there is no charge. Reverse-charge calls cannot be made to or from Iran.

In most cases the line into Iran sounds very clear but at the other end it is faint and crackly. It is not always easy to telephone Iran from abroad, even through the operator, and you shouldn't rely on receiving calls at prearranged times.

The Hotel Pirūzī is, among its other faults, also a little unprofessional about monitoring guests' telephone calls: one local call I made was audibly interrupted more than once by the hotel operator asking his colleague *chī goft?* ('What did he say?'). At more discreet places you usually only hear breathing in the background, or the line just becomes faint.

Telegram, Telex & Fax
From any telegraph office, you can send telegrams out of Iran in English, or within Iran in Persian. Charges to most Western countries are around 160 rials a word with a minimum of seven words. A word counts as a group of up to 10 letters or characters, and the words of the address are chargeable. International telegrams out of Iran rarely take more than a couple of working days to get through. Delivery into Iran is less reliable. The domestic telegram service is quite hopeless, and can take a week or more. Inland telegrams are absurdly cheap, but so they ought to be.

There are telex services, local and international, at the head telegraph offices in several Iranian cities. Some of the top hotels also run a machine for guests' use, at a price. Telex charges from telegraph offices are about 1500 rials a minute to most Western countries, with a minimum of three minutes but no service charge. Hotels charge about double that. You should be able to collect telexes sent to you care of a telex bureau if you leave your name and telephone number.

An international fax service has recently been started at the head telegraph office in Tehrān.

TIME
Iranians place no value on time. You will see very few public clocks, even in Tehrān, and many Iranians do not possess such a thing as a watch. Promises like 'I'll see you at seven' should not be taken literally, especially when the meeting is to be at your place. The Iranians' flexible sense of time does not always work both ways however, as Iranians generally expect foreigners to be punctual.

Time throughout Iran is 3½ hours ahead of GMT. In 1991 Iran introduced its own summer time system (daylight saving); clocks go forward one hour between mid-March and mid-September. The exact dates are determined each year.

When it's noon in Tehrān, it's 1 pm in

Kabul, 1.30 pm in Islamabad, 5.30 pm in Tokyo, 6.30 pm in Sydney, 8.30 pm in Auckland, 12.30 am in San Francisco, 3.30 am in New York and Toronto, 8.30 am in London, and 11.30 am in Ankara, Baghdad and Moscow, without allowing for summer time.

ELECTRICITY
When it's working, the electricity system is on 220 V, 50 cycles AC. The sockets have two circular holes. Be prepared for power cuts when you least expect them, such as in the middle of a hot shower or when listening to your favourite programme on the BBC. Imported batteries are expensive and the locally produced ones are short lived, so take spares with you. Since few hotels have a backup generator powerful enough to provide emergency lighting in guests' rooms, keep a torch or at least some candles in an easily accessible part of your luggage.

LAUNDRY
There are plenty of reliable laundries in most Iranian cities (but no launderettes) and you can also have your dirty shirts or skirts brought back to respectability at many of the better hotels. Charges are low: even at the Laleh International Hotel in Tehrān you can have a shirt laundered the same day for 400 rials, a pair of pants for 450 rials, or a handkerchief for only 100 rials. Dry cleaning works out at about 50% more. 'Where is there a laundry?' translates as *Rakht-shūkhūné kojāst?* in Persian. If you're doing your own washing, a universal bath plug is indispensable.

WEIGHTS & MEASURES
It used to be that various reaches of the Persian Empire would have their own system of weights and measures, but nowadays the metric system has permeated to almost every part of Iran. There is a standard conversion table at the back of this book. You may still come across the *sīr* (about 75 grams) and the *chārak* (10 sīr) in some remoter places. Gold and other precious metals are still measured by the *mesghāl*, equal to 4.7 grams. The *farsang* (sometimes known in English as the

parasang) is an old Persian measure of distance which always used to differ from place to place but is quoted in one recent reference book as measuring exactly 6.24 km. You may still hear the farsang used.

Feet and nautical miles continue to be used in aeronautical and naval circles.

BOOKS & MAPS
There is a good range of English language books on Iran, but finding copies of some of them is no longer easy. There have been no guidebooks written since the Islamic Revolution, except for this one. Iran has for many centuries held a particular appeal to British travellers, and I make no apologies for the national bias in this selection of authors.

Travel & Society
The Hon G N Curzon, MP (later Lord Curzon) – of whom it was most famously said 'My name is George Nathaniel Curzon, I am a most superior person' – in his two-volume *Persia and the Persian Question* (London, 1892) is characteristically scathing about all things Persian. It is authoritative as both a historical work and a travel book. The original is now very hard to come by, but there is a recent abridged reprint, *Curzon's Persia* (Sidgwick & Jackson, 1986, £9.95), which skips the heavier historical chapters.

Dame Freya Stark's *Beyond Euphrates* (John Murray, London, 1951; Century Hutchinson, London, 1989, £4.95) is packed with affectionate reminiscences from a fearless lone woman's travels through Luristan (roughly the present-day province of Lorestān) and other remote parts of Iran in the '30s. Her *Valleys of the Assassins* (London, 1934) describes a similarly uncompromising journey through the mountainous Caspian region of that name. Other books by Stark dwell briefly on various forays into Persia.

Written between 1933 and 1934, Robert Byron's *The Road to Oxiana* (Macmillan, London, 1937; Pan, London, 1981, £3.95) is widely acknowledged as one of the great travel books of its era. Recorded in Byron's admirably terse style, it is a vividly observed and often hilariously funny diary of a slow passage from England to the River Oxus in north-west Afghanistan, with lengthy jaunts through Iran en route. Although Byron has a scholarly preoccupation with Islamic architecture, the book remains a travel classic book more for its lively descriptive prose and for its often biting sketches of contacts with local people and encounters with disobliging officials. Byron is particularly critical of the heavy-handed British influence in Persia at the time.

Covering a haphazard 1950s jaunt by the author and friend from England to the Hindu Kush by way of Turkey and Iran, Eric Newby's *A Short Walk in the Hindu Kush* (London, 1972; Picador, London, 1982) is one of those gloriously eccentric travel books that could only have been written by an Englishman. Although more about Afghanistan than Iran, it does deserve a mention here as it is one of the funniest travel books I have ever read.

Accounts of Iran published in the West after the Islamic Revolution have tended to err on the sensationalist side. One of the best must be John Simpson's *Behind Iranian Lines* (Fontana, London, £4.99, A$14.95). Simpson shared Khomeinī's fateful Paris to Tehrān flight in 1979, and took full advantage of an unexpected invitation to return in 1987. A BBC correspondent, he writes perceptively and dispassionately about most aspects of Iranian life. The book may still be available at good bookshops in Pakistan for Rs 125.

A rare genuine modern travel book, Nick Danziger's *Danziger's Travels: Beyond Forbidden Frontiers* (Collins, London, 1987, £5.95, A$16.95) covers an overland and substantially illegal journey between 1984 and 1985 through Turkey, Iran, Afghanistan, Pakistan and China to Hong Kong, without much regard for tiresome formalities like visas, entry and exit stamps or travel permits. Loaded with enough hair-raising adventures to make all but the most seasoned traveller feel like a package tourist, Danziger's book proves that the age of the great traveller is not quite dead.

Out of Iran by Sousan Azadi 'with' Angela Ferrante (Macdonald, London, 1987, £4.99, A$12.95) is a revealing although one-sided autobiography of a member of the Westernised Iranian élite who stayed on after 1979, resolutely refusing to give up the pleasures of life proscribed under the Islamic Republic. The story closes with her harrowing escape from Iran in 1982, in the untrustworthy hands of Kurdish smugglers.

Archaeology & Architecture

A number of locally produced or foreign books in English about Iran's historical sites, nearly all of them published before the revolution, can be found in Iran or abroad in second-hand shops. Museum bookshops in Iran sometimes have something of interest in English, although not necessarily about the place you are actually visiting. If you see a book that might be of use, buy it, for you probably won't see it again anywhere else. At the shop at Ferdōsī's memorial in Tūs, I bought a very useful book entitled *A List of the Historical Sites and Ancient Monuments of Iran* (Nosratollah Meshkati, Ministry of Culture & Arts Press, Tehrān, 1974). It's scholarly and comprehensive although rather difficult to use due to its lack of an index.

The best concise introduction to the marvels of Iranian building styles through the ages is Arthur Upham Pope's *Introducing Persian Architecture* (Soroush Press, Tehrān, 1976). This short illustrated book is almost unobtainable in the West, but can be bought for 7200 rials at the bookshop of the Azadi Grand Hotel in Tehrān.

The superlative modern guide to Iranian archaeological sites is Sylvia Matheson's *Persia: An Archaeological Guide* (Faber & Faber, London, 1976, £4.95). Most of the information in this scholarly but very readable companion to almost every significant historical or ancient ruin in Iran is still valid, although some of the travel details have inevitably become outdated, and the book only covers sites up to the Seljuq era. Matheson's book is difficult and expensive to find in the West, but it is still sold at some of the hotel bookshops in Tehrān for around 14,000 rials. Although the 1972 first edition is much cheaper, the fuller 1976 edition is the one to buy.

Travel Guides

Apart from this book, there's virtually only one guidebook in English that's available in the West at all, and that's the out-of-print *Nagel's Iran* (Nagel, Geneva, 1977). Its coverage of archaeological and historic sites is mostly highly competent, but it is expensive and completely out of date for any sort of practical information. It also suffers from a very quirky translation from the original French and a very poor index. This guidebook is still available in Iran, most easily at the hotel bookshops in Tehrān, where it is decidedly cheaper than in the West. The old Fodor guide to Iran, available at some second-hand bookshops or libraries in the West but not very easily inside Iran, was aimed at a type of reader who is now least likely to have any use for it, the American tourist.

Philip Ward's highly anecdotal *Touring Iran* (Faber & Faber, London, 1971) gives some interesting or tangential insights into many of the main attractions.

Apart from the one you're reading now, there is no up-to-date guidebook on Iran available in English or any other European language. Some general business travellers' guides to the Middle East briefly touch upon Iran, but none is likely to be worth buying solely for its coverage of the Islamic Republic.

The official handout to English-speaking visitors to Iran, the 60-page *Tourist Guide of Iran* is occasionally given away to privileged customers at state tourist offices, or sold at a booth at Tehrān railway station. With chapter headings such as 'Iran as a Model in the Awakening of the Oppressed Nations' and 'Islamic Revolution and World Reaction', it is of high novelty value but very little practical use.

Language

Two excellent books for an introduction to the Persian language are LP Elwell-Sutton's *Elementary Persian Grammar* (Cambridge University Press, 1974) and John Mace's *Teach Yourself Modern Persian* (Hodder & Stoughton). Both are avaliable in Tehrān. There is no Persian phrasebook available which I can recommend.

Of the Persian-English and English-Persian dictionaries on the market, the most useful I found was S Haïm's two-volume set (Farhang-e Moaser Publishing Company, Tehrān, 1987). This is absurdly expensive in the West, but only about 15,000 rials in Iran.

Bookshops & Libraries

Iranians are not the world's most avid readers; traditionally the great works of Persian literature have been recited in public rather than read in private, and even today, reading for private pleasure is regarded as a somewhat antisocial habit. Paper shortages, press censorship and import restrictions have also helped to ensure that Iran has very few bookshops, but most towns have at least one, with a few shelves of books in English, one or two of which may actually be about Iran. In Tehrān nearly all of the bookshops are concentrated in the university district. Most of the international hotels also have a small shop selling books and maps in English, and although prices are high by local standards, there is at least a guaranteed supply. The British Council should reopen now that the British hostages are released from Lebanon, so there may be one good library open to the public. The British Institute of Persian Studies in the Gholhak British Embassy compound has an extensive library open for scholarly research.

Maps

There is no great need to bring any maps with you. Good, locally produced country, regional and city maps, adequate for most purposes, are fairly easily available inside the country. In any case it is very difficult to find them outside the country, and where available, they are extremely expensive.

Some maps are printed with Persian script only, some in English only, but the most useful ones have both together. The main cartographic publisher is Gītā Shenāsī of Tehrān, but the Ministry of Culture & Islamic Guidance also commissions maps of most provincial capitals and some provinces; the former can be bought at bookshops, street-stalls and Tehrān airport, and the latter can be picked up free at tourist offices throughout Iran. Information about the availability of regional, provincial and city maps is given in the main part of the book.

Country Maps If you can't wait until you get to Iran, the 1977 Bartholemew map (scale 1:2,500,000, English script only) is still available in some places. You could also try some of the specialist map sellers like Edward Stanford (☎ 071-836 1321), at 12 Long Acre, London WC2. If you can wait, a better and cheaper option is to pick up one of the free tourist maps of the country handed out at most tourist information offices. The standard *Tourist Map of Islamic Republic of Iran* is fairly detailed (scale 1:2,500,000) and clearly marks all the main and secondary roads, railway lines, driving distances and petrol stations, and labels all places in English and Persian script. It marks main physical features but doesn't give provincial boundaries. An identical map is also sold at bookshops for 200 rials under the title *Road Map of Islamic Republic of Iran* (published by Sahab Geographic & Drafting Institute). There is also a much more detailed map (scale 1:1,600,000) giving administrative divisions, published by Gītā Shenāsī under the title of *Map of Islamic Republic of Iran* (Map No 169, 1000 rials).

The largest map of the country you could hope to find is Gītā Shenāsī's *Naghshé-yé Omūmī-yé Jomhūrī-yé Eslāmī-yé Īrān* (scale 1:1,000,000), all in Persian, for only 2500 rials. It is the sort of thing you might find decorating the walls of Iranian embassies.

There are several road atlases of Iran, but none of them in English. If you know Persian, a useful pocket atlas is Gītā Shenāsī's new *Otō Atlas-é Īrān* (scale 1:2,200,000), which sells at around 600 rials. The larger version is so badly bound that my copy fell apart after a couple of days' use.

If you want to order maps from outside Iran, write and request a catalogue from Gītā Shenāsī Cartographic & Geographic Institute, PO Box 14155-3441, Tehrān, Iran (☎ (021) 679335; telex 213636).

MEDIA
Newspapers & Magazines
There are two English-language dailies published in Iran, *Tehran Times* (50 rials) and *Kayhan International* (25 rials), usually known in Persian as *Keihān-é Engelīsī*. Of these the latter is generally considered much more Hezbollāhī (Muslim fundamentalist), and consequently *Tehran Times* is often sold out well before noon. Both carry a fairly objective coverage of world affairs gleaned from Reuter and other Western press agencies, as well as a good number of reports and commentaries from a purely Iranian standpoint. You can buy them every day except Fridays and public holidays, from certain street newspaper kiosks or at a few of the international hotels in Tehrān. Outside Tehrān it's usually only yesterday's edition that you'll be able to pick up. You can subscribe to either paper from inside or outside Iran. For details write to *Tehran Times* (☎ 825023) at Kheyābūn-é Shahīd Ostād Nejātollāhī, Kūché-yé Bīmé 32, Tehrān; or

to *Kayhan International* (☎ 310251) at Kheyābūn-é Ferdōsī, Kūché-yé Shāh Cherāghī, Tehrān.

In some places you can occasionally find the *Financial Times* for 210 rials, a couple of weeks late but better than nothing. A few magazines known for their favourable coverage of the Iranian regime are also allowed in, but there is nothing of much general interest. *Time* used to be imported at the official exchange rate, but is now only available under the counter and usually several weeks late.

Radio & TV

Iranian radio and television are very heavily state-controlled, and are in fact under the control of a brother of President Rafsanjānī. Although there is extremely little editorial leeway on state TV, and religious programming is still very much a priority, viewing is not always quite as dull as one might imagine. Under Rafsanjānī, Iranian TV has become much more watchable than in the days when almost every programme had a propagandist theme. Some Iranians say that more interesting TV and radio are about the only good things to have come out of the present leadership.

During my most recent visit, the TV stations were doing a run of old British comedies, and one of the radio stations appeared to have been taken over by the Muzak Corporation. It is reported that President Rafsanjānī told a hardline mullah who was complaining about a particular piece of decadent Western music on TV that if he didn't like it, he was free to switch it off.

Game shows, cartoons and imported films and documentaries take up as much of the TV schedule as they would on many a Western station. Although foreign films are often shown on Iranian TV, they will be of little interest to most visitors as everything is rather clumsily dubbed into Persian, and in any case most potential threats to Islamic values are ruthlessly edited out with no regard for the plot. There is a short English-language TV news bulletin daily at 7 pm on Channel 2.

Short-Wave Radio Both the BBC World Service and Voice of America can be picked up clearly in most parts of the country. The BBC especially is listened to by millions of Iranians rightly distrustful of the state media network. Short-wave radios can be found in the most unlikely places, from the lowliest Afghan refugee's hovel to the bedside of the late Āyatollāh Khomeinī, who reportedly was an avid follower, if not supporter, of the BBC Persian Service. English-speaking friends tell me that the English-language services are much more objective on Iranian affairs than the Persian-language ones. Frequencies to try for the BBC English Service include 9410, 12095 and 15050 kHz.

The Islamic Republic of Iran Broadcasting External Service goes out in English to Europe at 7.30 to 8.30 pm GMT on 6035 and 9022 kHz; to East Asia at 11.30 am to 12.25 pm GMT on 9575, 9705, 11715 and 11790 kHz; to the Middle East at 11.30 am to 12.25 pm GMT on 1224 and 11940 kHz; and to West Asia at 2 to 3 pm GMT on 702 kHz. In Tehrān you can also hear it at 3 to 3.55 pm local time on FM 100.7 mHz, or at 11 pm to midnight on FM 97.7 mHz. For further information write to IRIB, PO Box 3333, Tehrān.

FILM & PHOTOGRAPHY

Although most towns in Iran have at least one photographic shop, and some have many more, the range of film and camera equipment available is rather limited. Try to bring any equipment or film that you are likely to need with you. By far the best selection of film and equipment is in Tehrān, where most of the camera shops are in or near Kheyābūn-é Nāser Khosrō.

Imported print film is widely available but the supply is largely random, and if you want a particular brand or film speed, take full advantage of your duty-free limit of five rolls. Kodak, Agfa and Fuji are the most commonly available film brands. Average prices are 3000 to 10,000 rials for a roll of 36 exposures, depending on the make and type of film. Always check the 'best before' date on the side of the box, as it may have been stored for ages in less than ideal conditions. Developing costs around 1500 to 3000 rials – more for certain types of film – and can take up to a week.

Slide film is generally about 50% more expensive than print film, but it is almost impossible to buy or have developed outside Tehrān. The only other place I found selling it was the small but well stocked shop in the Homa Hotel in Shīrāz.

All over Iran there are small backroom photographers specialising in portraits, recognisable by the samples displayed at the entrance. Many of them do passport photos very cheaply, about 1200 rials for four B&W shots ready to collect the next day. Most of them will also develop print film.

Lighting Conditions

In most places at most times of year lighting conditions in daytime are good, and you can usually afford to use very slow-speed film; I generally had the best daylight results using 50 ASA slide film. In fact one of the main problems is that the strong sunlight throws reflections on the lens (preventable with a lens hood) and casts very noticeable shadows which can spoil an otherwise good photograph. For this reason, buildings are often best photographed with the light directly overhead. For panoramic shots however, the very bright light at midday can make photos looked washed out and lacking in depth, and often you'll find better lighting conditions shortly after sunrise or just before dusk. Timing is critical, for the light can change completely in a few minutes at the start and end of the day.

Many mosques and other buildings are entirely unlit inside, and you'll need long exposures (several seconds), a powerful flash or faster film. A portable tripod can be very useful.

Photography Restrictions & Etiquette

Iranians are great shutter-bugs and you'll find them photographing each other all over the country. By and large they aren't very adventurous with their cameras and they were constantly mystified at my choice of such bizarre subjects as street scenes, traffic jams and farm animals.

You shouldn't have any problems photographing most of the things that tourists are expected to photograph, but be prepared for a lot of stares if you stroll around with a suspicious-looking camera slung over your shoulder. You'll look much less like the cinema-going Iranian's idea of a spy if you hide your equipment inside a bag of some sort. Video cameras are allowed, but you may attract unwelcome attention if you actually attempt to use one in public. Mile-long telephoto lenses are also bound to arouse intense curiosity.

Look out for and observe 'No Photography' signs with the symbol of a camera with a cross through it: these are nearly always marked in English as well as Persian. You don't want to be seen taking photos within range of any airport, naval dockyard, military installation, prison, train station, telegraph office or anywhere else with security implications, or anything within several km of any land border. Military and security personnel are also risky subjects.

There's still a certain amount of paranoia about foreign spies, and Iranians can get very suspicious of Westerners with cameras anywhere near anything sensitive. What seems like a perfectly innocent snapshot may take hours of explaining at the local Revolutionary Guards station. If in doubt ask first. Even seemingly innocuous subjects can be a problem if a forbidden building is within range. For example, the main square of Tehrān has the head telegraph office on it; photograph in the direction of this high-security installation and you are very likely to be arrested.

Most Iranians are only too delighted if you ask to photograph them, and quite often children will beg to be included in your photograph, though they do tend to strike up unnatural poses in front of the lens. As anywhere else, it's polite to ask before filming anyone close up. Never film women without permission, and respect any refusal. In some more conservative places people can get very touchy about this. Make sure you've got the OK before shooting if you don't want to risk having your camera smashed or stones thrown at you – don't think it doesn't happen.

Be sensitive about photographing people at docks and jetties, especially if they are handling cargo to which they would prefer not to attract attention. Ask permission first.

Under no circumstances photograph inside mosques during a service, and exercise caution at all other times. There are a few religious sites where photography is strictly forbidden, most notably the precincts of the Holy Shrine at Ghom and the Holy Shrine at Mashhad. It is not generally a good idea to photograph religious processions and other events on the Islamic mourning days.

Airport Security

If you are travelling on domestic or international flights, it is very common for guards to take batteries out of all electrical equipment, including cameras, and put them in a security box together with guns and other dangerous items. When you arrive at the other end you may have a long wait for your package to emerge.

Some but not all airports have X-ray machines for checking luggage. The operators always told me that they are safe for camera film, but they were ready to inspect my camera bag separately. If you too are suspicious of X-ray machines, keep any unexposed film somewhere where it can easily be removed for examination.

It is not a smart move to take photographs from aeroplanes, although I don't think it is strictly illegal.

HEALTH

Iran is not by the standards of West Asia an especially unhealthy country. Your chances of falling prey to some tropical disease are generally a lot lower than in places further east, although if you do want to come back with an interesting Oriental malady to liven up your dinner-table conversation, the opportunities are there.

Travel Health Guides

There are a number of books on travel health:

Staying Healthy in Asia, Africa & Latin America, Volunteers in Asia. Probably the best all-round guide to carry, as it's compact but very detailed and well organised.

Travellers' Health, Dr Richard Dawood, Oxford University Press. Comprehensive, easy to read, authoritative and also highly recommended, although it's rather large to lug around.

Travel with Children, Maureen Wheeler, Lonely Planet Publications. Includes basic advice on travel health for younger children.

Pre-Departure Preparations

No inoculations are compulsory, except against yellow fever for those coming from an infected country. Anti-malaria pills and vaccination against typhoid, polio and tetanus are recommended. Vaccinations against cholera, hepatitis, rabies and tuberculosis are also available, but offer less protection and are no substitute for good personal health care while you're travelling. The malaria risk is greatest between March and October; typhoid is most common in south-east Iran, especially in the Makrān. Vaccinations take a certain amount of planning ahead, and it is best to visit your doctor or local tropical disease centre at least two months before travelling.

Health Insurance A travel insurance policy to cover theft, loss and medical problems is a wise idea, although private doctors' fees are very low by Western standards and in practice basic medical attention on the state health service is likely to be free of charge. Iran does not have reciprocal health arrangements with other countries.

There are a wide variety of policies and your travel agent will have recommendations. The international student travel policies handled by STA or other student travel organisations are usually good value. Some policies offer lower and higher medical expenses options but the higher one is chiefly for countries like the USA which have extremely high medical costs. Check the small print:

1. Some policies specifically exclude 'dangerous activities' which can include skiing,

motorcycling, even trekking. If such activities are on your agenda you don't want that sort of policy.

2. You may prefer a policy which pays doctors or hospitals direct rather than you having to pay on the spot and claim later. If you have to claim later make sure you keep all documentation. Some policies ask you to call back (reverse charges) to a centre in your home country where an immediate assessment of your problem is made.

3. Check if the policy covers ambulances or an emergency flight home. If you have to stretch out you will need two seats and somebody has to pay for them!

4. Many policies exclude cover for travel in war zones, which may include Iran and other parts of the region.

Medical Kit A small, straightforward medical kit is a wise thing to carry. A possible kit list includes:

1. Aspirin or Panadol – for pain or fever.
2. Antihistamine (such as Benadryl) – useful as a decongestant for colds, allergies, to ease the itch from insect bites or stings or to help prevent motion sickness.
3. Antibiotics – useful if you're travelling well off the beaten track, but they must be prescribed and you should carry the prescription with you.
4. Kaolin preparation (Pepto-Bismol), Imodium or Lomotil – for stomach upsets.
5. Rehydration mixture – for treatment of severe diarrhoea; this is particularly important if travelling with children.
6. Antiseptic, Mercurochrome and antibiotic powder or similar 'dry' spray – for cuts and grazes.
7. Calamine lotion – to ease irritation from bites or stings.
8. Bandages and Band-aids – for minor injuries.
9. Scissors, tweezers and a thermometer (note that mercury thermometers are prohibited by airlines).
10. Insect repellent, sunscreen, chap stick and water purification tablets.

Ideally antibiotics should be administered only under medical supervision and should never be taken indiscriminately. Overuse of antibiotics can weaken your body's ability to deal with infections naturally and can reduce the drug's efficacy on a future occasion. Take only the recommended dose at the prescribed intervals and continue using the antibiotic for the prescribed period, even if the illness seems to be cured earlier. Antibiotics are quite specific to the infections they can treat; stop immediately if there are any serious reactions, and don't use an antibiotic at all if you are unsure if you have the correct one.

Medications If you require a particular medication take an adequate supply, as it may not be available locally. There is a minimal charge for medicines on prescription, more than 90% of which are made in Iran, but labelled in English and Persian.

You should, however, be careful when buying drugs as the expiry date may have passed, or correct storage conditions may not have been followed.

If you're looking for a particular medicine over the counter, try to find out its generic name rather than its Western trademark, which may not be used or understood in Iran. Take the prescription with you wherever you travel, to show you legally use the medication – it's surprising how often over-the-counter drugs from one place are illegal without a prescription or even banned in another.

Take a supply of sterile syringes with you if you are likely to need them. Since you may have problems in explaining these at Iranian customs, try to obtain a doctor's letter to go with them.

Dental Health There are over 5000 dentists in Iran, and many of them have been trained in the West and will speak good English. Nevertheless, it would be wise to make sure your teeth are OK before you leave.

Spectacles If you wear glasses, take a spare pair and your prescription. Losing your glasses can be a real problem, but replacement lenses are remarkably cheap in Iran. In Tehrān you can have one replaced for about 8000 rials in under a week. Private opticians charge about 2000 rials for an eye test.

Basic Rules

Food & Water The tap water is generally safe to drink, and bottled drinks, tea and coffee are practically always safe. Most bottled milk sold in Iran is pasteurised. The greatest health risk is probably from bootleg alcohol (although the stuff made by the Armenians is rarely a problem). Ice is often kept in less than ideal storage conditions and unless it has obviously come from an ice-making machine it may be best to avoid it.

If you have any doubts about the purity of the water, treat it by boiling for 10 minutes if possible, or with sterilising tablets or iodine solution (five to seven drops per litre of water, and leave for 10 minutes).

Standards of food hygiene are mostly satisfactory in all categories of eating-house, except for Iranian sausages which can cause stomach problems. In general most Iranian cooking is healthy and nutritious, and you shouldn't have much problem in keeping to a balanced diet. At street stalls it is advisable only to eat hot food that you have watched being cooked.

Everyday Health A normal body temperature is 98.6°F or 37°C; more than 2°C higher is a 'high' fever. A normal adult pulse rate is 60 to 80 per minute (children 80 to 100, babies 100 to 140). You should know how to take a temperature and a pulse rate. As a general rule the pulse increases about 20 beats per minute for each °C rise in fever.

Respiration (breathing) rate is also an indicator of illness. Count the number of breaths per minute: between 12 and 20 is normal for adults and older children (up to 30 for younger children, 40 for babies). People with a high fever or serious respiratory illness (like pneumonia) breathe more quickly than normal. More than 40 shallow breaths a minute usually means pneumonia.

Many health problems can be avoided by

taking care of yourself. Wash your hands frequently – it's quite easy to contaminate your own food. If you're unsure about the tap water, clean your teeth with purified water.

Avoid climatic extremes: keep out of the sun when it's hot, dress warmly when it's cold. You can get worm infections through walking barefoot. Cover bare skin when insects are around, by screening windows or beds or by using insect repellents. Seek local advice: if you're told the water is unsafe due to jellyfish, sharks or bilharzia, don't go in. In situations where there is no information, discretion is the better part of valour.

Cuts & Scratches Skin punctures can easily become infected in hot climates and may be difficult to heal. Treat any cut with an antiseptic solution and Mercurochrome. Where possible avoid bandages and Band-aids, which can keep wounds wet.

Coping with the Heat This is something you are going to have to do almost everywhere in Iran in summer, and in the far south for more than half the year. In the fierce midday heat, you won't see many Iranians out and about, and there's no reason why a visitor would be any less vulnerable to the heat. Heatstroke is a serious threat to health, and it can be fatal. If you aren't used to the heat, it's best to take life very easy for the first few days until your body has had a chance to adjust: take a siesta, a taxi, a Coke, anything to conserve your energy. Wear a hat (men only) or scarf over your head to keep the most vulnerable part of your body covered, and a pair of sunglasses if the sun is very bright.

Keep up your fluid intake; don't just drink when you feel thirsty, but whenever you have the opportunity. Hot sweet tea is as good as soft drinks. If you are travelling in conditions of extreme heat, it's very tempting to drink anything that's offered you, but it's a temptation worth resisting as an exhausted body is going to be even less able to resist water-borne infections.

Don't forget to keep up your intake of salt,

since you'll be losing a lot through sweat. Just 10 grams a day should be enough.

Pollution Air pollution is a major problem in Tehrān, most of all in summer. Tehrānīs tell the visitor almost with pride that theirs is one of the most polluted cities in the world. If you suddenly start spluttering and coughing, having headaches and stomach pains after a day or two in the capital, you're probably just reacting very naturally to the unhealthy air. Escape from Smog City and you'll stage a miraculous recovery. On some days of the year the radio station broadcasts warnings that people with heart conditions should stay indoors.

Medical Problems & Treatment

Self-diagnosis and treatment can be risky, so wherever possible seek qualified help. Although advice on treatment is given in this section, it is for emergency use only. Medical advice should be sought before administering any drugs. An embassy or consulate can usually recommend a good place to go for such advice. See the section on Medical Facilities.

Malaria Malaria is one of the world's greatest killer diseases in tropical and subtropical countries. In Iran the risk is not very great, but there is a slight danger between March and October. The malaria parasite is spread by certain species of mosquito, and quickly goes on to infect its new host's liver and bloodstream.

Symptoms include, in the first stage, severe chills, in the second, severe fever, diarrhoea, vomiting, headaches, nausea and rapid breathing, and in the third stage, severe sweating. These bouts last up to six hours altogether and recur every day to four days, according to the strain of malaria. If you have these symptoms, seek medical assistance.

There are good public malaria clinics in all those parts of Iran which are commonly affected by the disease.

No vaccination is available against the disease, but you are strongly recommended to take a course of anti-malaria tablets before, during and after your visit. There are several strains of malaria around, and because the situation in any given country can vary from year to year, it's best to discuss with your doctor or tropical disease centre which particular course is currently recommended for the places you are going to.

Obviously, steering well clear of mosquitoes is the surest way of not catching malaria. If you're camping out in a risk area, sleep under mosquito nets and/or burn mosquito coils. Most hotels in the malarial areas of Iran have screens over the windows. If yours doesn't, keep the window closed or sleep under a mosquito net. An insect repellent such as Autan is a good idea too. Take care especially after dark when the little bloodsuckers are at their hungriest.

Typhoid Typhoid fever is spread through food, milk, water and flies contaminated with infected human sewage. If allowed to enter your body, the typhoid parasite will home in on your small intestine, and after a week or two will go on to enter your bloodstream. It's often difficult to distinguish typhoid from other types of fever, but a few pointers include inflammation of the gut, a high temperature and rashes of pink spots. The real danger comes from the risk of internal bleeding: if allowed to get to this stage, typhoid can be fatal. Medical attention is essential and nearly always effective. Several anti-typhoid vaccines lasting up to three years are available and highly recommended. Some of them also give protection against paratyphoid and tetanus into the bargain. If time allows, take two injections four to six weeks apart.

There is currently a high typhoid risk in the western provinces of Iran where camps have been set up for large numbers of refugees from Iraq. You may be required to have a typhoid vaccination certificate to enter high-risk areas. There is also a permanent danger of typhoid in parts of Iran with poor standards of hygiene, especially rural areas. The Makrān is especially prone.

Top: View of northern Tehrān (DStV)
Left: Cable car (Telecabın) into the Alborz Mountains, overlooking Tehrān (RVD)
Right: Huge mural in a Tehrān street (RVD)

Top: Detail of eivān, Masjed-é Emām, Esfahān (DStV)
Left: Masjed-é Emām, Esfahān (DStV)
Right: Pol-é Shahrestān, Esfahān (DStV)

Polio Polio vaccine is entirely painless, has no side-effects and offers complete protection for 10 years. You probably had it as a child, and in that case will only need a booster every 10 years. Vaccination is highly recommended, and good sanitation should help keep this crippling disease at bay. It's at its worst in summer.

Yellow Fever This disease is not present in Iran, but if you're coming from an infected zone you'll need proof of yellow fever inoculation before being allowed into the country.

Cholera Cholera is an unpleasant and highly contagious disease usually spread in epidemics, and these are usually well publicised. There is a risk of catching it almost anywhere in West Asia, but particularly in areas of poor sanitation. Symptoms include watery and very frequent diarrhoea, vomiting, cramps and lack of urine, leading to a severe loss of water and salts and an upsetting of the chemical balance of the body fluids. Prompt medical attention is a must; untreated, cholera is often fatal. A vaccination of two injections is available against cholera, and it lasts for up to six months, but it is only partially effective and some doctors think it isn't worth bothering with. The best precaution is to give all potentially contaminated food and water a miss.

Rabies This is a serious disease which, if not treated very soon after contraction, is almost always fatal. Treatment at that stage is painful and protracted, but not always successful. Vaccination against rabies is available but rarely considered necessary for the average traveller with access to medical facilities. Rabies can be caught from infected dogs, cats, monkeys, bats, foxes, mice and other animals, especially carnivores. Keep well away from any animals showing signs of the disease: paralysis, agitation, any sort of abnormal behaviour, or, most obvious of all, foaming at the mouth. Don't touch any wild animal. If bitten or scratched or even licked by any animal, immediately wash the affected area very thoroughly with soap and water and, if there is the slightest risk of infection, seek immediate medical attention. Rabies is not a disease to be taken lightly.

Viral Hepatitis There are two common strains of this liver infection – hepatitis A and hepatitis B. The first is usually caught from eating contaminated food or from drinking (or swimming in) infected water. It has a long incubation period of about a month during which there may be no visible effects at all. Once hepatitis A has set in, symptoms include a high temperature, nausea, lack of appetite, lethargy, headaches, pain under the ribs and dark urine. Jaundice (a yellowing of the skin and the whites of the eyes) is also common. However, in less severe cases, there may be few or none of these symptoms. Hepatitis A isn't a life-threatening disease; it won't kill you but quite probably you won't feel like doing anything for a few weeks. And as it happens, the symptom is also the cure: complete rest for a week or so is the best – and only – medicine. Scrupulous sanitation is also a wise move, along with avoiding alcohol and antibiotics.

Hepatitis B is less common but more severe than type A. It is caught from contaminated syringes, kissing and sexual contact with infected persons, and from contaminated blood. It can take up to six months for the disease to appear. When it does, the symptoms are similar to those of hepatitis A, but there is a risk of permanent liver damage. Complete rest is the best cure, and a stay in hospital may be necessary.

An immunoglobulin vaccination against type A is available, but it only lasts a couple of months. Taking care over food and water is the best protection. There is also an inoculation against hepatitis B, but it takes up to six months to become fully effective. Abstinence from risky activities is your best bet; if you are likely to need syringes for personal medication, take a sterile supply with you.

Tetanus Tetanus can be a killer, but it is easily enough prevented. The bacillus spores which cause tetanus thrive in the earth and on dirty objects generally, and can enter the nervous system through open wounds, eventually causing painful muscular spasms. The anti-tetanus jab is very effective and lasts for up to 10 years. You may have had it when you first went to school, and if so you'll only need a booster injection. If you do get any cuts or grazes, wash the wound thoroughly and immediately; if there's a risk of contamination from any source, try to see a doctor. Antiseptic is worth packing.

Tuberculosis In its most common form tuberculosis or TB is a virulent lung infection spread from person to person by spitting and coughing or through infected food and milk. One strain is passed on through unpasteurised milk. Some of the symptoms are heavy coughing and spitting, chest pains, loss of appetite, lethargy, night sweats, weight loss, fever and coughing blood. Modern medicine can reduce the impact of TB but not, as yet, completely cure it, and the disease can easily recur. An inoculation – best taken three months before travel – is available, but it's no substitute for the standard precautions, which are scrupulous hygiene and proper nutrition, avoiding carriers and heavy spitters and coughers, and boiling any unpasteurised or doubtful milk before drinking. Any recurrent cough or heavy sweating at night is a good reason for a visit to the doctor. Most bottled milk in Iran is pasteurised.

AIDS Iran is not a high-risk area for AIDS, but even so you'd be well advised to take the usual precautions. Behave as is expected of you by the Islamic Republic and you shouldn't have any problems.

Diarrhoea & Dysentery These two are often confused: travellers with no more than a mild dose of the runs can easily panic themselves into believing that dysentery has struck. Sometimes it can happen the other way round. If you just have loose bowels – however frequently – without any other symptoms, then you've almost certainly got diarrhoea. Apart from severe cases, you don't really need to do anything about diarrhoea except to keep drinking and eat only basic, absolutely safe foods.

Lomotil (diphenoxylate loperamide), Dioralyte (dextrose chloride) or Imodium can be used to bring relief from the symptoms, although they do not actually cure the problem. (The first two are both available in Iran under the formulaic names.) Only use these drugs if absolutely necessary, eg if you *must* travel. For children Imodium is preferable, but do not use these drugs if the patient has a high fever or is severely dehydrated. Antibiotics can be useful in treating severe diarrhoea, especially if it is accompanied by nausea, vomiting, stomach cramps or mild fever. Ampicillin, a broad spectrum penicillin, is usually recommended.

Only if the runs keep on running, or if there are other symptoms, is there anything to worry about. If pus or blood makes an appearance, then it's probably telling you that you've got amoebic dysentery, especially if you also feel abdominal pain. The best remedy for amoebic dysentery is Flagyl (metronidazole). If you're also throwing up and feeling nauseous and constantly wanting to defecate but not producing anything, then the chances are that you've caught bacillary dysentery, which calls for a dose of tetracycline or ampicillin.

Bedbugs & Lice Bedbugs live in various places, but particularly in dirty mattresses and bedding. Spots of blood on bedclothes or on the wall around the bed can be read as a suggestion to find another hotel. Bedbugs leave itchy bites in neat rows. Calamine lotion may help.

All lice cause itching and discomfort. They make themselves at home in your hair (head lice), your clothing (body lice) or in your pubic hair (crabs). You catch lice through direct contact with infected people or by sharing combs, clothing and the like. Powder or shampoo treatment will kill the lice, and infected clothing should then be washed in very hot water.

Fungal Infections Hot weather fungal infections are most likely to occur on the scalp, between the toes or fingers (athlete's foot), in the groin (jock itch or crotch rot) and on the body (ringworm). You get ringworm (which is a fungal infection, not a worm) from infected animals or by walking on damp areas, like shower floors.

To prevent fungal infections wear loose, comfortable clothes, avoid artificial fibres, wash frequently and dry carefully. If you do get an infection, wash the infected area daily with a disinfectant or medicated soap and water, and rinse and dry well. Apply an antifungal powder like the widely available Tinaderm. Try to expose the infected area to air or sunlight as much as possible and wash all towels and underwear in hot water as well as changing them often.

Women's Health

Gynaecological Problems Poor diet, lowered resistance due to the use of antibiotics for stomach upsets, and even contraceptive pills can lead to vaginal infections when travelling in hot climates. Keeping the genital area clean, and wearing skirts or loose-fitting trousers and cotton underwear will help to prevent infections.

Yeast infections, characterised by a rash, itch and discharge, can be treated with a vinegar or even lemon-juice douche or with yoghurt. Nystatin suppositories are the usual medical prescription. Trichomonas is a more serious infection; symptoms are a discharge and a burning sensation when urinating. Male sexual partners must also be treated, and if a vinegar-water douche is not effective, medical attention should be sought. Flagyl is the prescribed drug.

Pregnancy Most miscarriages occur during the first three months of pregnancy, so this is the most risky time to travel. The last three months should also be spent within reasonable distance of good medical care, as quite serious problems can develop at this time. Pregnant women should avoid all unnecessary medication, but vaccinations and malarial prophylactics should still be taken where possible. Additional care should be taken to prevent illness and particular attention should be paid to diet and nutrition.

Medical Facilities

The standard of medical facilities varies greatly throughout the country. In Tehrān they are reasonably good, but in some less developed areas they are far from adequate. In many rural areas it is common for people to travel great distances for medical treatment. Although the health service is supposedly comprehensive and free of charge, some Iranians complain that they could not afford private treatment for common conditions that should have been covered by the public system.

After the revolution many of the best doctors emigrated to the West, and in an attempt to fill the gap the authorities send out newly qualified doctors to work in small towns and villages in place of their military service, and do not allow them to travel outside Iran for several years. They have started to employ some foreign doctors, largely in remoter areas.

A disproportionate number of doctors and medical establishments are in Tehrān, which is the best place to fall ill. Many of the doctors in Iran received their training in the West and in most large places you shouldn't have much problem in finding one who speaks English. Ask your consulate for a recommendation. Most private doctors have signs in English outside their practices.

WOMEN TRAVELLERS

Islam, and in particular the Iranian interpretation of Islam, does impose a number of strict constraints on women, and I would not advise any foreign woman to visit Iran unless she is prepared to fit in with the social code. You may not agree with all or any of it, but if you are not prepared to observe the rules you are going to have an extremely unpleasant time. Iran simply isn't the country to make a feminist statement. For information on appropriate dress, see the Culture section in the Facts about the Country chapter.

Cultural Background

A foreign journalist once asked if it would ever be possible for a woman to become president of the Islamic Republic of Iran. The official answer was that although a woman might not be intrinsically unsuited to the job, her work would suffer as a result of her needing to take time off to have babies. The general feeling is that a woman cannot achieve success in life without marrying and raising a family; if she can also rise to the top of her profession, it is to her credit, but the career must never be allowed to take precedence over her marriage or family. Furthermore, it is seen as shameful for a man not to be able to keep his wife on his own income, and having her go out to work is a sign of his neglect, not of his liberality.

Fathers should ensure that a daughter's bridegroom guarantees a *mahrīyé-yé mo'ajjal* (a fixed sum, often in the form of gold coins, payable by the husband in the event of divorce or his death), and ideally this is enough for her to live on for the rest of her life. Arranged marriages do exist, although nowadays few girls would be prepared to marry a man whom they did not know. The partners are not so much marrying each other as marrying into an extended family.

Women do work in offices and banks, sometimes as managers, and they are represented in the judiciary and politics and many other spheres of public life. Women can and do run their own businesses. However, there are some occupations that are closed to women, and some which are not closed but in which women are very unlikely to work. In general women who want to work tend to be pushed into certain types of job such as teaching, secretarial work and nursing. It is difficult for women to rise to the top of their profession, and when they do it is often as a result of exceptional qualities beyond those expected in a man in the same position, or through family connections or some other advantage.

Under Islam it is possible for a man to have up to four wives, but the rules concerning his treatment of them are very strict, and he is obliged to accord them all equal rights and privileges at all times. Islamic law does not permit him to simply dump one in favour of a younger woman and remain married to both. If he divorces the first in this case, he is expected to pay her a hefty dowry. In practice it is rare for Iranians in most urban areas to have more than one wife, and even in rural areas one is the rule and more than two has become an oddity. Mullahs however often have several wives.

General Advice

I have met a number of women who have visited Iran since the Islamic Revolution, some of them as solo travellers, and none had experienced the problems for which Pakistan and much of Turkey are notorious with female travellers. In fact most of their experiences were overwhelmingly positive. Nevertheless, travelling around Iran is more difficult for a woman than for a man in many ways, and you'll certainly have to make more of an effort in social and cultural terms. On the other hand unaccompanied women are treated with extra courtesy and indulgence because of their perceived vulnerability. When it comes to trying to find scarce hotel accommodation or aeroplane tickets, an unaccompanied woman is almost certainly at an advantage over a man in the same position. Under Islam a man is obliged to treat women with respect, and if he behaves otherwise it is not because the religion is bad, but because he is a bad Muslim.

In some matters a Western woman will be considered as an honorary male, accepted into all-male preserves like the teahouse in a way that no Iranian woman ever could be, but she can also enter female society more closely than any man could ever do. The problem is that you may feel isolated because of difficulties in making contact with local people, not because they don't want to be friendly but because they are afraid to make the first move. If you want to make contact with people, you are going to need self-confidence. You may find it easier to stick to making friends with Iranian women, at least until you have survived the initial culture shock, but few female Iranians speak much English (although some speak it very well) and you should try to learn some Persian. If you aren't prepared to make an extra effort, you may find yourself very marginalised and miss out on the best that Iran has to offer.

Many Iranian men are sexually repressed, and many of them do have distorted ideas about Western women, but it is very wrong to think that every male will be after your body. If you keep strictly to the dress and social codes, you will go a long way towards earning the respect of local people and you are unlikely to suffer any serious harassment. If you consistently break the sacred taboos many people will consider that, by showing your scorn for their traditions, you have lost any right to their respect and are fair game for any sort of attention. Never lead men on; they don't need much encouragement here, and in Iran it is the man alone who does the wooing.

If you do become a victim of harassment, tell your persecutor firmly but politely to desist (English will do), and try to enlist the sympathy of other Iranians around you. If they think that someone is behaving badly towards you, they are very likely to stop him out of shame. If you scream blue murder you won't gain anyone's sympathy and the situation may even get worse. If the problem persists, a mere mention of the word 'Komīté' can have an instantly sobering effect, although if you really do want to complain to the authorities, the police are the first people to go to. Thanks to social constraints, you will rarely be alone with an Iranian male unless you want to be (and perhaps not even then), but if a situation is likely to turn out that way, it is wise to exercise caution.

If you get stared at, approached by strangers with odd questions and generally treated like a creature from another planet, remember that all these things also happen to foreign men in Iran. In many places a male Westerner is just as much a novelty as a female one.

Many Western women will feel happier about going to Iran in a group or with a male companion, but neither is by any means necessary. It might be a good idea to wear a wedding ring, whether you're married or not, to ward off any unwelcome attention, and at times it may be sensible to say that your husband is travelling with you or about to join you, but in general people will respect your status because they know that Westerners have different rules. Iranian women can and do travel unaccompanied in their own country, though to a far lesser extent than women in the West, and there is no reason why a foreign woman prepared to fit in with Islamic values should not visit Iran alone if she wants to.

Some women have reported problems with local people and officials in eastern Iran, in conservative, undeveloped places like Zāhedān and Zābol. If you are coming from Pakistan, these may be your first impressions of Iran and it will be a shame if you are put off spending more time in the country as a result. The rest of Iran is a different place altogether.

DANGERS & ANNOYANCES

Although the Islamic Republic is notorious for certain sorts of excitements involving foreigners – and Westerners in particular – it has settled down considerably since the fanatical excesses of the early '80s. All the signs are that incidents such as embassy sieges, the arrest and imprisonment of Westerners without good reason and protest by incendiary device are things that the current leadership would prefer to belong to a closed chapter in the history of the Islamic Republic.

In February 1991 the Iranian authorities actually sent several armed guards to protect the British Embassy, rather than orchestrating anti-British protests as they had done so many times before. In April 1991 President Rafsanjānī brought the universally feared and previously semi-autonomous Islamic Revolutionary Guards into line by incorporating them into the police force.

While foreigners do still suffer occasional harassment from rogue elements of the law or, much more rarely, from individual

Iranians, there are certain precautions that every visitor can take to minimise the risk. As Iran opens up to tourism, the security situation will have to loosen up.

Precaution

Before entering Iran, *memorise* the address and telephone number of your diplomatic mission in Tehrān. (See the list in the Tehrān chapter; if yours isn't listed check with your foreign ministry. If your country doesn't have a mission in Iran, find out which embassy, if any, looks after your country's interests in in Iran.) Try to memorise the name of your country's consul or head of mission. Many Western consulates advise their nationals to register with them on arrival in Iran, in person or by telephone. In an emergency, the information you give when registering could prove vital. At a time of crisis, it may be impossible to find your embassy's address or telephone number.

Security

Iran has a reputation as a dangerous country for the Westerner to visit, but this is largely undeserved. In fact, open hostility towards Western visitors as individuals is very rare in Iran and, as noted above, has declined in recent years. I have been in the country twice when diplomatic relations between the UK and Iran were cut off, once at the height of the Rushdie affair, and not once did I encounter open hostility from Iranians because I was travelling on a British passport. The fundamentalists who chant with complete sincerity 'Death to America! Death to Israel! Death to Britain!' are declaring their hatred of the governments of those countries and not of their private citizens. Even the late Āyatollāh Khomeinī is on record as saying that he had nothing against Westerners as individuals, but only against their political leaders.

Many recent visitors to Iran have been constantly surprised at the kindness and generosity shown them by private Iranians of all political and religious hues, regardless of their own nationality. If you make an effort to fit in with local customs, it is unlikely that

you will be treated with anything but courtesy.

Police & Security Forces

The following is a brief rundown of the major police and security forces which you are likely to encounter in Iran.

Police Serving much the same role as any Western police force, the Iranian police have a far better reputation for probity and efficiency than their counterparts in some other countries of the region. In recent years there has been some resentment among the regular police at the power and prestige of the better-paid but generally less well-educated Revolutionary Guards. The police headquarters in each province is known as a *shahrbānī* (or more accurately *edāré-yé koll-é shahrbānī*), and each police station is a *kalāntarī*.

Traffic Police Occasionally seen directing pedestrians, they long ago gave up policing the traffic.

Highway Police The highway police have units patrolling each of the main intercity roads, attending to traffic accidents, manning checkpoints and informing drivers about road conditions.

Foreigners' Registration Department Operating under every shahrbānī but with ultimate responsibility to the ministry in Tehrān, this unit of the Ministry of Foreign Affairs, is empowered to issue visas, pass on deportation orders and deal in general with foreigners' passport matters.

Islamic Revolutionary Guards Having emerged early on as a channel of local revolutionary fervour, the Komītés of the Revolutionary Guard soon assumed responsibility, under their own extremely powerful ministry, for upholding every aspect of the Islamic Revolution. Their primary roles are the monitoring of internal security and the enforcement of Islamic law, but they have also helped the army, navy, air force, border guards, regular police and highway police. A uniquely Iranian outfit, the Revolutionary Guards are extremely powerful and, until very recently, all but autonomous. They are widely feared by the locals and best avoided by foreigners. When not in plain clothes, they are recognisable by short stubbly beards, black collarless shirts and green fatigues; their symbol is an arm with a bandaged hand clutching a rifle. Their favourite vehicle is the Nissan Patrol, with – look carefully – their emblem on the registration-plate.

The Revolutionary Guards are in fact two separate organisations. The less feared of the two, the *Sepah-é Pāsdārān* (literally 'Army of Guards'), is predominantly active in rural areas and is more of a paramilitary unit loosely linked to the regular army. The other organisation, the hated *Komīté (Komīté-yé Enghelāb-é Eslāmī*, literally 'Islamic Revolutionary Committee'), is most active in urban areas. It can best be described as half religious police and half secret police, like a combination of the Spanish Inquisition and the Gestapo.

In April 1991 President Rafsanjānī, in an attempt to curb the excessive power of the Islamic Revolutionary Guards, brought them under the control of the police organisation. Even before this move, they were widely believed to be on the retreat, but my guess is that the Revolutionary Guards are not going to lie down and die for some time to come. You have been warned.

Others There are other security outfits under various ministries, at least one of them specifically concerned with the activities of foreigners in Iran, and some of them very secret, but you are unlikely to have any direct contact with them. It is enough to know that they are there.

Security Checks

Virtually every significant public building in security-obsessed Iran demands at least two armed guards. Gun-toting Revolutionary Guards, soldiers and occasionally regular policemen also roam the streets and patrol the highways, checking on the movements of pedestrians and road-users. Passport and baggage inspections and body frisks are routine on entry to all train stations, ports and airports, and are to be expected at all public gatherings and, less commonly, outside post and telegraph offices, museums and other public buildings.

Foreigners are expected – although not legally compelled – to carry their passports with them at all times. If your visa is in order and nothing on your person is likely to inflict grievous bodily harm, you should have no fears. Sometimes cameras arouse suspicion.

Internal Customs Iran operates a system of internal security (or 'customs') checkpoints about 10 km outside most towns, and at irregular intervals along all major and most minor national highways. It would be difficult to travel 100 km by road in any direction without passing through at least one such checkpoint, or 50 km near any of the land borders. Triangular road signs marked 'Douane' give about a km's warning. Sometimes your car or bus is waved past, sometimes the Revolutionary Guards give the vehicle a once-over, maybe picking on the odd passenger to open his bags and show his ID card (women are usually ignored). Sometimes, if it's a bad day, you'll be stopped for hours and hours while everyone on board is quizzed about his or her travel plans, every piece of luggage is searched and every ID card or passport is thoroughly checked.

Foreigners are almost always the most fascinating passengers on board, their passports always the most intriguing. The guards who staff these checkpoints have been coached in pidgin English – 'What your name, meester?'; 'You like Islamic Republic, meester?' – for use in such rare encounters. It is unlikely that any reply in English apart from 'yes' or 'no' will be fully understood, but it is still very important that you answer any questions with complete politeness and calmness. These people do not muck around.

Political Crises

Iran is no stranger to political crisis. The best way to stay informed is to take a good short-wave radio.

Border Areas

Although a visa for Iran is officially valid for travel anywhere in the country, certain areas are off limits without special permission. It is often impossible to know for certain which areas these are without actually going to them, and by then it may be too late. As a general rule, anywhere within about 100 km of any land border will be heavily patrolled, and anywhere within about 50 km will be sensitive. The Afghan frontier is particularly sensitive. Don't assume that you can visit any border area not specifically mentioned in this book. Even locally you may have considerable problems in obtaining reliable advice, and tourist offices may not be qualified to give it. There are occasions when it will be wise to ask for written permission from the public security department of the relevant *ostāndārī* (provincial government office), even though technically it may not be required. Alternatively, go only with a local guide or don't go at all.

If You Are Arrested

Occasionally foreigners are subjected to arbitrary arrest by Revolutionary Guards, although less often than in the past. Technically, no-one in Iran has the right to arbitrarily arrest anyone, least of all a foreigner, but the point is likely to be difficult to argue. Nearly always the arrest is arbitrary, and it becomes obvious very quickly that you have attracted unwelcome attention merely because you are a foreigner. Nearly always you will be released after answering a few more or less innocent questions. However I would strongly advise any foreigner who is picked up for any reason at all to make every effort to contact his or her consulate in Tehrān *immediately*. The right of a foreigner to telephone his or her consul is not always observed in Iran, so insist on using the nearest available telephone to contact your consulate, or at least being

allowed to ask a reliable person to pass on a message, *before* being whisked away. If neither option proves possible, and you are taken off to the local Revolutionary Guards station, refuse to answer any questions before you have been allowed access to a telephone.

Unless you speak fluent Persian, do not reply to or appear to understand any questions in any language but English. Once an interpreter has been found, answer any questions politely, openly and diplomatically. Since the primary motives for arresting a foreigner without charge are usually curiosity, mild suspicion and the desire to appear very powerful, answer your interrogators in such a way that their curiosity is satisfied, their suspicion allayed and their self-importance flattered. Take special care not to incriminate yourself or anyone else, Iranian or not, by a careless statement. Drop the name of your consul as often as possible, perhaps mentioning that he/she will be worried about your safety because you haven't been in contact recently.

Although the Revolutionary Guards are supposedly under strict instructions not to hassle foreigners, treat any such encounters with extreme caution. It is very unlikely that any foreigner whose whereabouts are known to his or her consul and against whom there is no clear evidence to support criminal charges will be detained for any length of time.

Crime

The pervasive influence of Islam, with its duties of courtesy and hospitality towards guests, reinforced by the vigilance of the law in tracking down and punishing offenders, makes Iran one of the safest countries in Asia for the foreign visitor.

Of course crime does exist in Iran, in spite of some of the world's severest legal sanctions, so it pays to take the usual precautions. When travelling long distances by public transport, especially on international services, take your passport, money and camera as hand luggage and guard them at all stops – there is a slight possibility of theft by other passengers or at the frequent checkpoints en route, but mugging is extremely unlikely. It is said that there are small numbers of pick-pockets operating individually in some bazaars.

Theft of luggage from a room in a hotel or mosāferkhūné isn't very likely, since the staff keep such a careful watch over visitors and residents. Non-residents often have to leave their identity cards at reception if they want to go upstairs, and in many places they're strictly forbidden from any part of the hotel except the ground floor and restaurant. Hotels are securely locked or guarded at night. Most places also have a safe for guests' valuables.

Theft of motorcycles has become quite common recently, particularly in Tehrān. I wouldn't have thought many thieves would be brazen enough to go for a model with conspicuous foreign registration plates, but you should be careful – Iran would be one of the worst places to have a motor vehicle stolen: see the Driving section in the Getting There & Away chapter.

In most cases the most valuable possession which Westerners bring to Iran – and the hardest to replace – is a foreign passport. Largely because of the difficulties Iranians face in travelling legally to the West, but also partly because of certain undercover operations, there is a booming black market in forged, stolen or illegally issued foreign passports, visas and work permits.

There have been stories of unscrupulous Iranian officials trying to steal Western passports. To make matters worse, because impecunious travellers have been known to sell their passports, many consulates here may be extremely reluctant to replace missing travel documents. There is also the danger that a passport thief might try to bump off the previous owner to prevent any complications. At many hotels, even the most expensive ones, hotel receptionists try to hold on to your passport from check-in until check-out, and in some high-security areas you have to surrender your passport on entering and collect it on leaving. If you have to leave your passport anywhere – even at an embassy or consulate – insist on a valid receipt (lotfān man rasīd mīkhāham, 'I want a receipt, please'). At all other times keep a very tight grip on your passport.

Power & Water Cuts

Electricity blackouts are still a more or less daily occurrence throughout Iran. The maximum length is usually around two hours, most commonly in the early evening; early morning blackouts are very rare. Only the better hotels have generators, and the lobby may be the only place with emergency lighting. Some places have candles (but not always matches) in each room, but most don't. Take a torch with you at all times, or leave it where you can easily find it in the dark.

Water cuts are much less frequent, and there's not much you can do about them, except perhaps filling all available receptacles every night just in case.

WORK

Unless you have some skill which is in particular demand in Iran (such as engineering or medicine), are married to an Iranian or are a Shi'ite Muslim, your chances of finding legal paid work in Iran are negligible. Some Iranian companies, mostly state concerns, do take on foreigners on short-term contracts, but they do not recruit expatriates inside Iran. Even if you did get a job offer, the work permit is not a mere formality. For all practical purposes Westerners are only going to get one if a governmental or semigovernmental organisation is prepared to push the Ministry of Labour very hard on their behalf. There might also be an expectation that you become married to an Iranian and become a Muslim.

The many English language schools do not need casual labour, and even if you found one that did, you wouldn't get a work permit unless you had family ties in Iran. In any case wages in Iran are lamentable by Western standards, and only a limited amount can be repatriated at the official rate.

For foreigners who are already established in Iran, suitable job offers are regularly advertised in the two English-language newspapers in Tehrān. Embassies keep lists of foreign companies operating out of Iran.

ACTIVITIES
Beaches
There are a number of beaches on both coastlines, but activities on them are very low-key. The busiest beach I saw in Iran was at Bandar-é Abbās, which has pony rides and other typical seaside attractions, but I didn't see anyone actually swimming or sunbathing there, let alone surfing or waterskiing. The only people in swimming trunks were children; boys only of course. Occasionally young men would brave a few cm of water to paddle, but no-one dared risk the sharks and stinging jellyfish further out to sea. Do not swim anywhere in the Persian Gulf or the Sea of Oman unless there are locals in the water too; one reason for the decline in pearl fishing in recent years is the increase in the shark population.

The Caspian coast has a few hotels with private beaches, and there are some public beaches, but this is not the Mediterranean.

Sunbathing is not a preoccupation of Iranian holiday makers, and there's not much point for women who have to keep to the full hejāb at all times, even when in the water, unless they feel like going to private beaches well away from male eyes. Waterborne Iranian matrons, enveloped entirely in black and bobbing about like oil slicks, are one of those priceless sights unique to this country.

Skiing
Skiing is becoming very popular in Iran, and it is has the advantage of being one of the few sporting activities in Iran in which women can participate on equal terms with men. The season gets going in about the middle of January and lasts until a little after the Iranian New Year, about 21 March. The best skiing is at Dīzīn to the north of Tehrān. The 7½-km Tōchāl telecabin running from the far north of Tehrān to the slopes of Tōchāl is said to be the longest in the world.

Iran is one of the least expensive destinations for skiing in the world, although few people would go to Iran merely for alpine pursuits. Equipment can be rented very cheaply locally, but if you take skiing seriously, bring your own equipment. It's expensive to buy inside Iran and the range available is limited.

Waterskiing
There is a private club for waterskiing on the Karaj Dam to the west of Tehrān, and the sport is theoretically possible in many of the rivers and lakes, although you will have difficulty in arranging the equipment. Women must wear the full hejāb, which may not help with the aerodynamics.

Walking
Fridays in the spring, summer and autumn see great numbers of Tehrānīs flocking to the Alborz Mountains. Men and women can join in together, and the Revolutionary Guards who used to hide behind crags and assault any mixed groups who were having too much of a good time have now largely given up their spoilsport activities. Take a good pair of walking shoes. More details are given in the Tehrān Province chapter.

Others
If your aim in life is to go fishing, hunting, shooting or canoeing in Iran, or if you want to climb mountains or track down tigers, have a word with someone at your nearest Iranian embassy before making any plans. These are things not normally done by foreigners, and you can do with all the official support you can get.

HIGHLIGHTS & ITINERARIES
The most popular overland route from Turkey is east to Tabrīz and Tehrān, southeast to Esfahān and Shīrāz, then east again to Kermān and Zāhedān and on into Pakistan. Some people avoid Tehrān; the usual alternative is to turn south south at Tabrīz and go directly to Esfahān.

Although this standard and long-established route does take in many of the most interesting towns in Iran, and allows the opportunity to make a day-trip to Persepolis and Pasargadae, it does miss out on a very large chunk of Iran, including such culturally diverse areas as the Caspian provinces, the whole of west Iran and the Persian Gulf, and the vast province of Khorāsān.

Whatever you do, you should not miss the famous cities of Shīrāz and Esfahān, and the remains of the magnificent palace complex of Darius the Great at Persepolis, a short distance from Shīrāz. Esfahān was the glorious capital of Shāh Abbās the Great, and many of the buildings founded in his reign remain to make this architecturally the most stunning city in Iran. Shīrāz, once the capital of several Islamic dynasties and famed as a city of wine, poetry and song, has nowadays less immediate visual appeal than Esfahān, but its cultivated and artistic air makes it one of the most pleasant and relaxed cities in Iran.

The towns of Tabrīz and Zāhedān are of no outstanding interest, but they are almost inevitable features on the main overland trail. Yazd, midway between Esfahān and Kermān, is the centre of Zoroastrianism in Iran and also has a great number of Islamic and historical sites of interest, deserving at the very least a day's attention. Kermān, for centuries a poor and backward town, has preserved much of its cultural distinctiveness and also quite a few of its old buildings and its thriving historical bazaar.

Tehrān is an overcrowded and polluted capital, architecturally a tragedy and sociologically a mess, but it does have a number of things to see and, just as importantly, contains many of the best restaurants, shops and hotels in Iran. The people are friendly to foreigners and more Westernised than elsewhere in the country.

One of the most breathtaking sites in Iran is the ancient and amazingly well-preserved ziggurat of Choghā Zambīl, in the middle of a restricted military area in the south-west of the country and way off the main routes, but well worth a detour.

Don't let having a transit visa stop you spending more than a few rushed days in Iran, for you can very easily extend it inside the country. Go along the coast of the Caspian Sea, the favourite Iranian holiday destination and not spoiled by overdevelopment. If the weather is right go down to the shores of the Persian Gulf and visit some of the islands, all of which are quite different from anything you will find on the mainland. Make a personal pilgrimage to the awe-inspiring complex of the Holy Shrine of Emām Rezā in Mashhad, one of the most magnificent groups of buildings in the Islamic world. Glide along the 7½ km Tōchāl telecabin and go skiing at Dīzīn. Hear the president speak at Friday prayers in Tehrān. Travel to the hauntingly remote ancient church of St Thaddeus in the Kurdish enclave of Āzarbāyjān-é Gharbī, which has only one service a year, attended by Armenian pilgrims from all over Iran. Shake the Shaking Minarets of Esfahān.

Suggested Itineraries

If you only have a week to spend in Iran, it's probably best to restrict yourself to two or three main towns. Arranging long-distance transport can be difficult at short notice, and the hassle involved makes an extensive itinerary unworkable. Esfahān deserves at least three days and Shīrāz, with the nearby remains of Persepolis and Pasargadae, needs about the same. Tehrān is the sort of place that is easy to get to but difficult to extricate yourself from. It has less to offer in historical or architectural terms than many much smaller cities, and seeing everything takes a heavy investment in time and effort for the appalling traffic turns already long distances into day-trips.

If you have a couple of weeks to spend in Iran, book as early as you can to take advantage of Iran Air's incredibly low domestic fares and visit Kermān (minimum one day), Yazd (two days), Būshehr (one day), and Mashhad (one day). In spring, summer or autumn try to spend a few days touring along the Caspian littoral (avoiding any public holidays), enjoy the cool climate of Hamadān and check out the historical remains around Bākhtarān. In winter fly to Bandar-é Abbās, where the weather is pleasant, and take a tiny passenger boat out to the island of Hormoz, with its lonely red-stoned Portuguese fortress, once the centre of a thriving trading empire. Also visit the fascinating, unspoilt island of Gheshm, with its ancient ventilation-shafts and crude but charming architecture, soon to be changed beyond recognition under grandiose development schemes.

Those with more than a month to spare can work out a more extensive and rewarding itinerary, visiting most of the main regions of Iran. Much of the travelling involves long distances across desert, but you can avoid exhaustion if you make a plan and book some flights as soon as you arrive. Most flights are filled at least 10 days in advance, although exceptions are sometimes made for foreigners. For the first fortnight you can travel by land, and when you've had enough desert vistas and lousy meals at roadside cafés, you can make use of the Iran Air tickets you booked on arrival.

ACCOMMODATION

Accommodation in Iran is often in short supply, and it varies very widely in quality. Unfortunately, most places are now reported to be charging foreigners in dollars, so accommodation is not the bargain that it used to be.

Options range from the cheap and cheerful to the opulent and almost luxurious. Cheap and cheerful places are easy enough to find almost everywhere, but the opulent ones are restricted to Tehrān, the major provincial capitals and two or three outposts. Between the two there's something to suit almost everyone. Because there aren't always enough beds to go around you should book in early, preferably in the morning. If you turn up late at night in certain places at certain times of the year you will have trouble, but even if you front up in Mashhad at midnight at the peak of the pilgrimage season, someone would almost certainly take pity on you before you had to go looking for a park bench. I've tried to point out places where you might have problems finding a room.

All hotels and mosāferkhūnés (lodging houses) are categorised, regulated and

Lion and Bull motif at the Apadana, Persepolis

inspected by the Tourism & Pilgrimage Department of the Ministry of Culture & Islamic Guidance. Tourist offices in every provincial capital are supposed to display a list of all local places to stay, although not all of them actually do so. Hotels are classified according to a star system, with five stars for a luxury establishment with private bathrooms in every room, and one star for a place offering only simple accommodation, but with at least some bathroom or shower facilities and usually a few rooms with private bathrooms. There is also a grading system for mosāferkhūnés which classes them as 'superior', '1st class' or '2nd class'. In the last of these categories you can expect almost unimaginable deprivations. Prices within each category are fixed locally by the tourist office and are consistent within each province but not throughout Iran. Hotel taxes (generally around 250 rials) are also fixed locally.

I haven't used the star system much because it is not entirely reliable and it does not correspond to the classifications used in the West. As a rough guide, the places listed under 'bottom end' include mosāferkhūnés and one-star hotels, 'middle' are two-star and three-star hotels, and 'top end' are four-star and five-star hotels. Prices are generally lowest in the east and south-east of the country, and highest in Tehrān and the Caspian resorts. Esfahān is more expensive than Shīrāz. In small places with no hotels, mosāferkhūnés charge more because of the lack of competition.

When Iranian couples ask for a double room, they are always asked to provide proof that they are married. Since all guests have to show identity cards on checking in, there is no possibility of booking in anonymously as Mr and Mrs Smith. The rules may be relaxed for non-Muslim Westerners, but on the whole unmarried couples do not travel together and do not share rooms.

Camping

Camping on a regular basis is not really a viable accommodation option in Iran. Because of fears about security, the authorities don't like anyone pitching tents at unofficial sites except registered nomads, and least of all foreigners. Except for the very few government campsites, or private land which the owner has given you permission to use, almost everywhere in Iran counts as an unofficial campsite. Since many parts of the country are military or restricted zones, and it is not always immediately obvious when you are in or near one, there is a risk of unknowingly camping in an area where your mere presence would attract a great deal of suspicion.

In the days when Iran was a major feature on the Asian overland trail, a number of fairly well-equipped campsites sprung up outside most of the major cities of Iran (although never Tehrān). By the end of the Iran-Iraq War most of them had been closed altogether or converted to housing displaced persons, and those that remained open attracted few foreign travellers. Perhaps now that the refugees can return home, and tourism is officially a priority of the Iranian government, some of the old campsites may reopen.

In remoter parts of Iran where there is no alternative accommodation, camping out may be feasible and perhaps inevitable. Anywhere close to built-up areas is probably OK if a local says it is or gives you permission. Within a built-up area it is possible and not necessarily illegal, but not recommended. Camping anywhere within binocular range of a military zone or border area is very inadvisable.

If you do get stuck somewhere where you have no choice but to camp out for the night, try to ask someone where it is OK to do so, preferably someone with authority such as the police. You may even be offered use of someone's garden. If you are planning a long trek, hiking or mountaineering, and will have to camp out, it would be sensible to discuss your plans with the provincial tourist office first. They may be able to write a letter of introduction on your behalf, arrange a guide if you need one or help you in some other way. They can also warn you of any dangers such as wild animals or security problems. Bring any camping equipment you may need with you, as it is very difficult to find inside Iran.

Youth Hostels

There are no youth hostels in Iran.

Mosāferkhūnés

At the bottom end of the market is the mosāferkhūné (in classical Persian *mosāferkhāné*), literally 'traveller's house'. Conditions are either very primitive or else just primitive; if there's a hot shower in your room, it's probably not a mosāferkhūné at all. What you'll normally get is one of up to half a dozen beds in a male-only dormitory with a sink in the room, or else a small private room with a shared sink on the same floor.

If you can pay in rials, you're unlikely to have to fork out much more than about 800 rials a night for a dormitory bed, 1400 rials for a single room or 2100 rials for a double at any mosāferkhūné, and if you shop around you should be able to find somewhere to wallow in discomfort for quite a bit less. If the place is charging foreigners in hard currency, the minimum is US$5 to US$6 for a single in rock bottom places. Most mosāferkhūnés are almost clean, and a select few actually are so. Although few offer more than the most spartan of accommodation, they do have the advantage of intimacy, and they are usually excellent places for meeting friendly fellow-guests over a cup or two of tea from the bottomless pot constantly on offer at reception. Even if you can afford better, it is worth staying in at least one mosāferkhūné just for the cultural experience. If the thought of a day without a shower puts you off, you can always head for the nearest backstreet public bath-house *(hammūm)*. Some of the better mosāferkhūnés do have bathroom facilities, usually shared but occasionally private, but if there is hot water at all, it will only be available at certain fixed times of the day.

If you are looking for the cheapest place to stay in any town, you should learn to recognise the Persian script for mosāferkhūné. Some places which are officially classified as mosāferkhūnés have signs with the word 'hotel' in the name (sometimes in the English sign but not the Persian one) and it is not always obvious from the outside that they are not proper hotels.

It is not true that women have to stay at more expensive places – I met a number of unaccompanied female Westerners who were happily resident at the grottiest of mosāferkhūnés. However, at the bottom end places they may be more reluctant to have a Western woman as a guest than a Western man. In general I would not advise foreigners, female or male, to stay at the real cheapies unless they have some understanding of the local culture and a smattering of Persian. In the east of Iran they are best avoided by women altogether.

Hotels

The indigenous word for hotel is *mehmūnkhūné* (*mehmānkhāné* in classical Persian), but nowadays the word hotel (from the French) is much more common. The two

are completely interchangeable. The name *mehmūnpazīr* (classical *mehmānpazīr*) is sometimes used to describe a basic one-star hotel which is still one step above a mosāferkhūné.

Hotels – bottom end Into this category come many of the places that would have been classified as two-star or three-star hotels before the revolution, but have since fallen upon hard times, as well as a lot of places which have always been bottom end. At almost any place which has been officially classified as a hotel rather than a mosāferkhūné you can expect the option of a room with a private bathroom, and probably a private telephone too serving at least for decoration. It will quite possibly have a receptionist who can make a stab at intelligible conversation in English. Most places will only have Asian lavatories. Typical prices are around 2000/3000 rials for a single/double, but much more if you have to pay in dollars.

Hotels – middle In a two-star or three-star hotel you should be able to enjoy an intelligent conversation in English with the manager or receptionist, a hot private shower with good water pressure all day long (power cuts permitting), a couple of chairs in the room, a hotel restaurant or tea-room at least, and a telephone in the room, although probably without direct dialling facilities. Most hotels in this category will have Western lavatories in some rooms. Few will have a backup generator powerful enough to light up anything more than the lobby and perhaps the corridors, but there should be a supply of candles in each room. Typical prices are from 2500/4000 rials to 6000/9000 rials for a single/double, but much more in dollars.

Hotels – top end At the top end, you used to pay a pittance for the most sumptuous accommodation the Islamic Republic can offer, unless you had to pay in dollars (see below). The top half dozen or so hotels in Iran are still almost luxurious by international standards, although you do get the feeling that hardly any maintenance work has been done on them since the revolution, and probably none at all on the plumbing or telephone wiring. Most hotels in this category will have some boutiques in the lobby, a restaurant and teahouse or coffee-room, room service most hours of the day, and an overnight laundry service. A few also have bookshops, private taxi services, hairdressers and swimming-pools.

At one supposedly five-star hotel in Tehrān, while I was half-way through shampooing my hair, the water supply was suddenly and completely cut off without any warning. It took me over half an hour of constant redialling to get through to reception to complain, and while I was speaking to them the room was plunged into utter darkness as the electricity went on sympathy strike. And although the telephone was theoretically equipped to make outgoing calls, it only worked for certain Tehrān numbers beginning with the number '2'.

This sort of inconvenience is mildly annoying and sometimes even amusing if you are paying in rials, but it is intolerable when you have to pay in hard currency at around US$100 a night. Five-star hotels in Iran are definitely an Iranian experience, and not a facsimile of a thousand other international hotels. Where else but Iran might you find a luxury hotel with a 'Death to America!' coffee-room, or a souvenir shop which refuses to accept American Express?

Hard-Currency Pricing

After the revolution some of the best hotels in Iran passed into the ownership of certain state organisations such as the Martyrs' Foundation. Thanks to lacklustre management and indifferent service, the standards at these places, which include the famous and now sadly run-down Abbasi in Esfahān, rapidly began to fall. The controlling bodies persuaded the government that the reason for their failure was lack of money. In the summer of 1990 the central authorities decided to allow these hotels to set their prices in rials but require foreign guests to pay in dollars at a very unfavourable exchange rate. Since the best private hotels

charged only in rials and offered far better standards at about one-tenth of the price, hardly any foreigners stayed at the outrageously overpriced establishments, and they actually lost custom as a result.

On 21 January 1991 the Governor of the Central Bank of Iran gave an interview, broadcast on Iranian radio and TV and reported in *Tehran Times*, stating that with immediate effect:

All hotels in Iran are now obliged to charge their (foreign) customers in rials...With the implementation of the said plan, Tehrān which is now known as the most expensive capital will eventually be viewed as one of the most inexpensive cities of the world.

However some months later, the same hotels were still charging foreigners in dollars, and foreigners were still avoiding them. In 1991 there was even talk of making all hotels of a category higher than one star charge foreigners in hard currency, in spite of the new foreign exchange regulations then in force.

Late Update Reports from Iran in March 1992 indicate that all hotels and even mosāferkhūnés are charging foreigners in hard currency at highly unfavourable exchange rates. This means that a foreign visitor is expected to pay perhaps 10 times the price an Iranian is charged.

The research for this book was done before hard currency pricing became a general practice, and the prices given are those current at that time, in rials. The prices should still give an idea of the relative cost of various accomodation options in each place, but given the level of inflation in Iran, and the probability that you will have to pay in dollars, the actual cost is quite uncertain.

This is hardly good news for the individual traveller, or for Iran's tourist industry in general, but there are few avenues of protest. If a price you are quoted seems outrageous, bargain hard or go elsewhere. Hopefully competition between hotels will eventually result in more realistic prices, and if you find a place that offers good value for money, please let us know.

Reserving a Room

Many hotels in all categories are used to accepting reservations. Since hotels may be booked up weeks or even months ahead, it is advisable to do a certain amount of planning, and perhaps reserve some accommodation. Many hotels will give priority to a foreigner, but not usually in Tehrān. Conversely some places refuse to accept foreigners, especially the cheapest mosāferkhūnés.

There are several ways of booking a room, but the only sure one is to pay a deposit in advance against a written receipt. You can make a prepaid reservation for any hotel in the Homa chain (in Bandar-é Abbās, Mashhad, Shīrāz or Tehrān) at any other Homa Hotel or, at least in theory, through any Iran Air office. This is legally binding and if the hotel is double-booked or refuses you, you can go to the police. Some travel agencies can make hotel reservations, but they will usually only do so as part of a tour or package. Tourist offices may also be willing to arrange a room booking, but probably only within the same province.

If you plan to return at a particular date to the town where you're staying, it's a very good idea to book a hotel room in person before you leave. If you're travelling to another city at a fixed date, ask the receptionist at the hotel where you're staying to make a telephone booking at a hotel on your behalf. Some hotels have special arrangements with hotels in other cities, and they may be able to make bookings over the telephone.

Some hotels accept reservations over the telephone, or at least will do so for a foreigner, but the room will usually only be held until about 6 pm. If you have already reserved a room by telephone and are going to arrive later than this, ring the hotel the same day and say that you are going to be late. Otherwise, if you haven't paid a deposit, they may give the last room to someone else.

If you've just arrived at a city airport or station, it might be worth telephoning around to see which places have rooms, although some hotels are wary about agreeing to take strangers before they turn up in person. If you can't find anywhere at all you can ask at the tourist office or, outside their short opening hours, the police. You won't have much say over what sort of accommodation you get.

Hotel staff sometimes keep rooms back in case a special customer (such as a Revolutionary Guard or bigwig) turns up without notice, and they may be taking a risk in filling up the last free room. A generous tip may induce the receptionist to take the risk and offer you an otherwise unavailable room.

Since most hotels have a shortage of single rooms, there are often double rooms occupied by only one person. Sometimes the manager will ask a guest to allow someone of the same sex to use the spare bed, but of course no-one will be forced to share a room with a stranger against his or her will. Expect a discount if you are asked to share a room.

Registration

At all hotels and mosāferkhūnés every guest is required to fill out a registration form on arrival. There is usually an English translation, but some places only have forms in Persian which the receptionist will be happy to fill out on your behalf. It is not permitted to leave any part of the form blank. Every so often, sometimes daily, a man from the local Komīté comes to the hotel to inspect the registration forms, and has the right to make any further enquiries he likes about any particular guest. You will nearly always be asked to show some form of identification with your photograph on it (this does not have to be your passport) and the receptionist will usually keep this overnight. Sometimes the management tries to hold on to your passport or ID for more than one night, or even for the whole of your stay, on the grounds that the Komīté may come at any time and ask to see it.

If the reception is holding your passport and you need it for any reason, you may be asked to give some other form of identification in its place. Often you will be asked to pay a deposit on checking in, which may be equal to, or even more than, the total charge for your stay.

At Zāhedān and a few other places all overnight visitors have to go in person to register with the Komīté, but this is only a formality. First of all you have to find a hotel which is willing to give you a room.

FOOD

At its best the Iranian cuisine is very good indeed. With its emphasis on the freshest ingredients, especially vegetables and fruit, and its relatively low levels of red meat and fat, it is also remarkably healthy. The problem, in these difficult postwar days, is that to enjoy the full range of Iranian cooking you need to be invited to a good number of Iranian houses or else stick to only the most epicurean of restaurants. For the traveller it's all too often a choice of the same two or three standard dishes that you'll find almost anywhere in Iran, and sometimes you are simply told what you are having and there's no choice at all. Because of austere rationing the less well-off Iranian housewife, always heavily dependent on rice, bread and vegetables, often has to make do with the most meagre scraps of meat or fish, although no self-respecting Iranian hostess is going to give a foreign guest the slightest evidence of food shortages in her house.

It is not the custom for Iranians to talk much at meals. Cutlery is normally a fork and spoon rather than a knife and fork, except in high-class restaurants and Westernised households. Other than with snacks and kebabs served with bread, eating with the hands is less common than in the Arabic countries or Pakistan, but where this is the custom you should never put your left hand into a communal food dish; the left hand is used for something else.

The Persian diet is heavily based on rice, bread, fresh vegetables, herbs and fruit. Meat, usually minced or cut into small chunks, is used to add flavour but is rarely the dominant ingredient. The standard meat is lamb or mutton, although beef and veal also turn up from time to time. For religious reasons, pork never turns up. Chicken is

cheap and widely available, and it is often spit-roasted and served whole or by the half. Duck is sometimes used and goose, pigeon, pheasant, grouse and all manner of game are also available but rarely standard fare. Goat, camel and buffalo meat are eaten in rural areas, but are only sold in small quantities in the towns. Camel meat is considered something of a delicacy, but goat and buffalo are more of an acquired taste.

A large number of fresh herbs and spices is used in Iranian cooking, often with great subtlety, and very few settlements in Iran are without their spice market. Some mainstays are tumeric and saffron, nutmeg and cardamon. Nuts and fresh or dried fruit are commonly included in meat and poultry dishes to create a peculiarly Iranian blend of the sweet and the savoury.

The concept of vegetarianism is not widely understood in this country where meat is still a luxury for many people. Unless you are cooking for yourself, it would be hard to maintain a healthy diet in Iran without eating some animal products. If you're invited to dinner, it would be difficult to avoid meat without offending your host. Many restaurants will serve at least one vegetable dish, but sometimes small pieces of meat will be used in them for flavouring. The Persian for 'I am a vegetarian' is *geyāh khār hastam*.

Note

For a list of the items which may be on offer for meals and snacks, with Persian script, see the menu translator in the language section at the back of the book.

Rice

You had better love rice, for in Iran it is served in vast helpings with almost every main dish, and very few of the main dishes would be considered complete without it. Iranian rice from the rainy plains of Māzandarān is considered by many – not only Iranians – to be some of the world's best, but much of the rice sold in the country today is imported from Thailand and elsewhere. *Chelō* is rice prepared in several stages over 24 hours, boiled and steamed and served separately, while *polō* is rice cooked with the other ingredients. Rice in general is *berenj*. The rice is always fluffy and tender, never sticky and soggy. Often the cook will steam chelō rice with yoghurt or an egg yolk to make a crunchy golden crust at the bottom of the pan, which is broken up and served on top of the rest of the rice. Saffron is very frequently used to flavour and colour rice.

Bread

Iranian bread (*nūn*, in classical Persian *nān*) is excellent. It is always sold very fresh, and it is baked in front of you in nearly every bakery (*nūnvā ī*). There are four main varieties of Iranian bread, which are either baked in cavernous clay furnaces, or briefly plunged into the flames of a pit-oven.

Lavāsh is a flat and very thin type of bread which is folded twice into a square. It keeps for months. *Sangak* is a thicker bread, oval-shaped and pulpy, which is baked on a bed of stones to give it its characteristic dimpled look. Make sure all the stones are removed before putting your teeth into it. *Taftūn* (or *taftān*) is crisp, about a cm thick and oval-shaped, with a characteristic ribbed surface. *Barbarī* is the elite of Iranian breads: crisp and salty, with a glazed and finely latticed crust, it's best when hot from the oven. Bread is sometimes sold by weight, but usually it's 10 rials a round, except for barbarī, which is 20 rials. Some shops and bakeries sell French bread.

Yoghurt

Another great Iranian staple is yoghurt (*māst*), similar to Greek or Turkish yoghurt. Sometimes it is served on its own with lavāsh bread, sometimes as a side-dish, and sometimes as a cooking ingredient. It is also mixed into rice, often with diced cucumber or other vegetables, fresh herbs and spices stirred in.

Soup & Stew

Iranian soup (*sūp*) is thick and filling. Even thicker is *āsh*, more of a pottage or broth, and thicker still is *ābgūsht*, almost a stew, which is served as a first course or more commonly as a main dish. Ābgūsht is the only dish at many of the cheaper restaurants and tea-houses, where it is also known as *dīzī*. A thick brew of potato chunks, fatty meat and lentils, ābgūsht is mashed in a bowl and served with sangak bread: it makes a filling and inexpensive meal. The best ābgūsht is served in Tabrīz. The dividing lines between sūp, āsh and ābgūsht can be hazy.

Khōresh, or more colloquially *khōresht*, is a blanket term for any kind of thick meaty stew with vegetables and chopped nuts. It's a more sophisticated version of ābgūsht.

Chelō Kabāb

The other dish served in eating-houses throughout Iran is *chelō kabāb*, a long thin strip of lean lamb, marinated overnight in seasoned yoghurt, grilled at a high temperature for a few minutes and served with a mound of chelō rice. Chelō kabāb is usually sprinkled liberally with sumac (*somāgh*) and accompanied by a raw onion, a pat of butter and a bowl of yoghurt to stir into the rice. When it's made with lamb fillet, it's known as *fillé kabāb* and is invariably delicious. *Chelō kabāb-é makhsūs* ('special' chelō kabāb) is a larger strip of meat than average and is also made of good quality lamb; *chelō kabāb-é barg* ('leaf' chelō kabāb) is thinner and varies in quality, but is usually good. A vastly inferior version known as *chelō kabāb-é kūbīdé* ('ground' chelō kabāb) is made of minced meat of some description with bone and heaven knows what else, and I've never had a good one.

If you travel around Iran, you will have plenty of opportunity to carry out your own research. I suspect that many Western visitors blanch at the thought of chelō kabāb because they have been forced to eat kūbīdé, and have not known that better varieties were on offer.

Another Iranian favourite is *jūjé kabāb*, marinated chicken kebabs served in the same way as chelō kabāb. Sometimes it's very good and sometimes not so good.

Other Dishes

Kūkū is a very thick Iranian omelette cut into

wedges and served hot or cold. Spinach kūkū is a regular feature of Iranian home cooking. *Dolmé*, like Turkish *dolma*, is a stuffed vegetable, fruit or vine leaf, with a mixture of rice and vegetables or meat (or both) as the filling. *Ghormé-yé sabzī* is an occasionally rather bitter stew of lamb, spinach and dried lime. *Koftē* are meatballs, similar to Turkish *kofta*.

One of the prizes of Iranian cooking is *fesenjūn* (or *fesenjān*), a stew of duck, or sometimes goose or chicken, in a rich sauce of pomegranate juice and chopped walnuts. It's quite an honour to be served fesenjūn at an Iranian's house. Some restaurants serve it too, but the quality isn't the same.

There are few exciting fish dishes. Although a reasonable catch does come in from the Caspian Sea and the southern coast, and from some rivers and lakes, the distribution network is not good and very little fish is eaten away from these areas. What fish does get to the inland cities is expensive and sometimes past its best. If you get the chance to try it, Iranian sturgeon makes a magnificent meal; baked sturgeon is a traditional offering at Iranian wedding receptions. Shrimps and prawns are good and cheap along the Persian Gulf, but very little other seafood is available. The excellent Iranian caviar is now almost unobtainable inside the country.

Western-inspired dishes, especially steaks, are available at some of the better restaurants, but they don't always get them right. Snack food such as hamburgers, salad sandwiches, sausages and meatballs is sold at snack-bars. Iranian sausages are always suspect: give them a miss. Brightly decorated restaurants selling 'fast' food such as pizzas, hamburgers and fried chicken are very popular with hip young locals of either sex. They are often surprisingly good – but expect anything but fast service.

Desserts, Sweets & Snacks
Most Iranian meals end with a fruit-bowl rather than a dessert, and most of the pastry dishes listed below are much more commonly found in confectioners' shops than in restaurants or private houses. Nuts and fruit are passed round Iranian houses all day long, and eaten in copious quantities. Most Iranian fruit is good, some of it among the best in the world. There are very few fruits which will not grow in Iran; even pineapples and bananas can be found in southern Balūchestān. Particularly recommended are pomegranates, peaches and watermelons, and rosy-fleshed grapefruit which are perfect to eat without sugar. Iranian almonds and hazelnuts are highly edible, and the pis-

Iranian Chocolate Bar Wrapper

tachios are really excellent, though not as cheap as they used to be.

Iranian confectionery tends to err on the sickly side of sweet, but if yours is a sweet tooth, the cakes and puddings are worth a try, especially the delicious and refreshing *pālūdé* (also called *fālūdé*), tooth-breaking *gaz* and the wide range of ice creams.

Restaurants

The standard of restaurants and range of food available vary considerably throughout Iran. In smaller provincial towns, there may be only one or two eating-houses serving no more than three or four different main dishes between them, while in larger towns there may be several excellent restaurants. In Tehrān there are all manner of restaurants offering a wide range of Iranian and foreign food. There is a restaurant of some description in almost every airport, and there is usually somewhere to eat at the larger bus stations. There are roadside cafés along all main intercity highways. On many routes these will be a great distance apart and untroubled by competition so standards are not particularly high.

It is a good rule not to judge a restaurant by its decor. Some of the flashest places are very disappointing, while many plain and unprepossessing restaurants have excellent food and service.

If you don't know Persian it is sometimes rather difficult to recognise a restaurant. Many places are invisible from the main road, and others are in basements or upper storeys with only a sign in Persian at street level. The fact that a restaurant has a sign in English doesn't necessarily mean that there will be a menu in English or that anyone there will understand English. Conversely, the lack of a sign in English doesn't mean that foreigners are not welcome inside. Try to learn the Persian script for the words that mean a place to eat – most commonly either *restōrān* or *chelō kabābī*, although some places are marked *sālon-é ghezā* ('food hall'). A *kabābī* is someone or somewhere specialising in kebabs, served with bread.

Although some places do have English menus, most don't and many restaurants don't have even a menu in Persian. Even if there is a menu in Persian, the waiter may not bring it to you because it will probably be assumed that you cannot read Persian. Many of the flasher restaurants list about five times as many dishes as they ever serve at any one time.

At restaurants where there is a man sitting at a desk by the entrance, you either give him your order and pay at the same time, or the waiter takes your order and brings the bill to your table, you pay the waiter and leave a tip of 10 to 15% if it's warranted. If no-one brings you a bill, you pay at the desk before leaving. At roadside cafés you usually pay in advance and are given some tokens to take to the serving area in exchange for your meal – there is no need to tip. If the food is going to take a few minutes to prepare, you take a seat and wait for a waiter to bring the food to you. At restaurants where there is no-one at the front desk, you sit down at a spare table and the waiter will serve you and bring you the bill. You pay the waiter, along with any tip. If you don't have the exact change and you offer an amount not very much higher than the bill, the waiter may assume that the change is a tip.

Breakfast

Breakfast is usually lavāsh bread with goat's milk cheese, yoghurt, jam or honey, sometimes with a fried egg or two thrown in, and always washed down with tea. Cornflakes and the like are available, but very expensive and a luxury or an irrelevance for most Iranians. Many hotels serve breakfast, but it is not usually included in the room charge.

DRINKS
Tea

Tea (*chāy*) has to be the national drink of Iran. It's served scalding-hot, black and strong, sometimes with lemon, and traditionally in a small glass cup with a detachable metal holder. Tea is probably the first thing you'll be offered anywhere in Iran if you stay more than five minutes. By the stringent laws of Persian hospitality, any host is honour-bound to offer a guest at least one cup of tea before even considering any sort of business, and the guest is expected to drink it. To the outsider it may seem that the greatest decision most Iranians make all day long is how many lumps of sugar to have with their tea. Iranian tea is so bitter that almost no-one drinks it without sugar.

The traditional Persian way of drinking tea is to clench a chunk of crudely-broken sugar (*ghand*) between the front teeth while sipping the brew through it; it's quite a feat to pick up this trick, and in the mouth of a novice the sugar-lump lasts a matter of seconds. An Iranian can keep it going for a whole cup or more. As sugar is rationed, you should ask for a teaspoon rather than practise with this scarce commodity. The tea is not usually made from the choicest of leaves, and those that do reach the pot tend to be stewed rather than merely scalded; it's perfect for anyone suffering from a tannin deficiency but hard to enjoy without sugar. Certainly tea is one of the best, and safest, drinks that you can have on a hot day.

The Teahouse The *chāykhūné* (in classical Persian *chāykhāné*), or teahouse, is a great Persian institution. It's an all-male retreat where the regulars sit all day drinking pot after pot of chāy, pausing only to chat or smoke the hubble-bubble. The *chāykhūné* used to be, and still is in some places, a centre for social life and also for the exchange of news, information and gossip.

Until recent years many chāykhūnés regularly offered poetry recitals, story telling,

animal shows and other cultural or semi-cultural performances to pull in the crowds, but nowadays only a few places cling to the old traditions. Unfortunately for the foreign visitor, there's no *What's On In Village X* guide to check out the local scene, but if you hear on the grapevine that there's going to be a recital or other traditional cultural event on at the local, you'd be well-advised to drop everything and grab a seat.

Coffee

Iranian coffee (*ghahvé*) is the same as Turkish coffee. Remember to let the brew settle and then only drink the top three-quarters of it. Iranian coffee is served strong, black and sweet, with a spoon to stir the sugar. Coffee is generally considered something of a luxury, and is usually only served at the end of a meal. Nescafé has made its impact on Iran, and because it is very expensive you'd better look jolly pleased if anyone presses a cup on you. It is often served with milk or sometimes made into a rather good milk shake. If you ask for *café au lait*, expect the coffee to be instant and the milk to be sour. I have occasionally seen coffee with cream listed on menus, but never actually available.

Fruit Juice

Several sorts of delicious fruit juice are served at ice-cream parlours, cafés and street stalls throughout Iran, all very fresh and often squeezed while you wait. Orange, pomegranate and carrot juice are the three standards, although a few more adventurous establishments offer watermelon, lemon,

---

Smoking the Hubble-Bubble

Even if you're not in on a big cultural occasion, you should at least pop in to a tea house and try a drag or two on the hubble-bubble (*nārgīlé* or *ghalyān*). Sitting and puffing on the pipe, oblivious to the outside world, will acclimatise you to the normal Iranian state of mind. It is perhaps the greatest act of cultural integration that a foreigner can make in Iran, short of becoming a Shi'ite Muslim. You'll also get a mild buzz as you draw in the tobacco smoke and make that satisfying bubbling noise in the water-pipe.

Smoking the hubble-bubble is taken very seriously and you're bound to get it wrong the first few times, but not for lack of friendly advice. At only about 150 rials for 10 to 20 minutes' worth of tobacco, it has to be worth a try. No Iranian woman would consider entering the teahouse, but there's no reason why a Western woman shouldn't treat herself as an honorary male for the purpose, although she should not expect to go unnoticed. ∎

mango, cherry or grape juice. Some of these are packaged under the name 'Sundis'.

Water

I've never had any problems drinking the water anywhere in Iran. Tehrānīs claim that theirs is some of the purest tap water in the world – it comes straight from springs in the Alborz Mountains and is clean and excellent. Outside Tehrān the water varies widely in quality, although it's generally safe to drink in all the cities. In Esfahān it is notoriously murky and sour-tasting, but I don't think anyone would claim it's actually bad for you. In remoter places, if in doubt it's wise to treat the water (see the Health section). Alternatively, there is almost always bottled mineral water, soft drinks, tea or coffee, all of which are safe. Unless it has obviously come from an ice-making machine, ice is to be treated with caution.

On the islands in the Persian Gulf there is a limited supply of drinking water, and much of the tap water is not desalinated.

Other Drinks

Dūgh is made of churned sour milk or yoghurt, mixed with either sparkling or still water and often flavoured with mint and other ground herbs. It is probably the favourite Iranian cold drink and it's good stuff. In summer it's available in bottles at any snack-bar, café or restaurant. Another Iranian speciality, made with all sorts of chopped nuts and chilled milk, is good if the milk is fresh.

Even in Islamic Iran you can't get away from the Coca Cola influence. Cans of Coca Cola imported from Dubai are available at anything from 500 rials to over 1000 rials. Although not quite the Real Thing, two or three acceptable local imitations are around. The market leader is known as Zam Zam, after the name of the sacred spring outside the holy city of Mecca. Lemonade is also popular, including a fizzy mixture sold in ancient bottles marked 7 Up. Orangeade is known euphemistically as Fanta. Soft drinks are typically about 80 rials a small bottle.

'Islamic beer' or 'Iranian beer' (*mā'-osh-sha'īr*) tastes none too bad, but of course it

does lack alcohol. It is, however, the favourite mixer for home-brewed hooch, as the manufacturers must well know.

Alcohol

Iran is officially a dry country. Alcohol is strictly forbidden to the overwhelming majority of Iranians who are Muslims, and the rules concerning non-Muslims are not entirely clear. Although alcohol is permitted for religious uses, such as communion wine in churches, no official position has ever been made to clarify whether Christians, Jews, Zoroastrians and Sikhs are allowed to drink in private.

The black market in alcohol is controlled by Armenians, and most urban Iranians know someone who can sell bootleg vodka. Until recently patrols of Revolutionary Guards used to roam through towns, acting on tip-offs or looking out for flats and houses where parties seemed to be in progress. The best organised parties always used to have a relay of lookouts; whenever the red alert was raised, the music was turned off, all females present would make sure they were dressed properly, while the men would head off for another room or even a neighbour's flat. The host would then make sure that anything incriminating was either extremely well hidden or flushed down the lavatory. This frequently rehearsed routine could be performed in under two minutes.

This appears to have come to an end in Tehrān and many other places, but in places still heavily in the grip of Revolutionary Guards, party-busting still goes on, and the punishment for possessing or drinking alcohol remains severe.

ENTERTAINMENT

Unsurprisingly, Iran offers very little in the way of organised entertainment or nightlife. Qoran recital contests are about the only cultural activity to have flourished under the Islamic Republic. They can be quite interesting for the sheer range of contestants, from haggard old men and mullahs to boys of about seven, and for the amazing powers of memory they demonstrate.

Cinemas, theatres and concert-halls do still operate, but only under strict ideological constraints which have loosened very little since Khomeinī's death. In order, for instance, to listen to a Beethoven recital, the audience might first have to sit through half an hour of Islamic martial music. Western films and plays (very rarely in the original language) are sometimes shown, but only of certain types and often trimmed to fit in with Islamic values. Until quite recently one of the most prolific Iranian movie producers was the film unit of the Islamic Revolutionary Guards, which brought out unsubtle propaganda efforts loosely based on episodes from the Iran-Iraq War and the popular struggle against the Mojāhedīn and other enemies of the Islamic Republic. They were livened up with such a quota of action scenes that no knowledge of Persian was required.

Iranians have always entertained at home, but more so in the years since 1979, when banned activities such as dancing, drinking, boy meets girl and listening to Western pop music continued to be enjoyed behind closed doors. Favourite activities for young Iranians at a loose end include eating out, drifting between friends' and relatives' houses, window-shopping, playing street-football, and walking, motorcycling or driving in no particular direction for no particular reason. These activities are usually carried out in groups, for most Iranians feel lonely in a party of fewer than three. On Fridays, most Iranians who can, visit or entertain friends and relatives, or else go into the country; many Tehrānīs flock to the lower slopes of the Alborz.

Many younger Iranians listen to bootleg recordings of vaguely recent Western music, especially pop. For several years Madonna, Michael Jackson and Modern Talking (a German 'Europop' outfit largely spurned in the West, with good reason) have been fave raves. Those who can, watch pirate copies of illegally imported videos, though the equipment is still technically outlawed in most parts of Iran. Iranian music, much of which became legal again early in 1989, is more to the Western taste than Arabic or Turkish music. Most of the famous Iranian singers and musicians moved to the West around 1979, and it is still easier to find recordings of the best Iranian artists in the West than in Iran.

So what does the foreigner do for evening entertainment in Iran? Probably the best option is to make some local friends and tag along with them. The second possibility is to find a good restaurant and linger over your meal. The third is to get out that novel you have always been meaning to read and which you sensibly packed in your bag.

THINGS TO BUY

There is a whole host of worthwhile souvenirs to buy in Iran. Thanks largely to the shortage of tourists, mass-production is rare, prices are low and quality is high, even at the bottom end of the market. Iran is a buyers' market for souvenirs, and you will find it hard not to pick up a bargain or two.

Some of the more obvious buys include:

miniatures (*mīnyātūrhā*); decorative swords (*shamshīrhā*) and daggers (*khanjarhā*); tribal caps (*kolāhā-yé īlātī*); calligraphy (*khōsh nevīsī*); spices (*adveyé*); toy camels (*shotorān*) from Balūchestān made with genuine camel hair; Persian slippers (*kafsh-é sarpā'ī*); prayer-rugs (*sajjadehā*); pipes (*pīphā*) and hubble-bubbles (*nārgīlehā*); ceramics (*sefālgarī*); leatherwork (*charmīné*); glassware (*shīshé ālāt*); mosaics (*mōzā'īk-hā*); cashmere (*termé*) and mohair (*marghoz*); silk (*abrīshom*); pyjama-trousers (*pījāmehā*); copper (*mes*) and bronze (*beronz*) articles; items made of mother-of-pearl (*sadaf*) such as key-rings (*halghehā-yé kelīd*) and jewellery (*javāher ālāt*); marquetry (*monabbat kārī*) such as inlaid boxes (*ja'behā*) from Esfahān; henna (*hannā*) and saffron (*za'farān*); books (*kotob*); picture-frames (*ghābhā-yé aks*); stamps (*tambrhā*); coins (*sekkehā*) and banknotes (*eskenās*); tea-sets (*servīs-hā-yé chāy*) and coffee services (*servīs-hā-yé hahvé*); chādors and table-clothes (*sofrehā*).

There used to be quite a scam in Mashhad where credulous tourists would be talked into paying a small fortune for turquoises in the belief that they were worth a large fortune outside Iran. They weren't, and they still aren't. As Iran reopens to tourists there are bound to be plenty of similar cases of overzealous sales techniques. If you get caught out, please write and let me know so that I can warn future visitors.

Carpets

It is possible to export Persian carpets, but for the time being you can't just take one out in your suitcase, and there's no point in trying – you have to go to an agent who can make the arrangements for you. Quite a few carpet dealers in Tehrān, Shīrāz, Mashhad, Tabrīz, Esfahān and elsewhere make a good business of exporting carpets, and will be happy to have your custom however small the shipment.

The whole business of clearing a carpet through customs and getting it to your doorstep takes two to three months on average and adds roughly 20% or 30% to the cost. Some of the older and more valuable carpets cannot be exported legally, so check that yours doesn't belong to this category before paying for it. Also make absolutely sure whether you'll have to pay any transport costs or duties on delivery, and get everything down on paper. If in doubt, it's better to arrange to pay on delivery, so you don't risk being charged twice. The service is generally reliable, but it's up to you to work out a fail-safe agreement with the agent.

The Persians have had over a thousand years to perfect the art of carpet-making, and as long to master the art of carpet-selling. With hundreds of distinctive types of carpet around, it's going to take the Western novice several years of study to be on equal terms with the shrewd Iranian carpet dealer and Mercedes owner. If you don't know your warp from your weft, your Kermān from your Esfahān or your Turkish knot from your Persian, it might be worth reading up a little before visiting Iran. If you know what you're doing you might just be able to pick up a relative bargain in Iran, but it is worth remembering that dealers in the West often sell Persian carpets for little more than you'd pay in Iran – they know the market, bargain better, buy in bulk and save on transport costs. You are also much less likely to be ripped off by your local warehouse dealer than by some Persian bazaar merchant.

Unless you're an expert, don't buy a carpet as an investment – buy it because you like it, and even then only if you have some idea of what sort of price you'd pay for a similar piece back home.

If you're thinking of buying a carpet, lie it flat on the floor and check for any bumps or other imperfections. Small bumps will usually flatten out with wear, but if you find a big hump it is probably there to stay; if you're still sold on the carpet, look very disappointed and expect a generous price cut. To check if a carpet is handmade, turn it over. On a handmade piece the pattern will be distinct on the underside, the more distinct the better the quality. The fineness of any carpet is measured by the number of knots per sq cm. As a rough guide, an everyday carpet will have up to 30 knots per sq cm, a medium-grade piece 30 to 50 knots per sq cm, and a fine one 50 knots per sq cm or more. On a real museum piece you might have 500 or more knots per sq cm, but nowadays a museum is about the only place you will find such an attempt at perfection. The commonest pile material is wool, which is tough and practical, and the best wool is Iranian. Silk carpets are magnificent but they're largely for decoration and hardly very practical. Synthetics? Ugggh!

If you're in any doubt about a particular piece, or about your own bargaining ability, ask an Iranian friend to see it with you. Not only are Iranians often very knowledgeable about their own carpets, but they can always bargain a better price than Joe Tourist. For an introduction to Persian carpets, the National Carpet Museum in Tehrān is a must. It's not amazingly large, but the collection really is magnificent. They sell postcard-sized photos of many of the exhibits, which you can show to carpet dealers to demonstrate what sort of thing you are looking for.

Socio-Politico-Religious Souvenirs

If bizarre religious items grab you, you're in for a treat in the Islamic Republic. What about a flail (*shallāgh*), as used by some of the more devout (or exhibitionist) Shi'ites to publicly scourge themselves during Moharram. The bazaars of Mashhad and Ghom are the best places to track down these unusual souvenirs.

The Ministry of Culture & Islamic Guidance churns out a plethora of keepsakes with everyone's favourite āyatollāh on them – from Khomeinī postcards and Khomeinī wall-hangings to Khomeinī mirrors and even Khomeinī watches – all of which are very cheap and of great novelty value. The public has not fallen in such a big way for any Rafsanjānī cult, and I saw very few shops selling even postcards with the president's photo.

Iran's paper shortage has yet to make any impact on the Guidance Ministry, which continues to publish a profusion of politicoreligious treatises and pamphlets, for sale at any good bookshop. The office outside the former US Embassy boasts a particularly good line of propaganda in English, for sale at giveaway prices. There are other outlets too.

Export Restrictions

Bear in mind the restrictions on exporting certain items from Iran listed in the Customs section. Nobody has a satisfactory definition of how old an 'old' manuscript or how 'original' an original painting must be for it to be a forbidden export, nor exactly how an 'antique' is classified. You certainly mustn't take the word of some bazaar merchant. If you are worried about an expensive purchase being confiscated at the border, it's worth having a word with the local customs office (edāré-yé gomrok) first. The Iranians are particularly sensitive about the export of old or valuable Qorans. It is very common for keepers of handicrafts shops, well aware of the 50,000 rials duty-free limit, to offer to undervalue the price of goods on a receipt issued to foreigners.

Getting There & Away

It is possible to enter or leave Iran by air, road, rail or sea. Very few Western travel agencies have a clue about anything but full-fare air tickets. Most business visitors arrive by air, while most private travellers enter by road. The train service from Moscow is a challenging experience not often tackled by Westerners. The sea routes are mostly used by Iranians or Gulf Arabs. As a rule, visitors with transit visas are meant to enter and leave by land in different directions, but those with tourist visas can arrive and leave by other means, unless their visas are specifically marked otherwise. Even if your visa says that you are entering or leaving by a particular border or means of transport, it is usually possible to have it changed at the visa office in Tehrān.

AIR

There is a steadily increasing number of services to Iran with Iran Air and a few other airlines. There are at present five international airports in Iran. Tehrān Mehrābād is the main one and the only airport used for intercontinental services. There are also some flights to the Arab states from Shīrāz, Bandar-é Abbās, Mashhad and Esfahān, and there is a weekly PIA flight between Mashhad and Quetta.

At the time of writing there are flights to/from Iran on the following routes:

To Tehrān

From	Flights/Week	Airline
Bombay	1	Iran Air
Damascus	1	Iran Air
Doha	1	Iran Air
Dubai	3	Iran Air
	1	Emirates Air
Frankfurt	4	Iran Air
	4	Lufthansa
Geneva	1	Iran Air
Istanbul	2	Iran Air
	1	Turkish Airlines
Karachi	1	Iran Air
	1	PIA
KualaLumpur	2	Iran Air
Larnaca	1	Iran Air
London	3	Iran Air
	3	British Airways
Moscow	2	Aeroflot
Paris	3	Iran Air
Peking	2	Iran Air
Rome	1	Iran Air
	1	Alitalia
Sharjah	3	Iran Air
Tokyo	2	Iran Air
Vienna	1	Iran Air
	1	Austrian
Zurich	1	Swiss Air

To Bandar-é Abbās

From	Flights/Week	Airline
Dubai	2	Iran Air
	2	Emirates
Sharjah	1	Iran Air

To Esfahān

From	Flights/Week	Airline
Dubai	1	Iran Air

To Mashhad

From	Flights/Week	Airline
Quetta	1	PIA
Sharjah	1	Iran Air

To Shīrāz

From	Flights/Week	Airline
Abu Dhabi	1	Iran Air
Doha	2	Iran Air
	1	Gulf Air
Dubai	2	Iran Air
Sharjah	1	Iran Air

Iran Air plans to start flights to Canada and other countries over coming years, and other airlines are likely to establish or resume links with Iran. JAT has recently started a weekly service between Belgrade and Tehrān. There are also indirect connections between Tehrān and many cities around the world, mainly via Dubai, the regional transit centre.

Airlines have few problems in filling seats

to and from Iran, so there are few discounted fares. Iran Air and most other airlines only sell tickets at full IATA rates, although Apex fares are applicable on most routes, and bucket shops in London have some better deals. All international tickets purchased by foreigners inside Iran must be paid for in hard currency. Discounted tickets are not sold anywhere in Iran, nor does there even seem to be any market for them.

In countries with a thriving bucket shop industry or with a large Iranian community, you may be able to find discounted tickets for indirect flights to Iran. You can fly via London, where you can buy fairly cheap tickets to Tehrān. Another possibility is to get one of the many discounted fares to Dubai and then cross the Persian Gulf to Bandar-é Abbās with Emirates or Iran Air (370/740 UAE dirhams – roughly US$100/ 200 – one-way/return) or take a ferry from nearby Sharjah (much less expensive). From some places Aeroflot may have special deals via Moscow.

Iran Air

Iran Air, the national carrier, is not at all a bad airline, although it doesn't serve alcohol, female passengers have to wear the hejāb, and all seats are economy class. Its one concession to luxury is that it serves caviar to passengers on Tokyo flights. Most foreigners prefer to go by other airlines, while Iranians choose Iran Air because they can pay for tickets in rials at the official exchange rate.

Iran Air has sales offices in many major cities in Europe, the Middle East and Asia.

To/From the UK

There are a few small and specialised bucket shops in London selling discounted tickets to Tehrān. Agencies to try include Facts Travel (☎ 071-603 1246), House of Travel (☎ 075-3 832666), Sam Travel (☎ 071-434 9561) and Instyle (☎ 0784 24039). Facts Travel was quoting £570 return with British Airways, the only direct service apart from the much more expensive Iran Air. There are lower fares with Air France (via Paris), Aus-

trian Airlines (via Vienna) and Syrian Arab Airlines (via Damascus), but the cheapest of all is Aeroflot (around £230 one-way, £400 open return, depending on season) if you don't mind dismal service and having to spend a night in Moscow at your own expense. There are also special deals with Turkish Airlines (via Istanbul) and PIA (via Karachi). With the exception of Syrian Arab Airlines (☎ 071-491 8155), these discounted tickets are sold only through agencies and not direct from the airline.

To/From Europe

There are indirect connections, with various airlines, between Tehrān and Amsterdam, Barcelona, Berlin, Brussels, Budapest, Cologne, Copenhagen, Dusseldorf, Hamburg, Hanover, Madrid, Munich, Oslo and Stockholm.

Iran Air Boarding Passes

To/From Turkey

There are direct services from Istambul and indirect connections between Tehrān and Ankara and Izmir. There may soon be direct services between Erzurum and Tabrīz.

To/From the Arabian Peninsula

There are several flights between the Arab states and Iran with Iran Air, Emirates and Gulf Air. These are very popular with well-to-do Iranians on shopping sprees and tend to be booked up well in advance. Emirates, by far the best airline of the three, has return services from Dubai to Tehrān on Tuesday and Saturday at 1030/2060 UAE dirhams one-way/return, and there is an excursion fare of 1480 UAE dirhams for stays of at least seven nights but not more than 23 days. To Bandar-é Abbās it has return flights on Monday and Wednesday at 370/740 UAE dirhams one-way/return. Gulf Air has flights from Doha to Shīrāz at US$102/204 one-

way/return. It may be possible to get cheaper fares in Qatar if you ask at any branch of Cleopatra Travel or Qatar National Travel Agency, and there may also be some special deals in the UAE.

To/From East & Central Asia

There are indirect Tehrān connections with Osaka, Seoul and Singapore. The most convenient connection with Hong Kong is via Bombay with Air India. There are plans to introduce a service between Baku in (ex-Soviet) Azerbaijan and Tabrīz and Tehrān at some time in 1992. There is a new service every Sunday with PIA between Mashhad and Quetta. Ariana Afghan has started a service on Mondays between Kabul and Bandar-é Abbās.

To/From North & South America

There are no direct flights at present between Iran and either continent, but there are con-

Baggage Tickets

nections from most major cities, usually via Frankfurt or London. Iran Air is trying to set up a service to Canada.

To/From Australia/New Zealand

There are no direct flights from Australasia. PIA flies from Melbourne or Sydney to Tehrān via Bangkok and Karachi (A$1782 return). There is a weekly connection from Sydney via Kuala Lumpur with Malaysian Airlines and Iran Air. You can go to Dubai with Singapore Airlines from Melbourne (about A$2000) or with Gulf Air from Sydney (A$2150), and then cross the Persian Gulf to Bandar-é Abbās.

LAND

For over a decade the traditional overland passage (the 'Hippy Trail') between Europe and Kathmandu has been difficult, but it has never been impossible. While excitements in Iran, Afghanistan and other places have frightened off many overlanders and closed some borders altogether, the '80s and '90s have seen the opening of several new routes, some of them passing through Iran.

There are no longer any Iranian buses going further west than Istanbul, and the stencilled wordings on the sides of buses advertising such faraway destinations as Munich and London are for decoration only. There are very occasional (about monthly) Turkish buses between Istanbul and New Delhi via Iran.

Bringing Your Own Vehicle

To drive your own vehicle into Iran you need to be 18 years old or over and have a current International Driving Permit. For the vehicle you'll need a *carnet de passage en douane*, a *diptyque* or a *triptyque*, any of which can be obtained from your national motoring organisation. Alternatively, you can lodge a cash deposit or a bank guarantee for 300% of the new vehicle value, plus the full customs duties, commercial tax and other levies due on the import of a motor vehicle. The deposit is fully refundable if the vehicle is re-exported within a stipulated period, usually three months.

In any case, Iranian customs will note the vehicle details in your passport to make sure you don't leave the country without it. Crashing a vehicle in Iran, or having it stolen, is only recommended for those who love bureaucratic hassles.

Third party insurance is compulsory for foreign drivers, and you can obtain this outside Iran (make sure the policy is valid for Iran and accredited with Iran Bimeh, the Iranian Green Card Bureau) or at the border.

At various times since the revolution, the authorities have required that foreigners on transit visas travelling in their own vehicles be accompanied from entry to exit by a customs officer, usually as part of a convoy. The rule has never been strictly enforced, and may no longer apply at all. It was usually applied only to travellers whose dress or behaviour disqualified them from travelling unescorted. Some travellers have said that the customs official doubled as a guide and actually enhanced their visit. When you get your transit visa, enquire if this rule will apply to you. Better still, get a tourist visa.

Most visiting motorists will come via Turkey, crossing the border at either Bāzargān or Serō. Be prepared for a long wait and a thorough vehicle search at the border, especially at Bāzargān, where the queue of waiting vehicles can stretch to the horizon.

Crossing points at other borders include Mīrjāve (Pakistan), Eslām Ghal'é (Afghanistan), Khosravī (Iraq) and Āstārā (Azerbaijan), though entry to any of these countries, especially with your own vehicle, may be problematic. You may be able to have your vehicle transported via Jolfā on the Moscow to Tehrān railway line, or across the Persian Gulf to the Arabian Peninsula (see the section below on getting to Iran by sea) or across the Caspian between Baku and Bandar-é Anzalī.

To/From Turkey

Bus The Erzurum-Bāzargān-Tabrīz road is the main artery into Iran. The Bāzargān border crossing is one of the most congested bottlenecks in West Asia, and the delay at the border can be very wearisome. There are two main options by public transport on this route. The easier way is to take a direct bus to Tehrān or Tabrīz from Istanbul, Ankara or Erzurum. Several companies, Iranian and Turkish, operate direct buses between Istanbul and Tehrān, of which by far the best is Cooperative Bus Company No 1. The best Turkish operator is probably Van Gölü. Full fare is payable even if you do not go the full journey.

Alternatively, like many regular travellers, you may prefer to do the journey in two or three legs, changing buses at the border to avoid waiting for up to 50 fellow-passengers to clear customs. Also, it can be very difficult to buy a ticket at short notice for the direct bus. From Istanbul you can take a bus to Erzurum or to Dogubayazit. Make sure the bus you catch has a sign on the front with the name of your destination. Dogubayazit is the last main town, and there is a bus from there to the Iran border at 7 am every day, though minibus drivers will tell you that this bus doesn't exist or that it won't go today.

Expect considerable delays in winter as the high mountain passes near the frontier are frequently snowbound. For two or three weeks around Nō Rūz, when the domestic demand for transport becomes very heavy, no Iranian buses are allowed to operate international services and only Turkish buses serve this route. See also the Mākū and Tabrīz entries, and LP's *Turkey – a travel survival kit*.

A border-post has been reopened at Serō (see under Orūmīyé) to the south, and another may open in the near future. It is possible for foreigners to travel between Orūmīyé and Van (Turkey) via Serō, but the route is not much used except local people. This part of Turkey can be a little unpleasant for foreigners.

Warning Beware that for various mostly political reasons much of east and especially south-east Turkey is unsafe for Western travellers. After decades of oppression of the Kurds by the Turkish regime, certain splinter groups of the KDP (Kurdish Worker's Party) have taken to kidnapping foreigners travel-

ling in Turkish-controlled Kurdistan without KDP permission. At the same time, many eastern Turks are becoming increasingly antagonistic towards Westerners, and even a large town like Erzurum is not entirely safe. Bus passengers travelling direct to Ankara or Istanbul are not in any great danger, but those intending to travel independently should first consult their own country's representative in Tehrān or Istanbul, or one of the Kurdish information centres existing in some of the Western capitals.

Train Services between Ankara and Tehrān have recently resumed, departing Ankara at 10.40 am Tuesday, arriving Tehrān 5.30 am Friday. In the other direction, trains leave Tehrān at 10.15 pm Tuesday, arriving Ankara 3.05 pm Friday (45,000 rials return).

To/From Pakistan
One day there will be a railway running way from Tehrān to Quetta, and it will be possible to go by train all the way from London to Calcutta. For the time being however, about 600 km of track between Kermān and Zāhedān has yet to be laid, though the service from Zāhedān to the border has recently resumed. There are two trains a week between the Pakistani border and Quetta, one of which connects with the Zāhedān train. The two railheads are connected by regular buses through Zāhedān. There is also an Iran Air link between Kermān and Zāhedān. See the Zāhedān entry in the East & South-East Iran chapter.

To/From Azerbaijan & Russia
It is possible to enter Iran from the former USSR republic of Azerbaijan. The train crosses the border between Julfa (Azerbaijan) and Jolfā (Iran). You can also cross by land between Āstārā (Iran) and Astara (Azerbaijan), which has a rail connection to Baku. For information on connections to Āstārā, see that section in the Āzarbāyjān chapter. No other routes are currently open. Transport options in the former Soviet republics are subject to rapid and substantial change.

Train The train from Moscow to Tehrān is certainly an interesting alternative route into Iran, although organising the ticket and transit visa may be a considerable hassle. In Moscow you can book a ticket at the exasperatingly inefficient Intertourtrans office, 15 Ulitsa Petrovka (open 9 am to 9 pm daily except Sunday) or, on the day of departure only, at the Intourist office of Leningradskaya station. In Baku (Azerbaijan) you go to Intourist (if it still exists) in the Hotel Azerbaijan. In Iran tickets can be bought at the train station in Tabrīz, preferably at least a week in advance, and in Tehrān at the booth marked 'Moskva' preferably at least two weeks in advance. In other countries you should be able to book a ticket through Intourist, through an representative office (such as Ibusz in Budapest) or perhaps through a good travel agent. Now that the USSR has ceased to exist, Russians transit visas are a mere formality, and it is not clear what documents are required to pass through Azerbaijan.

There are two classes of sleeping accommodation, but only the very rugged should brave 2nd class. The 1st-class fare is very cheap at 17,000 rials or 124 roubles; foreigners do not have to pay in hard currency for tickets bought in Iran, but may have to, at least theoretically, in Moscow or Baku. Book tickets all the way through, not just to the border, as foreigners aren't allowed to stay in Jolfā and it's a very big hassle to get tickets at the train station here. If you're staying in Julfa (one very simple rouble hotel), tickets to Tehrān can be bought at the train station on the morning of the day of departure for 35 roubles (1st class). Foreigners are not allowed to cross the border here except by train.

From Moscow Kurski station (platform 4) there are trains on Wednesday (currently at 7 pm) and from Tehrān on Saturday (currently at 4.10 pm). From Moscow, the three carriages for passengers to Jolfā are at the rear of the train, marked only in Russian. The line goes through Rostov-on-Don, Baku and Tabrīz, and because of the difference in gauges you have to change trains at Jolfā. In theory trains arrive after about 3½ days but they are regularly delayed for days (mine arrived two days late). Customs formalities on either side of the border are time-consuming but relaxed. Do not count on being able to change money or make a telephone call here.

On the 'Soviet' side there are very few facilities on board, although the 1st-class compartments are comfortable. Some snacks (and occasionally vodka or beer) are touted at train platforms along the way, but the dining car is disgusting so you should take enough food for the whole journey. Since palatable food may not be available at an affordable price in Moscow, bring some with you. The Iranian train is much better, and food is available on board.

To/From Afghanistan

Foreigners are very rarely given permission to enter Afghanistan by land, though the border-post at Eslām Ghal'é on the Mashhad to Herat road is still open. The crossing at Dūst Mohammad east-north-east of Zābol is now closed. Although the Afghan frontier has always been a permeable one, alternative routes cannot be recommended for the time being. Further information is given in the Tāybād entry in the East & South-East Iran chapter.

To/From Iraq

Although the frontier is no longer closed, there is no organised transport between the two countries, and there is not likely to be any for some time to come.

At the time of writing the usual crossing into Iraq, at Khosravī in Bākhtarān Province, was mostly being used by Kurdish and other refugees coming from Iraq. In normal times, there is a bus to the border from the Iraqi side, but none from the Iranian. Further details are available from any Iraqi consulate or tourist office, at the Iranian Consulate in Baghdad or at the tourist office in Bākhtarān.

To/From Syria & Lebanon

There is a regular bus service between

Damascus and Tehrān. In the Syrian capital you can book tickets at the station on Shari'a Shoukri Kouwatli, just east of Martyrs' Square. In Tehrān, book at the west bus terminal. From Tehrān it is usually only possible to buy a return ticket, currently at a fare of 60,000 rials. From Damascus there are shared taxis to Beirut. Tehrān is probably the best place anywhere to apply for a Lebanese visa.

SEA

Valfajre-8 Shipping Company (Sherkat-é Kashtīrānī-yé Vālfajr Hasht), a subsidiary of the Islamic Republic of Iran Shipping Line (IRISL), operates passenger services in the Persian Gulf, and intends also to open or reopen routes to Karachi, Muscat and perhaps Baku (from Bandar-é Anzalī). At the time of writing Valfajre-8 has mostly overnight sailings between Būshehr and Doha, Qatar (nine weekly), Būshehr and Manama, Bahrain (two weekly) and Bandar-é Abbās and Sharjah, UAE (six weekly). Most are afternoon departures; for exact times enquire locally.

There are three classes of accommodation; 1st class (cabin), 2nd class (cabin) and 3rd class (seat). Fares are very reasonable, eg 9600 rials for 1st class between Bandar-é Abbās and Sharjah. There are few facilities on board, and in summer conditions may be a little too hot for many people. Cars can be shipped on some services. Valfajre-8 can arrange tours to Sharjah and also UAE visas for those who need them, payable partly in US dollars and partly in rials.

Inside Iran all tickets are payable in rials only and can be bought from any Valfajre-8 sales office (see the Getting Around chapter). Outside Iran fares are payable in hard currency, and correspond to about half the airfare, eg 230 UAE dirhams for 1st class between Bandar-é Abbās and Sharjah.

The UAE agent in Dubai is Oasis Freight Company (☎ 525000; telex 47720 OSFRT EM), Sharaf Building (next to Ramada Hotel), Shari'a al-Mankhool; in Sharjah (☎ 596321) the address is Kayed Ahli Building, Shari'a Jamal Abdul Nasser. In other countries tickets can be ordered through IRISL offices (ask the nearest Iranian commercial attaché for addresses).

There is little likelihood of travelling as a passenger on one of the many cargo ships plying in and out of the Persian Gulf (especially through Bandar-é Abbās), and even if you did you might have problems at Iranian customs. Dhows are a vague possibility for the very adventurous. It is possible to hire small fishing-boats at dead of night from ports on the Strait of Hormoz, but this is highly illegal and rather dangerous for foreigners.

TOURS

Not many Western companies sell tours to Iran, and very few do so on a regular basis. All such tours are organised by semigovernment tourist authorities in Iran and then sold at a vast mark-up. Although they do not include anything that independent travellers could not arrange themselves, they may be worthwhile for people with plenty of funds who have a limited amount of time, or who are wary of visiting the country alone. The great advantage of these tours is that visa applications for the participants are handled by the tour operator.

The main contact in Iran is the Azadi International Tourism Organization (AITO). This organisation has links with several travel agencies inside the country, especially one called Iran Air-Tours (no relation of Iran Air), which has branches in several cities. According to a recent advertisement, Iran Air-Tours has seven, 10 and 14-day inclusive tours covering up to five centres. They also offer a customised Mashhad pilgrimage tour and a range of 'affordably-priced' special interest group and individual tours covering 'archaeology, architecture, the arts, climbing, hiking, skiing and walking'. These can be arranged either in Tehrān or from overseas. These tours are a very recent innovation and so far largely untested.

In the UK, Jasmine Tours (☎ (06285) 31121; fax 29444), High St, Cookham,

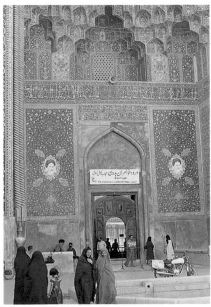

Top Left: Masjed-é Emām, Esfahān (DStV)
Top Right: Masjed-é Emām, Esfahān (DStV)
Bottom left: Entrance to covered market on Meidūn-é Emām ('polo field') , Esfahān (RVD)
Bottom Right: Entrance to Masjed-é Emām, Esfahān (RVD)

Top: Masjed-é Sayyed, Ja'far, Yazd (DStV)
Left: Kuché in Yazd (RVD)
Right: Ceiling of Masjed-é Sayyed, Ja'far, Yazd (DStV)

Maidenhead, Berkshire SL6 9SQ, was offering a 12-day guided tour with single/twin accommodation at £1617/1296. To find out if there is a travel agency in your country arranging tours to Iran, telephone the nearest Iran Air office. Alternatively you can get in touch directly with Azadi International Tourism Organization (☎ 298064; telex 212845 HYTT IR; fax 298072), Azadi Grand Hotel, Bozorgrāh-é Shahīd Doktor Chamrān, Tehrān 19395, or Iran Air-Tours (☎ 890298; telex 213956 IRAT; fax 895884), Chahārrāh-é Hojjat-ol-Eslām Doktor Mofatteh, 191 Kheyābūn-é Ostād Motahharī, Tehrān 15879.

LEAVING IRAN
Departure Tax
There is an airport tax of 1500 rials, payable by foreigners on all international departures. It is not included in the price of the ticket and has to be paid in cash at the airport. Check the current amount when buying your ticket. Iranians have to pay very heavy taxes for the privilege of leaving their country, but foreigners are of course exempt from these.

Getting Around

Although the Iranian transport system isn't as developed as those in most Western countries, it's considerably better than in many other countries in the region, and reasonably cheap. Most people travelling long distances prefer to go by air or train, but many end up going by bus. For shorter distances shared taxis and *savārīs* (private cars which take paying passengers) supplement bus or minibus services. There are a few passenger shipping and boat services in the Persian Gulf. Whichever form of public transport you take, try to book tickets as early as possible. One frustrating aspect of long-distance travel is the number of security checkpoints en route or at the points of arrival and departure (see Dangers & Annoyances in the Facts for the Visitor chapter).

AIR

There are two national civil airlines in Iran, Iran Air and Iran Asseman. Iran Air has a fairly modern fleet of Boeing 727s, 737s, 747s and the like, while Iran Asseman is more of a flying museum than an airline. If you have the choice, Iran Air is the one to go for. There is also a military airline operated by Sepah-é Pāsdārān, known as Saha (Sāhā), which has recently started offering spare seats to civilian passengers. Tickets for these can be bought at some airports.

Since boarding procedures are far from streamlined, try to check in for domestic flights 1½ hours before departure.

Foreigners do not have to pay in hard currency for domestic flights; the airport tax (1500 rials) is included in the price of the ticket. Tickets can only be booked for a particular flight, and you can only change the time or date by cancelling the original ticket and buying a new one. If you are unsure, it is better to buy more than one ticket and later cancel the ones you don't require. Tickets are not transferable. Full details of conditions are given in English on tickets. All the main Iran Air offices are computerised, but in some smaller places tickets have to be booked by telex, and can be collected after a few hours. There are children's fares, but no student discounts. Return tickets cost exactly twice the single fare, and have to be booked for a specific flight in both directions. Fares rise annually at around Nō Rūz.

Airfare Increases All domestic airfares were tripled at the Nō Rūz price review on 21 March 1992, though they are still cheap by international standards. The prices given in the text were current when this book was researched, before the 1992 increases.

Iran Air

Its full Persian name is Havāpeimā'ī-yé Jomhūrī-yé Eslāmī-yé Īrān, but it's also known as Homā, after the mythical bird used as the airline's symbol. It has frequent scheduled services (see the Domestic Air Routes map) and details are given in the entries for the various destinations. Although these are subject to change, services are more likely to expand than contract. Iran Air has at least one sales office in each of the places it serves, as well as one in Rāmsar. Tehrān is the hub of the air network, but there are many direct flights between other destinations.

Iran Air has very little in the way of in-flight service, particularly on domestic routes. There are no magazines or videos, but the staff are generally hospitable towards foreigners and can usually spirit up a current copy of the *Tehran Times*.

Because fares are so incredibly low, flying is the preferred means of travel for many, so the most popular flights are often booked up weeks ahead. One solution is to go to the airport the day you want to fly and just stand around looking lost: Iranian hospitality being what it is, someone will probably arrange for your name to be put on the waiting-list eventually, although you should not rely on this method. As a foreigner, you can quite often arrange tickets at relatively short notice from Iran Air offices, although rarely less than about a week in advance. Some travel agencies sell a small quota of tickets which may be unobtainable directly from Iran Air offices.

Iran Air reserves a certain number of seats on every flight for special customers until a few hours before boarding, and foreigners often count as special customers. Managerial authority is generally required for issuing such tickets. Unless you have some clout, you're most likely to get these otherwise unobtainable tickets from offices in Jazīré-

yé Kīsh, Rasht, Būshehr and Rāmsar. Places like Shīrāz, Mashhad, Bandar-é Abbās, Tabrīz and especially Tehrān and Esfahān are not good places to ask.

NIOC

The National Iranian Oil Company charters several flights from Iran Air between the mainland (Ahvāz, Esfahān, Shīrāz and Tehrān) and the islands of Khārk, Sīrrī and Lāvān. Tickets are intended for NIOC personnel and guests and can only be obtained from NIOC offices.

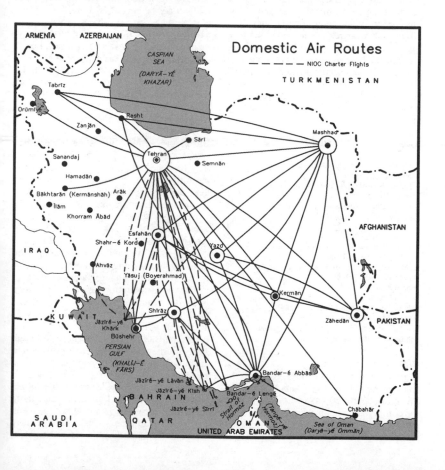

100 Getting Around

Iran Asseman

Also known as Sherkat-é Āsemān, this is one of the world's more hopeless airlines. At the time of writing it only had two small, anti-quated and noisy aeroplanes in service, and another undergoing repair in Switzerland. Asseman has a few services operating out of Tehrān, but since timetables change almost weekly and tickets can only be bought at the point of departure or arrival, few people rely on their services. It does, however, fly to some small places not served by Iran Air and, since Iran Asseman is so much a last resort, it often has tickets available at very short notice, even sometimes for the same day. The airline is not computerised, and sales offices only have reliable information about flights to and from the city they serve. I have not generally given information about Iran Asseman flights because no timetable would be reliable for more than a few days. As a very unreliable guide, at the time of writing Iran Asseman was flying on the following routes:

Route	Number of Flights Weekly
Tehrān-Ahvāz-Būshehr-Ahvāz-Būshehr	1
Tehrān-Ahvāz-Būshehr-Jazīré-yé Lāvān-Būshehr-Ahvāz-Tehrān	1
Tehrān-Ahvāz-Tehrān	10
Tehrān-Esfahān-Ahvāz-Esfahān-Tehrān	6
Tehrān-Esfahān-Shīrāz-Būshehr-Shīrāz-Esfahān- Tehrān	1
Tehrān-Esfahān-Tehrān	5
Tehrān-Khorram Ābād-Tehrān	5
Tehrān-Mashhad-Tehrān	11
Tehrān-Mashhad-Zābol-Mashhad-Tehrān	2
Tehrān-Nōshahr-Tehrān	2
Tehrān-Rāmsar-Tehrān	3
Tehrān-Shīrāz-Lāmard-Lār-Lāmard-Shīrāz-Tehrān	2
Tehrān-Shīrāz-Lāmard-Shīrāz-Tehrān	2
Tehrān-Shīrāz-Tehrān	7
Tehrān-Zāhedān-Īrānshahr-Zāhedān-Tehrān	2
Tehrān-Zāhedān-Tehrān	2

BUS

If you can't get somewhere by bus, the chances are that *no-one* wants to go there. There are nearly 20 bus companies linking the country and the business is highly competitive. Buses are the way most Iranians travel most of the time, and going by bus is a good way to meet them. You'll nearly always find someone wanting to practise English.

Since the revolution, bus companies have been organised into cooperatives, and they are usually referred to simply as Cooperative Bus Company No X (Sherkat-é Ta'āvonī Shomāré X), or whatever number it is. On most routes by far the best, and the most popular, is Cooperative Bus Company No 1 (also called Īrān Peimā; 'Iran Peyma'). Next best are No 15 (Tī Bī Tī; 'TBT'), and No 2 (Tī Em Tī; 'TMT') and No 5. Different companies cover different routes, and even major routes may be served by only one or two companies. You may have to enquire at half a dozen bus offices to find a company that serves your destination, has a bus at the right time, and has seats available.

There are two classes of long-distance bus: 'lux' (*lūks*), the regular class, and 'super' (*sūper* or *sūper lūks*), which is better than 'lux' and about 50% more expensive. 'Super' is only run on certain routes and tickets is in short supply. Most Cooperative Bus Company No 1 buses are 'super'. Bus fares are fixed by the government and – since they have not risen in step with inflation – absurdly cheap. Travelling 'lux' you could get from the Pakistani border to the Turkish border for little more than 6000 rials.

Note that bus passengers to intermediate stops normally have to pay the full fare to the final destination. Any vacant seats are quickly filled by paying passengers picked up along the way, and their fares are presumably a perk of the underpaid bus crew.

The most frustrating aspect of bus travel is the large number of security checkpoints. On nearly all routes there is at least one every 100 km. Don't count on averaging more than 60 km an hour on most routes. Although many journeys run overnight, it's difficult to sleep well on the buses, and they are not a recommended way of cutting down on accommodation costs. Some of the longer journeys, eg Mashhad to Ahvāz, take more than a day. It can get very cold at night, even in spring and autumn, so make sure you have warm clothes. Try to get a seat at the front, because the heater is usually only powerful enough to keep the driver and the front row or two of passengers happy.

On long hauls the buses are never overloaded and usually clean, while the seats are the comfortable reclining variety. If you take a 'super' bus you get more legroom and you really will travel comfortably, even if you are taller than average. The drivers are generally good, safe and polite, and the crew and passengers try to make travelling by bus a civilised affair. Smoking on board is permitted in moderation; Iranian buses are almost never the nicotine-filled chambers endured by Turkish bus passengers. There is a rubbish bucket for every row of seats, so you don't finish your journey with other people's spat-out nutshells all over your clothes and fag ends all over the floor. Buses stop for meals at roadside cafés, where you used to get a rather bad sort of kūbīdé and nothing else, but the variety and quality of food at these places have improved since the end of the Iran-Iraq War.

Seating is generally so arranged that women sit next to women, men next to men, but exceptions are sometimes made for travelling couples, especially foreigners. If in doubt, ask at the time of booking. Under no circumstances is it acceptable for a man to sit next to an unrelated woman, even if there's only one spare seat on the bus. Tickets are numbered and correspond to particular seats. Seats at the very front are the most highly prized, and they are very often reserved for special customers. Foreigners are often given front-row seats even without asking for them.

Buying Tickets

In many cities the bus companies have ticket offices in town but, except sometimes in Tehrān, it's almost always easier to get a ticket at the bus station itself. Travel agencies do not handle bus tickets. In some cities there's more than one bus station. Sometimes companies have their own stations, and occasionally a company will run buses from more than one station. There is a move towards rationalising bus services, and in some cities new bus stations have been opened at the edge of town to replace a number of separate facilities; other cities will do so in coming years. If in doubt, it's best to ask locally which is the right bus company or bus station for a bus to a particular place. Negotiating bus stations can be difficult when you can't read or speak Persian, but you will rarely have to look lost for more than a minute or two before Iranian hospitality comes to the fore and someone shows you the ropes.

Getting a seat at short notice, especially for longer journeys, can be a real ordeal, and it's certainly worth booking ahead if you can. Sometimes it is even possible to reserve a seat by telephone. Some companies will only accept same-day bookings and in this case make sure you book early in the morning. Most offices generally open at around 8 am, but in small places with only a few services they work for only a few hours before a bus is about to depart.

Occasionally you can get a seat at short notice if you approach the driver before the time of boarding, even if all seats are supposedly taken, but this method largely depends

Iranian Bus Ticket

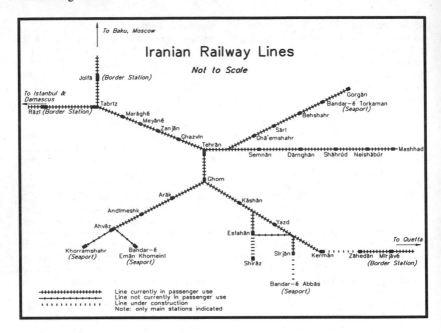

To Baku, Moscow

Iranian Railway Lines
Not to Scale

Jolfā (Border Station)

To Istanbul &
Damascus

Tabrīz

Rāzī (Border Station)

Marāghé

Meyāné

Zanjān

Ghazvīn

Tehrān

Ghom

Arāk

Andīmeshk

Ahvāz

Khorramshahr
(Seaport)

Bandar-é
Emān Khomeinī
(Seaport)

Kāshān

Esfahān

Shīrāz

Sīrjān

Bandar-é Abbās
(Seaport)

Yazd

Kermān

Zāhedān

Mīrjāvé
(Border Station)

To Quetta

Gorgān

Bandar-é Torkaman
(Seaport)

Behshahr

Sārī

Gha'emshahr

Semnān Dāmghān Shāhrūd Neishābūr Mashhad

++++++++++++++++ Line currently in passenger use
---------------- Line not currently in passenger use
. . . . Line under construction
Note: only main stations indicated

on someone who has booked a seat failing to turn up. There is often an extra seat in the middle of the back row, and many buses have odd little extra seats right at the front of the bus, which are sometimes made available to persistent last-minute bookers.

Information

There are few written timetables, even in Persian, and bus companies are surprisingly reluctant to give details of services. Even if you speak Persian information often has to be prised out piece by piece. The details of services, journey times, fares and distances given in the text were as far as possible correct at the time of writing, but the journey times and fares in particular should only be taken as a guide. Allow for considerable delays in winter or when road conditions are bad, or if the Komīté is being more than usually vigilant with its checks. Sometimes the fare in one direction is different from that in the return direction.

Ramazān

Transport is a problem during Ramazān; Iranian bus companies are not allowed to operate international services at this time and have to divert spare buses to extra domestic services. However Turkish buses still run in and out of Iran.

TRAIN

Islamic Republic of Iran Railways (Rāh-é Āhan-é Jomhūrī-yé Eslāmī-yé Īrān) run trains that are comfortable, efficient and reasonably fast and, because public transport is heavily subsidised, extremely cheap. Although the service is not extensive, and there are several large cities without a train link (most notably Shīrāz), it is impressive if you consider the mountainous terrain that the lines have to pass through: the great Trans-Iranian Railway built in the 1930s to connect the Caspian Sea at Bandar-é Torkaman with the Persian Gulf at Bandar-é Emām Khomeinī is one of the greatest engineering achievements of the 20th century. Some of the routes pass through very dramatic countryside.

More often than not there's someone in your compartment who can speak English. The guard will come round and take orders for tea and meals – reasonably good and inexpensive – to be served some time later in your compartment, but many passengers prefer to bring their own food. Iced water is also available. If you object to sharing glasses, bring one of your own. There are, at least theoretically, smoking and no-smoking compartments, but the latter are rarely respected even by guards. There are no left-luggage facilities at train stations.

There are 1st, 2nd and 3rd class seats, but not all trains have all three. First and 2nd class sleeping compartments are provided on overnight services. Most services are express, for which a small supplement is payable. As a rough guide, a 2nd class seat costs about 50% more than the corresponding 'lux' bus fare, while a 1st class sleeper is a little less than the airfare. Express services are not much faster than regular, and sometimes no faster at all. Children under seven travel free and those under 14 pay half-fare. There is a 10% student discount.

Tehrān is the hub of the network, with passenger trains running to the east (Mashhad and Gorgān), south-east (Esfahān, Yazd and Kermān), south-west (Ahvāz) and west (Tabrīz and Jolfā, for Baku and Moscow). Travellers heading to Pakistan can get as far as Kermān by train, and have to continue by bus or air to the Pakistani border. From Tabrīz the line turns north to the USSR and west into Turkey. There are plans to open a service between Shīrāz and Esfahān in 1992. A line between Sīrjān and Bandar-é Abbās is already near completion, and other lines are under construction.

All trains originate from Tehrān; there are no through services. To get from Tabrīz to Kermān you would have to buy a second ticket and change trains in Tehrān. Trains are not very practical for short-distance transport, for example between Yazd and Kermān.

Buying Tickets
It can be difficult to buy train tickets. In most cases it is only possible to buy tickets at the train station itself, although Esfahān has a city booking office. Travel agencies do not handle train tickets. They will nearly always find a seat for a single foreigner, although not necessarily for the class or time of departure of first choice. It's not possible to book a return ticket. It's a wise precaution to book tickets as early as possible.

Times & Services
It's almost impossible to find a train timetable in Iran and, at least until recently, it could be said that Iranian trains run to no timetable. There are usually several trains a day in each direction from Tehrān (except for the Kermān, Rāzī-Ankara and Jolfā-Moscow lines). For details, see the table on the next page. For the most recent information, phone Tehrān ☎ (021) 556114-5.

Details of international services, to Ankara, Moscow and Quetta, are given in the Getting There & Away chapter.

TAXI
Outside some bus and train stations you can find drivers offering intercity transport by private car. Fares are very expensive by Iranian standards, but they're sometimes worth considering if you can't get a ticket at short notice by any other means. A private car that takes paying passengers along certain intercity or rural routes, at a more or less fixed rate, is known as a savārī. Savārīs may be owned by either a private person or a cooperative. They take up to six passengers (four in the back, two in the front), and usually supplement a bus service, though sometimes they are the only option. They are not much faster than buses, no more comfortable and much more expensive, but they have the advantages of frequency and availability. Along the Caspian coast they are the commonest means of public transport. In a few places, seats on savārīs can be booked in advance at agencies. Along almost any main intercity road you can catch a savārī or shared taxi at least to the nearest town.

Destination	Frequency		Journey Time		Fare*		Express
	(per week)		max	min	1st class	2nd class	Supplement
	regular	express	hrs mins	hrs mins	(rials)	(rials)	(rials)
Ahvāz	7	21	17 30	15 55	3400	1870	1110
Andīmeshk	7	28	14 40	14 10	2800	1540	910
Arāk	7	28	6 45	5 30	1400	710	460
Bandar-é Torkamān	7	21	10 00	10 00	2000	1100	650
Behshahr	7	21	10 51	10 51	1800	990	590
Dāmghān	7	28	8 20	7 05	1600	880	520
Esfahān		3	9 45	9 45	3200	1760	1040
Gha'emshahr	7	21	5 00	5 00	1600	880	520
Ghazvīn	7	17	3 35	2 50	600	330	200
Ghom	7	24	3 20	2 55	800	440	260
Gorgān	7	21	10 45	10 45	2000	1100	650
Jolfā		2	20 15	20 15	3600	1981	1170
Kāshān		3	4 40	4 40	1200	660	390
Kermān		3	17 35	17 35	4600	2530	1500
Khorramshahr**					3800	2090	520
Marāghé	7	^ 17	13 20	12 15	2460	1350	800
Mashhad	7	***29	18 25	***11 00	3800	2090	1520
Meyāné	7	17	9 35	8 25	1800	990	590
Neishābūr	7	28	16 05	13 45	3200	1760	1040
Sārī	7	21	7 45	7 45	1600	880	520
Semnān	7	28	3 45	3 05	1000	550	330
Shāhrūd	7	28	8 05	7 05	1800	990	590
Sīrjān		3	16 45	16 45	4600	2530	1500
Tabrīz		****16	14 15	13 50	3000	1650	980
Yazd		3	12 20	12 20	3200	1760	1040
Zanjān	7	17	6 50	6 05	1400	710	460

* exclusive of 5% tax and 20 rials insurance fee.
** service temporarily suspended
*** weekly *tūrbōtren* (superexpress); (express 15 hours 40 minutes)
**** including two services weekly to Jolfā

Agency taxis (see Local Transport) can be hired for intercity journeys. I even jokingly asked one driver if he could drive me from Tehrān to Istanbul, and after a short pause he said that it would be possible for a not unreasonable 200,000 rials.

CAR & MOTORCYCLE
For a list of the documents you'll need to get your vehicle into Iran, see the Getting There & Away chapter. If you're driving in Iran, one book worth a place in your glove compartment is *Overland and Beyond* by Jonathan & Theresa Hewat (Roger Lascelles, London, 1981).

Rationing for petrol has been lifted, and a litre currently costs 70 rials. Iranian atlases and maps clearly mark the locations of petrol stations, which may be more than 100 km apart on some routes. Vehicle repair shops are also marked on city maps. Most spare parts for most cars are available, and improvisation and ingenuity usually make do where they aren't. Several multinational car producers have authorised service centres in Tehrān or elsewhere.

Road Rules

In theory, the rule of the road is to drive on the right, but in practice you'll find that quite a few motorcyclists and some others consider themselves exempt from the convention. Driving your own vehicle across Iran is not a task to be taken lightly. Take 10 Iranian car drivers and an otherwise deserted open road and you can be sure that all 10 will form a convoy so tightly packed that each of the rear nine can read the speedometer of the car in front. The expression 'braking distance' has no meaning in Iran. Any vehicle going less than 100 km/h is probably driven by a foreigner. Iranian motorists regard traffic lights as a challenge, unless they are actually being guarded by a detachment of traffic police. Bus lanes are considered a sort of VIP channel for Revolutionary Guards, mullahs, traffic police, regular police, or anyone driving a Mercedes. Mere buses rarely get a look in.

If you consider the Iranians' hair-raising driving habits and the often advanced state of disrepair of their vehicles, it's amazing that there aren't more serious accidents. For the recently arrived foreigner, motoring across Iran can be positively scary. Vehicle insurance is a must, and not just for legal reasons.

Road signs mostly conform to international conventions, although I did encounter one unorthodox sign depicting a skull and crossbones with the words 'Danger of Death' underneath. Most important signs on intercity roads are marked in English, but within towns directions are often given only in Persian script.

Only foreigners wear motorcycle helmets or use safety-belts in Iran.

Rental

There are no longer any car rental agencies in Iran.

BICYCLE

Why not? But don't follow the example of one Westerner I heard of cycling through Iran who was nearly stoned to death by zealous villagers for wearing shorts.

HITCHING

Hitching as commonly understood in the West hardly exists in Iran. Although you will often see travellers standing beside intercity roads hoping for a lift, they will nearly always be expected to pay at the going rate. Hitching in this manner is not so much an alternative to the public transport system but a part of it, as in many other Middle Eastern countries. Occasionally foreigners will be given lifts free of charge by private drivers, in return for English practice or simply out of hospitality, but you won't get very far if you set out intending to avoid paying for transport. Lone women should avoid accepting lifts in private cars, although taxis and savārīs should be safe.

BOAT

There are several passenger ferry services between the mainland and some of the islands of the Persian Gulf. At the time of writing Valfajre-8 Shipping Company has ferries between Bandar-é Abbās and Jazīré-yé Kīsh (nine a week), Būshehr and Jazīré-yé Kīsh (two a week), and Bandar-é Lengé and Jazīré-yé Kīsh (12 a week).

Tickets can be bought from Valfajre-8 sales offices in Tehrān (☎ 899288), Ahvāz (☎ 34081), Bandar-é Abbās (☎ 29095), Bandar-é Lengé (☎ 3448), Būshehr (☎ 2314), Bandar-é Kong (☎ 3632), Jazīré-yé Kīsh (☎ 27973) and Shīrāz (☎ 25103).

There are also a few private services, by motor-launch or tiny motor-boat, to Jazīré-yé Hormoz and Jazīré-yé Gheshm from Bandar-é Abbās (and vice versa) and between Bandar-é Chārak and Jazīré-yé Kīsh.

There are currently no passenger services in the Iranian part of the Caspian Sea, or along the Rūdkhūné-yé Kārūn, the only navigable river in Iran. You can take a boat across the Daryāché-yé Orūmīyé, Iran's largest inland lake: see that section for information.

LOCAL TRANSPORT
To/From the Airport

In most cases, airport transport is by taxi. There are airport bus services at Shīrāz and

Jazīré-yé Kīsh. In some other places it is possible to take a combination of city buses or shared taxis into town, but this is generally more trouble then it's worth, especially if you are arriving in a town for the first time. In most cases you will be greeted at the airport when you arrive by drivers of shared taxis, or else a porter will take you to one; if you are the only passenger you may be overcharged. Usually you can share with others going in roughly the same direction at a more or less fixed fare agreed in advance. Some cities have official airport taxis, marked in English. To get from a town to the airport it is usually advisable to book an agency taxi at an agreed fare at least 30 minutes in advance. You are unlikely to save much money by trying to hail a taxi in the street, and you may even miss your flight.

Bus & Minibus

There are local bus services in most Iranian cities. Depending on the city, tickets cost 10, 15 or 20 rials regardless of distance, and you have to buy them in advance at special roadside kiosks. Buses are difficult to use unless know exactly where you and the bus are going, or you can speak Persian and preferably read it as well. Bus numbers and destinations are marked only in Persian, and there are no published timetables. Bus stops are not always clearly marked even in Persian, buses do not always set out and return by the same route, services change frequently without notice and drivers are not always helpful about telling passengers where to get off.

There are also some desperately crowded minibuses on which you pay the driver something like 25 rials in cash regardless of distance. Quite often they are so crammed with passengers that you can hardly see out of the window to tell where you are going. Minibuses also run on some shorter rural routes, often picking up passengers from outside the local bus station. Seats cannot normally be booked on these, and the fare (rarely more than 100 rials) is paid in cash to the driver.

Shared Taxi

In cities and on some urban routes shared taxis often duplicate or even replace bus services. They usually take up to five passengers, occasionally more. Shared taxis do not keep to fixed routes, and the driver will take passengers anywhere that it is worth his while to take them. Official shared taxis are painted either orange and white or blue and white, according to city. There are also many private cars operating an unofficial taxi service, which are difficult for the foreigner to recognise. A shared taxi, official or unofficial, will nearly always be a Paykan, the locally produced car based on a British Hillman.

The custom is to stand in the road, preferably in a main road or at an intersection, and shout out your destination to every passing taxi. Don't be offended if the driver goes straight on without acknowledging your existence; this is the accepted practice, intended to keep journey times to a minimum. If you're in a hurry or there aren't many taxis around, you might offer to pay more than the usual fare, saying for example, *'Dah tōmān, Hāfez'* (10 tōmān (100 rials) to Kheyābūn-é Hāfez). If you start offering two or three times the normal fare, it's amazing how easy it is to find a taxi going to your destination, and it's still very cheap. Once you've learnt how to use them, shared taxis are an excellent and inexpensive way to get around. When you want the driver to stop you simply say *kheilī mamnūn* ('thank you very much'). You are expected to have the fare ready, preferably in coins; sometimes passengers pay before the car stops.

Often you'll have to take a number of taxis to get from one part of a city to another (especially if you're not prepared to offer more than the going rate) and having a map is almost essential. Fares are fixed by the government depending on distance. Although there are no meters, disputes are rare as passengers usually know what the fare should be. At the time of writing, the minimum fare is 20 or 30 rials depending on the place (but usually 50 rials in Tehrān), and the average fare is 50 rials. For a journey of up to about five km anywhere except Tehrān, if you're asked to pay more than 100 rials, you're probably being cheated. The rules are to speak Persian if you can, to fix and pay the fare when there are other passengers in the taxi (they will spring to your defence if you are being overcharged), and to carry plenty of small change. If you board a taxi as a solo passenger and you want to pay shared-taxi rates, make it clear that the driver can follow an indirect route and pick up other passengers; otherwise he may take you directly to your destination and he would be perfectly entitled to charge you at agency taxis' rates.

Agency Taxi

These are private or 'telephone' taxis, which don't stop to pick up other passengers and which you have to order either by telephone or at an agency office. There are taxi agency offices in even the smallest of towns, and hundreds in Tehrān. Some of the top hotels run their own taxi services, and any hotel or mosāferkhūné can order a taxi for a guest.

As a rule, hourly rates for any number of passengers are officially fixed at between 1500 and 2000 rials (1800 rials in Tehrān) within city limits, and 2000 to 3000 rials outside, depending on the place. In practice these are negotiable upwards or, less often, downwards. These rates do not usually apply to journeys lasting less than an hour. It is also possible to hire a taxi for long journeys at a flat fare. Foreigners very frequently end up paying more than Iranians, especially in Tehrān or Esfahān. On Jazīré-yé Kīsh taxis charge a uniquely high 5000 rials an hour. Once a fare has been fixed, it has to be honoured by both parties regardless of traffic or road conditions, which are sometimes offered as excuses for raising the agreed fare. However it is good practice to tip a driver who goes out of his way to be helpful. If you are going to be spending much time in a place, it is worth noting the name and telephone number of any driver you find helpful

in case you want to hire a taxi for a long journey or a tour at a later date.

On arrival at a bus or train station or airport, don't accept a lift from the first taxi driver who approaches you, as you are almost bound to be overcharged. If possible, arrange to share a taxi with some Iranians going in the same direction, keep out of sight of the driver and get them to fix the fare. Beware of arrangements where you end up as the only passenger in a taxi without having first arranged the fare directly with the driver. It's almost a point of honour among Iranian private taxi drivers to overcharge foreigners, although there are exceptions.

Even the poorest of Iranians will take a taxi from the station or airport: there is rarely an alternative. At some places you can buy tickets in advance to pay for your fare at a more or less fixed rate, for example at Tabrīz bus station or Tehrān airport.

There are said to be a few female drivers at some of the taxi agencies in Tehrān, but I've never seen one. Perhaps they only take female passengers.

TOURS

There are few organised tours in Iran, and very few, if any, are arranged specifically for foreigners. For most people, a tour is the best way to get to Jazīré-yé Kīsh, but otherwise most travellers make their own arrangements. If you really want to take a guided tour somewhere, a travel agency could probably arrange something for you at a price, but there wouldn't be much point. A company called Iran Air-Tours (no relation to Iran Air) organises tours of Mashhad, Shīrāz, Esfahān and Sārī, but these only include accommodation and airport transfers, sometimes with a short excursion thrown in, and they are really designed for Iranians.

If you need an English-speaking guide, the local tourist office may be able to put you in touch with one. You can then hire a taxi for the day as well, and arrange your own tour.

Tehrān Province

استان تهران

Tehrān Province, at the southern edge of the Alborz Mountains and the northern edge of the Dasht-é Kavīr, has an area of 29,900 sq km. The population is now well over 10 million, and it is the most densely populated province in Iran. The city of Tehrān is capital of both the province and the whole nation.

Tehrān

تهران

Iran is not blessed with one of the world's loveliest capitals. Pollution, chronic over-crowding and a lack of any responsible planning have all helped to make Tehrān a city which even a travel agent would have difficulty in praising. If you're expecting an exotic crossroads steeped in Oriental splendour, you'll be sadly disappointed. Though Tehrān is aesthetically a mess, it does deserve a day or two.

For a start, Tehrān is the undisputed capital of Iran, by far the largest city and a leader in almost every field of Iranian life. In addition, Tehrān was the centre of the Iranian Islamic Revolution – the first of its kind in the world. More than a decade on it is still, in many ways, a revolutionary city. There are a fair number of things to do and see here which you won't find elsewhere, including several excellent museums. The hotels, restaurants and shops are all by far the best in Iran.

Tehrān became the national capital at the end of the 18th century. Since then an almost complete lack of architectural vision has produced a city of very little beauty. Buildings owe more to the dour East European school of architecture than to the classical lines of Safavid Esfahān. Little evidence remains of Tehrān's two centuries as capital, and anything over 50 years old qualifies as historic. Although sightseers may find little to see on the streets, sociologists will find the city fascinating for its amoeba-like population growth. Go to the teeming slums in the south of Tehrān and see for yourself.

Another drawback is the heavy smog which permanently hovers over the capital. At some times of the year, especially in summer, it descends with unbearable effect and drives people out of Tehrān in coughing wheezing droves, while the radio warns those with a heart condition not to leave their houses.

For all its frenzy and bustle, Tehrān seems to cast an irresistible inertia on visitors, and people meaning to spend only a few hours here often end up staying for a week, a fortnight or even longer. The distances are vast, the traffic's appalling and the main sights are spread out all over the place. You really need the best part of a week just to make a start, and by that time you begin to appreciate the city's better points. The hotels are good, the variety of restaurants is impressive, the facilities are far ahead of those anywhere in the provinces, and the Tehrānīs are really quite friendly, hospitable people. In the northern suburbs at any rate, they are far more Westernised than the conventional media image would have you believe. The people here are, for the most part, fascinated

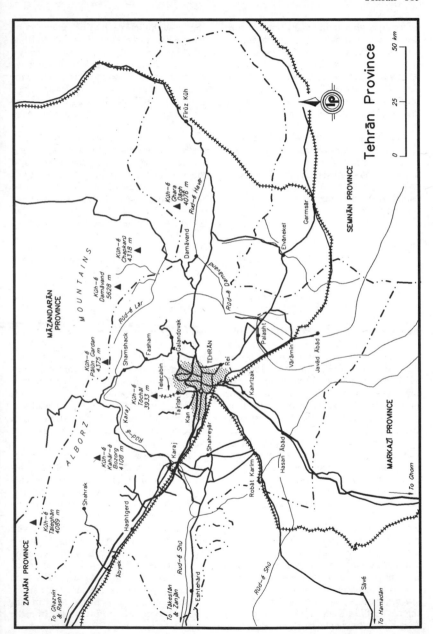

Tehrān Province

by foreigners but, unlike many Iranians, they don't stare or intrude. The atmosphere has loosened up very markedly over the last two or three years and within reason, you can do what you want here and people don't bother you. As recently as 1989 the Komīté would routinely stop foreigners on the street and demand identification, but now you might not see one patrol car in a week.

At an altitude of 1191 metres, Tehrān can get pretty cold in the winter and snow is not at all uncommon. Precipitation of any kind is rare in summer, when Tehrān can get far too hot for comfort. Autumn and spring are usually pleasant enough, though spring is the rainiest season.

History

Tehrān started as a small village in the foothills of the Alborz Mountains. Human settlement of the region dates to Neolithic times, but the development of Tehrān was very slow and its rise to prominence largely accidental. A succession of visitors to Tehrān from the 10th to as late as the 13th century described it as a village of half-savages who lived in underground dwellings and earned their livelihood from highway robbery. In 1197, after Mongols sacked the neighbouring town of Rei, then the major urban centre of the region, Tehrān began to develop in its place as a small, moderately prosperous trading centre.

In the mid-16th century, Tehrān's attractive natural setting, many trees, clear rivers and good hunting brought it into the favour of the early Safavid king, Tahmāsb I. Under his patronage, gardens were laid out, brick houses and caravanserais were built and heavily fortified walls were erected to protect the town and its steadily increasing population of merchants. It continued to grow under the later Safavid kings, and European visitors wrote of its many enchanting vineyards and gardens, but it was never a town of any great size or importance.

As a result of the Ghajar threat to his throne, in 1758 Karīm Khān-é Zand transferred his army here from his capital at Shīrāz, with the intention of moving in on his enemy. At the same time he refortified Tehrān and began the construction of a royal residence. Perhaps he had intended to move his capital here, but when his army killed the Ghajar chieftain, Mohammad Hasan Khān, and captured his young son Āghā Mohammad, Karīm Khān abandoned the unfinished palace and returned to Shīrāz.

In the chaos that followed Karīm Khān's death in 1778, Āghā Mohammad, now chieftain of the Ghajar tribe, escaped from Shīrāz and raised an army. With great brutality he came to subdue the whole of Persia from his base at Tehrān, killing Lotf Alī Khān, the last representative of the Zand dynasty. In 1789 he declared Tehrān his capital, and six years later he had himself crowned as shāh of all Persia. He destroyed the city walls of Shīrāz, disinterred the corpse of Karīm Khān and carried it back to Tehrān in a final act of revenge. At this time, Tehrān was no more than a dusty town of around 15,000 souls.

The town continued to grow slowly under Fath Alī Shāh and Mohammad Shāh, and few buildings of great merit were built. The majority of the population continued to live in adobe houses similar to those still found in Yazd. In 1807 it was recorded by one visitor as having a population of at least 50,000. Under Nasr-od-Dīn Shāh and his minister Amīr Kabīr, a new city wall was built with 12 great monumental gates and a moat, but these were taken down in the early part of this century.

From the early '20s the city was extensively modernised on a grid system, and this period marked the start of the phenomenal population growth that continues to this day. In 1887 the population was 250,000, and by 1930 had only increased to 300,000. By 1939 it had rocketed to half a million, with the city's rapid expansion only slowing during WWII. In the '50s, with increasing prosperity especially during the oil boom, Tehrān developed beyond recognition, with modern tower blocks, expressways, constantly expanding suburbs and an unstoppable population influx, mostly from the rural areas of Iran. In 1956 the population was 1,800,000; in 1966 it was 2,720,000, and by 1976 it had risen to 4,530,000.

The city was the main centre of uprisings against the last Shāh and remained pivotal throughout the Islamic Revolution. The great social upheavals caused by the Iran-Iraq War only hastened the population shift from the countryside to the larger urban areas, especially Tehrān. Large numbers of internal refugees from the western border provinces also fled here. Literally millions of villagers came here in search of work, cheap housing and a better life. By the 1986 census, Tehrān's population was over 8.7 million, and six years later it is certainly more than 10 million, and according to some estimates approaches 13 or even 14 million.

If the current population growth continues – and it shows no signs of abating – Tehrān will soon be one of the five or six most populous cities in the world.

Orientation

Tehrān is so vast and devoid of landmarks that getting hopelessly lost at least once is a near certainty whatever form of transport you take. Walking is futile unless you know exactly where you are going. It takes a long long time to get to know your way around, and because of the lack of landmarks there is no substitute for a good map, a compass and enough words of basic Persian to ask for directions and be able to understand the reply. The best advice is to buy a good map of Tehrān as soon as you arrive, and to take taxis everywhere. If you're really stuck, try to spot the Alborz Mountains, the 'North Star' of Tehrān, through the clouds of smog. The urban area slopes upwards from the south to the north, but the gradient is only noticeable in the very far north, and the rest of the town is pancake flat.

Officially the centre of town is Meidūn-é Emām Khomeinī. While many of the government offices are still around here, this part of town has changed over the decades into a dirty, run-down and unfashionable district. The smarter residential and business areas have gradually shifted northwards, and in practical terms there is no centre at all to speak of.

Tehrān is bisected by Kheyābūn-é Valī-yé Asr, which runs north-south for miles, from the railway station right up into the hills, and Kheyābūn-é Enghelāb, which runs west to east from the Āzādī Monument.

For many people arriving by land or air, the vast Meidūn-é Āzādī with its towering Āzādī Monument is the first thing they see of the town. The airport and the west bus terminal, the city's busiest, are both just off this square, and the traffic here is phenomenal. From here you can get into the centre of town by road in about an hour on the main east-west street, Meidūn-é Enghelāb, eventually reaching a busy crossroads, Chahārrāh-é Valī-yé Asr. If you turn left here, heading north, the first main square you'll come to is Meidūn-é Valī-yé Asr, from where you can easily take a shared taxi to almost anywhere in the northern part of Tehrān. The greatest concentration of hotels is around this square in a radius of about 1½ km.

The east bus terminal is at the far east of Kheyābūn-é Damāvand, the extension of Enghelāb. The train station and the south bus terminal are about five km further south. These are both way, way out of the centre, miles from the nearest hotel, and you'll save a lot of time and effort if you take a taxi direct to wherever you're going.

The smarter residential areas are all in the north of Tehrān, the closer to the Alborz the better. The main east-west street, Kheyābūn-é Enghelāb, is a fairly accurate division between the classes. The fact that some of the older embassies, palaces and ministries are in the now distinctly unsmart official centre of Tehrān, south of Enghelāb, is a hangover from the days when the area was a leafy outer suburb of a much smaller capital. Tehrān has no real centre, but officially it is the large and utterly shambolic Meidūn-é Emām Khomeinī (previously Meidūn-é Tūbkhūné). The area around here and Kheyābūn-é Amīr Kabīr used to be the centre of all the cheap hotels, but it has become even seedier since the revolution. Many of the old travellers' hostels have disappeared altogether or simply stopped taking foreigners.

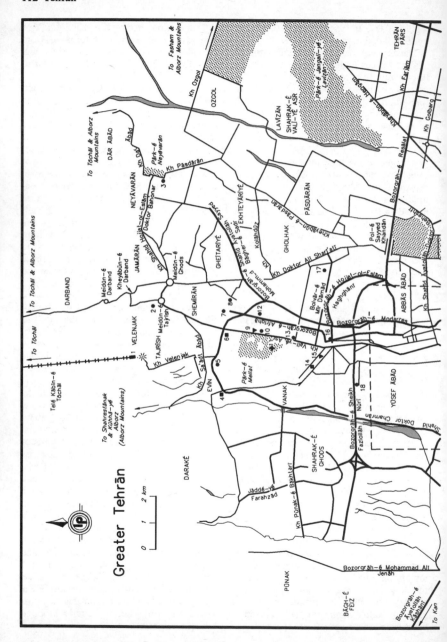

Greater Tehrān

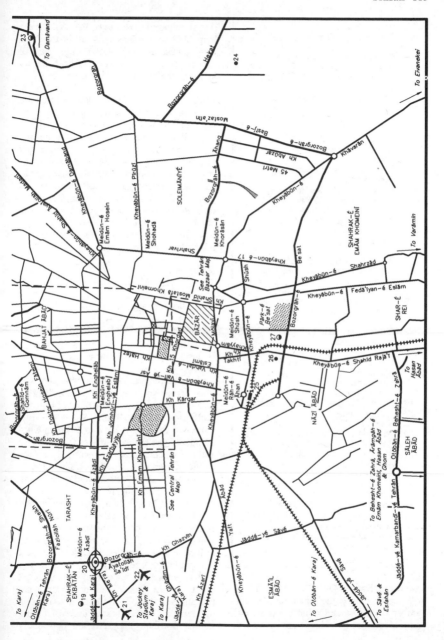

■ PLACES TO STAY

4 Grand Azadi Hotel (ex-Hyatt)
 (Mehmūnkhūné-yé Bozorg-é Āzādī)
6 Esteghlal Hotel (ex-Hilton) (Hotel-é
 Esteghlāl)
14 Homa Hotel (ex-Sheraton) (Hotel-é
 Homā)

▼ PLACES TO EAT

4 Grand Āzadi Hotel
6 Esteghlal Hotel
9 Restōrān-é Sūrnā ('Sorrento
 Restaurant')
14 Homa Hotel (Hotel-é Homā)
15 Restōrān-é Serīnā ('Seryna
 Restaurant') & Restōrān-é Chini
 ('Chinese Restaurant')

 OTHER

1 Īstgāh-é Avval-é Telé Kābīn-é Tōchāl
 (1st Station of Tōchāl Telecabin)
2 Majmū'é-yé Farhangī-yé Sa'd Ābād
3 Mūzé-yé Kākh-é Neyāvarān
5 International Trade Fair (Mahall-é
 Dā'emi-yé Namāyeshgāhhā-yé
 Bein-ol-Melali)
7 Belgian Embassy
8 Swiss Embassy
10 Bāzārché-yé Valī-yé Asr
11 Shahīd Rajā'ī Hospital (Bīmārestān-é
 Shahīd Rajā'ī)
12 Qatar Embassy
13 UAE Embassy
16 KIDO (Sāzmān-é Omrān-é Kīsh)
17 Irish Embassy
18 Kish Island Services Company
19 Termīnāl-é Gharb (West BusTerminal)
20 Borj-é Āzādī (Āzādī Monument)
21 Airport (International Terminal)
22 Airport (Domestic Terminal)
23 Termīnāl-é Shargh (East Bus Terminal)
24 Takhtī Sports Stadium (Estādyūm-é
 Varzeshī-yé Takhtī)
25 Train Station & Tourist Office
26 Export Customs Office (Edāré-yé
 Gomrok-é Sodūrhā)
27 Termīnāl-é Jonūb (South Bus
 Terminal)

New Street Names One disorienting legacy of the revolution is the renaming of a vast number of streets and other features with more ideologically sound names. Valī-yé Asr, for example, used to be Pahlāvī. On the maps and street-signs you will just see the new names, but in conversation people still use the old ones, and even the locals hardly know all the new ones. (See the table.)

Addresses When giving addresses that are on minor streets, Iranians often give the name of a more important road off which it runs. Sometimes, especially in Tehrān, the address may contain as many as three street names, starting from the most important street, then a smaller street which runs off it, and then the street running off that on which you'll find the building you want. An address on a *kūché* (lane) is nearly always given in combination with the name of the street it runs off. The word *kheyābūn-é* (street) is often ommited from addresses.

Information
The ostāndārī (provincial government office) is on the east side of Bozorgrāh-é Modarres 100 metres north of its intersection with Kheyābūn-é Ostād Motahharī. The shahrdārī (municipal government office) (☎ 81011, 530144) is on Kheyābūn-é Behesht, south of the Pārk-é Shahr.

Visa & Residence Permit Extensions The visa office (marked in English 'Police Department of Foreign Affairs') is on the north side of Kheyābūn-é Sakhā'ī, a few blocks north-west of Meidūn-é Emām Khomeinī. All the relevant offices for both visa and residence permit extensions are on the 1st floor, marked in English 'USA and W & E Europe', 'Asia' and 'Middle East and Africa', and, ominously, 'Executions & Interrogations'; Canadians, Australasians and South Americans can take their pick. There is a small snack-bar on the same floor.

It usually takes three or four working days to have a visa extension issued, although if you only want a few days extra to give you time to get a ticket out of Iran you might get it done in two. The office is open from 8 am to 2 pm, Sunday to Wednesday, and till noon on Thursday, but it is best to arrive first thing in the morning. The staff are reasonably

Streetnames

Old name	New name
Bolvār-é Elīzābet-é Dovvom (Elizabeth II)	Bolvār-é Keshāvarz
Bozorgrāh-é Anōshīravān-é Dādgar	Bozorgrāh-é Be'sat
Bozorgrāh-é Ayyūbī	Bozorgrāh-é Sheikh Fazlollāh Nūrī
Bozorgrāh-é Dāryūsh	Bozorgrāh-é Resālat
Bozorgrāh-é Jordan	Bozorgrāh-é Afrīghā
Bozorgrāh-é Kamāl Ātātürk (Kamal Atatürk)	Bozorgrāh-é Āyatollāh Kāshānī
Bozorgrāh-é Rezā Shāh-é Kabīr	Bozorgrāh-é Basīj-é Mostaz'afīn
Bozorgrāh-é Shāhanshāhī	Bozorgrāh-é Modarres
Bozorgrāh-é Shahbānū Farah	Bozorgrāh-é Afsarīyé
Bozorgrāh-é Shahyād	Bozorgrāh-é Āyatollāh Sa'īdī
Bozorgrāh-é Tarasht	Bozorgrāh-é Sheikh Fazlollāh Nūrī
Kheyābūn-é Amīrābād	Kheyābūn-é Kārgar
Kheyābūn-é Ārāmgāh	Kheyābūn-é Shahīd Rajā'ī
Kheyābūn-é Āyzenhāver (Eisenhower)	Kheyābūn-é Āzādī
Kheyābūn-é Bū Alī Hosein Karīmī	Kheyābūn-é Shahīd Amīr
Kheyābūn-é Būzarjomehrī	Kheyābūn-é 15 Khordād
Kheyābūn-é Cherchīl (Churchill)	Kheyābūn-é Nōfl Lōshātō(Neauphle-le-Château)
Kheyābūn-é Daryā-yé Nūr	Kheyābūn-é Shahīd Javād Sarāfrāz
Kheyābūn-é Dōlat	Kheyābūn-é Shahīd Kolāhdūz
Kheyābūn-é Estāmbōl (Istanbul)	Kheyābūn-é Jomhūrī-yé Eslāmī,
	Kheyābūn-é Mīrzā Küchek Khān and
	Kheyābūn-é Shahīd Hasan Akbarī
Kheyābūn-é Farah	Kheyābūn-é Sohrvardī
Kheyābūn-é Farahābād	Kheyābūn-é Belāl Habeshī , Kheyābūn-é Shahīd Abbās
	Sābūnyān and Kheyābūn-é Pīrūzī
Kheyābūn-é Farānsé (France)	Kheyābūn-é Nōfl Lōshātō (Neauphle-le-Château)
Kheyābūn-é Forūghī	Kheyābūn-é Sheikh Abd-ol-Hamīd Küshk-é Mesrī
Kheyābūn-é Kākh	Kheyābūn-é Falastīn
Kheyābūn-é Kāmrān	Kheyābūn-é Shahīd Dībājī-yé Jonūbī
Kheyābūn-é Khorāsān	Kheyābūn-é Khāvrān
Kheyābūn-é Khōrshīd	Kheyābūn-é Shahīd Homāyūn Nāteghī
Kheyābūn-é Mohammad Rezā Shāh	Kheyābūn-é Yākhchī Ābād
Kheyābūn-é Mokhtārī	Kheyābūn-é Yāser
Kheyābūn-é Nāder	Kheyābūn-é Shahīd Sayyed Amīn Kāj Ābādī
Kheyābūn-é Nāderī	Kheyābūn-é Jomhūrī-yé Eslāmī
Kheyābūn-é Nārmak	Kheyābūn-é Shahīd Doktor Āyat
Kheyābūn-é Neyāvarān	Kheyābūn-é Shahīd Hojjat-ol-EslāmDoktor Bāhonar
Kheyābūn-é Pahlavī	Kheyābūn-é Valī-yé Asr
Kheyābūn-é Rūsevelt (Roosevelt)	Kheyābūn-é Shahīd Hojjat-ol-Eslām Doktor Mofatteh
Kheyābūn-é Sepah	Kheyābūn-é Emām Khomeinī
Kheyābūn-é Sevvom-é Esfand	Kheyābūn-é Sargord Sakhā'ī
Kheyābūn-é Shāh	Kheyābūn-é Jomhūrī-yé Eslāmī
Kheyābūn-é Shāhābād	Kheyābūn-é Dārābād and Kheyābūn-é Rezvān
Kheyābūn-é Shāhpūr	Kheyābūn-é Vahdat-é Eslāmī
Kheyābūn-é Shāhpūr Alīrezā	Kheyābūn-é Āzarbāyjān
Kheyābūn-é Shahrdārī	Kheyābūn-é Shahīd Doktor Āyat
Kheyābūn-é Shāh Rezā	Kheyābūn-é Enghelāb-é Eslāmī
Kheyābūn-é Shāh Rokh	Kheyābūn-é Kamīl
Kheyābūn-é Sīrūs	Kheyābūn-é Shahīd Mostafā Khomeinī
Kheyābūn-é Takht-e Jamshīd	Kheyābūn-é Āyatollāh Tāleghānī
Kheyābūn-é Takht-e Tāvūs	Kheyābūn-é Ostād Motahharī
Kheyābūn-é Varzesh	Kheyābūn-é Shahīd Doktor Fayyāz Bakhsh
Kheyābūn-é Villā	Kheyābūn-é Shahīd Ostād Nejātollāhī
Kheyābūn-é Yūsefābād	Kheyābūn-é Sayyed Jamāl-od-Dīn Asad Ābādī

Old Name	New Name
Meidūn-é 24 Esfand	Meidūn-é Enghelāb-é Eslāmī
Meidūn-é 25 Shahrīvar	Meidūn-é Haft-é Tīr
Meidūn-é Ark	Meidūn-é 15 Khordād
Meidūn-é Farah	Meidūn-é Resālat
Meidūn-é Kākh	Meidūn-é Falastīn
Meidūn-é Sepah	Meidūn-é Emām Khomeinī
Meidūn-é Shāh	Meidūn-é Gheyām
Meidūn-é Shahnāz	Meidūn-é Emām Hosein
Meidūn-é Shahyād	Meidūn-é Āzādī
Meidūn-é Zhālé	Meidūn-é Shohadā

helpful and courteous and a few speak English. Some travellers have been offered the wrong passport when they came to collect their visas. If you have any problems, get in touch with your consulate.

The visa office has moved twice in the last three years and there's no guarantee it won't do so again. No photography is permitted around this building as it is opposite the presidential residence.

Useful Addresses Most of the following organisations are referred to in the text:

Archaeological Organisation
    Kheyābūn-é Ostād Motahharī, 60 Kheyābūn-é Lārestān (☎ 896223)
Azadi International Tourism Organization
    Azadi Grand Hotel, Bozorgrāh-é Shahīd Doktor Chamrān (☎ 298064; telex 212845 HYTT IR; fax 298072)
Iran Air-Tours
    Chahārrāh-é Hojjat-ol-Eslām Doktor Mofatteh, 191 Kheyābūn-é Ostād Motahharī (☎ 890298; telex 213956 IRAT IR; fax 895884)
Iranian Red Cross & Red Crescent Association
    Kheyābūn-é Shahīd Ostād Nejātollāhī (☎ 897335)
Kish Island Development Organization (KIDO)
    Bozorgrāh-é Afrīghā, Chahārrāh-é Shahīd Haghghānī, 3 Kheyābūn-é Kīsh (☎ 681491)
Ministry of Foreign Affairs
    Kheyābūn-é Sheikh Kūshk-é Mesrī (☎ 3211)
Ministry of Labour & Social Affairs
    Kheyābūn-é Āzādī (☎ 930033)
National Iranian Oil Company (NIOC)
    Kheyābūn-é Tāleghānī (☎ 6151, 933110; telex 212514)
Office of the Presidency
    Kheyābūn-é Falastīn, intersection with Kheyābūn-é Pāstör (☎ 6161)

Press & Mass Media Department
    Ministry of Culture & Islamic Guidance (Building No 2), Kheyābūn-é Valī-yé Asr (☎ 892725, fax 890695)
Ministry of Foreign Affairs
    Kheyābūn-é Sheikh Kūshk-é Mesrī (☎ 313304; fax 313149)
Statistical Centre of Iran
    Kheyābūn-é Doktor Hosein Fātemī (☎ 655061; telex 213233)
United Nations Representative Office
    74 Meidūn-é Arzhāntīn (☎ 4162811)
Valfajre-8 Shipping Company
    Kheyābūn-é Karīm Khān-é Zand, Kūché-yé Ābyār (☎ 899288)

Tourist Office The not particularly useful tourist office (☎ 892212 ext 29; telex 214256 IRIR; fax 893464) is in Kheyābūn-é Valī-yé Asr, 11 Kheyābūn-é Demeshgh, about 300 metres south of Meidūn-é Valī-yé Asr, on the 5th floor of the Department of Tourism & Pilgrimage of the Ministry of Culture & Islamic Guidance. The building is marked clearly in English, but they hardly ever see any foreigners. The postal address is PO Box 41-2334, Tehrān 14167.

There is an information booth (☎ 667785) at the international terminal of Tehrān airport where you might find someone who speaks English, and another (☎ 555067) at the train station which is occasionally open.

Money Plenty of banks in central Tehrān offer an exchange service: just look for a sign outside in English marked 'Exchange'. Most deal with both cash and travellers' cheques fairly efficiently. Rates are the same everywhere. Among many exchange branches, the central branch of Bank Melli Iran is on Kheyābūn-é Ferdōsī opposite the German Embassy, and the central branch of Bank Sepah is just north-west of Meidūn-é Emām Khomeinī. Probably the best and most popular place to go is the bank in the lobby of the Laleh International Hotel, open on weekdays from 9 am to 4 pm (9 to 11 am on Thursday). A few Western banks have representative offices in Tehrān, but they don't cater for private customers, even those with an account at the bank in their home country. To have money transferred in or out, you have to go to an Iranian bank or one of the private exchange offices. Most of the exchange offices are on the east side of Kheyābūn-é Ferdōsī; rates are typically about 5% above bank rates, but they're unlisted and negotiatiable.

Post & Telecommunications The main post office is behind gates on the north side of Kheyābūn-é Emām Khomeinī, 150 metres west of Meidūn-é Emām Khomeinī. Although it's not marked in English, you can recognise it by the postboxes outside. The poste restante counter (usually not staffed) is at the far right as you enter. Although this is not the only post office in Tehrān with a parcel delivery service, it is by far the most efficient. There are a few public telephone booths, less busy than most, just inside the entrance to the building.

The main telegraph office (for telegrams, telexes, faxes and telephone calls) is behind a guarded barbed-wire fence on the south side of Meidūn-é Emām Khomeinī. This is one of Tehrān's landmarks, with its satellite towers visible several km away. To reach it from Meidūn-é Emām Khomeinī, turn south into Kheyābūn-é Nāser Khosrō and take the first turning to the right. The very crowded telephone office is straight ahead as you enter, the telegram office is to the left and the telex and fax offices are on the 1st floor. This is the only telegraph office in Iran open 24 hours a day.

There are other post, telegraph and telephone offices all over town, but not all have international services. Most of the larger and

better hotels can put international calls through in under an hour, and sometimes almost immediately. Only a few places have a telex machine for the use of guests. The only public fax bureau is in the main telegraph office.

The following are useful telecommunications numbers:

Telegrams	☎ 120
Telephone Enquiries	
international	☎ 311041
domestic	☎ 118
Telephone Operator	
international	☎ 195
long-distance	☎ 126

Foreign Embassies The embassies of what were once called the Great Powers are all within walking distance of Meidūn-é Ferdōsī. Most of the others are within a few hundred metres either side of the northern half of Kheyābūn-é Valī-yé Asr. Since embassies keep odd and often very undemanding hours, always telephone to check on opening times before making a visit. All are closed for normal business on Friday, and most also close on Saturday or Sunday. However the larger embassies usually have someone on duty, at least to answer the telephone, 24 hours a day.

Embassy is *safārat* and interests section *daftar-é hāfez-é manāfe'*, so the Afghan Embassy is the *Safārat-é Afghānestān* and the US Interests Section is the *Daftar-é Hāfez-é Manāfe'-é Eyālāt-é Mottahedé-yé Āmrīkā*.

Consulates charge visa fees in rials at the official exchange rate.

Afghanistan (Afghānestān)
  Kheyābūn-é Shahīd Āyatollāh Doktor Beheshtī, Kheyābūn-é Pākestān, corner of Kūché-yé Chahārom (near the petrol station) (☎ 627531) (also consulate at Mashhad).
Australia (Ostralyā)
  Kheyābūn-é Sarvān Khāled Eslāmbōlī, 123 Kūché-yé Nōzdahom, (☎ 626202/23)
Austria (Otrīsh)
  78 Meidūn-é Ārzhāntīn (☎ 620180, 828431)

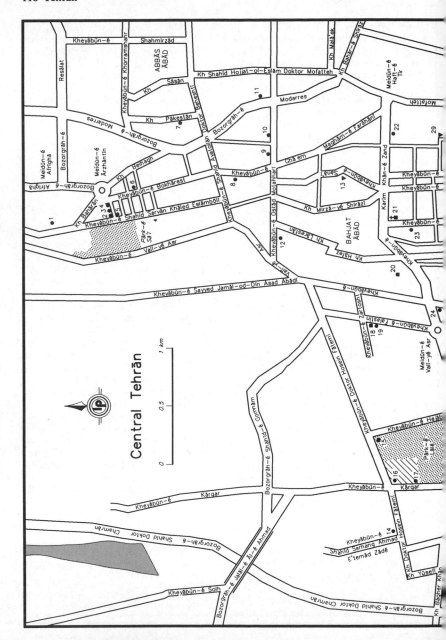

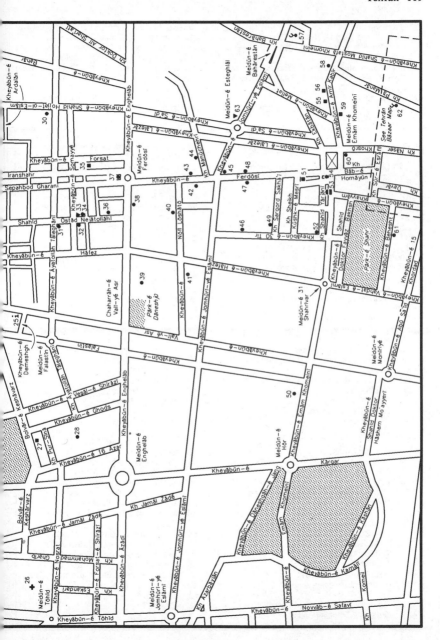

Bahrain (Bahrein)
 Kheyābūn-é Sarvān Khāled Eslāmbōlī, 16
 Kūché-yé Sī o Yekom (☎ 682079)
Belgium (Belzhīk)
 Kheyābūn-é Shahīd Sayyed Mortazā Feyyāzī,
 Kheyābūn-é Shahīd Āghā Bozorgī, 3 Kūché-yé
 Bābak (☎ 294574)
Canada (Kānādā)
 Kheyābūn-é Ostād Motahharī, 57 Kheyābūn-é

Shahīd Javād-é Sarāfrāz, corner of Kūché-yé
 Dovvom (☎ 622623, 623548)
Denmark (Dānmārk)
 Bozorgrāh-é Modarres, intersection with
 Bozorgrāh-é Afrīghā, 40 Kūché-yé Bīdār
 (☎ 297371)
Finland (Fanländ)
 Kheyābūn-é Gāndī, Kūché-yé Nōzdahom
 (☎ 684985)

■ PLACES TO STAY

15 Laleh International Hotel (ex-Intercontinental) (Hotel-é Lālé-yé Bein-ol-Melalī)
18 Hotel-é Keyān
20 Hotel-é Īrān
27 Hotel-é Bolvār
35 Hotel-é Īrānshahr
51 Hotel-é Bozorg-é Ferdōsī
55 Mosāferkhūné-yé Tūs (closed)
56 Mosāferkhūné-yé Ghasr-é Shīrīn, Mosāferkhūné-yé Īrān-é Nō, Mosāferkhūné-ye Masārrat & Mehmūnsarā-yé Markaz
59 Mosāferkhūné-yé Tehrān Gol

▼ PLACES TO EAT

13 Restōrān-é Epīkūr
15 Laleh International Hotel (Tiare Polynesian Restaurant and Rôtisserie Française)
29 Restōrān-é Tandūr ('Tandoor Restaurant')
33 Restōrān-é Nāder
63 Javān Chelō Kabāb

OTHER

1 Bahrain Embassy
2 Lufthansa
3 Australian Embassy
4 Alitalia
5 Interests Section of the United States of America
6 Saudi Arabian Embassy
7 Afghan Embassy
8 New Zealand Embassy
9 Canadian Embassy
10 Turkish Airlines
11 Ostāndārī
12 Netherlands Embassy
14 Pakistan Embassy
16 Mūzé-yé Farsh
17 Mūzé-yé Honarhā-yé Mo'āser
19 Gulliver's Travels (Gālī Tūr)

21 Kelsā-yé Hazrat-é Sarkīs (Armenian Cathedral of St Sarkīs)
22 Zand Bookshop (Ketābforūshgāh-é Zand)
23 Iranian Handicrafts Organisation Shop
24 Iraqi Embassy
25 Tourist Office (Ministry of Culture & Islamic Guidance (Vezārat-é Farhang va Ershād-é Eslāmī)
26 Emām Khomeinī Hospital (Bīmārestān-é Emām Khomeinī)
28 Tehrān University (Dāneshgāh-é Tehrān)
30 Former US Embassy
31 Swissair
32 PIA
34 Gulf Air
36 Aeroflot
37 Iran Air (Meidūn-é Ferdōsī Office)
38 British Airways
39 Iran Asseman
40 Russian Embassy
41 French Embassy
42 British Embassy
43 Moneychangers
44 Moneychangers
45 Turkish Embassy
46 Mūzé-yé Ābgīné
47 Bank Melli Iran (Central Branch); Mūzé-yé Javāherāt
48 German Embassy
49 Visa office (Police Department of the Ministry of Foreign Affairs)
50 Takht-é Marmar (present Majles Islamic Consultative Assembly)
52 Mūzé-yé Īrān-é Bāstān
53 Main Post Office (Edāré-yé Koll-é Post)
54 Bank Sepah (Central Branch)
57 Madrasé va Masjed-é Sepahsālār (Masjed-é Shahīd Motahharī)
58 Bank Melli Iran (Amīr Kabīr Branch)
60 Main Telegraph Office (Edāré-yé Koll-é Mokhābarāt)
61 Shahrdārī
62 Pā Manār

France (Farānsé)
83-5 Kheyābūn-é Nōfl Lōshātō (☎ 676001)
Germany (Ālmān)
324 Kheyābūn-é Ferdōsī, opposite Bank Markazi Iran (central branch) (☎ 314111-3)
India (Hendūstān)
Kheyābūn-é Āyatollāh Tāleghānī, 166 Kheyābūn-é Sabā-yé Shomālī (☎ 894554). Tourist visas are issued here.
Iraq (Erāgh)
494 Kheyābūn-é Valī-yé Asr, opposite Kūché-yé Nasr (50 metres south of Meidūn-é Valīyé Asr)
Ireland, Republic of (Īrländ)
Bolvār-é Mīr Dāmād, 8 Kheyābūn-é Rāzān-é Shomālī (☎ 222731)
Italy (Ītālyā)
81 Kheyābūn-é Nōfl Lōshātō (☎ 672107, 672333)
Japan (Zhāpon)
Kheyābūn-é Bokhārest, 12 Kūché-yé Panjom (☎ 623396, 623974)
Lebanon (Lobnān)
Kheyābūn-é Shahīd Ostād Nejātollāhī, 31 Kheyābūn-é Kalāntarī (☎ 898451) (consulate entered by an unmarked entrance in Kūché-yé Afshīn).
Netherlands (Holand)
Kheyābūn-é Ostād Motahharī, Kheyābūn-é Sarbedārān, 36 Kūché-yé Jahānsūz (☎ 896011)
New Zealand (Zelānd-é Nō)
Kheyābūn-é Shahīd Āyatollāh Doktor Beheshtī, Kheyābūn-é Mīrzā-yé Shīrāzī, 29 Kūché-é Mīrzā Hasanī (☎ 625061, 625083, 896011)
Pakistan (Pākestān)
Kheyābūn-é Doktor Fātemī, 1 Kheyābūn-é Shahīd Sarhang Ahmad E'temād Zādé (☎ 934331/2) (also consulates at Zāhedān and Mashhad). Tourist visas are issued here within two or three days.
Qatar (Ghatar)
Bozorgrāh-é Afrīghā, 4 Kheyābūn-é Gol Āzīn (☎ 221555). UK and Gulf Cooperation Council (GCC) nationals can enter for one month without a visa; others usually need a sponsor.
Russia (Rūs)
39 Kheyābūn-é Nōfl Lōshātō (☎ 671161).
Saudi Arabia (Arabestān-é Sa'ūdī)
59 Kheyābūn-é Bokhārest (☎ 624294). Pilgrimage (Hajj) visas to Mecca and Medina are issued according to the latest bilateral agreements and quotas of the Saudi authorities. No tourist visas are issued. Transit visas apply for entry and exit by land only along certain transit routes.
Sweden (Sū'ed)
78 Meidūn-é Ārzhāntīn (☎ 620514, 4162526)
Switzerland (Sū'īs)
Kheyābūn-é Elāhīyé, 13 Kheyābūn-é Būstān (☎ 268226)

Syria (Sūrīyé)
Kheyābūn-é Bokhārest, 42 Kūché-yé Dahom (☎ 229032)
Turkey (Torkīyé)
314 Kheyābūn-é Ferdōsī, diagonally opposite British Embassy (☎ 315299) (also consulates at Tabrīz and Orūmīyé). UK nationals need a visa which is only issued at the border (UK£5 in exact change). Some other nationalities require visas, but telephone enquiries here may not be fruitful.
UAE (Emārāt-é Arabī-yé Mottahedé)
Kheyābūn-é Valī-yé Asr, Kheyābūn-é Shahīd Sartīp Vahīd Dastgerdī (☎ 221333, 295029) (also consulate in Bandar-é Abbās) – UK and GCC nationals can stay for one month without a visa; others usually need a sponsor.
UK (Engelestān)
143 Kheyābūn-é Ferdōsī (☎ 675011) – also deals with nationals of Commonwealth countries not directly represented in Iran.
USA (Eyālāt-é Motahhedé-yé Āmrīkā)
(Interests Section): Kheyābūn-é Sarvān Khāled Eslāmbōlī, 5 Kūché-yé Hefdahom (☎ 625223)

Travel Agencies Most of the travel agencies are on or just off Nejātollāhī and are fairly helpful. Gardesh Travel Agency (☎ 836167) at 56 Kheyābūn-é Sepahbod Gharanī is recommended. There are no bucket shops.

Bookshops Most of the bookshops are around Tehrān University. No one place specialises in foreign literature, but most have at least one shelf of English-language books. Although you may well find some bargains here, a lot of shopping around is involved. More expensive bookshops with a better selection include the Zand on the south side of Kheyābūn-é Karīm Khān-é Zand, until recently import agent for *Time* magazine, and the well-stocked but relatively expensive bookshops inside the Homa, Grand Azadi and Esteghlal hotels. These are the best places to find most of the main prerevolutionary books on Iran in English; although the prices are very high by Iranian standards, they're well below what you'd pay in the West. The bookshop by the building marked 'Church Center' next to the Mūzé-yé Ābgīné also has a fairly small but good selection.

Maps The 1:20,000 Gītā Shenāsī *Complete*

Map of Tehran lives up to its name and is ideal for the foreign resident but a little bulky for the short-time visitor. The same company also publishes some smaller maps of Tehrān and an atlas (3000 rials) called *Tehran Today*, compiled in December 1990. The atlas includes a brief guide to the city, a few photographs, and a list of some useful addresses and telephone numbers. There is no tourist office map of Tehrān.

Medical Services Tehrān has by far the largest concentration of doctors and hospitals in Iran, and the quality of medical care is reasonably high by international standards. There are no services specifically set up to serve the foreign community, but your consulate in Tehrān should be able to recommend a doctor or hospital. Most doctors in Tehrān received training in the West, and you should have few problems in finding one who speaks English. If you need to see a doctor (or dentist), your consulate in Tehrān should be able to recommend one. One good place is the Emām Khomeinī Hospital (Bīmārestān-é Emām Khomeinī) (☎ 930040) on Bolvār-é Keshavarz.There are plenty of pharmacies all over town.

Emergency Hopefully you won't need to use any of these numbers:

Air Raid & Rocket Attack	
Emergency Assistance	☎ 198
Ambulance	☎ 123, 827815
Fire Brigade	☎ 125, 955555
General Emergencies	☎ 123
Komīté	☎ 310010
Police	☎ 110, 301081
Traffic Accidents	☎ 197, 342443

Mūzé-yé Ābgīné
The 'Glass & Ceramics Museum of Iran' standing in a small walled garden on the east side of Kheyābūn-é 30 Tīr, just north of the building marked in English 'Church Center', is one of the most impressive museums in Tehrān, not only for its exhibits but as a historic monument in its own right. This large two-storey building is perhaps the most interesting example remaining from the

Ghajar period open to the public anywhere in Tehrān, if not Iran. It was built in about 1910 as a private residence for a member of one of the leading families in Iran, later housed the Egyptian Embassy, and was then sold to the Iranian government, which converted it into a museum.

The building marks a move away from purely Persian traditions and exhibits a wide range of Eastern and Western styles, in this case a successful blend. The graceful wooden staircase and the classical stucco mouldings on the walls and ceilings are particularly impressive, and there are many delicate carvings and other decorations.

The worthwhile illustrated guide in English to the museum available here for 400 rials not only explains the exhibits but gives a general history of glassware and ceramics in Iran, which go back some 5000 and 10,000 years respectively. The museum has many hundreds of exhibits dating from the 2nd millennium BC and organised chronologically into galleries, including various items showing the early development of glassblowing from the 1st century BC, a technique then unknown outside the region. Unlike most museums in Iran, this one is very professionally organised and each piece is labelled in English. There is a small library with some art books in English in the basement. The museum is open from 9 am to 5 pm daily except Monday and mourning days, and entry is 50 rials. You'll have the place to yourself.

Namāyeshgāh-é 13 Ābān
This small museum (not marked in English) on the north-west corner of Meidūn-é Emām Khomeinī behind the newspaper stall is crammed solid with various bronze figures by the famous modern Iranian sculptor Sayyed Alī Akbar San'atī. All are life-size or larger and the subjects include such notables as the poets Ferdōsī, Sa'dī and Kamāl- ol-Molk, a crucified Christ, Shāh Abbās I, Nāder Shāh, and Mahatma Gandhi. Immediately to the left as you enter there are two sealed cases with peepholes through which you can see amusing tableaux of heav-

en and hell. This very muddled exhibition also has some Mexican carvings, a couple of Iran-Iraq War martyrs' tombs, a group sculpture of a human sea of prisoners in chains, and watercolours by San'atī. Nothing is labelled in English, but it doesn't really matter. It's open daily except mourning days from 8 am to 7 pm; entry is 50 rials. A resident photographer will take your portrait if you like.

Mūzé-yé Īrān-é Bāstān

The Archaeological Museum of Iran (not marked in English) is on Kheyābūn-é Shahīd Yārjānī at the intersection with Kheyābūn-é 30 Tīr. This is with little doubt the finest museum in Iran, and there's so much to see from so many periods that it's impossible to take everything in over one visit. The contents have been shifted about a bit over the last few years and now only the building nearest the entrance is used as a museum. The ground floor has exclusively pre-Islamic objects; all later items are on the 1st floor. It's best to visit each floor on separate occasions. Unfortunately many of the cases and exhibits aren't labelled in English, and there is no guide or map available in English.

You'll roughly follow a chronological progression if you go anticlockwise around both C-shaped floors. On the ground floor you'll start with ceramics from the 5th and 4th millennia BC, especially from Persepolis, Seyalk, Esmā'īl Ābād (125 km west of Tehrān), Susa, Rei and Tūrang Tappé, and a small number of 4th and 3rd millennium seals. Next you come to some delightful pitchers and vessels in animal shapes, mostly from Susa, Choghā Zambīl and Tūrang Tappé and dating from the 2nd millennium; clay tablets from Susa; various bead necklaces from the 1st millennium; bronze objects from the 2nd and 1st millennia; alabaster, gypsum, stone and bronze maceheads and axeheads from the 5th to 1st millennia; and various other weapons including spearheads, swords, daggers and bronze arrowheads from the 3rd to 1st millennia. Another case contains 1st millennium pottery from Seyalk and other sites. There

are some 2nd and 1st millennium bronze animal figurines from Marlik, Gīlan and other sites, and some very charming ceramic cows (one 1st millennium piece even on wheels) and other animals. You will come to some more 1st millennium BC seals and then to a 1st millennium Urartian stone tablet from Mākū inscribed in cuneiform.

Turn left now and enter the Achaemenian period. In the corridor between the two halls are two very valuable pieces by the wall: a stone capital of a winged lion from Susa, probably 5th millennium BC, and a 6th century BC audience hall relief of Darius I from the Treasury at Persepolis. In the west hall you come first to some ceramic plates and other domestic utensils from Persepolis; a frieze of glazed tiles from the Apadana at Persepolis (5th century BC); contemporary glazed bricks decorated with double-winged mythical creatures from Susa; the lower two-thirds of a human figure on a base with cuneiform inscriptions, also from Susa (5th century); a glazed tile with an archer figure from Susa (5th century); and the fragment of a staircase from Persepolis (5th century). Next there are several pieces from Persepolis, including a very famous trilingual Darius I inscription, a human-headed capital and a 5th century staircase, four foundation tablets inscribed in cuneiform (5th century BC), a stone capital and the base of a column, a marble statue of Penelope from the Treasury, and the the stone paw of a lion. Further on is a column base from Susa (6th to 5th century BC), a tall column with a double bull-head capital of black stone, a case of various coins from the 6th century BC to the 3rd century AD, tablets from Persepolis and Susa, a bronze statue of a Parthian prince, two large Sassanian stucco reliefs – one from Tehrān Province (5th century) and another from Dāmghān (6th century) – then a ceramic tomb box from Susa, some smaller 5th century stucco reliefs from Tehrān Province, and finally some 3rd century mosaic decorations from Shāpūr I's palace at Bīshāpūr (Fārs).

On the 1st floor, immediately to your right if you also take the anticlockwise route, are some stucco reliefs from Neishābūr (9th to 10th century AD) and Rei (12th century), then some semiglazed pottery from Soltān Ābād and Takht-é Soleimān from the 14th century AD, some large 11th-century inscribed bricks, and various large items of carved plaster and stucco reliefs from Rei, Esfahān, Neishābūr and Torbat-é Jām (Khorāsān). Farther along are tombstones from Hamadān, Kāshān and Ghom, two fine large stucco mehrābs from Esfahān, tiles from Sāvé (13th century), Gorgān (11th to 13th centuries), Takht-é Soleimān (about 13th century) and Kāshān (14th century), carved wooden doors from Fārs, Māzandarān, Lāhījūn and Esfahān dating from the 11th to 19th centuries, a large inlaid *membar* (mosque pulpit) from Fārs, a case containing inscribed books and other calligrapy from the 14th to 19th centuries, cases with brocades and items of clothing, some carpets, some more coins, and some small paintings from the 15th to the 19th centuries.

The museum is open daily from 9 am to noon and from 1 to 4 pm except on Friday and public holidays when it opens from 8.30 to 11 am only, and Tuesday and mourning days, when it's closed.

Presidential Palace

Right behind this museum there is a large old stone building behind a high-walled courtyard, unmarked, completely inconspicuous and not visibly guarded from the street, which happens to be the presidential palace. As is clearly the intention, it is not likely to attract the attention of any casual passer-by. Do not linger.

Mūzé-yé Honarhā-yé Mo'āser

The large, modern Tehrān Museum of Contemporary Art just south of the Mūze-yé Farsh is worth at least an hour. There are regular temporary exhibitions here featuring Iranian and foreign artists and photographers. The museum is open from 9 am to noon and from 1 to 5.30 pm daily except mourning days. There is a café in the museum which ought to be a popular hang-out for arty types but isn't. Entry to the museum is 50 rials; there is no extra charge for special exhibitions. There are some rather odd modern sculptures in the garden.

Parks

Tehrān has a number of attractive parks, mostly quite far north of the centre. Some of them are very secluded, and courting couples, forbidden from seeing each other alone in public, often arrange illicit liaisons in them; the Komīté used to hide behind bushes waiting for the chance to pounce. Some of the best are the Pārk-é Sā'ī at the top of Valī-yé Asr which is thick with tall trees and within sight of the Alborz, the large very popular Pārk-é Mellat, and the Pārk-é Shahr to the south.

Majmū'é-yé Farhangī-yé Sa'd Ābād

In the grounds of what used to be the Shāh's summer residence in Shemīrān in the far north of Tehrān there are several museums forming the 'Sa'd Ābād Cultural Complex', not all open at the same time. They are all clearly marked and signposted in English. No photography is permitted.

What is now called the **Nation Palace Museum** was the last Shāh's palace. The two stone boots outside are all that remains of a giant statue of Rezā Shāh Pahlavī. Upstairs in the Ceremonial Dining Room, the 145 sq metre carpet, a copy of a famous rug from the shrine of Sheikh Safī-od-Dīn in Ardabīl, is said to be one of the largest ever made in Iran, but it is not as large as the monster weaving downstairs in the Ceremonial Hall, which measures an incredible 243 sq metres.

The **Shāh's Mother's Palace** is now inexplicably known as the 'Reversion & Admonition Palace'. As a comment on the wicked ways of the Shāh the curators have kept open the 'Gamble Room' along with a photograph of a miserable pauper surrounded by backgammon sets and playing-cards.

The palaces seem homely rather than royally extravagant and much of the decor looks decidedly dated, even tasteless – an incongruous mixture of classical Persian and garish Western styles. As evidence that the Shāh squandered the national oil wealth on his own personal pleasure, these museums could hardly be less effective. Still, as one Iranian who had been to the palace when the original occupants were still there told me, all the best stuff was nicked in the revolution.

From there you can walk or take a courtesy bus uphill to what is now known as the **Jambazan Foundation Museum** and was the palace of the last Shāh's nephew Shahrām, who was only 16 at the time of the revolution. Appropriately this is the smallest palace of the lot, with a dining-room designed for only two persons.

In the same grounds there is an interesting **Military Museum** with a collection of hand-weapons including a 1979 present from President Saddam Hussein of Iraq to the Shāh. The Shāh's Rolls-Royce stands outside, looking very much in need of a wash.

To the right of the entrance is the **Fine Arts Museum** which has some charming Persian oil-paintings dating back to the 18th century, including several portraits, a rare form in Islamic art, and some very beautiful inlaid furniture.

In the grounds are some other museums, which are occasionally open. They include a small **Natural History Museum**, a short walk up from the Shahrām Palace and easily mistaken for a gasworks, with various stuffed animals and hunting trophies, and the nearby **Museum of Athnological Research** (sic) with a few waxworks, as well as something called the **Rejeat and Ibrim Museum**.

The complex is open daily from 8 am to 12.15 pm and from 1 to 4 pm: you pay 50 rials at the gate for a ticket to each museum that is open at the time, and just follow everyone else. Usually three or four are open on any one day. The grounds are quite extensive and it takes two or three hours to visit your quota of museums. Cameras are very strictly forbidden inside the complex. To get here take a blue and white shared taxi northwest from Meidūn-é Tajrīsh for 50 rials.

Bazaar

Far more than just a market-place, the bazaar district is traditionally the Wall St of Tehrān and hence Iran, where the prices of staple commodities are fixed. The powerful *bāzārī* class also wields a lot of political clout and forms a large part of the current president's power base. The bazaar is, however, in decline, and many merchants have moved their businesses north of the bazaar. Each corridor specialises in a particular trade: copper, paper, gold, spice and carpets, among others. In the last of these expect to be pounced on and whisked off on a tour that inevitably ends with a highly professional demonstration of hard-sell carpet marketeering. Tehrān's bazaar, never much of an architectural jewel, has grown haphazardly and is nowadays rather sleazy, but it's worth spending an hour or two there if you can ever find your way out again. It's a city within a city, encompassing over a dozen mosques, guesthouses and banks, one church and its own fire station. You can even buy a map of the bazaar. The main entrance is in Kheyābūn-é 15 Khordād.

Mūzé-yé Farsh

The Carpet Museum, 400 metres west of the Laleh International Hotel at the north-west corner of the Pārk-é Lālé, houses over 100 pieces from all over Iran, from the 18th century or earlier to the present day. Although the exhibition is not particularly vast it more than makes up in quality what it lacks in quantity. This is a must for carpet-lovers.

Between the Mūzé-yé Honarhā-yé Mo'āser and the Mūzé-yé Farsh is a large new open-air bazaar with some handicrafts on offer.

Borj-é Āzādī

Built in 1971 to commemorate the 2500th anniversary of the Persian Empire and originally known as the Borj-é Shahyād, this extraordinary inverted Y-shaped 'Freedom Monument' is close to Tehrān airport and the west bus terminal. Upstairs there's a historical museum of Iran, the Mūzé-yé Āzādī, and

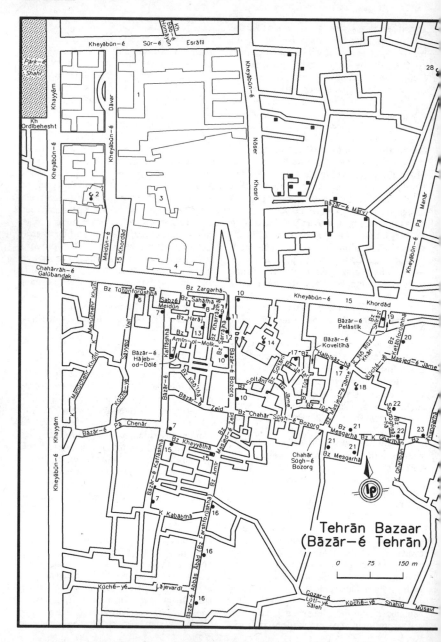

Tehrān Bazaar
(Bāzār-é Tehrān)

0   75   150 m

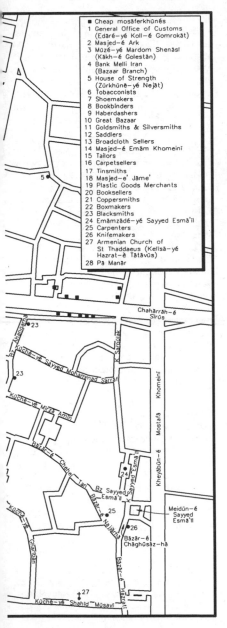

- ■ Cheap mosâferkhūnēs
1 General Office of Customs
  (Edārē−yé Koll−é Gomrokāt)
2 Masjed−é Ark
3 Mūzé−yé Mardom Shenāsī
  (Kākh−é Golestān)
4 Bank Melli Iran
  (Bazaar Branch)
5 House of Strength
  (Zūrkhūnē−yé Nejāt)
6 Tobacconists
7 Shoemakers
8 Bookbinders
9 Haberdashers
10 Great Bazaar
11 Goldsmiths & Silversmiths
12 Saddlers
13 Broadcloth Sellers
14 Masjed−é Emām Khomeinī
15 Tailors
16 Carpetsellers
17 Tinsmiths
18 Masjed−e' Jāme'
19 Plastic Goods Merchants
20 Booksellers
21 Coppersmiths
22 Boxmakers
23 Blacksmiths
24 Emāmzādé−yé Sayyed Esmā'īl
25 Carpenters
26 Knifemakers
27 Armenian Church of
   St Thaddaeus (Kelīsā−yé
   Hazrat−è Tātāvūs)
28 Pā Manār

you can take a lift to the top for a lofty view of Tehrān, smog permitting.

Mūzé-yé Mardom Shenāsī
Inside the Kākh-é Golestān (Rose Garden Palace) 800 metres south of Meidūn-é Emām Khomeinī, this ethnographical museum has a colourful exhibition of traditional Iranian dress with wax dummies as models, as well as a folk art exhibition. When you visit the provinces you'll see that many of these costumes are by no means relics of a bygone age. The building became the palace of the Ghajars a few years after Tehrān became the capital and is set in a formal Persian garden.

Former US Embassy
Not open to the public, this vast complex a third of the way up Kheyābūn-é Shahīd Mofatteh is currently used as a computer training centre for Islamic Revolutionary Guards. Nowadays it's predictably called the US Den of Espionage. There is a kiosk right on the corner outside selling propaganda in English, particularly copies of secret incriminating documents painstakingly pieced together from the shredder after the revolution. Don't photograph or linger here.

Mūzé-yé Javāherāt
The Iranian crown jewels are hidden beneath the Bank Melli Iran in Ferdōsī, close to the German Embassy. The vaults have been closed to the public for several years, though there are vague plans to reopen the museum soon: get a Persian-speaker to telephone the curator (☎ 310100) for the latest information.

The most famous piece of the original collection, the Kūh-é Nūr (Koh-i-Noor, 'Mountain of Light') diamond, was pilfered by the Brits, so you'll have to go to the Tower of London to see that. Remaining treasures include the Daryā-yé Nūr ('Sea of Light') diamond weighing 182 carats and said to be the largest uncut diamond in the world, the Peacock Throne encrusted with 26,000 gems and carted off from Delhi by Nāder Shāh, the jewelled globe (just to use up 51,366 spare precious stones), and enough crowns for all the queens and kings in the world.

Ārāmgāh-é Emām Khomeinī

The Resting-Place of His Holiness Emām Khomeinī, when completed, will be one of the greatest Islamic buildings in modern history. At the Islamic Republic's final send-off to its founder and inspiration – the largest funeral ever held in the world – the crush of an estimated 10 million mourners twice made it physically impossible for the hearse to reach the cemetery. Even when a helicopter hastily brought into service the next day landed, no amount of armed Revolutionary Guards could prevent the crowd from pushing forward to rip pieces off the shroud as holy relics. The shrine is assured of its place on the Shi'ite map. It is appropriately on the road between Tehrān, the town that launched the Islamic Revolution, and Ghom, the town where the great man underwent his theological training. It is not far from the southern edge of Tehrān, near the Behesht-é Zahrā, and can be reached by bus No 434 from Meidūn-é Emām Khomeinī, or you can stop there on any bus or shared taxi to Ghom (from the south terminal). An underground line will also operate to the shrine from south Tehrān.

Behesht-é Zahrā

This vast expanse of land, stretching as far in any direction as the eye can see, is the main cemetery for those who died in the Iran-Iraq War. It will be familiar to many from the moving TV and newspaper pictures taken of hysterical mourners by Western journalists during the height of the conflict. It is probably the world's largest graveyard. On the Ghom road nine km beyond the southern edge of Tehrān and a short distance north of the Ārāmgāh-é Emām Khomeinī, it is best reached by shared taxi from outside the south terminal.

Madrasé va Masjed-é Sepahsālār

Built between 1878 and 1890 during the Ghajar dynasty, the Commander-in-Chief's Theological College and Mosque is one of the most noteworthy examples of Persian architecture of its period as well as among the largest. It's on Meidūn-é Bahārestān, 500 metres north of Kheyābūn-é Amīr Kabīr. If you ask politely you might be allowed to climb its minarets or cool down in its shaded courtyard. The tilework is especially lavish and there is a marble-pillared room with an amazing echo.

Kelīsā-yé Hazrat-é Sarkīs

In case you think that Islam has a monopoly on Iranian life, go to the north end of Kheyābūn-é Shahīd Ostād Nejātollāhī and visit the impressive Armenian cathedral built between 1964 and 1970, impressive not so much for any great beauty but because of what it is and where it is. This is by far the most visible and important non-Islamic religious building in Tehrān. It's open free of charge to visitors daily except Sunday, and you can often find an Armenian who speaks English willing to show you around. The area immediately to the south is the Armenian quarter of Tehrān, centre of a still very thriving community. Every year on the anniversary of one of the many Armenian massacres in Anatolia thousands of Armenians form a solemn procession from there to the gates of the Turkish Embassy.

Other Churches

Although most of the Christians in Iran are Armenians, there is also a sprinkling of Protestants, Assyrians, Catholics and Orthodox, and all have their churches in Tehrān, mostly in the same district as this cathedral. Your consulate can give you some addresses. The modern Episcopal (Anglican) **Church of St Paul** (Kelīsā-yé Hazrat-é Pūlos) is on the east side of Kheyābūn-é Hāfez, not far north of Karīm Khān.

Pā Manār

This simple free-standing single minaret from the early 19th century is on Kheyābūn-é Pā Manār which runs south from opposite the Amīr Kabīr branch of Bank Melli Iran.

Top: Shepherd with flock, Ghalé-yé Sāng (DStV)
Left: Kūh-é Khājé (DStV)
Right: Arg-é Bam (DStV)

Top: Haram-é Motahhar-é Emām Rezā, Mashhad (DStV)
Bottom: Preparing buffalo for slaughter in street, Kūh-é Khājé (DStV)

Mūzé-yé Kākh-é Neyāvarān

In the far north-east of Tehrān, this concrete monstrosity complete with rooftop helicopter pad and private cinema used to be the Shāh's winter residence when Sa'd Ābād was covered in snow. Unlike the much larger Sa'd Ābād compound, the Neyāvarān Palace grounds only have one building open to the public. Hours are 8 am to 4.30 pm daily and a ticket costs 100 rials. It's opposite the south-east corner of the Pārk-é Neyāvarān and can be reached by shared taxi going east from Meidūn-é Ghods or Meidūn-é Tajrīsh.

Shūsh & Mōlavī

The busy area around the train station, particularly in and between Kheyābūn-é Shūsh and Kheyābūn-é Mōlavī, is the traditional working-class district of Tehrān. It is one of the few old parts of the city to have remained more or less intact throughout the years of boom, turmoil, development and creeping uniformity that have changed the face of the rest of the city beyond recognition. It is regarded by many if not most Tehrānīs as the ultimate no-go area, far worse than Kheyābūn-é Amīr Kabīr and Kheyābūn-é Nāser Khosrō, and it actually can be quite dangerous. The swaggering toughs traditionally associated by other Tehrānīs with this area are not merely a figment of the imagination, and fights do break out here at the slightest provocation.

Yet this frantically crowded, bustling and chaotic area is really the closest you can get to the old Oriental character of Tehrān that has all but vanished from the rest of the city. The narrow lanes are open to cars but once you drive in it's very difficult to get out again because of competition from the contraptions used by the bazaar merchants to transport their wares; everywhere there is a crush of humanity. Much of the economic life of Tehrān would grind to a halt were it not for the porters who shift the stock from A to B. For their backbreaking work they are very well paid by Iranian standards, perhaps 5000 rials for each local delivery. There are quite a few buildings from the early or middle Ghajar period, including several

mosques, and in many places you can still see the traditional balconied dwellings of old, protected behind carved and studded doors set into high walls. Most people prefer merely to drive through this part of town.

Masjed-é Emām Khomeinī

The Masjed-é Emām Khomeinī (ex-Masjed-é Shāh) is very much a working mosque, one of the largest and busiest in Tehrān, even having cigarette vendors inside. The building itself, although dating from the very early 18th century, is not the attraction: you go here to see Islam at work. Since the courtyard is not cut off from the surrounding area and hundreds of people hourly pass through on their way to and from the bazaar, it's no problem at all for non-Muslims to stand and watch the faithful performing their ablutions, praying and professing their belief in the one true God. This mosque is near the Kākh-é Golestān, in the bazaar and just opposite the southern extremity of Kheyābūn-é Nāser Khosrō. There is an inscription of Fath Alī Shāh's name on one wall as you approach from the bazaar, but it is very difficult to find.

Emāmzādé-yé Sayyed Esmā'īl

This small mausoleum in a private courtyard just west of Kheyābūn-é Mostafā Khomeinī is quite attractive, with its two sturdy cylindrical minarets.

Takht-é Marmar

Now the Majles or parliament building, this 'Marble Throne', two km west of Meidūn Emām Khomeinī, was founded by Karīm Khān and enhanced by Āghā Mohammad Khān. You can't go inside and photography is strictly forbidden.

Shopping Districts

Kheyābūn-é Valī-yé Asr is claimed to be the longest avenue in the world (so don't try walking from one end to the other), and it's one of the major shopping districts of

Tehrān. Foreign visitors to Iran are often struck by the range of Western goods openly available in the country, from the latest French fashions to the most expensive Japanese video machines. Even in the worst days of the Iran-Iraq War it was business as usual for Tehrān's shopkeepers. To many Tehrānīs the idea of a perfect night out is to go window-shopping, and the northern part of Kheyābūn-é Valī-yé Asr is one of their favourite places to do it.

Traditionally all the shopkeepers specialising in a particular trade or service would be grouped together in the same street or district, and buying a shop in that area would be almost akin to joining a guild. Nowadays of course the pace of development is so great that even if they wanted to all the fishmongers or cobblers, for example, could never fit onto one street, but certain addresses are still strongly associated with a particular product. Jomhūrī-yé Eslāmī (Estāmbōl) is still the preserve of the fishmongers, clothes are sold in Valī-yé Asr, expensive clothes in Gāndī, tools and spare parts in Ekbātān, and the carpet shops and money changers are concentrated in Ferdōsī. Old habits die hard, and even relatively modern trades often group in one area; there are three photographic shops on Nāser Khosrō and the airlines and travel agencies are around Nejātollāhī.

There are Iranian Handicrafts Organisation shops in Kheyābūn-é Valī-yé Asr (opposite the Pārk-é Mellat) and near the top of Kheyābūn-é Nejātollāhī, as well as in the Azadi Grand Hotel. Another good place to buy handicrafts is the Bāzār-é Valī-yé Asr (Pāsāzh-é Safavīyé) opposite the Pārk-é Mellat, just north of the state shop. You can also find imported goods such as chocolates and cosmetics relatively inexpensively here, especially during the sales before Nō Rūz and Christmas. There are many other places around Nejātollāhī, Karīm Khān Tāleghānī and Ferdōsī, and more or less throughout the rest of Tehrān. You can buy almost anything in Tehrān, imported or home-produced, licit or illicit, and if you don't know where to look, just ask around

locally. When shopping for goods at negotiable prices, especially carpets and handicrafts, it may help to take an Iranian friend.

Telé Kābīn-é Tōchāl

Iran has the world's longest and highest telecabin, the Telé Kābīn-é Tōchāl, which runs from a station at the far north of Kheyābūn-é Velenjak (reached by shared taxi from Meidūn-é Tajrīsh) right up to the peak of Tōchāl, 7.5 km, seven stations and 35 minutes away.

Walking

One very popular weekend activity with the Tehrānīs, especially in the warmer months, is walking in the foothills of the Alborz. They tend to go in small groups, but even if you go on your own this is an excellent way to meet people. The climb is not very arduous, although a good pair of shoes is advisable, and there are some pleasant cafés and water-fountains along the way. Most people stick to one or two main trails; on Fridays the traffic in both automobiles and humans can be very heavy. You can start off at Meidūn-é Darband, easily reached by bus or shared taxi from Tajrīsh, and then just follow everyone else.

Sports

There are many public swimming-pools, but they tend to be very crowded and foreigners usually get stared at. Some of the larger hotels have pools open to the paying public. There are also a few saunas, such as the one at the Keyān Hotel. You can go waterskiing in the Karaj Dam.

The best equipped sports club is the Enghelāb, near Pārk-é Mellat, which has 14 tennis courts, indoor and outdoor swimming-pools, a golf course and even a cricket field: try to find an Iranian willing to give you an introduction. There are twice-monthly televised car races on a circuit at the Pārk-é Eram and regular horse races at the Jockey Stadium. Soccer is very popular and there are more than 10 stadiums in Tehrān. Traditional Iranian wrestling can be watched at any of the zūrkhūnés in town, of which the most famous is probably that of the Bank Melli Iran.

Skiing is possible at Shamshak, north of Tehrān, and you can hire skiing equipment there for around 5000 rials a day. Get there by shared taxi from Evīn. Skiing conditions are best in winter and early spring.

Trade Fairs

Every spring an international trade fair is held in permanent purpose-built grounds near Evīn. Ask the commercial attaché of your consulate in Tehrān, or of your nearest Iranian consulate, for details some time in advance. All of Iran's major trading partners have stands, and it is sometimes possible for participants to obtain visas on arrival at Tehrān airport. Alternatively you can write direct to the Export Promotion Centre of Iran, PO Box 11-48, Tajrīsh (☎ 21911). An annual international book fair is held in about May: for details, contact the Secretariat of Tehrān International Book Fairs, PO Box 11365-3457, Tehrān (☎ 660238).

Places to Stay

Tehrān has a chronic shortage of hotel accommodation which shows no sign of improving. Unless you make a reservation at least several days in advance or are happy to go to one of the top hotels that charge foreigners in US dollars at an exorbitant rate, you are very unlikely to get into the place of your first or even second choice. Sometimes hotels give priority to foreigners, but increasingly even middle-bracket hotels refuse to take Westerners, apparently on the instructions of the tourist office. On one occasion I had to give up looking after being turned away at 15 hotels in a row. The tourist authorities appear bent on forcing foreigners to stay only at hotels that charge in US dollars, even though this was supposedly outlawed in February 1991.

If you have not arranged accommodation beforehand, try telephoning your chosen hotel from the airport or station on arrival. There are a couple of telephones from which you can call free of charge within Tehrān inside the domestic arrival lounge. It's hopeless to arrive in Tehrān without a reservation within the three weeks before or the week after Nō Rūz, or within a couple of days before any public holiday, and you will pay a fortune to cruise around Tehrān by airport taxi trying to find a room.

In view of the distance between hotels and the problems in finding a room, it really is worthwhile to hire a taxi if you have any amount of luggage. Taxi drivers also have a good idea of which places are likely to have a vacancy and can sometimes persuade a hotel to take you even if it's 'full' to anyone else.

Very few hotels in Tehrān have enough single rooms to go around, so if you're travelling unaccompanied you should expect to have to pay for a double room.

Places to Stay – bottom end

Most of the real cheapies are around the official centre of Tehrān, especially around all roads leading from Meidūn-é Emām Khomeinī within a radius of about two km. However most of these places are only really used to taking Iranians on zero expense accounts and you'll be lucky to find one that isn't 'full'. The bottom line in this area is about 800 rials, but it's as well to remember that many Tehrānīs consider this part of town a no-go area at night. You certainly see some desperate types, and evidence that despite all the bus searches drugs still get to Tehrān. On the other hand, plenty of Western travellers have stayed here over the years without coming to any harm, and most places are no worse and often a lot better than you would find in the cheaper parts of large Turkish or Pakistani towns. By and large the people at the mosāferkhūnés – so long as they let you in at the door – are friendly to foreigners.

Three of the old favourites with backpackers travelling the Asian overland route have closed – the Ferdōsī youth hostel, the grotty Amīr Kabīr and the Tūs (although the Tūs may reopen in the future).

If you stay somewhere without a bathroom, there are plenty of public bathhouses charging around 100 rials a shower throughout this part of Tehrān: you take your own soap, towel and shampoo.

There is no one place to stay in this area, but probably the best place to start looking is still Kheyābūn-é Amīr Kabīr. By far the best, cleanest and friendliest mosāferkhūné is the fairly large Tehrān Gol (marked in English 'Flor') on the south side of Amīr Kabīr, which charges 1500 rials for a single room with breakfast and shared bathroom. You shouldn't have any problems getting in if you don't look too scruffy. Otherwise there are several grotty places over the road, mostly just off the street, including the Ghasr-é Shīrīn ('Ghasreshirin') at 3000/3500 rials a double/triple, the Īrān-é Nō ('Iranno') at 2000/2900/3500 rials a single/double/triple with shared bathroom, the Masārrat ('Maserret') at 2000/3000 rials a single/double and the so-called Mehmūnsarā-yé Markazī at 3000 rials a double with shared bathroom. You can also try Kheyābūn-é Nāser Khosrō, Kheyābūn-é Emām Khomeinī and the area immediately southwest of the main post office, but you're unlikely to find one that accepts Westerners.

Places to Stay – Middle

For no more than twice the price of the cheapies you can easily find somewhere with 10 times the comfort level. This is well worth considering, as Tehrān is exhausting enough without having to deal with a ratty hotel. Along Ferdōsī, just north of Kheyābūn-é Amīr Kabīr, there are dozens of hotels which will or at least may take Westerners; the further you go the better the standard. Kheyābūn-é Valī-yé Asr is also a happy hunting-ground for hotels, most of them charging around 3000 rials a single. There are also many good mid-range hotels in or just off Kheyābūn-é Karīm Khān, Kheyābūn-é Īrānshahr, Kheyābūn-é Nejātollāhī and Kheyābūn-é Sepahbod Gharanī, all of them marked in English and within walking distance of each other. The only good place in the centre of Tehrān is the recently opened three-star Hotel-é Bozorg-é Ferdōsī ('Ferdowsi Grand Hotel') near the Foreign

Ministry which charges 3000/4000 rials a single/double with private bathroom.

There is little point in giving recommendations since the best places are understandably extremely popular and tend to be almost permanently booked up, but the Hotel-é Īrān (☎ 893161) on Kūché-yé Kāryābī off Kheyābūn-é Valī-yé Asr, the Hotel-é Īrānshahr (☎ 820518) on Kheyābūn-é Īrānshahr and the Hotel-é Bolvār (☎ 658546) ('Bulvar Hotel') in Bolvār-é Keshāvarz, each at around 3200/4800 rials a single/double with private bathroom, are all very good.

Beware that these places may start charging foreigners in US dollars in the near future, and many people will have no choice but to look for a bottom-end place. I can't imagine that the authorities would ever make the mosāferkhūnés start charging that way.

Places to Stay – top end

There are many four and five-star hotels in Tehrān, but only a few of them are luxurious by international standards. Generally you get the best service from the places most used to foreigners, including the Keyān, (☎ 650237) Esteghlal (☎ 290011), Laleh International (☎ 655024), Homa (☎ 683029) and Grand Azadi (☎ 835133); the Keyān is popular with long-term residents, the Esteqlal with diplomats and business people on expense accounts, the Laleh with journalists. The Homa and Laleh used to charge in rials (around 15,000 rials a double) and as a result often had more foreign guests than Iranian, but now all the top hotels charge in US dollars and represent poor value for money.

Typical charges are US$50 a double for the Keyān, US$92 for the Homa and up to US$150 at the Esteqlal and Grand Azadi.

Rental The best people to see for renting places are the estate agents who advertise in Tehran Times as specialising in rental or sale to foreigners.

Places to Eat

Most places stop serving between 9 and 10 pm, sometimes even earlier. The top hotels do have 24-hour restaurants and coffee rooms, but they are open at night more for the convenience of the guest who has a plane to catch at 5 am than for the pleasure of the late-night socialite.

Alcohol is not sold anywhere legally and openly, although there is no sound religious reason why non-Muslims should not be allowed to drink in their own company, as they can in other Muslim countries.

Chelō kabābīs Chelō kabāb is definitely the standard ration at most of the cheaper restaurants in Iran and Tehrān is no exception. If you're staying in central Tehrān you won't have to look far, as even richer Tehrānīs head south if they're looking for a good chelō kabāb. At almost any restaurant in this area you can fill up for 1500 rials or less, and at the snack bars for less than half that. Avoid Iranian sausages at all costs, however. There are dozens of almost identical restaurants in and around Meidūn-é Emām Khomeinī.

There is a slightly better class of chelō kabābī along Ferdōsī (as with the hotels, the further north you go the better the quality). One of the best and certainly most popular chelō kabābīs in this area is the *Javān* in Kheyābūn-é Bāgh-é Sepahsālār off Kheyābūn-é Jomhūrī-yé Eslāmī, where the kebabs are grilled in front of you and cost 450 rials a skewer. The *Restōrān-é Dīzī* in Kheyābūn-é Īrānshahr is the place to go for ābgūsht, at 1000 rials or less.

Restaurants There are hundreds of restaurants in Tehrān, few of which are actually bad, and the following is only a short personal selection. At weekends it's often a good idea to make a reservation.

At all but the most expensive restaurants it would be difficult to spend more than 4000 rials a person, so it is worth splashing out. You won't find anything like the same variety anywhere else in Iran.

One good and inexpensive place popular with thrifty Iranians looking for a good meal out is the *Nāder* in Kheyābūn-é Nejātollāhī, where 2000 rials should be more than

enough. It also has good value three-course set lunches for around 1300 rials.

One of the best gastronomic bargains in Tehrān has to be the eat-as-much-as-you-like lunch served at the excellent *Epīkūr* ('Epicure') in Kheyābūn- é Sanā'ī. With a charge of only 2000 rials it's difficult to see how they can make any profit. The à la carte menu is none too expensive either.

Mininimally more expensive, the *Tāndūr* ('Tandoor') (☎ 825701) in the Hotel-é Tehrān Sarā on Kūché-yé Ardalān off Shahīd Moffateh (the first street on the left north of the old US Embassy), is one of the few foreign-owned restaurants in Tehrān, and very good too. There are a few other less successful Indian restaurants in the same area.

Perhaps the most expensive restaurant in town is the Japanese *Serīnā* ('Seryna' (☎ 683735) at 3 Kūché-yé Abdō, near Meidūn-é Vanak. The indoor water-garden, Japanese prints, sunken tables and waiters in Japanese dress all add to the atmosphere, but with the cheapest main course costing more than 5000 rials and a minimum charge per person of something like 9000 rials I didn't think it was worth the money. It advertises – but does not provide – Japanese Suntory lager. It is open throughout the week except for lunch on Friday.

There is also a Chinese restaurant (☎ 890714), the first in Tehrān, at the same address.

The coffee lobbies in the luxury hotels are very popular with the locals, especially at the Laleh International where they go to watch, albeit very discreetly, the foreigners, a favourite Iranian pastime. Chocolate cake is 500 rials, coffee 250 rials.

The best two restaurants are both on the 13th floor of the Laleh International Hotel. The excellent *Tiare Polynesian Restaurant* commands a panoramic view of north Tehrān and also offers very good food which struck me as owing more to Chinese than Polynesian influences. Unless you suffer from vertigo, ask for a window table. In its prerevolutionary posters dotted around the hotel it advertises cocktails and exotic drinks, but sadly the most exotic beverage I was offered was a glass of orange juice. The more private *Rôtisserie Française* on the same floor is one of the best in Iran for Continental food and it manages to get the sauces right. At both places count on around 5000 rials a person, money very well spent.

The smart *Sūrnā* ('Sorrento') in Kheyābūn-é Valī-yé Asr opposite the Pārk-é Mellat is fairly good, and in summer it serves meals on the rooftop terrace. Chateaubriand is 2800 rials and chicken Kiev the same.

There are many very good, even luxurious restaurants in the far north of Tehrān, right up to the foothills of the Alborz, but they are expensive and very difficult to get to from the centre without private transport.

Tehrān also has some excellent cakeshops and confectioneries. Many of the best are owned by Armenians, and the greatest concentration is in Kheyābūn-é Nejātollāhī. This is also the place to buy pistachios or luxury foods. Almost any food not forbidden by Islam can be found in Tehrān, even mangoes and kiwi fruit, and the selection available here rivals that in most capitals in the region.

Along Kheyābūn-é Valī-yé Asr there are some so-called fast-food restaurants where you'll wait anything up to 30 minutes to be served. They have odd names like *Kentuky Fried Chicken* and *Macdonalds*, but in most of these places the food is actually much more wholesome than the American equivalents they strive to imitate.

Many foreign food restaurants or restaurants catering to foreigners advertise in *Tehran Times*: look out for any new ones.

Entertainment

Although the rigid social and religious constraints imposed by the Khomeinī brand of Islam have undoubtedly loosened recently, there is very little to do in the evenings in Tehrān. There certainly aren't any nightclubs, bars or discos (except perhaps very deep underground).

Cinemas & Theatre Unless you know Persian or have well-informed friends loc-

ally, it is rather difficult to get a listing for plays and films currently running in Tehrān, and most of them probably wouldn't in any case be of much immediate appeal to most foreigners. Although there are foreign plays and films to be seen in Tehrān, nearly all of them will have been translated into Persian. Foreign language students at the universities do occasionally perform plays in the original script, such as Shakespeare, and in period dress; if you're interested just ask one of the English students who are bound to approach you if you spend any time in Tehrān.

Music Music has only recently been resuscitated by the Iranian authorities, and organised public performances are still thin on the ground. Again, your best bet is to rely on the guidance of an Iranian friend. Until Iran is ready for something different, most concerts will be extremely traditional, such as a solo male performer playing the dulcimer, with or without singing. It is very rare to hear music on the street, and busking is out of the question.

Buying Caviar

In Tehrān caviar is difficult to find even on the black market. Nowadays nearly all the Iranian caviar is exported, and practically all

Lid of an Iranian Caviar Tin

the domestic trade is under the counter. Shopkeepers who do have a private supply line are very wary of official attention, and may well say that they don't have any caviar even when they do, especially to a foreigner. However, if you are prepared to pay the going price which has escalated rapidly of late, you should be able to find a supplier for your expensive taste somewhere in the area of the fishmongers' stalls in Kheyābūn-é Manūchehrī and Kheyābūn-é Jomhūrī-yé Eslāmī. You'll probably achieve success more quickly if you can take an Iranian with you. The price for good quality caviar is 100,000 rials a kg, and it is not often sold in quantities less than 250 grams, although I did once find some tiny 50 gram tins at 5000 rials apiece. There is a small risk of being given poor quality or imitation caviar, so ask for a tasting first.

Getting There & Away

The problem with travel in Iran is not how to get to Tehrān but how to avoid it. Tehrān is the hub of the national air, bus and train services. Every city of any size in Iran has a direct connection by bus and usually by air too. Generally it's a lot easier to get a ticket into Tehrān than out, and it's a good idea to book a ticket as soon as you arrive. See the relevant city sections of this book for details of bus fares and journey times to and from Tehrān.

Air Iran Air flies from Tehrān to:

Ahvāz (daily, 5.15 am, 5.45 and 9.30 pm, 1¼ hours, 7280 rials)

Bākhtarān (Tuesday and Saturday, 5.45 am; daily at noon; all one hour, 5280 rials)

Bandar-é Abbās (Saturday, 5 am, 2¾ hours; Sunday, Tuesday and Thursday, 7 am, 2¾ hours; Monday, Wednesday and Saturday, 7.30 am, 1¾ hours; Sunday, Wednesday and Friday, 12.45 pm, 2¾ hours; Tuesday, 4 pm, 2¾ hours; daily, 8.10 pm, 1¾ hours; daily, 8.45 pm, 2¾ hours; all 8850 rials)

Bandar-é Lengé (daily, 6 am, 2¾ hours, 8850 rials)

Būshehr (daily, 1.50 pm, 1½ hours; Wednesday, 5.40 pm, 3¼ hours; all 8330 rials)

Chābahār (Monday, Wednesday and Saturday, 7.30 am, 3¼ hours; Sunday, Tuesday, Thursday and Friday, 7.30 am, 3¼ hours; all 10,530 rials)

Esfahān (daily, 5 and 9.10 am and 6.45 pm; daily except Monday and Tuesday, 12.45 pm; daily except Tuesday, 2.30 pm; Tuesday, 4.30 pm; Wednesday, 5.40 pm; Wednesday and Friday, 6.30 am; Sunday, 6 pm; all 50 minutes, 5180 rials)

Jazīré-yé Kīsh (Sunday, Tuesday and Friday, 5.30 am; Tuesday, noon; all 1¾ hours, 8850 rials; tickets for these scheduled flights can only be bought at the Iran Air office in Meidūn-é Ferdōsī; chartered flights are sold through KIDO, but tickets are very difficult to get (see also Jazīré-yé Kīsh entry in the South Iran & the Islands of the Persian Gulf chapter)

Kermān (Wednesday and Friday, 8.30 am, 2½ hours; daily, 9.20 am, 1½ hours; Tuesday, 4 pm, 1½ hours; all 7280 rials)

Mashhad (daily except Tuesday, 8 am and 2.30 pm; Monday, Tuesday and Wednesday, 4.30 pm; daily, 3.35, 5 and 6.30 pm; all 1¼ hours, 8010 rials)

Orūmīyé (daily, 10 am and 2 pm, 1¼ hours, 6230 rials)

Rasht (Sunday, Tuesday, Thursday and Friday, 7.45 am; Wednesday and Saturday, 9 am; all 45 minutes, 4970 rials)

Sārī (Tuesday and Friday, noon, 55 minutes, 5120 rials)

Shīrāz (daily, 5 and 6 am, and 8.45 pm, 1¼ hours; Monday, Wednesday, Friday and Saturday, 7 am, 1¼ hours; daily except Tuesday, 2.30 pm, 1¾ hours; Tuesday, 4.30 pm, 1¼ hours; Tuesday and Friday, 4.30 pm; Wednesday, 5.40 pm, 2¼ hours; Monday, Wednesday and Friday, 9 pm, 1¼ hours; all 7070 rials)

Tabrīz (daily, 7.50 and 11.10 am, 3.15 and 5.45 pm, 1¼ hours, 5810 rials)

Yazd (Saturday, 5 am; Sunday, Monday, Wednesday, Thursday and Friday, 5.30 am; daily, 6.30 am; Tuesday, 9 am; all 1¼ hours, 6540 rials)

Zāhedān (daily, 5.45 am 1¾ hours; Sunday, Tuesday, Thursday and Friday, 7.30 am, 1¾ hours; Wednesday and Friday, 8.30 am, 2¾ hours; Tuesday, 9 am, three hours; Thursday and Saturday, 12.45 pm, 2¾ hours; all 8010 rials).

For information on domestic flights, telephone ☎ 91027.

International Services See the Getting There & Away chapter. For international flight information, telephone ☎ 91028.

Airline Offices Most of these are in or

very near Kheyābūn-é Nejātollāhī. Foreign airline offices are generally open from 9 am to 4 pm, Saturday to Thursday, except Aeroflot which is open from 8.30 am to 12.30 pm only. Iran Air opens from 9 am to 4.30 pm, but only the head office is open on Friday. Iran Asseman is open from 9 am to 1 pm. Not all the following airlines actually operate flights into or out of Iran.

Aeroflot
    Kheyābūn-é Shahīd Ostād Nejātollāhī (☎ 836164)
Air France
    Kheyābūn-é Enghelāb, 200 metres west of Meidūn-é Ferdōsī (☎ 674116)
Alitalia
    Meidūn-é Ārzhāntīn (☎ 621889)
Austrian Airlines
    Kheyābūn-é Ostād Motahharī, Kheyābūn-é Shahīd Javād-é Sarāfrāz, cnr of Kūché-yé Panjom (☎ 622488)
British Airways
    cnr Kheyābūn-é Enghelāb and Kūché-yé Pārs, 100 metres west of Meidūn- é Ferdōsī (☎ 670100)
Emirates
    Kheyābūn-é Shahīd Ostād Nejātollāhī, Kheyābūn-é Fallāh Pūr (☎ 835057)
Gulf Air
    Kheyābūn-é Shahīd Ostād Nejātollāhī (☎ 827865)
Iran Air
    Kheyābūn-é Shahīd Ostād Nejātollāhī (head office) (☎ 829087)
    Meidūn-é Vanak, next to Homa Hotel; only place for tickets to Tokyo (☎ 683024)
    Kheyābūn-é Tāleghānī, intersection with Kheyābūn-é Forsat
    Meidūn-é Ferdōsī; only place for scheduled tickets to Kīsh (☎ 826532)
Iran Asseman
    Kheyābūn-é Enghelāb, 13 Kheyābūn-é Khārk (☎ 674073)
JAL
    Kheyābūn-é Shahīd Ostād Nejātollāhī (☎ 823089)
JAT (Yugoslav Airlines)
    (☎ 689915)
KLM
    Kheyābūn-é Ostād Motahharī, Kheyābūn-é Shahīd Javād-é Sarāfrāz (☎ 627562)
Kuwait Airways
    cnr Kheyābūn-é Shahīd Ostād Nejātollāhī and Kheyābūn-é Somayyé (☎ 835860)

Lufthansa
    Kheyābūn-é Sarvān Khāled Eslāmbōlī (☎ 623382)
PIA
    Kheyābūn-é Shahīd Ostād Nejātollāhī (☎ 824097)
Sabena
    Kheyābūn-é Shahīd Ostād Nejātollāhī (☎ 824027)
SAS
    cnr Kheyābūn-é Shahīd Ostād Nejātollāhī and Kheyābūn-é Āyatollāh Tāleghānī (☎ 892228)
Swissair
    cnr Kheyābūn-é Shahīd Ostād Nejātollāhī and Kheyābūn-é Āyatollāh Tāleghānī (☎ 835081)
Syrian Arab Airlines
    Kheyābūn-é Shahīd Ostād Nejātollāhī, Kheyābūn-é Fallāh Pūr (☎ 835057)
Turkish Airlines
    Kheyābūn-é Ghā'em Maghām Farāhānī (☎ 627464)

Bus There are three bus terminals in Tehrān. The busiest one, the west terminal (☎ 941044) (termīnāl-é gharb) is the one used for buses to and from Turkey and Syria, Tabrīz, Sanandaj, Hamadān, Bākhtarān, Orūmīyé and all other places west of the capital, as well as Rāmsar and Chālūs. The south terminal (☎ 550046) (termīnāl-é jonūb) covers buses to and from the south and south-east, eg Kermān, Yazd, Zāhedān, Shīrāz, Esfahān and Ghom. The east terminal (☎ 784010) (termīnāl-é shargh) caters for buses to and from all places in Khorāsān and the Caspian provinces except Chālūs and Rāmsar. Some bus companies have offices in town, especially on or around Kheyābūn-é Ferdōsī, but it is better to go to the terminal and ask around at least a few hours ahead. The terminals are bedlam even for Iranians, and it can take a long time to get a ticket. There are buses at least daily to virtually all major destinations inside the country, and there are several a week to Istanbul and occasional services to Damascus. There are no direct services anywhere further west than Istanbul or east of Zāhedān.

Train A list of destinations from Tehrān is given in the Getting Around chapter. The ticket office is in a separate building from the train station itself, just to the left of it as you face the station. Since all baggage has to be checked on entering the station, the queue to get in is impressively long; it is essential to arrive at least an hour early. There are no porters nor any facilities to speak of at the station. The platforms are clearly signposted in English according to destination.

For the latest information on trains, telephone ☎ 556115.

Shared Taxi & Savārī There are savārīs to Rasht (five hours, 2500 to 4000 rials) and a few other Caspian destinations from Meidūn-é Āzādī, but it is better to take a bus if possible.

Getting Around
To/From the Airport The only practical way to get from the airport into town or back again is by taxi. Outside the airport terminal you'll have no problem finding a taxi going in your direction, but it can be a long wait if you want to share a taxi and the expense. Sample fares are 1500 rials to Meidūn-é Emām Khomeinī for one passenger sharing a taxi with two others, 2000 rials to Meidūn-é Valī-yé Asr, and 3000 rials to Meidūn-é Vanak. Foreigners who take a taxi by themselves are almost always overcharged. There is an airport taxi office inside the arrival lounge where you can book a taxi at a more or less fixed rate, but this is usually closed. From Tehrān to the airport you will have to book an agency taxi. There is no airport bus.

Bus & Minibus Extensive bus services cover nearly all parts of Tehrān, but for a foreigner they are difficult to use, crowded and painfully slow, and information is non-existent. There's rarely any need to subject yourself to them because shared taxis are so plentiful and cheap. Tickets cost 10 rials for regular buses, 20 for the so-called expresses. Buses run roughly from 6 am until 10 or 11 pm, earlier on Friday and public holidays. Expect to wait up to half an hour for a bus, even longer on Friday or late at night. The only occasion where it might be worth taking a bus is if you get on at the point of departure, have a long distance to cover and know

exactly where both you and the bus are going, or if an Iranian is accompanying you.

The desperately crowded minibuses charge 20 rials and are not much fun except on the very shortest routes.

Bus Routes The following is a partial list of bus services in Tehrān, but they are liable to change without notice. These buses run in both directions but they do not always set out and return by the same route, and bus stops are not always marked with the number of the bus service stopping there, if at all. The city bus enquiries number is ☎ 799050.

111 – Pol-é Sayyed Khandān to Meidūn-é 15 Khordād
112 – Pol-é Sayyed Khandān to Chahārrāh-é Valī-yé Asr
113 – Pol-é Sayyed Khandān to Emām Khomeinī Hospital (Bīmārestān-é Emam Khomeinī)
115 – Meidūn-é Ghods to Pol-é Sayyed Khandān
116 – Meidūn-é Tajrīsh to Meidūn-é Emām Khomeinī
118 – Kheyābūn-é Ekhteyārīyé to Meidūn-é Emām Khomeinī
122 – Meidūn-é Resālat to Meidūn-é Emām Khomeinī
125 – Meidūn-é Tajrīsh to Kheyābūn-é Ferdōsi
126 – Meidūn-é Tajrīsh to Meidūn-é Ārzhāntīn
127 – Meidūn-é Tajrīsh to Pārk-é Shahr
128 – Meidūn-é Ārzhāntīn to Kheyābūn-é Ferdōsi
130 – Daraké to Kheyābūn-é Valī-yé Asr (for the Alborz Mountains)
131 – Meidūn-é Darband to Meidūn-é Ghods (for the Alborz Mountains)
132 – Jamārān to Meidūn-é Ghods
216 – Meidūn-é Enghelāb to Meidūn-é Emām Hosein
218 – Meidūn-é Emām Hosein to Meidūn-é Emām Khomeinī
412 – Train Station to Emām Khomeinī Hospital
413 – Train Station to Kheyābūn-é Karīm Khān
418 – Kheyābūn-é Khānī Ābād-é Nō to Pārk-é Shahr
423 – Meidūn-é 13 Ābān to Park-e Shahr
427 – Nāzī Ābād to Kheyābūn-é Enghelāb
434 – Ārāmgāh-é Emām Khomeinī to Meidūn-é Emām Khomeinī
511 – Airport to Kheyābūn-é Enghelāb (infrequent and impractical)
633 – Meidūn-é Tajrīsh to Kheyābūn-é Jamāl Zādé
635 – Meidūn-é Jomhūrī-yé Eslāmī to Meidūn-é Bahārestān

Underground Twenty years ago Tehrān's underground system was going to be finished in 10 years' time; 10 years ago it was going to be finished in 10 years' time: guess how long it is predicted to take now. A short section connecting south Tehrān and the Tomb of Emām Khomeinī should, however, be in operation shortly. It is planned to have one north-south line and one east-west line connecting in the centre.

Taxi The orange and white service taxis, although they take some getting used to, are really the best way of getting around the maze of Tehrān. See the Getting Around chapter for more details.

Taxi fares in Tehrān are considerably higher than in the rest of mainland Iran; they appear to be rising faster than the rate of inflation, and the current minimum fare of 50 rials will not get you very far. If you spend some time in Tehrān, avoid being a solo passenger and watch what other passengers are paying: you'll soon have a good idea of what the current rates are. In late 1991 an average journey of about five minutes was around 100 rials.

From the train station or any of the bus terminals it's best to arrange to share a taxi with Iranians going in the same direction, and to keep a low profile while they negotiate a fare with the driver; the mere sight of a foreigner is enough to double or treble it. As a rough guide, the fare should be not more than 1000 rials from any one of them to Meidūn-é Ferdōsī.

If you want to go to the airport or cover a long distance in a hurry, it's best to book a telephone taxi at one of the many agencies all over the town, or to get a hotel receptionist to order one for you. Officially the hourly rate is currently 1800 rials between 6 am and 10 pm, 2000 at other times. You can order a taxi on ☎ 840015. Some of the top hotels have their own taxi service, typically charging around 3000 rials an hour.

Most shared taxis are Paykans, but there are also some Peugeots. The fares are the same, but the Peugeots tend to be used for longer journeys and don't usually stop for passengers just going a few blocks. In some of the northern suburbs there are blue and white shared taxis which run along fixed local routes for around 50 rials a passenger.

Car & Motorbike The traffic in Tehrān is homicidal and no rules are observed. Traffic lights, indicators, footpaths and the like are totally ignored. In some parts of Tehrān it's not uncommon to find whole families clinging to one motorcycle riding on the pavement and sweeping pedestrians aside. Of all the cars in Iran, almost half are registered in Tehrān, and at times it seems like all of these are on the road at the same time. Most foreign drivers give up a losing battle very soon after arriving and quickly assimilate the lawless aggression of the natives. Drive with 100% attention at all times or, better still, don't drive at all.

Most of central Tehrān is a traffic exclusion zone from Saturday to Wednesday, and traffic police often check that drivers entering this zone have the necessary permit sticker, but foreigners nearly always get away with pleading ignorance, especially if the vehicle is foreign-registered.

There are no car hire agencies in Tehrān.

Central Iran

ایران مرکزی

This chapter covers the provinces of Markazī, Esfahān, Chahārmahāl va Bakhteyārī, Semnān and Yazd.

The dry and dusty plain of central Iran is relatively sparsely populated, with few large towns and little in between. The two great deserts of Iran occupy the east of the region, and even in the more hospitable parts to the west most of the settlements began as oases and largely remain so today. If you travel by land across this largely barren heartland you can begin to appreciate the appeal to travellers, since ancient times, of these settled oases with their caravanserais. Their inhabitants have sought throughout history to give them an air of security and stability, echoed in the many sturdy monuments that survive as a testament to their builders. For most visitors the main draw is Esfahān, but the towns of Yazd and Kermān also have their attractions. There are also quite a few interesting monuments scattered around the region and easily accessible from the main transit routes, although few are prehistoric sites. Camels are still very much in use in the western part of central Iran. The culture and language are almost entirely Persian, although there are several local dialects.

Markazī Province

استان مرکزی

Population: 1,092,000
Area: 29,080 sq km
Markazī (Central) Province isn't actually the central province of Iran – that position goes irrefutably to Esfahān Province – but evidently no-one could think of anything better to call it. The capital is Arāk, but for most purposes the great pilgrimage centre of Ghom is the main town.

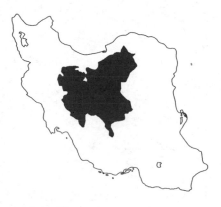

ARĀK
اراك

Population: 265,349
Arāk is a city not known for its great cultural or historical legacy. It has an altitude of 1759 metres above sea level, and quite cool average temperatures. The tourist office (☎ (02531) 34059) is in Bolvār-é Āyatollāh Ghoddūsī, just north of the train station. If you do get stuck here, you could try the *Hotel-é Kheibar*, in Kheyābūn-é 15 Khordād at the entrance to Arāk on the Tehrān road, or the *Hotel-é Lādan*, next to the tourist office.

Getting There & Away
Among other destinations, there are buses from Arāk to Mashhad (1212 km, 20 hours; several a week), Shīrāz (772 km, 12 hours; several a week) and Tehrān (288 km, five hours; at least one bus a day). There are also trains to Ghom, Tehrān and Ahvāz.

GHOM
قم

Ghom is just to the south of Tehrān, en route to Esfahān by train or bus. It's definitely Mullah City and you'll find a higher concentration of turbans here than anywhere else in Iran. Not many tourists make it here, but it's

Central Iran

0   50   100 km

certainly not off-limits to non-Muslims and I found that my infidel presence in this holy city was greeted with nothing more hostile than friendly curiosity. Ghom has a reputation among less devout Iranians for being the meanest and most Hezbollāhī of places, but it seems to have calmed down a lot of late. Perhaps the townspeople have had enough of a good thing.

Ghom has always been a leading centre of Shi'ism, and there's no chance of getting away from religion here. Khomeinī and countless other leading religious figures studied theology here, and the town took a particularly strong role in the anti-reformist movement against the last shāh, and throughout the revolution. It's a major pilgrimage site, aspirant mullahs come here for training, and it's a favourite weekend spiritual retreat with Tehrān-based religious big-wigs.

The town owes its initial development and subsequent eminence to its being the burial place of Fātemé, sister of Emām Rezā (whose shrine at Mashhad is the foremost Shi'ite pilgrimage site in Iran), who died and was interred here in the 9th century. The extensive complex of shrine buildings was constructed under Shāh Abbās and the other

Safavid kings, anxious to establish their Shi'ite credentials and to provide a counterweight to the sect's shrines at Najaf and Kerbala, then under alien Ottoman occupation. The magnificent golden cupola of the shrine was an embellishment built by Fath Alī Shāh.

Not surprisingly, most of the sights in the city are of a religious nature. The prime draw is the picturesque mosque in the sanctuary, the **Āstāné** – but non-Muslims are not welcome inside, and there are signs in English to that effect on all entrances. Photography is strictly forbidden. You can however see the entrance portal at a slight distance. Similarly, unless you're one of the faithful, you'll probably have to make do with peering from outside at the central **Masjed-é Jāme'** nearby, but it is worth a peek for its fine Safavid architecture. Visitors to Ghom should be reverent.

Information
There is supposedly a tourist office (☎ (0251) 32307) somewhere in town, but I couldn't find it. No maps of Ghom are available here or anywhere else in Iran.

Places to Stay
The *Hotel-é Gol* ('Roze Hotel'), in Meidūn-é Emām Khomeinī on the large square on the road from Tehrān, charges 3200/4400 rials a single/double with private bathroom. The staff here welcome foreigners and some speak English. There are dozens of mosāferkhūnés around the shrine, marked only in Persian, but they are there principally to cater for pilgrims and will almost certainly not take non-Muslim guests.

Places to Eat
There are dozens of restaurants along the main street, Kheyābūn-é Emām Khomeinī, and around the shrine.

Things to Buy
One thing you must try is the almost sinfully delicious pistachio-brittle known as sōhūn, which is produced locally and available in almost any main street of the town. Not sickly sweet like so much Iranian confectionery, sōhūn becomes an obsession once you've tasted it. A one-kg tin of sōhūn is about 1700 rials. Gaz is also widely stocked here.

Stalls around the Holy Shrine sell prayer-rugs, small tablets of compressed earth used in Muslim prayers, inscriptions from the Qoran, pictures of Mecca, and many other religious items. Flails wielded by the devout during flagellants' processions in Moharram are also on offer, if not always on display.

Getting There & Away
Buses to Ghom (250 rials, three hours) leave Tehrān more or less hourly from the south terminal, and return until about nightfall. From Ghom, near the bridge over the river from the main square, you can take a savārī to the same bus station in Tehrān for 1500 rials; I was offered a choice of cars – either a standard Iranian Paykan at 1500 rials or an Audi for 1700 rials. By car it is 1½ hours. This road is very busy with trucks and other traffic.

There are also buses from the Termīnāl-é Bozorg (easily accessible only by taxi) to various destinations as far away as Mashhad.

No aeroplanes are allowed to fly over the holy city of Ghom, a prohibition not even extended to Mashhad.

Ghom is an important railway junction, second only to Tehrān. At the time of writing there are services from the train station at the west of Ghom to the following destinations:

Ahvāz (via Arāk and Andīmeshk) – seven regular trains (14 hours 10 minutes) and 21 express trains (13 hours) a week, and seven extra expresses only as far as Andīmeshk

Esfahān (via Kāshān) – three express trains a week (six hours 50 minutes)

Kermān (via Kāshān and Yazd) – three express trains a week (14 hours 40 minutes)

Tehrān – seven regular trains (three hours 20 minutes) and 21 express trains (two hours 55 minutes) a week

SĀVÉ ساوه
Another important transit centre, Sāvé, on

one of the two main roads between Tehrān and Hamadān, was an important regional centre before its destruction by the Mongols in the 13th century. Nowadays the town is of interest principally for its two extremely fine Seljuq minarets, both outside mosques that have been extensively rebuilt. The minaret belonging to the **Masjed-é Jāme'** dates from 1110, has a well-preserved series of garters with intricate, raised geometric brickwork patterns and inscriptions, and is widely acknowledged as the finest such minaret in Iran. The minaret of the **Masjed-é Meidūn**, on the main square a few hundred metres to the north of the first, is less well preserved and much simpler in design, but it dates from 1061 and is also of interest.

The best pomegranates in Iran are said to come from Sāvé.

Esfahān Province

استان اصفهان

Population: 3,317,000
Area: 104,650 sq km
This vast province is the geographical centre of Iran, stretching from the Dasht-é Kavīr in the north-east to within 150 km of the Persian Gulf in the south-west, and is crisscrossed with many of the most important ancient and modern trade routes in Iran. Few travellers avoid it. Of all parts of Iran this is the most Persian in the sense that most foreigners understand the term. The capital is Esfahān and most of the population lives in urban areas. The province is renowned for its quinces and apples.

ESFAHĀN   اصفهان
Population: 989,000

The reputation of Esfahānīs amongst other Persians is not altogether enviable; avarice and niggardliness being accounted their chief characteristics. Thus it is commonly said of anyone who is very careful of his expenditure that he is 'as mean as the merchants of Esfahān, who put their cheese in a bottle, and rub their bread on the outside to give it a flavour'. Another illustration of this alleged stinginess is afforded by the story of an Esfahānī merchant, who one day caught his apprentice eating lunch of dry bread and gazing wistfully at the bottle containing the precious cheese; whereupon the merchant proceeded to scold the unfortunate youth roundly for his greediness, asking him if he 'couldn't eat plain bread for one day?'
Edward Browne,
A Year Amongst the Persians, 1893

Esfahān has the greatest concentration of Islamic monuments in Iran. The cool blue tiles of Esfahān contrast perfectly with the hot, dry Iranian countryside around it: Esfahān is a sight you won't forget. Not only is the architecture superb and the climate pleasant, but there's a fairly relaxed atmosphere here compared with many other Iranian towns. It's a city for walking, getting lost in the bazaar, dozing in beautiful gardens, and meeting people. The more time you have the better, because here it's easy to appreciate many of the best aspects of Persian culture.

For some pleasant views of Esfahān try to see the Pasolini film *Arabian Nights,* which was partly filmed on location in Esfahān and some other equally exotic parts. One amusing scene takes place in the courtyard of the Madrasé-yé Chahār Bāgh. The nearby Abbasi Hotel was elegantly converted from an old caravanserai and is worth a look around, even if a stay is out of the question.

Esfahān had long been an important trading centre, strategically situated in the south of modern Iran, but it came to its peak during the reign of Shāh Abbās I (1587-1629).

Iran had been in a period of decline until the early 1500s when the first rulers of the Safavid dynasty chucked the Mongols out of the country. Shāh Abbās the Great came to power in 1587 and extended his influence over rivals within the country, then pushed out the Ottoman Turks, who had occupied a large part of Persia. With his country once more united and free of foreign influence Shāh Abbās set out to make Esfahān a great and beautiful city. Its period of glory lasted for little over 100 years, for an invasion from Afghanistan hastened the decline and the capital was subsequently transferred to Shīrāz and then to Tehrān.

The power and breadth of Shāh Abbās' vision is still very much in evidence, although what remains is just a small taste of the city at its height. During the period of his rule Esfahān produced some of the most beautiful and inspiring architecture seen anywhere in the Islamic world.

The famous half-rhyme *Esfahān nesf-é jahān* (Esfahān is half the world) was coined in the 16th century to express the city's grandeur. You may well agree it has a ring of truth even today. Another popular saying, to the effect that Esfahān would be perfect were there no Esfahānīs in it, also has a great deal of currency to this day although it dates back to the time of Shāh Abbās and the reputation his strutting courtiers and hangers-on earned for their arrogance and loose morals. These days the town is better known as a citadel of inflexible Hezbollāhī thinking, filled with rude and unhelpful bureaucrats, scheming and tight-fisted private citizens and dishonest merchants. 'An Esfahānī buys a cucumber, paints it yellow and sells it as a banana' is one of many gibes.

The hype in the tourist office handout, claiming that the Esfahānīs are known throughout Iran for their friendly hospitality, is either self-delusion or disinformation. In view of the town's unrivalled visual legacy, it's surprising for the foreign visitor how little Iranians like this town and its people. However you shouldn't let this sullied reputation put you off, and many recent foreigner visitors have actually commented on the welcome they received from the local people. Just make sure you never commit yourself to anything without firmly fixing the price beforehand, expect the price to be raised when you finally come to pay it, and always check your change afterwards. Persian-speakers and even native Iranians aren't immune. Don't be deceived by the lack of Westerners here – Esfahānīs know all about taking their slice of the tourist trade.

Esfahān has pleasant weather for most of the year, but it can get rather cold in winter. Try not to visit around Nō Rūz as finding accommodation here then can be a hellish ordeal.

Orientation

The main street, Kheyābūn-é Chahār Bāgh (Four Gardens), runs north-south right through the main part of the city. If you use this to orient yourself, you can't go far wrong, although Chahār Bāgh does change its name slightly from north to south. Most of the main sights and the hotels are within easy walking distance, and it's a pleasure to wander along the tree-lined avenues. There are a few outlying sights that are most easily visited by hired taxi. Much of the city has been modernised over recent years and will continue to be so – there are plans to knock down the intrusive row of shops along the north side of Chahār Bāgh-é Abbāsī in order to open up the park behind to the street, and much has been done to preserve the city's historic buildings since the end of the Iran-Iraq War.

The Zāyandé Rūd river flows from west to east, and divides off Jolfā and some other suburbs from the main part of Esfahān, but most of the main attractions are to the north of the river. The new international and domestic airport is some 20 km to the east-north-east of Esfahān, and connected to it by buses and taxis, while the old airport marked on the local maps at the southern edge of town is now out of use. The train station is a long trek out of town and little used by tourists.

Information

The ostāndārī (☎ 22142) is on the west side of Kheyābūn-é Shahīd Āyatollāh Dastgheib, 400 metres to the east of Meidūn-é Emām Hosein (still widely known by its old name of Darvāzé-yé Dōlat) on Chahār Bāgh. The shahrdārī (☎ 22027) is on the east side of Meidūn-é Emām Hosein. There are no consulates in Esfahān.

There's an exceptionally unhelpful visa office in Kheyābūn-é Khōrshīd which enters Meidūn-é Emām at its south-east corner (near the Masjed-é Emām). If you're coming from the square, it's on the right at the beginning of the street; there's an unmarked gate in the wall, opening into a courtyard. Although some travellers have managed to get

Esfahān

0   1   2 km

PLACES TO STAY

2 Hotel-é Sepīd
4 Hotel-é Persepōlis
20 Kowsar Hotel
21 Hotel-é Su'īt
24 Hōtel-é Jolfā

OTHER

1 New Bus Station
3 Old Bus Station
5 Petrol Station
   (Pump-é Benzīn)
6 New Airport

7 Āteshgāh
8 Manār Jombān
9 Esfahān Hóspital
   (Bīmarestān-é
   Esfahān)
10 Pol-é Mārnān
11 Pol-é Felezzī
12 Pol-é Abūzar
13 Si o Sé Pol (Pol-é Pol
   Allāhvardī Khan)
14 Pol-é Ferdōsī
15 Bridge Under Construction
16 Pol-é Chūbī
17 Pol-é Khājū

18 Pol-é Bozorgmehr
19 Pol-é Shahrestān
22 Kelīsā-yé Beit-ol-Lahm
23 Kelīsā-yé Vānk
25 Mojtame'-é Pazīrā'ī-yé
   Negīn
26 Dr Sharī'atī Hospital
   (Bīmārestān-é
   Doktor Sharī'atī)
27 Golestān-é Shohadā
28 Stadium
29 Old Airport
30 Esfahān University
31 Petrol Station

a few extra days on a transit visa here, don't even bother asking if you've already had a first extension. I haven't been to every aliens' bureau in Iran, but I am sure there cannot be another one with staff so insufferably rude as this miserable lot.

Tourist Office The overstaffed tourist office (☎ 21555) is marked in English and diagonally opposite the Abbasi Hotel, next to the intersection of Chahār Bāgh with Kheyābūn-é Shahīd Āyatollāh Madanī. It is competent at answering the usual tourist enquiries. They have a visitors' book but the entries in it by foreign tourists that I saw were so glowing with unqualified praise that I couldn't help wondering quite how genuine they were.

Money There are several banks in Esfahān dealing with foreign currency transactions. Probably the most efficient is the Bank Melli Iran office in Kheyābūn-é Sepāh, which meets Meidūn-é Emām at its north-west corner. If you're coming from the square, it's on your left 100 metres from the beginning of the street. If you're staying at a hotel charging (illegally) in foreign currency, or buying an international aeroplane ticket, you'll have to change money here. The small bank next to the Hotel-é Pīrūzī is also helpful.

Post & Telecommunications The head post office is on the west side of Kheyābūn-é Neshāt, to the south-east of Meidūn-é Emām. The central telegraph office is on the west side of Kheyābūn-é Dastgheib, the street to the west of Meidūn-é Emām. There's also a small and efficient post office, for letters but not parcels, in Meidūn-é Emām near the Kākh-é Ālī Ghāpū. The dialling code for Esfahān is 031. As elsewhere in the provinces, international or even trunk calls are difficult to make, and it's worth paying a little extra to call from one of the larger hotels.

Travel Agencies Iran Tour & Travel Company (☎ 23010) is in the same arcade as Iran Air, opposite the Abbasi Hotel in Kheyābūn-é Shahīd Āyatollāh Madanī. It can arrange tours of Shīrāz, Mashhad or Esfahān itself for any number of persons, not including return transport, but it isn't currently fully geared up to deal with foreigners. In Mashhad and Shīrāz the accommodation is at the Homa Hotel, in Esfahān at the Abbasi Hotel (a foreigner would probably not be able to pay in rials). Before investing in one of these tours, read the entry under Organised Tours in the Mashhad section.

Books & Bookshops There are three bookshops in the same smart arcade as the Iran Air office near Meidūn-é Emām. They have some books in English, but few of them are likely to be of much appeal to the tourist. Unfortunately there are no recent guidebooks on Esfahān in English, and not as far as I know even in Persian. Those few travellers who have more than a week to spare in Esfahān and have visited all the sites mentioned here can get further information from the tourist office: there are plenty of other interesting buildings.

Maps The *Guide Map of Isfahan* I was given by the tourist office here was more than five years out of date and stated that it was printed 'on the occasion of the anniversary of the victory of the Islamic Revolution', but the most important details on it haven't changed much since then. On its reverse it also has some tourist hype about the city, and some useful information about the main sights. The Gītā Shenāsī *New Map of Esfahān City* (300 rials) in Persian and English is more detailed, but very many of the street names and listings are way out of date: don't be too disappointed if you can't find some of the places listed in its key, such as the Esfahān Night Club and the Moulin Rouge Cinema.

Medical Services There are several hospitals in Esfahān. For emergencies dial ☎ 118 or 43027. The former Anglican Hospital is next to the Church of St Luke in Kheyābūn-é Abbās Ābād.

Emergency The police headquarters
(☎ 24213) (shahrbānī) are in Kheyābūn-é
Khōrshīd off Meidūn-é Emām Hosein.

Meidūn-é Emām

Previously the Meidūn-é Shāh and sometimes also known as the Meidūn-é Naghsh-é
Jahān, this huge open square is one of the
largest in the world and is a majestic example
of town planning. Many of the most interesting sights in Esfahān are clustered around
the square, and it's a place you just keep
coming back to. It was laid out in 1612 and
measures 500 by 160 metres.

For all its daytime activity the Meidūn-é
Emām is almost deserted at night, and is very
beautiful when it's lit up in the evening for
the benefit of almost no-one but yourself.
The original goal posts from Shāh Abbās'
polo ground are still in place at the far ends
of the square, although nowadays table-
tennis is the only game played here.

Shops line the square: many specialise in
brasswork and there is some interesting stuff
among the gimcrack souvenirs and postcards. Times are hard and tourists are scarce,
but you'll still need all your bargaining
skills. The open-air prayer services held here
every Friday always attract a large number
of Muslim worshippers and are well worth
watching.

Masjed-é Emām

Previously the Masjed-é Shāh, this magnificent mosque lies at the southern end of the
Meidūn-é Emām and is one of the most
stunning buildings in the world. It's completely covered, inside and out, with the pale
blue tiles that became an Esfahān trademark.
The mosque is a particularly inspiring sight
at night when the tiles glow with a soft
ethereal sheen.

The main dome is double-layered and
although the entrance, with its twin minarets, faces squarely out onto the square, the
mosque itself is at an angle to face towards
Mecca. It was built in 26 years by an increasingly impatient Shāh Abbās I and was
completed in 1638.

The tiles of the mosque take on a different

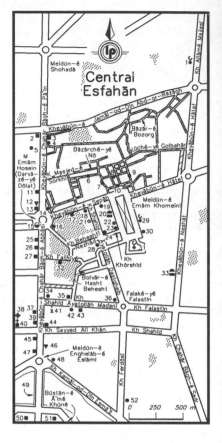

hue according to the light conditions, and
every hour brings a new face to this wonder
of the Islamic world. The magnificent entrance portal, some 30 metres tall, is a
supreme example of Safavid architectural
styles, combining sumptuous tilework and
calligraphy, complex stalactite mouldings
and a consummate use of colour and scale,
setting the scene for the interior and dwarf-
ing the visitor who passes through its
doorway, which is tiny in comparison.

Going through a short corridor you then
enter a hallway leading into the inner courtyard which is surrounded by four eivāns

■ PLACES TO STAY

2 Hotel-é Āzādī
3 Hotel-é Pershyā
11 Mehmūnsarā-yé Pīrūzī
13 Hotel-é Naghsh-é Jahān
25 Masāferkhūné-yé Parvāz
26 Masāferkhūné-yé Adālat
27 Hotel-é Īrān
35 Abbasi Hotel
37 Mehmūnkhūné-yé Pārs
39 Hotel-é ĀlīGhāpū
43 Hotel-é Āryā
45 Tūrīst Hotel
47 Mehmūnkhūné-yé Tūs
50 Kowsar Hotel
51 Hotel-é Sü'īt

▼ PLACES TO EAT

2 Hotel-é Āzādī
11 Mehmūnsarā-yé Pīrūzī
12 Sālon-é Ghezā-yé Nōbahar
35 Abbasi Hotel
39 Hotel-é ĀlīGhāpū
46 Restōrān-é Mahārājah
50 Kowsar Hotel

OTHER

1 Masjed-é Jāmé
4 Gaz-é Ālī Shop
5 Stadium
6 Dyers' Bazaar (Bāzār Rangraz-hā)
7 Carpetsellers' Bazaar (Bāzār-é Farsh Forūshhā)
8 Samovar-Smiths' Bazaar (Bāzār-é Samāvarsāz-hā)
9 Goldsmiths' Bazaar (Bāzār-é Zargarhā)
10 Shoemakers' Bazaar (Bāzār-é Kaffāshhā)
14 Petrol Station (Pomp-é Benzīn)
15 City Bus Station
16 Shahrdārī
17 Chehel Sotūn
18 Müzé-yé Tārīkh-é Tabī'ī
19 Bank Melli Iran (Central Branch)
20 Post Office
21 Ostāndārī
22 Kākh-é Ālī Fhāpū Ghāpū
23 Police Headquarters (Shahrbānī)
24 Visa Office
28 Main Telegraph Office
29 Masjed-é Sheikh Lotfollāh
30 Blacksmiths' Bazaar (Bāzār-é Āhangarhā)
31 Masjed-é Emām
32 Hasht Behesht
33 Main Post Office
34 Madrasé-yé Chahār Bāgh
36 Kanīsé-yé Esfahān
38 Eisā Ebn-é Maryam Hospital (Bīmārestān-é Eisā Ebn-é Maryam)
40 Anglican Cathedral of St Luke (Kelīsā-yé Hazrat-é Lūghā)
41 Tourist Office
42 Iran Tour & Travel Agency, Iran Air (Head Office) & International Bookshops
44 Iran Air
48 Train Ticket Office
49 Sīo Sé Pol (Pol-é Allāhverdī Khān)
52 Iran Asseman

(colonnaded halls). Three of them lead into vaulted sanctuaries, the largest to the south. The size of the complex is much less than the towering entrance portal might lead you to expect. In the east sanctuary, look out for a few black paving stones underneath the dome, which when stamped upon create seven clear echoes. Try it for yourself; everyone else does. To the east and west of the mosque there are two madrasés (theological colleges).

The whole mosque complex is lavishly decorated with tiles, and the design of the building combined with the lack of visitors gives the place a refreshing air of tranquillity and near-emptiness that could never be found in the mosque in Mashhad on which this complex was originally modelled. Three hours is hardly too long to spend here; an hour could be spent just staring at the portal. The best time to photograph is about 11 am when the sun is overhead.

It is currently undergoing extensive repairs, especially to the roof and upper levels, where structural damage and gaps in the tiling suffered from neglect following the earlier years of the revolution. Unfortunately visitors aren't normally allowed to go up to the roof level, but if you do manage to persuade someone to take you up there you can see the famous cupolas in close detail and the view is fantastic.

There is an entrance fee of 50 rials. The caretakers at the great mosque find it so incredible that Western visitors should comprehend even a few words of Persian that they have taken to using sign language.

Kākh-é Ālī Ghāpū

On the west side of Meidūn-é Emām, this seven-storey palace was built on a square plan as a functional seat of government. It has a huge pavilion from where royal spectators could watch the activities in the square below, where there was at one time a polo field.

Many of the valuable murals and mosaics which once decorated the many small rooms, corridors and stairways have been destroyed, partly in the Ghajar period and partly as a result of 'natural causes' (according to the caretaker) since the revolution – perhaps this natural process was hastened by the un-Islamic themes of the decorations. The beautiful fretwork stalactites on the top floor, chiselled out in the shapes of musical instruments, are quite unlike anything else you're likely to see in Iran. If it's open when you visit, the open terrace on the second floor commands a fine view of the Masjed-é Emām and the whole square.

The Kākh-é Ālī Ghāpū (entry 50 rials) is open from 8 to 11.30 am and 2 to 5 pm, Saturday to Thursday, and 2 to 5 pm only on Friday.

Masjed-é Sheikh Lotfollāh

This small mosque on the eastern side of the square is notable for not having any minarets. The reason is that it was built purely for family worship and so there was no need for the faithful to be called to prayer. Sheikh Lotfollāh was a sort of Islamic Billy Graham of his time.

Although it doesn't overwhelm you in the same way as the Masjed-é Emām, it is an architectural jewel, beautifully proportioned and decorated. The pale tiles of the dome change colour, from cream through to pink, depending on the light conditions.

The Masjed-é Sheikh Lotfollāh, no longer a functioning mosque, is open daily as a museum from 8 am to 5 pm (entry 50 rials). You will need a powerful flash to photograph inside the poorly lit dome-chamber with its tiled mehrāb.

Bazaar

Completing the fourth, northern end of the square, the bazaar is one of the highlights of Esfahān. It covers a simply enormous area and since Esfahān is the artistic and craft centre of Iran, this is one of the best places to make a shopping trip. There are something like five km of paths to stroll through so leave plenty of time. As you wander you will find shops that sell almost every imaginable item, not to mention mosques, teashops, bath-houses and even gardens. Like most Iranian bazaars, part of this one is loosely divided into several interconnecting corridors, each specialising in a particular trade or product, with samovar-makers, shoemakers, dyers, carpet-dealers and goldsmiths all having their own quarters.

Chehel Sotūn

Behind the Kākh-é Ālī Ghāpū there's a park with this interesting pavilion, built as a reception hall by Shāh Abbās I, who held some of his more notorious wild parties here. The name means The Forty Columns, although there are actually only 20. A reflecting pool is provided to see the other 20. A more mundane explanation is that 40 was once used synonymously with 'many' in Persian, and still is in some quarters.

There's a small museum inside the building, with a collection of ceramics, old coins, militaria, old clothes and several Qorans, including one said to be in the handwriting of the second emām. It's all quite out of keeping with the original purpose of this pleasure palace. There are six painted friezes here, but three of them are now obscured behind screens. The three friezes were covered after the revolution because they were deemed to be incompatible with

Islamic values, depicting as they do various uninhibited carousals. At least they weren't destroyed altogether. One of the interior domes is in a fairly good state of repair, but the other two have only a few traces of gold and other colours.

The Chehel Sotūn is open daily from 8 am to 5 pm (entry 50 rials). No photography is permitted inside the palace. If you visit on a cloudy day the 40 columns will only be visible as 20.

Mūzé-yé Tārīkh-é Tabī'ī

This natural history museum, recently established at the intersection of Kheyābūn é Sepāh and Kheyābūn-é Shahīd Āyatollāh Dastgheib, is open daily from 8.30 to noon and from 2.15 to 6 pm (entry 100 rials). It offers an interesting, if rather poorly housed and haphazardly displayed, collection of molluscs, stones and stuffed animals, some of them labelled with the Latin names. Look out for the model of a very contented-looking lion.

Hasht Behesht

The Safavid garden palace of Hasht Behesht (the Eight Paradises) is visible from the east side of Chahār Bāgh-é Abbāsī but approached from Kheyābūn-é Fathīyé. It has some charming and impressive mosaics and stalactite mouldings, and has been slowly undergoing renovation over the last 20 or so years. It isn't currently possible to climb up to see the first floor, but it will be reopened to visitors in the near future. The palace is open daily from 8 am to noon and from 2 to 5 pm (entry 20 rials).

Madrasé-yé Chahār Bāgh

The Madrasé, previously the Madrasé-yé Mādar-é Shāh (Theological School of the Shāh's Mother), is right on Chahār Bāgh. The courtyard is extraordinarily beautiful and restful but unfortunately the building is currently closed to non-Muslims.

Kanīsé-yé Esfahān

This is a small synagogue, easily missed, in a plain building behind some anonymous gates at the north-west corner of Falaké-yé Falastīn, 500 metres east of the Abbasi Hotel. A small building of modern construction and concrete and glass exterior, it is the focal point of the city's dwindling population of Jews, who go there at all times of the day to sit, chat and pray. There is believed to have been a Jewish colony in Esfahān from the early 5th century, when the Jewish wife of the Sassanian Yazdgerd I persuaded him to allow her people to settle freely both here and at Hamadān, but many left during or after the Islamic Revolution. It's OK for non-Jews to visit the synagogue, but take off your shoes first.

Masjed-é Jāme'

A brisk half-hour walk from the Meidūn-é Emām, the Masjed-é Jāme' is a museum of Islamic architecture. It displays styles from the 11th through to the 18th century, from the stylish simplicity of the Seljuq period, through the Mongol to the more baroque Safavid. It's difficult to unravel the historical complexities, but even so the building overwhelms the visitor with its age and beauty. There is no entry charge.

Kelīsā-yé Hazrat-é Lūghā

Headquarters of the Episcopal Church of Iran, the Church of St Luke is in Kheyābūn-é Abbās Ābād, the first main road to the north of Meidūn-é Enghelāb-é Eslāmī. If you're coming from Chahār Bāgh the church is at the corner of the first turning to the right, and recognisable by the cross on the gates. Knock hard. This used to be the seat of the Bishop of Esfahān but the present incumbent, Hasan Dehghānī Tāfté, went into exile more than a decade ago, when his son was killed here by a fanatical mob. Services are still held here, but the congregation has dwindled considerably since the revolution; one Anglican told me that many of them don't like to put all their eggs in one basket, and attend a service at the church one week and are seen praying at the mosque the next. On an earlier visit of mine, my hosts in Esfahān refused to take me to this church on the grounds that it was a nest of spies and that I must be a spy too if I wanted to visit it.

Bridges

Esfahān is famous for the old bridges which cross the Zāyandé Rūd, although there are a few modern bridges taking the place of older ones which are now closed to traffic.

Sī o Sé Pol The Sī o Sé Pol or Bridge of 33 Arches (also known as the Pol-é Allāhverdī Khān), which links the upper and lower halves of the Chahār Bāgh, was built in 1602 and is attractive, though not of any outstanding architectural merit.

Pol-é Khājū The Pol-é Khājū, some 1½ km downstream (east) of Sī o Sé Pol, is slightly smaller but even more attractive, with two levels of terraces overlooking the river. Built by Shāh Abbās in about 1650, it doubled as a dam and has always been as much a meeting place as a functioning bearer of traffic. The famous chāykhūné under the bridge is currently closed but may be re-opened soon: this used to be one of the most atmospheric places in Iran to sit and drink tea or smoke the hubble-bubble, surrounded by slumbering Esfahānī manhood.

Pol-é Shahrestān This most ancient of the bridges spanning the Zeyāndé Rūd is about three km east of the Pol-é Khājū and beyond the city limits, but well worth visiting and the walk is pleasant. Most of its present stone and brick structure is believed to date from the 12th century, although it stands on the foundations of a much earlier Sassanian bridge. Just before sunset is a very good time to visit or photograph it.

Jolfā

Jolfā, just south of the river over the Sī o Sé Pol, is the Armenian quarter of Esfahān. It dates from the time of Shāh Abbās, who set up this colony of Christians from the town of Jolfā (on present-day Iran's northern border), and named it 'New Jolfā'. The skills of these industrious merchants, vintners and entrepreneurs were coveted but it was pre-

ferred that they be kept in one area and away from the Islamic centres. As Esfahān expanded, Jolfā became another suburb, but the inhabitants have always been predominantly if not exclusively Christian. There are some interesting churches and a large cemetery, but the area is a maze of narrow alleys and more than a little difficult to explore without a guide. There are 14 churches here, of which the most impressive is the Vānk Cathedral; others of historic interest include the Kelīsā-yé Beit-ol-Lahm (Bethlehem Church), the oldest of all, and the Kelīsā-yé Hazrat-é Maryam (Church of St Mary).

Kelīsā-yé Vānk Vānk Cathedral in Jolfā, at the far eastern end of Kheyābūn-é Khāghānī, is open to visitors from 8 am to noon and 2 to 5 pm, Monday to Saturday. Built between 1655 and 1664 with the encouragement of the Safavid rulers, this is the historic focal point of the Armenian church in Iran, although it has to a certain extent been supplanted by the recent Armenian cathedral in Tehrān. The exterior of the church is unexciting, but the interior is richly, if rather tastelessly, decorated and shows the mixture of styles – Islamic Persian and Christian European – that characterises most churches in Iran. There is a small museum where you might be able to find a guidebook on Jolfā in English, or someone who speaks English, as most educated Armenians do.

Golestān-é Shohadā

The Rose Garden of Martyrs is a cemetery for those who died in the Iran-Iraq War. The rows of photographs on the tombstones are an unforgettable sight. By the entrance there is also a modern, domed mausoleum to Āyatollāh Shams Ābādī, who is said to have been assassinated by the Shāh's secret police shortly before the revolution. The cemetery is in Kheyābūn-é Karbalā about a km south of the Pol-é Khājū. To get there take a shared taxi from Pol-é Khājū to Meidūn-é Pīrūzī for 50 rials and walk east for 400 metres. Sad to say, most towns in Iran have at least one densely packed martyrs' cemetery similar to this one.

Manär Jombän

If you climb up the very narrow stairway to the top of one of these two 'Shaking Minarets' and lean hard against the wall it will start to sway back and forth. And so will its twin. Although by no means unique in this respect, the Shaking Minarets of Esfahän are probably the most famous of their kind. The minarets probably date from the Safavid period, although the mausoleum underneath was built in the 14th century.

The Manär Jombän are about seven km west of the centre and difficult to reach by public transport. You should resign yourself to chartering a taxi for 1000 to 1200 rials each way. Any taxi will do. If you were hell-bent on getting here by public transport, you could try taking a shared taxi west from Meidün-é Emäm Hosein to Meidün-é Montazerï, and then another to the minarets.

The Manär Jombän are open daily from 8 am to 5 pm (entry 100 rials).

Äteshgäh

This fire-temple is on your right about a km further out of town from the Manär Jombän on the same road. It is possible with only moderate difficulty and minor damage to skin and footwear to climb all the way up there from the road, making your way under a barbed wire fence surrounding the mud-brick remains above an ugly modern water-tank. Dating from Sassanian times, these ancient mud-brick ruins give you a good view back to the city. Along the road which passes the Manär Jombän and the Äteshgäh there are some old mud-brick houses, some with bädgïrs (wind towers).

Places to Stay

In Esfahän all the good hotels set their prices in rials, but charge foreigners in hard currency at a highly unfavourable exchange rate. If you find one that doesn't cost the earth, please let me know. I gave up the struggle.

Places to Stay – bottom end

Some of the cheapest hotels are near the old bus offices in the noisy Kheyäbün-é Masjed-é Sayyed. You get what you pay for here. The *Hotel-é Pershyä* ('Persia Hotel') (☎ 23274), on the east side of Chahärräh-é Takhtï, charges 1650/2500 rials a double/triple with a far from clean shared bathroom. The *Hotel-é Sepïd* ('Sepid Hotel') (☎ 63767) and the *Hotel-é Persepölïs* ('Persepolis Hotel') (☎ 31452) are in the same category.

There are several cheapies along the west side of Chahär Bägh-é Abbäsï. The *Mosäferkhüné-yé Parväz* (not marked in English) in Chahär Bägh, just south of Meidün-é Emäm Hosein, charges 700 rials for a dormitory bed with shared bathroom. The *Mosäferkhüné-yé Adälat* (not marked in English), a few metres to the south, charges 600 rials for a dormitory bed with a shared shower. A little further down, the *Mehmünkhüné-yé Pärs* (☎ 61018) ('Pars Hotel') charges 4000 rials a double with shared bathroom, radio and TV.

The *Mehmünkhüné-yé Tüs* (☎ 60068) ('Tous Hotel') just to the west of Meidün-é Engheläb-é Eslämï charges 3000 rials a double with bathroom, or 1500 rials for a dormitory bed; this hotel is a cut above the rest in its class and it also serves breakfast. The others are best avoided unless you're on a very tight budget. The *Türïst Hotel* ('Tourist Hotel') (38688), on Chahär Bägh at its intersection with Kheyäbün-é Abbäs Äbäd, is noisy but bearable and costs 1500/2250 rials for a single/double.

Just to the north of Meidün-é Emäm Hosein and isolated from the other bottom-end places, the *Hotel-é Naghsh-é Jahän* (☎ 32352, 38839) (not marked in English) has doubles for 1900 rials with clean shared showers.

A small step up takes you to the *Hotel-é Ïrän* ('Hotel Iran') (☎ 62070), 200 metres south of Meidün-é Emäm Hosein, which charges 2250/3400/4250 rials a single/double/triple with private bathroom, and 5100 rials for a room with four beds and a private bathroom.

Places to Stay – middle

The next step up is to hotels like the *Hotel-é Äzädï* (☎ 35056, 39011) ('Azady Hotel'), just off Chahār Bāgh-é Pā'īn, which has singles/doubles with private bathroom at 2400/3200 rials. It is clean and has recently been renovated. Two travellers wrote that the *Āzādī* was better than the famous Abbasi Hotel, at half the price. This place is quite popular with travellers arriving by bus.

The Armenian-owned *Hotel-é Jolfā* ('Hotel Julfa') (☎ 71003), near the Vānk Cathedral in Jolfā, charges 3000/4500/7650 rials a single/double/suite with private bathroom. This secluded hotel is reasonable value, although I had to wage war on the largest cockroaches I have seen in my life before braving the bath in my 'suite'. This place and its guests get a lot of attention from the Komīté. You can reach it by shared taxi from Meidūn-é Enghelāb-é Eslāmī for around 200 rials.

The *Hotel-é Āryā* ('Arya Hotel') (☎ 27242), which is in the same convenient and not too noisy street as the Abbasi Hotel, has adequate singles/doubles with private bathroom for 3300/3600 rials.

The state-owned *Mehmūnsarā-yé Pirūzī* (marked in English 'Piroozy Hotel') (☎ 61043) is on the west side of Chahār Bāgh-é Pā'īn a few metres north of Meidūn-é Emām Hosein. The hotel is OK, but is poorly maintained, has unfriendly staff, completely lacks personality, and does nothing to justify its charges of 4300/6300 rials a single/double with private bathroom.

Places to Stay – top end
The four best hotels in Esfahān all charge foreigners in hard currency, and most foreign tourists have joined an unofficial boycott of these outrageously overpriced establishments. If money is no object, read on.

The *Hotel-é Sūīt* (marked in English 'Suite Hotel') (☎ 43872), on the south bank of the river just to the east of the Sī o Sé Pol, would be reasonable value at the Iranian price of 3200/4800 rials a single/double with private bathroom, but not at the foreigners' dollar charge.

The *Hotel-é Ālī Ghāpū* ('Ali Qapu Hotel') (☎ 31283), on the west side of Chahār Bāgh-é Abbāsī, is good value at 4800/7200 rials a single/double with private bathroom, but it quoted a criminal sum in dollars.

The *Abbasi Hotel* (☎ 26014) (in Persian Mehmūnsarā-yé Abbāsī), on the north side of Kheyābūn-é Shahīd Āyatollāh Madanī about 100 metres east of the intersection with Chahār Bāgh, is rated five-star and undoubtedly the most romantic place to stay in Esfahān, with an air of faded elegance but few modern fittings in full working order. This hotel, which used to be known as the *Shah Abbas*, was luxuriously created in the shell of an old caravanserai and it's certainly worth visiting to see the extravagance of the decorations and the courtyard, or just to linger over a pot of tea in its chāykhūné. The nightclub is now shut but the restaurant is still there, although not the height of gastronomic excellence. The *Abbasi* is yet another in the sad catalogue of hotels which used to be good but were taken over by the Bonyād-é Mostaz'afīn (the Foundation for the Dispossessed). A few years ago I would have had no hesitation in recommending the place to anyone, but the elegance is now so faded and the service so indifferent that the hotel no longer deserves more than three stars, while the charge for foreigners is US$65/85 a single/double with private bathroom or up to US$250 a night for a suite – outrageous by Iranian standards, and more than 10 times what Iranian guests pay.

The *Kowsar Hotel* (☎ 40236) (Hotel-é Kōsar in Persian), in Būstān-é Mellat, is Esfahān's other five-star place. It's very good and comfortable with most of the modern fittings working and a fine view of Sī o Sé Pol and the river, but it lacks the character of some other luxury hotels in Iran. It is the most luxurious hotel in Esfahān, but few foreigners will be prepared to fork out US$70/104 for a single/double with private bathroom. Iranians pay 9850/14,500 rials, which isn't exceptionally high for a hotel of its class.

Places to Eat
There's a good selection of eateries in Esfahān, from the cheap and cheerful to the sophisticated and expensive, although some

of the grander establishments aren't all they're cracked up to be. The most famous speciality of the town is gaz, a delicious kind of nougat usually mixed with chopped pistachios or other nuts. It isn't generally served in restaurants or other eating-places, but is sold in confectionery shops to take away. The yoghurt is also especially good here, and often has a crust on it.

Surprisingly, there are no restaurants in Meidūn-é Emām itself, although there are some sandwich bars within walking distance, and teahouses in the bazaar. The nearest places for a sit-down meal are in the Chahār Bāgh.

Places to Eat – bottom end

There are plenty of sandwich-bars and chelō kabābīs along most of the length of Chahār Bāgh, and near most of the hotels. If you have some idea of what the correct price is, you can buy your own food in the bazaar.

Places to Eat – middle

The best restaurant I found in this category was the unpretentious underground *Sālon-é Ghezā-yé Nōbahār* in Kheyābūn-é Chahār Bāgh-é Pa'īn. This typical chelō kabābī is one of the less expensive, serving good, almost boneless jūjé kabāb without rice for 1200 rials, and excellent thickened māst.

The *Restōrān-é Mahārājah* ('Maharaja Restaurant'), on Meidūn-é Enghelāb, is a disappointing Indian restaurant. The steak is reasonable (1800 rials), but other Indian, Iranian and Continental dishes are not so good.

The restaurant at the *Hotel-é Āzādī* stays open for lunch later than others and is quite good. They make a fair attempt at chicken fesenjūn for 1400 rials, although nothing like the home-cooked version. Despite the enthusiastic service, the food at the restaurant in the *Mehmūnsarā- yé Pīrūzī* is none too good for the price: riceless and boneless jūjé kabāb with a strange taste to it costs an outrageous 2200 rials.

Places to Eat – top end

The *Mojtame'-é Pazīrā'ī-yé Negīn* ('Negin Restaurant Complex') (☎ 76977) is on the 1st floor of a shopping centre on the east side of Chahār Bāgh-é Bālā, just south of Chahārrāh-é Nazar. This is the expensive sort of place where music plays, conversation flows and boy meets girl, as far as the Komīté will allow. Service is professional and the decor is smart. It's a pity that the food (eg sturgeon kebabs 2000 rials, filet steak 2400 rials) isn't quite up to scratch.

At the restaurant in the *Abbasi Hotel* you are paying for the elegance of the decor and not for the quality of food, which is disappointing – the steak was tough, the peas tasted canned and the bill was startlingly high. Although the standard of food has slipped in recent years, this is still one of the most magnificent settings for any restaurant.

The food at the restaurant of the *Mehmūnsarā-yé Ālī Ghāpū* outranks that of the Abbasi Hotel in all but price, and offers the best value top-end eatery. Try the fried trout with almonds (2100 rials).

Sports

You can go canoeing in the Daryāché-yé Malek Shahr, the small lake to the south of the suburb of Malek Shahr at the far north of Esfahān, play table tennis in Meidūn-é Emām, watch football at one of the four city stadiums or, if you really want to keep fit, visit all the attractions in Esfahān on foot.

Things to Buy

There are several shops selling a selection of gaz (nougat) along Chahār Bāgh-é Pā'īn, and there are some good general confectionery shops along Kheyābūn-é Ferdōsī. Since it's difficult to get the best quality gaz outside Esfahān, buy as much as you could possibly want. The Gaz-é Ālī shop, a few metres south of the Hotel-é Pershyā in Chahār Bāgh-é Pā'īn, is probably the best place for gaz; one kg is 2400 rials for the best quality, or 1200 rials for the cheapest.

There are plenty of handicrafts shops around Meidūn-é Emām, mostly deserted and pining for the good old days of bus loads of free-spending foreign tourists. Even so, many of the salesmen speak good English and haven't forgotten their sales patter, and foreign customers still need all their wits about them to drive a hard bargain. Locally produced, hand-printed table-cloths and bedspreads, marquetry, miniatures, metal-work and carpets are the main items. Remember that Esfahān isn't the only place in Iran to buy handicrafts; almost everything for sale here can also be found in other large cities at similar or even lower prices, and you may be less likely to be cheated.

Getting There & Away

Air Iran Air has flights to the following destinations:

Bandar-é Abbās – Sunday, Wednesday and Friday at 2.10 pm (one hour 20 minutes)

Būshehr – Wednesday at 7 pm (one hour 50 minutes)

Kermān – Wednesday and Friday at 9.55 am (one hour five minutes)

Mashhad – Sunday, Tuesday, Thursday and Friday at 9.25 pm (one hour 25 minutes)

Shīrāz – Tuesday at 5.50 pm, Wednesday at 7 pm, other days at 3.50 pm (50 minutes)

Tehrān – several flights daily (45 minutes; 5180 rials)

Zāhedān – on Wednesday and Friday at 9.55 am (two hours 25 minutes) and Thursday and Saturday at 2.10 pm (one hour 25 minutes).

Iran Air also flies once a week to Dubai. Foreigners must pay in hard currency for tickets on this service.

NIOC charters flights at least weekly between Esfahān and Lāvān: see the Jazīré-yé Lāvān entry for details. For details of Iran Asseman's alleged services, see the Getting Around chapter.

Airline Offices All three airline offices in Esfahān achieve a similar level of unhelpfulness. The main Iran Air office (☎ 28200) is in the arcade opposite the Abbasi Hotel, and the second Iran Air office (☎ 27778), which doesn't deal with international tickets, is on the east side of Chahār Bāgh-é Abbāsī. Iran Tour & Travel Company (☎ 23010) is next to the main Iran Air office and acts as an Iran Air agent. The sleepy, uncomputerised Iran Asseman office (☎ 55014), on the east side of Kheyābūn-é

Ferdōsī, is open certain mornings of certain weekdays.

Bus

At the time of writing the bus company offices were spread out along Kheyābūn-é Masjed-é Sayyed and there were several terminals. However a new bus station, to accommodate all the bus companies, was being built on the northern edge of town in Kheyābūn-é Kavé about two km north of Meidūn-é Shohadā and should be in operation by the time you read this.

Most of the long-distance buses travel overnight, although they aren't a recommended way of saving on accommodation. Book seats as early as possible. Cooperative Bus Company No 1 is the best company to travel with out of Esfahān, and has 'super' buses to most of the major destinations. There are buses from Esfahān to:

Ābādān – 903 km, 15 hours, 1950 rials 'super'; at least one a day (Cooperative Bus Company No 1)

Ahvāz – 765 km, 14 hours, 1270 rials 'super'; at least one a day (Cooperative Bus Company No 1 and Cooperative Bus Company No 2)

Bākhtarān – 665 km, eight hours, 1025/1275 rials 'lux'/'super'; at least one a day

Bandar-é Abbās – 1082 km, 18 hours, 1510 rials 'super'; at least one a day (Cooperative Bus Company No 1)

Bandar-é Anzalī – 777 km, 13 hours; several buses a week

Kāshān – 209 km, 3½ hours; several buses a day

Kermān – 703 km, 12 hours, 950 rials 'super'; several buses a day (Cooperative Bus Company No 1)

Mashhad – 1338 km, 22 hours, 1800 rials 'super'; several buses a day (Cooperative Bus Company No 1)

Rasht – 737 km, 12 hours; several buses a day

Shahr-é Kord – 107 km, 1¾ hours; at least one bus a day

Shīrāz – 481 km, eight hours, 550 rials 'super'; several buses a day (Cooperative Bus Company No 1)

Sīrjān – 657 km, 11 hours; occasional buses (Cooperative Bus Company No 2)

Tabrīz – 1038 km, 16 hours, 1785 rials 'super'; several buses a day (Cooperative Bus Company No 1)

Tehrān – 414 km, seven hours, 615 rials 'super'; several buses a day (Cooperative Bus Company No 1)

Yazd – 316 km, five hours, 460 rials 'super'; one bus a day (Cooperative Bus Company No 1)

Zāhedān – 1244 km, 21 hours, 1825 rials 'super'; at least one a day (Cooperative Bus Company No 1); 1400 rials 'lux', at least one a day (Cooperative Bus Company No 15).

There is also a more or less weekly direct service with Cooperative Bus Company No 1 to Istanbul (around 15,000 rials 'lux', 22,000 rials 'super').

Train There are three express trains a week from Esfahān to Tehrān via Kāshān and Ghom (nine hours 45 minutes), but most people prefer to go by bus or plane. The railway station (☎ 45002) is near the airport and connected to the town by buses and shared taxis. You don't have to go all that way just to book a seat; there is a ticket office on the east side of Meidūn-é Enghelāb-é Eslāmī. There are plans to start a train service to Shīrāz.

Shared Taxi & Savārī Shared taxis and savārīs to Shīrāz – around 6000 rials away – leave from outside the central telegraph office. When the new bus terminal is operating, there may be savārīs to other destinations from outside it.

Getting Around
To/From the Airport Airport bus tickets (200 rials) are sold at an office outside the airport. The bus goes to and from Meidūn-é Enghelāb-é Eslāmī, from where you can easily continue your journey by city bus or shared taxi.

There is also a taxi office at the airport, but it is quicker and cheaper to take the bus if it goes in your direction. Shared taxis to the airport leave from the east side of Kheyābūn-é Sepāh near the main bazaar, or from Meidūn-é Shahīd Āyatollāh Sadūghī on the north-east side of town.

Bus & Minibus City bus tickets are 20 rials; minibuses charge 40 rials. There is a small city bus terminal at Meidūn-é Emām Hosein, with buses going in most directions. If you

speak Persian, you can ask for information at the ticket office on the south-west of the square.

Taxi Chahār Bāgh is the main city thoroughfare, and it is simple to catch a shared taxi *mostaghīm* (straight ahead) along it. On this same road there are two very busy junctions for shared taxis at Meidūn-é Emām Hosein and Meidūn-é Enghelāb-é Eslāmī. It's 50 rials by shared taxi between the two. The second one is the place to go if you want to go from the north to the south of the river. If you're not in a tearing hurry, you shouldn't have any great problems in getting almost anywhere in the city and back again by shared taxi, changing vehicle at junctions on the way. A map and a compass may help.

Esfahān is the only place in Iran where I was consistently cheated by taxi-drivers. Watch out, especially if you don't speak Persian, or if you start or finish your trip as the only passenger.

You can hire a taxi here for 1500 rials an hour within city limits. Hiring one for a few hours is definitely a good idea if you want to visit some of the outlying sights, and it's worth considering even for a tour of the main sights within the city.

KĀSHĀN كاشان

Dating perhaps from as early as the Sassanian era, prosperous from the time of the Seljuqs to the Safavids, and famous at various periods for its ceramic tiles, carpets and silk, Kāshān is an attractive oasis town. One of the most important archaeological sites in central Iran is on the edge of town. Kāshān is also of interest for its connections with Shāh Abbās I – it was a favourite town of his, and he beautified it and asked to be buried here in the mausoleum of a 13th century ancestor.

Interesting Buildings
The tomb of Shāh Abbās I is between two other tombs in the crypt of the **Zeyārat-é Habīb ebn-é Mūsā**, which was later used as a mosque. It's off Kheyābūn-é Emām Khomeinī, near the train station.

Another building worth visiting is the much-restored, Seljuq and Timurid **Masjed-é Jāme'**, with an 11th century mehrāb. It's approached by a short alley leading south-west from Kheyābūn-é Bābā Afzal. The Seljuq **Manār-é Zein-od-Dīn** is some 500 metres to the south-east. There is also a bewildering number of shrines throughout the city to various holies and worthies of later periods.

The town has many picturesque bādgīrs (wind towers), essential in the town's hot and airless summers before the introduction of air-con.

Bāgh-é Tārīkhī-yé Fīn

This famous and very beautiful garden, once known as the Bāgh-é Shāh or Bāgh-é Amīr Kabīr, is perhaps the finest surviving example in Iran. It is in the suburb of Fīn, eight km south-west of central Kāshān. Designed for Shāh Abbās I, this classical Persian vision of paradise has always been prized for its natural springs and still contains the remains of his two-storey palace set around a pool. The garden has other Safavid royal buildings, although they were substantially rebuilt, and others were added in the Ghajar period. There is also a small museum here. Fīn can be reached by shared taxi from central Kāshān via Kheyābūn-é Amīr Kabīr.

Tappé-yé Seyalk   تپه سیلک

Seyalk (Sialk) is four km to the north-east of Fīn, on the right of the road from Kāshān. It is probably the richest archaeological site so far uncovered in central Iran, although the most interesting finds have been moved to various institutes and museums, including Tehrān's Mūzé-yé Īrān-é Bāstān and the Louvre.

There are two mounds here, the larger of which is to the south. Excavated by the French Archaeological Service in the '30s and later, the site has revealed a large number and variety of pottery and domestic implements of clay, stone and bone from as early as the 4th millennium BC, and is believed to have been first settled in the 5th millennium or earlier. It appears to have been

sacked and deserted in about the 8th century BC. You can still see the outline of various mud-brick buildings and a large number of potsherds embedded throughout the two mounds. Perhaps the most interesting finds are some inscribed clay tablets dating from the late 3rd and early 2nd millennia BC. The remains here give an interesting record of the waves of immigrants and conquerors who passed this way, and settled near the abundant water supply at the site of present-day Fīn.

Places to Stay

The only hotels are the central *Hotel-é Sayyāh*, just to the north-west of Meidūn-é Emām Khomeinī, 1½ km west of the train station; and the large modern *Hotel-é Amīr Kabīr* at Fīn. Neither is at all distinguished.

Getting There & Away

A bus to Kāshān takes takes around 3½ hours from Esfahān (209km), four from Tehrān (258 km). There are three express trains a week to Tehrān, via Ghom (four hours 40 minutes) and to Kermān, via Yazd (12 hours 55 minutes). The train station is in the north-east of Kāshān, within walking distance of the centre.

ARDESTĀN   اردستان

Ardestān, on the road from Kāshān to Nā'īn, is worth visiting for its **Masjed-é Jāme'**, a large Seljuq mosque from the 10th century and later, with a brick dome, a beautifully ornamented prayer-hall and mehrāb and a simple brick minaret.

NĀ'ĪN   نائین

Slumbering Nā'īn, an important transit centre at the geographical centre of Iran, is famous for carpet making and also for its **Masjed-é Jāme'**. This rambling mosque from the early Islamic period still has some features from the 10th century, and is especially notable for its fine mehrāb and 14th-century membar, and for its innovative yet simple use of stucco decoration.

Buses passing through or originating in

Nā'īn can take you to Tehrān, Esfahān, Yazd or Tabas (602 km, 12 hours).

Chahārmahāl va Bakhteyārī Province

استان چهارمحال وبختیاری

Population: 637,200
Area: 14,870 sq km
This mountainous and comparatively tiny province was previously part of an even larger Esfahān Province. When Isabella Bird travelled here in 1890, she described much of her route as previously unexplored (see *Journeys in Persia and Kurdistan*). She gave the picture of a wild and inhospitable terrain inhabited by fiercely independent and warlike tribespeople (principally Lors and Bakhteyārīs) governed by feudal chieftains.

Except for the capital, Shahr-é Kord, which can be reached by bus from Esfahān (107 km, 1¾ hours) or Shīrāz (588 km, 10 hours), the province is still far from accessible and very few tourists make it here. There is a tourist office (☎ (0381) 24888) in Shahr-é Kord, as well as a two-star hotel, the *Mehmūnsarā-yé Shahr-é Kord* (☎ 4892).

Yazd Province

استان يزد

Population: 582,300
Area: 70,011 sq km
Bordered by the great land masses of Khorāsān, Kermān, Fārs and Esfahān provinces, Yazd Province is almost unrelieved desert except for the provincial centre of Yazd and a few other towns where most of the population lives.

YAZD
يزد
Population: 230,500
Midway between Esfahān and Kermān, Yazd is particularly interesting for its rela-

tionship with its desert environment. It stands on the border between the northern salt desert, the Dasht-é Kavīr, and the southern sand desert, the Dasht-é Lūt. At an altitude of 1230 metres, Yazd can be quite cold in winter, but it is very hot in summer, 42°C or more. There are 12 busy bazaars, a number of fine mosques and several other interesting buildings. Yazd was also an important religious centre for pre-Islamic Zoroastrianism, and there is still a substantial minority of Zoroastrians today – probably around 12,000, more than in the rest of Iran put together. It has always been a great weaving centre, known for its silks and other fabrics even before Marco Polo passed through on the Silk Road in the late 13th century. You can still see some traditional textile and carpet factories in the town. Yazd deserves a stay of several days.

Look out for the tall wind-towers or bādgīrs on rooftops, designed to catch even the lightest breezes and direct them down to the underground living rooms. In the hot summers they are very necessary, and far more healthy than modern air-conditioning. The adobe architecture here is of great interest, although it takes some time to explore and appreciate it. The building styles are simple, traditional and quite exotic compared with the uniformity of most of the other large towns of Iran. The whole town is the colour of clay, as memorable as the distinctive red ochre of Hormoz. The residential quarters appear almost deserted because of the high walls protecting the houses from the very narrow and labyrinthine kūchés (alleys) crisscrossing the town.

History
Although Yazd dates from Sassanian times, its history is fairly undistinguished. It was conquered by the Arabs in about 642, and subsequently became an important station on the caravan routes to Central Asia and India, exporting its silks, textiles and carpets far and wide. It was spared destruction by Genghis Khan and Tamerlane and flourished in the 14th and 15th centuries, but its commercial success and stability were never

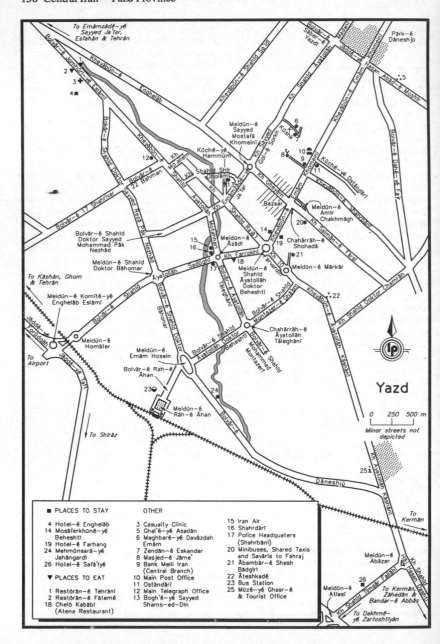

To Emāmzāde-yé Sayyed Ja'far, Esfahān & Tehrān

Pārk-é Dāneshjū

Meidūn-é Sayyed Mostafā Khomeinī

Kūché-yé Hammūm

Shahīd Shīr Gholamī

Bāzaar

Meidūn-é Amīr Chakhmāgh

Meidūn-é Āzādī

Chahārrāh-é Shohadā

Meidūn-é Shahīd Doktor Bāhomar

Meidūn-é Shahīd Āyatollāh Doktor Beheshtī

Meidūn-é Mārkār

To Kāshān, Ghom & Tehrān

Meidūn-é Komité-yé Enghelāb Eslāmī

Meidūn-é Homāfer

To Airport

Chahārrāh-é Āyatollāh Tāleghānī

To Shīrāz

Meidūn-é Emām Hosein

Bolvār-é Rah-é Āhan

Meidūn-é Rah-é Āhan

Yazd

0   250   500 m

Minor streets not depicted

To Kermān

Meidūn-é Abāzar

Meidūn-é Atlasī

To Kermān, Zāhedān & Bandar-é Abbās

To Dakhmé-yé Zartoshtīyān

■ PLACES TO STAY	OTHER	
4 Hotel-é Enghelāb	3 Casualty Clinic	15 Iran Air
14 Mosāferkhōné-yé Beheshtī	5 Ghal'é-yé Asadān	16 Shahrdārī
19 Hotel-é Farhang	6 Maghbaré-yé Davāzdah Emām	17 Police Headquaters (Shahrbānī)
24 Mehmūnsarā-yé Jahāngardī	7 Zendān-é Eskandar	20 Minibuses, Shared Taxis and Savārīs to Fahraj
26 Hotel-é Safā'īyé	8 Masjed-é Jāme'	21 Ābambār-é Shesh Bādgīrī
	9 Bank Melli Iran (Central Branch)	22 Āteshkadé
▼ PLACES TO EAT	10 Main Post Office	23 Bus Station
1 Restōrān-é Tehrānī	11 Ostāndārī	25 Mūzé-yé Ghasr-é & Tourist Office
2 Restōrān-é Fātemé	12 Main Telegraph Office	
18 Chelō Kabābī (Atena Restaurant)	13 Bogh'é-yé Sayyed Shams-ed-Dīn	

translated into political status. Like most of the rest of Iran, the town fell into decline after the end of the Safavid era, and remained little more than a provincial outpost until the extension of the railway line here under the last shāh. The town is known for its long line of distinguished historians and clerics, and also as the stronghold of the Zoroastrian community since the Arab Conquest, when many adherents of the old religion fled here from other parts of Persia. There has always been a certain amount of rivalry between the Zoroastrian and Muslim communities, but by and large the town has remained as free of persecution as it has of invasion.

Orientation

The centre of Yazd is Meidūn-é Shahīd Āyatollāh Doktor Beheshtī (still widely known by its old name of Meidūn-é Mojā-hedīn). From here to the train station in the south of Yazd, or the bus station almost next to it, is about three km. There are a couple of places to stay within walking distance of the main square, but most of them are some distance away and in various directions. Most of the main sights can be visited on foot, but it is very easy to get lost in the dense networks of kūchés and cul-de-sacs.

Information

The ostāndārī is in Kheyābūn-é Ostāndārī, off Kheyābūn-é Emām Khomeinī. The shahrdārī is at the north-west of Meidūn-é Āzādī. Visa extensions are dealt with at the police headquarters (shahrbānī), on the south side of Kheyābūn-é Sadūghī about 100 metres west of Meidūn-é Āzādī.

Tourist Office The utterly useless tourist office (☎ 35077) (daftar-é seir va seyāhat) is in the same building as the Mūzé-yé Ghasr-é Ā'īné in Kheyābūn-é Āyatollāh Kāshānī. It's marked in English, although the sign is craftily concealed from the view of the casual passer-by. No English is spoken, and the free map is a very poor photocopy, in Persian and without a key. Bus No 1 goes from Meidūn-é Shahīd Āyatollāh Doktor Beheshtī to the tourist office, but unless you are really stuck

for accommodation or want to visit the muddled museum in the same building, there is little point in forking out the bus-fare.

Money Bank Melli Iran is on the west side of Kheyābūn-é Emām Khomeinī at its intersection with Kheyābūn-é Masjed-é Jāme'.

Post & Telecommunications The head post office is a few metres north-east of the Bank Melli Iran in Kheyābūn-é Emām Khomeinī, and the main telegraph office is in Kheyābūn-é Shahīd Āyatollāh Motahharī. The dialling code for Yazd is 0351.

Maps The 300-rial Gītā Shenāsī map of Yazd is very detailed, with over 600 entries on its key, but there is no English translation. There is also a small sketch map at 180 rials, but it's in Persian and not reliable. The tourist office map is quite useless.

Medical Services For emergencies dial ☎ 118.

Āteshkadé

This important Zoroastrian fire temple is open to the public from 8 to 11 am and 2.30 to 4.30 pm Saturday to Thursday, except holidays. There is no entrance fee, but donations are welcomed. The sacred flame behind a glass case visible from the small museum inside has, according to the Zoroastrian elder in attendance here, been burning since about 470 AD and was transferred from its original site in 1940. This attracts Zoroastrians from around the world, and there will probably be someone who speaks English to explain things to you. There are also a couple of paintings here, including one of Zoroaster. The Āteshkadé is in a small walled garden on the east side of Kheyābūn-é Āyatollāh Kāshānī 500 metres south-east of Meidūn-é Mārkār.

The Zoroastrian district, the only one of any size remaining in Iran, is around this area. The men aren't easily distinguished from Muslims, although they tend to be close-shaven, but the Zoroastrian women can be recognised by their patterned head-scarves and embroidered dresses with white, cream or red as the predominant colour; they never wear chādors.

In the far north-east of Yazd is a more recent Zoroastrian building, the **Ghal'é-yé Asadān** (literally the 'Fortress of Lions'), which houses a Zoroastrian eternal flame moved here some 20 years ago. The building is usually closed. There are plenty of other Zoroastrian sites around Yazd, of which the most important is Chak Chak, 52 km to the north (see under that heading).

Zendān-é Eskandar

'Alexander's Prison' is hidden in a network of kūchés near the Masjed-é Jāme'. Probably the easiest way to get there on foot is to start off at Meidūn-é Sayyed Mostafā Khomeinī and walk north-east along Kheyābūn-é Gol-é Sorkh until you come to Kūché-yé Kūshk, about 800 metres on your right. Turn into this alley and walk straight ahead for about 300 metres and you will come to a small square, where you will find the prison. The ground floor is currently being rebuilt as a theological college, although the business end of the prison has been left in its original condition.

This prison must have been a pretty nasty place by any standards, and resembles the worst sort of mediaeval European dungeon. Approached by a steep set of stairs, it is simply a deep, circular, brick-lined pit about 10 metres in diameter, with a domed roof that lets in almost no light. There is no entrance charge, and the college being constructed above the old dungeon does not seem to keep fixed hours.

Maghbaré-yé Davāzdah Emām

The early 11th-century 'Tomb of the 12 Emāms' is almost next door to the Zendān-é Eskandar. It has a fine Seljuq inscription inside, with the names of each of the Shi'ite emāms, none of whom is buried here. Although the mausoleum is small, dusty and forgotten, it is nonetheless a well preserved building of the period. There are some interesting plaster mouldings on the mehrāb, and the brick dome is a good early example of its kind. The maghbaré is locked, but the doorkeeper at the Zendān-é Eskandar next door

will take you in; I suggest a tip of around 300 rials. This is one occasion when it might be useful to have a guide or taxi driver with you.

Masjed-é Jāme'

At the end of Kheyābūn-é Masjed-é Jāme', which runs off Kheyābūn-é Emām Khomeinī, this large, attractive mosque is a well preserved 14th-century structure built on the site of an earlier building, probably from the 12th century, which in turn was converted from an earlier fire-temple, no doubt without the Zoroastrians permission. It has a remarkably high, tiled entrance portal, flanked with two minarets and adorned with an inscription from the 15th century. The beautiful mosaics on the dome and on the mehrāb are also of interest. The interior of the mosque is cleverly ventilated and well lit and hosts a large bird colony.

Emāmzādé-yé Sayyed Ja'far

This mausoleum of the emāmzādé Sayyed Ja'far is on the south side of Bolvār-é Jomhūrī-yé Eslāmī. It is decorated inside with tens of thousands of modern mirror tiles of various colours illuminating the whole mosque. The outside of the mosque is also of interest, but like so many other Islamic buildings in Yazd it was undergoing extensive repair at the time of writing.

Ābambār-é Shesh Bādgīrī

The self-explanatory 'Water-Reservoir with Six Wind-Tunnels' is in an alley which branches off at angle, just north-west of Meidūn-é Mārkār.

Mūzé-yé Ghasr-é Ā'īné

The Mūzé-yé Ghasr-é Ā'īné in Yazd is a curious postrevolutionary ragbag of various objects including items of furniture, a matchbox collection, tea-services, guns and pistols, stamp albums, calligraphy, various tatty banknotes and coins of no great value or interest, including small change in several currencies, some labelled as donations from foreign visitors to the museum. This is your chance of immortality: no contribution is refused. The museum is open from 7.30 am

Top: Boy climbing palm tree, Bam (DStV)
Left: Emāzādé-yé Alī Ghal'é-yé Sāng (DStV)
Right: Young Iranian men, Kūh-é Khājé (DStV)

Top: Balūchī man, Chābahār beach (DStV)
Left: Porter carrying passengers from boat to land, Bandar-é Abbās beach (DStV)
Right: Part of Portuguese fortress, Hormoz (DStV)

to 7 pm Saturday to Wednesday and 7.30 to noon on Thursday. The tourist office is attached to the museum.

Places to Stay

Accommodation in Yazd is inexpensive, but there aren't enough hotel beds to go around. If you find all the hotels and mosāferkhūnés in town full, there is a heated waiting-room at the bus terminal where you can attempt to sleep the night in the company of many dozens of others.

Places to Stay – bottom end

The *Hotel-é Farhang* (☎ 35011) (literally 'Culture Hotel') is in Kūché-yé Farhang, off Kheyābūn-é Emām Khomeinī a few metres north-east of Meidūn-é Shahīd Āyatollāh Doktor Beheshtī. It charges 1270/1900 rials a single/double with shared bathroom, 1700/2550 rials with private bathroom. The hotel is clean and reasonable value, especially if you want to be woken in time for morning prayers by the muezzin at the mosque right next door. The *Mosāferkhūné-yé Beheshtī* ('Beheshty') opposite Kūché-yé Farhang is cheap at 600/1200 rials a single/double without bathroom, but no cheaper than it ought to be. If you get really stuck, there are a few places in Kheyābūn-é Āyatollāh Kāshānī that make an anthrax scab look hygienic .

Places to Stay – middle

The *Hotel-é Safā'īyé* (☎ 39812) is on the north side of Kheyābūn-é Shahīd Tīmsar Fallāhī in the far south of Yazd. It charges 1900/2890 rials a single/double with shared bathroom, 2250/3800 rials with private bathroom. The comfortable and popular *Mehmūnsarā-yé Jahāngardī* (☎ 32439), in Bolvār-é Dāneshjū, charges 2040/3060 rials for a single/double with shared bathroom, 2720/4100 rials with private bathroom. The *Hotel-é Enghelāb*, near Bolvār-é Jomhūrī-yé Eslāmī, isn't quite as luxurious as it appears from the outside but is still good value at 2100/3600 rials a single/double with shared bathroom, 2800/4200 rials with private bathroom.

Places to Eat

The chelō kabābī on the south side of Kheyābūn-é Farrokhī, marked in English *Atena Restaurant*, serves good chelō kabāb-é makhsūs and other old favourites.

Probably the best chelō kabābī in Yazd and certainly one of the most popular is the *Restōrān-é Tehrānī* in Bolvār-é Jomhūrī-yé Eslāmī; as well as the ubiquitous chelō kabāb, it serves good and inexpensive fish, chicken and khōresh dishes. The *Restōrān-é Fātemé* in the same street is also recommended. These places are a little difficult for public transport at night, but they're worth the taxi fare.

Things to Buy

The many bazaars here are probably the best places in Iran to buy silk, brocades and cloth, the products which brought the town its prosperity. Try to take an Iranian guide with you. Yazd is also a good place for cakes and sweets, although quite a lot of the tempting tooth-rotters on display aren't actually made in the town. There is a good cake shop next to the Hotel-é Farhang, selling sōhūn at 1500 rials a box. There are plenty of other places to try along Kheyābūn-é Emām Khomeinī. Almost everything in Yazd is cheap compared with the rest of Iran.

Getting There & Away

Air The Iran Air office (☎ 28030) is on the west side of Kheyābūn-é Shahīd Āyatollāh Motahharī, 50 metres north of Meidūn-é Āzādī. Iran Air flies from Yazd to:

Bandar-é Abbās – Saturday at 6.40 am (one hour 10 minutes)
Mashhad – Monday and Friday at 11.55 am (one hour 20 minutes)
Tehrān – two flights daily (one hour; 6540 rials).

Bus & Minibus The bus company offices are all in the same small building at the terminal near the train station. Usually no more than half of them are open at any one time. Buses serve the following destinations, but this list may not be complete:

Ahvāz – 1008 km, 20 hours, 1550 rials 'lux'; one a
day at 10 pm, (Cooperative Bus Company No 4):
1520/2045 rials 'lux'/'super'; several a week,
(Cooperative Bus Company No 2)
Bākhtarān – 1081 km, 16 hours; one a day at 2 pm
(Cooperative Bus Company No 12)
Bam – 581 km, nine hours; one a day at 3.30 pm
(Cooperative Bus Company No 12)
Esfahān – 316 km, five hours, 460 rials 'lux'; one a
day at 1 pm (Cooperative Bus Company No 1)
Karaj – 723 km, 11 hours, 1120 rials 'super'; one a
day at 6 pm (Cooperative Bus Company No 1)
Kermān – 387 km, six hours; at least one a day
Mashhad – 1306 km, 21 hours, 1600 rials; two buses
a day at 1 and 2.30 pm (Cooperative Bus
Company No 12)
Sanandaj – 968 km, 16 hours, 1680 rials; several
buses a week (Cooperative Bus Company No 12)
Shīrāz – 440 km, seven hours, 630 rials; one a day
(Cooperative Bus Company No 16); one a day at
6 pm (Cooperative Bus Company No 17)
Tabas – 419 km, eight hours; at least one a day
Tehrān – 677 km, 10 hours, 700/1120-1220 rials
'lux'/'super'; one a day at 5.30 pm (Cooperative
Bus Company No 12); one a day (Cooperative
Bus Company No 14); one a day at 6 pm (Coop-
erative Bus Company No 1)
Zāhedān – 928 km, 14 hours, 1030 rials 'lux'; one a
day at 3.30 pm (Cooperative Bus Company No
12)

There are no restaurants or hotels at all at the
bus terminal, but there is a small shop catering to passengers (don't have anything to do
with the dried-up pistachios it offers). There
is a heated waiting-room in the station open
24 hours a day.

Minibuses to Fahraj (30 km, 45 minutes)
leave from the south side of Kheyābūn-é
Salmān-é Fārsī about 75 metres south-east
of Chahārrāh Shohadā.

Train At the time of writing there are three
express trains a week from Yazd to Kermān
(five hours 15 minutes), and to Tehrān via
Kāshān (12 hours 20 minutes).

Shared Taxi & Savārī Shared taxis and
savārīs leave for Fahraj from the south side
of Kheyābūn-é Salmān-é Fārsī, about 75
metres east of Chahārrāh Shohadā. The fare
is around 150 rials.If you find a shared taxi
to Tabas, the fare is 5000 to 6000 rials per
person.

Getting Around

To/From the Airport There is no airport
bus service, but you can take a taxi into
town for around 750 rials as a single passenger. To get from Yazd to the airport,
book a telephone taxi through your hotel
or mosāferkhūné.

Bus Many of the city bus routes start from
and end up at Meidūn-é Shahīd Āyatollāh
Doktor Beheshtī. Tickets can be bought at
the kiosk here.

There is no direct service to or from the
bus station, but you can take a No 3 bus from
this square to Meidūn-é Emām Hosein, from
where you can walk or take a shared taxi to
the bus or train station for 50 rials at the
most.

Taxi A taxi into town from the bus or train
station is a reasonable 500 rials for a solo
passenger. Alternatively you can take a
shared taxi to Meidūn-é Shahīd Āyatollāh
Doktor Beheshtī for only 100 rials. Most
rides in town are a flat 50 rials, or even
less.

Taxi fares, like most things in Yazd, are
cheap. If you want to charter a taxi the
driver will probably tell you that the standard rate is at least 2000 rials an hour
within the city, or 3000 rials outside; the
correct charges are more like 1500 or 2000
rials respectively.

You'll find the taxi drivers in Yazd, especially the ones who hang out at the bus
terminal, are professionals when it comes to
dealing with foreigners, and you may have
to be quite firm about not letting a short ride
turn into a full tour. If you do want a tour
however, the ones I met weren't at all bad
company.

AROUND YAZD
Dakhmé-yé Zartoshtī   دخمه زرتشتیان
This revealing Zoroastrian site is about 15
km south-west of Yazd. It's a short walk up
two not very steep hills to the towers of
silence, which are no longer in use. You can
see the odd broken human bone on the very
top of the hill, where in the past the dead

were exposed to the attentions of passing vultures. Relatives of the dead would spend two or three days at the site. Beneath the hill there are several other disused Zoroastrian buildings including a defunct well, two small bādgīrs, an *ashpāzkhūné* (kitchen) and a lavatory.

The custom of exposing corpses in a tower of silence largely disappeared throughout the Zoroastrian world around 50 years ago, at about the same time that the eternal flame was transferred to the newly constructed āteshkadé in the centre of Yazd.

It is difficult to get to the Kūhhā-yé Dakhmé-yé Zartoshtī, except by taxi or private transport.

CHAK CHAK
چك چك

This important Zoroastrian fire-temple is on a hill 52 km to the north-north-west of Yazd. It attracts thousands of pilgrims for an annual festival which lasts for 10 days from the beginning of the third month after Nō Rūz. To visit, it's best to get the permission of the religious authorities at the āteshkadé in Yazd. The return trip, by a difficult stretch of road off the main route to Tabas, will cost around 10,000 to 12,000 rials by hired taxi. There are some other interesting Zoroastrian sites and villages in the countryside around Yazd.

Semnān Province

استان سمنان

Population: 418,200
Area: 90,958 sq km

This large province forms part of the commercially vital link between the central plateau and Khorāsān, thence to Central Asia. It is rendered almost entirely uninhabitable by the encroaching Dasht-é Kavīr desert, except for the settlements lying along the Tehrān to Mashhad road, to the south of the Alborz Mountains. The province grows the second best pistachios in Iran, after Rafsanjūn. The provincial capital is also called Semnān.

SEMNĀN
سمنان

An ancient town probably dating back to the Sassanian era, Semnān lies on the northern edge of the Dasht-é Kavīr, and owes its origins and mixed fortunes to its place on the historic trading route between Tehrān to Mashhad. The town has been occupied by a long succession of invaders, including the Mongols and the Timurids, who did nothing to enhance it. However, the attractive old part of the city hasn't been modernised much and there are still a few interesting historic buildings.

Orientation
Semnān is a flat and fairly small town, and most points of interest are in or near the central covered bazaar. The main east-west street, Kheyābūn-é Emām, leads on from the Tehrān road and bisects the bazaar, while Kheyābūn-é Ghods to the north joins onto the roads to Tehrān and Mashhad. The train station is 1½ km south-east of Meidūn-é Emām on Kheyābūn-é Emām, accessible by shared taxi.

Information
The ostāndārī is on the east side of Kheyābūn-é Motahharī to the north-west of the bazaar. The shahrdārī is on the east side of Kheyābūn-é Tāleghānī just to the north of the bazaar. The police headquarters (shahrbānī), where you go for a visa extension, is next to the head post and telegraph office.

Tourist Office The tourist office (☎ 4437) is on the north side of Kheyābūn-é 17 Shahrīvar, at the approach to Semnān on the Tehrān road.

Money Bank Melli Iran (central branch) is on the south side of Kheyābūn-é Emām to the east of the bazaar.

Post & Telecommunications The head post and telegraph office is at the intersection of Kheyābūn-é Rajā'ī and Kheyābūn-é Shohadā, opposite the north end of the bazaar. The dialling code for Semnān is 02231.

Masjed-é Jāme'

The present structure of the Masjed-é Jāme' dates from 1424 and has a plain but impressive entrance portal and some interesting stucco around its mehrāb. The Seljuq brick minaret known as the Manār-é Masjed-é Jāme', now freestanding but named for the nearby mosque, is in the bazaar on the south side of Kheyābūn-é Emām. It probably dates from the 11th century, and has a charming octagonal balcony with a Seljuq inscription slightly below it.

Masjed-é Emām Khomeinī

The Masjed-é Emām Khomeinī (formerly Masjed-é Soltānī), 200 metres east of the Masjed-é Jāme', is of considerable interest. Founded under Fath Alī Shāh in the 1820s, this large mosque is one of the best surviving buildings in Iran from this period. It has a very fine tiled mehrāb with stalactites. The high entrance portal is also very attractive; in the same clay colour as the whole of the old city, it has the ribs of its stalactites delicately picked out in contrasting colour, while there are some understated geometric motifs and inscriptions on the facade.

The Ghajar style marks the rather unhappy transition between the golden age of Persian architecture (culminating under the Safavid dynasty), and the creeping introduction of Western-inspired uniformity from the mid-19th century onwards. Now widely regarded as tasteless, flimsy and uninspired, the equivalent of icing-sugar sculptures on a wedding cake, the Ghajar style did nevertheless produce a few fine buildings, including this one and the Kākh-é Eram in Shīrāz. There are almost no structures of great beauty built in Iran after this period.

Other Buildings

There are several emāmzādés (shrines of descendants of emāms) in Semnān, mostly in the south-west of the city, and the covered bazaar is also of some interest.

Places to Stay & Eat

The three-star *Mehmūnsarā-yé Semnān* (☎ 2632) is on Jāddé-yé Mehdīshahr on the north-west outskirts of town. There are a couple of cheaper hotels on Kheyābūn-é Ghods to the south. There are several places to eat along Kheyābūn-é Emām.

Getting There & Away

Semnān is on the railway line between Tehrān and Mashhad, on which there are seven regular and 21 express trains a week. From Semnān to Tehrān it's three hours 45 minutes on the regular train, and three hours five minutes on the express. To Mashhad, via Dāmghān, Shāhrūd and Neishābūr, it's 14 hours 40 minutes regular, and 12 hours 35 minutes express. It is also possible to get here by road from either direction, but the tortuous route across the Dasht-é Kavīr to Nā'īn and Esfahān is not recommended.

DĀMGHĀN   دامغان

This historic town, settled at least since the 8th century, contains what is probably the oldest surviving mosque in Iran. There are also several interesting and very early minarets and tomb-towers here, similar to those built in Māzandarān Province, across the Alborz mountains to the north. About four km to the south-east of Dāmghān you can see the remains of the earlier prehistoric settlement.

Masjed-é Tārīkhūné

Dating from about 760 AD, the Masjed-é Tārīkhūné is on the south side of Kheyābūn-é Shahīd Motahharī, 500 metres to the south-east of the main square, Meidūn-é Emām. It is such an early example that it is almost entirely pre-Islamic Sassanian in appearance, although the plan is Arab. This small four-eivān mosque has an almost square inner courtyard, with three vaulted arcades supported by colossal round brick piers. The only Arab feature is the very slight pointing of the arches that later developed to become such a hallmark of Islamic architecture. Although it has been restored many times, most notably in the early 11th century when the single minaret was added, the original very simple design has been faithfully preserved. The towering 25-metre circular minaret adjoining the mosque is of great interest in its own right, and shows very skilful use of brickwork relief.

Manār-e Masjed-e Jāme'
The only remaining feature of a long-vanished mosque, this Seljuq minaret is one of the earliest examples of its kind, probably dating from the mid-11th century, and is notable for its vivid use of raised brickwork. To get there, turn left outside the Masjed-é Tārīkhūné and walk straight ahead for 300 metres, cross the road and turn into Kūché-yé Masjed.

Ārāmgāh-é Pīr Alamdār
This round tomb-tower, 100 metres north of the Masjed-é Jāme', dates from 1026. It was originally domed, and it is also remarkable for its innovative use of brick patterns, and its inscription, visible beneath the roof level.

Chehel Dokhtar
This slightly later structure, built in 1054-5, has a curious prototype onion dome, and beneath it three bands of brick reliefs and inscriptions that show a slight development from those on the Pīr-é Alamdar. To get to Chehel Dokhtar (the 'Four Daughters'), return to the main square and walk east along Kheyābūn-é Emām, past the bazaar, then turn into a courtyard very near this building.

Places to Stay
The central three-star *Mehmunsarā-yé Dāmghān* (☎ 2070) is set in a garden to the west of Bolvār-é Āzādī, which leads north-east from the west end of Kheyābūn-é Emām.

Getting There & Away
Dāmghān is on the rail route between Tehrān and Mashhad, on which there are seven regular and 21 express trains a week. The train station is at the south-east of town, 2½ km from the main square along Bolvār-é Shahīd Motahharī. The Semnān road leads south-west from the main square, and the road to Shāhrūd and Mashhad leads north-east.

SHĀHRŪD شاهرود
Near Shāhrūd, which is of no great interest in itself, you can visit the beautiful 14th-century **Masjed-é Jāme' at Bastām**. This mosque is decorated with some wonderful swirling stucco reliefs, especially in the mehrāb, and belongs to a large monastery complex, the **Sōme'é-yé Bāyazīd**, which has several other interesting Mongol structures, including a delightful circular tomb-tower.

Getting There & Away
There are several buses a day to Mashhad (517 km, 10 hours) and Tehrān (407 km, seven hours, 1200 rials 'lux'). Shāhrūd is also on the rail route between Tehrān and Mashhad, with seven regular and 21 express trains a week. The train station is at the south-east of Shāhrūd. Bastām is eight km from Shāhrūd on the Mashhad road.

This chapter covers Khorāsān, Sīstān va Balūchestān and Kermān, the three largest provinces in Iran, but also some of the most undeveloped.

With the qualified exception of Mashhad, you should not expect the highest standards of accommodation, restaurants or communications in this part of Iran. The east and south-east are very different from central Iran, less developed certainly but also steeped in archaeological and historical interest. If you have just arrived from the Indian subcontinent, east Iran will be a gentle introduction to Iranian culture; but if all your travelling has been spent in the rest of Iran, prepare yourself for something rather different.

The perennial excitements across the border in Afghanistan and the importance of the frontier provinces in the traditional Asian smuggling and trading routes do permeate the region and create a certain amount of tension in many places, only heightened by the legendary vigilance in these parts of the Islamic Revolutionary Guards, but by and large Westerners are treated with respect and often great generosity. There are some restrictions on travelling unannounced in the border zones and foreigners should exercise every caution about visiting areas off the tourist itinerary. The Iranian authorities have for some time been very concerned about drug trafficking and have few qualms in detaining suspects with or without evidence. In this part of Iran, especially in Sīstān va Balūchestān, the Komīté has become almost autonomous in dealing with offenders. It also has little concern for international human rights in its treatment of critics of the government or anyone perceived as a threat.

Throughout this part of Iran, look for *bādgīrs*, the wind towers designed to catch and circulate the merest breath of wind. In many places they are an essential architectural adaptation to the harsh and arid climate.

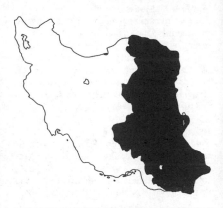

Khorāsān Province
استان خراسان

This immense province in the far north-east of Iran takes in the corridor between the Caspian Sea and the salt wastes of the Dasht-é Kavīr. This has been the funnel through which armies have passed from time immemorial. It is still remote and sparsely populated: at 313,340 sq km it is larger than the British Isles and by far the largest province in Iran, but the population is only 5.3 million. Mashhad, its capital, is famous as a centre for Shi'ite pilgrimage.

Although much of Khorāsān is mountainous, there are many fertile valleys, and the province produces large quantities of fruit, nuts, sugar-beet and cotton. Until fairly recently opium was also an important crop.

MASHHAD مشهد
Population: 1.5 million
This city in the far north-east of Iran used to be known for three things: religion, commerce and tourism. Now that transit trade with the former USSR and Afghanistan has

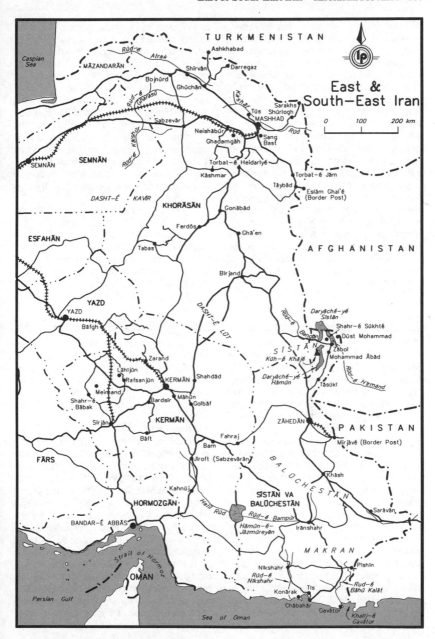

all but dried up, and tourism has collapsed, the one thing remaining is religion. However, Iran being Iran, this one commodity is more than enough to keep the city going.

Mashhad – or more correctly Mashhad-é Moghaddas (Mashhad the Holy) – literally means 'place of martyrdom' (or 'place of burial of a martyr'), and is sacred to Shi'ites as the place where their eighth emām, Rezā, died in 817. The story spread that Emām Rezā had been poisoned, and his tomb became a major Shi'ite pilgrimage site. What had been a small village by the name of Sanābād grew in time into a large city, the present-day Mashhad, capital of the mighty province of Khorāsān and the most important pilgrimage centre in Iran. In the late-July to mid-June pilgrimage season you're likely to develop an intense feeling of claustrophobia.

It can get very cold in winter and there is often snow on the ground for most of four or five months of the year.

Mashhad is a conservative city with a proud position as a pilgrimage centre, away from the main tourist trail now that the border with Afghanistan is more or less off limits. People may well assume you are a pilgrim even if you aren't, as few tourists now visit Mashhad. Even before the war in Afghanistan all but closed it as the gateway to Herat, the general consensus of travellers was that it was only worth visiting, if at all, for its holy precincts. However, the shrine of Emām Rezā and the surrounding buildings do together comprise one of the marvels of the Islamic world. Under certain constraints it is perfectly possible for even the non-Muslim to visit it; going to Iran and not doing so is a little like going to Italy and missing the Vatican. Little else in the town need detain you long, but a day or two here will not be wasted.

History
Mashhad grew around the legend of Emām Rezā, and the city's history is inextricably linked with that of his shrine. According to popular belief, Rezā, heir to the Abbasid caliphate and eighth of the Shi'ite emāms, died in what was then the village of Sanābād

in 817 after eating some grapes. The story spread, without any apparent evidence, that he had been poisoned on the orders of the Caliph Ma'mūn after having in some way aroused his resentment. Whatever the truth, Ma'mūn buried him in a tower in Sanābād next to the tomb of his own father, the famous Hārūn-ar-Rashīd, and in time this burial place began to attract Shi'ite pilgrims. What had been a small village grew around the shrine into a small town, later known as Mashhad, but for many centuries its development was slow and until much later it remained a pilgrimage centre of only regional importance.

In 944 the shrine was destroyed by the fervently Sunni Saboktagīn, founder of the Ghaznavid dynasty, only to be rebuilt by his son Mahmūd in 1009, but both it and the city were ransacked when the Mongols invaded in 1220. However, even in the dark years of the Mongol era, Mashhad developed enough to become capital of Khorāsān in the 15th century, in succession to the nearby town of Tūs, and the mausoleum of Emām Rezā was restored in the early 14th century.

In the early 15th century Shāh Rokh, son of Tamerlane, enlarged the shrine, and his extraordinary wife Gōhar Shād commissioned a mosque on the site. Even under this remarkable reign the city was troubled by Uzbek invasions, and the population fell dramatically.

Although it had always attracted pilgrims, Mashhad did not become a pilgrimage centre of the first order until the coming of the Safavid dynasty at the turn of the 16th century. Having established Shi'ism as the state creed, the most brilliant of the early Safavid rulers, Shāh Esma'īl I, Shāh Tahmāsb and Shāh Abbās I, gave the city and shrine the place they have held ever since on the Shi'ite map, frequently making pilgrimages there themselves and generously endowing the sacred complex. At the same time it was thought expedient to discourage the faithful from travelling to the holy sites which had now fallen to the Ottoman Empire, so although the tomb of Emām Rezā has never been the foremost Shi'ite holy site it was put

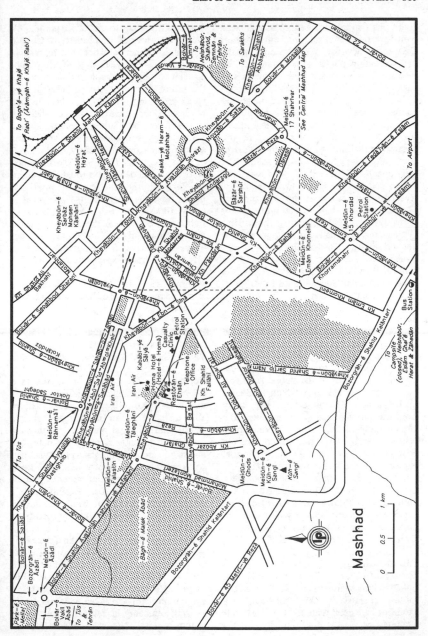

Mashhad

0   0.5   1 km

about that one pilgrimage to Mashhad was worth any number of pilgrimages to Mecca. Despite its new-found importance, Mashhad's location put it at constant risk of invasion, and it was attacked on several occasions in the 16th and 17th centuries by the Uzbeks (although they respected the shrine enough to leave it unscathed), and by the Afghans in 1722. In the early 18th century the shrine was firmly established as the greatest of the Shi'ite pilgrimage centres in Iran, and Nāder Shāh, although a Sunni of missionary zeal, generously endowed the shrine and restored Mashhad to stability. Eventually he was himself buried in the city. Several uprisings here in the 19th century were severely put down by the ruling Ghajars, but Mashhad returned to peace under the reign of Nasr-od-Dīn Shāh; it was modernised under Rezā Shāh, who built the ring road, and under the present regime its continuing importance, at least in religious matters, remains secure.

Orientation

As you might expect, all roads in Mashhad the Holy lead to the Holy Shrine of Emām Rezā. Almost everything of interest is within walking distance of this most unmistakable of landmarks, and all the public transport radiates from the ring road which delineates it, the Falaké-yé Haram-é Motahhar. Away from this physical and spiritual centre, the city is largely flat and characterless and there is little advantage to be gained by risking the near certainty of getting hopelessly lost exploring beyond the recognised sites.

Amazingly enough, Mashhad boasts a Coca Cola St: Kheyābūn-é Kōkā Kōlā in the far north-west of town (off the map) leads up to the city's soft drinks factory, although that great multinational company might not consider the product quite the Real Thing.

Information

The ostāndāri (☎ 42077) is in Kheyābūn-é Bahār and the shahrdāri (☎ 22178) is on the south-west side of Meidūn-é Shohadā. Visa extensions are dealt with at the police headquarters.

Tourist Office The tourist office (☎ 48288), on the 2nd floor of the Ministry of Culture & Islamic Guidance office (not marked in English) in Kūché-yé Eslāmī off Kheyābūn-é Bahār, is a little difficult to find but worth the effort. The staff are enthusiastic and speak good English, although the free map of Mashhad they gave me was not so helpful.

The officer here told me that no special permission was needed to visit any of the archaeological or historical sites in the province, except for the Holy Shrine itself which is strictly forbidden to non-Muslims without special authorisation from the mullahs' public relations department. However it is not at all advisable to try to visit Sarakhs, right on the Soviet border, without a letter of introduction, and there are sure to be other historical places near the border which are off limits without a special permit.

Money The central branch of Bank Melli Iran is on the east side of Kheyābūn-é Emām Khomeinī.

Post & Telecommunications The main post office is on the west side of Kheyābūn-é Emām Khomeinī, opposite Bank Melli Iran.

Consulates The Afghan Consulate (☎ 97551) (Konsūlgarī-yé Afghānestān) is in Kūché-yé Konsūlgarī just west of Kheyābūn-é Shahīd Doktor Bāhonar; it's not very clearly marked. It is possible to apply for permission to enter Afghanistan here, but unless you are applying for a press visa you will probably have a very long wait for a reply by telex from Kabul. Even if you do get a visa, it will almost certainly specify entry by air only and you won't be allowed in at the land border 225 km by road from Mashhad.

The Consulate of Pakistan (☎ 29845) (Konsūlgarī-yé Pākestān) is on the east side of Kheyābūn-é Emām Khomeinī opposite the Bāgh-é Mellī, and is clearly marked in English. Visa applications are accepted, but you will probably be asked why you didn't go to the embassy in Tehrān or your home country.

Travel Agencies There is a sluggish Iran Air-Tours office at the Homa Hotel. Part of the same organisation, the Adibian Travel Agency (☎ 98151-2) is at 56 Kheyābūn-é Pāsdārān; ask for Mr Alī Khatīb, the English-speaking guide. See also the Organised Tours section entry.

Maps The detailed Gītā Shenāsī map of Mashhad (300 rials) has all the main streets marked in English but no translation of any of the entries on the key. The smaller Sahāb map (200 rials) is entirely in Persian and lacks a key. The free map offered by the tourist office is fairly hopeless.

Medical Services For emergencies telephone ☎ 118. There is an emergency clinic on the north side of Kheyābūn-é Feizīyé.

Emergency The police headquarters (☎ 45026) is on the west side of Kheyābūn-é Emām Khomeinī.

Dangers & Annoyances Be especially careful about upsetting Muslim sensibilities in this most important of Iranian pilgrimage sites. Dress must be extremely conservative: no short sleeves for men or women, no bare legs, no loud colours. It is a privilege rather than a right for non-Muslims to visit here. Any incidents involving non-Muslims are likely to make life more difficult for subsequent visitors.

Mashhad used to be a centre of the now outlawed opium trade, and even today the production and sale of various kinds of narcotics still goes on. You may well be offered a joint here, but the penalties for being caught in possession are very severe.

Haram-é Motahhar-é Emām Rezā

حرم مطهر امام رضا

The shrine of Emām Rezā and the surrounding buildings of the *haram-é motahhar* (sacred precincts) comprise one of the marvels of the Islamic world. There is so much to see in such a confined area that it is impossible to take in everything in one visit. As well as the shrine itself, this large circular walled island in

the centre of Mashhad contains two mosques, 12 lofty eivāns (two of them coated entirely with gold), six theological colleges, two main and two lesser courtyards, several libraries, a small post office, two museums, a guesthouse, and many other religious and administrative buildings. Unlike Mecca and Medina in Saudi Arabia, which are completely off limits to non-Muslims, the holy precincts at Mashhad are open to infidels, although only under certain constraints. The shrine itself is strictly closed to non-Muslims (save under exceptional circumstances with the special permission of the religious authorities, applied for through the tourist office), but it is not generally a problem to visit the rest of the complex, so long as you don't try to enter any of the buildings. You will have to dress extremely conservatively and behave yourself impeccably, and you should avoid visiting during large religious gatherings or in the main pilgrimage season (late June to mid July).

Since non-Muslims are almost bound to feel a sense of guilt or embarrassment at visiting this most holy of Shi'ite pilgrimage sites in Iran, it is well worth considering taking a guide (see the Guided Tours entry), and in any case it is best to ask at the tourist office first. Photography is neither forbidden nor actively encouraged.

Much of the history of the shrine is directly linked to the rise of Mashhad. The original tomb chamber of Emām Rezā was built by the Caliph Hārūn-ar-Rashīd in the early 9th century, but later destroyed, restored and destroyed again, and the present structure in the centre of the complex was built by the orders of Shāh Abbās I at the beginning of the 17th century. Since then the collection of buildings has constantly been restored and enlarged, and even today a grandiose building project is underway in the north-west part of the compound. The tomb box is covered with a large gold latticed cage, and this is the object which pilgrims ritually touch or even kiss, often then retreating into a pitch of near frenzy. The mausoleum built over the tomb has a shimmering gilded cupola and single minaret and

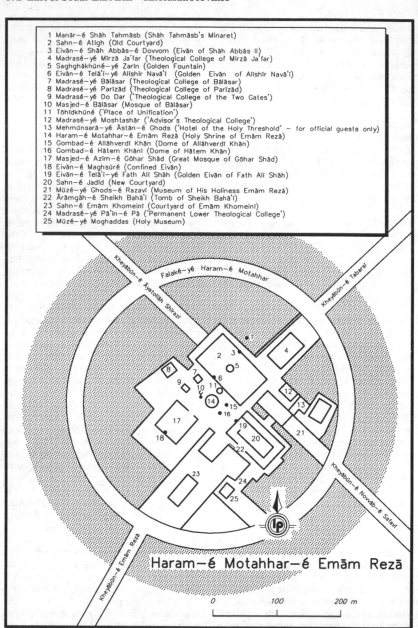

1 Manār—é Shāh Tahmāsb (Shāh Tahmāsb's Minaret)
2 Sahn—é Atīgh (Old Courtyard)
3 Eivān—é Shāh Abbās—é Dovvom (Eivān of Shāh Abbās II)
4 Madrasé—yé Mīrzā Ja'far (Theological College of Mīrzā Ja'far)
5 Saghghākhūné—yé Zarīn (Golden Fountain)
6 Eivān—é Telā'ī—yé Alīshīr Navā'ī (Golden Eivān of Alīshīr Navā'ī)
7 Madrasé—yé Bālāsar (Theological College of Bālāsar)
8 Madrasé—yé Parīzād (Theological College of Parīzād)
9 Madrasé—yé Do Dar ('Theological College of the Two Gates')
10 Masjed—é Bālāsar (Mosque of Bālāsar)
11 Tōhīdkhūné ('Place of Unification')
12 Madrasé—yé Moshtashār ('Advisor's Theological College')
13 Mehmūnsarā—yé Āstān—é Ghods ('Hotel of the Holy Threshold' – for official guests only)
14 Haram—é Motahhar—é Emām Rezā (Holy Shrine of Emām Rezā)
15 Gombad—é Allāhverdī Khān (Dome of Allāhverdī Khān)
16 Gombad—é Hātem Khānī (Dome of Hātem Khān)
17 Masjed—é Azīm—é Gōhar Shād (Great Mosque of Gōhar Shād)
18 Eivān—é Maghsūré (Confined Eivān)
19 Eivān—é Telā'ī—yé Fath Alī Shāh (Golden Eivān of Fath Alī Shāh)
20 Sahn—é Jadīd (New Courtyard)
21 Mūzé—yé Ghods—é Razavī (Museum of His Holiness Emām Rezā)
22 Ārāmgāh—é Sheikh Bahā'ī (Tomb of Sheikh Bahā'ī)
23 Sahn—é Emām Khomeinī (Courtyard of Emām Khomeinī)
24 Madrasé—yé Pā'īn—é Pā ('Permanent Lower Theological College')
25 Mūzé—yé Moghaddas (Holy Museum)

Kheyābūn—é Āyatollāh Shīrāzī

Falaké—yé Haram—é Motahhar

Kheyābūn—é Tabarsī

Kheyābūn—é Navvāb—é Safavī

Kheyābūn—é Emām Rezā

Haram—é Motahhar—é Emām Rezā

0   100   200 m

a vast tiled eivān. Do not enter unless you are a Muslim.

Architecturally perhaps even more impressive than the mausoleum itself is the **Masjed-é Azīm-é Gōhar Shād** or Grand Mosque of Gōhar Shād with its 50 metre high blue faience dome and cavernous golden portal. Queen of a mighty empire, wife of Tamerlane's eldest son Shāh Rokh, patron of the arts and powerful personality in her own right, Gōhar Shād was one of the most remarkable women of Islamic history. Although most of her major architectural commissions were at her capital Herat, this mosque in Mashhad is the best preserved testament to her genius. Constructed between 1405 and 1418, this stately mosque with its four eivāns and two minarets is remarkable in every aspect of its construction and decoration, and vast sums have been spent on its maintenance.

There are two museums attached to the holy precincts, both of them open to non-Muslims. Each displays a collection of precious articles donated by pilgrims to the shrine since the time of Emām Rezā. The larger **Mūzé-yé Moghaddas** or Holy Museum inside the precincts was closed for renovations at the time of writing, but among many other items it used to have a 16th century gold bas-relief door originally belonging to the mausoleum and, a recent addition, the **Carpet of the Seven Beloved Cities**, which is said to have taken 10,000 weavers 14 years to make and has 30 million knots. The museum used to be open from 8 am to 2 pm every day.

The smaller museum, the **Mūzé-yé Ghods-é Razavī** or Holy Rezā Museum, is approached from the Falaké-yé Haram-é Motahhar surrounding the shrine complex. You will have to take off your shoes and surrender your camera on entering. The ground floor has a display of carpets, many of them woven in Khorāsān, examples of calligraphy in Arabic and Persian and a collection of valuable donations by pilgrims, including a Qoran bound and cased in mother-of-pearl from Yasser Arafat. Now that the PLO leader is *persona non grata* in

Iran, the name of the donor is missing. Presidents Saddam Hussein of Iraq and Hafez al-Assad of Syria have also made their contribution; a chandelier each, both now hanging inside the shrine. The first floor houses a collection of over 100 hand-inscribed Qorans which is said to be the largest on public display in Iran. On the wall look out for one page of a Qoran said to be in the hand of Shāh Rokh. This museum is open daily except public holidays from 8 am to 2 pm, and entry is 50 rials.

Guided Tours I would strongly recommend that you consider taking a guide on any visit to the holy precincts. Not only is it difficult to get adequate information about the buildings in English, but most infidels will feel distinctly uncomfortable wandering through this most holy of Iranian religious sites unaccompanied, and as a result may rush through it without more than the briefest of glimpses at what it has to offer. See the Organised Tours entry for more details.

Bazaars

Around the shrine there are three bazaars, none of them of any overwhelming interest. The biggest, the **Bāzār-é Bozorg**, has the usual tacky merchandise and a few shops on the 1st floor selling Mashhad turquoises, and is open from 8 am to 8 pm, Saturday to Thursday. There are a few stalls in the bazaars selling handicrafts, but little if anything on offer warrants a ready wallet. The remains of several old caravanserais, now put to other purposes, can be seen. See also the Things to Buy entry.

Masjed-é 72 Tan Shahīd

مسجد ۷۲ تن شهید

In the Bāzār-é Bozorg, about 150 metres from the street, only the facade of the Mosque of the 72 Martyrs (previously the Masjed-é Shāh) can be seen . The blue dome of this 15th-century mosque can be seen from the Falaké-yé Haram-é Motahhar. The building behind the facade is now occupied by Sepah-é Pāsdārān and it is not possible to go behind the barbed wire fence protecting it. The mosque lacks a number of tiles at the base of the dome and the facade, and is in rather a sorry condition.

Gombad-é Sabz کنبد سبز

The Green Dome in the centre of its own small square – the Falaké-yé Gombad-é Sabz – on Kheyābūn-é Shahīd Doktor Bāhonar is probably the most interesting and best preserved historical building in Mashhad outside the Holy Shrine. A small quadrangular mausoleum used by Naghshbandī dervishes, and originally built in the Safavid era, but later partly rebuilt, it is in good condition except for a missing patch of tiles at the base of its green dome. The *gombad* (dome) is almost permanently closed, but inside it is the tomb of Sheikh Mohammad Hakīm Mo'men, author of a famous book on medicine.

Bogh'é-yé Khājé Rabī' بقعه خواجه ربیع

This fine octagonal 16th-century mausoleum, four km north of central Mashhad and now standing in the centre of a large four-walled martyrs' cemetery known as the Ārāmgāh-é Khājé Rabī', is worth a visit for its famous 16th-century inscriptions by Alī Rezā Abbāsī, one of the greatest Persian calligraphers. The cemetery was originally a park, and now the single monument to Khājé Rabī' seems a little extravagant in the midst of so many much simpler memorials. To get there take a No 30 bus from the north-west part of the Falaké-yé Haram-é Motahhar and get off at the last stop about 200 metres from the Ārāmgāh, which is probably where most of the other passengers are going too.

Ārāmgāh-é Nāder Shāh آرامگاه نادر شاه

This hideous concrete building, housing the tomb of Nāder Shāh and topped with his statue, is in Kheyābūn-é Āzādī in a small park on the north side of Chahārrāh-é Shohadā at the intersection of Kheyābūn-é Āzādī and Kheyābūn-é Āyatollāh Shīrāzī. It's open daily from 7.30 am to 12.30 pm and from 2 to 4.30 pm. The Nāder museum has a room containing a collection of guns, swords and other militaria, mostly from the

time of Nāder Shāh. The museum entrance is to the left of the building as you enter (tickets 20 rials). A smaller room to the right contains various prehistoric domestic implements from the Khorāsān region. Outside the museum building is a solitary bronze Spanish cannon, dated 1591 and later inscribed in Persian with the Persian date 1180. How it came to be here is a mystery.

Road to Neishābūr

There are several historical buildings on or near the road between Mashhad and Neishābūr, including the ruined 15th-century **Mosallā-yé Torāgh** (14 km from Mashhad) and the Ghaznavid minaret and gombad at **Sang Bast** (37 km).

Organised Tours

The Adibian Travel & Tour Company (☎ 91151) at 56 Kheyābūn-é Pāsdārān arranges private guided tours of the Holy Shrine with an English-speaking guide at 12,100 rials for one person, 7200 rials each for two, or 4800 rials each for three. Tours to Neishābūr leave at 9 am and return at 3 pm, and cost 31,000 rials for one person, 16,000 rials each for two and 11,000 rials each for three; there are also occasional coach tours for groups of 20 or more, for which the charge is 4000 rials per person.

If you want to arrange a private tour anywhere – not necessarily in Mashhad – there is a knowledgeable guide at the agency, Mr Alī Khatīb, who speaks excellent English. If you are apprehensive about visiting the Shrine of Emām Rezā on your own or want to visit Sarakhs, it is well worth considering taking him as your guide. However, if you are booking a tour of Mashhad from inside or outside the city, be very careful about making any payment before having all the details in writing, as confusion about prices and payment can arise easily.

Places to Stay

Nearly all the hotels are within a few minutes' walk of the Haram-é Motahhar-é Emām Rezā. Prices are relatively high, but so is the demand for rooms in this most important of

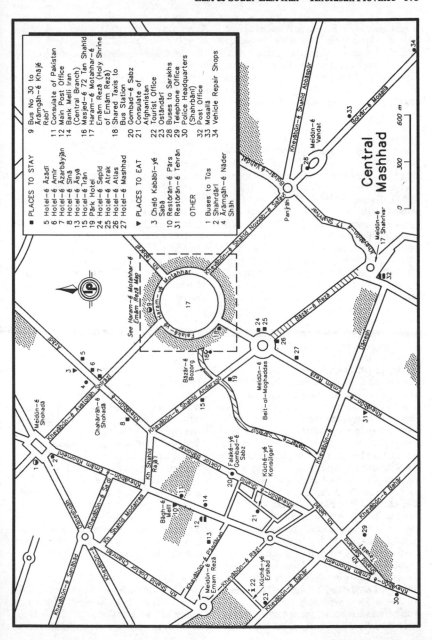

PLACES TO STAY

5 Hotel-é Āzādī
6 Hotel-é Amīr
7 Hotel-é Āzarbāyjān
8 Hotel-é Sīnā
13 Hotel-é Āsyā
15 Hotel-é Īrān
19 Park Hotel
24 Hotel-é Sepīd
26 Hotel-é Atrak
26 Hotel-é Atlas
27 Hotel-é Mashhad

PLACES TO EAT

3 Chelō Kabābī-yé Sabā
10 Restorān-é Pārs
31 Restorān-é Tehrān

OTHER

1 Buses to Tūs
2 Shahrdārī
4 Ārāmgāh-é Nāder Shāh
9 Bus No 30 to Ārāmgāh-é Khājé Rabī'
11 Consulate of Pakistan
12 Main Post Office
14 Bank Melli Iran (Central Branch)
16 Masjed-é 72 Tan Shahīd
17 Haram-é Motahhar-é Emām Rezā (Holy Shrine of Emām Rezā)
18 Shared Taxis to Bus Station
20 Gombad-é Sabz
21 Consulate of Afghanistan
22 Tourist Office
23 Ostāndārī
28 Buses to Sarakhs
29 Telephone Office
30 Police Headquarters (Shahrbānī)
32 Post Office
33 Mosallā
34 Vehicle Repair Shops

Central Mashhad

Iranian holy sites. For several weeks before and after the Iranian New Year (about 21 March) and again during the late June to mid-July pilgrimage season, finding a room anywhere can be a real problem, and enough of a trial to make you identify with the origins of the name Mashhad – place of martyrdom.

Places to Stay – bottom end

There are plenty of inexpensive places to stay close to the Holy Shrine itself. Acceptable hotels in the area in the lowest price bracket include the *Hotel-é Sīnā* (☎ 51361) in Kheyābūn-é Āzādī at 1800/2700 rials a single/double with private bathroom, the *Hotel-é Āzarbāyjān* (☎ 54002) on Chahārrah-é Shohadā at 1800/2700 rials, and the good *Hotel-é Mashhad* (☎ 22666) in Kheyābūn-é Emām Rezā, which charges 2000/3000 rials a single/double with private bathroom. There are literally dozens of other places within a few minutes' walk of the shrine – especially to the south and east – but the ones listed here are some of the most likely to accept Westerners. Although there are plenty of mosāferkhūnés around the shrine to cater for the throngs of pilgrims, getting into one as a non-Muslim is a mammoth exercise in persistence and probably more trouble than it's worth.

Places to Stay – middle

A small step up in quality if not in price takes you to the *Hotel-é Sepīd* (☎ 29053) on the east side of Meidūn-é Beit-ol-Moghaddas, at 2000/3000 rials. Slightly bigger steps up lead you first to the *Pārk Hotel* (☎ 26821) by the entrance to the Bāzār-é Sarshūr in Kheyābūn-é Shahīd Andarzgū, which charges 2400/3200 rials, and then to the *Hotel-é Amīr* (☎ 21301) on Kheyābūn-é Āzādī at 2800/ 4200 rials.

More expensive places within a few minutes' walk of the sacred precincts include the excellent *Hotel-é Īrān* (☎ 28020) in Kheyābūn-é Andarzgū, which is very reasonable at 3800/5700 rials a single/double with private bathroom, the not overwhelmingly friendly *Hotel-é Āzādī* (☎ 51927) in

Kheyābūn-é Āzādī and the more welcoming *Hotel-é Atlas* (☎ 45022) on the south side of Meidūn-é Beit-ol-Moghaddas, both at 3200/ 4800 rials.

Probably the best hotel in this category, and less noisy than many, is the comfortable *Hotel-é Āsyā* (☎ 20074) on Kheyābūn-é Pāsdārān, which charges 4400/6600 rials. The *Hotel-é Jam* (☎ 90045) on the same street charges 4000/6000 rials.

Places to Stay – top end

The *Atrak Hotel* (☎ 22044) on the east of Meidūn-é Beit-ol-Moghaddas does a good job for the price at 4800/7200 rials. However the uncompromising seeker after luxury will not hesitate to go straight to the *Homa Hotel* (☎ 32001) (in Persian, Hotel-é Homā), set in splendid isolation from all the other hotels in Mashhad within its own grounds north of Meidūn-é Tāleghānī. Prices start at 14,200 rials for a twin or double. Before the revolution this was one of the very few places in religiously conservative Mashhad licensed to serve alcohol.

The Homa may start to charge foreigners in dollars without warning.

Places to Eat – bottom end

Ābgūsht is fairly popular and especially cheap in Mashhad. One good place for it is the *Restōrān-é Tehrān* opposite the Hotel-é Tehrān in Kheyābūn-é Emām Khomeinī, charging only 700 rials. The *Kabābī-yé Sālyā* on Kheyābūn-é Ebn-é Sīnā serves excellent fīllé kabāb for 1100 rials, and there is a good self-service restaurant, the *Restōrān-é Pārs*, at 451 Kheyābūn-é Emām Khomeinī, with chelō kabāb from 1200 rials.

There are plenty of cheap eating-houses around the Holy Shrine – kabābīs, sandwich bars and places specialising in ābgūsht – which may appeal to the more adventurous. None of them is really used to Westerners.

Places to Eat – middle

The *Chelō Kabābī-yé Sabā* (marked in English 'Saba Chelo Kebabi') at the first turning to the north-east of the hideous Nāder statue is average, serving chelō kabāb-é makhsūs at 1600 rials. The subterranean *Chelō Kabābī-yé Ehsān* in Kheyābūn-é Feizīyé, opposite the entrance to the Homa Hotel, is excellent and serves good chelō morgh for 1200 rials.

Places to Eat – top end

The restaurant at the *Homa Hotel* has quite a few not particularly expensive dishes on the menu (spaghetti 1200 rials, beef stew 1500 rials, chicken schnitzel 2000 rials, filet steak 2400 rials; also hamburgers, eggburgers and cheeseburgers), although it also caters for those used to dining à la carte.

Things to Buy

It is best not to buy turquoises in Mashhad unless you have a clear idea of their international market value and can recognise a fake. In the boom days of tourism in the '70s, visitors to Mashhad would inevitably get a very convincing sales pitch about how much more they were worth outside Iran. Needless to say, they weren't, and they still aren't. Since Mashhad has for some years been generally off the tourist trail, the turquoise racketeers in the bazaar must be having a hard time. Not much has changed over the last century since Curzon wrote:

It would be quite a mistake to suppose that by going either to Meshed or to Nishapur, or even to the pit mouth [of the turquoise mine], the traveller can pick up valuable stones at a moderate price. Fraser tried several years ago, and was obliged to desist from the attempt by the ruthless efforts made to cheat him. Every succeeding traveller has tried and has reported his failure. All the best stones are bought up at once by commission agents on the spot and are despatched to Europe or sold to Persian grandees. I did not see a single good specimen either in Meshed or Teheran, though I made constant inquiries...

G N Curzon,
Persia and the Persian Question

If you do want to go in for a bit of honest speculation – Iranians do it all the time – probably the most profitable investment you can make is to buy sealed and clearly identifiable containers of saffron. The spice is commonplace in Iran and there's a lot of it available cheaply in Mashhad, but it's in-

credibly expensive in the West. Unlike many other exportable goods, there aren't any specific restrictions on taking saffron out of the country. Of course you would have to know someone who wanted to buy it at the other end.

Getting There & Away

The road between Mashhad and Gorgān is difficult in winter because of frequent snowfalls and ice. My journey took 11½ hours. It is, however, a spectacular drive, passing through and beside the forest of Māzandarān.

To/From Turkmenistan Despite what the maps may indicate, there is no legal crossing point into Turkmenistan from north-east Iran; the nearest routes into the former USSR are through Āstārā and Jolfā.

To/From Afghanistan The nearest border crossing is at Eslām Ghal'é, 245 km east of Mashhad (see the Tāybād entry in this chapter).

Air Iran Air flies from Mashhad to:

Bandar-é Abbās – Sunday and Thursday, 4.25 pm, 1¾ hours
Būshehr – Wednesday and Saturday, 4.25 pm, 1¾ hours
Esfahān – Sunday, Tuesday, Thursday and Friday, 7.10 pm, 1¼ hours
Kermān – Sunday and Thursday, 9.55 am, 1¼ hours
Rasht – Sunday and Thursday, 11 am, 1½ hours
Shīrāz – Monday, Wednesday and Saturday, 9.10 pm, 1½ hours
Tabrīz – Monday and Friday, 4.25 pm, two hours
Tehrān – Thursday at 12.25 pm, daily except Tuesday at 1.50 pm, daily at 5.40 pm, Monday and Tuesday at 6.20 pm, daily at 8.35 pm, daily except Tuesday at 9.30 pm and daily at 11.45 pm; all 1½ hours, 8010 rials
Yazd – Monday and Friday, 9.55 am, 1¼ hours
Zāhedān – Wednesday and Saturday, 9.55 am, 1½ hours

There is also an Iran Air service to Sharjah in the UAE once a week; foreigners must pay in hard currency for tickets on this flight. PIA has recently introduced a weekly service to and from Quetta in Pakistan: enquire locally for details.

Airline Offices The main Iran Air office
(☎ 30030) is on the south side of Kheyābūn-
é Sanābād. There is also a small and sluggish
branch in the Homa Hotel.

Bus & Minibus The bus station has moved
to a new site on the Bozorgrāh-é Shahīd
Kalāntarī at the far south of Mashhad. It
gives the outward impression of order, with
all the bus company offices arranged around
one courtyard and numbered bays, but the
inner reality is of chaos. It is even more
difficult here to gain information about bus
services and timetables than in most cities,
and people at the offices cannot understand
why anyone should want to know when a bus
leaves for a certain place without actually
wanting to buy a ticket on it at the same time.
Outside the company offices there is usually
someone shouting out the names of destinations for which tickets are immediately
available.

There are buses to most major cities,
although if you're going any further than
Tehrān or Zāhedān you'll probably wish
you'd flown or taken a train by the time you
get there. The one important place without a
direct service is Shīrāz. Destinations include:

Ahvāz – several a week, 1805 km, 30 hours,
    2500/3000 rials, Cooperative Bus Company No
    2
Arāk – several a week, 1212 km, 20 hours
Bākhtarān – at least one a day, 1449 km, 23 hours
Bandar-é Abbās – one a day, 1417 km, 22 hours
Bandar-é Anzalī – several a week, 1116 km, 18 hours
Bandar-é Lengé – one a day, 1662 km, 25 hours, 2000
    rials
Bīrjand – several a day, 514 km, 10 hours
Chālūs – several a week, 877 km, 14 hours
Esfahān – several a day, 1338 km, 22 hours, 2020 rials
    'super', Cooperative Bus Company No 1
Ghom – at least one a day, 1048 km, 17 hours)
Gombad-é Kāvūs – one a day, 471 km, eight hours
Gonābād – several a day, 294 km, six hours
Gorgān – two a day, 564 km, nine hours, 650 rials
    'lux', Cooperative Bus Company No 11; see also
    Gorgān entry
Kermān – at least one a day, 919 km, 15 hours
Lāhījūn – several a week, 1032 km, 17 hours
Neishābūr – several each morning from about 7.30

am, 114 km, 2½ hours, 230 rials 'lux', Cooper-
    ative Bus Company No 4
Rasht – at least one a day, 1075 km, 18 hours
Sārī – at least one a day, 695 km, 12 hours
Shāhrūd – several a day, 517 km, 10 hours
Tabrīz – at least one a day, 1548 km, 25 hours, 3430
    rials 'super'
Tāybād – each morning, about hourly from about 5.30
    am, 224 km, three hours, 300 rials 'lux', Coop-
    erative Bus Company No 16; see the Tāybād
    section for details
Tehrān – several a day, 924 km, 14 hours, 1280 rials
    'super'
Torbat-é Heidarīyé – 160 km, three hours
Torbat-é Jām – several a day, 162 km, 2½ hours
Yazd – two a day, 1306 km, 21 hours, 1600 rials 'lux',
    Cooperative Bus Company No 12
Zābol – one a day, 1149 km, 14 hours, 1320 rials,
    Cooperative Bus Company No 2
Zāhedān – at least two a day, 1001 km, 12 hours,
    1335/1880 rials 'lux'/'super', Cooperative Bus
    Company No 13.

If you are heading for Zābol (not a very wise
destination) or Zāhedān, you can expect a
higher than average number of tedious
checkpoints on the way.

Minibuses to Tūs (24 km, 30 minutes)
leave from Meidūn-é Shohadā, and buses to
Sarakhs (185 km, three hours) leave from
Meidūn-é Vahdat on Kheyābūn-é Mosallā.

Train There are four regular trains and one
express daily to Tehrān, stopping at Neishābūr, Shāhrūd and Semnān. There has been
talk of linking up with the Turkmenistan
railway system, at its closest point little more
than 100 km from Mashhad.

Getting Around
To/From the Airport Taxis are quite cheap
in Mashhad and you should be able to take a
taxi from the airport into town for not more
than 700 to 1000 rials as a single passenger.
The Adibian Travel & Tour Company
(☎ 91151) can organise airport transfers at
4500 rials for one, 2300 rials each for two
and 1600 rials each for three.

Bus Since most of the hotels are within easy
walking distance of the Shrine of Emām Rezā,
the Gombad-é Sabz and most of the main
offices, buses will not be much of an issue.

However there are several bus stops around Falaké-yé Haram-é Motahhar with the routes listed for each bus in Persian. If you hold up a map and look lost, someone will probably guide you to the right one.

No 3 or No 9 bus will take you between the bus station and Falaké-yé Haram-é Motahhar, but most people do not bother waiting and instead take a shared taxi for 100 rials. Alternatively you can take a taxi directly to any hotel in Mashhad for not more than 500 rials as a single passenger.

Taxi Taxi fares in Mashhad are low. Even the taxi service at the Homa Hotel charges only 1000 rials an hour within city limits and 1500 rials outside.

There are plenty of shared taxis passing by the train station; you should be able to get one from there into town for around 200 rials, or back again from Kheyābūn-é Tabarsī for 50 to 100 rials.

TŪS طوس

Sacked in 1389 and abandoned in the 15th century, Tūs was the regional capital before Mashhad. Parts of the walls of the citadel of the great city remain, but the present-day village is best known to most Iranians as the home town of the epic poet Ferdōsī, whose mausoleum lies here over what is believed to be his exact place of death.

Ārāmgāh-é Ferdōsī

Set in its own garden and dominating the village of Tūs, the pale stone mausoleum of Ferdōsī was built in 1933 in preparation for the celebration of the 1000th anniversary of the poet's death a year later, but rebuilt in 1934 because the first version was thought too plain. In *The Road to Oxiana*, Robert Byron wrote of the beauty of the original, and of returning to show it to a companion:

I was saying to Christopher that...he ought to see the Firdaussi memorial, because it proved that a breath of architectural taste still lingered in modern Persia. The words froze on my lips: a crowd of workmen were busy demolishing it. Iron railings hid the pool. Municipal flower-beds lay ready for cannas and begonias. And at the end, instead of the pleasant unostentatious pyramid I admired in November, rose half-built copies of the bull's-head columns at Persepolis.

There is a small museum in the grounds (entry 20 rials), which has a bookstand with some offerings in English not easily available elsewhere.

Bogh'é-yé Hārūnīyé

This large, crumbling, quadrangular domed mausoleum, about a km south of the present village on the Mashhad road, is the only remaining structure of the original city of Tūs. Although popularly associated by the locals with Hārūn-ar-Rashīd (whose remains are generally accepted to have been buried near those of Emām Rezā at Mashhad) no-one knows for whom it was built or at which date, and there are no clues inside or out.

Getting There & Away

Tūs is 23 km from Mashhad on a turning east off the road to Gorgān. Minibuses to Tūs (20 minutes, 100 rials) leave about hourly from Chahārrāh-é Shohadā in Mashhad, and make the return journey until about 5 pm. See also the Organised Tours entry under Mashhad.

NEISHĀBŪR نیشابور

The earliest recorded capital of Khorāsān, and at one time a thriving literary, artistic and academic centre, Neishābūr (better known in English as Nishapur) is famous as the home town of Omar Khayyām. The town fell into terminal decline in the 12th century and is no longer an inspiring place; very little of interest remains of the ancient city. Apart from Omar Khayyām's, there are two other tombs of famous men here, but neither of them is particularly attractive; it's a long drive from Mashhad, and for many it will be a disappointing one.

Ārāmgāh-é Omar Khayyām آرامگاه عمر خیام

The tomb of Omar Khayyām lies about a km south of the town, isolated in a sea of concrete. The very simple tombstone sits in uneasy contrast with the questionable modern structure towering above it, formed of several very tall and narrow tiled concrete lozenges linked at the edges and redeemed only by inscriptions from the works of the great man. In the 19th century the translator Edward Fitzgerald brought Omar Khayyām's quatrains to the attention of the West, and as a result he is probably the best known Persian poet outside Iran. In his native country, however, he's esteemed more for his abilities as a mathemetician and astronomer.

Bāgh-é Mahrūgh

Omar Khayyām is not the only famous son of Neishābūr: near his tomb, in a beautiful and historic garden, the Bāgh-é Mahrūgh, there are also monuments to the great 12th to 13th-century mystic poet Attār-od-Dīn and to the 20th-century poet Kamal-ol-Molk. Both monuments are modern but on a more human scale than Khayyām's. In the same grounds is the **Emāmzādé-yé Mohammad Mahrūgh**, a fine 16th-century domed mausoleum.

Bogh'é-yé Ghadamgāh   بقعه قدمگاه

This charming octagonal mausoleum, set in a small walled water-garden, is on the Mashhad road, 26 km from Neishābūr in the village of Ghadamgāh, the 'Place of the Foot', so named because inside the mausoleum there is a stone slab with what are believed to be the (very large) footprints of Emām Rezā, who stopped here on his way to Tūs. This 17th-century monument, which can hardly accommodate more than half a dozen pilgrims at a time, also has some fine inscriptions and stalactite mouldings. It is no problem for non-Muslims to visit or to photograph inside.

Places to Stay

The primitive *Mosāferkhūné-yé Rezā* (not marked in English) is in the centre of Neishābūr, and the slightly better *Mehmūnsarā-yé Neishābūr* is at the west of town. Stay in Mashhad.

Getting There & Away

Cooperative Bus Company No 4 in the main street has several buses a day to Mashhad

(114 km, 2½ hours, 230 rials 'lux'). It is possible to stop off at Ghadamgāh on the way, or to get there by shared taxi and continue by bus. For a whole-day round trip to Neishābūr from Mashhad the charge by private taxi is around 12,000 rials for one person. If you want to go at 6 am and return by noon, the charge is more like 10,000 rials. Alternatively you can hire a private taxi for 800 to 1500 rials an hour. For details of tours see the Organised Tours entry under Mashhad.

REBĀT-É SHARAF   رباط شرف

There is a very impressive 12th-century Seljuq *rebāt* (caravanserai) on the track leading south-east from the village of Shūrlūkh, 60 km before Sarakhs on the main road from Mashhad to Chakūdar; on a grander scale than the usual caravan station, this may once have been a palace complex including two mosques. You will need to ask at the shahrdārī in Sarakhs or at the ostāndārī in Mashhad to visit this one, as it lies in a sensitive military area. There are several other Seljuq and earlier remains off the Mashhad to Sarakhs road, but you will need a good guide and 4WD to visit them.

SARAKHS   سرخس

The town of Sarakhs, 178 km east-north-east of Mashhad by road, is right on the Turkmenistan border, although there is no legal crossing-point. Of course the border was not always drawn here and Sarakhs was once an important caravan station. You will need permission in writing to visit Sarakhs or even to get very far along the road to it, and this can be obtained from the public security department of the ostāndārī in Mashhad. The tourist office may be able to help, but don't believe them if they say that you don't need permission.

Gombad-é Sheikh Loghmān Bābā

Sheikh Loghmān Bābā was a famous 10th-century teller of fables, and this vast domed monument on the outskirts of Sarakhs was constructed as his mausoleum in the 14th century. One writer describes this as among the most remarkable historic buildings in

Iran, while another passes it over as merely 'interesting', but anyone who visits is unlikely to regret the slight difficulty involved in reaching it. For its scale and for the quality of its interior and exterior decorations in brick and plaster, what remains of this mausoleum makes it one of the most impressive surviving structures of its period in Iran.

Getting There & Away

Buses from Mashhad to Sarakhs (three hours) leave from Meidūn-é Vahdat on Kheyābūn-é Mosallā; but much the best way to get here is with a guide (who can obtain the necessary permit on your behalf and help you through checkpoints) and a sturdy vehicle (helpful if you want to visit the sites on the way): see the Organised Tours entry under Mashhad. Allow plenty of time to return to Mashhad, as you won't be allowed to stay in Sarakhs overnight.

TABAS   طبس

An oasis poised between the Dasht-é Lūt and the Dasht-é Kavīr, Tabas (earlier known as Golshan) is the only town of any size for hundreds of km in any direction, and since you can only get to it by land, no visitor can fail to appreciate its relationship with the desert environment. Camels are still the most common means of transport along the desert roads out of Tabas, where the few tiny villages, little more than mud hut settlements, are untouched by the 20th century and the terrain is as bleak and inhospitable as anywhere on earth. So when you arrive at the medium-sized town of Tabas with its palm trees, paved roads, bazaar and public gardens, you would be forgiven for thinking you had stepped into a mirage. No-one just passes through Tabas.

Even though a recent earthquake killed 25,000 people and destroyed much of the historical structure of Tabas, the city is still one of the most attractive towns of the desert border, and none of its fertile land is wasted. Dates are the primary crop here. It is easy to understand the Iranian passion for gardens if you visit the **Bāgh-é Golshan** with its lush variety of tropical trees, its pools and cascades, and its utter defiance of the desolate conditions at its edge.

The 11th-century citadel or **Arg-é Tabas** was already in ruins before the earthquake and has crumbled further since, but enough remains to give you a good idea of its

purpose. Unfortunately the **Madrasé-yé Do Manar** with its two Seljuq minarets was completely flattened in the earthquake, but an ancient domed **water reservoir** (*ābambār*) near the citadel still stands.

Places to Stay & Eat
Despite the official tourist office information, there is no guesthouse in Tabas 'offering suitable accommodations of an adequate nature to travellers'. The only place to stay or eat in town is the *Hātem* roadside café and service station in the north of the city, marked only in Persian, which has a few rooms. The restaurant is typical of its kind and the accommodation is very simple: there are only triple rooms at 1500 rials, and washing and lavatory facilities (no shower or bathroom) are shared with hundreds of transit passengers a day and afford few opportunities for personal hygiene. There is a bath-house in town: ask around for directions.

Getting There & Away
Tabas can be reached from Yazd or Mashhad, and all buses between the two cities stop at the Hātem service station. To get out of Tabas in either direction, you can go there and wait (perhaps up to an hour) until a bus passes through, or go to one of the two bus company offices in the centre and buy a ticket on a bus starting from Tabas. Most buses leave in the afternoon.

Buses originating in Tabas run at least daily to Yazd (in the afternoon or evening) (419 km, eight hours) and to Mashhad (521 km, 10 hours), and there is a service to Tehrān (1090 km, 20 hours) perhaps twice or three times a week. There are also buses running to Nā'īn (602 km, 12 hours), where you can probably flag down a bus to Shīrāz, Esfahān or elsewhere. In any direction the road will pass through almost unrelieved desert with practically no facilities of any kind for hundreds of km.

Partly because of a failed US air raid on Tabas shortly after the revolution, people here are sensitive about foreigners, and Westerners arriving in Tabas are likely to be greeted by curious and suspicious Revolutionary Guards, but left alone for the rest of their stay.

Shared Taxi & Savārī There are two telephone taxi companies in town, the Mīlād and the Golshan. As a foreigner you are more likely to strike a good deal with the second. The fare to Yazd (seven hours) for a single passenger is 25,000 or 30,000 rials.

TĀYBĀD   تایباد
Tāybād, 224 km south-east of Mashhad, is the nearest town to the border post with Afghanistan. There is an interesting Timurid mosque, the **Masjed-é Mōlānā**, but otherwise this is not a town you want to go to unless you're heading for Herat.

Getting There & Away
Contact the tourist office in Mashhad before venturing here, whether you want to go to Afghanistan or not.

To/From Afghanistan There is a border post at Eslām Ghal'é, 245 km east of Mashhad. Cooperative Bus Company No 16 at the bus station in Mashhad has buses about hourly every morning to Tāybād (224 km, three hours), the earliest leaving at about 5.30 am. From Tāybād there are minibuses and shared taxis to the border, 11 km (about 20 minutes) away. From the Afghan side of the border there is, according to the consulate in Mashhad, a bus to Herat some 206 km east.

In the unlikely event that you get a visa for Afghanistan that's valid for entry by land, I would strongly recommend that you visit either the Afghan Consulate in Mashhad or the embassy in Tehrān and ask for two letters in Persian – one a safe-conduct pass for you to keep with you on your dangerous journey and the other a letter of introduction to the ostāndārī in Zāhedān or Mashhad stating that you have permission from the Afghan authorities to enter Afghanistan by land from Iran. Zāhedān is better because the border post comes under the responsibility of the governor-general of Sīstān va Balūchestān. Take this letter to the relevant ostāndārī and ask for another letter confirming that you also have this permission from the Iranian authorities. If you have language problems, the tourist offices in Zāhedān or Mashhad should be able to help. The Afghan Consulate in Mashhad should be able to give up-to-date information about transport to and from the border.

If you don't have permission in writing from the Iranian authorities, you will probably encounter problems near or at the border, even though an Iranian visa is supposedly valid for the whole of Iran. If you are planning to cross by an alternative route, you will almost certainly need to have contacts in Mashhad, Zāhedān or Zābol or somewhere else near the border. You will be very likely to attract official suspicion if you try to make these contacts locally. Read Nick Danziger's *Danziger's Travels: Beyond Forbidden Frontiers* before making any moves.

If you are coming into Iran from Afghanistan, head directly to Mashhad or Zāhedān – or better still, further to the west – as quickly as possible, because otherwise you risk attracting unwelcome attention from the authorities.

Sīstān va Balūchestān Province

استان سیستان وبلوچستان

Sīstān va Balūchestān, the second largest province in Iran, with an area of 181,600 sq km and a population of 1.2 million, is also one of the most undeveloped and desolate. This province stretches from the southern border of Khorāsān to the Sea of Oman, bounded to the east by Afghanistan and Pakistan and to the west by the provinces of Kermān and Hormozgān. Sīstān, the northeast pocket of the province jutting into Afghanistan, was once a fertile agricultural area and the seat of many ancient kingdoms, but it is now largely barren and lawless, hampered by swamps and salt lakes and

prone to fierce blizzards which bend every tree permanently southwards. Balūchestān, the main part of the province, is exceptionally arid and inhospitable country supporting little more than bananas, dates and limes for cultivation. Its coastal strip is known as the Makrān.

Although the region of Sīstān especially is rich in ancient and prehistoric sites, this is not a province that attracts many travellers. All that most see is Zāhedān on the way to or from Pakistan, and few people would choose even to go there. The Komīté presence throughout the province is extremely heavy, occasionally even intimidating, few of the recognised sites are straightforward to visit, and facilities are primitive almost everywhere. Guns are openly paraded in the streets in Zābol, and there are motorcycles without any registration plates. Komīté patrols in 4WD vehicles do give a show of force along the border with Afghanistan, but still a lot of trafficking goes on with Afghanistan and Pakistan and people quite openly describe themselves to foreigners as smugglers. However, for the intrepid and adaptable the province does offer some travel experiences not found elsewhere in Iran, and in the south at least the locals, most of them Baluchis, are friendly and relaxed.

Female Westerners, accompanied or not, should stick to the better hotels in the larger towns, as there have been some problems for women travellers here. Unless you speak some Persian and have some understanding of and interest in the local culture, you will probably be much happier avoiding the province altogether or passing through as quickly as possible. I did not regret coming here, but I am not sure that I would have enjoyed it so much if I had just entered Iran for the first time from Pakistan.

Camel Races

Camel races are a traditional Baluchi activity, and their audience has increased in recent years thanks to Iranian TV. There is usually at least one important race meeting held each year in Zāhedān, and there may be other events elsewhere, but it is difficult to get information except locally. The tourist office in Zāhedān may be able to help. In Persian, 'camel race' is *mosābāghé-yé shotor-é davānī.*

ZĀHEDĀN

زاهدان

Population: 282,000

Zāhedān is not inspiring in any way. Its only claim to fame is the fact that it is the nearest town to the only legal crossing point into Pakistan at Mīrjāvé, which lies across the barbed wire from Taftan on the Pakistani side.

There is nothing at all remarkable to see in Zāhedān, but if this is your first stop in Sīstān va Balūchestān you may be interested to have a look at the mud-brick huts with their bādgīrs in the outskirts of the city, especially in the eastern quarter, which are typical of this region. There is a colourful mixture of people living or passing through here, Baluchis, Persians, Afghans, Pakistanis and naturalised Sikhs, but as far as the

locals are concerned no face or costume is as wondrous as a Westerner's, and children will actually turn round and follow you down the street giggling. Despite Zāhedān's proximity to the Afghan border, I found the atmosphere here fairly relaxed and the people friendly, and the streets at night much safer than I had been warned. However I have heard a few bad stories about the place from Iranians and foreigners, all of them involving the Komīté. In a place which is renowned for its trade in narcotics and contraband, it is inevitable that there is a certain amount of tension here (see the Dangers & Annoyances entry).

Orientation

Zāhedān is a flat, dusty and largely featureless town. Although there isn't any obvious centre as such, and the main offices are spread all over the place, most visitors will only worry about getting from the bus terminal to their hotel and back, and that is easily

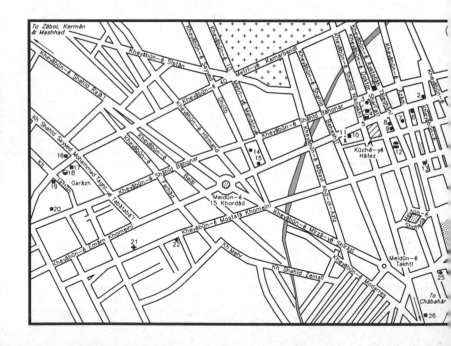

enough done. The airport is on the east edge of town, as is the train station. There are several basic hotels around the bus terminal area in the far west of town, but the better places are in the centre of town.

Zāhedān is divided by the main east-west street Kheyābūn-é Emām Khomeinī and the north-south artery, Kheyābūn-é Shahīd Nīkbakht. Although the whole of Zāhedān might be called one great marketplace with no particular focus, the official bazaar area is at the intersection of the two main streets, and this might be considered the centre of town.

Information

The ostāndārī (☎ 91091) is on Meidūn-é Āzādī, the shahrdārī (☎ 4065) is at the inter-section of Kheyābūn-é Āzādī and Kheyābūn-é Emām Khomeinī, and the pass-port office (*edāré-yé gozarnāmé*) – for visa extensions – is on the south side of Khey-ābūn-é Mostafā Khomeinī.

Tourist Office There is a not particularly helpful tourist office (☎ 20001) (not marked in English) in Kūché-yé Hāfez off Khey-ābūn-é Shahīd Nīkbakht, at which one man speaks some English. Here I was given some dangerously misleading advice about the wisdom of travelling to Zābol, as a result of which I was held prisoner by the Komīté in that town for three nights. Do not believe them if they say that Zābol or anywhere else in the province close to the Afghan border is safe and completely free to visit. Insist on a letter of introduction or else don't go at all.

Money Bank Melli Iran, the only bank in town which deals with foreign currency, is on the west side of Kheyābūn-é Āzādī. There is a small black market for Pakistani and Afghan currency (and even for passports) in the bazaar district.

Post & Telecommunications The main

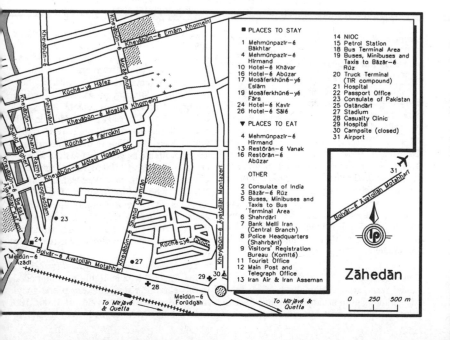

```
■ PLACES TO STAY
 1  Mehmūnpazīr-é
    Bākhtar
 4  Mehmūnpazīr-é
    Hīrmand
10  Hotel-é Khāvar
16  Hotel-é Abūzar
17  Mosāferkhūné-yé
    Eslām
19  Mosāferkhūné-yé
    Fārs
24  Hotel-é Kavīr
26  Hotel-é Sālé

▼ PLACES TO EAT
 4  Mehmūnpazīr-é
    Hīrmand
13  Restōrān-é Vanak
16  Restōrān-é
    Abūzar

OTHER
 2  Consulate of India
 3  Bāzār-é Rūz
 5  Buses, Minibuses and
    Taxis to Bus
    Terminal Area
 6  Shahrdārī
 7  Bank Melli Iran
    (Central Branch)
 8  Police Headquarters
    (Shahrbānī)
 9  Visitors' Registration
    Bureau (Komīté)
11  Tourist Office
12  Main Post and
    Telegraph Office
13  Iran Air & Iran Asseman

14  NIOC
15  Petrol Station
18  Bus Terminal Area
19  Buses, Minibuses and
    Taxis to Bāzār-é
    Rūz
20  Truck Terminal
    (TIR compound)
21  Hospital
22  Passport Office
23  Consulate of Pakistan
25  Ostāndārī
27  Stadium
28  Casualty Clinic
29  Hospital
30  Campsite (closed)
31  Airport
```

Zāhedān

0   250   500 m

post and telegraph office is on the east side of Kheyābūn-é Doktor Sharī'atī. The code for Zāhedān is 0541.

Consulates

The Consulate of Pakistan (☎ 23389) (Konsūlgarī-yé Pākestān) in Kheyābūn-é Shahīd Razmjū Moghaddam, is open from 8 am to 2 pm, Saturday to Thursday. The consul issues visas 'without undue delay'. The cost (in rials) varies according to nationality and type of visa. Take two photos.

The Indian Consulate (☎ 2337) (Konsūlgarī-yé Hendūstān) is on the north side of Kheyābūn-é Emām Khomeinī opposite the intersection with Kheyābūn-é Āyatollāh Kaf'amī.

Maps The free tourist office map of Zāhedān and Sīstān va Balūchestān has place names and most street names in English, but little other useful information in English. The Sahāb map of Zāhedān is the same as the Ministry of Culture & Islamic Guidance one but not as glossy, and costs 400 rials.

Medical Services For emergencies dial ☎ 118 or 4000. The medical emergency centre is a few metres east of the train station on Kheyābūn-é Āyatollāh Motahharī.

Emergency The police headquarters (shahrbānī) are on the west side of Kheyābūn-é Āyatollāh Tāleghānī.

Dangers & Annoyances There is an unofficial curfew in Zāhedān; you don't see many people out on the streets after dark, although you do sometimes hear gunfire.

Do not venture west of Zāhedān unaccompanied or on foot; gun law is in force there and the jagged hills visible from Zāhedān are not known as the 'Black Mountains' for their colour alone.

Camel Races

Camel races are occasionally held at Zāhedān, although not usually more than once a year: ask at the tourist office for details.

Places to Stay

Many travellers have had problems in finding a room in Zāhedān. As all the available beds in town can fill up very quickly, arrive in the morning if possible and try not to look too scruffy. Of course, if you're coming straight from Pakistan, it might be a little difficult to achieve either aim. At Mīrjāvé there seems to be a conspiracy to keep you at the border as long as possible. Make sure you get on the first available transport to Zāhedān. If you get really desperate, the tourist office or the police will probably find a room for you somewhere in town.

All foreign visitors staying overnight in Zāhedān must register with the Komīté, after being accepted at a hotel or mosāferkhūné. If this rule is still in force when you visit, you will be sure to know about it. The registration office, which is open all hours, is next to the police headquarters in Kheyābūn-é Tāleghānī; ask for the *Edāré-yé Amāken-é Komīté*. On registering, you have to say how many nights you will be staying and at what address; if you change hotels, leave Zāhedān and come back, or extend your stay you will have to return to the Komīté and register again.

Places to Stay – bottom end

If you want to make a quick getaway by bus, the *Hotel-é Abūzar* (marked in English 'Abuzar Hotel') is convenient and good value at 1300/1900 rials a single/double with a shared bathroom, although it is rather noisy. Cheaper options in the same terminal area that aren't as good include the *Mosāferkhūné-yé Nūr*, at 1500 rials for a triple with shared bathroom, or the *Mosāferkhūné-yé Fārs* in Kheyābūn-é Taftūn. The *Mosāferkhūné-yé Eslām* diagonally opposite the *Abūzar* has been recommended. However this is a noisy and not particularly attractive part of town and it is better to go to the centre of town.

The *Mehmūnpazīr-é Hīrmand* (☎ 22827) in the Bāzār-é Rūz is highly recommended in this class: the staff are very friendly and the place is reasonable value at 1900/2100 rials a single/double with very adequate shared shower facilities. It is also quite large and you are less likely to be given the knock-back here than elsewhere. The hotel is a few metres from the stop for buses from the bus terminal.

The *Mehmūnkhūné-yé Bākhtar* in Kheyābūn-é Doktor Sharī'atī charges 2500 rials for a double with shared bathroom: it is OK but not among the best. The *Hotel-é Kavīr* in Bolvār-é Āyatollāh Motahharī, over the bridge from Meidūn-é Āzādī, has gone downhill in recent years. It costs 1000/2000 rials a single/double with shared bathroom.

Places to Stay – middle
The two best hotels in Zāhedān, charging around 3000/4500 rials, are the *Hotel-é Khāvar* in Kheyābūn-é Emām Khomeinī and the lower category *Hotel-é Sāleh* in Kheyābūn-é Āzādī, but it is very difficult all year round to get a room in either of them without a reservation or a great deal of influence.

Places to Eat
There are several restaurants in the bus terminal area, of which the *Restōrān-é Abūzar* (marked on the window in English, 'Welcome to the Abuozar Restaurant') is the most popular and probably the best.

Closer to the centre of town in the *Mehmūnpazīr-é Hīrmand* is a good and inexpensive restaurant with friendly service. The *Restōrān-é Vanak* (previously the 'Gandhi') above the Iran Asseman office arcade in Kheyābūn-é Āzādī has seen better days but the food is still good.

All these restaurants charge around 1500 rials a person.

Things to Buy
Zāhedān is famous in Iran for its low prices on all manner of goods, especially cigarettes, which are imported from and often made in Pakistan (under Western names). The grand cigarette bazaar is in the bus terminal area.

Getting There & Away
The railway line to the Pakistani border has recently reopened. There has also been talk of linking up the railway system between Kermān and Zāhedān; of course there is a lot of talk about a lot of things in present-day Iran without a great deal of action. If it does happen it will theoretically be possible to go by train all the way from London to Calcutta. For the time being, however, you will have to travel between Zāhedān and Kermān by road or air.

The roads go north to Mashhad and Zābol, and south to Chābahār (for those with the constitution of a camel), but most travellers will only be interested in roads east to the Pakistani border and west to Kermān. Although Kermān is only seven hours and 600 rials away, many travellers go straight through to Shīrāz. This is a long journey (17 hours, 1560/2110 rials) but it does put an awful lot of desert behind you. It's about the same price and an extra five hours to get to Tehrān direct. There are other possibilities.

If you just can't face another bus, then it is possible to fly from Zāhedān to Tehrān, Kermān or Esfahān to the west, Chābahār to the south or Mashhad to the north.

To/From Pakistan Until the Afghanistan route became no-go, the route through Pakistan was only an alternative for overlanders. It was not much used in summer, when the temperature often soars to thermometer-bursting levels, but made a good winter alternative when the high passes in Afghanistan were blocked with snow. Transport schedules and conditions at the border are liable to change, so check the situation at the Pakistani Consulate in Zāhedān or the Iranian Consulate in Quetta. See also Lonely Planet's *Pakistan – a travel survival kit.* This is the latest information we have:

Whether crossing by road or train, you'll pass through the Iranian border post of Mīrjāvé and the Pakistani border post of Taftan (also known as Kuh-i-Taftan). Take food and water whichever way you go. All times given here are local and theoretical. If relations between Iran and Pakistan continue to improve, the journey should become easier, quicker and more comfortable with less hanging around at the border.

The train service between Quetta and Zāhedān was resumed late in 1991, with one service weekly going

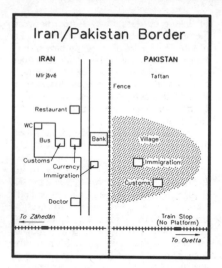

Iran/Pakistan Border

IRAN — Mīrjāvé — Restaurant — WC — Bus — Customs — Currency — Immigration — Doctor — Bank — To Zāhedān

PAKISTAN — Taftan — Fence — Village — Immigration — Customs — Train Stop (No Platform) — To Quetta

all the way in each direction, and another going only between Quetta and the Pakistani border. For the time being, by far the best overland option is to take the through service. However, tickets for it are often hard to come by at short notice and you may have to have to take the other train which stops at Taftan, and make the other half of the journey by bus.

Trains leave Zāhedān on Sunday at 9 am, arriving in Mīrjāvé at 11.35 am. At 2.15 pm, after you've completed the customs formalities, the train departs for Quetta, arriving at 11.10 am on Monday. The other weekly train leaves Taftan for Quetta at 2.20 pm on Wednesday, arriving at 11.55 am on Thursday. In the return direction, the direct Zāhedān service leaves Quetta at noon on Friday, reaching Taftan at 7.05 am, Saturday, leaving Mīrjāvé at 11.35 am and arriving in Zāhedān at 2.50 pm. The other train leaves Quetta at 10.45 am on Tuesday and reaches Taftan at 7.55 am, Wednesday. There are sleepers only, and the full fare from Pakistan is Rs 90 for 2nd class and Rs 320 for 1st class. Those with the right paperwork can claim a 25% tourist discount or a 50% student discount. Details of the fares from Zāhedān were not available.

Between Taftan and Quetta, the alternative to the train is a very dusty and unpleasant bus ride for Rs 85, but this would be better than staying in Taftan although probably not as good as staying in Quetta and waiting for the next train. There are several buses daily. From Quetta buses for Taftan leave from the New Quetta Bus Station on Sariab Road.

There are frequent bus services between Mīrjāvé and Zāhedān (96 km, about two hours thanks to the many checkpoints, 1000 rials for foreigners, plus 500

rials for each bag. Since Pakistani time is 1½ hours ahead of Iranian time, be sure to make an early start if you're taking the bus to Mīrjāvé.

At Mīrjāvé, first queue to get in and take your bag to the the customs shed for a thorough search. Then go back to immigration and finally hand in or fill out in your currency declaration. You can then walk the short distance across the border to the Pakistani village of Taftan or else to proceed to Zāhedān. If you are entering Iran, you may have to visit a doctor, who may inspect your international health card. There are banks on both sides of the border, and there's no need to change money on the black market.

Taftan is a depressing, fly-blown den of smugglers, and you can expect to spend a minimum of four hours here. In summer this would be murder. According to the Pakistani authorities, Taftan is to be developed into a township with a clean restaurant and even hotels, but until then, don't even think about spending the night there. Pakistani customs and immigration offices are a 10-minute walk apart, with immigration closer to the border. The train stops in the middle of nowhere, a short walk from a nondescript customs office where you're required to fill in a register. If it's hot, or if you have lots of luggage, share a taxi (around Rs 50): it will wait until you complete customs formalities, then take you on to immigration.

Drivers travelling between Europe and India often describe this as the worst leg of their journey. The road from Quetta to the Iranian border is barren and lonely, with virtually no facilities, and motorcyclists I met regretted not having booked their motorcycles as luggage and gone by train instead. If you're travelling between Quetta and the Iranian border in your own transport, it's advisable to travel in a convoy.

To/From Afghanistan There is no legal direct route into Afghanistan from Zāhedān, nor is there an Afghan Consulate in Zāhedān. You will have to go to Mashhad first.

Air Iran Air flies from Zāhedān to:

Chābahār – Sunday, Tuesday, Thursday and Friday, 9.50 am, 55 minutes
Esfahān – Wednesday and Friday, 12.55 pm, 2½ hours; Thursday and Saturday, 4.10 pm, 1¾ hours
Kermān – Wednesday and Friday, 12.55 pm, 50 minutes
Mashhad – Wednesday and Saturday, 11.55 am, 1¼ hours
Tehrān – daily, 8.15 am, 1¾ hours; Tuesday, 12.30 pm, 2¾ hours; Wednesday and Friday, 12.55 pm, 3¾ hours; Sunday, Tuesday, Thursday and Friday, 1.10 pm, 1¾ hours; Thursday and Saturday, 4.10 pm, three hours; all 8010 rials

The Iran Asseman timetable is a complete mystery, even I suspect to most of the airline's employees.

There are no longer connections from Zāhedān to Kabul, Karachi and Bombay.

Airline Offices Iran Air (☎ 20813) and Iran Asseman are next to each other in a small arcade on the east side of Kheyābūn-é Āzādī.

Bus & Minibus There is no station as such, but all buses leave from a small area in the north-west of Zāhedān generally known as the Gārāzh, where all the transport cooperatives have their offices. Buses and minibuses leave from outside the Mosāferkhūné-yé Fārs direct to the bazaar district, and return from next to the intersection of Kheyābūn-é Emām Khomeinī and Kheyābūn-é Shahīd Nīkbakht: listen for drivers, or more often young boys working as ticket-collectors, shouting 'Gārāzh! Gārāzh!' After dark you can take a shared taxi on the same route for around 200 rials.

There are buses from Zāhedān to:

Bam – at least two a day, 360 km, six hours, Cooperative Bus Company No 10
Bandar-é Abbās – one a day, 1039 km, 17 hours, 1200 rials, Cooperative Bus Company No 5
Bīrjand – several a day, 480 km, nine hours
Chābahār – four a day, 691 km, 12 hours, 1150 rials 'lux', Cooperative Bus Company No 5; one a day, 1500 rials 'super', Cooperative Bus Company No 1
Esfahān – at least one a day, 1244 km, 21 hours, 1400 rials 'lux', Cooperative Bus Company No 15
Gorgān – at least one a day, 1563 km, 26 hours)
Kermān – at least one a day, Cooperative Bus Company No 3; at least one a day, Cooperative Bus Company No 9; about four a day, Cooperative Bus Company No 11; all 541 km, seven hours, 600 or 625 rials 'lux'
Mashhad – at least two a day, 1001 km, 12 hours, 1335/1880 rials 'lux'/'super', Cooperative Bus Company No 13
Mīrjāvé – several a day from about 4 am, 96 km, two hours, 1000 rials 'super', Cooperative Bus Company No 2; see To/From Pakistan
Sarāvān – 331 km, five hours, 700 rials 'lux', Cooperative Bus Company No 13
Shīrāz – at least one a day, 1088 km, 17 hours, 1560 rials, Cooperative Bus Company No 5

Tehrān – several a day, 1605 km, 22 hours, 2100 rials 'lux'
Yazd – at least one a day, 928 km, 14 hours, 1030 rials 'lux', Cooperative Bus Company No 12
Zābol – four minibuses a day, 216 km, four hours, 360 rials, Cooperative Bus Company No 2; do not go before reading the Zābol entry in this chapter

There is no direct service to Tabrīz. If you are headed for Zābol or Mashhad, you can expect a generous number of checkpoints along the road.

Train The service has recently resumed, see under the To/From Pakistan heading for the latest information.

Car & Motorcycle The clearly signposted road between Zāhedān and Kermān is good but very short on facilities. Take plenty of water with you if you are driving, and make sure your vehicle is in good order or else you risk having a very long and unpleasant wait for a repair job. Fill up whenever you see a petrol station, as you may not otherwise make it to the next one.

Hitching If you want to try some long-distance hitching, you could ask around in the truck compound just west of the bus terminal area. Occasionally a few foreign trucks pass this way, although most of the vehicles are Iranian. You would be unlikely to save any time by hitching on a lorry to Pakistan.

Getting Around
There is a great shortage of taxis and buses in Zāhedān, and vans and private cars often duplicate their services. Much of the time it's easier to walk.

To/From the Airport A taxi between the airport and the town should be no more than about 600 rials for a single passenger. There is no airport bus service.

ZĀHEDĀN TO ZĀBOL
A road has recently been laid to connect Zābol with Mashhad – previously traffic had to make a long detour via Zāhedān. Zābol is still most easily reached from Zāhedān. On

either side of the Zāhedān to Zābol road there are many archaeological and historic sites, including a large number of prehistoric mounds around the village of **Shahr-é Sūkhté**, 163 km north of Zāhedān. The bus does not stop at Shahr-é Sūkhté, but you can ask to be dropped off at Mohammad Ābād, 17 km south of Zābol, and take a minibus or shared taxi south from there.

On the Zāhedān to Zābol road look out for the many bādgīrs which are an essential part of survival here in summer, and for the village of **Tāsūkī** 126 km north of Zāhedān, which is literally packed with hundreds of camels. At a remote point about 40 km north of Zāhedān, don't be surprised if the bus slows down to allow several passengers with sacks over their shoulders to jump out and run into the hills east of the road. From here it's only about five km to the point where the borders of Pakistan, Iran and Afghanistan converge.

ZĀBOL   زابل

This dusty overgrown village dangerously close to the border with Afghanistan is of no interest to the traveller except as a stepping-off point for Kūh-é Khājé. Zābol has earned a name as a town where there are only two things that matter – guns and money. It has all the mistrust and suspicion of foreigners that you might expect of a settlement close to the lawless frontier with Afghanistan, but none of the romantic appeal.

Gun law is in force in and around Zābol, the locals stare at visitors and don't answer their *salāms*, and the heavy Komīté presence is exceptionally intrusive and oppressive. In short, the atmosphere here is unpleasant and intimidating in the extreme.

On the dubious reasoning that Zābol is not a tourist place, the Komīté here held me prisoner here without any charge and denied me access to a telephone or anyone who spoke English, even though the tourist office in Zāhedān had supposedly cleared my visit. After three nights I was freed without any apology or explanation except the one I had originally been given, that Zābol is not a tourist place. Worse still, I was given the distinct impression that this sort of shabby treatment is routine for any foreign visitor

arriving without an official escort: no-one is immune, and there was recently even a case involving an accredited diplomat. The smiling guards in my prison told me that the unlucky diplomat who had been in my cell a few weeks earlier was surely *dīvāné* (crazy) because he kept on demanding the use of a telephone.

The problem is that, even though there is nothing to see in Zābol except for a few stones remaining from the **Manār-é Ghāsem Ābād** (a 12th-century minaret) and a few bādgīrs, it is difficult to reach the province's most famous historical site, Kūh-é Khājé, without passing through Zābol.

Apart from the insides of the Sepah-é Pāsdārān prison and the Komīté station, the most interesting thing I saw in Zābol was a public square displaying an unexploded Soviet missile.

Even Zābolīs curse this town.

Orientation & Information

Zābol is a small town, so you can easily make your depressing way around on foot. The focus of life here is the bazaar, which is hardly worth visiting.

Post & Telecommunications The post office and the telegraph office are in the bazaar district.

Places to Stay

Conditions in prison in Zābol are an affront to civilised values, but they are not very much worse than those in the city's grim collection of mosāferkhūnés. There is no good place to stay in Zābol. There is no hotel, and the mehmūnsarā mentioned in some official lists is no longer open. None of the following places is marked in English.

The *Mosāferkhūné-yé Valī-yé Asr*, about a km from the bus terminal and easy to reach from it by bus or taxi. It is convenient for a quick getaway, but extortionate at 2200 rials for a tiny and not quite clean single without either heating or air-conditioning. There's one shared shower with occasional hot water, and some heating in the dormitory rooms. Close to the bazaar, Kheyābūn-é Emām Khomeinī boasts three mosāferkhūnés in the same league as the Valī-yé Asr, namely the *Ahmadī*, the *Selūkī* and the *Nasīrī*: all are within sight of each other and none is recommended.

Places to Eat

Nor is there any good restaurant in Zābol. The chelō kabābī underneath the Mosāferkhūné-yé Valī-yé Asr is OK for chicken but not mutton. There are a few other places of similarly modest gastronomic standards around the bazaar.

Getting There & Away

Air The small airport near Zābol mostly deals with military aircraft; it may also be an Iran Asseman destination from Tehrān, depending on the week's timetable.

Bus & Minibus The one bus company, Co-operative Bus Company No 2, is to the right of the southern approach to Zābol on the Zāhedān road. Buses go to:

Gorgān – daily, 1.30 pm, 1713 km, 28 hours, 2100 rials 'lux'

Gombad-é Kāvūs – one 'lux' a day, 1621 km, 26 hours

Kūh-é Khājé – several minibuses a day between 7 am and 4 pm, 30 km, one hour, 100 rials

Mashhad – daily at 2 pm, 1149 km, 14 hours, 1320 rials

Zāhedān – minibus four times daily between 7 am and 4 pm, 216 km, four hours, 360 rials

Shared Taxi & Savārī From the same terminal there are also some private cars and shared taxis going to Zāhedān until quite late at night, as well as buses between Mashhad and Zāhedān which often pick up passengers at Zābol. There are also frequent savārīs (200 rials) and vans (100 rials) to Kūh-é Khājé.

To/From Afghanistan There is no legal crossing point into Afghanistan from Zābol, although the fact is not acknowledged by many of the locals.

Getting Around

There are regular buses (10 rials), minibuses (20 rials) and shared taxis (50 rials) between the terminal and the bazaar, and it's easy to reach the bazaar by shared taxi from anywhere in town for 50 rials at most. If you are coming from a stint in the Sepah-é Pāsdārān prison, turn right as you walk out until you reach the first crossroads: from there you can take a shared taxi (30 rials) to the bazaar, and then another to the terminal, where you take the first bus, car or donkey out of town.

To/From the Airport There is an airport taxi service.

KŪH-É KHĀJÉ كوه خواجه

The famous Kūh-é Khājé is a small hilly island with a number of ancient remains on its peak, rising out of a seasonal lake thick with reeds, the Daryāché-yé Hāmūn. It is especially beautiful between early spring and early autumn when the level of the lake rises and the causeway to the island becomes impassable; in winter and late autumn it is usually possible to walk across, but at other times you will probably have to take a *tūtan* (a tiny wickerwork punt) at a negotiable fare.

The best ascent is from the north of the island, approached by a 10-minute walk from the point where the causeway joins the island, but even this is steep and requires a good pair of shoes. When you reach the peak you will come first to the remains of a square Arsacid and early Sassanian complex containing a large square palace and an *āteshkadé* (Zoroastrian fire temple), both built of mud-brick. Although nothing now remains of the frescoes which originally decorated the palace, it is still possible to trace the outline of the interior and exterior walls, which survive to a height of more than two metres in places.

At the south and south-east of the peak are two fairly well-preserved forts overlooking the lake, and there are also the ruins of several other less important structures scattered around.

On the south shore of the island there is a tiny hamlet of single-roomed mud huts with a much reduced population of about 20, but otherwise the island is uninhabited.

The new village, also known as Kūh-é

Khājé, is 1½ km east of the island, and this is where you will be dropped off if you arrive by bus or shared taxi from Zābol. There is no accommodation or restaurant, and since you should count on at least 2½ hours to see the remains on the island and to get back to the village bus stop, it is best to leave Zābol in the morning. The last minibus back to Zābol leaves at about 4 pm, and there is very little transport of any kind later than that. It is not safe to spend the night or even stop in Zābol, but you should be OK if you just pass through its terminal on the way from Zāhedān. See also the Zābol entry.

CHĀBAHĀR   چابهار

Until very recently, the tiny Sea of Oman port of Chābahār (also Chāh Bahār or Bandar-é Chābahār) was extremely isolated, but since Iran Air opened a much-needed air link with the interior it is now the most accessible of all the towns of Balūchestān proper, although certainly not by road. The town is still predominantly Baluchi in population and character, culturally and economically allied with the Pakistani province of Baluchistan only 90 km to the east, and no-one seems to care very much about Pakistanis, Bangladeshis and others crossing here without a visa or passport.

Although there isn't a great deal to see or do, Chābahār is a small friendly place without the tenseness of some of the other towns along Iran's eastern frontier. The relaxed pace of life and the friendliness of the locals may well persuade you to spend some time here happily without bothering much with sights or activities. A surprising number of people here speak good English, albeit with a Pakistani accent.

The weather is very pleasant in winter, but horrifically hot in summer. Even in winter Chābahār hosts one of Iran's densest mosquito populations.

Orientation & Information
The airport is actually at Konārak, a typhoid-ridden settlement 61 km by road from Chābahār. Within Chābahār it's easy to walk anywhere as there is only one main road – Kheyābūn-é Ghods merging into Kheyābūn-é Be'sat at its eastern end – and nowhere in town is very far from it. At its east end it joins the road to Īrānshahr and Zāhedān and at its south it stops at Chābahār Bay, (Khalīj-é Chābahār).

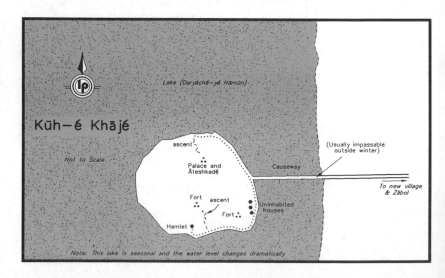

Top: Ship and dhows, at docks, Jazīré-yé Kīsh (DStV)
Bottom: View of Hormoz (DStV)

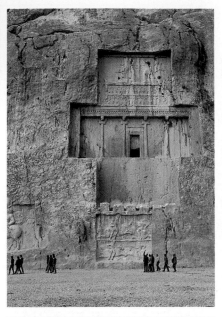

Top Left: Naghsh-é Rostam, Fārs (DStV)
Top Right: Takht-é Jamshīd, Persepolis (DStV)
Bottom Left: Relief, Apadana, Persepolis (RNE)
Bottom Right: Xerxes' Gateway, Persepolis (RNE)

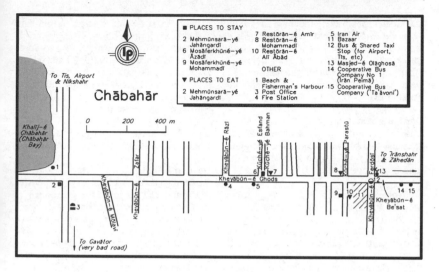

Chābahār

PLACES TO STAY
- 2 Mehmūnsarā–yé Jahāngardī
- 6 Mosāferkhūné–yé Āzādī
- 9 Mosāferkhūné–yé Mohammadī

PLACES TO EAT
- 2 Mehmūnsarā–yé Jahāngardī
- 7 Restōrān–é Amīr
- 8 Restōrān–é Mohammadī
- 10 Restōrān–é Alī Ābād

OTHER
- 1 Beach & Fisherman's Harbour
- 3 Post Office
- 4 Fire Station
- 5 Iran Air
- 11 Bazaar
- 12 Bus & Shared Taxi Stop (for Airport, Tīs, etc)
- 13 Masjed-é Olāghosā
- 14 Cooperative Bus Company No 1 (Irān Peimā)
- 15 Cooperative Bus Company ('Ta'āvonī')

Things to See

The **beach** (pelāzh) at the east of town, with its charming fishermen's huts of timber frames and walls of woven reeds, is worth visiting. The people, many of them in flowing Baluchi robes, are friendly, laid-back, and willing to stop their less-than-frenzied activities to chat to strangers. Apart from the low-key fishing activities, most of the shipping here is carried out between Iran and Pakistan on a small scale by private traders.

Walking east along the main road with its low-roofed stone shops you come to the intersection with Kheyābūn-é Ferdōsī at the east end of Kheyābūn-é Ghods. The **bazaar** west of Kheyābūn-é Ferdōsī lacks the bustle of the usual Iranian marketplace, and it is common to see merchants recumbent or even asleep on their stalls, and not only in the early afternoon siesta.

The small Sunni **Masjed-é Olāghosā**, to the north-east of the bazaar in Kheyābūn-é Be'sat, is made of white stone, very much in the Indian style.

Places to Stay

The *Mehmānsarā-yé Jahāngardī* (not marked in English or even Persian, but known to everyone) has a policy of nearly always finding a room for a foreigner, which is just as well since it is the only even remotely comfortable place in town. Even here running water, let alone hot water, cannot be expected 24 hours a day. It has no single rooms; the price for a double with/without bathroom is 4500/3400 rials; a triple with bathroom is 7900 rials. The grotty *Mosāferkhūné-yé Mohammadī* (not marked in English) charges 2500 rials for sole occupancy of a dormitory room with few distractions in the way of facilities for personal hygiene or air-conditioning. The *Mosāferkhūné-yé Āzādī* in the same class trusts foreigners to take up a place in a shared five-bed dormitory for 500 rials.

Places to Eat

Fish dishes are common in this part of Iran, as you might expect, and cheap. There is no spectacularly excellent restaurant in Chābahār, but if you don't mind the flies and uninspired decor the one at the *Mehmānsarā-yé Jahāngardī* is fairly good and inexpensive. There are several snack bars and chelō kabābīs along the main road. The *Restōrān-é Alī Ābād* (not marked in English) is good in a simple way with chelō gūsht (meat with boiled rice) for 1150 rials and other basic dishes. None of the restaurants I went to in Chābahār served drinks apart from water or tea.

Getting There & Away

Chābahār is still very isolated by land, and the most sensible way to get there is by air. There are bus services from Zahedān, but the road is far from good.

To/From Pakistan There is no legal route between Iran and Pakistan except at Mīrjāvé, but this is a long way to the north of Chābahār – too far for most of the locals. The land crossing into Pakistan through Pīshīn is not recommended for foreigners, even though there may be little government presence along the border, since much of the western part of the Pakistani province of Baluchistan is off limits to foreigners and is also fairly dangerous; if you were caught by the Iranians trying to cross the border illegally the consequences could be very regrettable.

Air Iran Air flies from Chābahār airport to Bandar-é Abbās (Monday, Wednesday and Saturday, 11.35 am, 55 minutes), Tehrān (daily, 11.35 am, 3¼ hours, 10,530 rials), and Zāhedān (Sunday, Tuesday, Thursday and Friday, 11.35 am (55 minutes).

Airline Offices Iran Air is on the south side of Kheyābūn-é Ghods, about 100 metres east of the fire station. Like most things in Chābahār, it keeps odd hours.

Bus & Minibus There are two bus company offices a short distance apart on the south side of Kheyābūn-é Be'sat, neither marked in English. One is Cooperative Bus Company No 1 (Īrān Peimā) and the other to the east is Cooperative Bus Company No 5 (known simply as Ta'āvonī). Cooperative Bus Company No 1 offers one 'super' bus a day to Zāhedān at 7.30 am (691 km, 12

hours, 1500 rials) and one 'lux' to Īrānshahr at 7 am (361 km, six hours, 710 rials), while Cooperative Bus Company No 5 runs buses daily to Zāhedān at 9, 9.30, 10 and 11 am (1150 'lūx', 1500 rials 'super') and to Īrānshahr at 9.30, 10 and 11 am and noon (710 rials 'lux'). All buses leave from the place in Kheyābūn-é Ferdōsī marked on the map.

Sea There are no passenger boats out of Chābahār.

Getting Around

To/From the Airport It is very inexpensive to travel the 61 km into Chābahār on any of the fleet of minibuses and shared taxis which attend the arrival of any flight: by minibus it is 300 rials to almost anywhere in Chābahār or only about 600 rials by shared taxi. Shared taxis to the airport go from the place marked on the map. Leave by 9.30 am at the latest. There is no X-ray machine at Chābahār airport, and luggage has to be checked laboriously by hand.

TĪS   چابهار

Tīs is a small oasis village about 9 km north of Chābahār along the coast road. At the Tīs petrol station, turn towards the sea and you will face the remains of a **Portuguese castle** (ghal'é Portoghālīhā) on top of a small hill. This fort is not recorded in any historical documents I have seen, but it is worth the short climb. The village of Tīs is well irrigated and even boasts a modest arboretum, known as the **Bāgh-é Tīs**, with a canopy of tamarind and pine trees. Bang on the gates many times if you want to rouse the ever-slumbering caretaker. There is a fine Sunni **mosque** of white stone colourfully decorated in the Indian style, not very different from the Masjed-é Olāghosā in Chābahār.

Getting There & Away

From Chābahār you can walk the 9 km along the coastal road, or else you can try taking a shared taxi from the taxi stop in Kheyābūn-é Ferdōsī to the petrol station at Tīs (*pomp-é benzīn-é Tīs*) for not more than 250 rials a person.

Kermān Province

گنبد شیح لقمان بابا

The province of Kermān is the third largest in Iran, with an area of 180,000 sq km, but its population is only 1.6 million. Its north-east takes in much of the Dasht-é Lūt, and most of the province is largely steppe or sandy desert, although there are some oases where dates, oranges, pistachios, cereals and arable crops are cultivated. In view of its barren nature, the province is very dependent on ghanāts (underground water channels) for its irrigation. Relatively isolated by land, its main outlet was for many centuries through the seaport of Bandar-é Abbās to the south, but trade in this direction has declined over recent years and the province is in a state of economic regression.

If you are planning to spend any time in Kermān province, try to take a copy of Anthony Smith's *Blind White Fish in Persia* with you. Whatever you do, don't miss the unique mediaeval citadel at Bam, 194 km south-east of Kermān city.

KERMĀN

کرمان

Population: 250,000

If you are coming from or going to the Pakistani border you are highly likely to pass through the desert city of Kermān, the terminus for the train to Tehrān. Between there and the Pakistani border you will have to depend at least partly on buses, unless you take the plane to Zāhedān. Although there are a few things to see in Kermān, there's not a vast amount to slow you down, especially if you're on a transit visa, and many travellers just keep on going.

The local Persian dialect, spoken with something approaching an Indian accent, is so different that one writer was prompted to record that Persian isn't spoken in Kermān. The Kermānīs do speak Persian, but my efforts to speak to the people in their own language were greeted with looks of complete incomprehension. People here also look different from other Persians, a little Indian perhaps.

The city and province of Kermān have long been known for their poverty and lack of development. People who become successful in Kermān don't tend to stay long in the city. For many centuries its livelihood depended on its place on the Asian trade routes, but from about the beginning of the Safavid dynasty it has relied more on the production of carpets. The barren nature of the surrounding terrain has never presented much scope for agriculture, and today the main activity of the town continues to be the manufacture of carpets and other handicrafts. It has a Zoroastrian minority, although much smaller than that in Yazd.

Thanks to the altitude, 1749 metres, Kermān's climate is not too hot in summer.

History

Kermān has a long and turbulent history, and it has only for short spells enjoyed peace and prosperity at the same time. Believed to have been founded in the early 3rd century AD by Ardashīr I, founder of the Sassanian dynasty, it was from the 7th century ruled in turn by the Arabs, the Buyids, the Seljuqs, the Turkomans and the Mongols, and then until the Ghajar dynasty by a further succession of invaders and local dynasties. Kermān was restored to security under central government in the last century, but its relative remoteness has denied it any great prosperity in recent times.

Orientation

There are two main squares in Kermān, Meidūn-é Āzādī to the west and Meidūn-é Shohadā to the east. Most of the important offices and things to see are on or close to the road between these two squares, or in the bazaar district south-west of Meidūn-é Shohadā. The train station is four km south-west of Kermān and the airport is also south-west, but the bus station is in the south.

There are two bottom-end places to stay at the bus terminal itself, and although there is nowhere else within comfortable walking

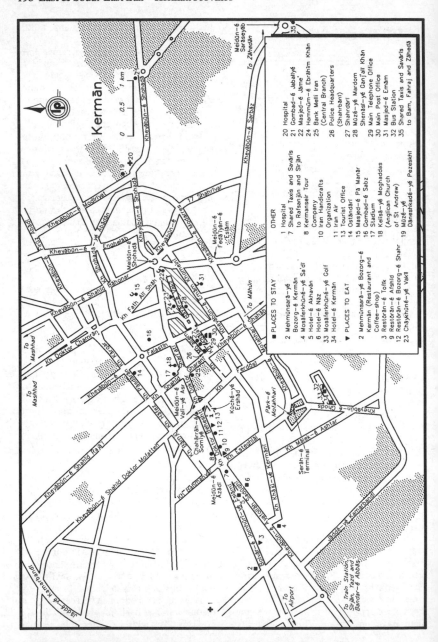

Kermān

0   0.5   1 km

PLACES TO STAY

2   Mehmūnsarā-yé
    Bozorg-é Kermān
5   Mosāferkhūné-yé Sa'dī
6   Hotel-é Akhavān
6   Hotel-é Naz
33 Mosāferkhūné-yé Golf
34 Hotel-é Kermān

▼ PLACES TO EAT

2   Mehmūnsarā-yé Bozorg-é
    Kermān (Restaurant and
    Coffee-shop)
3   Restorān-é Toflk
9   Restorān-é Afshīd
12 Restorān-é Bozorg-é Shahr
23 Chaykhūné-yé Vakīl

OTHER

1   Hospital
7   Shared Taxis and Savārīs
    to Rafsanjān and Sīrjān
8   Kermanseir Tour
    Company
10 Iran Handicrafts
    Organization
11 Iran Air
13 Tourist Office
14 Ostāndārī
15 Masjed-é Pā Manār
16 Gombad-é Sabz
17 Stadium
18 Kelīsā-yé Moghaddas
    (Anglican Church
    of St Andrew)
19 Mūzé-
    Dāneshkadé-yé Pezeshkī
20 Hospital
21 Gombad-é Jabalīyé
22 Masjed-é Jāme'
24 Hammūm-é Ebrāhīm Khān
25 Bank Mellī Iran
    (Central Branch)
26 Police Headquarters
    (Shahrbānī)
27 Shahrdārī
28 Mūzé-yé Mardom
    Shenāsī-yé GanjAlī Khān
29 Main Telephone Office
30 Main Post Office
31 Masjed-é Emām
32 Bus Station
35 Shared Taxis and Savārīs
    to Bam, Fahraj and Zāhedā

distance of the station, the three best hotels are fairly easy to reach by shared taxi.

Information
The aliens' bureau (☎ 22150) where you can try to get a visa extension is in the police headquarters in Kheyābūn-é Adālat. The ostāndārī (☎ 22222) is in Kheyābūn-é Pās-dārān and the shahrdārī (☎ 27030) is at the intersection of Kheyābūn-é Ghods and Kheyābūn-é Adālat.

Tourist Office The tourist office (☎ 25098) is in Kūché-yé Ershād off Kheyābūn-é Ferdōsī. The enthusiastic and cultivated man at the tourist office speaks excellent English and is a great authority on almost everything worth visiting in or near the province. He should be your first port of call, even though the office is a little difficult to find, and not marked in English. The *kūché* (lane) is the first on the right south-east of Chahārrāh-é Somīyé. It appears to lead nowhere, but at the end is a gate, and behind that a small compound. Tell the gatekeeper that you want the Daftar-é Seir va Seyāhat (tourist office) and he will direct you to the correct building. When you get there, turn left inside the entrance and you are at the tourist office.

Money For foreign exchange, go to the central branch of Bank Melli Iran on the south of Meidūn-é Valī-yé Asr.

Post & Telecommunications The telegraph office on the north side of Kheyābūn-é Adālat is open from 7 am to 10.30 pm; international calls – which cannot be made from any hotel in Kermān – must be booked at least two hours ahead. The main post office is diagonally opposite the telegraph office on the south side of Kheyābūn-é Adālat. The dialling code for Kermān is 0341.

Travel Agencies The Kermanseir Tour Company (☎ 28029) on the north side of Kheyābūn-é Doktor Beheshtī – the only travel agency in town – exists for the sole purpose of selling tours to the island of Jazīré-yé Kīsh. It takes shoppers and perhaps a few tourists to the island on the flights of the military airline Saha, arranges two nights' accommodation for them and flies them back again. For more information, see the Jazīré-yé Kīsh entry in the South Iran & the Islands of the Persian Gulf chapter.

Maps The glossy *Tourist Map of Province Kerman* issued free by the tourist office covers both the city and the province of Kermān. Like so many maps, this one gives an English transliteration of most of the main street names, but doesn't go any further. The not-so-glossy but more detailed Gītā Shenāsī map of Kermān (300 rials) is entirely in Persian.

Medical Services For emergency services, dial ☎ 118.

Emergency The police headquarters (☎ 110/22180) are in Kheyābūn-é Adālat.

Bāzār-é Vakīl
The extensive Regent's Bazaar (also known as the Bāzār-é Bozorg), constructed of beautiful and well-preserved brick, much of it from the Safavid period, is largely of interest for its architecture rather than for the range of goods, although there are a few metalwork shops selling brass trays and the like noisily hammered into shape on site. The 17th-century **Madrasé-yé Ganj'alī Khān** and the early 19th-century **Madrasé-yé Ebrāhīm Khān** now form part of this bazaar. There is a traditional and very atmospheric teahouse inside the Bāzār-é Vakīl: see the Places to Eat entry.

Mūzé-yé Mardom Shenāsī-yé Ganj'alī Khān
Look out for the Ganj'alī Khān Ethnological Museum in the Bāzār-é Vakīl. This building houses an interesting exhibition of good waxworks of men in various poses and costumes set in a traditional but no longer operational bath-house. Entry is 50 rials.

Hammūm-é Ebrāhīm Khān

Close to the Ganj'alī Khān museum, the Hammūm-é Ebrāhīm Khān is a working traditional bath-house for men only: try to go with a male Iranian friend, as you may have language or cultural problems.

Masjed-é Jāme'

The well-preserved and well-restored Masjed-é Jāme', at the end of a short road leading off from the west of Meidūn-é Shohadā, is worth visiting. This large mosque with its four lofty eivāns and shimmering blue tiles was founded in the 14th century, although much of the present structure dates from the Safavid period or later. It's no problem for non-Muslims to go inside.

Masjed-é Emām

The Masjed-é Emām (formerly the Masjed-é Malek) is aptly enough on Kheyābūn-é Emām Khomeinī. This quadrangular, domed mosque, part of which has been rebuilt, dates from the late 11th century, and original Seljuq structures include a mehrāb and the remains of a minaret.

Masjed-é Pā Manār

This 14th or perhaps 12th-century mosque in Kheyābūn-é Fath Alī Shāh is worth visiting for the fine original tilework in its portal.

Gombad-é Sabz

Although the Green Dome in the network of kūchés east of Kheyābūn-é Falastīn was once one of the most important monuments in Kermān, it was irreparably damaged in the 1896 earthquake and little more remains than its small doorway with some original tilework.

Mūzé-yé Dāneshkadé-yé Pezeshkī

There is a small medical museum in the Medical College (Dāneshkadé-yé Pezeshkī) in Kheyābūn-é Modīrīyat, open Saturday to Thursday mornings only.

Kelīsā-yé Moghaddas

The Anglican Church of St Andrew, a building easily missed from the street, is hidden in a garden behind a doorway in Kheyābūn-é Sharī'atī marked with the Persian cross characteristic of all the Anglican churches in Iran. The small flock seems largely to have been forgotten by headquarters in Canterbury except for goodwill cards at Christmas and Easter, and fellow believers are assured of a warm welcome.

The original building founded by British missionaries was destroyed in a recent earthquake, but with a great effort the tiny congregation built a new church in stone in the mid '80s. For a few years now they have had to do without a minister, so a small community of lay members sharing the priest's house take it in turn to lead the Sunday services (in Persian) with communion wine somehow imported from Jerusalem.

Gombad-é Jabalīyé

On the north side of Kheyābūn-é Shohadā just beyond the eastern edge of Kermān, this small and unadorned octagonal double-domed structure is of unknown age or purpose. It appears to predate the 2nd millennium AD and may have been a Zoroastrian building, and is remarkable because of it's constructed of stone rather than the much more usual brick. The door is permanently locked, although the tourist office might be able to find someone to open it for you if you really want to see inside. To get there, take a shared taxi for 50 rials from Meidūn-é Shohadā.

In the hills overlooking the martyrs' cemetery (the Golestān-é Shohadā) just south-east of the Gombad-é Jabalīyé look for some slogans painted in very large letters in Persian on the cliff, *Allāho Akbar* and *Marg bar Āmrīkā* ('God is most great!' and 'Death to America!'). These rocky outcrops offer a fine outlook over Kermān, if only you can manage to climb to the top.

Places to Stay – bottom end

There are two places at the bus terminal itself. The *Mosāferkhūné-yé Golf* (no telephone) is about as basic as you can get, while the *Hotel-é Kermān* (☎ 32999) is a step up and convenient if you're just passing through, but noisy and far from ideal if you are not. There are no other places to stay within comfortable walking distance of the bus station.

One of the best of the cheaper places in town is the *Mosāferkhūné-yé Sa'dī* (☎ 29340) in Kheyābūn-é Dokhānīyāt off Bolvār-é Āyatollāh Sadūghī, about 600 metres south-west of the Hotel-é Nāz.

The campsite is closed.

Places to Stay – middle

The *Hotel-é Nāz* (☎ 26786) (marked in English 'Naz Hotel') on the south side of Kheyābūn-é Shahīd Āyatollāh Sadūghī is adequate but overpriced, claiming to have no singles and charging 4400 rials for a double with private bathroom. The service can best be described as intrusive. On the other side of the road, the *Hotel-é Akhavān* (☎ 31411) ('Akhavan Hotel') is 3300/4700 rials a single/double with bathroom. This is a slightly better bet than the Nāz. You can reach either from Meidūn-é Āzādī by shared taxi for 30 rials.

The best hotel in town is the *Mehmūnsarā-yé Bozorg-é Kermān* (☎ 35203) ('Kerman Grand Inn') in Bolvār-é Jomhūrī-yé Eslāmī, not perhaps the height of luxury but still good value at 4000/6000/9000 rials a single/double/suite with private bathroom and Western-style lavatory. The tourist office can make a reservation here if necessary. You can get here from Meidūn-é Āzādī by minibus for 20 rials or by shared taxi for 30 to 50 rials.

Places to Eat

Without a doubt the most atmospheric place to eat or drink in town is the *Chāykhūné-yé Vakīl* (☎ 25989) inside the Bāzār-é Vakil. This subterranean teahouse and restaurant with its elegant brickwork arches and vaulting is known for its traditional Iranian and local dishes, and for its elegant decor, but since it is a state-owned operation it is not highly regarded for its service. It is open for lunch from about noon to 2 pm, or for good spiced tea (100 rials) and a puff or two at the hubble-bubble from about 10 am to 4 pm, every day except Friday and public holidays. Order and pay in advance at the desk by the entrance.

The *Restōrān-é Afshīd* (not marked in English) on the east of Meidūn-é Āzādī is inexpensive and OK if you like your chelō kabāb cooked rare. The better *Restōrān-é Bozorg-é Shahr* (marked in English 'Big Restaurant of City') on the south side of Kheyābūn-é Doktor Beheshtī is good and inexpensive, with friendly service. The chelō meigū comes recommended at 1200 rials.

The *Restōrān-é Tofīk* (not marked in English) on the south side of Bolvār-é Jomhūrī-yé Eslāmī serves average imitations of pizza and Kentucky Fried Chicken as well as traditional Iranian food.

The *Mehmūnsarā-yé Bozorg-é Kermān* has a teahouse and a good restaurant, but the menu is short and the bill high.

Things to Buy

The well-stocked Iran Handicrafts Organization shop is on the south side of Kheyābūn-é Beheshtī, opposite the Kermanseir Tour Company.

Getting There & Away

Air Iran Air flies from Kermān to:

Bandar-é Abbās – Tuesday, 5.55 pm, 45 minutes
Esfahān – Wednesday and Friday, 2.15 pm, one hour
Mashhad – Thursday and Sunday, 11.50 am, 1½ hours
Tehrān – daily, 11.30 am, 1¼ hours; Wednesday and Friday, 2.15 pm, 2½ hours; Tuesday, 8.25 pm, 1¼ hours; all 7280 rials
Zāhedān –Wednesday and Friday, 11.30 am, 50 minutes

Saha flies from Kermān to Jazīré-yé Kīsh, but you can only normally get tickets as part of a tour organised by the Kermanseir Tour Company.

Airline Offices Iran Air (☎ 35151) is in Kheyābūn-é Beheshtī. Saha is at the airport.

Bus & Minibus The bus station is on the east side of Kheyābūn-é Ghods in the south-east of Kermān. If you are arriving in Kermān by bus and don't have any business at the terminal, it is best to get off at the Serāh-é Termīnāl a little farther north, from where you can take a shared taxi to Meidūn-é Āzādī for 50 rials. All the bus company offices are at the terminal. Buses run from here to:

Ahvāz – several a week, 1265 km, 20 hours, 2090/2250 rials 'lux'/'super', Cooperative Bus Company No 2

Bam – two a day, 7 am and 1 pm, 194 km, three hours, 340/500 rials 'lux'/'super', Cooperative Bus Company No 2; several buses a day from 7 am, Cooperative Bus Company No 7; tickets can be bought an hour to half an hour in advance

Bandar-é Abbās – at least one a day, 498 km, eight hours

Esfahān – several a day, 703 km, 12 hours, 950 rials 'super', Cooperative Bus Company No 1

Mashhad – at least one a day, 919 km, 15 hours

Shahr-é Bābak – two a day, 238 km, four hours

Shīrāz – at least two a day, 797 km, eight hours, 830 rials

Tehrān – several a day, 1064 km, 18 hours

Yazd – at least one a day, 387 km, six hours

Zāhedān – at least one a day, Cooperative Bus Company No 3); at least one a day, Cooperative Bus Company No 9; about four a day, Cooperative Bus Company No 11; all 541 km, seven hours, 600 or 625 rials 'lux'

The best way to get to Māhūn is on one of the buses passing through the town en route to points further east such as Bam or Zāhedān. In this way you can get a seat on a 'super' bus from Kermān to Māhūn for 500 rials. Ask first at Cooperative Bus Company No 2. There are also some buses passing through Sīrjān. There are alleged to be minibuses to Shahdād (108 km) from just north of Meidūn-é Fedā'īyān-é Eslām at about 7 am and 1 pm.

Train There are daily express trains from Kermān to Tehrān via Yazd, Kāshān and Ghom (2.20 pm, 18 hours). The line east stops at Kermān, so if you are heading for

Pakistan you will have to continue your journey by road or aeroplane as afr as Zāhedān.

You can try getting a shared taxi to the train station from Meīdūn-é Āzādī, but it's much easier to order a telephone taxi for 1000 rials.

Shared Taxi & Savārī From the south-west of Meidūn-é Āzādī where it meets Kheyābūn-é Āyatollāh Sadūghī there are savārīs and shared taxis to Rafsanjūn (137 km, 1½ hours, 1000 rials) and Sīrjān (183 km, two hours, 1500 to 2000 rials), and even sometimes to Bandar-é Abbās.

Shared taxis and savārīs to Māhūn (42 km, half an hour, 200 rials) go from Meidūn-é Fedā'īyān-é Eslām (not Meidūn-é Shohadā as the tourist office told me) within daylight hours. If you arrive by taxi from Māhūn, this is where you will be dropped off.

Cars to Bam, Fahraj (269 km) and Zāhedān run from Meidūn-é Sarāseyāb at the far east of Kermān. The fare to Bam is 1500 rials a person.

It is a little difficult to get to Shahdād and back, and I did not see any shared taxis or savārīs going there. If you are desperate to go, your best bet is to hire a taxi for the round trip at around 1500 rials an hour.

Car & Motorcycle The clearly signposted road between Kermān and Zāhedān is good but very short of facilities. Take plenty of water with you if you are driving, and make sure your vehicle is in good order or else you risk having a very long and unpleasant wait for a repair job. Fill up whenever you see a petrol station, as you may not otherwise make it to the next one.

Getting Around

To/From the Airport There is no airport bus, but you can take a taxi to or from town for about 700 rials as a single passenger.

Bus & Minibus Most buses go through Meidūn-é Āzādī or Meidūn-é Shohadā, and several buses connect the two, but it is usually quicker to go by shared taxi.

Taxi Taxi fares in Kermān are fairly low. You can get from Meidūn-é Āzādī to Meidūn-é Shohadā for 100 rials, or around 200 rials at night. The main junctions for shared taxis are Meidūn-é Āzādī, Meidūn-é Valī-yé Asr and Meidūn-é Shohadā. From Meidūn-é Shohadā south to Meidūn-é Fedā'īyān-é Eslām is 30 to 50 rials, and from there to Meidūn-é Sarāseyāb is another 50 to 100 rials.

BAM بم

Bam is a pleasant tree-lined town famous for its dates, and even more famous with visitors for the remarkably well-preserved remains of a mediaeval town which sit on a hillock at the northern edge of town.

Arg-é Bam ارگ بم

The citadel and original town of Bam were probably founded in the Sassanian era, and some of the surviving structures must have

been built before the 12th century, but the greater part of what remains dates from the Safavid period. It is similar to a large mediaeval European castle, except that the material is not stone but brick. The high walls around the citadel are still intact and even today there is no way of entering it except through the small gatehouse at the south.

As you enter you walk up a steep pathway through the old bazaar, from where lanes lead past the remains of mosques, mansions, squares, military barracks and a caravanserai, all in sand-coloured mud brick. You can climb up steep and narrow stairways to the pinnacles of the outer walls for the definitive outlook over the old and new towns. The inner citadel dominating the town contains a fortified residence known as the **Chahār Fasl** ('Four Seasons'), an artillery yard, and another yard with stables. It is possible to climb right to the top of the citadel. In the Middle Ages a thriving commercial and

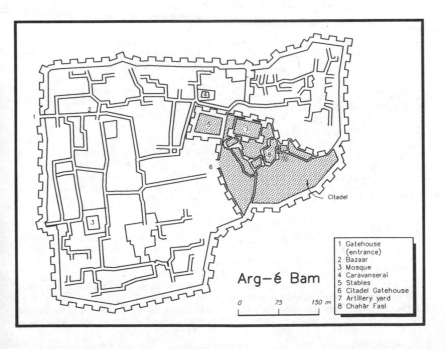

Arg-é Bam

0   75   150 m

1 Gatehouse (entrance)
2 Bazaar
3 Mosque
4 Caravanserai
5 Stables
6 Citadel Gatehouse
7 Artillery yard
8 Chahār Fasl

Citadel

artistic centre lay protected behind these all but impregnable walls.

The Arg-é Bam is open daily from 8 am to noon and from 2 to 5 pm, but you won't be admitted later than 30 minutes before either closing time; there is an entrance fee of 50 rials. The gatehouse has some information about the site in Persian, but nothing in English. An excellent English-speaking guide can be arranged through the tourist office in Kermān.

Places to Stay & Eat

The *Mehmūnsarā-yé Bam* (☎ 3323) (marked in English 'Bam Inn') just off Meidūn-é Farmāndārī charges 2250/3000 rials for a double without/with private bathroom or 6000 rials for a suite. It is a little run-down. The Mehmūnsarā-yé Bam's restaurant can best be described as unpretentious.

Things to Buy

The superb Bam dates, which are exported thoughout the world, cost 700 to 1200 rials a kg in town, depending on the season. The locals are contemptuous of the nearby town of Jīroft (Sabzevārān) which grows yellow dates considered by them vastly inferior to the black ones of Bam.

Getting There & Away

Bus & Minibus The bus companies are on Kheyābūn-é Emām Khomeinī in the south of Bam. There are buses from Bam to:

Īrānshahr – 352 km, seven hours, Cooperative Bus Company No 10
Kermān – two a day, 194 km, three hours, 340/500 rials 'lux'/'super', Cooperative Bus Company No 2; several a day, Cooperative Bus Company No 7
Tehrān – at least one a day, 1258 km, 21 hours, Cooperative Bus Company No 10
Yazd – one a day, 581 km, nine hours, Cooperative Bus Company No 12
Zāhedān – at least two a day, 360 km, six hours, Cooperative Bus Company No 10

Shared Taxi & Savārī There are also shared taxis and savārīs much more regularly from the Serāh-é Zāhedān south of town: to

Meidūn-é Fedā'īyān-é Eslām in Kermān six cramped passengers pay 1500 rials each. Alternatively you could stop off at Māhūn in either direction.

Getting Around

From the Cooperative Bus Company No 7 station (ask for the Gārāzh-é Herandī) in the south of Bam you can walk or take a taxi to the Arg, about two km to the north. It should cost about 300 to 500 rials for a single passenger.

MĀHŪN   ماهان

The small town of Māhūn (or Māhan), 35 km from Kermān on the road south-east to Bam, attracts visitors and pilgrims for its fine mausoleum, but it also has an attractive historical garden from the Ghajar period, the **Bāgh-é Tārīkhī**. The combination of delightful scenery and the charm of its mausoleum is very restful.

Ārāmgāh-é Shāh Ne'matollāh Valī

The dome over the tomb of Shāh Ne'matollāh Valī, a well-known Sufi dervish, dates from the early 15th century, but many of the other structures in the small enclosed complex of religious buildings around it were built in the reign of Shāh Abbās I or later. It is possible to climb up a stairway to the roof level for a better view of the two slender Ghajar minarets and the vast Safavid cupola.

Places to Stay – bottom end

The adequate *Mehmūnsarā-yé Māhūn* (☎ 2700) is on the outskirts of Māhūn, to the right of the road as you approach from Kermān.

Places to Eat

There is a state-owned teashop and restaurant open for lunch behind the mausoleum.

Getting There & Away

From Māhūn you can travel 35 km north-west to Kermān, 65 km north-east along a new asphalted road to Shahdād, or 164 km south-east to Bam. There are regular shared taxis and buses (about hourly until about 6.30 pm) from Meidūn-é Nem'atollāh right in front of the mausoleum to Kermān (30 to 45 minutes, 200 rials). There are also shared taxis and savārīs to Sīrjān (232 km, 2½ hours, 2000 rials a person) and Rafsanjūn (181 km, two hours, 1000 rials).

MEIMAND   ميمند

Meimand, 27 km north-east of Shahr-é Bābak, is a beautiful and well-preserved historical village perched on a hill. To get there, you will have to take a taxi from Shahr-é Bābak, which is accessible by bus from Kermān.

RAFSANJŪN   رفسنجان

Rafsanjūn (or Rafsanjān) is famous for its pistachios, which can be bought here more cheaply than anywhere else in Iran, and for its presidential son, Hojjat-ol-Eslām Alī Akbar Rafsanjānī, whose family owns a pistachio estate here, but for nothing much else of interest to the visitor.

Places to Stay

There is only one hotel, the adequate *Mehmūnsarā-yé Rafsanjūn* (☎ (03431) 2050).

Getting There & Away

From the south-west of Meidūn-é Āzādī in Kermān where it meets Kheyābūn-é Āyatollāh Sadūghī there are savārīs and shared taxis to Rafsanjūn (137 km, 1½ hours, 1000 rials).

SHAHDĀD   شهداد

An interesting archaeological site has recently come to light about five km east of this small town on the western border of the Dasht-é Lūt. This prehistoric mound, known as the **Tappé-yé Kohné**, has revealed many fascinating metal implements with animal motifs and clay human figurines from the 3rd millennium BC. Some of the latter are on display on the ground floor of the Mūzé-yé Īrān-é Bāstān in Tehrān. In the town of Shahdād itself there is an impressive mausoleum, the **Emāmzādé-yé Mohammad Ebn-é Zeid**.

There is no hotel in Shahdād.

Getting There & Away

There is a good asphalted road from Māhūn to Shahdād, but it is still a little difficult to get there by public transport. There are alleged to be minibuses to Shahdād (108 km) from just north of Meidūn-é Fedā'īyān-é Eslām in Kermān at about 7 am and 1 pm, but your best bet is probably to hire a taxi for the return trip at around 1500 rials an hour from Māhūn or Kermān.

SĪRJĀN   سيرجان

Midway between Yazd and Bandar-é Abbās, the town of Sīrjān is also an important transit stop between Kermān and Shīrāz. There is an interesting 13th-century brick monument in the town, and a number of historical remains have been unearthed, but the excavations were abandoned some time ago and there is almost nothing to see at present.

Ghal'é-yé Sang

At Ghal'é-yé Sang ('Stone Fortress') on the outskirts of Sīrjān there rest the remains of a walled town on the northern and eastern flanks of a small hill. You can see fragments of pottery in the very crumbly mud-brick walls of this village and all around the site. It is possible to climb up the hill from the south side to trace out the indistinct remains of a stone fortress on the hilltop. Ghal'é-yé Sang lies on the main local shepherds' route, and you may have your sightseeing disturbed by hundreds of ewes and rams.

This settlement was in the early Islamic period the provincial capital occupying a strategic position on the road between the interior and the Strait of Hormoz. It was captured after a long siege by the Timurids at the end of the 15th century and appears to have been abandoned soon afterwards. Although the town and citadel are nowhere near as well-preserved as those at Bam, the remains have excited many archaeologists.

Tappé-yé Yahyā

This ancient mound is in a valley south-east of Sīrjān in the direction of Jīroft (Sabzevārān). It has been of great interest to archaeologists, but it is very difficult to get to from either town.

Places to Stay

The good *Mehmūnsarā-yé Sīrjān* (☎ (03452) 7887) in the centre of town charges 3000 rials a double with bathroom.

Places to Eat

There is a good restaurant, the *Sālon-é Ghezā-yé Khazarī-yé Nāz* (not marked in English), in the main street about 250 metres from the Kermān taxi station on the other side of the road.

Getting There & Away

Cooperative Bus Company 2 and Cooperative Bus Company No 6 are in Kheyābūn-é Sayyed Jamāl. From the Kermān station (at the north-east approach of Sīrjān) you can take a taxi or bus (300 rials 'lux', 500 rials 'super') to Kermān until late at night: flag down any passing bus.

Bus Cooperative Bus Company No 2 has buses from Sīrjān to Būshehr (683 km, 11 hours), Esfahān (657 km, 11 hours) and Shīrāz (381 km, six hours). Both Company No 2 and Company No 6 have buses to Tehrān (1037 km, 17 hours).

Getting Around

To get to the Ghal'é-yé Sang from Sīrjān, take a shared taxi to the Polīs-é Rah (highway police station) for 100 to 200 rials and from there charter a taxi at a negotiable sum between 500 and 1000 rials. To get back to Sīrjān, walk a km to the Emāmzādé-yé Alī (the large walled compound with garish modern mirror tiles around the tomb) and take a shared taxi, truck or savārī or any other transport to the Polīs-é Rāh: it is much easier to find transport in this direction than it is from the Polīs-é Rāh to Ghal'é-yé Sang, although even so you may have to wait a long time.

It might be worth chartering a taxi to take you from Sīrjān to Ghal'é-yé Sang and back for around 1500 rials an hour.

South Iran & the Islands of the Persian Gulf

ایران جنوبی وجزائر خلیج فارس

This chapter covers the provinces of Hormozgān, Fārs, Būshehr, Boyerahmad va Kohgīlūyé and Khūzestān. The three coastal provinces – Hormozgān, Būshehr and Khūzestān – are hot and humid all year round. The only truly pleasant time to visit them is November to March. Fārs is more agreeable, and it is rarely excessively hot or cold. Boyerahmad va Kohgīlūyé is of little interest and is not discussed in this chapter.

The indigenous people of the Iranian shores of the Persian Gulf are often loosely known as Bandarīs, from the Persian word for 'port'. Of Arab, Negro or mixed stock, the Bandarīs are darker-skinned than the Persians, and although they have become Persianised in many ways, they preserve their own Arabic dialect and culture; many are Sunni. The Bandarī women have their own dress, quite unlike any other in Iran: colourful embroidered or printed layers of wraps over loose trousers, leg-bracelets and sandals or flip-flops, and, because of the heat, owlish face-masks instead of veils. Many of the men still wear the *abā* (a long, sleeveless, usually white robe), sandals or flip-flops and sometimes a turban. The traditional Bandarī dress is most common in Hormozgān, especially on the islands.

The people of Fārs are mostly Persian, although there are still some migratory tribes whom even Genghis Khan and Tamerlane never tried to pacify.

Because of the excessive heat in the Gulf region, the siesta is taken very seriously here, even in winter, and very little except public transport functions between noon and late afternoon. Offices and shops close throughout the afternoon and reopen for a few hours at about 6 pm.

Although the region is largely desert, semidesert or mountainous, limes and other citrus fruits, cotton, tobacco and dates are grown here. There are more than 200 varie-

ties of fish, among other marine life, in the Gulf, but there is surprisingly little variety in the markets and restaurants, although excellent shrimps and prawns are widely available.

Since illicit traffic in goods and humans alike does go on quite a lot in the Gulf and especially around the Strait of Hormoz, it is not wise to travel along the coast, and most especially not to any of the islands, without a passport bearing a valid visa to show that you have entered the country legally. If you must leave your passport somewhere, take a photocopy and a receipt.

Islands of the Persian Gulf

There are several sizeable islands in the Persian Gulf, of which all but Khārk (in Būshehr Province) belong to Hormozgān. With the exception of Kīsh, a thriving free port, none is equipped to entertain tourists, and few if any are tourist destinations in the conventional sense. Even so, they are of great interest, and there are preserved in them pockets of a way of life almost vanished from the mainland and in danger of disappearing from the islands too. Pearl

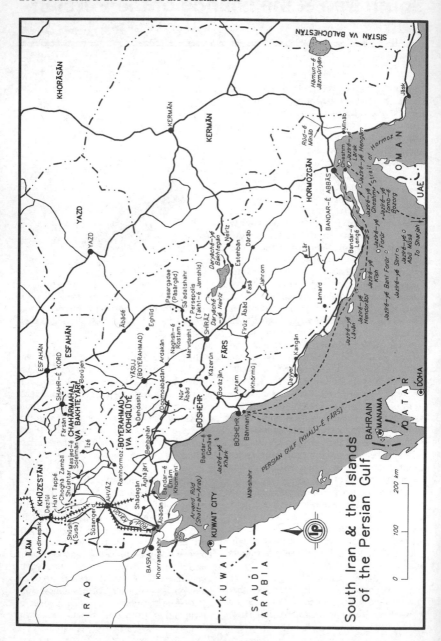

South Iran & the Islands of the Persian Gulf

diving used to be a very important activity, but the trade has gone into decline over recent years with the increasing popularity of cultivated pearls and a rise in the local shark population.

Because of the heat and a shortage of drinking water, winter is the sensible time to visit.

Although it is not true, as some people on the mainland will tell you, that foreigners need special permission to visit the islands, the authorities are not used to foreigners making casual visits to them, so exercise caution and avoid attracting excessive suspicion, especially at times when there is military activity in the region.

Hormozgān Province

استان هرمزگان

The hot, humid and largely barren Hormozgān Province, named after the Strait of Hormoz which it guards, has an area of 66,870 sq km and a largely rural population of 760,000. It's best visited only between November and March. The provincial capital is Bandar-é Abbās.

BANDAR-É ABBĀS
بندر عباس

Population: 201,600

This city overlooking the Strait of Hormoz is the busiest port in Iran. In the summer it gets sizzling hot and very humid here, but it's pleasant enough to visit in winter. Despite its links with Shāh Abbās I who founded the town in 1622, about the only thing you'll find to remind you of the origins of Abbas' Port is its name. There's not a lot of reason to hang around here, but Bandar-é Abbās – simply Bandar to the locals – is a stepping-off point for Jazīré-yé Hormoz and the other islands.

Its population is largely of Arab, Negro or mixed stock, with a large Sunni minority. The small but long-established Hindu community has its own temple here.

History

Until 1622 no more than a fishing village by the name of Gāmerūn, this strategically important site was chosen as Persia's main southern port and naval dockyard after the decline of nearby Hormoz. The British East India Company was granted a trading concession here, followed later by Dutch and French traders, all of whom established factories; by the 17th century Bandar-é Abbās became the chief Persian port and the main outlet for the lucrative trade in Kermān carpets. However, the port went into decline after the end of the Safavid dynasty; in 1759 the East India Company moved to the recently founded port of Būshehr after its factory at Bandar-é Abbās was destroyed by the French, and by 1793 the fortunes of Bandar-é Abbās, already supplanted as chief port by Būshehr, had fallen so low that it passed into the hands of the Sultan of Oman. In 1868 it returned to Persian control, but its role in maritime trade was only peripheral until the second half of this century.

Ironically, its hour of glory came during the Iran-Iraq War, when the rival ports of Būshehr, Bandar-é Emām Khomeinī and Khorramshahr to the west became too dangerous for regular shipping, and it is still the only truly active international port on the northern shores of the Persian Gulf. The city has grown remarkably over recent years, and vast sums have been invested in the building of a large modern port, Bandar-é Shahīd Rajā'ī, three km west of Bandar-é Abbās.

Orientation

Bandar-é Abbās stretches out along a long and narrow coastal strip. The main east-west thoroughfare changes its name from Bolvār-é Shahīd Doktor Mohammad Hosein Beheshtī to Kheyābūn-é Emām Khomeinī and then to Bolvār-é Pāsdārān. The main docks (the Esklelé-yé Shahīd Bāhonar) are in the west of town, the airport and bus station to the east and the main road out of Bandar-é Abbās in all directions extends eastward from Bolvār-é Shahīd Doktor Mohammad Hosein Beheshtī.

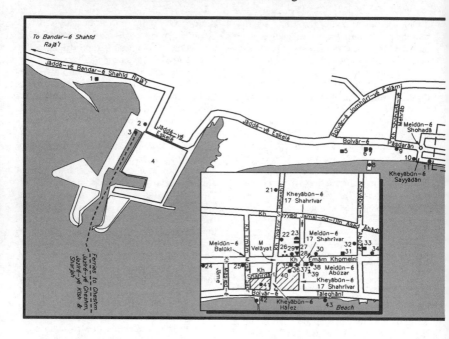

Information

The shahrdārī (☎ 23022) is in an alley on the north side of Kheyābūn-é Emām Khomeinī 250 metres west of Meidūn-é Enghelāb. The ostāndārī (☎ 27002) is on the seafront in Kheyābūn-é Doktor Chamrān, about a km from Meidūn-é Enghelāb.

The visa office is on the ground floor of the police headquarters on the south-east side of Meidūn-é Valī-yé Asr. The police are more than a little laid back – the sun affects everyone here – but if you give them a week they should be able to oblige with a visa extension. No English is spoken.

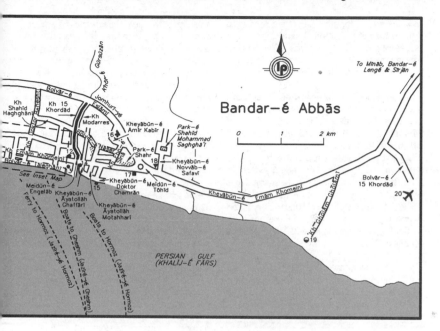

Bandar–é Abbās

PERSIAN GULF
(KHALĪJ–É FĀRS)

13	Stadium
14	Main Telephone Office
15	Ostāndārī
16	Emergency Clinic
19	Bus Station
20	Airport
21	Cooperative Bus Company No 1
22	Telephone Office
23	Main Post & Telegraph Office
24	Iran Air & Valfajre-8 Shipping Company
25	Balooki Travel Agency
26	Hindu Temple (Mābad-é Hendūhā)
29	Cooperative Bus Company No 8
30	'House of Culture' (Khūné-yé Farhang)
32	Cooperative Bus Company No 15
34	NIOC (National Iranian Oil Company)
36	Bank Melli Iran (Central Branch)
37	Police Headquarters (Shahrbānī)
38	Shared Taxis and Savārīs to Mīnāb
39	Tourist Office
40	Fruit Market (Bāzār-é Mīvé)
41	Bāzār-é Shahrdārī
42	Old Jetty (Eskelé-yé Ghadīm) & Ferry to Hormoz (Jazīré-yé Hormoz)
43	Boats to Hormoz (Jazīré-yé Hormoz) & Gheshm (Jazīré-yé Ghesh)

Tourist Office The tourist office (☎ 23012) is in a kūché behind the police headquarters (shahrbānī) – don't confuse it with the 'House of Culture' (Khūné-yé Farhang) building across the main road. Not marked in English, it's impossible to find unless you ask for directions (ask for Ershād-é

Eslāmī). Like most things around here, it closes at about noon.

Money Bank Melli Iran (central branch) is on the south-west of Meidūn-é Valī-yé Asr. When I went here to ask about cashing a travellers' cheque, the clerk told me I would have to wait a month while they sent it to Tehrān for authorisation. There's a thriving black market for UAE dirhams and other foreign currencies in the bazaar district and on the street near Bank Melli Iran.

Post & Telecommunications The main post office is on the west side of Kheyābūn-é Bohādor-é Shomālī, 150 metres north of Meidūn-é Valī-yé Asr, and the main telephone office is on the south side of Kheyābūn-é Emām Khomeinī at the intersection with Kheyābūn-é Āyatollāh Ghaffārī. Trunk calls can also be made at the telephone office on the east side of Kheyābūn-é Doktor Beheshtī. International and even trunk telephone calls are fraught with difficulty. The dialling code for Bandar-é Abbās is 0761.

Foreign Consulate The UAE Consulate (☎ 23063, 27531) (Konsūlgarī-yé Emārāt-é Mottahedé-yé Arabī) is on the south side of Bolvār-é Pāsdārān, midway between Meidūn-é Shohadā and the Homa Hotel.

Travel Agency The Balooki Travel Agency on the south-west side of Meidūn-é Balūkī handles bookings for aeroplane tickets, and is worth trying if the Iran Air office claims that all flights are full.

Maps The tourist office has a free map of Bandar-é Abbās and Hormozgān with some entries in English. The Gītā Shenāsī map (200 rials) is more detailed but entirely in Persian.

Medical Services The emergency clinic (☎ 115, 22055) is at the intersection of Bolvār-é Jomhūrī-yé Eslāmī with Kheyābūn-é Amīr Kabīr.

Emergency The police headquarters (shahr-bānī) is on the south-east side of Meidūn-é Valī-yé Asr.

Things to See & Do
The most pleasant walk, along Bolvār-é Tāleghānī, takes you from the daily early morning fish market (Bāzār-é Māhī) in the west, past the busy beach (pelāzh) with its boatmen, smugglers and seaside attractions on one side and the no less bustling main bazaar to the other. There's quite a long sandy beach and it's possible to walk or paddle much of the way along it, but swimming isn't a good idea because of the sharks and stinging jellyfish.

The old quarter (shahr-é ghadīm) of Bandar-é Abbās, around the Homa Hotel, has been largely rebuilt and is no longer of much interest unless you get a thrill out of being stared at by everything on two or four legs.

Places to Stay
There's an acute shortage of accommodation in Bandar-é Abbās in winter, which is when nearly everyone wants to visit. If you do make the mistake of arriving at that time of year without a reservation, your only options are bribery and corruption or an appeal to the tourist office or the police, who can employ the same methods of persuasion on an unsuspecting hotel manager. None of the hotels is anything to write home about, even the supposedly luxurious Homa, but at least you shouldn't have any problem finding a room with air-con or a fan in the hotter months of the year, when most places are almost empty.

Places to Stay – bottom end
There are some mosāferkhūnés around the main bazaar district, but a lack of air-con makes these places harsh options for at least six months of the year. One of the better ones is the Mosāferkhūné-yé Hormozgān (☎ 24856) (marked in English 'Hotel Hormozgan') in Bolvār-é Sayyed Jamāl-od-Dīn Asadābādī. Among others in the same area, cheaper places include the Mosāferkhūné-yé Īrān (☎ 22707) on the south side of Kheyābūn-é Emām Khomeinī 100 metres west of Meidūn-é Valī-yé Asr, the Mosāferkhūné-yé Eslāmī (☎ 22584) ('Islami') and the Mosāferkhūné-yé Chahār Fasl (☎ 22158) ('Chahar Fasl'), both in Kheyābūn-é Bahādor-é Jonūbī.

If you can't find anywhere in town which will give you a room, a discreet tip (say 1500 rials) to the receptionist will probably find you a room at the *Hotel-é Naghsh-é Jahān* (☎ 28640) about a km west of Shahīd Bāhonar Docks. It's not marked in English and you'll have a very long trek from the centre, so it's best to take a taxi: from the centre pay 500 to 1000 rials as a single passenger. Although far from ideal and surely in danger of structural damage from the constant rumble of heavy juggernaut traffic along the main road outside, this truckers' dive does have reasonably clean rooms with fans and private showers. Rooms cost 2200/3300 rials a single/double.

Places to Stay – middle
Probably the second best hotel in town is the central *Hotel-é Ghods* (☎ 22344) ('Hotel Ghods') in Kheyābūn-é Emām Khomeinī, which is comfortable if not luxurious and charges 2250/3400 rials a single/double with private bathroom. Slightly cheaper places are the *Hotel-é Hamzé* (☎ 23771) ('Hotel Hamza') in Kheyābūn-é Doktor Sharī'atī, the *Hotel-é Āzādī* on the south side of Bol-

vār-é Pāsdārān, a long way from the centre but offering a good view over the Gulf, and the almost equally isolated *Hotel-é Sa'dī*, opposite the Pārk-é Shahr on the south side of Kheyābūn-é Emām Khomeinī.

Places to Stay – top end
With its tennis courts and swimming pool, the *Homa Hotel* (☎ 23082) (Hotel-é Homā, but equally well known by its old name of Gāmerūn), on the south side of Bolvār-é Pāsdārān overlooking the Gulf, must once have been a good hotel, but today gives the impression of not having seen any mainte-nance or a lick of paint since before the revolution. With its cramped and antiquated lifts, flaking paintwork, seatless lavatories, surly receptionists and a deservedly low rep-utation for service, this sadly run-down establishment can no longer be considered in the luxury class. Rooms do at least have an air-con system over which the guest has little or no control. Quite rightly the cheapest in the otherwise excellent Homa chain, this one

Dhow

charges 6200/7800/10,000/17,000 rials a single/double/triple/suite. Unfortunately it doesn't face any sort of competition, and in winter it's essential to book a room here some weeks ahead for the exact number of nights required.

Places to Eat

Despite its abundance of fresh fish and seafood, there's no really good restaurant in Bandar-é Abbās, and it would only take a day or two here for eating out to become monotonous. The best thing to try in Bandar-é Abbās is chelō meigū – battered prawns or shrimps with boiled rice – which is cheap, fresh and served almost everywhere. At night there are some kebab stalls around Meidūn-é Valī-yé Asr.

On Meidūn-é Valī-yé Asr, the *Chelō Kabābī-yé Shahrzād* (not marked in English, but next to the Shahrzad Cinema, which is) serves good chelō kabāb-é barg with dūgh, māst and tea, all for 1200 rials. The *Restōrān-é Sajjād* ('Sadjad Restaurant'), on the north side of Kheyābūn-é Emām Khomeinī 400 metres east of Meidūn-é Emām Khomeinī, has chelō meigū for 1500 rials and good chelō kabāb. There's an adequate canteen in the *Hotel-é Naghsh-é Jahān*.

The *Homa Hotel* has the city's smartest restaurant, although its minimalist menu isn't up to the chain's usual standards.

Lādan Bastanī Forūshī (not marked in English) on the north-west side of Meidūn-é Valī-yé Asr, caters to the hot and thirsty visitor's need for ice cream, fālūdé, milk shakes, coffee or tea.

Things to Buy

All manner of imported goods are traded here, many of them brought over from the UAE and mostly sold at prices lower than on the rest of the Iranian mainland. You won't buy as cheaply here as in Jazīré-yé Kīsh, but the range of goods is wider. If you're a fan of European chocolate you'll probably find it cheaper and fresher here than elsewhere in Iran. Cigarettes are cheap too.

If you're looking for indigenous souvenirs, some handicrafts unique to the region include abās, coarse rugs and carpets, woollen blankets, brocade, and various tools and implements woven from the fibres of the date palm leaf.

Getting There & Away

Air From most points this is the most sensible way of reaching Bandar-é Abbās. Iran Air flies from Bandar-é Abbās to:

Chābahār – Monday, Wednesday and Saturday, 9.55 am, 1 hour
Esfahān – Sunday, Wednesday and Friday, 4 pm, 1½ hours
Jazīré-yé Kīsh – Monday and Saturday, 9.35 pm, 40 minutes (tickets very difficult, and only obtainable from Iran Air main office)
Kermān – Tuesday, 7.10 pm, 45 minutes
Mashhad – Sunday and Thursday, 6.50 pm, 1¾ hours
Rasht – Tuesday and Friday, 11.55 am, 2¼ hours
Shīrāz – daily, midnight, 45 minutes
Tehrān – daily, midnight, 2½ hours
    Saturday, 8.20 am, 2¾ hours
    Monday, Wednesday and Saturday, 1.10 pm, 1¾ hours
    Sunday, Tuesday and Thursday, 1.40 pm, 1¾ hours
    Sunday, Wednesday and Friday, 4 pm 2¾ hours
    Tuesday, 7.10 pm, 1½ hours
    daily, 10.45 pm, 1¾ hours (8850 rials)
Yazd – Saturday, 8.20 am, 1¼ hours.

International Services Iran Air flies to Dubai on Sunday and Tuesday at 9.50 am (one hour) and Sharjah on Thursday at 9.50 am (one hour). Return flights leave at 11.15 am the same day. Emirates (probably a better airline) flies to and from Dubai every Wednesday and Friday. Although foreigners have to pay in hard currency for seats, these services are the cheapest ways of leaving or entering Iran by air. They're also very popular with well-to-do Iranians on shopping sprees and tend to be booked up some weeks ahead, although priority is usually given to foreigners. Both airlines charge US$100/200 one-way/return, or 370/740 UAE dirhams if you're paying in the UAE. Ariana Afghan has weekly flights to Kabul. See also the Getting There & Away chapter.

Airline Offices There's a not-terribly-useful Iran Air office opposite the entrance to the Homa Hotel. Even though the staff at the main Iran Air office (☎ 26250), on the south side of Kheyābūn-é Emām Khomeinī 500 metres east of Meidūn-é Shohadā, are blighted by the general air of lethargy so prevalent in the Persian Gulf, this is the place to go for domestic and international tickets. If they claim all flights are full, go to the Balooki Travel Agency. Emirates (☎ 22142) is at the west end of Bolvār-é Tāleghānī.

Bus Although Bandar-é Abbās enjoys better road communications with central Iran than anywhere else along the southern shores, heavy truck traffic, poor facilities along the road, endless expanses of desert and punishing temperatures for most of the year mean that few people would willingly take the long and dusty bus trip here. Any such journey could only lead to disappointment. The best road is from Kermān.

The bus station is near the airport to the far east of town, about 500 rials by shared taxi from the centre. The bus companies are spread out around the centre of town. The one to try first, Cooperative Bus Company No 1, is on the west side of Kheyābūn-é Doktor Beheshtī 600 metres north of Meidūn-é Velāyat. Cooperative Bus Company No 15 is 100 metres north of Meidūn-é Abūzar on the west side of Kheyābūn-é Doktor Sharī'atī, and Cooperative Bus Company No 8 is on the north side of Kheyābūn-é Emām Khomeinī, just west of Meidūn-é Valī-yé Asr. There are buses from Bandar-é Abbās to:

Ahvāz – several buses a week, 1169 km, 19 hours, 1620/2550 rials 'lux'/'super' (Cooperative Bus Company No 2)
Bākhtarān – at least one a day, 1748 km, 28 hours, 3215/3855 rials 'lux'/'super' (19 to 21 hours)
Bandar-é Anzalī – several a week, 1864 km, 32 hours
Bandar-é Lengé – several a day, 253 km, four hours, 600 rials 'lux'
Būshehr – several a day, 921 km, 16 hours, 1650 rials
Esfahān – at least one a day, 1082 km, 18 hours, 1510 rials 'super' (Cooperative Bus Company No 1)
Kermān – at least one a day, 498 km, eight hours
Mashhad – one a day, 1417 km, 22 hours
Shīrāz – at least two a day, 601 km, 10 hours
Zāhedān – one a day, 1039 km, 17 hours, 1200 rials.

Train The partially completed line to Sīrjān marked on some maps is only for cargo; in any case it's liable to buckling.

Shared Taxi & Savārī Shared taxis and savārīs (2000 to 2500 rials) to Mīnāb leave from the south side of Kheyābūn-é Emām Khomeinī, just east of the shahrdārī.

Sea Valfajre-8 (☎ 29095) is above the main Iran Air office. There are nine sailings a week to/from Jazīré-yé Kīsh, and six weekly to/from Sharjah (cars can be shipped on this ferry). Other destinations such as Jāsk and Muscat are planned for the near future. Check fares (payable in rials) and exact times locally.

Valfajre-8 can also arrange inclusive tours to Sharjah, payable partly in US dollars and partly in rials.

To/From the Islands The best way to get to the islands is to take one of the constant relay of small motorised skiffs from the main beach. The dangers of piracy, sharks and assaults by lawless boatmen on their passengers have been much exaggerated, and a trip to one or other of the islands is highly recommended for anyone jaded with the mainland culture.

During daylight hours, and currents permitting, the small boats take around six passengers (fewer with heavy luggage) every few minutes from the main beach east of the old jetty. Ordinarily they only go to Hormoz or Gheshm, according to the destination called out by the pilot, but if there are enough passengers or the price is right you could charter one further afield. To Hormoz, about 30 minutes away, the fare's 500 rials a passenger, and to Gheshm, about 45 minutes away, 1000 rials. Don't wear any clothes that are likely to be damaged by the inevitable seepage of salt-water into the boat. Hold on very tightly to anything likely to blow away. It's best to leave from Bandar-é Abbās in the morning, leaving plenty of time to catch the last boat back, and to keep a watch on the current, or else you risk being stranded on one of the islands for the night. There are even porters at Bandar-é Abbās beach, who wield extraordinary contraptions designed to carry passengers from the shore to the boat or back without getting their feet wet: pay 100 rials a head for this luxury.

There are also occasional ferries, perhaps one every day or two, to Jazīré-yé Hormoz from the old jetty (Eskelé-yé Ghadīm) opposite the bazaar, and to Jazīré-yé Gheshm from the main docks (Eskelé-yé Shahīd Bāhonar) west of town.

Getting Around

There's a shortage of taxis in Bandar-é Abbās, and crowded vans are often the only option. The Homa Hotel, however, has a 24-hour taxi service.

To/From the Airport To the airport is 1000 to 1500 rials for a solo passenger, or 500 to 700 rials in a shared taxi; there's no airport bus.

MĪNĀB ميناب

Although Mīnāb was one of the earliest large settlements in the area, it's famous above all for the exceptionally luxuriant date plantations which dominate the town. On the left as you approach from Bandar-é Abbās there's a historic tower on a hilltop with houses perched all the way up to it. It's the custom that couples from the town must walk once around this fortress in the company of their families before taking their marriage vows.

Mīnāb is one of the closest towns to the UAE, and it's well-known for its open trade in cigarettes smuggled over the Strait of Hormoz. A carton of genuine Marlboro is only 8700 rials here. However, the Komité have checkpoints on all roads out to prevent anyone from taking more than two or three cartons. The remarkably dark-skinned Mīnābīs are not especially friendly towards foreigners. There's a mehmūnsarā (government rest house) in the main street.

Getting There & Away

The road from Bandar-é Abbās is demanding, often being waterlogged at one point

after rain, and the road east is exceptionally dire. Mīnāb can be reached by bus from Bandar-é Abbās and Shīrāz.

BANDAR-Ē LENGÉ بندر لنگه

The main port for Jazīré-yé Kīsh, Bandar-é Lengé (simply Lengé to the locals) was until quite recently a very sleepy little fishing village. It has now grown into a very sleepy little town, its rise in the world marked by the introduction of an air link to Shīrāz and Tehrān. The population is half Sunni and half Shi'ite, and Arabic enjoys equal currency with Persian.

Lengé is an infectiously lethargic place, and although there isn't a great deal to do here even outside the rigidly observed five or six-hour siesta, it's a pleasant overnight stop before or after visiting Jazīré-yé Kīsh in the cooler season. Things to see include several colourful white or pale stone mosques, with single minarets decorated in the Arab style, and a few old and largely derelict Bandarī buildings of mud brick.

Orientation & Information

The beach is more or less closed off from the town. None of the roads is, as far as I could tell, marked in Persian, let alone English; probably no-one could be bothered to put up the signs. The main streets are Bolvār-é Emām Khomeinī (the coast road) and Kheyābūn-é Enghelāb, which runs at a right angle to it opposite the harbour. The exceptionally unanimated bazaar is to the east of Kheyābūn-é Emām Khomeinī.

Places to Stay – bottom end

A much-needed hotel is being built in Lengé and may be completed within the life of this book. The *Mehmūnsarā-yé Jahāngardī* is now closed, so you're left with a choice of four mosáferkhūnés in the centre of town. In terms of rooms there isn't much to choose between the best three – the *Amīd*, the *Bābū* (☎ 2170, 2350) and the *Īrān* – but the Amīd is the best, even if overpriced at 4000 rials a double (no singles), because it has hot showers and the others don't even have showers. The other two – both friendly to foreigners – charge 2400/3000 rials a double/triple. Even simpler accommodation can be had at the *Mosāferkhūné-yé Vīllā*.

Places to Eat

There are a few teahouses (chāykhūnés) in the bazaar where the hubble-bubble is without a pipe, for the mouthpiece leads directly into the water jug. Opposite the harbour there's a popular pavement teahouse where it's pleasant to sit at night. It's open until late, and doubles as a boarding-point for buses along the coast road.

The *Restorān-é Shafā'īgh* on the east side of Kheyābūn-é Emām Khomeinī is a bit of a fly sanctuary but serves good fried prawns at 1500 rials. The *Restorān-é Mosāferkhūné-yé Bābū* has good kabāb-é gūsht (shīshlīks) for 1200 rials for four skewers and bread, and is less troubled by flies. There are several other similar restaurants along the main road and along the coast road west of the harbour.

Getting There & Away

Air Iran Air flies from Bandar-é Lengé to Shīrāz daily at 9.15 am (one hour) and to Tehrān daily at 9.15 am (2½ hours, 8850 rials). The unbelievably lethargic Iran Air office (☎ 2799) is on the east side of Kheyābūn-é Shahrdārī. Foreigners cannot buy international tickets here because there's no exchange office in town.

Bus The Vālfajr Bus Company (not to be confused with the shipping company) has buses to:

Bandar-é Abbās – hourly from early morning to evening, 253 km, four hours, 600 rials 'lux'
Būshehr – one daily, 656 km, nine hours, 1250 rials 'lux'
Mashhad – one daily, 1662 km, 25 hours, 2000 rials
Shīrāz – one daily, 654 km, 12 hours, 1400 rials

Sea Valfajre-8 Shipping Company (☎ 3438, 3632, 3448) on the south side of Kheyābūn-é

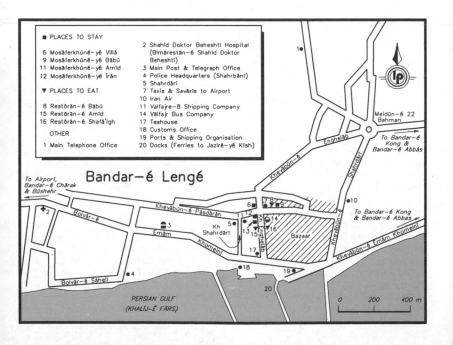

PLACES TO STAY
6 Mosāferkhūné–yé Vīllā
9 Mosāferkhūné–yé Bābū
11 Mosāferkhūné–yé Amīd
12 Mosāferkhūné–yé Īrān

PLACES TO EAT
8 Restorān-é Bābū
15 Restorān-é Amīd
16 Restorān-é Shafā'īgh

OTHER
1 Main Telephone Office
2 Shahīd Doktor Beheshtī Hospital (Bīmārestān-é Shahīd Doktor Beheshtī)
3 Main Post & Telegraph Office
4 Police Headquarters (Shahrbānī)
5 Shahrdārī
7 Taxis & Savāris to Airport
10 Iran Air
11 Valfajre–8 Shipping Company
14 Vālfajr Bus Company
17 Teahouse
18 Customs Office
19 Ports & Shipping Organisation
20 Docks (Ferries to Jazīré–yé Kīsh)

Bandar–é Lengé

Pāsdārān is open Saturday to Wednesday, from 8 am to 12.30 pm and 4 to 6 pm, and Thursday from 8 am to 12.30 pm. There are 12 sailings a week to and from Jazīré-yé Kīsh, and the single fare is 5000 rials for the five-hour journey. Tickets are in short supply, but foreigners are given priority. Alternatively you can go by motor launch from Bandar-é Chārak for 7500 rials, but you'll only be allowed to take the very minimum of hand luggage. Ships to Jazīré-yé Kīsh no longer leave from Bandar-é Kong, the port and ship-building town five km east of Lengé.

Getting Around
To/From the Airport A taxi to the airport west of Lengé costs 1000 rials for a solo passenger; hail one at the place marked on the map. From the airport there are plenty of savārīs (no more than 500 rials) but no taxis.

JAZĪRÉ-YÉ HORMOZ   جزیره هرمز
Area: 42 sq km
Population: 3900
Hormoz Island is well worth a visit, easily made from Bandar-é Abbās. It is some seven km from the mainland and 18 km south-east of Bandar-é Abbās or north-east of Jazīrē-yé Gheshm. There's one small town, Hormoz, on the northern promontory; the rest of the island is uninhabited. Its interior is hilly and infertile, although some of its mineral resources are exploited. The island is famous for the reddishness of its soil and some of its stone, both of which are used for building materials in Hormoz. The temperature here generally hovers two or three degrees above that in Bandar-é Abbās. In summer even some of the locals find the heat and humidity unbearable and retreat to the mainland.

Despite its smallness, Jazīré-yé Hormoz was for around 300 years a thriving and opulent trading centre of the Persian Gulf, supporting a population of up to 40,000, and it has the most historical interest of any of the Iranian islands.

History
The island was, until the 14th century, known as Jazīré-yé Jarūn, or sometimes Zarūn, while Hormoz was the name of a famous and long-established commercial town on the mainland, probably at an unknown site on the Rūd-é Mīnāb. Around 1300 the damage caused by repeated raids by Mongol horsemen made the 15th Amīr of Hormoz shut up shop and move with many of his subjects first briefly to Jazīré-yé Kīsh and then to Jazīré-yé Jarūn. It's not recorded whether the place was previously inhabited, but it is known that after a short time the same *amīr* (emir; ruler) founded a great city on the northern tip of the island and named both the city and the island Hormoz. This new Hormoz soon became the main emporium of the Persian Gulf, attracting immigrants from the mainland and trade from as far away as India, even though the sole product of the island was salt, and water had to be imported. Visitors to Hormoz described it as heavily fortified, bustling and opulent. There's evidence that some other Persian Gulf islands, and even a coastal strip of Oman, came under the suzerainty of the amīrs of Hormoz.

In 1507 the talented Portuguese admiral and empire-builder Affonso de Albuquerque, Affonso the Great, in an attempt to establish by force a network of Portuguese bases in Goa, Aden, Malacca (present-day Melaka, Malaysia) and Hormoz, besieged the island and, after a battle, conquered it. The castle of Hormoz, which he started the same year, was completed in 1515; in the meantime he took Goa in 1510 and Malacca in 1511. In 1515 he returned from Hormoz to Goa only to be informed by the ungrateful Portuguese authorities that he was out of a job; later the same year he died at Goa.

With Jazīré-yé Hormoz as their fortified base, the Portuguese, keeping on the amīrs as hereditary rulers, quickly extended their gains and came to hold sway over all shipping in the Gulf. Virtually all trade with India, the Far East, Muscat and the Gulf ports was funnelled through Hormoz, to which the Portuguese, under an administration known for its justice and religious tolerance, brought great prosperity for over

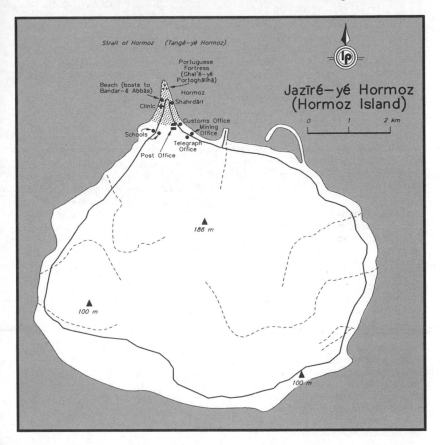

a century. But Portugal's stranglehold over vital international trading routes could hardly fail to arouse the resentment of Persia and the other rising imperial powers of the day, and in 1550 Ottoman forces besieged the fortress of Hormoz for a month but failed to take the island. Early the next century, Shāh Abbās I granted the British East India Company trading rights with Persia through the port of Jāsk, thus enraging the Portuguese. He cajoled the English into sending a force to assist him, and in 1622 the joint expedition, despite a brave defence by the Portuguese, succeeded in gaining the island.

Abbās I selected the small coastal town of Gāmerūn to be the new outlet for Persian trade, changing its name to Bandar-é Abbās after himself, and Hormoz quickly fell into a period of decline from which it has never recovered, with most of its former splendours in ruins within a few years. The British general Sir Percy Molesworth-Sykes, who made a visit to the island in 1893, reported that Hormoz was no more than a miserable little village of some 200 souls whose livelihood depended entirely on fishing and smuggling.

Today, the town of Hormoz is still an

impoverished outpost where foraging goats and barefoot children are rarely disturbed by motorised traffic, though some of the traditional mat huts have been replaced by low-roofed stone dwellings. In summer the exceptionally high temperatures on the island drive many of its inhabitants onto the mainland, especially to work in the date harvest at Mīnāb. Hormoz hosts a sizeable Bangladeshi community. Salt and red ochre are extracted from mines on Jazīré-yé Hormoz and shipped from the commercial port to the east of Hormoz. The only other main activities are fishing and smuggling.

Portuguese Castle
Towering some 750 metres to the north of the beach at Hormoz, and easily reached by foot from it, is the famous Portuguese castle (ghal'é-yé Portoghālīhā) of Hormoz. Although almost entirely neglected by travellers and locals alike since the revolution, it is without doubt the most impressive colonial fortress in Iran. Constructed of reddish stone on a rocky promontory at the far north of the island, the castle was originally cut off from the rest of the island by a moat, traces of which remain. Although most of the roofing long ago caved in, much of the lower part of the very substantial outer walls are intact, with the remains lying on different levels of the site. Allow at least an hour for visiting the castle, which is unattended and open all hours without charge.

Hormoz   هرمز
The present town of Hormoz is of interest, although there's nothing actually to do except ramble through the small maze of kūchés and be stared at by awe-struck children. The focus of activity lies along the thin strip of beach to the west of town, where boats and passengers with their various small private shipments, some of them licit, compete in trying to avoid the attention of the solitary soldier patrolling the sands. Away from this one hive of excitement, Jazīré-yé Hormoz may well strike you as a prime contender for the title of most indolent

place in Iran – unless you happen to have been to one of the other Iranian islands.

In the northern part of Hormoz is the **Masjed-é Jom'é-yé Emām Shāfe'ī**, a small Sunni mosque with a fine single minaret of pale stone.

Other Sites
Little but rubble remains of the great mediaeval settlement around present-day Hormoz: you'll see this rubble when passing from the town to the fortress. The Islamic palace of the former amīrs of Hormoz was demolished by the Portuguese, and a fine 15th-century mosque, which stood in part until the last century, stands no more.

The rocky crags of the interior of the island are said to be worth visiting, but I wouldn't know as I was pursued along the road out of Hormoz by a none-too-friendly *shahrdār* (mayor) and expressly forbidden from venturing any further. It may be that there are secret goings-on at the strategic southern tip of the island. If you do want to travel outside Hormoz, it might be worth asking the ostāndārī in Bandar-é Abbās for an introduction to the Hormoz shahrdārī.

Places to Stay & Eat
There are no places to stay on the island. Take a picnic. I did see a bakery and one shop selling some scraps of food, but there's no public eatery of any other kind on the island.

Getting There & Away
Small motorised skiffs ply between the beaches of Bandar-é Abbās and Hormoz, whenever they have their full complement of about half a dozen passengers, or their equivalent with luggage. The 30-minute journey costs 500 rials. There are several boats an hour in either direction between about one hour after dawn and about an hour before dusk, weather permitting. At other times or to other destinations you can charter a boat from Hormoz. On arrival at Hormoz beach expect to be asked to show your passport to the soldier on guard; you'll be detained by Islamic Revolutionary Guards if, as I did,

you visit the island without a passport and a valid visa and entry stamp.

Getting Around

Walk.

JAZĪRÉ-YÉ GHESHM جزیره قشم

Population: 51,000

Area: 1335 sq km

Gheshm is by far the largest island in the Persian Gulf, more than twice the size of Bahrain but with less than 15% of its population. The island is mountainous, with a largely rocky coast dotted with villages and small towns but few settlements of any size in the interior. There are deer, snakes and scorpions here as well as various types of birds – pelicans are found in the mud-flats off the north-west shore of the island. There are many freshwater streams throughout the island, and there's some scope for subsistence agriculture. Salt mines on the south-east coast complete the picture.

The main town and administrative centre is Gheshm. The best time to visit is between October and March.

Despite the island's highly strategic position on shipping lanes of great historical and current importance, at the very gateway to the Persian Gulf and close to some of the world's richest sources of crude oil and natural gas, it is astoundingly undeveloped. Cows, goats and fat-tailed sheep roam freely even in the centre of the main town, and the population is overwhelmingly poverty-stricken, illiterate and malnourished. Fishing, pearl diving, shipbuilding and smuggling remain the main occupations. Most of the islanders are Sunni and of Arab origin.

However, according to the island's first postrevolutionary five-year plan, launched on 31 January 1990, grandiose schemes have emerged for it to become a free area (on the same lines as Jazīré-yé Kīsh), under its own ministerial council chaired by no less than the President of the Republic, and with its own executive president. This council will be called the Qeshm Free Area Authority. The islanders will not be consulted.

Under these plans Jazīré-yé Gheshm will become the entrepôt of the Persian Gulf, with a superport on its south coast and a causeway connecting its north coast with the mainland. The vast untapped natural gas reserves in the strait will be sold off cheaply to Iranian and foreign companies, who will set up energy-intensive industries on the island. Supporting a large community of mainland Iranians and expatriates there will be international schools, a 'Hormoz International University', hotels, telecommunications, fully-equipped hospitals, good roads and an international airport, among other facilities at present very much lacking. Eventually Jazīré-yé Gheshm will be a 'major international economic and financial centre' and the 'largest free zone between Europe and Japan'. It's also planned to market the island as a tourist attraction, emphasising its natural facilities and potential for water sports.

These plans have not gone down at all well with the islanders, for although their current standard of living is deplorably low and several of them told me to write that there's not enough food or drinking water there, they're worried that the development will lead to the demolition of their houses and a mass resettlement. Furthermore they're worried that any new jobs and investment in the island won't come to them, and they would far prefer to carry on with their present way of life, hard as it is, than become a ghetto population on their own island. Even their traditional livelihood from fishing would be taken away by large companies. Their fears are undoubtedly justified, but as some of them told me, they have no means of complaining.

The time to visit is now.

History

Although the island has been referred to briefly in documents as early as the Achaemenian era, and has for many centuries been a trading centre between the continents and subcontinents, it lacks the historical status of the much smaller Jazīre-yé Hormoz, and very little is known of its early development.

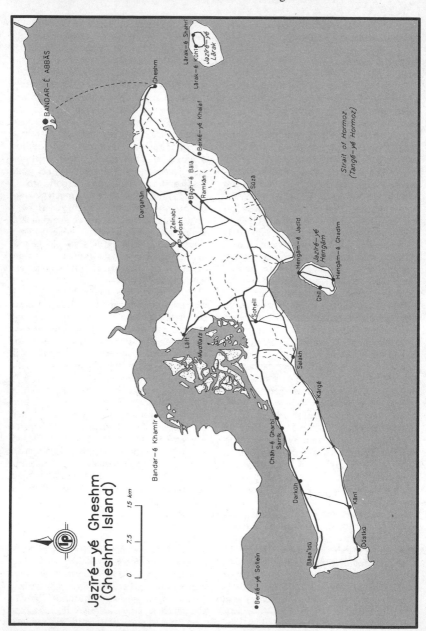

Jazīré–yé Gheshm
(Gheshm Island)

0   7.5   15 km

BANDAR–É ABBĀS

Gheshm

Lārak–é Shahri
Lārak–é Kūhi
Jazīré–yé Lārak

Berké–yé Khalaf

Strait of Hormoz
(Tangé–yé Hormoz)

Sūzā

Bāgh–é Bālā
Ramkān

Dargahān
Zeinabī
Peiposnt

Hengām–é Jadīd
Jazīré–yé Hengām
Hengām–é Ghadīm

Ghīl

Soheilī

Lāft
Mudflats

Salakh

Kārgé

Chāh–é Gharbī
Sarrīk

Kānī

Darkoh

Dūstkū

Bāsa'īdū

Bandar–é Khamīr

Berké–yé Soltein

Archaeologists have yet to give the world the benefit of their wisdom about the prehistoric and other sites so far uncovered on Jazīré-yé Gheshm. The island was mentioned by Marco Polo, and later marked out for colonial potential by Vasco da Gama. The Portuguese built a castle in the east of Gheshm during their occupation of Hormoz, and the island came under the sway of the Dutch, the East India Company, the French, Germans and British in turn, and it was only brought back firmly into Iran shortly after WWI. Until the Islamic Revolution the island was off limits to foreigners, and they were not entirely free to visit until the end of the Iran-Iraq War.

Orientation & Information

Gheshm is the largest town (officially a city) on the island, with wide roads and a main square, but it's tiny by mainland standards. The second town and port, Dargahān or Bandar-é Dargahān, is 22 km west of Gheshm. There are no other settlements of any size. Road communications around the island are very poor, and it would take several days to explore the whole of Jazīré-yé Gheshm even superficially. The only road out of Gheshm leads north-west from the main square, Meidūn-é Jehād-é Sāzandegī. There's nowhere to change money legally, and telecommunications are best forgotten.

Before visiting the island, you can check the latest state of development from the Secretariat, Qeshm Free Area Authority (☎ (021) 824456, 8107265, 8107267; fax (021) 820635), 248 Kheyābūn-é Somayyé, Tehrān.

Things to See

The conical **water reservoirs** (ābambārhā) are scattered all over the island, with the highest concentration around Gheshm. They have small holes at the top of the dome to let rain in, two narrow doors, and pools from which the islanders previously gathered water for washing. Many of the buildings in Gheshm are modern and of little interest, although the older flat-roofed cubic houses with their heavy, carved wooden doors

bearing metal studs and their simply decorated bādgīrs have a great deal of charm. It would be a cultural tragedy if development destroyed these living memorials of hundreds of years of island history. There are a few mosques, both Sunni and Shi'ite, of Arab style. Actually in the middle of one pavement is an ancient tomb with a fence around it. The kūchés in all the villages and towns except for Gheshm are apt to be very muddy after rainfall. There are remains of a **Portuguese fortress** (ghal'é-yé Portoghālīhā) in Gheshm, but they're nothing like as impressive as those at Hormoz.

Places to Stay & Eat

There's only one hotel on the island, the not-very-luxurious *Mehmūnsarā-yé Gheshm* (☎ (07625) 2001) in Gheshm; there's also a mosāferkhūné in Dargahān and one in Gheshm. Take any food and drinking water needed with you, as both are very scarce throughout the island, although you might find a bakery, snack bar or teahouse open in Gheshm.

Things to Buy

Japanese TVs and various other electrical goods, which are smuggled in from Dubai and suddenly become legal on arrival, are sold here in the many small shops throughout the island, but especially in Gheshm and Dargahān. As long as the trade carries on at its present low level, the authorities seem quite prepared to turn a blind eye to it. Apart from the small range of electrical goods sold at prices lower than those on the mainland, very little is available on the island. All shops are closed throughout the very long siesta.

Getting There & Away

The main jetty (the eskelé-yé Jazīré-yé Gheshm) is on the north coast of Gheshm town: there are regular boats from there to Bandar-é Abbās (45 minutes, 1000 rials) until just before dusk; they wait until they have their full seaworthy capacity of about eight passengers before sailing. Services depend on tidal and lighting conditions, and it's a good idea to check on sailings out as

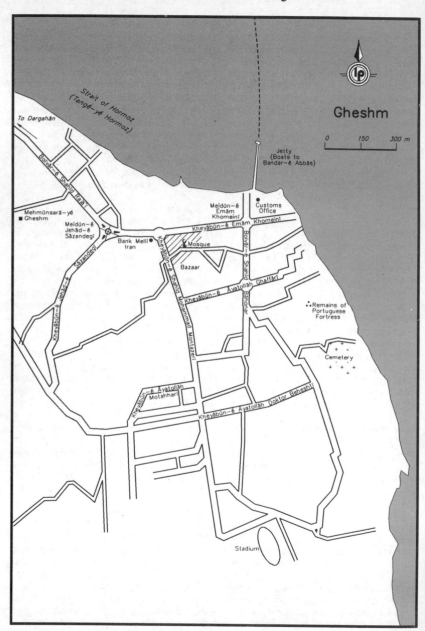

Gheshm

Strait of Hormoz
(Tangé-yé Hormoz)

To Dargahān

Bolvār-é Shahīd Rajā'ī

Mehmūnsarā-yé
Gheshm

Meidūn-é
Jehād-é Sāzandegī

Kheyābūn-é Jehād-é Sāzandegī

Bank Mellī
Iran

Kheyābūn-é Shahīd Mohammad Montazerī

Meidūn-é
Emām
Khomeinī

Customs
Office

Jetty
(Boats to
Bandar-é Abbās)

Kheyābūn-é Emām Khomeinī

Bolvār-é Shahīd Bāhonar

Mosque

Bazaar

Kheyābūn-é Āyatollāh Ghaffārī

Remains of
Portuguese
Fortress

Cemetery

Kheyābūn-é Āyatollāh
Motahharī

Kheyābūn-é Āyatollāh Doktor Beheshtī

Stadium

0   150   300 m

soon as you arrive. Gheshm's small customs post doesn't usually trouble private travellers. There are also occasional services to Bandar-é Abbās from Dargahān.

Boats to and from other destinations, such as Jazīré-yé Hormoz or Jazīré-yé Lārak, are arranged as required, according to the number or wealth of passengers. You can hire a boat to Jazīré-yé Hengām from one of the villages on the south coast of the island.

Getting Around

There's no organised public transport, but vans take passengers along the coastal road: between Gheshm and Dargahān the fare's 200 rials a person. You might also be able to hire a van in Gheshm for a tour of the island.

JAZĪRÉ-YÉ KĪSH   جزیره کیش

Population: 760

Area: 77 sq km

Kīsh Island is largely flat, sandy and uncultivated, with a high point of 45 metres. It's very hot and humid in summer, and only pleasant from about November to March. It has no known oil wells. Despite the forbidding climate and lack of oil wells, Kīsh Island is that great oddity in postrevolutionary Iran, a runaway economic success story. In effect semiautonomous under its own council, the Kish Island Development Organization (KIDO, or Sāzmān-é Omrān-é Kīsh), which in turn is directly responsible to the President of the Republic. Kīsh is Iran's first and, so far, only free port.

In the Middle Ages Kīsh became an important trading centre under its own powerful Arab dynasty, and at one time it supported a population of 40,000. The island was known for the quality of its pearls; when Marco Polo was visiting the imperial court in China and remarked on the beauty of those worn by one of the emperor's wives, he was told that they had come from Kīsh. The island fell into decline in the 14th century when it was supplanted by Hormoz. It remained obscure until just before the revolution, when it was developed as an almost private retreat for the Shāh and his privileged guests, with its own international airport,

palaces, luxury hotels and restaurants and even a grand casino. Shortly after the revolution the new regime appointed a very able team of managers under KIDO to establish Kīsh as a free port, taking advantage of the facilities already in place. The pace of development over recent years has been remarkable, outstripping anything found on the mainland, but without the usual concentration on building great numbers of new mosques.

Nowadays the east coast of the island resembles a vast building site, and already KIDO readily admits to having made more money than it knows what to do with. It's also intended to develop Kīsh as a top-class regional holiday centre, and a grand five-star Yugoslav-built hotel complex is planned for completion within the next five years. At present its main attraction to Iranians is the availability of electrical goods imported from Dubai and sold at prices far lower than anywhere on the mainland. Kīsh has become such a popular destination that the government has had to introduce a lottery for air tickets to the island, as there would be no means of accommodating all the visitors.

Kīsh is a place apart: it has its own distinctive flag, and even the vehicle registration plates are marked in both English and Persian, unlike anywhere else in Iran. In fact almost everything's marked in English, in preparation for what's hoped will be a great influx of foreign visitors in the near future. Since almost every necessity of life except fish is imported from the UAE, prices are higher than anywhere on the mainland, but this island is unlike anywhere else in Iran. The bulk of the developments should be

KIDO Slogan

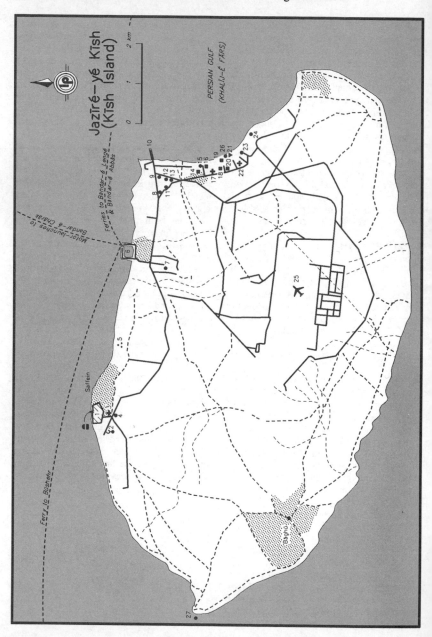

■ PLACES TO STAY

14 Kīsh Hotel (Hotel-é Ksh)
16 Villas (Vīlāhā)
18 Villas (Vīlāhā)
19 Villas (Vīlāhā)
20 Villas (Vīlāhā)

▼ PLACES TO EAT

14 Kish Hotel
15 Sākhtemān-é Sāhel (Coast Building)
    (Former Casino)
21 Restōrān-é Mr Mohannā

OTHER

1   Bāzār-é Saffein (Bāzār-é Arab) &
    Post Office
2   Mosque
4   Bakhshdār
5   Historical Remains
6   New Jetty (Eskelé-yé Jadd) &
    Customs Office
7   Petrol Station
8   Telephone Office
9   KIDO, Valfajre-8 Shipping Company
    & Iran Air
10 Old Jetty (Eskelé-yé Ghadm)
11 Bāzār-é Ksh
12 Bank Melli Iran
13 Supermarket
15 Coast Building (Sākhtemān-é Sāhel)
    (Former Casino)
17 Clinic
22 Clinic
23 Aquarium (Ākvāreyom)
24 Kākh-é Shāh (Shāh's Palace)
25 Airport
26 Beach
27 Greek Ship (Kasht-yé Yūnān)

completed by 1994, but until then, and until KIDO is able to lift the stringent quota of flights and sailings to the island, most Iranians will go green with envy if you tell them you're going to Kīsh.

Orientation & Information

There's no centre to Kīsh, and there are no addresses as such. Kish Hotel, the main place to stay, and the major area of tourist development are in the north-east of the island, the area favoured by the last Shāh and his court-

iers. The Arab settlements are at the town of Saffein on the north coast and the small oasis village of Bāghū in the south-west of the island. The airport's to the south of the centre of the island, and the new jetty's between Saffein and the tourist area. The main offices of importance – KIDO, Iran Air and Valfajre-8 – are all in the same building about 10 minutes' walk north of the Kish Hotel.

You can make trunk or international calls at a very extortionate rate from the Kish Hotel. The telephone office is near Iran Air, and there's a small post office in the Bāzār-é Arabī (Arab Bazaar) of Saffein. The dialling code for Jazīré-yé Kīsh is 07653.

Little or no information in English is available from KIDO (although many of the workers on the island do speak English); it's best to get help from the public relations department on the 1st floor of KIDO in Tehrān (☎ 681491, 687085, 687086, 864079) before visiting Kīsh. Its address is Bozorgrāh-é Afrīghā, Chahārrāh-é Shahīd Haghghānī, 3 Kheyābūn-é Kīsh, Tehrān. This organisation can give you a booklet in English entitled *Kish Island*, a priceless piece of extraordinary hype couched in florid and, in places, incomprehensible tones.

Things to See & Do

Although for most visitors the main attraction of Kīsh is its duty-free shopping, there are quite a few things to see here aside from the bazaars. There are sandy, uncrowded **beaches** around much of the coast, the most pleasant of which is on the north-east coast near the Restōrān-é Mīr Mohannā. There's a wide range of decorative fish around the coral reefs off Kīsh, including the rare emperor fish, but diving is difficult unless you bring your own equipment, and there are dangers from sharks and poisonous fish. It's easier to see the **turtle colony** (*dasté-yé lāk-é posht- é ābī*) off the island, for which you can hire a boat at the jetty at a negotiable rate.

Many of the buildings constructed under the former regime now have other uses: the casino is now the **Coast Building** (*Sākhtemān-é Sāhel*), containing shops, a restaurant and a café (obviously formerly a bar), while the **Shāh's Palace** (*Kākh-é Shāh*) itself, a villa-type building of surprisingly modest proportions, is being reconstructed as a bazaar for electrical equipment. Near the palace there's a small **aquarium** (*ākvāreyom*) nearing completion. The ruins of an 11th or 12th century **palace complex** and other historical structures of the old city are on the north coast, between the town of Saffein and the new jetty, but very little remains. Very close to the west coast there's the wreck of a Greek ship (*Kashtī-yé Yūnānī*). The **new jetty** (*eskelé-yé jadīd*) has a number of interesting dhows, the sailors of which are very sensitive about being photographed without permission. Efforts have been made to green the island, and there are already several small parks of tropical trees.

Other facilities will be established over the next few years as tourism grows in importance, but even now it's a pleasant enough place to explore on your own for two days.

Places to Stay

There's only one hotel open in Kīsh, the five-star *Kish Hotel* (Hotel-é Kīsh) in the north-east of the island. On the dubious reasoning that Kīsh is a free port, it charges foreigners US$107 a double, while Iranians pay only 15,000 rials. It's probably good value by international standards, and the rooms are truly palatial, the equivalent of suites anywhere else, with colour TVs, balconies, noiseless air-con and far more, but by Iranian standards it's overpriced. Other hotels are under construction or renovation. Alternatively you can hire a small villa, cabin or flat for 10,000 to 15,000 rials a day from the *Daftar-é Vīllāhā-yé Seyāhatī-yé Morvārīd*, which can be reached in Kīsh on ☎ 2743 or in Tehrān on ☎ 667398, but there's a shortage of available rooms in winter. Visitors without prearranged accommodation often to have to sleep in the open, and even the *Kish Hotel* is very busy. If possible, arrange your accommodation in advance as part of a tour (see below).

Places to Eat

There are three restaurants in Kīsh, all air-conditioned and good but expensive, since except for fish practically everything, even the paper napkins, is imported. Soft drinks alone are cheaper than on the mainland, around 500 rials for an imported can, compared with around 1000 rials in Tehrān. Count on at least 4000 rials a person for a meal at any of the following restaurants.

There's a restaurant on the ground floor of the *Kish Hotel*, and a café in the basement. There's another, less formal, restaurant on the ground floor of the Coast Building, and there's perhaps the plushest café in Iran on the 2nd floor, with excellent ice cream, coffee, milk shakes and cakes. Probably the best restaurant is the *Restōrān-é Mīr Mohannā*, by the beach about five minutes' walk south-east of the Kish Hotel. Its extraordinary but tasteful decor – Jolly Rogers, trellises, hanging ropes and nets, palms, cane furniture and other pieces of carefully chosen flotsam and jetsam – comes straight out of a desert island fantasy. You have to come here if only to experience one of the most unusual restaurants in Iran, obviously very little changed since the time of the Shāh. The food's good but very expensive: soup, jūjé kabāb with rice, three cans of Miranda, and tea come to 14,000 rials for two, far higher than anywhere on the mainland.

Duty-Free Shopping

Almost no-one goes to Kīsh without buying a colour TV. According to the latest rules, all visitors to the island are allowed to purchase one colour TV, one vacuum cleaner and one stereo per year with complete exemption from duty or taxes in return for paying 50,000 rials to KIDO, while smaller goods can be taken out freely. By taking advantage of this duty-free arrangement, visitors can resell these goods legally on the mainland at a profit of around 50% and more than repay their travelling expenses. Return flights from Kīsh are often met by traders offering to buy TVs from passengers. Ask at KIDO or the airport on arrival about how to apply for exemption, and check the latest prices with Iranians before buying anything.

The cost of a standard colour TV is around

400,000 rials, compared with more than 600,000 rials on the mainland, but both prices fluctuate. There are more than 130 shops on the island, including the basement of the Kish Hotel, on the ground floor of the Coast Building, in the Bāzār-é Saffein (Bāzār-é Arabī) and in the Bāzār-é Kīsh. There's also a supermarket near the Bāzār-é Kīsh. There is little of interest to the consumer except for electrical goods, and most pearls are exported.

You aren't allowed to take any duty-free goods out of Kīsh if you leave by motor launch for Bandar-é Chārak or by other private transport, but otherwise passengers returning to the mainland are subject to customs examination as if arriving from abroad, and you'll have to show your KIDO permit if you have bought a TV, vacuum cleaner or stereo.

Getting There & Away
Air Air tickets to Kīsh are very difficult to arrange. For most Iranians there's regularly a waiting-list of three or four months, especially in summer or whenever shopping prices on the island are low. Foreigners, however, are often given priority.

Scheduled Flights You can try asking the marketing manager of any Iran Air office for a ticket on a scheduled flight a few days ahead, but unless you have a certain amount of clout or luck you'll have to try for a chartered ticket, probably as part of a tour. As a counter to black-market and under-the-counter ticket deals, tickets to Kīsh can only be bought at the Iran Air office in Meidūn-é Ferdōsī in Tehrān, and at the main Iran Air offices in Shīrāz and Bandar-é Abbās.

Once you get to Kīsh, the manager of the Iran Air office (☎ 2274) on the island is exceptionally helpful, and this is one of the best places in Iran to buy otherwise unobtainable tickets. Even so it's not at all a good idea to arrive in Kīsh on a one-way ticket. Unlike most Iran Air offices, this one's open every day of the week.

Iran Air flies from Jazīré-yé Kīsh to: Bandar-é Abbās (Monday and Saturday, 8

am, 40 minutes); Shīrāz (Sunday and Thursday, 8 am, 55 minutes); and Tehrān (Tuesday and Friday, 8 am, 2¾ hours; Sunday, 11.20 am, 1¾ hours; Tuesday, 2.30 pm, 2¾ hours; all 8850 rials).

Chartered Flights & Tours KIDO charters three flights weekly between Tehrān and Kīsh from Iran Air, and at least one weekly between Kermān and Kīsh from Saha. In Tehrān these tickets can be bought with some difficulty on a flight-only basis (15,000 rials one-way) from Kish Island Services Company (☎ 681052-3) (Sherkat-é Kharmātī-yé Kīsh) at Kheyābūn-é Yūsefābād, Kheyābūn-é Shahīd Alī Khānī, 10 Kuché-yé Haftād o Yekom, or as part of a tour from Gulliver's Travels (☎ 659116), 12 Kheyābūné Falastīn-é Shomālī. If you have any difficulties, go to KIDO. In Kermān tickets can only normally be bought as part of a tour from the Kermanseir Tour Company (see the Kermān entry). Tours currently cost 60,000 rials, and include two nights' villa or hotel accommodation, return flights from Tehrān or Kermān, and airport transfers. For most visitors, a tour is the best and most economical way of travelling to Kīsh.

Sea Valfajre-8 sails to and from: Bandar-é Abbās (298 km, nine times weekly); Bandar-é Lengé (93 km, five hours, 5000 rials, 12 times weekly); and Būshehr (twice weekly). Alternatively, you can take a motor launch to or from Bandar-é Chārak (1000 rials by shared taxi from Bandar-é Lengé) for around 7500 rials but, because of customs restrictions on passengers leaving the island, you won't be allowed to take more than a tiny amount of luggage with you, and certainly not a TV. If at all possible, take the ferry. There are no longer sailings from Bandar-é Kong. If you want to sail by dhow to Dubai with some island traders, you can ask at KIDO for permission, but you're unlikely to get it.

Valfajre-8 in Tehrān is very reluctant to sell foreigners tickets to Kīsh, but there's no great problem in Bandar-é Lengé, which is the best place to try. (See the Getting Around chapter for the addresses of all Valfajre-8 offices in Iran.)

Getting Around

Chartered Iran Air flights are met by a courtesy bus, and even if you aren't on a tour you can take a free lift. A minibus around the island costs 100 rials; private taxis charge 5000 rials an hour.

JAZĪRÉ-YÉ LĀVĀN   جزيره لاوان

Population: 650
Area: 76 sq km

Until 1968 known as Jazīré-yé Sheikh Sho'eib, this island is best-known for its important oil refinery. It's also of interest for the historical guns on the island dating from the time of Nāder Shāh and known as the **Tūphā-yé Nāderī** or Nāder's Cannon.

Getting There & Away

NIOC has flights between Lāvān and Tehrān and Shīrāz at least three times weekly, and at least weekly between Lāvān and Esfahān. Enquire at NIOC in Tehrān for details.

OTHER ISLANDS   جزائر ديگر

According to the latest available official information, foreigners and Iranians are free to visit any of the islands listed below without special permission, except for Jazīré-yé Abū Mūsā, which is an important naval station. However, it's wise not to go to any island without written authority from the ostāndārī or tourist office in Bandar-é Abbās. Abū Mūsā and the two Tomb islands were previously claimed by the UAE, but they're now firmly under Iranian control, though very difficult to get to from the mainland. Except for Sīrrī (which can be reached by NIOC flights at least weekly from Shīrāz and Tehrān) and Abū Mūsā, none of the following islands is on any regular passenger transport route, although some of them can be reached by hired fishing boat from other islands.

If you really want to go, don't be put off by the difficulty of touring the islands, as they're undoubtedly of vast and largely undocumented ethnological and zoological

interest, and as far off the tourist trail as one can get. The tourist office in Bandar-é Abbās is probably the best place to get any practical information. You would probably have to charter a boat for several days from Bandar-é Abbās, and it would be advisable to take an Iranian guide with you. Good luck!

Jazīré-yé Abū Mūsā – population 420; 12 sq km
Jazīré-yé Forūr-é Bozorg (Forūr) – no permanent population; 26 sq km
Jazīré-yé Forūr-é Kūchek (Banī Forūr) – uninhabited; 1.5 sq km
Jazīré-yé Hendorābī – population 33; area 21 sq km
Jazīré-yé Hengām – population 420; area 33 sq km
Jazīré-yé Lārak – population 430; area 49 sq km
Jazīré-yé Shatvar – uninhabited; area 0.8 sq km
Jazīré-yé Sīrrī (Serrī) – population 225; area 17 sq km
Jazīré-yé Tomb-é Bozorg – population 220; area 10 sq km
Jazīré-yé Tomb-é Kūchek – uninhabited; area 1.5 sq km

Fārs Province   استان فارس

Fārs, which in its historical sense extends far beyond its present boundaries and covers much of the southern region of Iran, is where the Persians or Fārsīs first settled and the great Achaemenian and Sassanian empires were once centred. Persepolis was the greatest city of the region and is the principal attraction today, but it's far from the only reminder of Persia at its peak. Shīrāz, the provincial centre since the 7th century AD, claims its own glory as a capital of several Islamic dynasties and, perhaps more importantly, an artistic centre. The province has an area of 133,300 sq km and a population of 3.3 million. It has the largest number of nomads of any province in Iran (67,000), most from the Ghashghā'ī tribe.

SHĪRĀZ   شيراز

To the three weeks which I spent in Shīrāz I look back with unmixed pleasure. The associations connected with it are familiar to every student of Persian; its natural beauties I have already feebly attempted to depict; its inhabitants are, amongst all the Persians, the most subtle, the most ingenious, the most vivacious, even as their speech is to this day the purest and most melodious.

Edward Browne,
A Year Amongst the Persians, 1893

Shīrāz was one of the most important cities in the mediaeval Islamic world and was the Iranian capital during the Zand dynasty from 1753 to 1794. Many of its most beautiful buildings were built or restored in that period. The two most famous Persian poets were born and lived in Shīrāz – Hāfez (1324? to 1389) and Sa'dī (1207? to 1291?). Both have a famous mausoleum here. Through its many artists and scholars, Shīrāz has been synonymous with learning, nightingales, poetry, roses and, at one time, wine.

To many, Shīrāz is simply the most pleasant of the large Iranian cities, with relaxed, cultivated and generous inhabitants who don't try to cheat visitors, wide tree-lined avenues, and monuments to two of the greatest poets in the Persian language. It's easy to like Shīrāz and its friendly, unassuming people. It's a city that captivates most visitors, although its charm is less immediately perceptible than that of Esfahān – more poetic and less visual.

There are a number of imposing buildings from various periods of Iranian architecture, but especially from its days as capital under Karīm Khān. Something of the tranquillity of its wide boulevards has been lost since the revolution and the subsequent mass influx of population, but it's still a fairly relaxed place. People are far less Hezbollāhī than in Esfahān, and it's an important university town with lots of students eager to speak English. The medical faculty is the most prestigious in Iran, and the only one in the country where students are lectured in English rather than Persian. In many ways Shīrāz continues to justify its former epithet of Dār-ol-Elm ('House of Learning').

Shīrāz lies at an altitude of 1491 metres in a fertile valley once famed for its vineyards (the Shīrāz grape is still known to winegrowers throughout the world) and has one of the most agreeable climates in Iran; it's espe-

cially pleasant between February and May and between October and November.

History

There was a settlement at Shīrāz at least as early as the Achaemenian period, and it was already an important regional centre under the Sassanians. However, it did not become provincial capital until about 693 AD, after the Arab Conquest, following the capture of Estakhr, the last Sassanian capital (eight km north-east of Persepolis, but now completely destroyed), in 684 AD. As Estakhr fell into decline Shīrāz grew in size and importance under the Arabs and then under a succession of local dynasties, and by the time Estakhr was eventually sacked in 1044, Shīrāz was said to be the rival of Baghdad.

The city grew further under the Atābaks of Fārs, and under their rule Shīrāz became an important artistic centre in the 12th century. It was spared destruction by the invading Mongols when the province's last Atābak monarch offered tributes and submission to Genghis Khan. Shīrāz was again spared by Tamerlane when, in 1382, the local monarch Shāh Shojā' agreed to submit to his armies, even offering the hand of his granddaughter in marriage to a grandson of Tamerlane. After the death of Shāh Shojā', there was a turbulent succession of rulers for several years, until Tamerlane appointed his own son as ruler.

The Mongol and Timurid periods marked the peak of Shīrāz's development. The encouragement of its enlightened rulers, the presence of Hāfez, Sa'di and many other brilliant artists and scholars, and the city's natural advantages helped it to become one of the greatest cities in the Islamic world throughout the 13th and 14th centuries and a leading centre of calligraphy, painting, architecture and literature. For several centuries, even after the end of the Mongol period in Iran, its artists and scholars went out as cultural emissaries both inside and outside the country, beautifying Samarkand (a district of which Tamerlane named Shīrāz) and many of the Mogul cities of India. The most noteworthy was Ostād Īsā, a 17th-century Shīrāz architect who provided the design for the Taj Mahal.

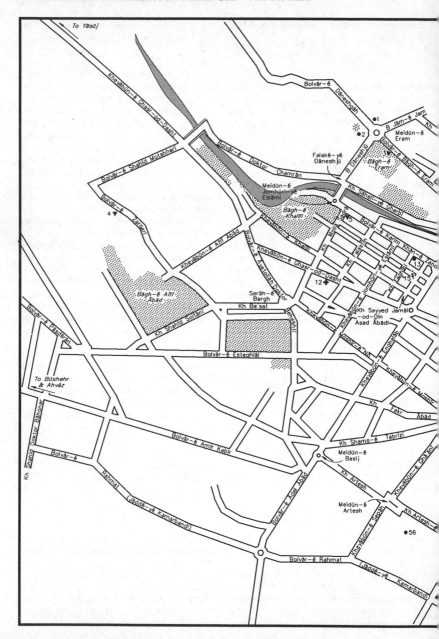

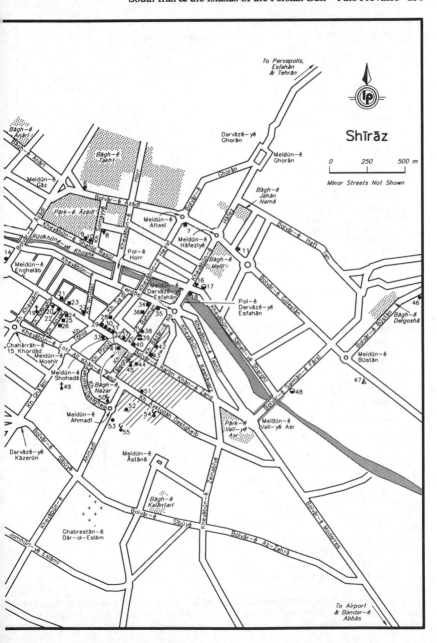

To Persepolis,
Esfahān
& Tehrān

Darvāzé–yé
Ghorān

Meidūn–é
Ghorān

Shīrāz

0   250   500 m

Minor Streets Not Shown

Bāgh–é
Anārī

Bāgh–é
Takht

Meidūn–é
Gāz

Bāgh–é
Jahān
Namā

Park–é Āzādī

Bolvār–é Āzādī

Meidūn–é
Atlasī

Bāgh–é
Melli

Meidūn–é
Hāfezīyé

7

Pol–é
Horr

11

Rūdkhūné–yé Khoshk

Meidūn–é
Enghelāb

14

16

17

Meidūn–é
Darvāzé–yé
Esfahān

Pol–é
Darvāzé–yé
Esfahān

18

46

Bāgh–é
Delgoshā

21

23

34

35

36

Meidūn–é
Būstān

19

20

24

22

25

26

28

29

30

38

39

40

42

47

33

Chahārrāh–é
15 Khordād

Meidūn–é
Moshīr

31

43

44

Meidūn–é
Shohadā

49

45

48

Bāgh–é
Nazar

50

51

52

54

Meidūn–é
Ahmadī

53

55

Meidūn–é
Vali–yé Asr

Darvāzé–yé
Kāzerūn

Park–é
Vali–yé
Asr

Meidūn–é
Āstāné

Bāgh–é
Kalāntarī

Bolvār–é Āz–Zahrā

Ghabrestān–é
Dār–ol–Eslām

To Airport
& Bandar–é
Abbās

■ PLACES TO STAY

7   Hotel-é Atlas
9   Homa Hotel (Hotel-é Homā)
21 Hotel-é Eram
23 Hotel-é Kōsar
24 Mosāferkhūné-yé Kesrā
25 Mehmūnpazr-é Sāsān
26 Mosāferkhūné-yé Anvar
28 Pārk Hotel
34 Mosāferkhūné-yé Srūs
35 Mosāferkhūné-yé Māh
36 Mosāferkhūné-yé Pāyām
47 Campsite (Ordūgaāh-é Jahāngard)

▼ PLACES TO EAT

4   Restōrān-é Sonnat-yé Sūf
5   Restōrān-é Bahārān
6   Sālon-é Sambūsé-yé Jalāl
8   Restōrān-é Eram
9   Homa Hotel
11 Ārāmgāh-é Hāfez (Teahouse)
20 Restōrān-é Golestān
21 Hotel-é Eram
27 Sālon-é Ghezā-yé Khōrāk-é Habb
28 Pārk Hotel

    OTHER

1   University Stadium (Estādyūm-é
    Dāneshgāh)
2   Shrāz University (Dāneshgāh-é
    Shrāz)
3   Kākh-é Eram
10 Iran Air (Homa Hotel Office)
11 Ārāmgāh-é Hāfez

12 Casualty Hospital
13 Iran Air (Main Office)
14 Ostāndār
15 Tourist Office
16 Emāmzādé-yé Al Ebn-é Hamzé
17 Minibus Terminal for Marvdasht, etc.
    (Termnāl-é Hāfez)
18 Taxi Terminal for Marvdasht, etc.
19 Kelsā-yé Moghaddas-é Sham'ūn-é
    Ghāyūr (Anglican Church of St
    Simon the Zealot)
22 Gulf Air
29 Mohajeri Air Tours
30 International Bookshop
    (Ketādforūshgāh-é Bein-ol-Melal)
31 Shahrdār
32 Police Headquarters (Shahrbān)
33 Iran Air (Meidūn-é Shohadā)
37 Arg-é Karm Khān
38 Telephone Office
39 Main Post Office
40 Bank Melli Iran (Central Branch)
41 Mūzé-yé Pārs
42 Bāzār-é Nō
43 Bāzār-é Nō
44 Bāzār-é Vakl
45 Masjed-é Vakl
46 Ārāmgāh-é Sa'd
48 Bus Station
49 Kelsā-yé Arāmané (Armenian Church)
50 Masjed-é Shohadā
51 Madrasé-yé Khān
52 Bogh'é-yé Sayyed Mr Mohammad
53 Bogh'é-yé Shāh-é Cherāgh
54 Masjed-é Nasr-ol-Molk
55 Masjed-é Jāmé-yé Atgh
56 Artesh Stadium (Estādyūm-é Artesh)

Under Shāh Abbās I, Emām Gholī Khān, the governor of Fārs, constructed a large number of palaces and other ornate buildings on the lines of the royal capital at Esfahān. But while Shīrāz remained a provincial capital under the Safavids, even attracting a number of European traders who exported its famous wine, it quickly fell into nearly a century of decline which was worsened by several earthquakes, the Afghan raids of the early 18th century, and an uprising led by its governor in 1744, which was put down after a siege by Nāder Shāh.

At the time of Nāder Shāh's murder in 1747, most of Shīrāz's historical buildings were damaged or ruined and its population had fallen to 50,000, a quarter that of 1500. Shīrāz soon returned to prosperity under the enlightened Karīm Khān, first of the short-lived Zand dynasty, who made Shīrāz the national capital in 1750. Even though master of virtually all Persia, Karīm Khān refused to take any higher title than *vakīl* ('regent'). He was determined to raise Shīrāz into a worthy capital, the equal of Esfahān under Shāh Abbās I.

Karīm Khān was a benevolent and wise ruler and one of the greatest patrons of the arts in Iranian history. Employing more than 12,000 workers, he founded a royal district in the area of the Arg Karīm Khānī and commissioned many fine buildings including the finest bazaar in Iran. He had a moat built around the city, constructed a clever irrigation and drainage system, and rebuilt the city walls. However Karīm Khān's heirs failed to secure his gains, and when Āghā Mohammad Khān, the cruel founder of the Ghajar dynasty, eventually came to power after killing Lotf Alī Khān, the last of the Zand dynasty, he wreaked his revenge on Shīrāz by destroying the city fortifications and, in 1789, moving the national capital to Tehrān, taking with him the remains of Karīm Khān. Although lowered to the rank of provincial capital, Shīrāz maintained a level of prosperity as a result of the continuing importance of the trade route through Būshehr, and its governorship was a royal prerogative throughout the Ghajar era.

The city's role in transit trade greatly diminished with the opening of the trans-Iranian railway in the 1930s, when the bulk of its custom passed to the ports of Khūzestān. Much of the architectural inheritance of Shīrāz, and especially the royal district of the Zands, was either neglected or destroyed as a result of irresponsible town planning under the Pahlavī dynasty. Lacking any great industrial, religious or strategic importance, Shīrāz is now largely an administrative centre, although its population has grown considerably since the revolution.

Orientation

The bus station is just north of the river, on the east side of Bolvār-é Salmān-é Fārsī, the best part of an hour's walk from the centre but well connected by shared taxi. It is no longer at the place marked on all the local maps. The airport is south-east of Shīrāz, connected to the city by Bolvār-é Modarres.

The main street of Shīrāz is the wide tree-lined Bolvār-é Karīm Khān-é Zand, the name of which no-one has ever dared change. It's often abbreviated simply to 'Zand'. This boulevard runs about as far east and west as you would want to go without actually leaving Shīrāz, and since most of the things to see and nearly all the hotels, are along it or within walking distance of it, this is a street you'll keep coming back to. The

old city and the commercial centre of Shīrāz is south of the river, while the smarter residential areas are to the north. The modern university buildings and dormitories are on a steep hill in the north of Shīrāz. The city centre is at Meidūn-é Shohadā (still widely known as Meidūn-é Shahrdārī) on Bolvār-é Karīm Khān-é Zand.

The river – the Rūdkhūné-yé Khosk – which was almost dry when I last visited, is crossed by seven bridges, none of them of any great historical interest.

Information

The ostāndārī (☎ 38028) is on the north side of Meidūn-é Enghelāb and the shahrdārī (☎ 23624) is on the north side of Meidūn-é Shohadā. The visa office is on the 1st floor of the police headquarters to the north-east of Meidūn-é Shohadā. The senior police officer in the aliens' bureau is helpful and speaks good English; the others are less so.

I had to go for an interview with a very Hezbollāhī security bigwig here before being granted a visa extension. After quizzing me about my opinions of the achievements of the Islamic Republic and asking with an air of disbelief if it was really interesting for me to visit all the tourist sites in Shīrāz for the second time in three years, he gave me the one-month visa extension I had asked for, even though he was at first only willing to make it two weeks.

Tourist Office The tourist office (☎ 34080) doesn't exactly advertise its presence and is a little far out from the centre. To get there, head north-east from Meidūn-é Enghelāb, take the first turning to the left (Kheyābūn-é Sayyed Jamāl-od-Dīn Asādābādī, not marked in English) then walk straight ahead for about 100 metres, past the first turning to the left but before the second. On your right you'll see a tall ugly building with some desks on the ground floor visible through a glass front, and several maps on the wall. This is the tourist office. Although the building is only marked in Persian, the staff inside speak English.

Money Probably the most efficient bank for exchanging foreign cash and travellers' cheques is the palatial Bank Melli Iran on the north side of Bolvār-é Karīm Khān-é Zand, just east of the Arg. If you are buying an international aeroplane ticket for hard currency, this is where you'll be sent. Most of the other banks have their main branches around Meidūn-é Shohadā. The private exchange offices – which may not be legal for foreigners to use – are on the north side of Bolvār-é Karīm Khān-é Zand between Meidūn-é Shohadā and Kheyābūn-é Sa'dī.

Post & Telecommunications The main post and telegraph office is in an alley behind the Bank Melli Iran central branch. The main telephone office is a few metres north, on the east side of Kheyābūn-é 22 Bahman (not at the place marked on the tourist office map). If you want to try making a long-distance call yourself, there's a rank of public telephones behind the Arg; you can ask for change at the telephone office. The easiest place to make an international call is at the Homa Hotel, booked an hour or two in advance. A call to the UK costs 1650 rials a minute there. The dialling code for Shīrāz is 071.

Consulate The Indian Consulate (Konsūlgarī-yé Hendūstān) can be contacted on ☎ 31254.

Travel Agencies There are several travel agencies along Bolvār-é Karīm Khān-é Zand, not many of which I found particularly helpful. One of the best is Mojahari Air Tours (☎ 26366) at the intersection with Kheyābūn-é Sa'dī.

Books & Bookshops The International Bookshop (Ketābforūshgāh-é Bein-ol-Melalī) – formerly the BBC bookshop – immediately west of the shahrdārī has, by Iranian standards, a large collection of English-language books. Although most of them are aimed at the student market, you can buy copies of Ali Sami's guidebooks *Shiraz* or *Persepolis* here for 800 rials, or a day-old copy of *Kayhan* (English edition). At the smaller bookshop in the Homa Hotel the price for either guidebook is 1500 rials.

Medical Services Shīrāz is famous for the standard of its medical training, so this is probably the best place to fall ill outside Tehrān. Of the three casualty hospitals in town, the most central is on the south side of Kheyābūn-é Ghasr-od-Dasht. For emergencies dial ☎ 31027.

Emergency The police headquarters (shahr-bānī) (☎ 22576) is a few metres to the north-east of Meidūn-é Shohadā, opposite the west corner of the Arg.

Arg-é Karīm Khānī

The imposing structure of the Citadel of Karīm Khān is on the north side of Bolvār-é Karīm Khān-é Zand, just to the east of Meidūn-é Shohadā. Now belonging to the police headquarters and inaccessible to visitors, this well-preserved fortress with four circular towers was in the time of the Zand dynasty part of a royal courtyard which Karīm Khān had intended to rival that of Esfahān, but it's no longer recognisable as such.

Mūzé-yé Pārs

Built by Karīm Khān opposite his Arg in a garden originally twice the size of the present one (the Bāgh-é Nazar) this small octagonal pavilion was originally used for official receptions. It later became his tomb for a short time until the vengeful Āghā Mohammad Khān removed the royal remains to his new capital of Tehrān, out of spite for the dynasty he overthrew. This century it became the Pārs Museum, and it now contains a small exhibition of items relating to the life of Karīm Khān and other historic artefacts displayed in cases set into four alcoves. Much of the interest lies in the building itself, with its charming tiled panels outside and its painted roof and unusual carved marble pool inside. The museum and gardens are open from 9 am to noon, daily except Monday.

Bāzār-é Vakīl & Bāzār-é Nō

Bāzār-é Vakīl (Regent's Bazaar), on the south of the eastern end of Bolvār-é Karīm Khān-é Zand, was constructed by Karīm Khān as part of a plan to make Shīrāz into a great trading centre. The vaulted brick ceilings ensure that the interior is cool in the summer and warm in the winter, and it has often been described as the finest bazaar in Iran. As in so many Iranian bazaars, the interest lies mainly in the architecture and the whole atmosphere rather than the goods. This bazaar has its own bath-house, the **Hammūm-é Vakīl**, dating from Karīm Khān's time. Bāzār-é Nō (New Bazaar) is north of the eastern end of Bolvār-é Karīm Khān-é Zand.

Masjed-é Vakīl

The Regent's Mosque, built in 1773 by Karīm Khān at one of the entrances to his bazaar is worth visiting, but only on a Friday, as it's inexplicably closed to visitors every other day of the week. The mosque has two vast eivāns (open rectangular halls) to the north and south, a magnificent inner courtyard surrounded by beautifully tiled alcoves and porches, and a vaulted mehrāb room with 48 impressive columns as well as a remarkable 14-stepped marble membār (pulpit). Although the structure of the mosque dates from 1773, most of the tiling with its predominantly floral motifs was added in the early Ghajar era.

Masjed-é Shohadā

Although the Martyrs' Mosque (previously the Masjed-é Nō), at the end of a short lane leading north from Meidūn-é Ahmadī, is one of the largest ancient mosques in Iran (its vast rectangular courtyard alone covers more than 11,000 sq metres), it attracts nowhere near as many visitors, especially pilgrims, as the Boghé-yé Shāh-é Cherāgh. Founded at the start of the 13th century, it has since been partially rebuilt many times and now has very little in the way of tiling or other decorations, although it does have some impressive barrel vaulting.

Bogh'é-yé Shāh-é Cherāgh

This famous tomb of the 'King of the Lamp' houses the remains of Sayyed Mīr Ahmad, brother of Emām Rezā, who died or was killed in Shīrāz in 835. A mausoleum was first erected over the grave in the mid-14th century, and ever since this has been an important Shi'ite place of pilgrimage. The shoe repository outside the doorway is as hectic as any in Iran, and it's fascinating to see the hordes of supplicants and the piles of money and gold they give every day. Non-Muslims should ask for permission before entering. One traveller wrote that his socks were smelled before he was allowed in.

The multicoloured reflections from the vast numbers of minute mirror tiles inside the shrine are quite dazzling. The large bulb-shaped glazed dome has been retiled recently.

This shrine is in a large square leading south-east from Meidūn-é Ahmadī. At the main entrance to the courtyard there's a small but interesting museum, marked in English, with a display of fine china and glassware, exquisitely inscribed old and modern Qorans, and some old coins. Entry is 50 rials.

Bogh'é-yé Sayyed Mīr Mohammad

Some 200 metres east of the Masjed-é Shāh-é Cherāgh in the same courtyard there's a mausoleum to Sayyed Mīr Mohammad, brother of Mīr Ahmad, who also died at Shīrāz. This shrine has intricate mirror tiling and some inscriptions in the dome, but is of less interest than the other one.

Masjed-é Jāme'-é Atīgh

This ancient mosque, first built in 894, is in an alley 400 metres south-east of the Bogh'é-yé Shāh-é Cherāgh. Virtually all the original structure has disappeared as a result of various earthquakes, and most of the building dates from the Safavid period or later. It's of interest for a very unusual, rectangular turreted building in the centre of its courtyard. Known as the Khodākhūné ('House of God'), it was built in the mid-14th century as a repository for valuable

Qorans, and is believed to be modelled on the Kaaba at Mecca. Although most of it was very skilfully rebuilt earlier this century, the House of God still bears an original and unique inscription in raised stone characters on a tiled background.

Madrasé-yé Khān

Near both the Masjed-é Shohadā and the Masjed-é Shāh-é Cherāgh on the north side of Kheyābūn-é Shahīd Āyatollāh Dastgheib is the impressive Madrasé-yé Khān. The *khān* in question was Emām Gholī Khān, governor of Fārs, who founded this theological college for 100 students in 1615. The original building was much damaged by earthquakes and only a small part remains, but the mullahs' training college (as it still is today) has a fine stone-walled inner courtyard set around a small garden. This is approached from the street through a very impressive portal with an unusual type of stalactite moulding inside the outer arch and some very intricate mosaic tiling in the inner doorway.

Masjed-é Nasīr-ol-Molk

Further down Kheyābūn-é Shahīd Āyatollāh Dastgheib from the Madrasé-yé Khān is the modern Masjed-é Nasīr-ol-Molk of the Ghajar period, currently undergoing extensive repairs and open to visitors only in the morning. It has some fine stalactite moulding in the not-very-large outer portal, but it's not as intricate or stunning as that of the earlier religious buildings mentioned above.

Kelīsā-yé Moghaddas-é Sham'ūn-é Ghayūr

The Church of St Simon the Zealot, on the west side of Kheyābūn-é Nōbahār off Bolvār-é Karīm Khān-é Zand, is Anglican, although the old building itself is very Iranian in character. It is known for its very valuable stained glass windows. According to local tradition, St Simon was martyred in Persia together with St Thaddeus, another of the 12 apostles. The great metal door bearing a Persian cross is usually closed, but if you come at the right time and knock hard enough someone will let you in. The building behind the church used to be the Anglican Hospital.

Kelīsā-yé Ārāmāné

The 17th-century Armenian Church is in an alley off Kheyābūn-é Ghā'ānī: if you are coming from Meidūn-é Moshīr this is the first kūché to your left.

Ārāmgāh-é Hāfez

The tomb of the celebrated poet Hāfez is north of the river, in a small garden diagonally opposite the east corner of the Bāgh-é Mellī. The marble tombstone, engraved with a long verse from the poet's works, was placed here inside a small shrine by Karīm Khān in 1773. In 1935 an octagonal pavilion was put up over it, supported by eight stone columns beneath a tiled dome. Karīm Khān also built an eivān close to the shrine, which was enlarged at the same time as the pavilion was erected. The garden with its two pools is very pleasant and restful, especially in the warmer months when the flowers are in full bloom, and the mausoleum itself is simpler and more attractive than that of Sa'dī. The grounds are open daily from 7 am to 6 pm, and entry costs 20 rials. There's a wonderfully atmospheric teahouse in a private walled garden of the grounds (see Places to Eat). You can get there by shared taxi from the Ārāmgāh-é Sa'di (about 50 rials).

Khājé Shams-ed-Dīn Mohammad, or Hāfez ('one who can recite the Qorān from memory') as he became known, was born in about 1324. Since his father died while he was still young, the boy had to rely on the education of some of the leading scholars in Shīrāz, so apart from learning the Qorān by heart at an early age he became deeply interested in literature. He wrote many verses which are still used in everyday speech today, and much of his poetry, known as the *Dīvān-é Hāfez*, has a strong mystical and untranslatable quality which has always appealed to the Persian mind, although at an another level much of it was about wine, nightingales and courtship. Although he lived in turbulent times, Hāfez refused many very generous invitations to some of the great courts of the day inside and outside Iran because of his love for his birthplace. His poetry helped to make Shīrāz famous well beyond his lifetime and it's fitting that his tomb is still one of the city's most popular attractions. Hāfez died in 1389.

Ārāmgāh-é Sa'dī

In the far north-east of Shīrāz, at the end of Bolvār-é Būstān, the Tomb of Sa'dī is set in a tranquil garden with a natural spring in a valley at the foot of a hill, but the monument itself is a rather unfortunate piece of modern architecture. The previous and simpler mausoleum, which was the result of a long succession of renovations by various patrons since the death of Sa'dī, including Karīm Khān, was replaced in 1952 after being deemed unworthy of the great man by a learned committee. Now part of a rather grandiose complex, the marble tomb-box itself, which dates from the 1860s, is in an octagonal stone colonnade inscribed with various verses from Sa'dī and supporting a tiled dome, while a metal chandelier hangs over it. The grounds are open daily from 7.30 am to 5.30 pm, with an entry fee of 20 rials.

The tombs of Hāfez and Sa'dī are some way out of the centre and the walk is not particularly rewarding. Instead you can take bus No 7 to the Ārāmgāh-é Sa'dī from Meīdūn-é Ahmadī, or a shared taxi from anywhere north of the river.

Sheikh Mohammad Shams-ed-Dīn, known by his pen-name of Sa'dī, lived from about 1207 to 1291. Like Hāfez, he lost his father at a tender age and his education was entrusted to some of the leading teachers of Shīrāz. However, unlike Hāfez, Sa'dī spent a large part of his life travelling to many countries, even becoming involved in the Crusades, before he settled down to writing in his home town. Many of his elegantly phrased verses reflect the philosophy of humility and compassion which he developed during his travels, and they are still commonly used in conversation. His most famous work is the Golestān ('Rose Garden'), which has been translated into many languages. Before he died Sa'dī moved to this retreat which was then well beyond the edge of Shīrāz. Ever since he was buried here on what's said to be the exact place of his death, his tomb has been an important pilgrimage site.

Bāgh-é Eram

Shīrāz used to be famous for its many large parks thick with cypress trees, but today this small and well-tended 'Garden of Paradise'

north of the river near the university has probably the best and tallest collection remaining. There's also a charming 19th-century Ghajar palace, the **Kākh-é Eram**, in the gardens.

Other gardens worth a stroll include the ancient **Bāgh-é Afīf Ābād** and **Bāgh-é Delgoshā** as well as the more recent **Bāgh-é Khalīlī**.

Emāmzādé-yé Alī Ebn-é Hamzé

This mausoleum's just north of the river, on the east side of Kheyābūn-é Hāfez. Virtually all the original 10th-century structure has disappeared after several earthquakes and successive repairs and extensions, but there are some interesting tombstones making up the forecourt, and the tiled dome is of some appeal.

Places to Stay

There are plenty of places to suit all budgets, including one luxury hotel that's one of the best for value in Iran. Apart from the campsite, there are no places close to the bus station, but it's easy enough to get to any of the hotels by shared taxi.

Places to Stay – bottom end

There are plenty of mosāferkhūnés and cheap hotels in the small streets running from the south side of Bolvār-é Karīm Khān-é Zand, especially on Kheyābūn-é Anvarī and Kheyābūn-é Tōhīd, and some even cheaper places along Kheyābūn-é Lotf Alī Khān-é Zand and around Meīdūn-é Ahmadī. There's a slightly better and quieter class of place along Kheyābūn-é 22 Bahman.

In Kheyābūn-é Anvarī you could try the Mosāferkhūné-yé Kesrā (marked in English 'Kasra Guest House'), charging 2000 rials a triple without bathroom, the Mosāferkhūné-yé Anvarī ('Madaen') or the Mehmūnpazīr-é Sāsān. Places in Kheyābūn-é 22 Bahman include the Mosāferkhūné-yé Sīrūs, the Mosāferkhūné-yé Māh and the Mosāferkhūné-yé Pāyām, which charges 1650 rials a double with shared bathroom.

The campsite, with its partly equipped huts, is about 10 minutes' walk from the bus station. There's no hot water, and the site is so run-down that the manager begged me in my own interests to stay elsewhere. You could take a shared taxi going north-east from the bus terminal for 50 rials, or walk to the crossroads and turn right. Ask for the *ordūgāh-é jahāngardī*.

Places to Stay – middle

The *Hotel-é Atlas* (☎ 29225, 47748) ('Hotel Atlas') on the south-east of Meidūn-é Atlasī to the north of the river charges 2400/3200 rials a single/double with bathroom and is recommended by one traveller as clean, very comfortable and even having piped music in the rooms, if that is a good thing. On the north of Bolvār-é Karīm Khān-é Zand there are two good and not particularly expensive hotels, the *Hotel-é Kōsar* ('Kowsar Hotel') which charges 2700/4050 rials with private bathroom or 2400/3050 rials with shared bathroom, and the *Hotel-é Eram* ('Eram Hotel') a few metres to the west charging 2700/4050 rials with private bathroom.

Places to Stay – top end

The large *Pārk Hotel* in an alley north of Meidūn-é Shohadā is popular with Iranians and foreigners and closer to the city centre than the Homa. Rooms are 4600/7000 rials with private bathroom. Although the hotel's a little off the main road, its sign in English – 'Park Hotel' – is clearly visible from Kheyābūn-é Karīm Khān-é Zand.

If you stay at only one top-end hotel in Iran, choose the *Homa Hotel* (☎ 28000) (Hotel-é Homā) on Kheyābūn-é Shahīd Rasūl, north of the river. Not only is this one of the best places in Iran for service, food and accommodation but, at only 8000 rials a twin room, also one of the world's least expensive luxury hotels. The Homa is understandably very popular with Iranians, but the friendly receptionists can usually manage to find room for a foreigner. The hotel has an excellent restaurant, good coffee shop, expensive private taxi service with Buicks and English-speaking drivers, barbershop, small bookshop, shoeshine booth, overnight laundry and dry-cleaning service, handi-crafts shop, photographic shop and Iran Air office. Despite the notices throughout the lobby warning foreign guests to change money at the hotel bank before making any purchases, the Bank Mellat branch on the ground floor has never had any dealings with foreign currency. The Homa is a little difficult to reach by shared taxi unless you offer to pay more than the usual fare, perhaps 200 rials from Bolvār-é Karīm Khān-é Zand. From the bus station 50 to 100 rials should be enough.

Places to Eat

There are plenty of places to eat in the centre of Shīrāz, although there are few fully fledged restaurants outside the hotels. Most of the cheaper chelō kabābīs and kabābīs are around Meidūn-é Shohadā, especially behind the Arg. Most of the best establishments are some way out of the centre. North of the river there are several good but rather expensive restaurants around the Homa Hotel and Meidūn-é Gāz. If you are entering or leaving Shīrāz, the restaurants at the bus terminal and the airport are better than most of their kind.

The *Sālon-é Ghezā-yé Khōrāk-é Habīb* (not marked in English) at the intersection of Bolvār-é Karīm Khān-é Zand with Kheyābūn-é Rūdakī, next to the cinema marked in English 'Hafez Cinema', has good khōresh for 800 rials. Another good and inexpensive place is the *Restōrān-é Golestān*; if you're going west along Bolvār-é Karīm Khān-é Zand, this is in the first arcade on the left past the intersection with Kheyābūn-é Anvarī.

Iran may not be a country that you would immediately associate with samosas and pakoras, but they are very popular in the southern provinces, and both can be found at the *Sālon-é Sambūsé-yé Jalālī* off Meidūn-é Gāz in the north of Shīrāz. Very good large samosas with a spicy sauce are only 120 rials.

Shīrāzīs take the art of liquid refreshment very seriously. Although the world-famous Shīrāz grape is, in Iran, no longer made into the wine that inspired Omar Khayyām to poetry, there are several substitutes that won't leave you with a hangover, such as tea, ice-cream and fruit juice. All along Bolvār-é Karīm Khān-é Zand places serve these answers to a hot summer's day. The most atmospheric teahouse in Shīrāz is the small outdoor one set around a rectangular pool in the grounds of the Ārāmgāh-é Hāfez, with cushioned niches in each of its four walls where you can rest and drink tea for 100 rials a throw, or puff at the hubble-bubble to your heart's discontent. It also serves ice-cream and cakes. Although it ought to be thronging with tourists, the place hardly sees a single foreigner and remains for the time being one of the most idyllically private of teahouses, open only from 9 to 11 am and from 4 to 5.30 pm.

Don't forget to try the local fālūdé (also known as pālūdé), a difficult-to-describe sweet chilled dish, half drink, half pudding, made of rosewater and vermicelli, working out as something like a cross between a sorbet and a rice pudding and very refreshing. There are several places behind the Arg to sample it for around 150 rials.

The flash but disappointing *Restōrān-é Bahārān*, at the intersection of Bolvār-é Karīm Khān-é Zand with Kheyābūn-é Mollā Sadrā, serves overpriced bony and not-too-good jūjé-kabāb for 2100 rials. The restaurant at the *Hotel-é Eram* is a much better option. The restaurant in the *Pārk Hotel* is not much cheaper than that at the Homa Hotel but it lacks in personal service and isn't nearly as good.

The *Restōrān-é Sonnatī-yé Sūfī* on Bolvār-é Zargarī, a long way out from the centre and hopeless for public transport, has good food and the right atmosphere for a top restaurant (with lift music thrown in). Menus are in English but do not list prices, which are high. This is the nearest thing you'll find in Shīrāz to a romantic dinner rendezvous for two. It even has a salad buffet table – very unusual in Iran.

If you want to splash out and still get good value for money, the ground-floor restaurant in the *Homa Hotel* is without doubt one of the best places around. The French might not be convinced, but the restaurant serves some

of the best Continental food in Iran, as well as traditional Iranian dishes such as excellent boneless fish kebabs (2100 rials) or quail kebabs (3200 rials). I had orange juice, 'Islamic beer', good onion soup, a special salad, and chicken in tarragon sauce with carrots and fried potatoes, all for 3620 rials. The restaurant, although expensive by Iranian standards, is cheap in dollar terms and is as highly recommended as the hotel itself.

Things to Buy

Most of the items you can find in Esfahān are available in Shīrāz, although not in the same quantity or variety. On the other hand, you are much less likely to be cheated here. Good buys in the bazaar include metalwork and printed cottons, especially tablecloths and tribal rugs woven by Fārs nomads.

Getting There & Away

Air Iran Air flies from Shīrāz to:

Bandar-é Abbās – daily, 10.35 pm, 55 minutes
Bandar-é Lengé – daily, 7.50 am, 50 minutes
Būshehr – Wednesday, 8.20 pm, 30 minutes
Esfahān – daily except Tuesday, 5.10 pm; Tuesday, 7.10 pm; Wednesday at 10.30 pm; 45 minutes
Jazīré-yé Kīsh – Sunday and Thursday, 9.40 am, 55 minutes (tickets very difficult)
Mashhad – Monday, Wednesday and Saturday, 8.25 pm, 1½ hours
Tehrān – daily, 1.25 am, 7.10 am, 10.40 am, 1¼ hours; Monday, Wednesday, Friday and Saturday, 1.40 pm, 1¼ hours; daily except Tuesday, 5.10 pm, two hours; Tuesday, 7.10 pm, two hours; Tuesday and Friday, 10.30 pm, 1¼ hours; Wednesday, 10.30 pm, two hours; Monday, Wednesday and Friday, 11 pm, 1¼ hours (all 7070 rials).

International Services Iran Air flies to the UAE (Abu Dhabi weekly, Dubai twice a week, Sharjah weekly) and Qatar (Doha once a week), and Gulf Air has one flight a week to Doha and one to Manama. Foreigners must pay in hard currency for tickets on these flights, which cost £102/204 one-way/return (no excursion fare).

Airline Offices There are three Iran Air

ticket offices in town, but the only one dealing with refunds or international flights is the main one (☎ 30045), on the south side of Bolvār-é Karīm Khān-é Zand about 150 metres north-west of Meidūn-é Enghelāb; there's another sales office on the same side of the same street a few metres north-west of Meidūn-é Shohadā, and a third in an annexe to the Homa Hotel.

Gulf Air (☎ 35030) is at 308 Bolvār-é Karīm Khān-é Zand, on the south side near the intersection with Kheyābūn-é Anvarī.

Bus & Minibus The main bus station is on Bolvār-é Salmān-é Fārsī north of the river. This is where to go for most intercity buses. If you're going there by taxi, ask for the Termīnāl-é Bozorg. From Bolvār-é Karīm Khān-é Zand take a shared taxi to Meidūn-é Valī-yé Asr and another one north to the station.

The terminal for buses to Marvdasht and some other places in Fārs, known as the Termīnāl-é Hāfez, is in Kheyābūn-é Hāfez and is easy to reach by shared taxi. There's no city bus from or passing by the main bus terminal, but taxis are very cheap from there. At the gates of the station there's an office (with separate windows for men and women) for booking seats on shared taxis at more or less fixed prices. They arranged a lift for me in a van to Meidūn-é Shohadā for only 50 rials.

This is the most well-organised bus station I have seen in Iran, with numbered bays for the coaches, comprehensive signs – some of them even in English – and the bus company offices all in two large rooms, with boards above each desk giving the names in Persian of the available destinations. The terminal boasts a teahouse and eating room as well as lavatories, shops and a prayer-room. If this recently completed terminal is the shape of things to come with Iranian transport planning, it's a good sign. Even if you don't read or speak Persian, you shouldn't have much problem here if you pass around the name of your intended destination. There are buses to most major destinations, with the important exception of

Mashhad, but no international services at present. Buses leave from the main bus terminal for:

Ābādān – at least one a day, 615 km, 10 hours
Ahvāz – several a week, 568 km, 10 hours, 1085/1300 rials 'lux'/'super' (Cooperative Bus Co. No 2)
Arāk – 772 km, 12 hours
Bākhtarān – at least one a day, 1077 km, 18 hours, 1820 rials 'lux'
Bandar-é Abbās – at least two a day, 601 km, 10 hours
Bandar-é Lengé – one daily, 654 km, 12 hours, 1400 rials
Būshehr – several a day, 320 km, five hours, 550 rials 'lux'
Dezfūl – 730 km, 12 hours
Esfahān – several a day, 481 km, eight hours, 830 rials 'super'
Karaj – 943 km, 17 hours
Kermān – at least two a day, 797 km, eight hours, 830 rials
Lāmard – 503 km, nine hours
Lār – 358 km, six hours, 535 rials
Mīnāb – 685 km, 12 hours
Rafsanjūn – 563 km, nine hours
Sanandaj – at least one a day, 1133 km, 20 hours, 1550/1970 rials 'lux'/'super'
Shahr-é Kord – 588 km, 10 hours
Sīrjān – 381 km, six hours (Cooperative Bus Company No 2)
Tabrīz – several a day, 1519 km, 24 hours, 1915 rials 'lux'
Tehrān – several a day, 895 km, 16 hours, 1650/2390 rials 'lux'/'super'
Yāsūj – 258 km, four hours
Yazd – two a day, 440 km, seven hours, 630 rials; (Cooperative Bus Companies Nos 16, 17)
Zāhedān – at least one a day, 1088 km, 17 hours, 1560/2110 rials 'lux'/'super' (Cooperative Bus Company No 5).

Shared Taxi & Savārī The main terminal for shared taxis and savārī to destinations throughout the province and further afield is across the road from the minibus station – the Termīnāl-é Hāfez – by the bridge.

Getting Around

To/From the Airport Tickets for the new airport bus service cost 100 rials at the office in the arrivals lounge; there are several routes into town. A taxi between the airport and town costs 1500 rials for a solo passenger, or 500 to 700 rials in a shared taxi.

Bus & Minibus There are city bus terminals outside the Arg, in Meidūn-é Ahmadī and in front of the Ārāmgāh-é Sa'dī.

Taxi You can take a shared taxi to the north of the river from Meidūn-é Valī-yé Asr, Meidūn-é Shohadā or Meidūn-é Enghelāb for 50 to 100 rials, or from one end of Bolvār-é Karīm Khān-é Zand to the other for around 50 rials. Most of the sights south of the river can easily be visited on foot.

PERSEPOLIS (TAKHT-É JAMSHĪD)

تخت جمشید

The earlier capital of the Achaemenians was at Pasargadae, further north, but in about 512 BC, Darius I (the Great) started construction of this massive and magnificent palace complex. It sits on a plateau on the slopes of Kūh-é Rahmat and at one time it was surrounded by a wall 18 metres high. In Persian the site is known as Takht-é Jamshīd, or Throne of Jamshīd, after one of the mythical kings of ancient Persia, although the original name was Pārsā; the first known reference to it by its Greek name Persepolis – meaning both 'city of Pārsā' and 'Persian city', but also 'destroyer of cities' – dates only from after its sacking.

In 331 BC, Alexander the Great, in an uncharacteristic act of wanton destruction, burnt Persepolis to the ground – fortunately

Part of Frieze at the Apadana

not without first having the enormous library translated into Greek. The ruins you see today are just a shadow of Persepolis' former glory, even though they are much more revealing than the few surviving traces of the much less well preserved Achaemenian administrative capital at Shūsh. As you survey the barren land around it, remember that this area was once far more fertile than it is today.

The only entrance to the palace was by the four flights of steps of the **Grand Stairway**. At the top they led to **Xerxes' Gateway**, with three entrances flanked on the east and west by two seven-metre-high stone bulls.

The southern door leads to the immense **Apadana** where the kings once held audiences and received visitors. The roof was supported by 36 stone columns each 20 metres high, but the main interest today is in the superb reliefs that decorate the stairways. Altogether they are over 300 metres long; in Persepolis' heyday they were brightly coloured and must have been an amazing spectacle. The quality of the work is still astounding today. The **Parade of Nations** shows people and animals bearing tribute to the Persian king. Other reliefs show the 10,000-man palace guard, called 'the Immortals' because as soon as one man fell he would immediately be replaced by another from an apparently limitless reserve.

Behind the Apadana are the smaller **Palace of Darius** and **Palace of Xerxes**, and a small but interesting **museum**, most of the exhibits at which are labelled in good English (50 rials; no photography). The eastern door from Xerxes' Gateway leads to the **Hall of 32 Columns**, behind which is the now demolished **Treasury of Darius**.

Below Persepolis there are the remnants of a **tent city** which was assembled for the 2500th anniversary of the Persian Empire in 1971, a swansong of the Shāh, attended by a glittering array of ambassadors and international royalty that outstripped even the parades of supplicants depicted in the Achaemenian bas-reliefs.

Persepolis is well worth the effort to visit: the lack of visitors is very pleasant, as you

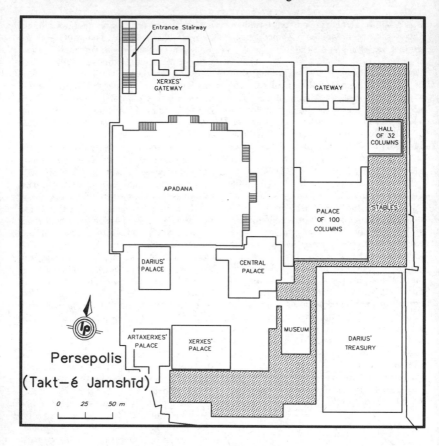

Persepolis
(Takt—é Jamshīd)

have the site virtually to yourself, except on Fridays and public holidays when it's just busy enough to support touts offering donkey rides outside the entrance. In summer it's wise to visit the area early in the morning or late in the afternoon, avoiding the intense midday heat. There's an entrance charge of 50 rials, and for some reason foreigners have to fill out their passport details in a ledger. The site is open daily from 7 am to 12.30 pm and from 1.30 to 5 pm. No information in English is available at the site, except for the labels in the museum, and there are no resident guides, although you may come across a visiting Iranian archaeological student eager for the chance of being an unpaid one to a rare foreign visitor, especially on Friday. Much has been written about Persepolis by many, but the only book in English easily available locally is Ali Sami's helpful and illustrated 160-page *Persepolis* (Musavi Printing Press, Shīrāz, 1976), which can be picked up in Shīrāz for 1500 rials at the Homa Hotel, or for 800 rials at the International Bookshop.

Places to Stay & Eat

The *Homa Hotel* (Hotel-é Homā) at Persepolis (illustrated on the back cover of some Iran Air tickets) has for several years been rented out to the military, but there are vague rumours that it may soon reopen to the public. Ask at the Homa Hotel in Shīrāz or the tourist office there for the latest information. There's a fairly good restaurant, the *Restōrān-é Takht-é Tāvūs*, a short distance to the right of the main entrance to Persepolis as you walk out, but no others.

Getting There & Away

Since Persepolis and the two following sites (Naghsh-é Rostam and Pasargadae) can be visited in one trip, this information applies to all three.

Persepolis (Takht-é Jamshīd to Iranians) is 57 km from Shīrāz, just off the Esfahān road. Naghsh-é Rostam is about three km north of Persepolis, and Pasargadae (Pāsārgād in Persian) is 130 km from Shīrāz, in the same direction as the other two sites but rather further off the main road. Getting to these sites and back again isn't as straightforward as it would be in a country more geared towards tourism. Allow a whole day for the round trip from Shīrāz. If you can afford to hire a taxi for the trip, you could easily see everything in one day, leaving not much later than 10 am. If you're going by public transport, don't leave Shīrāz any later than about 8 am if you want to see all three without having to rush, and try to avoid going on a Friday or public holiday when transport is always a problem. Alternatively you could visit Persepolis and Naghsh-é Rostam one day and Pasargadae another.

Public Transport The cheapest method to make the trip is to catch a minibus to Marvdasht, taking a shared taxi from there to Persepolis, from where you could either walk or take a shared taxi to Naghsh-é Rostam. Return by shared taxi to Marvdasht and then take another shared taxi to Sā'adatshahr and then another to Pasargadae. When returning to Shīrāz you might be lucky and catch a direct bus; otherwise you have to take a succession of shared taxis via Sā'adatshahr or Marvdasht, or both.

It's difficult to find any transport out of Pasargadae after dark. Alternatively, you could visit the sites in chronological order by taking a direct bus from Shīrāz to Pasargadae and from there going to Persepolis and Naghsh-é Rostam via Marvdasht.

Minibuses for Marvdasht (40 minutes, 100 rials) leave Shīrāz about hourly, not from the main bus station but from the smaller Termīnāl-é Hāfez. Much more frequent shared taxis or savārīs (300 rials, 30 minutes) leave from the taxi terminal across the road from the minibus station and about 100 metres west.

You'll be dropped off in Marvdasht at the bus stop and taxi bay known as the Darvāzé-yé Shīrāz. You can catch a taxi to Persepolis from across the road about 100 metres away. The correct fare by shared taxi is 100 rials (500 rials as a single passenger), but foreigners are not always eligible for this. You can also charter a taxi to take you to Persepolis and Naghsh-é Rostām and back to Marvdasht for 1000 to 1500 rials an hour, with a guided tour in Persian by the driver thrown in.

To get from Persepolis to Naghsh-é Rostam you can hitch a lift for 50 rials, or turn right outside the gates as you leave and walk along the road straight ahead for about 20 minutes. It's difficult and expensive to take a taxi from Persepolis or Naghsh-é Rostām to Pasargadae: I was quoted 10,000 rials for a return trip. Instead you should return to Marvdasht and either try to take a shared taxi direct from there for probably not less than 1000 rials a person or, more likely, take a shared taxi to Sā'adatshahr (500 rials a person) and from there to Pasargadae (150 rials). If you are coming direct from Shīrāz, there are regular direct buses or minibuses to Pasargadae and Sā'adatshahr for 400 rials from the Hāfez station.

Hired Taxi To save a lot of time, if not money, you could charter a taxi for a complete tour of Persepolis, Naghsh-é Rostam and Pasargadae. In Shīrāz, the Homa Hotel taxi service quoted 20,000 rials for this with an English-speaking driver and Buick, but other taxi companies may be cheaper. It's probably better to charter a taxi by the hour rather than for a flat fare, so that there's less incentive for the driver to rush you on from one site to another. Some of the travel agencies along Bolvār-é Karīm Khān-é Zand may be able to offer an English-speaking guide.

NAGHSH-É ROSTAM   نقش رستم

About four km north of Persepolis, hewn out of a cliff at a lofty height from the ground, the four tombs of Naghsh-é Rostam are believed to be those of Darius I, Xerxes, Artaxerxes and Darius II, but only that of Darius I (the second from right as you face the cliff) has been positively identified. There are also eight reliefs from far later in the Sassanian dynasty, cut into the stone below the facades of the Achaemenian tombs, depicting various scenes of imperial conquests and royal investitures, as well as a probable fire-temple from Achaemenian times. There's a custodian, but there's no entry charge, and there's no fence or other way of preventing you visiting at any time of night or day. See the Persepolis entry for details of how to get to this site.

PASARGADAE (PĀSĀRGĀD)   پاسارگاد

The capital of Cyrus the Great is 130 km from Shīrāz and rather further off the main road. It's nowhere near as visually interesting as Persepolis, and what remains is fairly widely scattered. Begun under Cyrus the Great in about 546 BC, it was succeeded soon after his death by Darius I's magnificent palace; some historians suggest that the construction of Persepolis may actually have started under Cyrus.

The first structure you'll come to is the Tomb of Cyrus itself, known incorrectly by the locals as Ghabr-é Mādar-é Soleimān or Tomb of Solomon's Mother. Constructed on a stone platform, Cyrus' impressive stone cenotaph was originally much taller than its present height, but even so this now empty tomb is the best preserved of the remains of Pasargadae. The lonely custodian at this tomb will charge you 20 rials for a ticket and can direct you to the other sites along a deserted road to the north-east. After about 1200 metres you come to the insubstantial remains of three Achaemenian palaces, and a short distance to the north to the ruins of a tower on a plinth known as the Zendān-é Soleimān or Prison of Solomon. A little to the north-east again you reach a large stone platform on a hill known as the Takht-é Mādar-é Soleimān or Throne of the Mother of Solomon, and finally about a km to the north-west are two stone plinths which originally formed part of a pair of altars within a sacred precinct.

Pasargadae is open from 7.30 am to 6 pm every day, but it's better not to arrive later than about 3 pm in winter (it gets surprisingly cold and windswept soon afterwards) or 4 pm in other seasons, and it's difficult to get transport out after dark. Unless you arrive here by private transport, you'll have to walk between the remains.

Getting There & Away

Minibuses and taxis will drop you off at the small village of Pāsārgād, a short walk south of the Tomb of Cyrus and the other remains, now approached through a gateway across the road. For details of getting to this site, see the Persepolis entry.

Būshehr Province
استان بوشهر

Occupying a narrow coastal strip north and south of the town of Būshehr, this province is a modern and largely artificial creation. It has an area of 27,650 sq km and a population of 579,000.

BŪSHEHR   بوشهر

Without a doubt Būshehr (Bandar-é Būshehr, sometimes known in English as Bushire) is the most pleasant of the larger towns along the Iranian shores of the Persian Gulf. It lacks the frantic bustle of Bandar-é Abbās (even before the Iran-Iraq War the shipping trade was in decline here) and is free of the

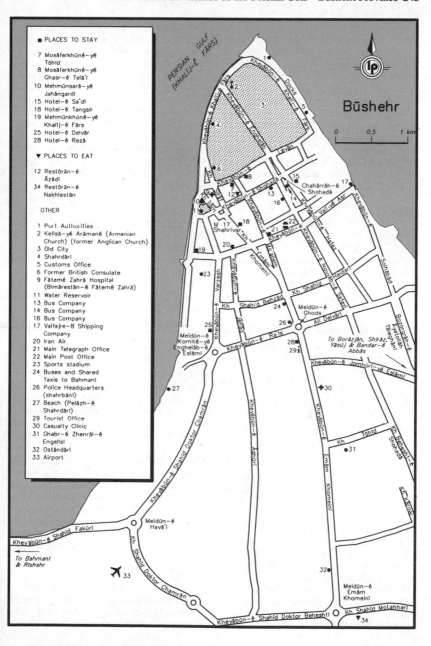

Būshehr

0   0.5   1 km

■ PLACES TO STAY

7   Mosāferkhūné–yé
    Tōhīd
8   Mosāferkhūné–yé
    Ghasr–é Telā'ī
10 Mehmūnsarā–yé
    Jahāngardī
15 Hotel–é Sa'dī
18 Hotel–é Tangsīr
19 Mehmūnkhūné–yé
    Khalīj–é Fārs
25 Hotel–é Delvār
28 Hotel–é Rezā

▼ PLACES TO EAT

12 Restōrān–é
    Āzādī
34 Restōrān–é
    Nakhlestān

    OTHER

1   Port Authorities
2   Kelisā–yé Arāmané (Armenian
    Church) (former Anglican
    Church)
3   Old City
4   Shahrdārī
5   Customs Office
6   Former British Consulate
9   Fātemé Zahrā Hospital
    (Bimārestān–é Fātemé Zahrā)
11 Water Reservoir
13 Bus Company
14 Bus Company
16 Bus Company
17 Valfajre–8 Shipping
    Company
20 Iran Air
21 Main Telegraph Office
22 Main Post Office
23 Sports stadium
24 Buses and Shared
    Taxis to Bahmanī
26 Police Headquarters
    (shahrbānī)
27 Beach (Pelāzh–é
    Shahrdārī)
29 Tourist Office
30 Casualty Clinic
31 Ghabr–é Zhenrāl–é
    Engelīsī
32 Ostāndārī
33 Airport

menace of Mīnāb or the total lethargy of Bandar-é Lengé. Būshehr has an interesting history, much of it tied up with the colonial era, and a fair number of little-known attractions. The people have time to talk to foreigners, the pace of life is relaxed, the food is good, hotels aren't permanently full in winter and the old part of town stands more or less untouched by the developers. Its indigenous population is predominantly Arab in origin.

Būshehr is very hot and humid in summer, although sea breezes give some relief near the coast, but very pleasant in winter.

History

Although Curzon described Būshehr as a 'town without history', the peninsula on which it stands is in fact the site of one of the earliest ports of the Persian Gulf. The original settlement at Rīshahr, 12 km south of modern Būshehr, may have been founded in the time of Ardashīr, or even as early as the Elamite era.

During the early Islamic period until at least the 16th century, Rīshahr was one of the chief trading centres of the Persian Gulf, but it lost its importance after the establishment of Bandar-é Abbās in the early 17th century. In 1734, the site of Būshehr, then only a small fishing village, was chosen by Nāder Shāh for the principal port and naval station of Persia, in response to increased colonial activity in the area, and the bricks of the soon-to-be-forgotten Rīshahr went into building this new town. Its prosperity was assured when in 1759 the British East India Company, then the dominant power in the Persian Gulf, moved its base to Būshehr after its factory at Bandar-é Abbās was destroyed by the French.

Although initial development was slow and ultimately Nāder Shāh's naval ambitions came to nothing, Būshehr grew under Karīm Khān-é Zand, who had established his capital at nearby Shīrāz. By the end of the 18th century Būshehr became not only the main outlet of Fārs but the chief port of Persia.

Under Karīm Khān, Būshehr, together with the surrounding region and even Bahrain, remained peacefully and prosperously within the domain of their hereditary Arab ruler, Sheikh Nasr, who maintained trading relations with Muscat and India. However, his son was on bad terms with Lotf Alī Khān, and after a long period of tension and misrule the area returned to central Persian control by the mid-19th century. At about the same time, Būshehr became the seat of the British Political Residency on the Persian Gulf, and the town was even occupied by the British from 1856 to 1857 and during WWI.

With the completion in the '30s of the trans-Iranian railway, which bypassed Būshehr in favour of the ports of Khūzestān, Būshehr began to decline. The British moved the Political Residency to Bahrain in 1946, and the consulate which took its place was closed in 1951 after the nationalisation of the Anglo-Iranian Oil Company. The town was of some importance to the navy in the Iran-Iraq War, but most of its commercial activities collapsed, to the benefit of the less exposed Bandar-é Abbās to the east, and the port is still largely idle.

Orientation

The town juts out like a shark's fin into the Persian Gulf, at the northern tip of a peninsula connected to the interior by a narrow neck of land prone to waterlogging. The old town is at the northern tip of Būshehr, enclosed by Kheyābūn-é Khalīj-é Fārs (Persian Gulf St). In winter it's one of the best promenades in Iran. Būshehr is a manageable size for exploring, unlike some Iranian ports which stretch for miles along the coast. Most of the attractions and the hotels, restaurants and bus terminal are in the northern part of Būshehr. Even the airport is as close as it could be to the centre.

Information

The ostāndārī (☎ 33023) is on the west side of Kheyābūn-é Emām Khomeinī just north of Meidūn-é Emām Khomeinī. The shahrdārī (☎ 23314) is in Kheyābūn-é

Khalīj-é Fārs. The visa office is at the police headquarters in Meidūn-é Ghods.

Tourist Office The tourist office (☎ 22828) is on the west side of Kheyābūn-é Emām Khomeinī a few metres south of the Hotel-é Rezā.

Money The main banks are along Kheyābūn-é Leyān.

Post & Telecommunications The main post office and the central telegraph office are almost next to each other on the north side of Kheyābūn-é Valī-yé Asr. The dialling code for Būshehr is 0771.

Maps The tourist office has a helpful combined map of Būshehr town and province, Bahmanī and Borāzjān, typically with a key entirely in Persian. This is the only published map of the town.

Medical Services For emergencies dial ☎ 115. There's a casualty unit at the hospital on the east side of Kheyābūn-é Emām Khomeinī, south of the intersection with Kheyābūn-é Jomhūrī-yé Eslāmī.

Emergency The police headquarters (shahrbānī) (☎ 23035) is on the north-west side of Meidūn-é Ghods.

Old City

The old city (*shahr-é ghadīm*) on either side of Kheyābūn-é Enghelāb represents one of the largest living museums of traditional Bandarī architecture. Unlike so many other ports in the Persian Gulf, the old city has been spared the destructive effects of development, although little has been done in the way of renovation and few buildings last long under such harsh climatic conditions. Most of the way along Kheyābūn-é Khalīj-é Fārs and in the maze of narrow alleys on either side of Kheyābūn-é Enghelāb you can see examples of characteristic Bandarī building.

One of the best-preserved and largest examples is the two-storey, columned old **shahrdārī** building on the seafront, still used

as municipal headquarters. Most of the old houses in the narrow winding kūchés and blind alleys are still inhabited by families, many of the women dressed in the traditional brightly coloured layers of clothing unique to the Persian Gulf. The houses are made of mud brick covered with a thin layer of sand-coloured plaster, with tall facades, latticed glassless windows, arched balconies, sturdy wooden doors with metal studs and carved jambs, protruding joists, overhanging balconies on flat roofs (where the residents sleep out in the hottest months), flaking plaster and rudimentary plumbing systems. Few tourists make it to the old city, so one of the ragged boys native to the old city may break off his game of alley football for the far more interesting and prestigious pursuit of taking a genuine foreigner on a tour of the neighbourhood and, if you are lucky, show you inside one of the old houses. There are four mosques in the historical quarter.

Most Iranians are far more impressed by modern imported styles of architecture than in the traditional indigenous methods of building, with their elegant yet essentially functional answer to the harsh climatic challenges. The feeling is rather one of embarrassment at the shanty status which housing of this kind has assumed in recent years, and it's probable that within little more than a generation almost nothing will remain of the distinctive Bandarī style of architecture.

The slumbering docks are east of the old city. Look out for traditional shipbuilding activities: ask for the **Kārgāh-é Lenjsāzī**. Private fishing and transport boats operate out of the strip of coast to the south of the docks.

Ābambār

This small, traditional drinking-water reservoir is between the Hotel-é Khalīj-é Fārs and the Mehmūnsarā-yé Jahāngardī in Kheyābūn-é Khalīj-é Fārs.

Kelīsā-yé Arāmané

The former Anglican church (Kelīsā-yé Engelīsīhā) is in Kheyābūn-é Enghelāb, just north of the intersection with Kheyābūn-é Khalīj-é Fārs. This small, typically English, stone building, concealed from the street by a high wall, was established in 1819 by members of the then vibrant British community. It has since been taken over by the Armenians and is presently marked in English 'Armenian Church (Apostolic)'. Although the congregation only numbers about a dozen, they have gone to great efforts to renovate and redecorate the small stone church, and the results so far are impressive. There's a small graveyard (entered through the church) with tombs of a cosmopolitan mixture of parishioners spanning the history of British missionary activity, including one rejoicing in the name of Mackertich Goolzad (RIP 18 May 1915). Some of the tombs are still in good condition, but a number are missing their headstones.

There's a small **Adventist Church** (Kelīsā-yé Zohūr) in Kheyābūn-é Fārs, so inconspicuous that I was unable to find it.

Ghabr-é Zhenrāl-é Engelīsī

When I visited Būshehr I was told that, as an Englishman, I had almost a duty to visit this, the 'Tomb of the British General', but I would have been happier if I hadn't. Once standing in its own small plot of land, the tomb and statue, in an advanced state of neglect, are now completely surrounded and obscured by hundreds of pot plants in a small walled nursery, difficult to find without a guide. The memorial has been parted from its plinth, so that only a military historian could establish the identity of this forgotten soldier, unfortunate enough to die at Būshehr.

Beach

There's a small beach, the **Pelāzh-é Shahrdārī**, west of Meidūn-é Komīté-yé Enghelāb-é Eslāmī, not near the shahrdārī at all. It's equipped with huts but does not boast much in the way of sand. Men at least can swim a short distance out to sea here, apparently immune from the dangers of sharks and jellyfish.

Places to Stay – bottom end

Most of the mosāferkhūnés are in the old quarter of Būshehr, on or near Kheyābūn-é Leyān and Kheyābūn-é Enghelāb. Having visited what are claimed to be the best two such lodging houses, I decided that I couldn't face seeing the worst. If money really is a problem, just ask around in this part of town. The *Mosāferkhūné-yé Ghasr-é Telā'ī* (☎ 23418) (marked imaginatively in English 'Golden Palace Inn') is on the south side of Kheyābūn-é Leyān. Looking inside remarkably like a prison, it has dormitory rooms only, none remotely palatial. The *Mosāferkhūné-yé Tōhīd* (☎ 23193) (not marked in English), a minute's walk south-west on the same side of the same street, is a much better option and has some smaller rooms at around 1500 rials.

The adequate *Hotel-é Sa'di* (☎ 22607), on the east side of Kheyābūn-é Hāfez, charges 2400/3100 rials a single with shared/private bathroom.

The old *Mehmūnkhūné-yé Khalīj-é Fārs* (not clearly marked in English but also known in English as the 'Persian Gulf Hotel') is in its own garden at the far west of Kheyābūn-é Valī-yé Asr. This was once at least a middle-range hotel and still has the best setting of any hotel in Būshehr, but it's now rather run down and the staff are surprised by anyone turning up. It has no singles and charges 3000 rials for a double with private bathroom.

Places to Stay – middle

Your choice of hotel in this category depends largely on whether you want a place overlooking the Persian Gulf but a slight distance from the centre, or one in the heart of town but lacking the sea view. Opinion is divided over which of the two is the best hotel in town.

The one in central Būshehr is the *Hotel-é Rezā* (☎ 27171) (marked in English 'Reza Hotel'), on the west side of Kheyābūn-é Emām Khomeinī a minute's walk south of Meidūn-é Ghods. The hotel, which has no singles, charges 4800 rials a double with bathroom, fridge, air-con and telephone.

There is hot water only from 6 to 8 am and 7 to 10 pm. The manager is helpful, speaks good English and is used to foreigners. In the lobby there's a large colour TV and free self-service tea. If you are in Shīrāz you can book a room here through the reservations office in the Homa Hotel (although not from any other Homa Hotel).

The alternative accommodation with the more dramatic view is the quietly efficient *Mehmūnsarā-yé Jahāngardī* (☎ 22346), also known as the Mehmūnsarā-yé Būshehr, by the park south of Kheyābūn-é Khalīj-é Fārs. This state-owned hotel is about the same standard and price as the *Hotel-é Rezā* but highly rated, largely because it overlooks the Gulf.

The *Hotel-é Tangsīr* in Kheyābūn-é Emām Khomeinī was closed some years ago and shows no signs of an imminent relaunch, and the *Hotel-é Delvār* (☎ 26108), intended to be the top hotel in town when completed, is still under construction north-west of Meidūn-é Komīté-yé Enghelāb-é Eslāmī.

Places to Eat

Food is very good in Būshehr, especially seafood. The small *Restōrān-é Āzādī* (not marked in English), in Kheyābūn-é Shohadā at the intersection of Kheyābūn-é Shohadā with Kheyābūn-é Mo'allem, prides itself on the quality of the ingredients; it's probably the best place in the province. I recommend chelō meigū-yé sūkhārī (fried prawns in a spicy tomato sauce, served with boiled rice) at 1800 rials, but the place is also good for kebabs, chicken and fish. To get here from Meidūn-é Ghods for 50 rials, take a shared taxi north going to the *bīmārestān* (hospital) and ask to be dropped off or pointed towards the restaurant.

The *Restōrān-é Nakhlestān* (marked in English 'Nakhlestan Restorant'), on the south side of Kheyābūn-é Shahīd Motahharī, 200 metres east of Meidūn-é Emām Khomeinī, is fairly big and offers uniformed waiters and good jūjé kabāb for 1700 rials. There are other restaurants along Kheyābūn-é Novvāb-é Safavī north of its intersection with Kheyābūn-é Valī-yé Asr.

Getting There & Away

Air At the time of writing Iran Air flies from Būshehr to:

Esfahān – Wednesday, 9.25 pm, 1¾ hours
Mashhad – Wednesday and Saturday, 6.50 pm, two hours
Shīrāz – Wednesday, 9.25 pm, 35 minutes
Tehrān – daily, 6.10 am, 1½ hours; Wednesday, 9.25 pm, three hours (all 8330 rials).

The staff at the Iran Air office (☎ 22041) on the north side of Kheyābūn-é Valī-yé Asr are helpful beyond the call of duty: one of them even arranged and collected a bus ticket for me when all the flights were full.

Bus Buses leave from outside the bus company offices in Kheyābūn-é Shohadā and Kheyābūn-é Novvāb-é Safavī between Kheyābūn-é Shohadā and Kheyābūn-é Valī-yé Asr. Cooperative Bus Company No 1 (☎ 24525) is in Kheyābūn-é Shohadā, just south-west of Chahārrāh-é Shohadā. Among other destinations there are buses from Būshehr to:

Ābādān – several times a week, 691 km, 11 hours
Ahvāz – at least one a day, 626 km, 10 hours, 1050 rials 'lux' (Cooperative Bus Company No 9)
Bandar-é Abbās – several times a day, 921 km, 16 hours, 1650 rials
Bandar-é Lengé – one a day, 656 km, nine hours, 1250 rials
Bandar-é Māhshahr – several a day, 359 km, six hours
Kāzerūn – several a day, 169 km, 2½ hours
Shīrāz – several a day, 320 km, five hours, 550 rials 'lux'.
Sīrjān – 683 km, 11 hours (Cooperative Bus Company No 2)

Buses (50 rials) and shared taxis (100 to 200 rials) go to Bahmanī (seven km, 20 minutes) from the bus stop on the west side of Kheyābūn-é Mo'allem about 250 metres north of Meidūn-é Ghods.

Sea Valfajre-8 sails in both directions between Būshehr and Doha in Qatar (nine weekly), Jazīré-yé Kīsh (two weekly) and Manama in Bahrain (two weekly).

Check the latest sailing times, which can change very frequently, with Valfajre-8

(☎ 2314) at the Valfajre-8 Passenger Terminal, Kheyābūn-é Solhābād. See also the Getting Around and Getting There & Away chapters. There may also be occasional NIOC supply vessels between Būshehr and Jazīré-yé Khārk: enquire at NIOC in Ahvāz at least a week ahead.

Getting Around

To/From the Airport
A taxi from Būshehr airport into town costs 800 to 1000 rials for a single passenger. There's no airport bus service. To get to the airport it's safest to order a telephone taxi, but you could try taking a shared taxi from Meidūn-é Komīté-yé Enghelāb-é Eslāmī for around 200 rials.

Bus & Minibus
Nobody bothers with buses much here, not even the city transport authorities.

Taxi
Getting around the new part of town is simple enough by shared taxi, using the main squares and crossroads as junctions, but not so easy in the old city, which is in any case best explored on foot.

AROUND BŪSHEHR

Bahmanī
بهمنى

Bahmanī is seven km south of Būshehr. The **British Cemetery** (Ghabrestān-é Engelīsīhā) in the centre of the town was one of the most sickening sights I encountered in Iran. Standing in what appears to be a temporarily abandoned building site, and itself reduced to little more than rubble, this graveyard has been systematically vandalised since the Islamic Revolution to such a degree that almost none of the flagstones is now intact, and many of the tomb chambers have been emptied. Had it not been for the directions given by an apologetic local, I would probably never have recognised this heap of gravel, looking like a public lavatory destroyed in an earthquake, for what it was. The only undamaged tomb was that of a Sri Lankan sailor buried in 1981, with the inscription apparently etched by finger in wet cement.

A local tried to tell me a fanciful story

about a crazed Westerner single-handedly doing the damage. The site is by no means secluded, and it's hard to imagine that its desecration can have been carried out without the knowledge of the authorities.

Getting There & Away Buses (50 rials) and shared taxis (100 to 200 rials) go to Bahmanī (20 minutes) from the bus stop on the west side of Kheyābūn-é Mo'allem in Būshehr.

Rīshahr
ريشهر

Despite its historical importance, very little remains of the ancient city of Rīshahr, and in any case the site now stands within sight of no fewer than three top-security coastal installations and is not very easy to explore. However, on the 12 km of road between Būshehr and Rīshahr, especially south of Bahmanī, there are quite a few carved tombstones from the early Islamic era and some perhaps even earlier, and excavations along the same road have revealed a more or less continuous line of buried earthenware vases believed to contain the remains of Zoroastrians after the vultures had done their work.

Getting There & Away Rīshahr can be reached on foot or by taxi from Bahmanī.

JAZĪRÉ-YÉ KHĀRK
جزيره خارك

Thirty-one nautical miles north-west of Būshehr, this small coral island, also known in English as Kharg, is the only island of any size in this part of the Persian Gulf. Although Khārk is best known today as one of the world's most important crude oil pumping stations, and for the devastation wreaked on it during the Iran-Iraq War, the island does have a history of some importance and there are quite a few historic remains.

From the earliest days the island has held an important place on the main trading routes between the Far East and Europe by way of Mesopotamia. It's believed to have been under Elamite control from the 3rd millennium BC, and it was later settled by a succession of communities. It's likely that a temple of Neptune mentioned in the 1st century AD by Pliny referred to the one on Khārk. At some time it was settled by Palmyrenes, who established a flourishing trading community here, and from about the 3rd century until the Arab Conquest the island was an early base of Christianity under a Nestorian colony.

After the introduction of Islam the island was known for its large pearling industry, but with the increase in colonial activity in the Persian Gulf from the 16th century, Khārk was picked out by several powers as a strategic naval and trading station. It was controlled by the Dutch for some years until 1766, when it was recaptured by Persian forces but seized in turn by the British in 1838. The oil terminal was extensively damaged by Iraqi bombardments during the Iran-Iraq War, but a new refinery is being built and output is already nearing pre-war levels.

Things to See
In the centre of Khārk are the remains of the staircase of a temple of Poseidon, probably the one referred to by Pliny. Over this a fire-temple was constructed in the Sassanian era, and later, in the Arab period, a mosque. Around these remains are some largely damaged Christian tomb-chambers. To the north there's a charming tomb tower of unknown date, typical of the northern Persian Gulf region with its white sugar-loaf dome of 15 layers. On the west coast of Khārk are the ruins of a Nestorian church and monastery, probably from around the 5th century AD. Other pre-Islamic remains found on the island include traces of an early irrigation system and a number of ancient graves.

Getting There & Away
Although technically part of Būshehr Province, Khārk is for most purposes under the control of NIOC, and visitors need to have permission from the oil company. On no account travel there independently. You can apply at least 10 days in advance at NIOC in Ahvāz (☎ (061) 7711, 7545; fax 672787) or Tehrān (☎ (021) 6153789; fax 672787). If permission is granted they can arrange air

transport to and from Khārk. NIOC has flights at least weekly to and from Shīrāz, Esfahān and Ahvāz, and at least twice weekly to and from Tehrān. There may also be occasional supply vessels to and from Būshehr. It helps to have a friend or sponsor working at NIOC, but work on a new refinery on the island has meant that permission has not been granted very easily to casual visitors, although Khārk is no stranger to expatriates. The tourist office in Ahvāz or Būshehr may be able to help. There's an NIOC guesthouse on Khārk. English is widely understood on the island.

Khūzestān Province

استان خوزستان

Population: 2.7 million
Area: 67,300 sq km
The province of Khūzestān in the far south-west of Iran is probably best-known for its oil, but this vast plain is also an important agricultural area with many date and sugar plantations. Although the indigenous population is largely Arab in origin and language, the Arab culture only predominates in the smaller places outside the provincial capital of Ahvāz. The main attractions of Khūzestān are the remains of the ancient capital of Shūsh (Susa) and the breathtaking Elamite ziggurat of Choghā Zambīl. The province is still recovering from the devastating effects of the Iran-Iraq War and the Kuwait War.

AHVĀZ
اهواز
This sprawling industrial city spanning both banks of the Rūdkhūné-yé Kārūn owes its prosperity to the discovery of oil at nearby Masjed-é Soleimān in 1908. Ahvāz is not in any way beautiful but it is the best place from which to explore the many historical sites of Khūzestān, and it does have plenty of what might be called sociological interest. All over Ahvāz there is evidence of the oil trade, but it isn't an obviously affluent place – for the city which should be the Dallas of Iran,

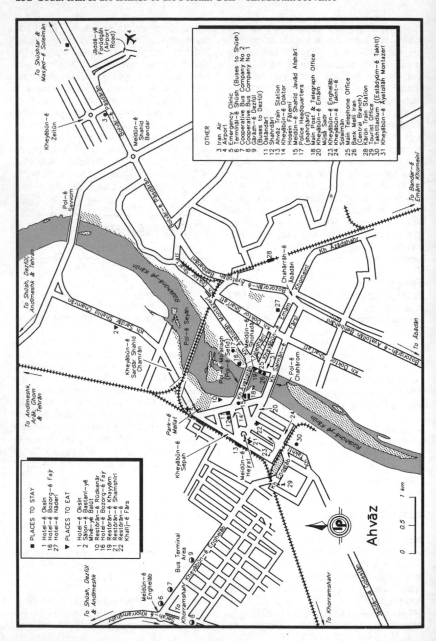

OTHER
3 Iran Air
4 Airport
5 Emergency Clinic
6 Terminal-é Shush (Buses to Shush)
7 Cooperative Bus Company No 2
8 Garazh-é Dezfūl
9 Cooperative Bus Company No 1
(Buses to Dezfūl)
11 Shahrdāri
13 Ahvāz Train Station
14 Kheyābūn-é Doktor
15 Hosein Fātemi
16 Meidūn-é Shahid Javad Afshari
17 Police Headquarters
(Shahrbāni)
18 Main Post & Telegraph Office
20 Kheyābūn-é Emām
23 Mūsā Sadr
24 Kheyābūn-é Enghelāb
25 Kheyābūn-é Takht-é
Soleimān
25 Main Telephone Office
26 Bank Melli Iran
(Central Branch)
28 Kārūn Train Station
29 Tourist Office
30 Takhtistadium (Estādyom-é Takhit)
31 Kheyābūn-é Āyatollāh Montazeri

PLACES TO STAY
■ 1 Hotel-é Oksin
16 Hotel-é Bozorg-é Fajr
27 Hotel-é Nāderi

PLACES TO EAT
▼ 1 Hotel-é Oksin
2 Sālon-é Bastani-yé
Shabnam
10 Restorān-é Rādksenār
16 Hotel-é Bozorg-é Fajr
19 Restorān-é Khayyām
21 Restorān-é Shamshiri
22 Restorān-é
Khalij-é Fārs

Ahvāz

0   0.5   1 km

you don't see many Rolls Royces on the streets.

Although the origins of the city date back to Parthian times, there's no longer anything of historical interest in the town, and it was devastated by unremitting Iraqi bombardments throughout much of the Iran-Iraq War. The only aspect of Ahvāz that anyone has thought worth making into a postcard is the modern suspension bridge, and that only by night. To be fair, a great deal of work has been done on rebuilding the city after the Iran-Iraq War. The priorities do, however, seem to have been the oil industry and mullahs, for whom a vast number of new mosques have been erected, which many locals feel are completely surplus to requirements.

Ahvāz is very pleasant in winter, but not at all so in summer.

Soon after the first of the Iraqi bombardments, the town of Ahvāz became almost a ghost town as most of the inhabitants sought refuge in towns to the west, property prices in Ahvāz plummeted and vast numbers of people from the rural areas of Khūzestān who had always dreamed of moving to the big city, took advantage of this opportunity to do so. Now that the war is over and the oil refineries are back in service, many of the original inhabitants have moved back, and the city which before the war had a population of about half a million now bursts with perhaps three million. Locals complain in private that the authorities are spending vast sums of money on building second or third mosques in every suburb when there is only one university and the city urgently needs new hospitals and schools.

Orientation
Ahvāz is sprawling and featureless, with nothing to orientate you but the Rūdkhūné-yé Kārūn, which flows north-east to south-west through the middle of Ahvāz, and the modern bridges spanning it. The main square is Meidūn-é Shohadā just to the east of the suspension bridge – Pol-é Mo'allagh or Pol-é Sefíd – and the main shopping district is south-east of this square. The airport is on the north-east edge of Ahvāz, south of Bolvār-é Pāsdārān, and the bus terminal area is at the far west of town on Kheyābūn-é Enghelāb.

The most notable landmarks aren't in Ahvāz at all, but a short distance north of the city. To the right of the road to Shūsh are several blazing towers which light up the night sky, burning off waste gases from oil refining. It's difficult to miss these giant beacons after dark.

Information
The ostāndārī (☎ 31072) and the shahrdārī (☎ 30037) are next to each other on the north side of Kheyābūn-é Doktor Hosein Fātemī at the north-west of Meidūn-é Javād Afshārī. For visa extensions go to the police headquarters opposite the west corner of the Bāgh-é Mellī. NIOC is in the Kārūn Industrial Area: for visits to Khārk you should apply to the head of the Materials, Order & Inventory Control Department (☎ 7711, 7545; fax 672787; telex 616007).

Tourist Office The tourist office (☎ 32725) (not marked in English) is west of the river, on Kheyābūn-é Enghelāb: ask for Ershād-é Eslāmī. The enthusiastic and helpful officer here speaks good English and is a fount of reliable information. Enquire here before venturing to Ābādān, Khorramshahr or Choghā Zambīl.

Money Bank Melli Iran (central branch) is on the west side of Kheyābūn-é Āyatollāh Montazerī 200 metres south of Meidūn-é Shohadā. There are also several licensed exchange offices on the other side of the road from the Bank Melli Iran; the one at the corner of Kheyābūn-é Emām Khomeinī marked in English 'Jalal Money Exchanger' has good rates.

Post & Telecommunications The main post office is on Meidūn-é Javād Afshārī and the main telephone office is on the west side of Kheyābūn-é Āyatollāh Montazerī, at the intersection with Kheyābūn-é Emām Khomeinī. The dialling code for Ahvāz is 061.

Maps The tourist office had only an out-of-date map of Ahvāz and Khūzestān entirely in Persian, but a version in English script should be out by the time you read this. One of the best-stocked map shops I saw in Iran is on the north side of Meidūn-é Shohadā.

Medical Services The emergency clinic (☎ 118) is opposite the Pārk-é Mellat on the west bank of the river.

Emergency The police headquarters (☎ 22231) (shahrbānī) is opposite the west corner of the Bāgh-é Mellī, 150 metres north of Meidūn-é Shohadā.

Things to See & Do
Although there's very little actually to do here, this is one of the few cities in Iran which doesn't practically shut down for the night after dark, and the streets are busy far later than in other towns. The weather must have something to do with it. It's possible to take a short pleasure cruise along the river in a small motor-boat for about 200 rials, but beware that the boats tend to be overladen, and seven passengers recently drowned in one. If you want to take the risk, boats leave from a tiny jetty near the Restōrān-é Rūdkenār. It's quite pleasant to walk along the riverbanks at night when the bridges are illuminated.

Places to Stay
The best hotel in town in terms of facilities is the conveniently located *Hotel-é Bozorg-é Fajr* (marked in English 'Fajr Grand Hotel'), on the east bank of the river 200 metres north of the Pol-é Mo'allagh. It has a restaurant, outdoor swimming-pool, coffee room and shop, but the service is a little grudging. Single/doubles with private bathroom are 5000/7500 rials.

On Bolvār-é Pāsdārān the smaller and more friendly *Hotel-é Oksīn* (☎ 42133) (marked in English 'Hotel Oxin') is used to foreigners and is highly recommended. The one drawback is that, although very convenient for the airport, it is a long way from the centre of town. It charges 3400/5100 rials with private bathroom.

One cheaper place that has been recommended is the *Hotel-é Nāderī* on the north

side of Kheyābūn-é Emām Khomeinī, at 2000/3000 rials with private bathroom. There are several mosāferkhūnés along the same street.

Places to Eat
The river-fish here is among the best in Iran. There are the usual sandwich bars and several good chelō kabābīs around Meidūn-é Shohadā. There are a few unspectacular restaurants around the bus terminal area and near Ahvāz train station, such as the large and not particularly good *Restōrān-é Shamshīrī* (curiously marked in English 'Shamshiri Mess Hall'), opposite the Ahvāz train station, with an unsatisfactory combination of barg and kūbīdé for 1350 rials. The *Restōrān-é Khalīj-é Fārs* just around the corner in Kheyābūn-é Enghelāb is slightly better.

The *Restōrān-é Rūdkenār* ('Riverside Restaurant') on the west bank of the river, a pleasant 300-metre walk north of the suspension bridge, is popular on Fridays and holidays, being the nearest thing to a touristy eating place in town; it's quite good for fish, but perhaps a little overrated because of its setting.

The *Restōrān-é Khayyām* at the east end of Pol-é Mo'allagh has delicious fried whitefish (māhī-yé sefīd) with boiled rice for 1500 rials, although the yoghurt has a curiously burnt flavour.

The restaurant at the *Hotel-é Oksīn* is less expensive and elegant than the one at the *Hotel-é Fajr-é Bozorg*, but also less complacent about standards of food and service. Fīllé kabāb is 1700 rials. Both hotels have coffee lounges.

The *Sālon-é Bastanī-yé Mīvé-yé Balūt* saloon (not marked in English) is very good for fruit ice cream and samosas, and a popular hangout for young trendies of both sexes, but it's a long trek out of the centre.

Getting There & Away
To/From Ābādān & Khorramshahr To get to Ābādān (148 km) or Khorramshahr (130 km), take a minibus or taxi (two to 2½ hours, 200 rials) from Chahārrāh-é Ābādān, the

intersection of Kheyābūn-é Emām Khomeinī with Bozorgrāh-é Āyatollāh Behbahānī, in the south-east of Ahvāz.

To/From Dezfūl, Shūsh, Haft Tappé & Choghā Zambīl Buses for Dezfūl (151 km, two hours) leave from the Gārāzh-é Dezfūl on the north side of Kheyābūn-é Enghelāb. The Termīnāl-é Shūsh for buses and minibuses to Shūsh (116 km, 250 rials) and Serāh-é Haft Tappé (10 km from Haft Tappé) is about 400 metres west of the Gārāzh-é Dezfūl. The bus is comfortable and the trip to Shūsh takes about 1½ hours. Buses leave about hourly from early morning until 5 pm.

If you want to visit the three main sites on the same day, you'll have to leave Ahvāz at about 7 am; and since you'll need written permission to visit Choghā Zambīl from the archaeological office in Shūsh, there's no point in going on a Friday or a public holiday, and even Thursday is a little risky.

It's difficult to get to the Termīnāl-é Shūsh or any of the bus company offices from the centre of town by shared taxi in under an hour, and there's no convenient bus service. A telephone taxi will take 20 to 30 minutes and set you back 1500 rials. Alternatively you can take a shared taxi (100 rials) from Falaké-yé Sā'at near the Ahvāz train station, or a minibus from Kheyābūn-é Salmān-é Fārsī to Serāh-é Khorramshahr.

Air Iran Air flies to Tehrān daily at 8 am, 8.50 and 10.15 pm (1¼ hours, 7280 rials). NIOC has flights at least weekly to Jazīré-yé Khārk: see the Jazīré-yé Khārk entry for details. The Iran Air office (☎ 42094) is on the north side of Bolvār-é Pāsdārān, just west of the airport road. If you're going there from the centre, you'll save a lot of time if you take a telephone taxi.

Bus & Minibus The bus company offices with their own terminals are mostly spread out along Kheyābūn-é Enghelāb in the unlovely north-west outskirts of town. Cooperative Bus Companies Nos 1 and 2 are the ones to try first: No 1 (☎ 31253) is just south of Serāh-é Khorramshahr on the east

side of the road, and No 2 (☎ 34678) is on the north side of Kheyābūn-é Enghelāb. The bus company offices are open from about 7 am to 6 pm, sometimes with one or more breaks; there's little point in visiting after about 4 pm.

Since most buses running from Ahvāz originate elsewhere, timetables aren't generally fixed until the day of departure, and you can't buy tickets more than a few hours ahead. It's best to arrive at Kheyābūn-é Enghelāb early in the morning, and ask around at the bus offices until you find one offering the right service. This search will be a nuisance if you have heavy bags with you since the offices are rather spread out, and if you must carry them with you, it's easiest to take a telephone taxi and get the driver to help you find a ticket, or else to get someone to make telephone enquiries first thing in the morning and reserve a seat for you: Cooperative Bus Company No 2 will accept phone reservations for a foreigner.

There are buses from Ahvāz to:

Bākhtarān – at least one a day, 509 km, nine hours, 915/1225 rials 'lux'/'super'
Bandar-é Abbās – several a week, 1169 km, 19 hours, 1620/2550 rials 'lux'/'super' (Cooperative Bus Company No 2)
Būshehr – at least one a day, 626 km, 10 hours, 1050 rials 'lux' (Cooperative Bus Company No 9)
Esfahān – at least one a day, 765 km, 14 hours, 1270 rials 'super' (Cooperative Bus Companies Nos 1 and 2)
Gorgān – several a week, 1262 km, 22 hours, 2250/2550 rials 'lux'/'super' (Cooperative Bus Company No 2)
Kermān – several a week, 1265 km, 20 hours, 2090/2250 rials 'lux'/'super' (Cooperative Bus Company No 2)
Mashhad – several a week. 1805 km, 30 hours, 2500/3000 rials 'lux'/'super'; (Cooperative Bus Company No 2)
Rasht – several a day, 1049 km, 17 hours
Sanandaj – several a week, 645 km, 10 hours, 1250/1550 rials 'lux'/'super' (Cooperative Bus Company No 2)
Sārī – several a week, 1131 km, 18 hours, 1210/1900 rials 'lux'/'super' (Cooperative Bus Company No 2)
Shīrāz – several a week, 568 km, 10 hours, 1100/1300 rials 'lux'/'super' (Cooperative Bus Company No 2)

Tabrīz – at least one a day, 1087 km, 18 hours
Tehrān – several a day, 881 km, 14 hours, 1250/1450
rials 'lux'/'super' (Cooperative Bus Company
No 2)
Yazd – at least one a day, 1008 km, 20 hours,
1550/2045 rials 'lux'/'super' (Cooperative Bus
Company Nos 2 and 4).

Train There are two train stations in town, the Ahvāz station (Īstgāh-é Rāh-é Āhan-é Ahvāz) west of the river and the Kārūn station to the east, but the second is used only for commercial traffic to Bandar-é Emām Khomeinī. Although the line from the Ahvāz station runs in two directions, there are no services south to Khorramshahr; the train will only take you north to Tehrān via Andīmeshk, Arāk and Ghom. Demand for seats to Tehrān far outstrips supply, and I saw queues outside the station which would have been better suited to Moscow. Perhaps the situation will improve now that the airport has reopened. There are three express trains (15½ hours) and one regular train (18½ hours) daily to Tehrān.

Shared Taxi & Savārī Along the east end of Kheyābūn-é Enghelāb and at Serāh-é Khorramshahr, or more conveniently from Kheyābūn-é Āyatollāh Tāleghānī where it meets Meidūn-é Shohadā, you'll find taxis and savārīs to Shūsh and other places.

River/Sea Although the Kārūn is the only navigable river in Iran, there are no regular passenger boat services to or from Ahvāz. It may one day again be possible to sail to Ābādān or even Basra. Valfajre-8 (☎ 34081) is at Serāh-é Khorramshahr.

Getting Around
To/From the Airport There's no airport bus service, but you can take a taxi to or from the centre for around 1200 rials as a single passenger.

Taxi From Meidūn-é Shohadā you can take a shared taxi easily in any direction, but the distances to be covered are very great, and if you're only staying a short time you may well save your sanity by paying extra to go by telephone taxi. All the hotels can book one and there are agencies all over town. Charges are about 1500 rials an hour.

SHŪSH (SUSA) شوش
Although Shūsh (Susa in English; biblical Shushan) was one of the great ancient cities of Iran and is one of the earliest to have been explored by archaeologists, there's no longer very much to see compared with the much better preserved site of Persepolis.

While probably best known as an Achaemenian capital, Shūsh was in fact a prehistoric settlement from at least the 4th millennium BC, and an important Elamite city from about the middle of the 3rd millennium. It reached its first peak under the reign of Untash Gal, who built Shūsh up as his administrative capital and founded Choghā Zambīl as his religious centre. Shūsh was burnt around 640 BC by the Assyrian King Ashurbanipal, at about the same time he destroyed Choghā Zambīl, but it came back to prominence in 521 BC when Darius I set it up as his winter capital, with Ecbatana (modern Hamadān) as the summer capital. Persepolis became the spiritual centre, just as Choghā Zambīl had been under the Elamites. Darius fortified Shūsh and built palaces and other buildings, so that at one time Shūsh must have been similar in grandeur to Persepolis.

In 331 BC Shūsh fell to Alexander the Great, and its days of greatness were over, although it was occupied by the Seleucids and later by the Parthians. It became in turn the Sassanian capital, and in Shāpūr I's reign in the 4th century AD an important centre of Christianity, later extirpated by Shāpūr II. Although the Arabs later settled and built a mosque here, Shūsh faded away after about 1200 and didn't come back to attention until 1852 when W K Loftus, a British archaeologist, was the first to survey the site; his work was continued by the French Archaeological Service from 1884 more or less continuously until the revolution.

Many fine examples of pottery from various periods showing the development of the typically Persian highly stylised animal

Top: Masjed-é Shāh-é Cherāgh, Shīrāz (DStV)
Bottom: Bandarī architecture, old city, Būshehr (DStV)

Top: Masjed-é Jāme', Hamadān (DStV)
Bottom: Ruins of Ecbatana (Hekmatāné, Hamadan) (DStV)

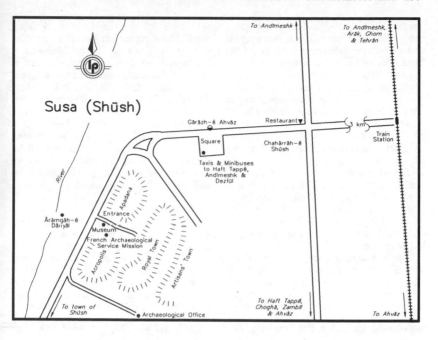

motif, as well as bronzes, have been found here, and some examples are on display at Tehrān's Mūzé-yé Īrān-é Bāstān, while a famous 4th century BC bulls'-head capital from Shūsh is now in the Louvre.

Things to See

The site is built on four small mounds. If you enter at the gate from the street, the only official entrance, you cannot fail to notice the **fortress** on top of the tallest mound, the **Acropolis**. This castle, quite unlike any other archaeological camp, was built by the French Archaeological Service at the end of the 19th century as a necessary defence against the unpacified Arab tribes of the region, and is now probably the most imposing structure at Shūsh. The 'château', as it was known, was occupied by the archaeological team until the revolution and, although I was probably the first foreigner to see inside it in over a decade, it's still the property of the French, and its solitary care-

taker is still paid through their embassy in Tehrān. Quite recently the owners blocked a potentially disastrous plan to build a bypass road on the very edge of the site that threatened structural damage to the remains. Almost nothing remains of the buildings of the Acropolis on which the castle stands, which was the site of the earliest prehistoric settlement and later of the main Elamite royal buildings and then of the Achaemenian citadel.

Next to the Acropolis is the largest mound, the **Royal Town**, once the quarter of the court officials, which has revealed the remains of many periods from the Elamite to the Arab. North-west of the Royal Town is the **Apadana**, where Darius I built his residence and two other palaces. Two very well preserved foundation tablets found beneath the site of Darius' Palace, one in Elamite and the other in Babylonian, record the noble ancestry of its founder and the far-flung origins of its materials and workers – from

as far east as India and as far west as
Abyssinia – as a piece of propaganda to show
the might of the Achaemenian Empire at the
time. The tablets are now in the Mūzé-yé
Īrān-é Bāstān. The remains of 72 columns
and bulls-head capitals here show that the
palace was built on the same lines as that at
Persepolis, constructed soon afterwards.

The **Artisans' Town** mound dates from
the Parthian and Seleucid eras. Traces of an
Arab mosque were found here, but little else
of substance remains.

The **museum** between the entrance and
the Acropolis was closed for renovation at
the time of writing. The fanatical, xenopho-
bic caretaker takes exception to foreigners
visiting the remains after lunchtime, even
though Iranians are free to wander around at
all times of day.

The **Ārāmgāh-é Dānyāl** ('tomb of the
Prophet Daniel') is a short walk west of the
entrance to the archaeological site. This
building, with its characteristic white sugar-
loaf tower, does attract pilgrims, almost all
Muslim, but it isn't otherwise of any great
interest and has been rebuilt several times.

The small town of Shūsh is to the west of
the archaeological site. It's appropriate that
Shūsh has given its name to one of the grottiest main streets in Tehrān, for this is a
miserable and cheerless place, rightly
regarded as having some of the least friendly
inhabitants of anywhere in Iran. There's no
acceptable hotel or any other reason to hang
around here. The archaeological office
(daftar-é mīrās-é farhangī), where you go to
apply for a permit to visit Choghā Zambīl, is
at the far end of the narrow first turning to
the left as you walk south-west from the
entrance to the archaeological remains. It's
open from 7 am to about 2.30 pm (7 am to
noon on Thursday), daily except Friday.
Take your passport.

Getting There & Away
Shūsh is 116 km north-north-west of Ahvāz
via a very busy and, especially at night,
dangerous road. Although it's on the Tehrān
to Ahvāz railway line, it's not practical to get
there by train. Buses and minibuses to Ahvāz

(1½ hours, 250 rials) run about hourly from
the Gārāzh-é Ahvāz until about 4 pm; after
that you'll have to go to the Chahārrāh-é
Shūsh, about two km to the west of the centre
of Shūsh (50 rials by taxi) and either take a
shared taxi or savārī (1000 rials by day or
1300 rials by night), or wait up to an hour for
a bus or minibus (200 or 250 rials) passing
through on the way to Ahvāz. There are also
minibuses to Haft Tappé (70 rials) and other
local destinations from opposite the Gārāzh-
é Ahvāz, but Choghā Zambīl can only be
reached by private taxi. See also the Ahvāz
and Choghā Zambīl entries.

CHOGHĀ ZAMBĪL   چتا زنبیل
The remarkably well preserved ziggurat of
Choghā Zambīl is the best surviving example of Elamite architecture anywhere and
one of the most memorable sights in Iran.
Originally it had five concentric storeys but
only three remain to a total height of some
25 metres. It's hard to believe that such an
imposing landmark could have been lost to
the world for over 2500 years, as it was until
accidentally discovered in 1935 during an
Anglo-Iranian Oil Company aerial survey.

In ancient times the inhabitants of Iran
attached great religious importance to the
mountains, and where, as in the plains of
Khūzestān, they had no mountains, they
made their own imitations, so creating this
distinctive pyramidal style of building. This
ziggurat was the raison d'être of the town of
Dur Untash founded by King Untash Gal in
the middle of the 13th century BC as the
chief pilgrimage site of his Elamite realm,
while Shūsh remained the royal seat and
political centre. It reached its peak towards
the start of the 12th century BC, when it had
a large number of temples and priests, but it
was later sacked by the Assyrian King
Ashurbanipal around 640 AD at about the
same time as he destroyed Shūsh.

The ziggurat, which is now the most
imposing structure of Dur Untash, was dedicated to Inshushinak, the chief god of the
Elamites and patron of Shūsh; there was
originally a quadrangular temple to him on
the summit of the ziggurat, accessible only

to the élite of Elamite society. Unlike the more familiar Mesopotamian ziggurats, few if any of which are as well preserved as Choghā Zambīl, this one was built on a square plan, with its sides measuring 105 metres, and its storeys were erected vertically from the foundation level as a series of concentric towers, rather than one on top of another like a wedding cake. The height is believed to have been over 50 metres. You can still climb the surviving three storeys of the ziggurat by a steep staircase on the north-west side which, like the other three staircases, was originally partially vaulted, with lofty brick doorways flanked with animal figures. The ziggurat was built on a low base as a precaution against flooding, for once this was a fertile and forested area, although nowadays the setting is bleak, barren and windswept, and hot even in winter.

You can still clearly see the cuneiform inscriptions on many of the surviving bricks, bearing the name of Untash Gal, although the original blue and green mosaic tiles are no longer in place. There was originally a complex of chambers, tombs, tunnels and water channels in the lowest storey, as well as two temples to Inshushinak on the south-east side. The ziggurat was surrounded by a paved courtyard protected behind a wall, outside which were the living quarters of the town, as well as 11 temples dedicated to various Elamite gods and goddesses, of which only the largest, to the north-west, remains in fair condition.

The rest of the city is not well preserved, but there are still the remains of three simple but well-constructed royal palaces in the eastern corner of the town. One of these was the king's residence and another probably the harem, and a royal gate. It's still possible to walk down to a vaulted tomb chamber under the remains of the king's palace, but you'll need a powerful torch to see anything. There are also traces of an ingeniously designed water and drainage system. North-west of the ziggurat there's a brick platform which appears to have been an altar. Very little remains of the rest of the town, but

some of the artefacts found here and at the ziggurat are now on display in Tehrān's Mūzé-yé Īrān-é Bāstān.

Getting There & Away
Choghā Zambīl is 45 km south-east of Shūsh along a very bad road which deteriorates into a heavily rutted mud track beyond Haft Tappé. Since the very remote area around Choghā Zambīl is a restricted military zone (an obvious site during the Iran-Iraq War after UNESCO declared it a cultural site of international importance, hence off-limits to Iraqi bombers) visits can only be made with the written permission of the archaeological office in Shūsh, although nowadays this is granted routinely in a few minutes. Therefore it makes sense to visit Shūsh first thing in the morning, collecting the permit there and hiring a taxi to take you to Choghā Zambīl and back (there's no other way of reaching it). The flat return fare is around 6000 rials, or around 7500 rials if you also want to stop off in Haft Tappé. Allow at least four hours for the trip.

There are several military checkpoints between Shūsh and Choghā Zambīl. Unfortunately you cannot take photographs at Choghā Zambīl; all cameras have to be surrendered at the last checkpoint but one, where you also pick up an armed escort who doubles as a guide (mine was courteous, informative and enthusiastic, although he spoke no English).

HAFT TAPPÉ   هفت تپه
To the left of the road as you leave Choghā Zambīl for Shūsh (about 24 km), look out for the remains of this 2nd-millennium BC Elamite town, which once had several ziggurats as well as various royal buildings, tombs and temples. Although there's less to see than at Choghā Zambīl or Shūsh, the site here is much more spread out than the other two.

ĀBĀDĀN   آبادان
The Iran-Iraq War made this front-line city, within a grenade's throw of Iraq, out of bounds to all foreigners not belonging to the

press corps. Nowadays it's still not entirely accessible, and the rare Western sightseer is likely to be treated with suspicion for some time to come.

A tiny village until 1910, Ābādān doesn't rank very highly in the history and culture stakes, but it would deserve a chapter of its own in any book about the international oil industry. For one thing, prerevolutionary Ābādān was one of the most important places in Iran for foreign influences, as thousands upon thousands of Westerners came to exploit its new-found oil wealth. For another, Ābādān really did look the most un-Iranian of cities, built up as if overnight in a highly ordered fashion, with clearly defined quarters for each rank of refinery worker (with foreigners of course bagging the best residences). When the war started, the remaining foreigners packed up and left, and waves of locals also sought to escape from the incessant Iraqi bombardments. If you take a look at what remains of Ābādān you'll see that they had good reason to leave. The Iran-Iraq War largely destroyed Ābādān, and virtually razed the neighbouring city of Khorramshahr to the ground. Rebuilding work had hardly begun when the Kuwait War brought Ābādān back to the front line. Conflict over the border in Basra and in Kuwait, only 50 km to the south-west, threatened to spill over. Ask at the tourist office in Ahvāz for reliable advice about whether to visit yet.

Getting There & Away

The railway branch line between Ahvāz and Khorramshahr is no longer open, and Ābādān international airport is still closed. Ābādān can be reached from Ahvāz by minibus or taxi (see the Ahvāz entry), from Esfahān by bus (at least one a day, 903 km, 15 hours, 1950 rials 'super', Cooperative Bus Company No 1) and from Shīrāz by bus (at least one a day, 615 km, 10 hours).

West Iran

ایران غربی

This chapter covers the provinces of Lorestān, Īlām, Bākhtarān, Hamadān, Kordestān and Zanjān.

Because the region is dominated by the Zāgros Mountains, winter is very harsh in many parts, while summer is very mild and pleasant weather. The scenery is a dramatic combination of wild and rolling mountains, valleys and rivers.

There is evidence of settlement in west Iran as early as the 6th millennium BC, and many of the earliest empires and kingdoms in Persia had their capitals there. Standing at the frontier with Mesopotamia, much of the region has been vulnerable to incursions from the west throughout history. The towns guarding the mountain passes have seen many invaders and would-be occupiers. During the Iran-Iraq War the region was thrown into turmoil, its towns bombed and occupied by Iraqi forces. Refugees from Iraq fled into west Iran throughout that war and, to an even greater extent, after the Kuwait War and the widespread oppression of the Kurds in Iraq – their homecoming may be delayed for many years.

With the exception of Zanjān and Hamadān provinces, most of the population of west Iran is not Persian, so the national language is seldom heard. Kurds are predominant in Kordestān and Bākhtarān provinces, and Lors in Īlām and Lorestān provinces. Tribal dress is still very much in everyday use. There are also many Āzarīs throughout the north-west part of the region. The 1986 census found a nomadic population of around 37,000 (0.6% of the total population of the region), with the highest numbers in Lorestān (15,140) and Īlām Province (14,160), but a very improbable zero for Kordestān.

Most of the region is not well documented, although some more intrepid explorers have been attracted to it for its very remoteness. Anyone interested in travelling in the region is strongly recommended to

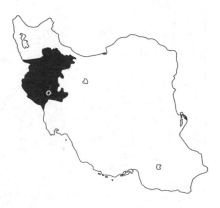

pick up a copy of Dame Freya Stark's *The Valleys of the Assassins* (John Murray, London, 1951; Century, London, 1983), which she had originally intended to entitle *A Treasure Hunt in Luristan*. Also recommended is *Journeys in Persia and Kurdistan* (written in 1889 but republished by Virago, London in 1989 in two volumes) by the redoubtable Victorian Isabella Bird.

There are few facilities outside the main towns. Only two towns are connected by air to the rest of Iran, and the railways will not get you far. The ancient royal highways connecting the central plateau with Mesopotamia are still very much in use, and you can see the remains of many ancient caravanserais along the road. As a result of the refugee crisis there is a small risk of typhoid and cholera in the western border regions, and some travellers have been turned back on the road to Sanandaj for not having the required vaccinations.

There are several important archaeological sites, especially in what is known as the Golden Triangle linking the ancient towns of Khorram Ābād, Hamadān and Bākhtarān. Unfortunately the most interesting parts, the mountain villages of the Kurds and Lors, are

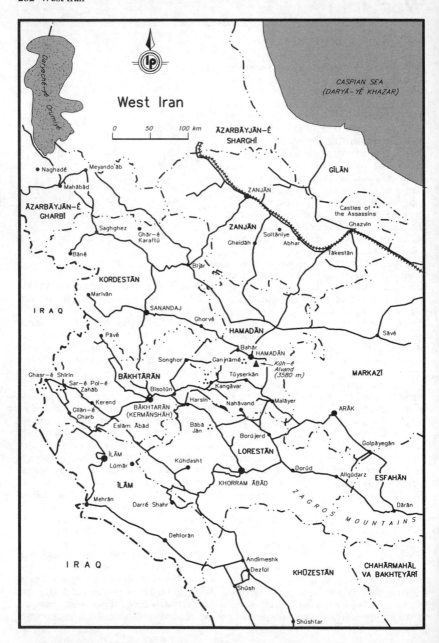

West Iran

CASPIAN SEA
(DARYÃ-YÉ KHAZAR)

Daryacheh-yé Orumiyé

0   50   100 km

ÃZARBÃYJÃN-É
SHARGHÍ

• Naghadé   Meyando'ab
Mahãbãd

GÍLÃN

ÃZARBÃYJÃN-É
GHARBÍ

ZANJÃN

Castles of
the Assassins

Ghazvin

Saghghez   Ghãr-é
Karaftú

ZANJÃN

Soltãníye

Bãné

Gheidãh   Abhar   Tãkestãn

KORDESTÃN

Bíjãr

Marivãn

IRAQ

SANANDAJ

Ghorvé

HAMADÃN

Sãvé

Pãvé

HAMADÃN
Bahãr

Songhor   Ganjnãmé   ▲ Kúh-é
Alvand
(3580 m)

MARKAZÍ

Ghasr-é Shírín   Tüyserkãn

BÃKHTARÃN

Bísotún   Kangãvar

Sar-é Pol-é
Zahãb   Harsin   Nahãvand   Malãyer   ARÃK

Kerend   BÃKHTARÃN
(KERMÃNSHÃH)

Gílãn-é
Gharb

Golpãyegãn

Eslãm Ãbãd   Bãbã
Jãn   Borújerd

LORESTÃN   ESFAHÃN

ÍLÃM   Kúhdasht   Dorúd   Alígúdarz

Lúmãr •

ÍLÃM   Dãrãn

KHORRAM ÃBÃD

Mehrãn   Z A G R O S

Darré Shahr   M O U N T A I N S

Dehlorãn

CHAHÃRMAHÃL
VA BAKHTEYÃRÍ

IRAQ

Andímeshk

Dezfúl   KHÚZESTÃN

Shúsh

Shúshtar

inaccessible to most visitors, even if the threat of brigandry is much exaggerated.

Lorestān Province
استان لرستان

Lorestān has a population of 1.4 million, a little over half of whom live in rural areas. The provincial centre is Khorram Ābād. The province is omitted from the official tourist handout, strongly suggesting that foreign tourists neither visit it nor are expected to do so, but the Lors themselves have attracted a small number of distinguished, intrepid travellers, foremost among them women such as Isabella Bird and Dame Freya Stark.

KHORRAM ĀBĀD
خرم آباد
Population: 209,000
Picturesque at a distance beyond any Persian town that I have seen... [Khorram Ābād] successfully rivals any Persian town in its squalor, dirt, evil odours, and ruinous condition. Two-thirds of what was 'the once famous capital of the Atabegs' are now 'ruinous heaps.' The bazars are small, badly supplied, dark, and rude; and the roads are nothing but foul alleys, possibly once paved, but now full of ridges, holes, ruins, rubbish, lean and mangy dogs, beggarly-looking men, and broken channels of water, which, dribbling over the soil in the bazars and everywhere else in green and black slime, gives forth pestiferous odours in the hot sun.

Isabella Bird
Journeys in Persia and Kurdistan, 1891

Orientation & Information
The tourist office in the main Ministry of Culture & Islamic Guidance building is on ☎ (0661) 6054. Khorram Ābād is rather milder in winter than most of the region, and often uncomfortably hot in summer.

Things to See
Khorram Ābād is chiefly of interest for the Black Fortress, or **Dez-é Seyāh**, after which the town was known until about the 14th century. This strong and still very impressive structure, standing on a rocky prominence which dominates the town, was the citadel of the Atābaks, the powerful rulers of

Lorestān, from the 12th century until about 1600, when the last Atābak king was defeated and killed by Shāh Abbās I. A tall Seljuq brick minaret, the **Manār-é Masjed-é Jāme'**, probably dating from the 12th century, now stands without its original mosque on the southern outskirts of town.

Khorram Ābād is famous for its handicrafts, including bronzes and painted glass and china items such as charming cordless hubble-bubbles and decorative smoking pipes.

Places to Stay – middle
The *Hotel-é Shahrdāri* (☎ 4044) is probably the best hotel in town.

Getting There & Away
Apart from any flights to Tehrān on the Iran Asseman timetable (supposedly five a week each way), there are buses or minibuses from Khorram Ābād to:

Ahvāz – at least one a day, 390 km, six hours
Bākhtarān – at least one a day, 197 km, three hours
Hamadān – several a day, 252 km, four hours
Īlām – at least one a day, 405 km, seven hours
Tehrān – at least one a day, 491 km, eight hours, 1310 rials 'lux'

BORŪJERD
بروجرد
The town of Borūjerd, on the main Hamadān road out of Khorram Ābād, is of interest for its substantially rebuilt **Masjed-é Jāme'** which has an original Seljuq dome and mehrāb room containing an inscription from the same period. The Ghajar **Masjed-é Soltānī** and the perhaps 12th-century **Emāmzādé-yé Ja'far** are also worth visiting.

BĀBĀ JĀN
بابا جان
Among the many pre-Islamic mounds uncovered in the province, the most interesting is that of Bābā Jān, 93 km north-west of Khorram Ābād by road in the direction of Harsīn. It is accessible from the village of Nūr Ābād by a rough track. Occupied from at least the 3rd millennium BC, this large mound shows the indistinct remains of a town partly burnt in the 7th century BC and

abandoned 200 years later. Its fortifications have excited archaeologists, although there is no longer that much to see.

Īlām Province استان ایلام

With a largely rural or nomadic population of 384,000, Īlām is the least populous province in Iran and also one of the most remote. There is almost nothing to be seen of the ancient Elamite empire that flourished in this region in ancient times, although some archaeological surveys were started before the revolution.

ĪLĀM ایلم
Īlām sits on a high plateau fringed to the north-east by mountains. Until just before WWII this town remained the seat of the Vālī Khāns, the Lor chieftains of the region. The remains of their palaces can still be seen near the northern edge of Īlām at a site called the **Ghal'é-yé Vālī**; but otherwise the town is of more drabness than interest. The proximity to the Iraqi border, only some 45 km to the west, has only added to its isolation in recent years.

Orientation & Information
The tourist office (☎ (0438) 2337) is in north Īlām at the intersection of Kheyābūn-é Resālat with Bolvār-é Modarres. The main post office and the telephone office are on central Meidūn-é 22 Bahman, and Bank Melli Iran is 100 metres east.

Places to Stay
The best hotel in town, the *Mehmūnsarā-yé Jahāngardī*, is on Bolvār-é Jonūbī at the southern approach to Īlām; more central places include the *Hotel-é Ferdōsī* and the *Hotel-é Dālāhō* on Kheyābūn-é Ferdōsī, the main east-west street. Visitors must register with the Komīté.

Getting There & Away
Cooperative Bus Company No 1 is on the south side of Kheyābūn-é Ferdōsī. Some destinations are:

Ahvāz – one a day, 505 km, nine hours
Bākhtarān – several a day, 208 km, 3½ hours, 500 rials
Khorram Ābād – at least one a day, 405 km, seven
    hours
Sanandaj – at least one a day, 344 km, six hours

There is no legal crossing into Iraq from this province.

Bākhtarān Province
استان باختران

Bākhtarān Province has some of the most interesting and famous archaeological sites in this part of Iran, dating from before recorded history through the Median, Achaemenian, Parthian and Sassanian dynasties to the Islamic era. The climate is pleasant for most of the year, the largely mountainous scenery is stunning, and the soil fertile. The province has an area of 23,700 sq km and a population of 1.47 million.

BĀKHTARĀN (KERMĀNSHĀH)
باختران (کرمانشاه)
Population: 561,000
An important station on the ancient trading route to Baghdad, Bākhtarān is by far the largest, most populous and busiest of the towns of west Iran, but it no longer has any buildings of much interest. First built on a site a few km from the present town, it probably dates from the 4th century AD. Its vulnerable position has always rendered it liable to incursions, and it was in turn captured by the Arabs in 649 AD, the Buyids in the 10th century, soon after by the Seljuqs, and then sacked by Mongols in the early 13th century. After several centuries of relative peace and prosperity, its strategic position on the road to Baghdad brought trouble in the form of very heavy Iraqi missile and bomb attacks during the Iran-Iraq War.

The town has, throughout its history, usually been known as Kermānshāh or

Kermānshāhān – the city of the 'king (or kings) of Kermān' – because its founder had formerly been governor of Kermān Province. After the revolution this name was dropped from official use because of the supposed hatred of the Iranian people for the word 'shāh'. However, Rafsanjānī recently conceded that since the ancient name had no connection with the ousted Pahlavī dynasty there was no reason why the name Kermānshāh should not be used alongside Bākhtarān.

Its main importance for visitors is as a base for exploring the famous carvings at Bīsotūn and Tāgh-é Bostān, but the predominantly Kurdish inhabitants are very friendly to visitors and they, together with the lively bazaar, make this a pleasant enough overnight stop. It is also the only town in western Iran on Iran Air's schedule.

At an altitude of 1322 metres, it has a beautiful setting, framed by permanently snow-clad mountains. Bākhtarān is best avoided in winter, but the climate is very pleasant for most of the rest of the year.

Orientation & Information

The new airport is about 10 km out from the new bus terminal at the east edge of town, both on the Tehrān road. The visa office is in the police headquarters on Kheyābūn-é Modarres between Serāh-é Safavī and Meidūn-é Āzādī, and initial extensions are normally granted straightforwardly in two days. The ostāndārī is on Kheyābūn-é Kāshānī. The tourist office (☎ 20095, 24572, 24573) is on Kheyābūn-é Beheshtī near Serāh-é 22 Bahman, a few metres from Iran Air. The main post office is on Meidūn-é Sepah, and the main telephone office is on Kheyābūn-é Madanī. The dialling code for Bākhtarān is 0431.

Places to Stay

In Kheyābūn-é Modarres, 20 metres north of Meidūn-é Āzādī (by the old bus terminal or Gārāzh), there are several mosāferkhūnés with dorm beds (300 to 800 rials) and single rooms (1400 to 1700 rials): none of them can be recommended.

On Meidūn-é Āzādī there are two hotels, the *Hotel-é Āzādī* at 2100/3300 rials a double/triple and the *Hotel-é Tōhīd* at 2100/2800 rials a double/triple.

The best hotel in Bākhtarān is the average *Hotel-é Ferdōsī* (☎ 24056) (also known as Hotel-é Resālat) on Meidūn-é Ferdōsī, 300 rials by taxi from the bus station: it charges 2400/3200 rials a single/double without a private bathroom, or 2850/4300 rials with one.

Places to Eat

There is a restaurant in the *Hotel-é Ferdōsī*, and there are some chelō kabābīs around the centre. Try some of the excellent rice cakes for which the town is known. There are several pleasant restaurants at Tāgh-é Bostān, a popular weekend and holiday destination with the locals, and cafés at Bīsotūn.

Getting There & Away

To/From Iraq See the Getting There & Away chapter.

Air Iran Air flies from Bākhtarān to Tehrān on Tuesday and Saturday at 7.15 am and daily at 1.30 pm (one hour, 5280 rials). Their office (☎ 53814) is on Kheyābūn-é Beheshtī, by Serāh-é 22 Bahman.

Bus & Minibus At the time of writing the bus companies were in Meidūn-é Āzādī (the Gārāzh), but a new station by Meidūn-é Emām Khomeinī on the Tehrān road, at the intersection of two rivers, was nearing completion: ask locally for the latest information. The locals call this place Lab-é Āb ('Water's Edge'). From the new station to Meidūn-é Ferdōsī is 300 rials by shared taxi. Buses or minibuses go to:

Ahvāz – at least one a day, 509 km, nine hours, 915/1225 rials 'lux'/'super'
Bandar-é Abbās – at least one a day, 1748 km, 28 hours, 3215/3855 rials 'lux'/'super'
Bandar-é Anzalī – several a week, 636 km, 12 hours
Esfahān – at least one a day, 665 km, nine hours, 1025/1275 rials 'lux'/'super'
Gorgān – at least one a day, 906 km, 18 hours, 2250 rials 'super'

Hamadān – several a day, 189 km, three hours, 500 rials

Īlām – several a day, 208 km, 3½ hours, 500 rials

Khorram Ābād – at least one a day, 197 km, three hours

Mashhad – at least one a day, 1449 km, 23 hours

Orūmīyé – at least one a day, 596 km, 11 hours, 1335/1505 rials 'lux'/'super'

Sanandaj – several a day, 136 km, two hours

Sārī – at least one a day, 775 km, 15 hours, 2180 rials 'super'

Shīrāz – at least one a day, 1077 km, 18 hours, 2065/2255 rials 'lux'/'super'

Tabrīz – at least one a day, 578 km, 11 hours, 1265/1670 rials 'lux'/'super'

Tehrān – at least one a day, 525 km, nine hours, 1145/1355 rials 'lux'/'super'

Yazd – one a day, 1081 km, 16 hours, Cooperative Bus Company No 12).

On some routes there are also some 'super super lux' buses which have fewer seats and more legroom than the regular 'super' and cost about 300 rials more.

Shared Taxi & Savārī From outside the bus terminal you can take a blue shared taxi to Hamadān for 1500 rials. Shared taxis on other routes cost around 100 rials every 30 km.

Getting Around
To/From the Airport There is no airport bus but there are shared taxis into or out of town at around 800 rials a person. Inside the town there are shared taxis and minibuses (10 rials).

AROUND BĀKHTARĀN
Bīsotūn   بیستون
Some 32 km from Bākhtarān overlooking the main Hamadān road, the famous bas-reliefs of Bīsotūn (also Behīstūn) are carved out of the cliff of Kūh-é Bīsotūn, a dramatic mountain imbued with religious significance in pre-Islamic times. The fact that the rock was also on the ancient royal road between Iran and Iraq made it an ideal location for these tablets, the precursors of the propaganda hoardings that accost the present-day traveller along many of Iran's highways. Their significance cannot have been lost on Alexander the Great when he passed this way in 324 BC.

Things to See The tablet of Darius I is high up on the side of the cliff over the village of Bīsotūn which stands next to a large pool. Below the tablet is a staircase up to a platform, from which you can see a shallow recess containing an inscription in Greek and a rather worn mid-2nd century BC **sculpture of Hercules** (Heracles) on the back of a lion.

Above and about 50 metres to the right of Hercules are two heavily eroded Parthian **bas-reliefs**. The one on the left shows King Mithradites standing before four supplicants. The one on the right depicts several scenes relates to the later Gotarzes II: one of him on horseback spearing an enemy, another of him at his investiture and third of a religious ritual. A much later Safavid inscription in Arabic has defaced these.

The **tablet of Darius I** is a relief which represents Darius' hard-won final victory over several rebel princes, principal among whom was the pretender Gaumata who had passed himself off as Cyrus the Great's second son Bardiya, who had in fact been secretly assassinated by his brother Cambyses. Symbolically and typically, the figure of the king is taller than any other mortal presence, and is only overshadowed by the symbol of the deity Ahura Mazda hovering above the whole group.

The trilingual inscription elaborates on the same theme, also recording a list of the lands then under Darius' control. The central one is in Old Persian (Pahlavī), the one on the left Neo-Babylonian (Akkadian) and the one on the right Neo-Elamite. These texts were first studied in recent times by Sir Henry Rawlinson in 1833 and 1834. He had himself suspended by a rope from the summit of the cliff in order to copy and later decipher the script, using it to uncover the key to the lost Akkadian language. Unless you wish to emulate Rawlinson's methods, it is not possible to get closer than about 50 metres to the tablet, so most of the details will be lost on the visitor without binoculars or a telephoto lens.

In the cliffs above this tablet, about 40 metres to the left, there is a vast unfinished **stone panel** which is exceptionally smooth and, as my Iranian companion put it, shows the advanced level of 'Iranian technology' at the time. Probably started in about the early 7th century BC by order of Khosrō II, its intended purpose remains a mystery.

There are plenty of other remains at this site, which has probably been settled continuously since Neolithic times. Within easy reach of the cliff there are a Median citadel, the walls of a Parthian settlement, a stone block carved with three Parthian figures, the foundations of a Sassanian bridge, and a grotto with evidence of occupation in Neanderthal times.

It would take the best part of a day to explore everything, although most visitors are happy merely to see the famous reliefs. There are several places to eat there.

Getting There & Away Bīsotūn can be reached by shared taxi from Meidūn-é Āzādī or elsewhere in Bākhtarān for around 200 rials, or you can stop there on any bus going between Bākhtarān and Hamadān. Because of the lighting conditions, it is better to visit this site in the early morning and then move on to Tāgh-é Bostān.

Tāgh-é Bostān   طاق بستان
North of the road to Bīsotūn, the bas-reliefs and carved alcoves at Tāgh-é Bostān (the 'Arch of the Garden') overlook a large pool and a pleasant garden. The first one you come to depicts the investiture of Ardeshīr II, at the same time celebrating a victory over the Romans, by the deities Ahura Mazda to the right and Mithras, holding a symbolic sacred bunch of twigs, to the left. The next is a small arched recess carved out of the cliff in the 4th century AD, showing Shāpūr II and his grandson (later Shāpūr III), created by the latter as a testament to his own dynastic credentials. The third is a larger grotto, with a lower panel depicting an armoured figure holding a lance and seated on a now-headless horse, and an upper panel showing a royal investiture. Both are believed to represent Khosrō II, a contemporary of the Prophet Mohammad. The inner walls of this remarkable monument are decorated with reliefs of royal hunting scenes, together with a much later addition, a coloured picture of three royal princes added at the time of Fath Alī Shāh. On the symmetrical facade are two winged angels above some simple floral reliefs.

Originally decorated in bright colours, the figures are rather more formal and stylised than those on the Darius relief at Bīsotūn. The site is fenced off and attended by a curator from the Ministry of Culture & Islamic Guidance. There is an entry fee of 50 rials. It is open more or less throughout the hours of daylight, but it is best to come in the mid-afternoon, after visiting the site at Bīsotūn.

There are many pleasant restaurants with a selection of fried chicken, kebabs and sometimes fish. Bīsotūn is a popular destination with daytrippers from Hamadān.

Getting There & Away Tāgh-é Bostān can be reached by shared taxi from Meidūn-é Āzādī in Bākhtarān for 100 rials. See also the Bīsotūn entry.

GHASR-E SHĪRĪN   قصر شيرين
There are several interesting if rather primitive rock carvings, dating from around 3000 BC to the Median period, in the grottoes in and around Ghasr-é Shīrīn and nearby Sar-é Pol-é Zahāb, as well as the ruins of several palaces and other structures. Ghasr-é Shīrīn is the nearest Iranian town to the main border post at Khosravī 20 km to the south-west. Perhaps it's too close to the Iraqi border for comfort: between 1976 and 1986 its population fell from 102,000 to 107.

KANGĀVAR   كنگاور
Ma'bad-é Ānāhītā
Recent excavations of the famous Parthian Temple of Ānāhītā (Artemis) at Kangāvar have revealed two staircases, and a number of massive columns of what must once have been a truly colossal monument to this ancient goddess of the waters. The columns

are now restored to their correct vertical positions. These impressive remains are believed to date from about 200 BC.

Getting There & Away
Kangāvar is 93 km from Bākhtarān and 96 km from Hamadān, on the main road between the two and accessible by public transport from either.

Hamadān Province
استان همدان

Hamadān has a predominantly rural population of 1.5 million and an area of 19,800 sq km.

HAMADĀN
همدان

Hamadān sits in a high plain below the peak of Kūh-é Alvand at an altitude of 1747 metres. Originally called Ecbatana, this is one of the oldest continually inhabited towns in the world, but almost nothing remains of the original settlement which is presumably buried beneath the present, rather featureless, city. This was the summer capital of the Achaemenians when Shūsh was their winter capital. To this day Hamadān is a very popular retreat with Iranians during the warmer months when the climate in autumn and spring is one of the most pleasant in the country, but winters are long and severe.

Visitors do not seem to be put off by the Hamadānīs' popular reputation for slow wits and tight fists, nor by the lack of good hotels.

Hamadān has, like Bākhtarān, always been a major stop on the ancient royal road to Baghdad, and it remains an important trading and transit centre. Unlike Bākhtarān, the population is largely Persian, with a large Āzarī minority. In the '70s it was said to have 4000 Jews, but the present figure is not recorded; a sizeable Jewish colony has been there at least since the 5th century AD, and possibly as early as the time of Xerxes I.

The town has several interesting shrines and two hideous modern ones, and is (or at least used to be) an important place of Jewish pilgrimage.

History
According to one legend this town was founded by the mythical King Jamshīd, and has been inhabited at least since the 2nd millennium BC. Under Cyrus the Great it became the Median capital in the 6th century BC, when it was known as Ecbatana or Hagmatāné. When it reached the height of its glory as the Achaemenian summer capital it was described at the time as one of the most opulent of cities, with splendid palaces, buildings plated with precious metals, and seven layers of town walls, the inner two coated in gold and silver. Some valuable finds from the ancient town have come to light this century, but the lower layers of settlement have not so far been explored, nor could they be without uprooting the present city. Later occupiers included Seleucids, Parthians, Alexander the Great, and the Sassanians. Hamadān faded in importance after the Arab Conquest in the mid-7th century, but again became the capital for some 60 years under the Seljuqs in the late 12th century AD. It was devastated by the Mongols in 1220 and again by Tamerlane in 1386, but soon returned to relative prosperity and remained so until the 18th century, when it fell into a serious decline from which it did not recover until the mid 19th century, once again becoming an important trading centre.

Orientation & Information
Despite its history, Hamadān is a rather drab town. In this century it was relaid around a main square, now Meidūn-é Emām Khomeinī, with six straight avenues radiating from it and a ring road encircling most of the town. The bazaar is immediately north of the main square, and on the road leading south from it, Kheyābūn-é Bū Alī Sīnā, a large square of the same name encloses the unmistakably ugly Ārāmgāh-é Bū Alī Sīnā. Most of the main offices and all the hotels are in this central district.

The ostāndārī and shahrdārī are respec-

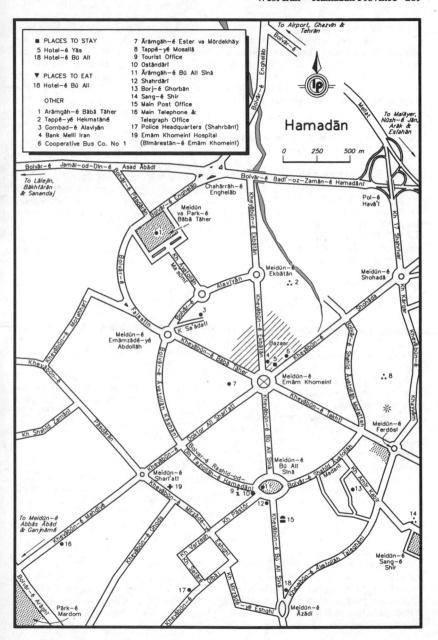

PLACES TO STAY
5 Hotel-é Yās
18 Hotel-é Bū Alī

PLACES TO EAT
18 Hotel-é Bū Alī

OTHER
1 Ārāmgāh-é Bābā Tāher
2 Tappé-yé Hekmatāné
3 Gombad-é Alaviyān
4 Bank Mellī Iran
6 Cooperative Bus Co. No 1
7 Ārāmgāh-é Ester va Mördekhāy
8 Tappé-yé Mosallā
9 Tourist Office
10 Ostāndārī
11 Ārāmgāh-é Bū Alī Sīnā
12 Shahrdārī
13 Borj-é Ghorbān
14 Sang-é Shīr
15 Main Post Office
16 Main Telephone & Telegraph Office
17 Police Headquarters (Shahrbānī)
19 Emām Khomeinī Hospital (Bīmārestān-é Emām Khomeinī)

Hamadān

0   250   500 m

tively on the west and south sides of Meidūn-é Bū Alī Sīnā, and the visa office is in the police headquarters on Kheyābūn-é Dībāj, a km south-west of the meidūn.

Tourist Office The tourist office (☎ 25065) is 200 metres west of the Ārāmgāh-é Bū Alī Sīnā.

Money Bank Melli Iran is on the north side of Meidūn-é Emām Khomeinī.

Post & Telecommunications The main post office is on the east side of Kheyābūn-é Bū Alī Sīnā, 200 metres south of Meidūn-é Bū Alī Sīnā, and the main telephone and telegraph office is on the south side of Kheyābūn-é Mahdīyé, two km south-west of Meidūn-é Emām Khomeinī. The dialling code for Hamadān is 0261.

Ārāmgāh-é Ester va Mōrdekhāy

Significantly no longer marked on the official maps, the Shrine of Esther and Mordecai, in a small walled garden in Kūché-yé Tābātabā'ī 200 metres west of Meidūn-é Emām Khomeinī, is the most important Jewish pilgrimage site in Iran. Popularly believed to contain the corpses of Esther, the Jewish wife of Xerxes I, who is credited with organising the first Jewish emigration to Persia in the 5th century, and her uncle Mordecai. In fact it more probably covers the grave of a much later Jewish queen, Shūshān, who is said to have persuaded her husband Yazdgerd I to allow a Jewish colony at Hamadān in the early 5th century AD. The remains lie in a crypt visible through a small gap between the two heavily draped tombs in a small chamber of this mausoleum, the walls of which are inscribed in Hebrew.

Gombad-é Alavīyān

The well-preserved probably 12th century mausoleum of the Alavī family – the pre-eminent family in the town during the Seljuq era – is the most noteworthy monument in Hamadān. This magnificent square tomb tower may have been a monastery in the Mongol era, and may at one time have been intended as a mosque. It is notable for the outstanding quality of its stucco ornamentation, with whirling floral motifs on the exterior walls and intricate geometric designs on its mehrāb. The tombs are in the crypt, reached by a spiral staircase. The shrine stands in a small square at the end of Kūché-yé Sa'ādatī, which leads east from Bolvār-é Alavīyān.

Sang-é Shīr

The famous stone lion in the square of the same name in south-east Hamadān is the only distinct monument of the ancient Ecbatana that is visible. Dating from the 4th century, this now seriously eroded statue originally guarded a city gate and may have been carved at the behest of Alexander the Great.

Ārāmgāh-é Bū Alī Sīnā

This sad testament to the decline of Iranian architecture in the 20th century stands over the tomb of Bū Alī Sīnā (died 1307), the renowned philosopher and physician who is best known in the West as Avicenna, the name under which his widely respected medical encyclopaedia was published in Europe. The towering monstrosity can be politely described as a concrete fluted obelisk beneath a conical dome. There is, however, an interesting museum relating to the life and works of Bū Alī.

Ārāmgāh-é Bābā Tāher

Another modernist atrocity, this 20th-century mausoleum to the mystic poet Bābā Tāher, grandson of Omar Khayyām, resembles a rocket before lift-off or a giant petrified spider. It's in a park in north-west Hamadān, south of Bolvār-é Enghelāb.

Borj-é Ghorbān

This conical 13th-century tomb tower is in a kūché of the same name, approached from Kheyābūn-é Amīr Kabīr which runs from the Sang-é Shīr to Bolvār-é Shahīd Āyatollāh Madanī.

Tappé-yé Hekmatāné

The far from overwhelming ruins of the ancient city can be seen at this mound east of Meidūn-é Ekbātān. Some small items found here and elsewhere in Hamadān have been put on display at Tehrān's Mūzé-yé Īrān-é Bāstān. The mound here should not be confused with the even more insubstantial heap of rubble at **Tappé-yé Mosallā** ('Mound of the Place of Prayer') to the south-east.

Places to Stay

Accommodation in Hamadān is bad news. There are some mosāferkhūnés along Kheyābūn-é Ekbātān in the bazaar district, such as the *Rāsī*, the *Ordībehesht* and the *Ekbātān*, all charging around 800 rials for a dorm bed. The best of a bad lot is the *Hotel-é Yās* on the north of Meidūn-é Emām Khomeinī, which charges 2500 rials a double with shared bathroom. The *Hotel-é Bū Alī* ('Bou Ali Hotel') on the east side of Kheyābūn-é Bū Alī Sīnā, 200 metres south of the square and mausoleum of the same name, is outrageously overpriced, even at the Iranians' rate of 10,000 rials a double with private bathroom (no singles).

Places to Eat

There's a quiet and reasonably good restaurant in the cellar of the *Hotel-é Bū Alī*, but its menu is minimalist. There are several chelō kabābīs nearby and around the bazaar. There are also quite a few pleasant cafés and restaurants at Ganjnāmé, 35 km away, that are very popular with Hamadānīs.

Things to Buy

Apart from its famous carpets, Hamadān is known for its ceramics and leather and copper wares.

Getting There & Away

There are no passenger flights to or from Hamadān airport. Occasionally Hamadān can be cut off by snowdrifts in winter. When it's not snowing, Hamadān is only about five hours from Tehrān by either the expressway via Tākestān or the more direct road via

Sāvé. If you continue on to Bākhtarān you'll go through the dramatic Asad Ābād Pass.

The bus companies are around Meidūn-é Emām Khomeinī. Try first at Cooperative Bus Company No 1 on the north side of Kheyābūn-é Shohadā, 200 metres north-east of the main square; they'll tell you who, if anyone, has a service going in the right direction. Buses tend to leave in the afternoon and tickets should be bought early the same day. Some destinations, each with several buses or minibuses a day, are:

Bākhtarān – 189 km, three hours, 500 rials
Ghazvīn – 234 km, four hours
Khorram Ābād – 252 km, four hours
Sanandaj – 176 km, three hours
Tehrān – 336 km, five hours, 680/800 rials
  'lux'/'super'

AROUND HAMADĀN

Ganjnāmé   گنجنامه

Some 35 km south-west of Hamadān by road, near the small town of Asad Ābād, the rather misleadingly named 'treasure book' is in reality a pair of famous Achaemenian-dynasty rock carvings of Darius I (on the left) and his son Xerxes I. Inscribed in Old Persian (Pahlavī), Elamite and Neo-Babylonian (Akkadian), these tablets list the kings' titles and hence the extent of their empires at the time. Take a shared taxi from Meidūn-é Abbās Ābād in Hamadān.

There is seasonal skiing in the area behind the cliffs (entry 50 rials). There are also several pleasant outdoor cafés.

NŪSH-E JĀN   نوش جان

This mound, about 50 km south of Hamadān in the district of Malāyer, contains the remains of a Median fire-temple dating from the 8th century BC, one of the earliest discovered in Iran. It is between the tiny villages of Nakmīl Ābād and Shūshāb, 20 km north-east of Malāyer, and is most easily reached by hired taxi from Hamadān.

LĀLEJĪN   لالجين

This village 32 km north of Hamadān is famous for its pottery industry, with more than 40 workshops producing all kinds of designs of ceramics, but particularly in the turquoise glaze for which the region is known. Get there from Hamadān on the Bākhtarān road, and after 16 km turn right and hitch the rest of the way.

Kordestān Province

استان کردستان

Kordestān has a mostly rural population of 1.1 million and an area of 25,000 sq km. Although its name translates as Kurdistan, this province's borders by no means mark the limits of Kurdish settlement in Iran; there are many Kurds throughout Āzarbāyjān and as far south as Īlām Province.

SANANDAJ

سنندج

Population: 205,000

Although Sanandaj, the rather ramshackle capital of Kordestān, dates back at least to the Middle Ages, it is not of any great architectural or historical interest, but some travellers are attracted to it for a glimpse into the Kurdish way of life. It has gradually emerged as the chief market town of the Kurds and in recent years many of the pastoralists and nomads who used to drive their flocks and bring their wares here have settled in the town. It is still predominantly Kurdish in character, as are its people in their dress and language.

At the time of writing the town was awash with Kurdish refugees from Iraq, the better off of whom were staying in hotels, and consequently accommodation is likely to be a problem for some time to come. Another problem was the fear of a typhoid or cholera epidemic, and some travellers have reported being turned back on the road to Sanandaj for not having the required jabs.

Orientation & Information

The two main squares are Meidūn-é Enghelāb and Meidūn-é Āzādī to the south, connected by Kheyābūn-é Ferdōsī. The bazaar district is east of Meidūn-é Enghelāb.

The airport is south-east of town, reached from Meidūn-é Āzādī along Bolvār-é Pāsdārān.

Tourist Office The tourist office (☎ (0471) 22700) is a minute's walk down Kheyābūn-é Hammūm, a short road leading east from the north side of Meidūn-é Āzādī. It's advisable to check there before venturing into the interior of Kordestān.

Money

Bank Melli Iran is just north of Chahārrāh-é Shohadā; to get there, turn north-west at Meidūn-é Enghelāb, then take the first main turn to the right into Kheyābūn-é Shohadā.

Post & Telecommunications

The main post office is on Kheyābūn-é Keshāvarz, 150 metres north-west of Meidūn-é Āzādī, and the main telephone office is on Kheyābūn-é Zhāndārmerī, 250 metres east of the same square.

Things to See

The city museum, the **Mūzé-yé Sanandaj** is on the south side of Kheyābūn-é Emām Khomeinī, 400 metres north-west of Meidūn-é Enghelāb. The large **Masjed-é Jāme'** (also known as the Masjed-é Dār-ol-Ehsān), almost opposite on Kheyābūn-é Emām Khomeinī, dates from 1813 and has some attractive Ghajar tilework.

Places to Stay & Eat

The best hotel, the *Mehmūnsarā-yé Sanandaj* (5813, 5814), which has its own restaurant, is some distance out from the centre on Bolvār-é Pāsdārān, the airport road. The two other hotels, the *Ābīdar* and the *Hedāyat*, are on the west side of Kheyābūn-é Ferdōsī. For the time being, all visitors have to register with the Komīté.

Getting There & Away

There are no passenger flights to Sanandaj airport, although Iran Asseman may resume services from Tehrān in the future.

The main bus station is west of town on the Tehrān road, but the station for buses to

Bākhtarān is on the east side of Bolvār-é Pāsdārān 900 metres south-east of Meidūn-é Āzādī. Cooperative Bus Company No 1 is 300 metres north-west of Meidūn-é Enghelāb on the north side of Kheyābūn-é Emām Khomeinī. Most companies only accept same-day bookings: try to arrive no later than 7 am.

Among other destinations, there are buses or minibuses to:

Ahvāz – several a week, 645 km, 10 hours, 1250/1550 rials 'lux'/'super', Cooperative Bus Company No 2
Bākhtarān – several a day, 136 km, two hours
Hamadān – several a day, 176 km, three hours
Īlām – at least one a day, 344 km, six hours
Orūmīyé – one every other day, 4 pm, 460 km, nine hours
Shīrāz – at least one a day, 1133 km, 20 hours, 1550/1970 rials 'lux'/'super'
Tabrīz – at least one a day, 442 km, eight hours
Tehrān – several a day, 512 km, nine hours, 1565 rials 'lux'
Yazd – several a week, 968 km, 16 hours, 1680 rials

GHĀR-É KARAFTŪ غار کرفتو

If you take a powerful torch you can explore the labyrinthine grotto of Karaftū about 115 km north of Sanandaj. Among other traces of what must once have been a sanctuary carved out of the cliff, there is a Greek inscription mentioning the name of Heracles (Hercules), to whom there was a cult in this region during the Parthian era, as well as several chambers and passageways.

Zanjān Province

استان زنجان

Between Tehrān and Āzarbāyjān provinces, Zanjān Province has an area of 36,400 sq km and a largely rural population of 1.6 million. It is famous for its seedless grapes. The town of Zanjān itself is of no interest to travellers.

GHAZVĪN قزوین
Population: 249,000
Famous for its carpets and seedless grapes,

the large town of Ghazvīn has always been an important transit centre between Asia Minor and Mesopotamia, and it was briefly the Persian capital under Shāh Tahmāsb I in the 16th century. The Ghazvīnīs have a reputation among Iranians for homosexuality and stupidity.

History
Founded by the Sassanian King Shāpūr I in the 3rd century BC, the town was prosperous under the Seljuq rulers who erected many fine buildings. It again briefly rose to prominence much later, when the Safavid Shāh Tahmāsb I (reigned 1524-1576), a great patron of the arts, transferred the Persian capital here from Tabrīz, which was at the time vulnerable to Ottoman incursions. He embarked on an ambitious architectural plan for Ghazvīn, but the fine buildings founded here were only a dress rehearsal for Esfahān, where his indirect successor Shāh Abbās I set up court in 1598. Ghazvīn has been devastated by earthquakes more than once, and what remains is only a shadow of its former splendour, although there are still some fine Safavid and Seljuq structures intact.

Information
The tourist office (☎ (0281) 3363) is in the Ministry of Culture & Islamic Guidance office: ask for Ershād-é Eslāmī.

Ālī Ghāpū
Some 500 metres south of the main square, this charming pavilion dates probably from the time of Tahmāsb and is notable for its fine southern facade. Originally this portal formed the entrance to the royal palace of the Safavids, nothing of which remains. The pavilion of the same name in Esfahān may have been inspired by it.

Masjed-é Jāme'
In an alley leading west from the main road, 600 metres south of the Ālī Ghāpū, this ancient mosque with four eivāns has some features dating back to the early Islamic era, and some even claim it was founded by the Abbasid Caliph Hārūn-ar-Rashīd in the late

8th century. The dome dates from the Seljuq era (early 12th century), as does the main prayer hall beneath with its fine marble mehrāb, beautiful inscriptions and geometric plaster mouldings. The two minarets and the imposing southern eivān were added in the Safavid era.

Madrasé-yé Heidarīyé

This theological college was built around a small, 12th-century Seljuq mosque, but most of it dates from the much later Ghajar period. The fine plaster mehrāb is original, and there are some exquisite Seljuq inscriptions and floral and geometric ornamentations in and around the dome-chamber. It's in an alley 250 metres south-east of the Ālī Ghāpū.

Places to Stay

There are two reasonably good hotels in central Ghazvīn, the *Hotel-é Alborz* (☎ 6631) and the *Hotel-é Ghods* (☎ 7437).

Getting There & Away

Ghazvīn can be reached by bus or shared taxi from Zanjān (180 km, three hours), by bus from Tehrān (150 km, 2½ hours, 700 rials 'lux'), Hamadān (234 km, four hours) or Tabrīz (474 km, eight hours), or by train from Tehrān or Tabrīz.

Getting Around

Some of the main sites are in a dizzy maze of narrow alleys, so for a tour of the town it is best to hire a taxi, for around 1800 rials an hour.

SOLTĀNĪYÉ سلطانیه

This once great Mongol city of the early 14th century is now no more than a large village with only one important building of the period remaining intact, but for this alone it warrants any detour. Soltānīyé – the 'town of the Sultans' – is six km along a road which turns south off the main road from Zanjān to Ghazvīn, 46 km south-east of Zanjān. The Y-junction (the Serāh-é Soltānīyé) can be reached by bus from Ghazvīn or Zanjān, and from there you hitch.

Gombad-é Soltān Oljeitū Khodābandé

The building for which Soltānīyé is deservedly famous is the great Mausoleum of the Mongol Soltān Oljeitū Khodābandé. Visible from far across the surrounding plain, the mausoleum's very striking egg-shaped dome is said to be the largest Islamic version ever built. The octagonal brick building on which it stands is also imbued with a grand sense of scale, measuring over 50 metres in height and nearly 25 metres in diameter. Very little remains of the eight minarets or the vast portals once in place, but through the main entrance on the east side is a chamber stunningly decorated with the most exquisite plaster mouldings, brickwork, inscriptions and mosaic tilework all dating from the early 14th century and recently restored. The intricate raised inscriptions on its stucco mehrāb are among the finest extant in Iran.

The mausoleum was originally built as the final resting place of Alī, the son-in-law of the Prophet Mohammad – Soltān Oljeitū was anxious to prove his Shi'ite credentials after being converted to the creed during a visit to Najaf. However, Alī was already buried in Najaf, and the people there were loath to hand over the saint's mortal remains, which had brought prominence to their town. The Mongol sultan was left with a vast mausoleum and no-one to occupy it. So the building which was intended to be a great religious shrine was converted to become the sultan's own tomb, and he was buried here in about 1317.

This unforgettable sight proves that the Mongols, usually associated with savagery and destruction by both Iranians and Westerners, were in fact capable of the highest forms of cultural expression.

There is a less interesting 14th-century octagonal Mongol tomb tower in the village. Like the Gombad-é Oljeitū nearby, it was spared destruction by the Timurids when they sacked the town in 1384.

CASTLES OF THE ASSASSINS دژهای حشیشیون

In the remote valleys north-east of Ghazvīn, on the southern foothills of the Alborz

Mountains, are the historic fortresses known as the Castles of the Assassins (Dezhā-yé Hashīshīyūn). They were first brought into European literature by the returning Crusaders, and made famous this century in Dame Freya Stark's classic *Valleys of the Assassins*.

The castles were the heavily fortified lairs of the adherents of a bizarre religious cult, based loosely on the precepts of the Ismaili sect. The cult was founded in the 11th century by by Hasan Sabah (1040-1124), known in Western folklore as the 'Old Man of the Mountains'. This heretical and widely feared sect sent out killers throughout the region to murder leading political and religious figures. Its followers, the Hashīshīyūn, were so called because of their leader's cunning ruse of taking them into beautiful secret gardens (filled with equally enticing young maidens), getting them stoned on hashish and then sending them out on their homicidal assignments under the illusion that Hasan Sabah had the power to transport them to paradise. The word 'assassin' comes from the name of this sect.

The cult at its height extended from Syria to Khorāsān. Until 1256, when the Mongols captured its castles, the Assassins spread fear throughout the region, although some scholars claim that their reputation was exaggerated.

As one might expect, the outlaw mountain hideaways were designed to be impregnable and inaccessible, and to this day it is still extremely difficult to visit them; a complete tour of the castles in this region would take about a week on horseback with a local guide. Many of them are only accessible to experienced and well-equipped mountaineers. However, the castle of **Alamūt**, one of the most famous of all, is nowadays more or less accessible by 4WD in dry weather, if you can find a guide or driver in Ghazvīn willing and able to take you there. It was originally built in about 860, and captured in 1090 by the Assassins, who occupied it until 1256.

The best book to take (apart from Freya Stark's) is Peter Willey's long-out-of-print *The Castles of the Assassins* (Harrap, London, 1963) which covers all the known sites. His *The Assassins of Central Asia* (Harrap, London, 1971) also gives an interesting historical background.

Getting There & Away

Alamūt is reached by an unsealed road heading east-north-east from the outskirts of Ghazvīn to the settlement of Mo'allem Kalāyé (73 km), then by a rough mud track leading south, east then north to the village of Gāzor Khān (another 21 km). The castle stands on a relatively easily climbed hill at the edge of this village. Allow at least six hours for the return trip, which could conceivably be made by a hired taxi in good shape.

If you have the determination, time and equipment to explore the other castles, visit the tourist office in Zanjān (☎ 28023) or Ghazvīn; they may be able to organise a guide.

Āzarbāyjān

آذربایجان

Āzarbāyjān is the north-west corner of Iran, squeezed between Turkey to the west, the former USSR republics of Azerbaijan and Armenia to the north, the Tālesh coastal strip of Gīlān Province to the east, and the provinces of Kordestān and Zanjān to the south. The province is united by one thing above all others, namely Āzarī, a tongue grammatically descended many centuries ago from Anatolian Turkish, but now a language in its own right. The signs are in Persian, and in the towns at least most people do at least understand the national language even if they prefer not to use it, but Āzarī is the mother tongue of the vast majority. Some of the Kurds of the western border country have three working languages – Kurdish, Āzarī and Persian – and many of the Christians have their own language too.

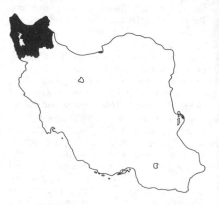

The geography is varied, and the countryside is largely a mixture of broken mountain ranges and steppe, with many oases and one extensive fertile basin west of the large salt lake known as Daryāché-yé Orūmīyé. The highest peaks are on Kūh-é Sabalān (4811 metres) and Kūh-é Sahand (3707 metres). To the north it is bordered by the Rūd-é Aras (Araxes), the river that also marks the frontier with Azerbaijan and Armenia. Agricultural products include cotton, tobacco, grapes, fruit, cereals and sugar beet. The good quality wool from the region goes to make the famous Tabrīz carpets.

In summer the region is very hot and dry, and in winter it is often bitterly cold, with frequent snowfalls which sometimes close the narrow mountain passes, even on the main international road, for days at a time. Spring and, to a lesser extent, autumn are the best times to visit.

Culturally the place has a great deal in common with Azerbaijan to the north. After a few years of bad relations following the Iranian Islamic Revolution, there is now more contact between the two Azerbaijans, although private visits by Āzarīs in either

direction are still few. The Āzarīs are related to the Anatolian Turks, but they are divided in religion; the Iranian Āzarīs are almost entirely Shi'ite, whereas the Anatolian Turks are predominantly Sunni. Older Āzarī men traditionally wear brimmed felt hats, and Tabrīz, the main town of the region, is one of the few places in Iran where it is not uncommon to see men wearing ties, still branded un-Islamic and un-Iranian by the central religious authorities.

Many of the villages in the western border country are Kurdish, some of them extremely isolated and poor, without running water, electricity or any facilities whatsoever. There are also many Chaldean Christian settlements west of Lake Orūmīyé. Armenians, Assyrians and other Christians live in many of the towns.

In the wild western border area you will see armed patrols of soldiers or Revolutionary Guards along the roads. There are lookout towers all along the western side of the Daryāché-yé Orūmīyé. During the Iran-Iraq War and immediately after the revolution there were many attempts by dissenters and military deserters to escape from Iran over the Turkish border, and some

Āzarbāyjān

0   25   50 km

tension still lingers.There have been recent reports of Revolutionary Guards being killed on deserted roads by Āzarī separatists.

Āzarbāyjān is divided into two provinces. Āzarbāyjān-é Gharbī (West Āzarbāyjān) lies to the north-west, west and south of the Daryāché-yé Orūmīyé and has an area of 38,850 sq km and a population of 2 million. Its capital is Orūmīyé. Āzarbāyjān-é Sharghī (East Āzarbāyjān) lies to the north-east, south and east of the Daryāché-yé Orūmīyé and has an area of 67,100 sq km and a population of 4.2 million; its capital is Tabrīz, the largest town in the region. The lake itself is not in either province, and until early this century it was a Russian concession and not part of Iran at all.

History

The region now known as Āzarbāyjān has always been an important funnel between Asia and Europe, the gateway taken by a succession of invaders and settlers. Part of the Urartian Empire and later the Median Empire, it was the centre of one of the earliest civilisations in Persia. In 330 BC it was taken by Alexander the Great, who appointed his general Atropates as governor.

Atropates soon established his own autonomous dynasty, and the land was given the name Atropatene, from which the present Āzarbāyjān is derived. This kingdom lasted until about the time of the Sassanian era, when it came back under central Persian government and became an important centre of Zoroastrianism. Later it fell to Arabs, Turks and then Mongols, until the Safavid dynasty, its own roots firmly entrenched in Āzarbāyjān, recovered it.

Under the Ghajar shāhs, themselves of Āzarī origin, Āzarī influences became very important in Persian life, and Tabrīz was established as the seat of the crown prince, but at the same time Āzarbāyjān began to come under the Russian influence. In WWI it was invaded by the Turks, who attempted to attack the Russians through Persian territory. Until the Bolshevik Revolution, Russians also occupied much of northern Persia, building a railway line from Tabrīz to the border at Julfa. During WWII the Soviet army occupied Āzarbāyjān and much of the north of Iran in an attempt to secure the supply route through the Persian Gulf. They proved reluctant to leave in 1945 and tried to set up a puppet government in Āzarbāyjān, provoking the Tehrān government to send a force to expel them in December 1946.

Since then Āzarbāyjān has been secure within Iranian borders, and for the most part the Āzarīs have been able to retain their cultural and linguistic integrity. The region continues to depend on its transit routes, although trade with Turkey and the former USSR has gone through a number of ups and downs in recent years.

DARYĀCH-YĀ ORŪMĪY

دریاچه ارومیه

This lake, the largest one wholly within Iran, is technically in neither of the provinces of Āzarbāyjān. It has an average area of 4686 sq km and a mean depth of around five metres, both of which vary according to season. The lake is far too salty for anything but the most primitive marine life, and with its jagged rocky islands and barren shores, it is not the most enticing of places. The waters are said to have therapeutic values and to be excellent for relieving rheumatism.

There are a few ports and several hotels and low-key resorts along the shore.

Jazīré-yé Kabūdī

The largest of the many islands in the lake, Jazīré-yé Kabūdī is 32 sq km in area, has a high point of almost 1600 metres, and is covered in trees. Also known as Jazīré-yé Ghoyūn Dāghī or 'Sheep Mountain Island', it has a spring which supports a small village and a few wild sheep. The island also hosts a wide variety of birds, including flamingo, wild duck and migratory pelican.

It is on this island that Hulagu Khan, grandson of Genghis Khan, sacker of Bagh-

dad and founder of the Il-Khanid dynasty, set up his treasury. In 1265 he was buried there with – as was demanded by the Mongol custom of the time – the ritual slaughter of virgins.

For many years hunting has been forbidden on Jazīre-yé Kabūdī and it is now a conservation area of considerable interest to naturalists. It is only possible to visit the island with the permission of the Department of the Environment office in Orūmīyé, which can also help to arrange transport there and back.

Getting Around the Lake

Although Tabrīz and Orūmīyé, the two provincial capitals of Āzarbāyjān, are only some 115 km apart as the crow flies, the land journey along one of the poor roads skirting the lake covers more than 320 km and takes around five hours even in dry weather. A causeway across the narrowest part of the lake was begun in the 1970s, but the project was abandoned soon after the revolution and the road from the west side still ends two thirds of the way across.

There are some small craft taking passengers and cargo between the few ports, but the only car-ferry, which connects Bandar-é Golmānkhūné, the port for Orūmīyé, and Sharafkhūné, the port for Tabrīz, sails about twice a week and is not generally used by public transport. This ferry takes passengers and up to 50 cars at a fare of 1200 rials, but no buses. The sailing takes about 30 minutes and more or less halves the journey time between Tabrīz and Orūmīyé. Ask around locally about the latest timetable.

Āzarbāyjān-é Gharbī Province

استان آذربایجان غربی

ORŪMĪYÉ

ارومیه

Population: 301,000

Orūmīyé lies at an altitude of 1312 metres on a large and fertile plain to the west of the lake of the same name, and is famous for its white seedless grapes; apples, other non-citrus fruit and tobacco are also grown in the region. Despite its relatively remote position, cut off from the interior by a vast salt lake, it does lie on a trade route with Turkey that is increasing in importance and helping to relieve the pressure on the overburdened main road between Erzurum and Tabrīz.

Orūmīyé may date back to the middle of the 2nd millennium BC. It is one of the many places claimed to have been the birthplace of Zoroaster, but evidence of its early history is very scant. It fell to the conquering Arabs in the mid-7th century AD, and subsequently came under the control of the Seljuqs and the Mongols, and from then on its history has been less eventful and more peaceful than that of Tabrīz.

Also known as Ūrmīyé, and sometimes in English as Urmia, and from 1930 to the Islamic Revolution as Rezā'īyé (in honour of Rezā Shāh), the town has few historic buildings of great importance but it is of considerable interest as the centre of a large and long- established Christian community. It is said that Christians make up something like one third of the population of Orūmīyé, probably the highest proportion of any large town in Iran. The town's population is a mixture of Āzarīs, Kurds, a few Persians and the various Christian denominations. In the last century and the first half of the present one, foreign missionaries were particularly active in Orūmīyé, and many of the Christians were converted to Protestantism or Catholicism, but the largest churches are those of the Chaldeans, Armenians, Assyrians and Nestorians.

In 1918, most of the Christian population fled Orūmīyé in the face of an Ottoman invasion, mindful of the appalling massacres of Armenians in Turkey that are still remembered with anger and horror by Iranians. Most of those who remained were brutally slaughtered, but the Christian community soon reestablished itself, free of the Turkish threat.

In contrast to the Tabrīzīs, the inhabitants of Orūmīyé are known for their hospitality,

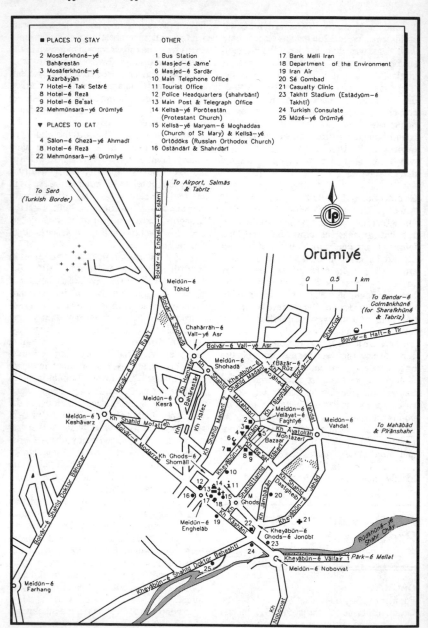

■ PLACES TO STAY

2 Mosāferkhūné–yé
   Bahārestān
3 Mosāferkhūné–yé
   Āzarbāyjān
7 Hotel–é Tak Setāré
8 Hotel–é Rezā
9 Hotel–é Be'sat
22 Mehmūnsarā–yé Orūmīyé

▼ PLACES TO EAT

4 Sālon–é Ghezā–yé Ahmadī
8 Hotel–é Rezā
22 Mehmūnsarā–yé Orūmīyé

OTHER

1 Bus Station
5 Masjed–é Jāme'
6 Masjed–é Sardār
10 Main Telephone Office
11 Tourist Office
12 Police Headquarters (shahrbānī)
13 Main Post & Telegraph Office
14 Kelīsā–yé Porōtestān
    (Protestant Church)
15 Kelīsā–yé Maryam–é Moghaddas
    (Church of St Mary) & Kelīsā–yé
    Ortōdōks (Russian Orthodox Church)
16 Ostāndārī & Shahrdārī

17 Bank Melli Iran
18 Department of the Environment
19 Iran Air
20 Sé Gombad
21 Casualty Clinic
23 Takhtī Stadium (Estādyūm–é
    Takhtī)
24 Turkish Consulate
25 Mūzé–yé Orūmīyé

To Serō
(Turkish Border)

To Airport, Salmās
& Tabrīz

Orūmīyé

0   0.5   1 km

To Bandar–é
Golmānkhūné
(for Sharafkhūné
& Tabrīz)

Meidūn–é
Tōhīd

Chahārrāh–é
Valī–yé Asr

Bolvār–é Vali–yé Asr

Meidūn–é
Shohadā

Bāzār–é
Rūz

Meidūn–é
Kesrā

Meidūn–é
Velāyat–é
Faghīyé

Meidūn–é
Vahdat

To Mahābād
& Pīrānshahr

Meidūn–é
Keshāvarz

Kh Shahid Mofatteh

Kh Hāfez

Kh Ayatollāh
Montazerī

Bāzār

Kh Ghods–é
Shomālī

Meidūn–é
Enghelāb

Meidūn–é
Nobovvat

Rūdkhūné–é
Shahr Chāy

Pārk–é Mellat

Kheyābūn–é
Ghods–é Jonūbī

Kheyābūn–é Vālfajr

Meidūn–é
Farhang

and the atmosphere is quite pleasant. The main problem for the visitor is the shortage of hotel accommodation – arriving in the evening without a reservation can easily turn into a desperate situation.

Orientation & Information
Orūmīyé is a flat and smallish city. The Rūdkhūné-yé Shahr Chāy, a river that drains into the Daryāché-yé Orūmīyé, is south of the main part of the city. The main square is the Meidūn-é Velāyat-é Faghīh, and the main street of interest is Kheyābūn-é Emām, which runs south-west from the main square. The main shopping district, most of the hotels, mosāferkhūnés and restaurants are found along or near this road. The airport (☎ 22206) is about 25 minutes by road north of Orūmīyé. There is no train station. The bus station is near the north-east edge of town.

For visa extensions, go to the police headquarters.

The Department of the Environment office (Edāré-yé Koll-é Hefāzat-é Mohīt-é Zīst) (☎ 40620, 40629) is on the south side of Kheyābūn-é Shahīd Keshtgar, the first turn right if you walk south-east from the tourist office. This is where you go to apply for permission to visit Jazīré-yé Kabūdar in Daryāché-yé Orūmīyé.

Tourist Office The tourist office (☎ 20241) is helpful, although little English is spoken. It is on the 2nd floor of the Ministry of Culture & Islamic Guidance building (not marked in English) on the north side of Kheyābūn-é Ghods-é Jonūbī.

Money Turkish lira can be bought and sold either at Bank Melli on Kheyābūn-é Kāshānī or in the bazaar, but US dollars are, as usual, the preferred unit of currency.

Post & Telecommunications The main post office is next to the petrol station at the southern end of Kheyābūn-é Emām. For long-distance telephone calls go to the telephone office (mokhābarāt) a little further up, just north of the intersection with Kheyābūn-é Ghods. To get the operator, dial ☎ 116; for directory enquiries, ☎ 118. The dialling code for Orūmīyé is 0441.

Consulate The Turkish Consulate (☎ 28970) (Konsūlgarī-yé Torkīyé) is at 30 Kheyābūn-é Shahīd Beheshtī.

Maps The only map of Orūmīyé is produced by the Ministry of Culture & Islamic Guidance, but it is in Persian script. Pick it up free at the tourist office.

Medical Services The casualty unit (markaz-é ūrzhāns) is quite close to the stadium in the south of town, but a little difficult to get to by public transport: take a private taxi. For emergencies dial ☎ 118, 24081 or 24082.

Emergency The police headquarters (☎ 110) are on the north side of Meidūn-é Enghelāb.

Masjed-é Jāme'
This large quadrangular Seljuq mosque in the bazaar district has some very fine plaster mouldings in its original 13th century mehrāb, and a dome of very generous proportions. Much of the present structure dates from later than the Seljuq period, but this sand-coloured mosque is still an impressive sight.

Sé Gombad
This late 12th-century circular Seljuq tomb tower is notable for its stucco and stalactite decorations; it is in Kūché-yé Sheshom which leads east off Kheyābūn-é Jāmbāzān in the south-east of town.

Mūzé-yé Orūmīyé
The city museum in Kheyābūn-é Shahīd Doktor Beheshtī has a small display of historical and archaeological exhibits from the region, and some examples of calligraphy and the local decorative arts. It is open daily from 9 am to noon and 2 to 4 pm; entry is 50 rials.

Churches
The various communities here – Assyrian,

Armenian, Nestorian, Protestant, Orthodox and Roman Catholic (Chaldean Rite) – all have their own places of worship, and Orūmīyé is the seat of a Chaldean archbishopric. The most noteworthy church is that of St Mary, the **Kelīsā-yé Maryam-é Moghaddas**, in Kheyābūn-é Ghods-é Jonūbī opposite the tourist office. This low-roofed old building of white stone stands on the site of a much older church and has some interesting tombs inside, one of them inscribed in Russian and Persian. Next to St Mary's is a large modern church built in the 1960s and used by the Orthodox community, most of whom are remnants of a White Russian influx earlier this century. The two churches are entered by a blue metal gate with a cross on it, diagonally opposite the tourist office; anyone inside should be able to find the required keys. Immediately to the left as you walk out is a modern Protestant church; the priest, who speaks good English, said that any visitors intending to see the church need a letter from the tourist office over the road.

Places to Stay

Since Orūmīyé regained its place on the transit route to Turkey the volume of traffic through the town has increased markedly without any corresponding growth in the number of hotel beds, so finding somewhere to stay can be difficult; if you arrive at night you may have to ask the police to help. The dirt cheap places appear to be under instructions not to accept foreigners.There are no places close to the bus station, but buses and long-distance taxis, especially ones arriving after dark, often drop passengers off in Meidūn-é Velāyat- é Faghīh, which is within easy walking distance of most places.

Places to Stay – bottom end

The uninspiring *Mosāferkhūné-yé Āzarbāyjān* and *Mosāferkhūné-yé Bahārestān* are on the east side of Kheyābūn-é Emām, between Meidūn-é Velāyat-é Faghīh and Kheyābūn-é Be'sat. Neither is marked in English and neither is likely to accept foreigners.

The *Hotel-é Be'sat* (marked in English 'Hotel Be'sat') (☎ 36128), in Kheyābūn-é Be'sat about 100 metres to the right as you walk out of the Hotel-é Rezā, is friendly and reasonable value at 2200/3300 rials a single/double. There is another hotel in the same street about 200 metres further down on the other side of the road at the corner. The clean and comfortable *Hotel-é Tak Setāré* (marked in English 'Hotel Taxsetareh') is reasonable value at 2000/3000 rials a single/double with private bathroom. This is in a short unmarked dead-end street about 200 metres south-west of the Hotel-é Rezā, on the other side of Kheyābūn-é Emām.

Places to Stay – middle

The *Hotel-é Rezā* (marked in English 'Hotel Reza') (☎ 26580) is at the intersection of Kheyābūn-é Emām and Kheyābūn-é Be'sat. It has no single rooms and charges 6200 rials a double with private bathroom. Although the best hotel in the centre of town, it is reported to have gone seriously downhill in recent years. When I arrived at 7 pm I was told that my reservation was only good until 6 pm.

The best hotel in town, the *Mehmūnsarā-yé Orūmīyé* (☎ 23080, 23085), on the north side of Kheyābūn-é Kāshānī close to the river, is quite comfortable although heavily indebted to modern Soviet architecture. It is very popular with Turkish truck drivers who help to keep it full most of the time. A single/double with private bathroom costs 4300/4400 rials.

The *Hotel-é Jomhūrī* (☎ 22260) in Kheyābūn-é Emām has been closed for repairs. When it reopens it is likely to charge around 2500/4000 rials a single/double with private bathroom.

Places to Eat

There isn't a great deal of scope for the discerning gourmet in Orūmīyé, and places close early. The flashest restaurant in town is in the *Hotel-é Rezā*. You can also get a bite to eat in the *Mehmūnsarā-yé Orūmīyé*.

There are some chelō kabābīs and snack bars along Kheyābūn-é Emām. The *Sālon-é Ghezā-yé Ahmadī* (marked also in Turkish

'Yasasin Islamiyet') is OK for humble cooking, charging 1400 rials for average boiled knuckle of mutton. A place in an alley nearby serves ābgūsht.

A certain amount of imported alcohol gets smuggled through to Orūmīyé, where it is cheaper than in most of Iran, but of course I wouldn't advise you to take the risk.

The excellent sweet white grape juice of Orūmīyé is packaged under the name Sundis; the juice used to be put to an even better use, but wine is no longer openly produced here.

Things to Buy

Various goods, many of them cheap clothes and trinkets imported from Turkey, can be picked up in the bazaar. Indigenous souvenirs include excellent wood carvings and other handicrafts.

Getting There & Away

To/From Turkey The border post at Serō, 50 km north-west of Orūmīyé by road, is not much used except by locals, although it is open to foreigners. There is no bus or minibus service to Serō from Orūmīyé or anywhere else, and you will have to take a taxi or savārī for around 1000 rials from the bus station or hitch a lift. By car the journey time is about an hour, road checks and weather conditions permitting. Count on at least five hours to get through both customs posts.

From the Turkish side of the border head for Van (240 km) via Yüksekova (40 km) and Sivelân (77 km). Although there may be occasional buses and shared taxis direct to Van, you will more probably have to hitch at least as far as Yüksekova (40 km). If you were truly desperate for somewhere to stay for the night, you could risk staying in Hakkâri, 124 km from the border, but it is not at all a good idea to spend more than the minimum possible time in the area southeast of Van, which is notorious for strife. Foreign trucks passing through eastern Turkey are regularly held up by the infamous 'Marlboro controls', where Turkish soldiers and policemen relieve drivers of their duty-free cigarette allowance and other inconveniences. If you left Orūmīyé early in the morning you should be able to get to Van the same day, and vice versa. Take a packed lunch, breakfast and dinner.

Although buses between Tehrān and Damascus pass through Serō, they don't normally pick up passengers on the way.

Since this route has only recently been reopened, check the latest situation with the Turkish Consulate in Orūmīyé. If you're coming from Turkey, ask at the tourist office in Van (☎ (061) 12018). See also Lonely Planet's *Turkey – a travel survival kit*.

Air There is no X-ray machine at this small airport, so luggage has to be examined by hand: arrive in good time. Iran Air flies from Orūmīyé to Tehrān daily at 11.45 am and 3.45 pm (1¼ hours, 6230 rials). Try to get a window seat on the left side of the aeroplane for this flight, and look out for the causeway across the Daryāché-yé Orūmīyé which was abandoned after the revolution only two-thirds completed. It is sometimes possible to get standby tickets to Tehrān with Saha.

The Iran Air office (☎ 27777) is on the south side of Kheyābūn-é Kāshānī, between Meidūn-é Enghelāb and the Mehmūnsarā-yé Orūmīyé. Saha has an office at the airport (☎ 22206).

Bus & Minibus All the bus companies operating out of Orūmīyé have offices at the station (Termīnāl-é Bozorg) in Bolvār-é Haft-é Tīr on the eastern approach to the city. Among other destinations, there are buses to:

Bākhtarān – at least one a day, 596 km, 11 hours, 1335/1505 rials 'lux'/'super'
Bandar-é Golmānkhūné – several minibuses a day, 17 km, 20 minutes; see also Daryāché-yé Orūmīyé section
Ghara Zeyā'-ed-Dīn – two in the afternoon, 189 km, three hours, Cooperative Bus Company No 8; see also Ghara Kelīsā entry
Marāghé – several a day, 224 km, four hours
Rasht – at least two a day, 803 km, 13 hours
Sanandaj – every other day, 460 km, nine hours
Tabrīz – five or six a day, 322 km, five hours, 400/500 rials 'lux'/'super'

For most destinations further afield you will probably have to change at Tabrīz.

Shared Taxi & Savārī There are frequent shared taxis and savārīs to Tabrīz (four hours, 2500 rials) and Bandar-é Golmānkhūné (15 minutes, 100 to 200 rials) from outside the bus station. See also the Daryāché-yé Orūmīyé section.

Getting Around
To/From the Airport A taxi to or from the airport is 1500 rials for a single passenger. Allow at least 25 minutes. There is no airport bus service.

Taxi Shared taxis run along all the main roads of Orūmīyé, with the greatest concentration in Kheyābūn-é Emām. Fifty rials should be enough for most journeys.

TAKHT-É SOLEIMĀN   تخت سليمان
Although Takht-é Soleimān ('Throne of Solomon') is one of the most interesting archaeological sites in this part of Iran, few but the most determined of travellers get to it, as it's a long way from any sort of overnight accommodation, and public transport is out of the question.

If you do make it, you will see the fairly well preserved remains of a large fortified settlement, built around a small lake on a hilltop. It is entered through a large arched gateway hollowed out of the very thick circular stone wall surrounding the settlement. The original 38 fortified towers along the wall have worn away to the same height as the wall, but the wall itself is largely intact and the south gateway is still in remarkably good condition. There are remains of buildings from the Parthian, Achaemenian, Sassanian and Islamic periods, many of them rebuilt or enlarged several times, but the walls themselves probably date from the 3rd century AD. The oldest remaining structures are the ruins of a Sassanian palace and a substantial fire-altar which once formed part of a temple complex, now largely in ruins. This was an important religious site in Sassanian times, but the reason for its importance is not known; it is one of the many places claimed to be the birthplace of Zoroaster.

Getting There & Away
Takht-é Soleimān is 29 km by road north of Takāb. Takāb is a small town in the extreme south-east of Āzarbāyjān-é Sharghī. Probably the most sensible way of getting to Takht-é Soleimān is to charter a taxi for the day for a return trip from Marāghé 228 km to the north-west. Even then you would need to set out not much later than 6 am and bring some food with you. The road from Marāghé to Takāb is fairly straightforward, and most of the road from there to Takht-é Soleimān has recently been sealed, but the final few km are still not good. The return trip from Marāghé will probably take 10 to 12 hours and, if you spend two hours at the site including a break for lunch, you are looking at a taxi fare of around 25,000 rials.

HASANLŪ   حسنلو
Hasanlū, another important archaeological site, is a little easier to reach than Takht-é Soleimān. This tappé is about 5 km west of the small town of Mohammad Yār, just south of the southernmost tip of the Daryāché-yé Orūmīyé on the main road between Marāghé and Orūmīyé.

Hasanlū was an important Iron Age settlement and later citadel, first settled as early as the 6th millennium BC. You can still see the the outer walls of the citadel and the outline of the original town, with its alleys, mud-brick houses, store-rooms and various administrative and other buildings dating back over four distinct periods. The centre of the site gave way, at the beginning of the 1st millennium BC, to a hefty citadel with walls of great thickness and height. In times of peace the residents lived in a settlement beyond the outer walls of the stronghold. Despite Hasanlū's impressive fortifications, the skeletons of people who died here under violent circumstances suggest that the town was destroyed by the Urartians in the 9th century BC. It is perhaps best known for a priceless golden chalice from the 11th century BC, uncovered during excavations here.

ORŪMĪYÉ TO GHARA KELĪSĀ
Bastām
بسطام

Bastām is probably the most important of the many Urartian archaeological sites yet found in Iran. At the time of writing it was reported to be closed to the public: ask at the tourist office in Orūmīyé or the Archaeological Department in Tehrān. If it is open, you can get there by taking the first turning to the left after leaving Ghara Zeyā'-ed-Dīn on the road west to Seyah Cheshmé, and driving straight ahead for six km along a bad road until you come to the tall hill on which Bastām stands.

A mighty Urartian citadel, larger than any other yet discovered in Iran, with great stone walls, two large gateways and the remains of a hall, has been unearthed, together with a number of interesting ceramics and other finds. The settlement is believed to have lasted until a Median attack in about the 5th century BC, and much later to have been the site of an Armenian village.

GHARA KELĪSĀ
قره کلیسا (کلیسای تادی مقدس)

This church, the Church of St Thaddaeus, though now very remote, is probably the most interesting and remarkable Christian monument in Iran. If you visit only one place in Āzarbāyjān, this should be it. Despite the difficulty involved in reaching it, it is worth every rial of the taxi hire fare.

This famous monastery church is clearly visible from afar, at the edge of a promontory, behind a fortified wall with buttresses. Both the church and the tiny Muslim Kurdish settlement next to it are known as Ghara Kelīsā (Āzarī for 'Black Church'), but the church itself is more accurately known as Kelīsā-yé Tātāvūs, or Kelīsā-yé Tādī, the Church of Thaddaeus.

Little is known of Thaddaeus, one of Christ's disciples who was also called Judas or Jude, and there are only passing references to him in the Bible. According to legend, he and another disciple, Simon the Zealot, were

martyred in the area of present-day Āzarbāyjān (perhaps at Sūfeyān, between Tabrīz and Marand), and a church dedicated to St Thaddaeus was built on the present site of Ghara Kelīsā as early as 68 AD (although other sources say that it was not founded until the 7th century). Among the Armenians he is revered as an apostle of the Christian church in Persia and one of its first martyrs.

Little or nothing remains of this original church, which was largely rebuilt after extensive earthquake damage in the 13th century, and subsequently repaired many times, but there are some older parts, perhaps from the 10th century, around the altar. Although the original building was constructed of black and white stone, giving it the name Ghara Kelīsā or Black Church, the present structure, most of which dates from the 17th century, is the colour of sand. The church is protected behind a thick wall, which also forms the outer wall of the monastery buildings. There are two small chambers behind unlocked doors to either side of the altar, one of which may cover the tomb of St Thaddaeus.

The church has one service a year, on the feast day of St Thaddaeus (around 19 June), when Armenian pilgrims from all over Iran camp for three days to attend the ceremonies. At other times, this isolated church is rarely visited. Enter through a south gateway, the key for which is kept in the hamlet: ask for the *kelīd-é kelīsā*. The keys to the outer monastery buildings are not kept in Ghara Kelīsā. When approaching this hamlet, be extremely wary of the exceptionally ferocious mastiffs keeping guard duty over it, and do not photograph any of the colourfully dressed Kurdish women in the hamlet without permission.

There are some other almost entirely neglected Armenian churches of less interest in the area. To find them you will have to ask the villagers for directions. The priests at the Protestant Church in Orūmīyé, or St Mary's Church in Tabrīz may be able to give you details.

Getting There & Away
Reaching Ghara Kelīsā is impossible by

public transport, and is not straightforward even by private transport. You will have to hire a taxi from Orūmīyé, the driver of which may get completely lost on the way, and probably make the journey there and back into a day-trip (10 am to 7 pm with a brief stop for lunch at Khoy). In view of the very demanding road conditions, the correct fare for this trip is probably something like 25,000 rials, but you will be lucky to get away with less than 40,000 rials. You could also take a chartered taxi from Mākū, Khoy, Salmās, Marand or Tabrīz at greater or lesser expense, but whatever route you take you are almost certain to pass through Ghara Zeyā'-ed-Dīn, which is itself clearly signposted on all approach roads. From there you follow the main road to Seyah Cheshmé 65 km to the west. Nine km before Seyah Cheshmé you come to a T-junction with a sign marked in English 'Ghareh Kelisa', where you turn right into a very poor mud track (difficult in rainy weather). Drive straight ahead, ignoring any tracks to either side, and after about 10 km on the right side of the road you come to the unmistakable church on a promontory overlooking a tiny village. Since your taxi driver may well not have a clue how to get to Ghara Kelīsā, make sure that he follows the route given here.

The alternative would be a combination of several changes of infrequent public transport and a walk of about 10 km, with the genuine risk of being savaged by mastiffs on the way. The Cooperative Bus Company No 8 buses from Orūmīyé to Ghara Zeyā'-ed-Dīn (daily, 2.30 and 3 pm) are only of much use for inhabitants of Ghara Zeyā'-ed-Dīn, as there is no return service until the next morning. In any case it would take at least two hours to reach Ghara Kelīsā from there by taxi and there is nowhere to stay in Ghara Zeyā'-ed-Dīn.

MĀKŪ ماكو

The little town of Mākū, 22 km from the Turkish border is of no great interest although it is a not unattractive place, straggling along either side of a mountain gorge at an altitude of 1634 metres. It is the place

where travellers following the main highway into Turkey bid farewell to civilisation until Erzurum, 342 km to the west.

There are a few Urartian sites around Mākū and to either side of the road between there and Orūmīyé to the south, but none of importance can be easily reached from Mākū. If you are interested, you could hire a taxi to the small Urartian citadel of **Sangar** about 10 km to the west of Mākū, just to the north of the road to Bāzargān.

Although Ghara Kelīsā is only 23 km south of Mākū as the crow flies, there is no direct road or track between the two.

Places to Stay & Eat

There are several small but adequate hotels in Mākū, all on the main east-west road, Kheyābūn-é Emām, of which probably the best are the central *Hotel-é Alvāné* (☎ 3491) and the *Mehmūnsarā-yé Mākū* (☎ 3185) at the western approach to town. There are plenty of chelō kabābīs around.

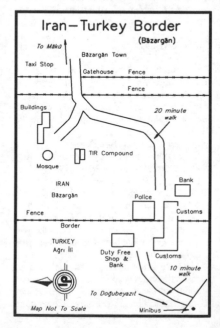

Iran–Turkey Border
(Bāzargān)

To Mākū
Taxi Stop
Bāzargān Town
Gatehouse   Fence
Fence
Buildings
20 minute walk
Mosque
TIR Compound
IRAN
Bāzargān
Bank
Police
Fence
Customs
Border
TURKEY
Āgrı İli
Duty Free Shop & Bank
Customs
10 minute walk
To Doğubeyazıt
Map Not To Scale
Minibus

Getting There & Away
Although you could conceivably find a shared taxi or savārī going from here to Orūmīyé, almost all the traffic from Mākū is headed for Tabrīz or Bāzargān. There are several buses a day to Tabrīz (242 km, four hours, 400/500 rials 'lux'/'super'). See the Tabrīz entry and the Getting There & Away chapter for more details.

Most people arriving in Iran at Bāzargān tend to head straight to Tabrīz, as often as not arriving there exhausted at dead of night. If you're heading in the opposite direction it's worth bearing in mind the considerable journey time between here and Erzurum, the first even remotely hospitable place to stay west of Mākū, not to mention the inevitable delays and hassles at the border. Spending all night going through customs, as you almost certainly will if you arrive later than about 6 pm, is not a recipe for a happy introduction to either country.

Āzarbāyjān-é Sharghī Province
استان آذربایجان شرقی

TABRIZ
تبریز

The natives of Adharbáyján...with their scowling faces and furtive gray eyes, are not popular among the Persians, whose opinion about the inhabitants of their metropolis, Tabríz, is expressed in the following rhyme:

...From a Tabrízí thou wilt see naught but rascality: Even this is best, that thou shouldst not see a Tabrízí.'
Edward Browne,
A Year Amongst the Persians, 1893

Tabrīz has had a spell as the Persian capital and was for many years, until quite recently, the second city of Iran. Today it's a sprawling industrial and commercial centre of 971,000 people, and not a particularly attractive city.

The capital of Āzarbāyjān-é Sharghī is an oasis town in an enclosed valley, but after the beauty of the mountains Tabrīz itself is an anticlimax. Tabrīz has a decidedly Russian air about it, and architecturally resembles a

Russian provincial town which went to seed around the turn of the century. Moreover, the Tabrīzīs are not known for their hospitality.

In winter the town (at 1360 metres) is miserably cold and often thick with snow, while in summer it's often far too hot for comfort. Spring and autumn are sometimes pleasant. It is possible to ski near Tabrīz in winter: ask at the tourist office for details.

Most travellers just pass through or spend the minimum possible time here, but for many people arriving in Iran from Turkey, Armenia or Azerbaijan, this is the first place they can rest their boots.

History
Tabrīz has for many centuries lain on the main trade corridor between the northern part of Iran and the outside world, but its outlying position and vulnerability to foreign invasion, which makes its history interesting, also stunted its development. It has been particularly prone to earthquakes, which have all but destroyed the city more than once.

Although the early history of Tabrīz is shrouded in legend and mystery, the town's origins are believed to date back to distant antiquity, perhaps even before the Sassanian era. It was the capital of Āzarbāyjān in the 3rd century AD and again under the Mongol Il-Khanid dynasty, although for some time Marāghé supplanted it.

In 1392, after the end of Mongol rule, the town was sacked by Tamerlane. It was soon restored under the Turkoman tribe of the Ghara Ghoyūnlū, who established a short-lived local dynasty. Under the Safavids it rose from regional to national capital for a short period, but the second of the Safavid kings, Shāh Tahmāsb, moved the capital to Ghazvīn because of the vulnerability of Tabrīz to Ottoman attacks. The town then went into a period of decline, fought over by Persians, Ottomans and Russians and stricken by earthquakes and disease.

Tabrīz was the residence of the crown prince under the Ghajar shāhs, themselves of Turkish stock, but the town did not return to prosperity until the second half of the 19th

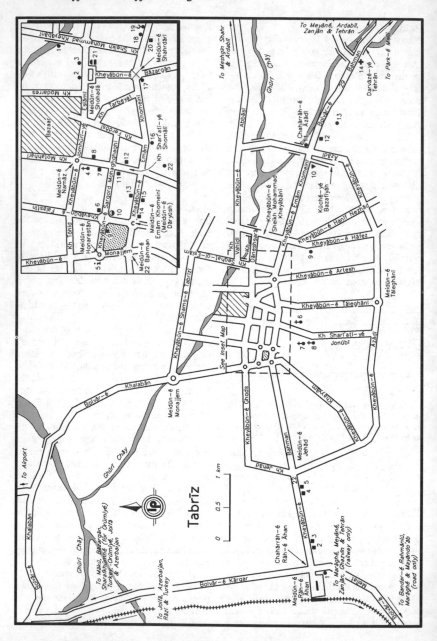

Top: Kurdish village, Āzarbāyjān-é Sharghī (DStV)
Bottom: Ghara-Kelīsā (Church of St Thaddaeus) (DStV)

Top: Detail of moulding, Emāmzādé-yé Nūr, Gorgān (DStV)
Left: Caspian Sea from Nōshahr (DStV)
Right: Emāmzādé-yé Soltān Zein-ol-Ābedīn, Sārī (DStV)

INSET KEY

■ PLACES TO STAY

6, 7, 8, 11 & 12 Dirt Cheap
  Mosāferkhūnés
13 Pārk Hotel
14 Hotel-é Morvārīd
15 Hotel-é Sepīd
20 Hotel-é Golshan

▼ PLACES TO EAT

6, 7, 8, 11 & 12 Very Cheap Restaurants & Tea-Houses

OTHER

1 Main Telephone Office
2 Bank Melli Iran (Central Branch)
3 Ostāndārī
4 Kelīsā-yé Maryam-é Moghaddas
  (Armenian Church of St Mary)
5 Tourist Office
9 Bāgh-é Golestān Park
10 Bus Station
16 Arg
17 Shahrdārī
18 Mūzé-yé Āzarbāyjān
19 Masjed-é Kabūd
21 Main Post & Telegraph Office
22 Police Headquarters (shahrdānī)

■ PLACES TO STAY

2 Hotel-é Daryā
3 Hotel-é Īrān
4 Mosāferkhūné-yé Khayyām
5 Mosāferkhūné-yé Īrān
12 Hotel-é Tabrīz

▼ PLACES TO EAT

12 Hotel-é Tabrīz
10 Chelō Kabābī-yé Ūldūz

OTHER

1 Customs Office
6 Kelīsā-yé Anjīlī (Evangelical Church)
7 Kelīsā-yé Sarkīs-é Moghaddas (Armenian Church of St Sarkis)
8 Kelīsā-yé Ādventīst (Adventist
  Church)
9 Takhtī Stadium (Estādyūm-é Takhtī)
11 Iran Air
13 Tabrīz University (Dāneshgāh-é
  Tabrīz)
14 Casualty Clinic

century. The greatest boost to Tabrīz came with the opening up of Persia to the West at the turn of this century, when it became the main staging post between the interior of Iran and the Black Sea and, for a short time, the economic capital. In 1908 it was the centre of a revolt against Mohammad Alī Shāh, which was only put down with the brutal intervention of the Russians. It was occupied by Russians several times in the first half of this century, including most of both world wars; it was they who built a railway line to the border at Julfa. The town fell even more rapidly into decline after the Russian Revolution, which all but closed its north-west corridor to Europe. The railway line into the former USSR was of little importance until recently, but it has increased in significance in the '90s as a result of Iran's friendlier relations with its northern neighbours. The line to Turkey was of operation for some years the Iranian revolution, but has recently reopened.

Tabrīz regained its commercial importance after WWII, but the air of faded elegance is beginning to look decidedly shabby.

Orientation
The main street is Kheyābūn-é Emām Khomeinī, which runs almost as far east and west as you could go without actually leaving the city. The centre is Meidūn-é Shahrdārī, on the south-west of which stands the imposing edifice of the shahrdārī. The large, modern railway station, with its own vast carpark and mosque, lies at the western edge of Kheyābūn-é 22 Bahman, the western extension of Kheyābūn-é Emām Khomeinī. The Ghūrī Chāy river runs through Tabrīz, draining into the Daryāché-yé Orūmīyé a

short distance to the west. Most places of interest to the visitor are to the south of this river, and along or north of Kheyābūn-é Emām Khomeinī. The exception is the train station, which is five km from the centre of town. There are plenty of hotels within easy walking distance of the bus station. The airport is about 20 minutes' drive to the north of Tabrīz.

Information

The ostāndārī (☎ 22696) is a few metres east of Bank Melli Iran on Meidūn-é Shohadā. For visa extensions go to the police headquarters in Kūché-yé Arg, near the Arg itself.

Tourist Office The tourist office (☎ 23841) is a little difficult to find, and you will not get to it by following the misleading signposts in English supposedly directing customers to it. Despite what they and the maps say, it is actually a few metres west of Meidūn-é Honarestān, which is 30 rials by shared taxi west of the bus station: ask for Ershād-é Eslāmī. It is not marked in English. Perhaps it will move to a more convenient site.

Money Bank Melli Iran (☎ 25251) is on the north side of Meidūn-é Shohadā. I had great problems in trying to change money here and eventually had to give up.

Post & Telecommunications The main post office (☎ 22084) is at the east side of Meidūn-é Shohadā, opposite Bank Melli Iran; the main telegraph office is in a turning off Kheyābūn-é Seghat-ol-Eslām immediately to the south of the river. The dialling code for Tabrīz is 041.

Consulate The Turkish Consulate (☎ 52417, 66474) is at 516 Kheyābūn-é Sharī'atī.

Maps The only complete map of Tabrīz available in the city is a sketch map in Persian with a very limited amount of out-of-date information. It's produced by the Ministry of Culture & Islamic Guidance and

is available at the tourist office and some hotels. In Tehrān I found a Gītā Shenāsī map of Tabrīz (300 rials) in English and Persian, but most of the listings on it dated from before the revolution.

Medical Services For emergencies telephone ☎ 118 or 35053. The casualty clinic is close to the Darvāzé-yé Tehrān on the far eastern edge of town. Flag down a taxi from the centre of town and offer 500 rials for the trip to the 'Markaz-é Ūrzhāns-é Tabrīz'.

Emergency The police headquarters (☎ 58035, 73032) is in Kūché-yé Arg, near the Arg itself.

Masjed-é Kabūd

The Masjed-é Kabūd (Blue Mosque), on the north side of Kheyābūn-é Emām Khomeinī, dates from 1465. Despite being damaged by earthquakes it is still notable for its extremely good tilework, although it is now in a rather sorry state, with the blue mosaics in its portal heavily damaged and half missing. Much of the rest of the mosque stands, but it is little more than a ruin. The mosque is now almost permanently closed, but renovation work and eventual reopening seem inevitable.

Arg-é Tabrīz

The Arg, a huge and crumbling brick citadel, is a notable landmark that was built in the early 14th century on the site of a massive mosque which collapsed over 500 years ago, and which must have been one of the largest ever constructed. In earlier times criminals would be hurled from the peak of the citadel into a ditch below, and it is said that one woman sentenced to this end was saved from death by the parachute-like effect of her chādor.

Mūzé-yé Āzarbāyjān

The Āzarbāyjān Museum, next to the Masjed-é Kabūd, has a small collection of items of sculpture and calligraphy.

Bazaar

This very large and labyrinthine 15th-century covered bazaar is much diminished in its variety of goods, but still a great place for getting hopelessly lost amid its dusty architectural splendours. Carpet making is still the main trade, but Tabrīz is also renowned for its silverwork and jewellery. The spice bazaar, one of the most pungent and impressive in Iran, is an excellent place for picking up henna. Look out also for the traditional Āzarī hats resembling those worn by the gypsies of Eastern Europe.

Churches

From the earliest days of Christianity there has been a sizeable Armenian community in Tabrīz, and the city boasts a number of churches, including one mentioned by Marco Polo on his travels. Probably the most interesting one is the old but substantially rebuilt **Kelīsā-yé Maryam-é Moghaddas** (Church of St Mary) on the south-west side of Meidūn-é Namāz.

Bāgh-é Mellī

This pleasant large park, around an artificial lake east of Tabrīz, is a popular weekend retreat for the locals.

Places to Stay

There are hotels and mosāferkhūnés from the train station to the eastern edge of town, along and near Kheyābūn-é 22 Bahman, Kheyābūn-é Emām Khomeinī and Bolvār-é 29 Bahman; the greatest concentration is west of Meidūn-é Shahrdārī. The best hotels are at the east and west of town, and the cheapies, which aren't recommended, are mostly near the bus station. Finding a room is not generally a problem.

About five minutes' walk due east from the train station are a couple of mosāferkhūnés, the *Mosāferkhūné-yé Īrān* (marked in English 'Passengers House', and not to be confused with the Hotel-é Īrān) (☎ 80792) and the *Mosāferkhūné-yé Khayyām* (not marked in English) (☎ 42480), both on the south side of Kheyābūn-é 22 Bahman: the Khayyām is closer to the station.

There are two good hotels within very easy walking distance of the railway station: the plush *Hotel-é Daryā* ('Darya Hotel') (☎ 44464) and the *Hotel-é Īrān* ('Iran Hotel') (☎ 49516), both on the south side of Kheyābūn-é 22 Bahman, straight ahead as you walk out of the station. They charge around 4000/6000 rials a single/double with private bathroom. The *Hotel-é Morvārīd* ('Hotel Morvarid') (☎ 56398) opposite the south-east corner of the Bāgh-é Golestān is a reasonable and friendly place with singles/doubles at around 2000/3000 rials; the *Pārk Hotel* ('Park Hotel') (☎ 51852) is slightly more comfortable than the Morvārīd, but not friendly and poorer value at 2500 rials for a single with private bathroom and – inexplicably – 6000 rials for a double with private bathroom.

The modern and comfortable *Hotel-é Tabrīz* (still generally known in English as the 'International Hotel') (☎ 31081-8) is some way east of the centre, diagonally opposite the Iran Air office in Chahārrāh-é Āzādī. The hotel no longer has a functioning swimming pool and is not really in the luxury class, but even so it's the best hotel in Āzarbāyjān. It charges 7800 rials for a double with private bathroom, and claims not to have any single rooms. Its restaurant is fairly good. The (unmarked) information desk at the airport can telephone to the hotel to see if there is a room available.

Places to Eat

Tabrīz is the best place in Iran for ābgūsht (also known as dīzī), a stew made of fatty meat, usually beef or mutton, thick chunks of potato and lentils, traditionally served in a pipkin and eaten in a bowl with a spoon. A pestle is provided for grinding up the meat and potatoes, and there is a great art to pouring the ābgūsht from the pipkin and in pounding the ingredients into just the right consistency without using up all the gravy too soon. It is a good idea to take a local with you the first time you try this triumph of Iranian cuisine.

Places to Eat – bottom end There are plenty of chelō kabābīs, sandwich bars, kabābīs, teahouses and ābgūsht places all along Kheyābūn-é Emām Khomeinī. The cheapest places are around Kheyābūn-é Sharī'atī-yé Shomālī though some of these look and smell distinctly unwholesome.

Places to Eat – middle
The subterranean *Chelō Kabābī-yé Ūldūz* (not marked in English) on the south side of Kheyābūn-é Emām Khomeinī, just west of Kūché-yé Bazafyān (the first alley to the west of Kheyābūn-é Āzādī) is worth tracking down. It has good veal schnitzel for 1700 rials, as well as steaks and some other Continental dishes. The restaurant of the *Hotel-é Tabrīz* is not at all bad either. Most of the middle-range hotels have their own restaurants.

Things to Buy
Items to look for in the bazaar include silverwork, jewellery, carpets and Āzarī hats. A wide range of Turkish goods, mostly cheap trinkets and trash, finds its way to the shops of Tabrīz.

Getting There & Away
To/From Azerbaijan Trains leave for Jolfā (the station for Baku and Moscow) on Sunday morning. I was assured at the station that foreigners would have no problem in buying a ticket on the morning of the day before, but it is better to buy one at least a week in advance. Take your passport and visa with you. See also the Getting There & Away chapter, and check all information locally.

To/From Turkey The usual route from here is via Mākū (several buses a day, 242 km, four hours, 400/560 rials 'lux'/'super') and the very congested border crossing at Bāzargān. There are occassional daily buses direct to Erzurum and Istambul. See the Getting There & Away chapter for details.

Air There is an unmarked information desk in the airport departure lounge (reached from the arrivals area by turning left and past the Iran Air security office). Iran Air flies from Tabrīz to Mashhad (Monday and Friday, 7 pm, 1¾ hours), Rasht (Wednesday and Saturday at 11.30 am, 45 minutes) and Tehrān (daily at 9.30 am, 1.10, 4.55 and 7.25 pm, one hour, 5810 rials).

An air link between Tehrān and Baku via Tabrīz should open in 1992, and there is also talk of starting up a direct service from Tabrīz to Erzurum and Istanbul, but details were not available at the time of writing.

The Iran Air office (☎ 52000) is in its own building on the north-east corner of Chahārrāh-é Āzādī.

Bus & Minibus The bus terminal (☎ 57132) is hidden from the street behind iron gates in Kheyābūn-é Jomhūrī-yé Eslāmī, opposite the north-east corner of Bāgh-é Golestān. It is rather chaotic even though the bus company offices are all in the same building. People are not helpful about showing you to the correct bay, which will only be marked with the name of the destination in Persian, so you should arrive in plenty of time. Buses usually leave punctually.

The ground floor houses the offices for buses to local destinations, but not Ardabīl. The ticket booths are marked only by the name of the destination in Persian and not by the number of the bus cooperative. Even on the ticket there is no mention of the name of the company. Among many other places, there are local services to:

Jolfā – several a day, 137 km, 2½ hours, 250/270 rials 'lux'/'super'
Mākū – several a day, 242 km, four hours, 400/560 rials 'lux'/'super'
Marāghé – several a day, 143 km, 2½ hours
Marand – several a day, 71 km, one hour
Orūmīyé – several a day, 322 km, five hours, 400/500 rials 'lux'/'super'
Sanandaj – at least one a day, 442 km, eight hours
Sharafkhūné – several a day, 97 km, 1½ hours

Upstairs are the ticket offices for long-distance buses. Destinations (at least one bus a day unless stated otherwise) include:

Ahvāz – 1087 km, 18 hours
Andīmeshk – 940 km, 15 hours
Ardabīl – 216 km, four hours, 430 rials 'lux'
Bākhtarān – 578 km, 11 hours, 1265/1670 rials 'lux'/'super'
Bandar-é Anzalī – 416 km, seven hours
Chālūs – 679 km, 11 hours
Esfahān – 1038 km, 16 hours, 2200 rials 'super'
Istanbul via Mākū, Bāzargān & Erzurum – occasional services; see the Getting There & Away chapter
Mashhad – 1548 km, 25 hours, 3430 rials 'super'
Rasht – 481 km, eight hours
Sārī – 861 km, 14 hours
Shīrāz – 1519 km, 24 hours, 2530 rials 'lux'
Tehrān – 624 km, nine hours, 1100/1400 rials 'lux'/'super'
Yāsūj – 1541 km, 25 hours

Train There are two overnight trains daily to Tehrān (around 15 hours) stopping at Marāghé, Meyāné, Zanjān, Ghazvīn and Karaj; 1st class sleepers are available. For information on trains to Jolfā for Baku and Moscow see the To/From Azerbaijan entry. The service to the Turkish border at Rāzī and beyond has recently resumed, see the Getting There & Away chapter for details.

Shared Taxi & Savārī There are shared taxis and savārīs to Orūmīyé from outside the bus terminal; the fare is 2000 to 2500 rials. By car it is about four hours; public transport does not generally use the ferry across Daryāché-yé Orūmīyé, but has to go the long route on either of the run-down roads around the lake. There are shared taxis and savārīs to other destinations according to demand.

Getting Around
To/From the Airport A taxi from the airport into town is 500 rials for a shared lift or 1500 rials for a single passenger. The airport police check the fares with the driver and his passengers before letting the taxi leave. Your chances of being overcharged, so long as you fix the fare before setting out, are therefore slimmer than at most airports. There is no airport bus.

Bus & Minibus There is no bus service directly from the centre to the train station. Buses and minibuses run along Kheyābūn-é

Emām Khomeinī, but you are better off taking a shared taxi.

Taxi You can take a taxi into town from outside the train station. For a shared lift into town the correct fare is something like 150 rials, or 600 rials for a solo passenger. Alternatively you can walk east about 100 metres from outside the station to Meidūn-é Rāh-é Āhan and take bus No 129 from the stop next to the stall on the south-east corner of the square (selling bus tickets at 15 rials each) to Meidūn-é Emām Khomeinī. From here take a shared taxi to Meidūn-é Shahrdārī for 30 rials.

Getting around is mostly a matter of saying 'mostaghīm' ('straight ahead') to shared taxi drivers and covering small distances on foot. From the centre of town you should have no problem in getting a lift as far west as the train station or as far east as Chahārrāh-é Āzādī. The bus station is easily reached too: just stand on the correct side of

the road and shout *'termīnāl'*. You may be dropped off at the bazaar.

JOLFĀ   جلفا

At one time, Jolfā was the major settlement of Armenians in Persia, until Shāh Abbās I moved them to 'New Jolfā' outside Esfahān. It is the border post where railway passengers between Moscow and Tehrān change trains because of the different gauges. See To/From Azerbaijan & Russia in the Getting There & Away chapter for details of this route. Foreigners are not allowed to stop in Jolfā without advance permission, although it is possible to stay in Julfa, across the border on the other side of the river.

Kelīsā Darré Shām   کلیسا دره شام

The Kelīsā Darré Shām (Church of St Stephanos) is a spectacular and very remote Armenian monastery in the hills about 18 km to the west-north-west of Jolfā. It is possible to visit if you have permission in writing, obtainable through the tourist office or the public security department of the ostāndārī in Tabrīz, though they might direct you elsewhere

The monastery is right on the Azerbaijan border at a point where two rivers, the Rūd-é Aras and the Rūd-é Āgh Chāy, meet. The earliest surviving part of the building dates back to the 14th century and the main part to the 16th. A church is said to been founded on the site by St Bartholomew (one of the earliest Christian apostles in Armenia) in around 62 AD – about the same time as the establishment of the Church of St Thaddaeus near Mākū. The well preserved, but now hauntingly isolated, stone building is remarkable for the very fine exterior reliefs, with Armenian crosses, angels and other Christian motifs.

Getting There & Away

You will need to charter a taxi to Jolfā (1500 to 2000 rials an hour) and pick up an official or military escort for the rough road skirting along the border.

ARDABĪL   اردبیل

Although Ardabīl is a town of great antiquity, it is best known for the **Bogh'é-yé Sheikh Safī-od-Dīn**, the shrine of Sheikh Safī-od-Dīn (1252 to 1334), forefather of the Safavid dynasty. A Sufi and a Shi'ite, his own religious beliefs were passed on by his descendant Shāh Esmā'īl I and became the othodoxy of Iran. As well as Sheikh Safī-od-Dīn and Shāh Esmā'īl I, this fine early 14th-century mausoleum, with its circular domed tower, contains the tombs of various other notables. Sheikh Safī-od-Dīn's father Sheikh Jebrā'īl is buried at a 16th-century mausoleum in the village of Kalkhōrān, three km north-east of Ardabīl. The shrine of

Safī-od-Dīn is in the north-west part of town in Kheyābūn-é Ālī Ghāpū.

Places to Stay

Among other, simpler, hotels, there is the good *Hotel-é Sheikh Safī* (☎ 4000) in Kheyābūn-é Sharī'atī which charges 3500/4800 rials a single/double with private bathroom. The *Āsyā Hotel* in Kheyābūn-é Emām Khomeinī charges 1500/2500 rials a single/double.

Getting There & Away

Ardabīl is the main junction between Āzarbāyjān and Gīlān. There is at least one bus daily from Ardabīl to Tabrīz (216 km, four hours, 430 rials 'lux') and there are several buses a week to Sārī (645 km, 11 hours). There are also regular savārīs and minibuses to Āstārā (68 km, 1½ hours). The best bus cooperative, No 15, is in Kheyābūn-é Emām Khomeinī.

MARĀGHÉ   مراغه

The ancient city of Marāghé, on the east side of the Daryāché-yé Orūmīyé, was for a short period the capital of the Mongol Il-Khanid dynasty which ruled from Āzarbāyjān; the name Marāghé means 'wallowing-place for a beast', and it is said that the Mongols favoured this site for the pastures it afforded their horses. To this day Marāghé remains fertile, and the area around the town is known for the excellence of its seedless grapes.

Although almost nothing remains of the famous *rasadkhūné* (observatory) that Hulagu Khan established in a cave outside Marāghé in the 13th century, there are four interesting brick tomb towers surviving in the town. The Gombad-é Sorkh, the Gombad-é Kabūd and the Borj-é Mādar-é Holākū Khān) are 12th century, and the Gombad-é Ghaffārīyé, dates from the early 14th century. The earliest and probably most important of these is the Gombad-é Sorkh, which is noted for the glazed tiling used to decorate its exterior walls, one of the earliest known examples of this in Iran. The tomb towers are difficult to find and it is worth hiring a taxi driver as guide.

You can see many old pigeon towers in the town of Bonāb, 17 km to the west of Marāghé.

Getting There & Away

Each day there are two express trains (11 to 13½ hours) and one regular train (14 hours) from Marāghé to Tehrān (via Meyāné, Zanjān, Ghazvīn and Karaj), and two express trains to Tabrīz (2¾ hours). The train station is south of town.

There are also buses to Orūmīyé (several a day, 224 km, four hours) and Tabrīz (143 km, 2½ hours).

The Caspian Provinces

ایران شمالی (استانهای گیلان و مازندران)

The provinces of Gīlān and Māzandarān occupy the coastal belt between the Alborz mountain range and the southern shores of the Caspian Sea (Daryā-ye Khazar). To Iranians the Caspian region, known as Shomāl ('The North'), is a tourist area favoured above any of the dry and dusty towns of the central plateau usually visited by foreign tourists. No-one can claim to have seen Iran if they have not travelled through this geographically and culturally unique northern enclave, and the locals are very kind people.

The terrain is varied, but in general the two provinces are thickly forested and have a coastal plain up to 100 km wide. The main exception is Māzandarān, which is mostly steppe in the north-east. Gīlān and Māzandarān are very rainy for much of the year; they're mild in winter, pleasant in spring and autumn, and cooler than central Iran in summer, but exceptionally humid.

The forest, especially that of southern Māzandarān, is rich in wildlife. Much of it is all but impenetrable and it gives cover to a wide range of animals, including wild boar, jackal, leopard and tiger. Recently there was even an alleged sighting of a Persian lion, a beast long believed extinct.

Nowadays the Caspian coastline is one of the most densely populated regions in Iran, but it hasn't always been so. There have been small settlements in both provinces from the earliest times, but until fairly recently the area was too unhealthy because of its malarial swamps and too thick with forest to permit settlement on a large scale. Although much of the forest has been cleared and the swamp reclaimed over the centuries, to make way for settlement and agriculture, the southern parts of both provinces are still sparsely populated and lack communications.

The rainy Caspian plateau is ideal for growing rice, which is the main agricultural crop of the region; cotton is also harvested in both provinces, and oranges and other citrus fruits are becoming increasingly important in Māzandarān. Many varieties of sea and river fish are found here, most notably sturgeon, salmon-trout, perch and pike. Caviar processing has become very lucrative now that nearly all the produce is able to find a foreign market once more.

The Caspian Sea itself is surprisingly peripheral to the activities of most of the inhabitants of the coast, and it isn't even put to much use by the tourists and holiday-makers who come here in large numbers. There are few beaches or other seaside attractions, and tourism, although important, is very much a do-it-yourself business. There's remarkably little in the way of organised activities for visitors, and most Iranian holidaymakers come here by private car, very much making their own entertainment.

The whole of Iran's Caspian coast is very undeveloped for tourism. How much you like the region will depend very much on whether you view this lack of development as an advantage or a disadvantage. Because of the general shortage of water in Iran, and the great Iranian love of parks, gardens and greenery, Gīlān and Māzandarān naturally have a draw on the inhabitants of the dry and dusty plains.

Where you go depends on your reasons for visiting. If you have come for the scenery and change of air, it's best to stick mainly to the narrow, central coastal strip, roughly between Rāmsar and Nōshahr. If you are more interested in historic or archaeological sites, visit Sārī, Gorgān, Behshahr and Āmol and the surrounding areas. Whatever your incentive for coming, there are three places you should not miss: the spectacular 11th-century tomb tower of Gombad-é Kāvūs in the town of the same name, the breathtakingly beautiful mountain village of Māsūlé, and the small coastal town of Rāmsar, the most attractive of all the resorts.

Probably the most interesting historical structures in the Caspian provinces are the many surviving tomb towers, which reached their peak in Māzandarān during the 15th century. This chapter includes the more interesting and accessible ones, but there are many others worthy of attention.

Although public transport isn't well developed in this part of Iran, and there are very few east-west bus services within the two provinces, getting around by shared taxi or savārī is simple along the main roads that link all the towns and skirt the coast; sometimes you can travel hundreds of km without changing car. On the other hand, transport is difficult away from the main roads, and many of the villages are still extremely remote. There are no passenger shipping services anywhere along the coast, and it isn't easy to hire a boat.

Except in the peak holiday season and on public holidays, accommodation is rarely a problem; there are hotels, motels and mosāferkhūnés along all the main roads, especially in the main tourist areas of the coastline. Try to avoid visiting in or near any public holidays at any time of year, because without firm reservations you are going to have a terrible time finding anywhere to stay. Charges are higher than elsewhere in mainland Iran, but the standard is better than average. The better and more expensive places tend to fill up most quickly. Weekends in good weather can also be busy.

Gīlān Province   استان گیلان

Population: 2.1 million
Area: 14,700 sq km

The largely rural province of Gīlān was independent until the 16th century and still has its own distinctive dialect and dress. Because of Gīlān's later development, there's less of archaeological interest than in Māzandarān, and nothing of architectural greatness in the towns. Although Gīlān is less of a tourist area than Māzandarān, there are many routes of great scenic attraction, even on the main roads.

The province extends from the Caucasus in the north-west of Iran to the western edge of Māzandarān, and is bordered on the west by Āzarbāyjān-é Sharghī, and on the south by Zanjān province. The coastal strip is widest in the centre, where it is more densely populated. Gilān's capital is Rasht, the most important city in the whole region, and its main port is Bandar-é Anzalī, a town at the mouth of the Mordāb-é Anzalī lagoon. The most important river is the Sefīd Rūd, which runs from the Sadd-é Sefīd Rūd (Sefīd Rūd Dam), on the border with Zanjān province, to the Caspian Sea. This is the wettest part of Iran, and it produces rice, silk cocoons and tea, which is nowadays the major agricultural speciality of Gīlān.

A road crosses into the former Soviet republic of Azerbaijan at Āstārā, but the Caspian passenger ferry between Bandar-é Anzalī and Baku has been out of operation for some years.

1990 Earthquake

Iran is especially prone to earthquakes, but there has never been such a devastating one recorded so far north as that which occurred in Gīlān in 1990. Early in the morning of 21 June a series of tremors, measuring 7.7 on the Richter scale, struck just north of Rasht.

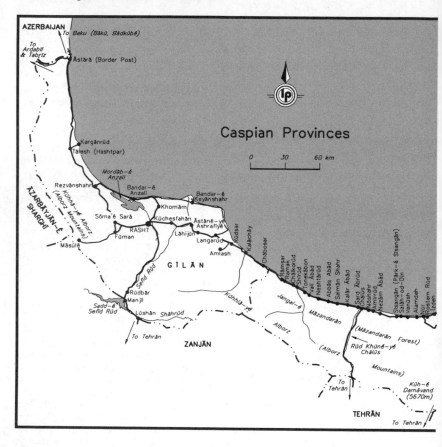

The scale of the devastation surprised seismologists. The shallow initial tremor, only about 10 km below the earth's crust, would have caused considerable damage, but it is thought that the effect was exacerbated by further tremors shortly afterwards.

Even though the Iranian emergency services had proved their ability to cope with disasters many times since the beginning of the Iran-Iraq War, they had never had to deal with such a large operation. Rescue efforts were hampered by the inaccessibility of many of the mountain villages and by the reluctance of the authorities to accept assistance from abroad. Although some foreign rescue teams did get in, there was a backlash from hardliners in the government who insisted that it would be better to bow to the will of God and allow thousands of people to die, than to drink the poison cup of Western aid. In the end the leadership agreed that it was willing to accept assistance from any country except Israel or South Africa, but many foreign volunteers complained of a lack of local coordination.

More than 40,000 people were killed and many more were injured or made homeless. Much of the damage has yet to be cleared,

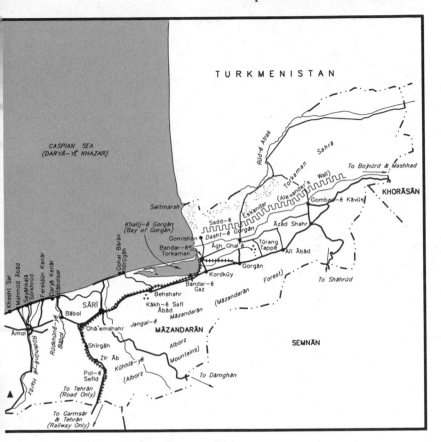

and there's a certain amount of barely concealed resentment among the victims that more has not been done for them by the government. Although the flimsiness of much of the housing in the area was a major factor in the heavy casualty toll, it isn't clear whether any architectural lessons have been learned by local planners.

If you want to gain a true picture of the scale of the human tragedy caused by the earthquake, visit the excellent photographic exhibition in Tehrān at the Mūzé-yé Honarhā-yé Mo'āser, which has both Iranian and foreign contributions taken at the scene;

this looks likely to become a permanent exhibition.

RASHT
رشت

Seven metres below sea level and 15 km inland from the Mordāb-é Anzalī (Anzalī Lagoon), to which it is connected by the Seyāh Rūd, Rasht is the largest settlement of the southern Caspian and the industrial centre of the region. Rasht is one of the wettest places in Iran, and can be very humid. The city has sprawled enormously over recent years, sacrificing some of its charm for the sake of development. Only 324

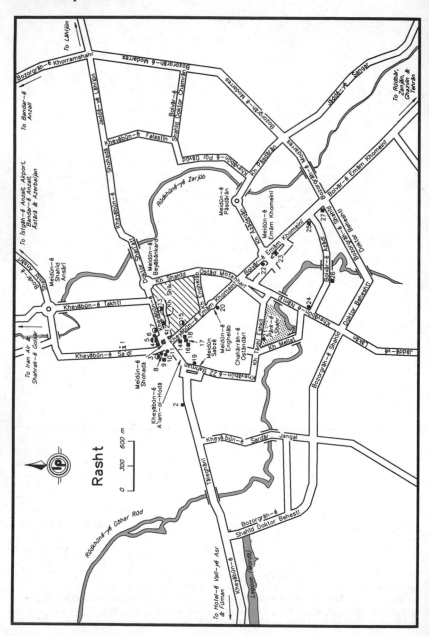

and Rashtī jokes are as much part of the national culture as Irish jokes in England. Much fun is made of the curiously lisping Rashtī accent, which can sound a little comical to the outsider. Some jokes run on the lines of 'There's this Rashtī and there's this Esfahānī...', poking fun at the meanness and cleverness of the Esfahānī and the naivety and unquestioning generosity of the Rashtī.

History
Rasht grew into a town around the 14th century, soon becoming the major settlement in Gīlān. The city has been occupied by Russians several times in its history, most ruinously in 1668 when almost the whole population was massacred by the rebel forces of the Cossack brigand Stenka Razin, who had already destroyed the Persian navy in the Caspian Sea, and whose sole aims in life appear to have been rape and pillage. During WWI the city was again occupied by Russians, and in 1920 Bolsheviks destroyed much of the bazaar, driving many of the inhabitants into temporary exile. Nowadays Rasht is the centre of distribution for the local rice and silk cocoon industries, although the cocoon industry has declined in recent years.

Orientation
Rasht is a flat and fairly featureless city. The three main streets, Kheyābūn-é Doktor Sharī'atī, Kheyābūn-é Sa'dī and Bolvār-é Emām Khomeinī, converge at the main square, the vast Meidūn-é Shohadā. Most of the major points of interest are within walking distance of this square, to the north, south or east, although the hotels are spread out at some distance. Most people arriving by public transport will end up in or near Meidūn-é Shohadā. Two rivers meander through Rasht, the Rūdkhūné-yé Zarjūb and the Rūdkhūné-yé Gōhar Rūd. The airport (☎ 2001) is a short distance north of Rasht on the Bandar-é Anzalī road. Main roads out of Rasht are all clearly signposted in English.

km north of Tehrān along a good motorway, Rasht is a very popular weekend or holiday destination for Tehrānīs, for whom the change in climate and scenery is enough in itself, but the city has little to offer the sightseer. For most foreigners Rasht is no more than a convenient staging post for a tour of the region.

The people of Rasht are popularly believed to be the kindest and most hospitable in Iran, but also the most slow-witted,

Information

The ostāndārī (☎ 32233, 32085-8) is in the north-west corner of the Pārk-é Shahr. For visa matters enquire at police headquarters on the north-east side of Meidūn-é Shohadā. The shahrdārī (☎ 22166) is on the west side of Meidūn-é Shohadā.

Tourist Office The tourist office (☎ 22006, 22284), as usual not marked in English, is on the east side of Kheyābūn-é Sa'dī, about five minutes' walk north from Meidūn-é Shohadā, in a block next to the Bank Tejarat. The staff do not speak English, and they were unable to hide their mystification at my managing to track them down.

Money Bank Melli Iran is on the south of Meidūn-é Enghelāb. Black market roubles can be bought here; ask around at the bazaar.

Post & Telecommunications The main post office is the large building on the north side of Meidūn-é Shohadā, and the telegraph office is on the west side of Meidūn-é Emām Khomeinī. There's also a small, inefficient telephone office for trunk (but not international) calls next to the Hotel-é Ordībehesht on the west side of Meidūn-é Shohadā. Directory enquiries are on ☎ 118. The dialling code for Rasht is 0231.

Maps The tourist office has a combined map of Rasht, Gīlān, Lāhījūn and Bandar-é Anzalī, but it isn't much use unless you can read Persian, for only the roads are marked in English. There's also a more detailed Gītā Shenāsī map for 300 rials, but again most of the information is in Persian only.

Medical Services For emergencies telephone ☎ 118 (the same as the directory enquiries number). The casualty clinic is just south-west of Meidūn-é Emām Khomeinī.

Emergency The police headquarters (☎ 22101, 22105) are on the north-east side of Meidūn-é Shohadā.

Mūzé-yé Rasht

The Rasht Museum (☎ 27979), on the north side of Kheyābūn-é Tāleghānī about 250 metres to the west of Sabzé Meidūn, holds a small collection of archaeological exhibits. It's open from 9 am to 4 pm Tuesday to Sunday (entrance 50 rials).

Bazaar

The uncovered bazaar is bounded by Kheyābūn-é Emām Khomeinī and Kheyābūn-é Doktor Sharī'atī. Little of any great antiquity remains, since most of the bazaar was burned by the Bolsheviks in 1920.

Places to Stay – bottom end

More than 20 mosāferkhūnés are listed in Rasht, so you should be able to find some inexpensive hideaway easily enough. The greatest concentration is around the central bazaar district, which is also the most convenient place to stay.

The *Mehmūnpazīr-é Kārvān* ('Carvan Hotel') (☎ 22362), 50 metres south-east of Meidūn-é Shohadā, is friendly and charges 2100 rials for a clean triple with shared bathroom, having no smaller rooms. There are a couple of mosāferkhūnés in the same league in Kūché-yé Yūsefī (the first kūché after the Kārvān): the *Mosāferkhūné-yé Golestān* (not marked in English) and the *Mosāferkhūné-yé Fārs*.

There are several hotels in the official one-star category, offering simple accommodation with better personal hygiene facilities than the mosāferkhūnés: the *Hotel-é Valī-yé Asr* (☎ 27907), at the far west of Rasht on the road to Fūman, is only convenient if you have your own transport; the *Hotel-é Keivān* (☎ 22967), is in Kūché-yé Yūsefī off Kheyābūn-é Emām Khomeinī; and the *Hotel-é Pāmchāl* (☎ 33822) is in Bolvār-é Emām Khomeinī. One other place that has been recommended is the *Hotel-é Īrān-é Javān* (☎ 22362), in Kheyābūn-é Shīk just off Meidūn-é Shohadā.

Places to Stay – middle

Most foreigners end up at the *Hotel-é Ordībehesht* (marked in English 'Hotel

Ordibehesht') (☎ 22210/29211), in Meidūn-é Shahrdārī immediately west of Meidūn-é Shohadā. Very convenient if you arrive in town by shared taxi or savārī and only too visible from the main square, this monstrous carbuncle of a tower block isn't half as bad as it looks, although it is a little draughty. It charges 4800/3600 rials a double with/ without private bathroom. A slightly cheaper place and less of an eyesore is the *Hotel-é Pardīs* (☎ 31177/31188) at the intersection of Bolvār-é Emām Khomeinī and Bolvār-é Āzādī.

Places to Stay – top end
The modern *Mehmūnsarā-yé Bozorg-é Gīlān* (also known as the *Kādūs*) (☎ 30991, 30992) is on the south side of Bolvār-é Āzādī. It tends to fill up quickly in the tourist season.

Places to Eat
Chicken and fish are very common ingredients in Rashtī cooking, as well as pickles of various kinds. Many restaurants serve fesenjūn.

There are plenty of snack bars, fast food places and chelō kabābīs along Kheyābūn-é Doktor Sharī'atī, Kheyābūn-é Ostād Motahharī and Kheyābūn-é Taghī Eshkīl, and especially around Sabzé Meidūn. Some of the fast food joints along Kheyābūn-é Taghī Eshkīl are quite good. The restaurant at the *Hotel-é Ordībehesht* is rather expensive for what it offers, such as shishliks (not the world's best) without rice for 1700 rials. There's a better restaurant in the *Mehmūnsarā-yé Bozorg-é Gīlān*.

Things to Buy
A tiny drapery shop on Sabzé Meidūn, not marked in English but recognisable by the loom behind the window, sells woollen gloves and colourful thick socks in traditional Gīlān designs. A pair of plain, thick, white woollen gloves is quite a bargain at only 1500 rials, and a pair of decorated thick woollen socks is the same price. Some other items are partly synthetic. The shopkeeper speaks English.

If you are looking for caviar (officially a state monopoly), persistent but discreet enquiries at the bazaar may be rewarded. Iranians told me that this was the best place to buy it in Iran, but I didn't have any luck. Prices here should be a little lower than in Tehrān.

Getting There & Away
Rasht is better set up for public transport than anywhere else in the Caspian provinces, but not very developed compared with most of Iran. Aeroplane and bus tickets are in short supply, and many passengers have to resort to shared taxis and savārīs.

The road to Tehrān is good, and one of the most scenic drives in Iran, although much of it passes through some of the areas worst affected by the 1990 earthquake. Traffic is heavy on most roads out of Rasht.

Air Iran Air (☎ 29705) flies from Rasht to Bandar-é Abbās (Tuesday and Friday, 9.10 am, two hours), Mashhad (Sunday and Thursday, 9 am, 1½ hours), and Tehrān (Wednesday and Saturday, 12.45 pm; Sunday and Thursday, 1.10 pm; Tuesday and Friday, 2.40 pm; all 45 minutes, 4970 rials). Its office recently moved to a new building in Shahrak-é Golsār, some way out from the centre. To get there take a shared taxi north from the main post office to Shahrak-é Golsār (100 rials) and ask to be dropped off at the airline office.

Bus & Minibus Cooperative Bus Company No 7 (☎ 22599) is about 50 metres north of Meidūn-é Shohadā on the west side of Kheyābūn-é Sa'dī. Although the office is often very chaotic, this is the first place to ask; if they don't have a bus going where you want, they'll tell you who does. Cooperative Bus Company No 8 is on the east side of Kheyābūn-é Emām Khomeinī 250 metres south-east of Meidūn-é Shohadā. Cooperative Bus Company No 11 is immediately east of Meidūn-é Shohadā, and Cooperative Bus Company No 1 is 200 metres further east on the south side of Kheyābūn-é Doktor Sharī'atī.

Among other destinations, there are several buses daily to:

Ahvāz – 1049 km, 17 hours
Esfahān – 737 km, 12 hours
Fūman – 25 km, 30 minutes
Gorgān – 511 km, nine hours
Mashhad – 1075 km, 18 hours
Orūmīyé – 803 km, 13 hours
Sārī – 380 km, seven hours
Tabrīz – 481 km, nine hours
Tehrān – 324 km, six hours, 500 rials 'lux'

To get to places along the Caspian littoral east of Rasht, take a bus to Sārī, Gorgān or Mashhad and ask to be dropped off on the way.

Buses leave from the relevant bus company office. Tickets can be bought the same day, but it's better to ask the day before as demand is very high and many passengers who don't book early are forced to pay extra to go by savārī in no greater comfort.

Minibuses to Bandar-é Anzalī (40 km, 1¼ hours, 200 rials) and Āstārā (190 km, three hours) leave from a small station at the northern edge of Rasht, the Īstgāh-é Anzalī. To get there, take a shared taxi from the main post office for 50 to 100 rials. If your destination is Bandar-é Anzalī, it's much easier and only a little more expensive to go by shared taxi or savārī from the post office.

Shared Taxi & Savārī Savārīs to and from Rāmsar (116 km, 2¾ hours, 1000 rials) and other points on the Caspian littoral leave from and arrive at Meidūn-é Shohadā. There are regular shared taxis and savārīs to Bandar-é Anzalī (one hour, 250 to 400 rials) from outside the main post office. Savārīs to Tehrān (five hours, 2500 to 4000 rials) and other destinations to the south leave from the west side of Kheyābūn-é Sa'dī about 100 metres north of Meidūn-é Shohadā. You'll have to pay in advance, but there's no need to pay the first price you are asked. Savārīs to Āstārā (2000 rials) leave from the Istgāh-é Anzalī at irregular intervals.

Getting Around
To/From the Airport There's no airport bus

service. Count on around 1000 rials by taxi for a single passenger.

Minibus The minibuses are infrequent and desperately crowded, so you should stick to shared taxis.

Taxi Most shared taxi routes radiate from Meidūn-é Shohadā. However this square is extremely crowded with both traffic and passengers waiting for taxis, so it takes a certain amount of aggression or patience to catch a lift. About 50 rials is enough for most journeys. Most of the taxis in Rasht are blue and white.

ĀSTĀRĀ   آستارا
This small town is in the far north of Gīlān, on the border which divides it from the town of Astara in the republic of Azerbaijan. This is the only legal road crossing between Iran and its northern neighbour. Gun-toting border guards can clearly be seen from Āstārā.

Although devoid of any great historical interest, Āstārā is not unattractive, and there are worse places to spend the night. Due to its proximity to the border, you're not entirely free to travel around this part of Iran; enquire with the police or at your hotel.

Places to Stay
There are some mosāferkhūnés around Meidūn-é Shahrdārī charging around 700 to 1000 rials, all much the same. The best of the cheapies is the *Hotel-é Aras* at 1500 rials.

A step up takes you to the good *Meh-mūnsarā-yé Āstārā* (☎ 2135), in Kheyābūn-é Hakīm Nezāmī by the sea. There's also a very comfortable motel a short distance out of Āstārā which charges 5500 rials for a double with private bathroom.

Getting There & Away
There are three main routes from Āstārā: north to the republic of Azerbaijan, west to Iranian Āzarbāyjān, and south to central Gīlān. The road south is appalling, but the road west is scenic and reasonably good. There are savārīs and minibuses to Rasht

(190 km, three hours), Ardabīl (68 km, 1½ hours) and Tālesh (76 km, two hours), but there's no direct service to Bandar-é Anzalī.

To/From the Republic of Azerbaijan This route isn't much used by foreigners, although Iranian and Azerbaijani citizens from the immediate area can cross visa-free with only a special permit. You will need to have a visa stating Astara as the point of entry or exit, and all sorts of extra documentation if you are also going by private car. Most people will find it much more straightforward to take the train via Jolfā/Julfa (see the Āzarbāyjān chapter).

With the collapse of the old Soviet infrastructure, no facilities of any kind can be guaranteed in Astara or anywhere between there and Baku, 220 km north-north-east, although there's supposed to be one train a day connecting the two towns, and there may or may not be other travel options. It's difficult to get up-to-date information except locally, although the Azerbaijan Embassy in Moscow or the Iranian or Russian Embassy in Baku may be able to help. As a last resort you could get a Persian speaker to contact the Ministry of Culture & Islamic Guidance office in Āstārā (☎ 3056).

See also the Jolfā entry in the Āzarbāyjān chapter, and the Getting There & Away chapter.

MĀSŪLÉ ماسوله
There are many traditional and unspoilt mountain villages throughout Gīlān and Māzandarān, but one of the most breathtakingly beautiful is Māsūlé, 56 km south-south-west of Rasht and 1050 metres above seal level. Approached from Fūman by a dramatic mountain pass and completely surrounded by forest, this perfectly preserved village appears to have grown out of its surroundings like a limpet clinging to a rock. It's formed of several irregular levels of terraced, pale cream houses with grey slate roofs, interspersed with evergreen trees. So steep is the slope that the familiar Iranian network of narrow alleys is entirely absent, and instead the flat roof of each level

of houses forms a pathway for the level above.

Māsūlé has few facilities to offer the visitor, but its inspiring setting makes it a perfect antidote to travel in the dry and dusty central plateau, and well worth a day trip from Rasht. It's bitterly cold in winter, with snow sometimes three metres deep, but the climate in summer is extremely pleasant and bracing.

Getting There & Away
Māsūlé can be reached from Rasht via Fūman by bus or, more likely, savārī. Allow at least 1½ hours for the journey each way.

BANDAR-É ANZALĪ بندر انزلی
This town came into prominence in the early 19th century as a result of the increasing Russian dominance over trade in the Caspian Sea. When traders from western Europe had been the most active in the region, the river port of Langarūd, 96 km to the east, was their main outlet to northern Persia. Around 1800 the Russians established their trading post at Bandar-é Anzalī, taking advantage of its unrivalled natural harbour. Since then it has been the only major port along the southern Caspian coast, and today is the only one active in trade with the former Soviet states.

The Russian influence over Anzalī has been strong, and the city bears a remarkable physical likeness to the Azerbaijani port of Baku, its main trading partner in the north Caspian Sea. There's a provincial Russian air about the town, from its shop displays to its crumbling architecture and lonely promenade, and fair-skinned visitors were usually assumed to be 'Soviet'.

Anzalī has a major caviar-processing factory (although you can't easily buy caviar in town) and is a resort town, albeit a very low-key one. There are some crumbling old ruins of buildings from the 19th century, very Russian in character, around Meidūn-é Emām Khomeinī and the bazaar. Anzalī is the only Iranian Caspian port with a real promenade, but otherwise its tourist potential is rather limited.

Orientation & Information
Bandar-é Anzalī is divided in two by the outlet of the Mordāb-é Anzalī (Anzali Lagoon); a bridge connects the town to a small undeveloped island, Jazīré-yé Beheshtī, just inside the mouth of the lagoon. The docks and customs house are on the east side of the outlet, but the main commercial centre is on the opposite bank, reached by a single bridge called the Pol-é Ghāryān. There's a wide and often wind-swept promenade along the west bank, facing the harbour. The main square, Meidūn-é Emām Khomeinī, is five minutes' walk west from there, past the bazaar. The shahrdārī is in a small park off the promenade, and the main hotel, the Hotel-é Īrān, is two minutes' walk north from there.

Money There was a black market in roubles at the time of writing – ask around in the bazaar, or pick on a sailor.

Places to Stay
The *Hotel-é Īrān* (marked in English 'Iran Hotel'), on the north side of Kheyābūn-é Dādgostarī east of Meidūn-é Emām Khomeinī, is comfortable and has a good view over the harbour from some rooms. It charges 5000 rials a double with private bathroom (there are no singles).

Places to Eat
There are several restaurants in Meidūn-é Emām Khomeinī.

Getting There & Away
There are two roads out of Anzalī, a very poor one north-west to Āstārā and a better one, east veering south, to Rasht.

Bus & Minibus The bus companies are on the east side of Meidūn-é Emām Khomeinī. There are buses from Bandar-é Anzalī to:

Bākhtarān – several a week, 636 km, 12 hours
Bandar-é Abbās – several a week, 1864 km, 32 hours
Esfahān – several a week, 777 km, 13 hours
Mashhad – several a week, 1116 km, 18 hours
Tabrīz – at least one daily, 416 km, seven hours

Tālesh (Hashtpar) – at least two minibuses a day, 70 km, two hours
Tehrān – at least one a day, 365 km, seven hours

There's no direct service to Āstārā: it's best to go from Rasht or Tabrīz, or change at Tālesh (also called Hashtpar).

To/From Rasht From the west side of Meidūn-é Emām Khomeinī there are regular savārīs to Rasht (40 km, one hour, 250 to 400 rials). Alternatively, but less conveniently, you can take a minibus (200 rials) from the Īstgāh-é Anzalī on the eastern approach to the town, which you can reach by shared taxi from Meidūn-é Emām Khomeinī (100 to 200 rials). Although the road distance is short, traffic between Anzalī and Rasht is heavy: an hour is the normal journey time by car.

Sea The Islamic Republic of Iran Shipping Line (IRISL) (☎ 3772) is in the street opposite the customs office (take a taxi to Meidūn-é Gomrok). There are no passenger services from Bandar-é Anzalī; you can ship a car or any other cargo at US$21 a cubic metre (excluding collection and delivery) between Bandar- é Anzalī and Baku, but cannot travel with it. There are at present two or three ships a week to Baku. In Baku or Moscow ask at Morflot (Soviet) State Shipping Lines. With the right permits you can drive from Baku to Moscow if the local situation allows.

LĀHIJŪN لاهیجان
Lāhījūn (also Lāhījān), on the road between Rāmsar and Rasht, is a small town which tends to be a bottleneck for traffic. There are plenty of old traditional Caspian houses with sloping channelled brick roofs and walls of pastel shades including violet. Most of these old houses are rivalled by neighbouring modern houses of metal, plastic and cement.

Lāhījūn was at one time the only settlement of any size in Gīlān, but it fell somewhat into decline after the 14th century when Rasht grew into a town and eclipsed it. It does attract some tourists, but relies more on its many tea factories.

Masjed-é Chahār Ōleyā'

This Mosque of the Four Guardians (also known as the Masjed-é Chahār Pādshāh, 'Mosque of the Four Kings') is on the south of Meidūn-é Sardār Jangal in the west of Lāhījūn. This mausoleum, probably from the 13th century, is dedicated to four members of the Sādāt-é Keyā family, Rezā, Rāzī, Khōr and Alī, although there are only tombs visible for the first three. There are some excellent examples of wood carving inside the mausoleum; one of its carved wooden doors, among the finest surviving examples of its kind, is in the Mūzé-yé Īrān-é Bāstān in Tehrān.

Bogh'é-yé Sheikh Zāhed-é

A short distance east of Lāhījūn on the Langarūd road (100 rials by shared taxi or savārī) is this historic and typically Caspian mausoleum. The square building has a tiled roof surmounted by a sculptured pyramid-shaped painted dome, supported by white pillars on three sides. The inner vault is covered with colourfully tiled plaster mouldings and contains the tombs of Sheikh Zāhed and two other religious figures, Sayyed Rezā Keyā and Gholām Sheikh. The date on the carved wooden tomb of Sheikh Zāhed corresponds to 1419, although part of the original structure may have been built before this date.

Sheitān Kūh

Sheitān Kūh (also Kūh-é Sardār Jangal) – literally 'Devil Mountain' – is a tree-covered hill south of the eastern approach to Lāhījūn, with a natural pool and large park on its slopes.

Places to Stay

The average *Mehmūnsarā-yé Lāhījūn* (☎ 2987, 3051) is on Meidūn-é Sepah-é Pāsdārān, by the eastern approach to Lāhījūn, and the similar *Hotel-é Fajr* (☎ 3081) is four km from Lāhījūn on the Langarūd road. There are also a couple of mosāferkhūnés around Meidūn-é Shohadā.

Getting There & Away

There are several bus companies around Meidūn-é Shohadā with services east, north and west, or you can easily catch a savārī in the same central square going along the main coast road. Buses from other towns in the region stop at Lāhījūn, even if it isn't their final destination.

Māzandarān Province

استان مازندران

Population: 3.5 million
Area: 46,500 sq km
The largely rural province of Māzandarān stretches from the eastern border of Gīlān to the frontiers of Khorāsān Province and the former Soviet republic of Turkmenistan in the north-west, and is flanked to the south by the provinces of Zanjān, Semnān and Tehrān.

There are two distinct geographical regions in the province. The coastal strip, from the western border with Gīlān to about the Khalīj-é Gorgān (Bay of Gorgān) at the far east of the southern Caspian littoral, is fairly similar to Gīlān in its climate and terrain, although slightly drier. At its narrowest and most attractive point, roughly between Rāmsar and Sīsangān, the thickly forested northern slopes of the Alborz roll almost to the sea, but farther east the coastal strip is up to 60 km wide and supports many urban communities.

In the north-east region, where the southern edge is also marked by the Alborz mountains almost as far as the border with Khorāsān Province, the forest is less dense and the peaks are lower than further east. To the north, the country is largely inhospitable steppe and marshland. The Torkaman Sahrā, the harsh Turkoman desert, occupies the strip south of the Rūd-é Atrak which partly forms the border with Turkmenistan. The more fertile Dasht-é Gorgān (Gorgān plain), between the desert and the mountains, formed until recently the limit to settled population. The area is prone to fierce blizzards, snowfalls and avalanches in the winter. The population is largely Turkoman, and the threat posed to the settled communities by this previously wild and nomadic tribe only receded at the end of the last century.

The provincial capital is Sārī, which is of much less commercial importance than Rasht in Gīlān. Almost the whole length of the southern Caspian coast is very densely populated, with almost continuous settlement along many of the main roads. Because of its slightly more favourable conditions, Māzandarān was settled earlier than Gīlān, and the Dasht-é Gorgān in particular is believed to contain some of the most important archaeological sites in West Asia.

After the Arab Conquest the Muslim governors named the province Tabarestān (roughly corresponding to the present-day Māzandarān). It has only attracted settlement on a large scale in relatively recent times, and large areas of forest and swamp had to be cleared to make this what it is today, one of the most important agricultural areas of Iran. Rice and corn are the main crops but orange groves, visible along much of the coast, are becoming increasingly important. Tobacco is grown in some areas. Fishing is less widespread than in Gīlān, and shipping activities are very limited, even at the main port of Nōshahr.

The main tourist area in Māzandarān is the coastal strip between Rāmsar and Bābolsar, where facilities are well developed by Iranian standards. A few travel agencies may be able to organise tours of Māzandarān, but you are pretty much on your own. Foreign tourists are still something of a novelty, but not so much that you'll get constantly stared at, and in general the locals are extremely hospitable and helpful to visitors.

There's no legal crossing point into Turkmenistan from Māzandarān.

SĀRĪ ساری

Sārī is one of the smaller provincial capitals. It's not unattractive and there are a few not-particularly-ancient emāmzādés and some typical Māzandarānī houses with sloping timber roofs, but the unattractive modern buildings interrupt the views of the old ones. Sārī is much smaller and less developed than Rasht and attracts far fewer Iranian holidaymakers, but it does retain a certain charm that is fast disappearing from Rasht; I found Sārī a much more relaxed place. For many the major disincentive is the lack of a good hotel in the town itself.

The origins of Sārī (in ancient times Sārīyé) are lost in the mists of antiquity, but it is known to have been the first capital of the province (then known as Tabarestān) from perhaps as early as the Sassanian era until the 8th or 9th century. This was the last part of Iran to yield to Islam after the Arab Conquest. Some centuries after the capital was moved to Āmol, Sārī was sacked, first by the Mongols and later by Tamerlane. In 1937, Sārī was again made the provincial capital. Sassanian gold and silver pieces unearthed in the area of Sārī are on display in Tehrān, but archaeological work has more or less been abandoned since the revolution.

Orientation

The Rūdkhūné-yé Tajan runs north-south, to the east of the main part of the city. The main square is the small Meidūn-é Haft-é Tīr, almost universally known as Meidūn-é Sā'at ('Clock Square') because of the public clock in its centre – a rare landmark in Iran. The old part of Sārī and most of the modern points of interest are within walking distance of this square, and the bazaar is on either side of Kheyābūn-é Jomhūrī-yé Eslāmī immediately to the south-west. The train station (☎ 5062) is 1½ km south of the centre, and the bus station is in the north-east of Sārī on the city ring road. The main roads out of Sārī are all clearly signposted in English.

Information

The ostāndārī (☎ 4002-4) is behind the central telegraph office 400 metres south of the main square; the shahrdārī (☎ 4035, 5637) is on the east side of Meidūn-é Mostaz'afīn. For visa extensions enquire at the police headquarters.

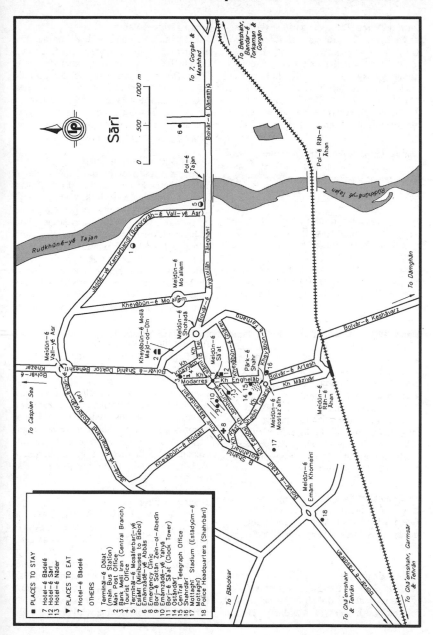

Sārī

PLACES TO STAY
7   Hotel-é Badelé
12 Hotel-é Sārī
13 Hotel-é Nāder

▼ PLACES TO EAT
7   Hotel-é Badelé

OTHERS
1   Terminál-é Dōlat
    (main Bus Station)
3   Main Post Office
4   Bank Melli Iran (Central Branch)
4   Tourist Office
5   Terminál-é Mosáferbarí-yé
    Eslāmí (Minibuses to Bábol)
6   Emāmzādé-yé Abbás
8   Emergency Clinic
9   Borj-é Soltān Zein-ol-Abedīn
10 Emāmzādé-yé Yahyā
11 Borj-é Sā'at (Clock Tower)
14 Ostāndārí
15 Central Telegraph Office
16 Shahrdārí
17 Mottaghī Stadium (Estādyóm-é
    Mottaghī)
18 Police Headquarters (Shahrbānī)

Tourist Office The tourist office (☎ 2007, 2008) is on the east side of Kheyābūn-é Khayyām, 600 metres north of Meidūn-é Sā'at. The people there do a good job producing glossy and unusually informative handouts advertising the province, and even distribute them to other tourist offices around Iran. Perhaps one day they will translate some of them into English.

Money Bank Melli Iran (for foreign exchanges) is on the east side of Kheyābūn-é Modarres at its junction with Kheyābūn-é Amīr Māzandarānī.

Post & Telecommunications The main post office is on the north side of Kheyābūn-é Mollā Majd-od-Dīn, 500 metres north-west of Meidūn-é Shohadā, and the central telegraph office is on the west side of Kheyābūn-é Enghelāb, 400 metres south of Meidūn-é Sā'at. The dialling code for Sārī is 02431.

Maps The tourist office has a combined map of Sārī, Māzandarān, Rāmsar, Āmol, Chālūs, Ghā'emshahr and Gombad-é Kāvūs, but none of the information is in English and the maps don't show any features except the main roads, hospitals and petrol stations. The Gītā Shenāsī map of Sārī (300 rials) is much more detailed but still has very little information in English; it's also very difficult to find. Try the bookshops and magazine stalls along Kheyābūn-é Enghelāb and Kheyābūn-é Jomhūrī-yé Eslāmī.

Medical Services For emergencies dial ☎ 118. The emergency clinic is on the east side of Kheyābūn-é Amīr Māzandarānī, just north of its intersection with Kheyābūn-é Rāzī.

Emergency The police headquarters (☎ 3020-2) is in the south-west of Sārī, on the south side of Bolvār-é Pāsdārān, 100 metres south-west of Meidūn-é Emām Khomeinī.

Emāmzādé-yé Yahyā
Yahyā's mausoleum is inside the bazaar district in a small square at the end of Kūché-yé Dahom 200 metres south-west of Meidūn-é Sā'at. This small and simple circular building with its tiled pyramid-shaped dome dates from the 15th century and is highly regarded for its original wooden doors and tomb box. It's normally possible to go inside only on Thursday afternoon and Friday.

Borj-é Soltān Zein-ol-Ābedīn
A few metres west of the Emāmzādé-yé Yahyā, the early 15th-century Borj-é Soltān Zein-ol-Ābedīn is a small square brick tomb tower with a lower roof leading up to a tiled octagonal dome. Apart from some plain arched brick friezes below the lower and upper roof levels, the exterior is unadorned. The main interest lies inside the building, but unfortunately the heavy wooden door is almost permanently locked, so you are unlikely to be able to see the interior tiling or the tomb itself, which is said to bear a superlatively carved inscription.

Emāmzādé-yé Abbās
The largest of the historical mausoleums of Sārī, the Emāmzādé-yé Abbās is east of the river some 300 metres north of Bolvār-é Dāneshjū (100 rials by shared taxi from Meidūn-é Sā'at). This brick tower features a conical dome and has only simple exterior decorations. It is attached to a low rectangular annexe of modern construction. According to the date on the tomb, which Abbās shares with two others, its box was carved in 1491.

Places to Stay
There's no good hotel in the town itself; the best place to stay is the *Hotel-é Bādelé* (marked in English 'Hotel Badeleh') (☎ 3128), 10 km from Sārī on the road to Gorgān. This place, which is more of a motel than a hotel, is very busy in the holiday season, so it's worth arriving in the morning or checking by telephone. It costs 6300 rials for a comfortable double with private bathroom (no single rooms). From the hotel into

town by shared taxi is 200 rials: just stand opposite the hotel and flag one down. The shared taxi will drop you off at Meidūn-é Sā'at. Getting back is more of a problem. You should avoid being a solo passenger if you don't want to be charged up to 2500 rials – the correct telephone taxi fare is about 1200 rials.

If you get stuck in Sārī itself, there are a couple of cheap hotels in the centre of town, far removed from luxury but adequate for one night. The *Hotel-é Sārī* (☎ 4077) is on the east side of Kheyābūn-é Enghelāb, 50 metres south of Meidūn-é Sā'at, and the *Hotel-é Nāder* (☎ 2357) is on the south side of Kheyābūn-é Jomhūrī-yé Eslāmī, 200 metres south-west of Meidūn-é Sā'at.

Places to Eat

The *Hotel-é Bādelé* has a reasonable restaurant, with good sturgeon kebab at 1600 rials, not-so-good shishlik at 1400 rials, and the most garlicky māst I have ever tasted. There are few, if any, restaurants in Sārī, but there are some snack-bars around Meidūn-é Sā'at.

Getting There & Away

Sārī is a little out of the way as far as public transport is concerned: the airport has only recently opened for passenger flights, the train from Tehrān goes by a slow and circuitous route, and there aren't even many buses.

Air Iran Air flies from Sārī to Tehrān on Tuesday and Friday at 1.25 pm (55 minutes, 5120 rials). The address of the new office in Sārī wasn't available at the time of writing.

Bus & Minibus The main bus station (Termīnāl-é Dōlat) is on the Jāddé-yé Kamarbandī (ring road) near the west bank of the river. There are minibuses to Bābol (40 km, 45 minutes, 100 rials) and some other local destinations from the Termīnāl-é Mosāferbarī-yé Eslāmī, west of the Pol-é Tajan, which can be reached for 50 to 100 rials by shared taxi from Meidūn-é Sā'at. From there to the main bus station is another

50 rials. Buses leave from the main terminal to:

Ahvāz – several a week, 1131 km, 18 hours, 1210/1900 rials 'lux'/'super', Cooperative Bus Company No 2
Ardabīl – several a week, 645 km, 11 hours
Bākhtarān – at least one a day, 775 km, 15 hours, 2180 rials 'super'
Chālūs – at least one a day, 180 km, 3¼ hours, 700 rials 'lux'
Gorgān – several a day, 137 km, two hours
Mashhad – at least one a day, 695 km, 12 hours
Rasht – several a day, 380 km, seven hours
Tabrīz – several a day, 861 km, 14 hours
Tehrān – several a day, 250 km, five hours

Train There's one regular (not express) train daily to Tehrān via Ghā'emshahr and Garmsār (8¾ hours), and to Gorgān via Behshahr and Bandar-é Torkaman (2¾ hours). Neither is an overnight journey, and only 2nd-class seats are available. The current departure time of 9.10 am may change without notice.

Shared Taxi & Savārī From Meidūn-é Emām Khomeinī there's a constant flow of shared taxis and savārīs to Bābol from early morning until about 7.30 pm (30 minutes, 200 rials). From Meidūn- é Sā'at you can take a taxi south-west to Meidūn-é Emām Khomeinī for 50 rials. Savārīs to and from Gorgān (1¾ hours, 1000 rials) leave from and arrive at Meidūn-é Sā'at.

RĀMSAR رامسر

Since the mountains stop only a few hundred metres short of the coast at this point, Rāmsar is squeezed into little more than one main street, and the natural limits to its development have helped to make this the most attractive of the seaside resorts. The last shāh built a palace in the thickly wooded hill overlooking Rāmsar; and who could blame him, for the setting is one of the most magnificent of anywhere along the Caspian coast.

There isn't much in the way of activities here, nor is there much of historical or architectural interest, but the breathtaking scenery is enough for most holidaymakers.

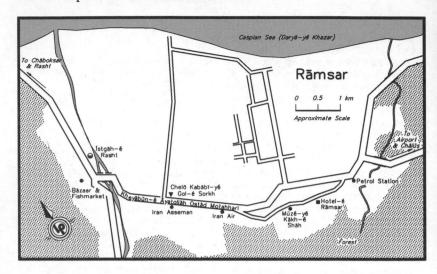

The more energetic could try walking in the hills. The people here are very friendly and like to see foreigners, remembering the boom years before the revolution.

Orientation & Information

Rāmsar stretches many km along the coast and a few blocks either side of the coast road. The main part of the road through Rāmsar is Kheyābūn-é Āyatollāh Ostād Motahharī, which passes the shahrdārī, the hospital, Iran Air and Iran Asseman (not marked in English), and is overlooked by the Hotel-é Rāmsar. To the north-west are two bridges, and beyond them the bazaar and fish market and the road to Chāboksar and Rasht. About 200 metres north of the bazaar, on the east side of the road, you come to the Rasht station (Īstgāh-é Rasht), from where there are minibuses, shared taxis and savārīs to Rasht. Rāmsar airport is about two km from town on the Chālūs road. There's no beach to speak of, nor is there a harbour.

Mūzé-yé Kākh-é Shāh

The Shāh's Palace is just behind the Hotel-é Rāmsar, approached through a gateway from the road. It is open as a museum in summer only.

Places to Stay

The four-star Hotel-é Rāmsar ('Hotel Ram ppposar') (☎ 3593) is set in a splendid hillside location overlooking the whole town and surrounded in all directions by evergreen trees. Although not in the same grand-luxe class as the Hotel Enghelab Khazar near Chālūs, it's perfectly comfortable and has probably the best view of any hotel in the Caspian provinces. Foreigners stopped staying here after the government ordered it to start charging them in dollars at an absurd exchange rate. The setting is so pleasant, even in winter, that you should check to see whether it still charges in dollars before looking elsewhere. Rooms start from US$53/64 (7700/9500 rials for Iranians) for a single/twin room with private bathroom in the new part of the hotel.

The Motel-é Khazar ('Khazar Motel'), which belongs to the hotel, costs US$41/52 a double/triple.

There's no other hotel in Rāmsar although there's a tiny mosāferkhūné in Kheyābūn-é Motahharī. If you ask at the reception of the

Hotel-é Rāmsar the receptionist may be able to arrange a private room or villa near the sea for you, payable in rials. Mine was in an annexe to a private house very close to the sea, with two beds and a bathroom for 8000 rials. Residents of Rāmsar told me that it was possible to rent a room elsewhere as cheaply as 2500 rials a night. You may be approached by people on the street offering such accommodation.

Places to Eat

The fairly large *Chelō Kabābī-yé Gol-é Sorkh* (not marked in English), on the north side of Kheyābūn-é Motahharī, is recommended. It has good fried māhī-yé sefīd with chelō sabzī (rice with green vegetables) for 2000 rials, and very good jūjé kabāb with chips and very garlicky yoghurt for 1500 rials. It's worth enquiring here, as elsewhere, about the availability of sturgeon and salmon-trout. The restaurant in the *Hotel-é Rāmsar* is good but expensive: chicken schnitzel without rice costs 2600 rials.

Getting There & Away

From the Īstgāh-é Rasht you can take a shared taxi or savārī to Rasht (1000 rials, 2¾ hours), or a less frequent minibus to Lāhījūn (200 rials, 2½ hours) or Rasht (300 rials, three hours). You can get off at points on the way by either means of transport.

Air Although Iran Air doesn't operate out of Rāmsar, it does have a small office in town. It's not computerised and bookings have to be requested at least a few hours in advance by telex, but the staff are helpful, perhaps because they don't have many customers. The Iran Asseman office is as hopeless as ever. It does fly between Tehrān and Rāmsar, but timetables and future services are anyone's guess. The nearest Iran Air flights are from Sārī, Rasht and Tehrān.

Getting Around

Getting around is easy: you just hail a taxi and say *'mostaghīm'* ('straight ahead'). Fares are 20 to 50 rials.

To/From the Airport The airport is within easy walking distance (without luggage) of the town of Rāmsar, and you should be able to get into town from the airport in a shared taxi for not much more than 100 rials.

NŌSHAHR & CHĀLŪS نوشهر چالوس

You can walk from one end of Nōshahr to the other in about 10 minutes. The port of Nōshahr has enlarged in the last two years to engulf what used to be a popular beach for paddling, but there's little shipping business as yet, so the town relies on internal tourism for its livelihood.

Chālūs is a small resort town only five km west of Nōshahr, now virtually a suburb of its larger neighbour. Its streets are lined with palm trees and the atmosphere is very relaxed, but there's very little to do. Since transport is no problem, even late at night, you can pick and choose between the hotels, restaurants and other facilities in either town. The best hotel is in Nōshahr, but the restaurants are better in Chālūs.

There are more trees in Nōshahr, and there's a grand new mosque, the Masjed-é Jāme', but it isn't of any great architectural interest. There's alleged to be a small beach somewhere near the edge of town, but I couldn't find it.

Orientation & Information

Chālūs is so compact that exact addresses are unnecessary. The Rūdkhūné-yé Chālūs flows through the town from south-west to north-east, and the main square is south of the bridge. The three roads from the square lead to Tonekābon, Nōshahr and Tehrān.

Places to Stay

The place to stay in Nōshahr is the *Hotel-é Shālīzār* ('Hotel Shalizar') (☎ 8139) which charges 6000 rials a double with private bathroom.

Accommodation in Chālūs is quite expensive, apart from a few grotty mosāferkhūnés in the Gārāzh area at the western approach to the town. The *Hotel-é Malek* ('Hotel Malek') (☎ 2627) and the *Hotel-é Jamshīd* ('Hotel Gamshid') charge around 4000 rials for a double with private bathroom; they are reasonably good, but not as good as the Hotel-é Shālīzār in Nōshahr.

The best place of all, however, is in the tiny coastal village of Namak Ābrū, 12 km west of Chālūs. The *Hotel Enghelab Khazar* (in Persian, Hotel-é Enghelāb-é Khazar) (☎ 2002), originally built as the Hyatt Regency, offers almost unimaginable luxury by Iranian standards. Anyone staying there would hardly need to leave the gates of this upmarket holiday complex with its top-class restaurants, exclusive boutiques, marina, golf-course, riding lessons and other leisure activities, not to mention its transparent lift and other novel features.

Unfortunately, this temple to Western hedonism is largely a preserve of the well-to-do Iranian, as its dollar charges for foreigners are US$119/136 a single with forest/sea view, and up to US$699 for a suite. Iranians pay about one-tenth of this amount, in rials.

Places to Eat
The best restaurants are in Chālūs. Try the *Restōrān-é Māzandarān* (not marked in English) which has good fried māhī-yé sefīd for 2000 rials, or else the good *Restōrān-é Gīlān-é Fard* (not marked in English either), in Kheyābūn-é Emām Khomeinī just southwest of the terminal, which serves quail fesenjūn with rice for 2500 rials. The restaurant in the *Hotel-é Shālīzār* in Nōshahr isn't at all bad.

Things to Buy
At Chālūs and Nōshahr, as at almost any other seaside resort in the world, shops sell inflatable beach toys at inflated prices, and all sorts of other dubious souvenirs. There are some acceptable locally made items of wickerwork and matting, but most of the stuff on offer could best be described as *dehātī* ('rustic', 'unstylish' or 'kitsch'). There's a busy outdoor fishmarket in Nōshahr where I tried in vain to find caviar.

Getting There & Away
Bus & Minibus A few long-distance buses

pass through Nōshahr, but it's easier to catch one from Chālūs. The bus company offices are in the area known as the Gārāzh, at the western approach to Chālūs (30 rials by shared taxi from the centre). There are occasional buses from Chālūs to Mashhad (877 km, 16 hours), Sārī (at least one a day, 180 km, three hours, 700 rials 'lux', Cooperative Bus Company No 12), and Tabrīz (679 km, 11 hours).

Shared Taxi & Savārī From Nōshahr there are shared taxis and savārīs to Tehrān (202 km, three to four hours). Just west of the Masjed-é Jāme' there's an agency office which organises cars to Tehrān for 2200 rials; in the holiday season you may have to book seats some time ahead, or take a private car for around 4000 rials a passenger. Shared taxis and savārīs also run to Rāmsar and other points along the coast.

From Chālūs, shared taxis and savārīs leave for towns in Māzandarān and Gīlān from the main square, and agency offices in the Gārāzh area operate savārīs to destinations further afield.

Sea Despite rumours to the contrary, there are no passenger shipping services to or from Nōshahr, although there may be in the future. Enquire at IRISL opposite the harbour customs office (both clearly marked in English).

Getting Around
There are frequent minibuses throughout the day until about 6 pm between Nōshahr (just west of the Masjed-é Jāme') and the main square of Chālūs (10 minutes, 20 rials). At other times you can take a shared taxi for 50 to 100 rials.

PĀRK-É SĪSANGĀN پارک سی سنگان
This small national park, 29 km east of Nōshahr on the coast road, is pleasant but really designed for motorists who only want to stretch their legs, perhaps have a picnic, or ride one of the tourist horses before getting back to the wheel. The pathways through the woods lead nowhere, and the

walker following one of the asphalt or dirt tracks through the park runs the risk of being mowed down, or at least sprayed with mud, by a speeding car.

Getting There & Away
From Nōshahr take a minibus from the crossroads next to the Masjed-é Jāme' and ask to be dropped off at the park (45 minutes, 100 rials). Getting back is more of a problem: I waited over an hour on the busy road passing the entrance to the park for someone to offer me a lift.

ĀMOL آمل
Āmol succeeded Sārī as the capital of Muslim Tabarestān in the 9th century, and became renowned for a distinctive style of glazed earthenware pottery which reached its peak between the 10th and 13th centuries. After the devastation of the Mongol invasions, Āmol reverted to relative obscurity. In 1888 Edward Browne described it as 'one of the chief cities of Mázandarán, a pictureque straggling town divided into two parts by a large river, which is spanned by a long narrow bridge built of bricks', but it's no longer of any great beauty.

Things to See
In Āmol itself there are two historic mausoleums, the largely rebuilt 12th-century Maghharé-yé Mīr Heidar and the 16th-century Emāmzādé-yé Ebrāhīm. The most interesting sight is another mausoleum, the **Mashhad-é Mīr Bozorg**, just outside the city. This 17th-century sanctuary of the martyred Mīr Bozorg lies a short distance north of Āmol on the west bank of the river. The large rectangular brick structure, with its red brick dome, was built on the site of an earlier shrine by Shāh Abbās I, and is known for the ornateness of its tomb and for the original interior mosaics, some of which have survived.

Place to Stay
The only hotel is the *Hotel-é Sadaf* (☎ 4450).

Getting There & Away
There are four main roads out of Āmol, all served by regular shared taxis and savārīs. North takes you to the small coastal town of Mahmūd Ābād (20 km); east to Bābol (29 km); south to Tehrān (174 km); and west to Nūr (45 km), the junction for Nōshahr and Chālūs.

BĀBOLSAR بابلسر
The port of Bābolsar was at one time the province's main international trading outlet, and more recently it was established as a fashionable resort town with a luxury seaside hotel complex. Nowadays the dock is dry, the hotel complex is closed, and Bābolsar is no longer an inspiring place, although Iranian tourists still go there.

Orientation
The main part of the town is four km inland, and the walk between it and the coast is a lonely and disappointing one. The beach area isn't by any means inspiring, consisting of a dead-end road looking out over a short and usually deserted stretch of sand, with a small children's playground at the junction of the road back into the centre. To share this excitement, you can take a shared taxi northeast from the main square (which is where you will be dropped off if you arrive by public transport) for 30 to 50 rials.

Places to Stay
There's a good modern hotel, the *Hotel-é Mīchkā* ('Hotel Michka') (☎ 24656), along the dead-end road opposite the beach, unusually built in the style of a Mediterranean villa. It charges 4500 rials for a double with private bathroom, and is apt to fill up very quickly in the holiday season.

Places to Eat
There are two restaurants, one attached to the *Hotel-é Mīchkā* (good but quite expensive) and the *Sālon-é Ghezā-yé Khān-é Kūchek*, at the corner of the same dead-end street, which is far less elegant but also good, with excellent whole grilled māhī-yé sefīd with rice for 2800 rials.

Getting There & Away

On the south side of the main square there's a small stop for regular minibuses to Bābol (20 km, 30 minutes, 40 rials). For places further afield you will probably have to change at Bābol.

BĀBOL بابل

Founded in the early 16th century on the main east-west route between the Caspian provinces, Bābol was once a busy river port with its outer harbour at Bābolsar. Since the early 19th century it has been one of the most important towns of Māzandarān, but nowadays it's a sprawling and drab commercial centre with only a few isolated ancient buildings.

Maghbaré-yé Soltān Mohammad Tāher

This late 15th-century tomb tower stands in an old cemetery in the village of Soltān Mohammad Tāher, four km from Bābol on the east road (not the main road to Ghā'emshahr). The exterior features a simple arched frieze beneath its polygonal tiled dome, shallow arched recesses on each outer wall, and a tall narrow portal over the original carved wooden door. Although the structure is simple, this structure marks the peak of the development of the tomb tower in Iran, and there are few good examples from later times. The carved wooden tomb box of Soltān Mohammad Tāher remains inside the mausoleum.

Places to Stay

There's no hotel in Bābol, although there are some mosāferkhūnés.

Getting There & Away

If you arrive by public transport, you will be dropped off at Meidūn-é Keshvarī. Right next to the taxi stop is the minibus station for Bābolsar: minibuses on this route are slow and crowded (20 km, 30 minutes, 40 rials). From the same square there are shared taxis and savārīs heading for Chālūs (128 km, two hours, 1200 rials) and Ghā'emshahr (20 km, 15 minutes, 100 rials) and sometimes as far afield as Rasht or Tehrān. There are also regular minibuses to Sārī (40 km, 45 minutes, 100 rials).

BEHSHAHR بهشهر

Behshahr is a small sleepy town on the main road between Sārī and Gorgān. The Khalīj-é Gorgān (Bay of Gorgān) lies 12 km to the north, and immediately south are hills and woodland which you can explore on foot. Behshahr is too far east to be much of a resort town, but it does have one site of historical interest, and is a pleasant enough stopover between the north-east steppe and the coastal plain.

Kākh-é Safī Ābād

On the Kūh-é Kākh, a tall hill thick with trees south-west of Behshahr, to your right as you approach the town from Sārī, are the remains of this Safavid palace. In about 1612, Shāh Abbās I set about building a palace complex in a royal water garden, the Bāgh-é Shāh, on this idyllic woodland perch. Many palaces and other buildings for the king and his court grew up on the same site, which gradually expanded to become the town of Ashraf (present-day Behshahr), but over the centuries they fell into ruin and today the only remaining structure is that of the Safī Ābād Palace itself, the Kākh-é Safī Ābād. The royal residence is surprisingly small, and what remains gives little indication of the magnificence of design employed by Shāh Abbās' architects in Esfahān, but the setting is still very dramatic.

The hill is easily accessible by foot from Kheyābūn-é Āyatollāh Tāleghānī, which leads south from the main east-west road, Bolvār-é Shahīd Hāshemī Nezhād.

Prehistoric Caves

There are two interesting caves near Behshahr which have revealed prehistoric pottery dating back perhaps to the 10th millennium BC, as well as evidence of some unusual ancient burial rites. To get to the caves, take a shared taxi and ask to be dropped off at the Serāh-é Torūjan-é Bālā, about three km west of Behshahr on the main road to Sārī. From there walk south for about

300 metres until you come to a small village (Torūjan-é Bālā), where you will see the Ghār-é Hōtū (Hōtū Cave) overlooking the road; the Ghār-é Kamarband (Kamarband Cave) is a very short distance south.

Places to Stay & Eat
You can take your pick of two simple hotels in Behshahr: the outlying *Hotel-é Behshahr* (☎ 3231), on Bolvār-é Shahīd Hāshemī Nezhād, on the right if you approach the town from Gorgān; or the central *Hotel-é Meyāngālé* (☎ 2151), on the same street at its intersection with Kheyābūn-é Emām Khomeinī. Both places have restaurants.

Getting There & Away
From anywhere along Bolvār-é Shahīd Hāshemī Nezhād you can take a shared taxi or savārī to Gorgān (91 km, 1¼ hours, 500 to 750 rials) or Sārī (46 km, 30 minutes, 200 to 400 rials). Alternatively you could try at the bus terminal on the south side of the same road near the western edge of Behshahr.

Train The train station (☎ 3822) is in the north of town, about 1½ km (50 to 100 rials by shared taxi) from the centre. There's one train a day to Gorgān (via Bandar-é Torka-man; 1¾ hours) and to Tehrān (via Sārī, Ghā'emshahr and Garmsār; 9¾ hours).

BANDAR-É TORKAMAN   بندر ترکمن
A coastal town just south of the narrow inlet to the Khalīj-é Gorgān (Bay of Gorgān), Bandar-é Torkaman is, at its name suggests, the Turkoman port of Iran. For a long time it was a major channel of trade with Russia, despite the attentions of Turkoman pirates who were a scourge to shipping on these shores until the last century. But with the establishment of the trans-Iranian railway in the 1930s it also became the sole railhead of the south Caspian coast. The decline in the shipping trade has left Bandar-é Torkaman a small and largely Turkoman settlement with something of the air of a frontier town.

Things to See
If you happen to be around this part of Iran on a Monday morning, it's worth coming to Bandar-é Torkaman for its traditional weekly market where you can buy local produce and tribal handicrafts. Sadly, the exciting polo matches which used to be held here are on the long list of un-Islamic activities banned since the revolution.

GORGĀN   گرگان
On the northern edge of the Alborz and at the southern frontier of the north-eastern steppe, Gorgān (formerly known as Aster Ābād) has, for much of its long history, been the last secure outpost of Persian civilisation. Settled since ancient times, it has, with the exception of a series of incursions in the last century, been in a geographical position to resist the threat of Turkoman raids, unlike Gombad-é Kāvūs and other Māzandarānī towns to the north and east. It has always represented the final frontier of settlement for camel caravans and everyone else who passed through it on the way to Central Asia or Khorāsān. The Turkomans started to give up their nomadic and pillaging ways at the turn of this century, and it's one of the twists of history that eventually they conquered Gorgān not by violence but by peaceful urbanisation. The final irony is that the town they made their own has now lost much of that Turkoman character enthused about by earlier visitors.

Gorgān become the new railhead of the Caspian provinces after a branch line was constructed in the '70s from Bandar-é Tor-kaman, but it is still little more than a provincial market town. Some of its individual personality has been replaced over recent years by Persian uniformity, and very few people now wear the distinctive Turkoman dress, but it's still a pleasant base for exploring the many archaeological and historical sites in the region, and contains a couple of interesting buildings itself.

The main square has a modern Persian character and isn't exciting architecturally, but in the network of narrow winding kūchés around it, especially around the ramshackle bazaar immediately to the west, there are many fine examples of traditional

Māzandarānī houses, with tiled sloping roofs and charming wooden balconies. Most of the historic structures in Gorgān have been destroyed by earthquakes, but there are two interesting and well preserved religious buildings behind the bazaar. Although both are very close to the main square, it's difficult to find them or describe how to get to them, so you should ask for directions.

Masjed-é Jāme'

Built around a quadrangle, this single-storey building has the traditional sloping tiled roof, but the most interesting and only original structure of the still-functioning mosque is an unusual Seljuq minaret. This circular brick tower, topped with a latticed open loft (for the muezzin), covered with a sloping corrugated tile roof, squat, sturdy and top-heavy, is quite unlike the more graceful needles of later Islamic architecture. Inside the mosque there's a 15th-century wooden membar (pulpit) as well as a number of later carved stone tablets.

Emāmzādé-yé Nūr

About 200 metres west of the Masjed-é Jāme', this small 14th or 15th century polygonal tomb tower has outer walls decorated with simple brickwork designs (possibly from the Seljuq period). On the exterior of the west wall you can see a good early example of the style of stalactite moulding that reached its zenith in the time of Shāh Abbās I. The mid-15th century wooden door is normally locked, but if you ask around someone will probably be found to open it for you. Inside there are some early mouldings around the mehrāb, and a priceless wooden tomb box.

Places to Stay

There are several simple hotels in Gorgān, of which probably the best is the central *Hotel-é Khayyām* (not marked in English) which charges 3000 rials a double, with a shower and basin but no lavatory in the room; it's clean and adequate.

Places to Eat

There are some chelō kabābīs and snack bars around the main street, Kheyābūn-é Emām Khomeinī.

Getting There & Away

The road east to Mashhad is often very treacherous in winter as a result of frequent blizzards and snowfalls. My journey took 11½ hours. It is, however, a spectacular drive, passing through dramatic forest scenery. The road to Sārī is slightly less prone to bad weather, but in winter allow for delays.

Gorgān airport doesn't currently have any passenger services.

Bus & Minibus The main bus station area, the Termīnāl-é Jorjān, is at the eastern approach to Gorgān on the Mashhad road: take a shared taxi from the centre (100 to 200 rials). Buses leave from there to:

Ahvāz – several a week, 1262 km, 22 hours, 2250/2550 rials 'lux'/'super', Cooperative Bus Company No 2
Bākhtarān – at least one a day, 906 km, 18 hours, 2250 rials 'super'
Gombad-é Kāvūs – minibuses about hourly until around 7 pm, 93 km, 1½ hours, 150 rials; alternatively you can catch the Mashhad bus
Mashhad via Gombad-é Kāvūs – two a day, 564 km, nine hours, 650 rials 'lux', Cooperative Bus Company No 11
Rasht – at least two a day, 511 km, nine hours
Sārī – several a day until about 8.30 pm, 137 km, two hours
Tehrān – at least two a day, 387 km, seven hours
Zābol – one a day, 1713 km, 28 hours, 2100 rials 'lux'
Zāhedān – at least one a day, 1563 km, 27 hours

A smaller terminal area, the Gārāzh-é Sāhel, on Kheyābūn-é Emām Khomeini, about a km (30 to 50 rials by shared taxi) west of the centre, has minibuses to Sārī (137 km, 2½ hours) via Behshahr (91 km, 1½ hours) about hourly until about 7 pm.

Train The recent extension of the railway here has opened one of the most scenic routes in Iran to the train passenger. There's one service to Tehrān daily, stopping at

Bandar-é Torkaman, Behshahr, Sārī, Ghā'emshahr and Garmsār and taking 11¾ hours. This isn't an overnight journey, and only 2nd-class seating is available (900 rials). Enquire at the train station (☎ 7911) on the northern edge of Gorgān for the latest departure times (trains supposedly leave at 6.20 am).

Shared Taxi & Savārī You can take a shared taxi or savārī to Sārī (1½ hours, 1000 rials) or Behshahr (45 minutes, 500 rials) from outside the Gārāzh-é Sāhel.

Getting Around
A taxi from the Termīnāl-é Jorjān to the centre is 500 to 700 rials for a single passenger or 100 to 200 rials in a shared taxi. Around the centre you walk.

NORTH OF GORGĀN
The Dasht-é Gorgān (the steppe north of Gorgān) and the even remoter Torkaman Sahrā (the Turkoman plain) together form potentially one of the richest archaeological regions in Iran. There must be a great number of undiscovered sites here, and the known sites have not all been excavated. However, the mounds which have come to light are often extremely difficult to reach, and an attempt at exploration is really only worthwhile for a dedicated archaeologist with a 4WD and a local guide. If you are interested, there's no harm in asking at the Ministry of Culture & Islamic Guidance office (☎ 4246) in Gombad-é Kāvūs. The most important mound yet discovered, Tūrang Tappé, is fortunately also one of the most accessible.

Tūrang Tappé
Tūrang Tappé, the Troy of Māzandarān, is north-north-east of Gorgān, 22 km by road and dirt track. Until it was destroyed in the Mongol period, this was a major caravan station and the main town of the region. It has been dug this century to reveal five distinct layers, the earliest dating back to the 6th millennium BC and the latest to the early Islamic era. Lapis lazuli beads and ceramic pieces indicate that this was a major pottery-producing centre, with its peak in the 2nd and 3rd millennia. You can still see the remains of mud brick structures from several periods, but the more important items of pottery are now on display in Tehrān at the Mūzé-yé Īrān-é Bāstān and the Mūzé-yé Ābkīné.

Getting There & Away Tūrang Tappé is impossible to reach by public transport, and even by private car it's almost inaccessible in bad weather: hire a taxi in Gorgān for around 1500 rials an hour (more if it's snowing).

Sadd-é Eskandar
The remains of a historical wall called Sadd-é Eskandar ('Alexander's Wall') lie within 30 km of Gorgān, stretching from just west of Gombad-é Kāvūs to within about five km of the sea. Built probably in the 6th century (and thus not by Alexander the Great) as a bulwark against warring tribes to the north, this equivalent of Hadrian's Wall has crumbled or been cannibalised for building materials along most of its length, but the foundations at least are clearly visible, and in places its original purpose can still be imagined.

Getting There & Away The wall is difficult to get to and, since it's near the Turkmenistan border, it isn't advisable to go there without permission in writing from the *farmāndārī* (district administrative headquarters) in Gorgān or Gombad-é Kāvūs or the Ministry of Culture & Islamic Guidance office (☎ 4246) in Gombad-é Kāvūs. After getting this permit, you can charter a taxi in either town for not more than 2000 rials an hour. It isn't at all safe to walk there.

GOMBAD-É KĀVŪS   گنبد کاووس
This otherwise featureless and unattractive Turkoman town on the Gorgān to Mashhad road is famous for, and named after, one thing; but for that alone it repays the very longest of detours. The Gombad-é Kāvūs (or Mīl-é Gombad-é Kāvūs) is a spectacular tomb tower built by Ghābūs ebn-é Vashmgīr

– the name Kāvūs is a corruption of Ghābūs. It's a remarkable memorial to a remarkable man. Famous as a poet, scholar, general and patron of the arts, Ghābūs was prince of the Ziyarid dynasty. He ruled the surrounding province of Tabarestān at the turn of the 11th century and decided to build a monument to last forever. The monument was completed in 1006, six years before Ghābūs died at the hands of an assassin.

This earliest of skyscrapers is a full 55 metres tall and can be seen on a clear day as far as 30 km away. The tower rests on a large earth mound formed around its substantial foundations, which are at least 12 metres deep. Built of brick, the circular structure has 10 buttresses rising from the base to the pointed dome, which itself measures 18 metres in height. There are two rings of inscriptions around the tower, one on a moulded cornice below the dome and the other about a metre above the doorway. Originally the glass coffin of Ghābūs hung from the dome of the tower, but it vanished long ago, and there's no longer anything to see inside. In any case, the arched doorway on its east side is permanently locked, and it has never been possible to climb to the top of the tower. A spiral pathway up to the base of the tower is only partly completed, and the climb is very slippery in the rain.

The whole tower is so perfectly preserved that it is hard to believe that it was built almost a millennium ago. In its imposing scale and simple but perfect construction, this first such tomb tower in the Persian empire set a precedent which was difficult to follow, and comes closer to immortality than any other secular building in Iran.

Places to Stay

There's alleged to be a hotel in Gombad-é Kāvūs, but it's better to stay in Gorgān.

Places to Eat

There's a simple, unmarked restaurant opposite the place where the bus from Gorgān drops you off. It serves good mutton khōresh

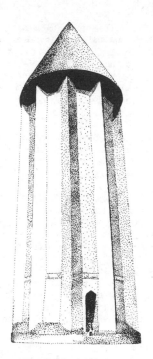

The Gombad-é Kāvus

for 730 rials and insists on not charging for tea.

Getting There & Away

Cooperative Bus Company No 2 (marked in English 'PMT') has buses to:

Gorgān – minibuses about hourly until about 7 pm, 93 km, 1½ hours, 150 rials
Mashhad – one a day, 6 am, 471 km, eight hours
Sabzevār – one a day, 8 am, 384 km, seven hours
Tehrān – several a day, 480 km, eight hours
Zābol – one a day, 9 am, 1621 km, 26 hours
Zāhedān – one a day, 9 am, 1460 km, 24 hours

Some of the company's buses also pass through Gombad-é Kāvūs on their way from Mashhad to Gorgān. You can take a seat on one of these for 200 rials.

To get to the tower itself, take a shared taxi

from opposite the Cooperative Bus Company No 2 office, where the bus from Gorgān to Gombad-é Kāvūs drops you off. Ask for the Mīl-é Gombad, as it's known locally. A shared taxi there and back is around 30 rials.

Glossary

Generally, the Persian words in this book are transliterations of colloquial usage. Other words are also given in the Language chapter, particularly in the Food and Drinks sections.

Ābambār – water storage tank
Āghā – sir; gentleman
Āghā-yé – the equivalent of Mr, but commonly used with the forename only
Allāh – Muslim name for God
Allāho Akbar – God is Most Great: a Muslim declaration of faith
Ārāmgāh – resting-place; burial-place; tomb
Arg, ark – citadel
Āstāné – sanctuary; threshold
Āyatollāh – literally a 'sign or miracle of God': Shi'ite cleric of the highest rank; used as a title before the name
Āzād – free; liberated
Āzādī – freedom

Bādgīr – wind-tower or ventilation shaft used to catch any breeze and funnel it down into a building for cooling
Bāgh – garden
Bandar – port; harbour
Bandarī – pertaining to a port; person native to a port: indigenous inhabitant of the Persian Gulf coast and islands
Basīj – mobilisation; Mobilisation Corps: an organisation set up in 1980 to dispatch volunteers of all ages to fight at the front in the war against Iraq
Basījī – someone mobilised by the *basīj*
Bāstān – ancient; ancient history; antiquity
Bāstānī – ancient; archaeological
Bāzār – bazaar; market; market place
Bāzārī – pertaining to a bazaar
Bāzār-é āzād – 'free' market; black market
Behesht – paradise
Bīmārestān – hospital
Bogh'é – mausoleum
Bolvār – boulevard
Borj – tower
Bozorg – big; large; great
Bozorgrāh – urban motorway; expressway

Chādor – literally 'tent'; a cloak, usually black, covering all parts of a woman's body except the hands, feet and face
Chahārrāh – intersection; crossroads
Chāy – tea
Chāykhūné – tea-house

Chelō – boiled rice
Chelō kabāb – lamb kebab served with rice: a staple at Iranian restaurants
Chelō kabābī – place serving *chelō kabāb*; restaurant in general

Daftar (*pl* **dafāter**) – office
Daftar-é belīt forūshī – ticket-office
Daftar-é hāfez-é manāfe' – interests section (of an embassy)
Daftar-é seir va seyāhat – tourist office
Darvāzé – gate, especially a city gate
Daryā – sea
Daryāché – lake
Dasht – plain; plateau; desert, specifically one of sand or gravel

Edāré – department; administration; office
Eivān – rectangular hall opening onto a courtyard
Emām – leader; title of one of the 12 descendants of Mohammad who, according to Shi'ite belief, succeeded him as religious and temporal leader of the Muslims
Emāmzādé – descendant of an *emām*; shrine or mausoleum of an *emāmzādé*
Enghelāb – revolution
Enghelāb-é Eslāmī – Islamic Revolution
Enshāllāh – God willing
Ershād – guidance; an abbreviation for the Ministry of Culture & Islamic Guidance
Eskelé – jetty; dock; harbour
Eslām – Islam: literally 'submission' (ie to the will of God)
Eslāmī – Islamic
Estādyūm – stadium

Falaké – round open space; roundabout
Farhang – culture
Farsh – carpet
Fārsī – Persian language or people
Forūshgāh – shop

Ghal'é – fortress; fortified walled village
Ghalyān – water pipe; hubble-bubble
Ghanāt – underground water channel
Gharb – west
Ghollé – summit; peak
Ghorān – the Qoran: the holy book of the Muslims
Gombad – dome; domed monument; tomb-tower

Hajj – pilgrimage to Mecca
Hajjī – one who has performed the *Hajj*, used as a title

before the forename; polite form of address for an old man

Halāl – permitted by Islamic law; lawful to eat or drink

Hammūm – bath; bath-house; bathroom

Hāmūn – plain; desert; salt waste; marsh

Harām – forbidden by Islamic law; unlawful to eat or drink

Hazrat-é – title used before the name of Mohammad, any other apostle of Islam, or a Christian saint

Hegira – see *Hejrat*

Hejāb – veil; the 'modest dress' required of Muslim women and girls

Hejrat – the flight of the Prophet Mohammad from Mecca on 16 July 622 AD; the starting-point of the Muslim lunar calendar and the Persian solar calendar

Hezbollāh – 'Party of God': a loose grouping of hardline Khomeinī-style fundamentalist Muslims

IRISL – Islamic Republic of Iran Shipping Line

Īstgāh – station (especially railway station)

Jāddé – road

Jāddé-yé kamarbandī – ring-road

Jahāngard – tourist

Jangal – forest; jungle (name used for the Māzandarān forest)

Jazīré – island

Jehād – holy war; crusade

Jom'é – Friday, the Muslim day of rest and worship

Jonūb – south

Kabāb – kebab(s): meat, fish, poultry or seafood grilled on a skewer

Kabīr – great

Kākh – palace

Kavīr – salt desert

Kelīsā – church (sometimes cathedral)

Khalīj – gulf; bay

Khān – feudal lord

Kheyābūn – street; avenue

Khūné – house; home

KIDO – Kish Island Development Organization

Komīté – committee, especially a local 'committee' of the Islamic Revolutionary Guards Corps

Konsūlgarī – consulate

Kūché – lane; alley

Kūchek – small; little

Kūh – mountain

Lotfān – kindly; please (when requesting something)

Lux – luxury; deluxe (regular class of bus)

Madrasé – school; Muslim theological college

Maghbaré – tomb; burial-ground

Manār – minaret: tower of a mosque

Markaz – centre; headquarters

Markazī telefon – main telephone office

Masjed – mosque: Muslim place of worship

Masjed-é jāme' – congregational mosque

Mehmūn – guest

Mehmūnkhūné – hotel

Mehmūnsarā – government-owned rest house or hotel

Mehrāb – chevron-shaped niche inside a mosque indicating the direction of Mecca, often ornately decorated with tiling and calligraphy

Meidūn – town square; open space

Membar – pulpit of a mosque

Moharram – first month of the Muslim lunar calendar, Shi'ite month of mourning

Mojāhed – soldier of the *jehād*

Mosāfer – traveller; passenger

Mosāferkhūné – lodging-house or hotel of the cheapest and simplest kind, sometimes offering only dormitory accommodation

Mostaghīm – straight ahead: the usual answer to any request for directions

Muezzin – functionary at a mosque who calls Muslims to prayer

Mullah – Islamic cleric; sometimes used as a title

Mūzé – museum

NIOC – National Iranian Oil Company, a state monopoly

Nō – new

Nō Rūz – Persian New Year's Day, celebrated on the vernal equinox (about 21 March)

Ostān – province: Iran is divided into 24 *ostānhā*

Ostāndārī – office of the provincial government

Otōbān – motorway

Pā'īn – down; downwards; low; of low status

Pārs – Persia; Iran

Pāsāzh – passage; shopping arcade

Pol – bridge

Polō – rice cooked together with other ingredients

Qoran – see *Ghorān*

Ramazān – ninth month in the Muslim lunar calendar; month of fasting

Rūdkhūné – river; stream

Rūz – day

Sahn – court; courtyard

Sahrā – desert

Salām – 'peace': a greeting

Sālon-é ghezā – food-hall; simple restaurant

Savārī – private car, sometimes operated by a cooperative, taking up to five or six paying passengers on fixed intercity or rural routes

Sayyed – male descendant of Mohammad, used as a title before the forename

Serāh – 'three roads': Y- junction or T-junction

Sepah-é Pāsdārān – 'Army of Guards': paramilitary unit of the Islamic Revolutionary Guards, mainly active in rural areas

Shāh – king; the usual title of the Persian monarch

Shahīd – martyr; used as a title before the forename of a fighter killed during the Islamic Revolution or the Iran-Iraq War

Shahr – town or city

Shahrbānī – the police; provincial police headquarters

Shahrdārī – administrative headquarters of a *shahr*; municipal office; town hall

Shargh – east

Shomāl – north; the Caspian provinces of Gīlān and Māzandarān

Sūper lux – super deluxe: the superior class of bus

Takht – throne

Tappé – hill; mound

Termīnāl – terminal; bus station

Tōmān – unit of currency equal to 10 rials, no longer in official use but the usual unit in speech

Ziggurat – pyramidal temple with a series of tiers on a square or rectangular plan

Persian Language Guide

Persian grammar is refreshingly simple, and what few rules there are have few exceptions. For most people the greatest barrier to learning Persian is the script, but even this is relatively easy to decipher, at least in the printed form.

In the transliterations, proper nouns which would otherwise look odd in English have been capitalised, with no change in the pronunciation. Where an apostrophe occurs at the beginning of a Persian word, it has not been included since it makes no difference to pronunciation. Hyphens have been used before the *ezāfé* (see below), between compound words which are pronounced as one word but written as two, and where a combination of consonants would otherwise be mispronounced.

In most cases the colloquial pronunciation or word is used. Colloquial Persian, as spoken most of the time by most Iranians, is not the equivalent of slang, although many slang expressions are used. Classical Persian is not the language of everyday speech; it is oratorical or written Persian, which would be used for reading a speech or writing a book.

PRONUNCIATION

In general, the last syllable of a multisyllable word is stressed, unless it is a short vowel at the end of a word eg *emĀm* but *bAlé* (with the stress on the capital letter).

Vowels & Dipthongs

A macron over a vowel (ā, ī, ō and ū) indicates a longer vowel sound. This is very important in Persian as the wrong vowel length can completely change the meaning of a word, or make it incomprehensible. For example, *māst* (rhyming with 'passed') means 'yoghurt', while *mast* (rhyming with 'gassed') means 'drunk'. Fortunately no sounds in Persian are completely alien to the English-speaker, and it should not take very long to pick up a workable pronunciation.

a	as in map, but slightly more rounded
ā	between the *a* in *class* and the *a* in *what*
e	similar to *e* in *beg*
é	*e* with a slight rising tone; as in *café*, often a mere glide or even inaudible
ī	similar to *i* in *Fiji*
o	between the *o* in *god* and the *oo* in *good*
ō	similar to the *o* in *bone*
ū	similar to the *u* in *ruse*; never as in *use*
ei	similar to *ei* in *rein*
oi	similar to *oy* in *boy*

Consonants

The letters **b, d, f, j, m, n, p, sh, t** and **z** are pronounced as in English.

ch	as in *rich*
g	hard *g* as in *bag*, never as in *age*; at the end of a word or before *ā, e, é, ei* or *ī* the *g* is palatised, rather like the *gg* in *egg yolk* read quickly
gh	soft gargling sound, sometimes pronounced as a *g* from the back of the throat
h	never silent; always unvoiced as in *harm*, not *hit*

k	as in English; at the end of a word or before *ā, e, é, ei* or *ī* the *k* is palatised, rather like the *ck* in *backyard* read quickly	
kh	as *ch* in Scottish *loch* or German *achtung*	
l	as in *leg* not *roll*, even when doubled (but see note below)	
r	trilled *r* as in Italian or Russian, never silent or diphthongised	
s	always as in *sad*, never as in *rise*	
v	as in English, but tending towards *w*	
y	always consonantal *y* as in *yak*	
zh	as *zh* in *Zhivago* or *g* in *mirage*	
'	very weak glottal stop, as in Cockney *bo'l* for *bottle* or in *go away*	

Note that doubled consonants are always pronounced distinctly as in *hat trick* not *battle*; the sole exception is the word for God, *Allāh*, in which the *l*s are swallowed as in English *doll*.

GRAMMAR

The verb usually comes at the end of the sentence or clause. Punctuation is not always used, or at least not as often as in English. For most purposes, it is only necessary to learn two tenses of each verb, the present (also generally used for the future) and the past, and verb endings are regular in all verbs.

To ask a question it is usually enough merely to alter the intonation, as in English: in writing a question mark is usually used. To be certain, you can use the question word *āyā* at the beginning of the sentence.

There is no gender (he and she are the same word in Persian), although inanimates and lower animals are treated differently in some cases from rational beings.

I	*man*	من
you (singular)*	*to*	تو
he/she	*ū*	او
it	*ān*	آن
we	*mā*	ما
you (plural)*	*shomā*	شما
they (of people and higher animals)	*īshān*	ایشان
they (of things and lower animals)	*ānhā* ·	آنها

*In Persian *shomā* is the formal, polite form of the second person singular pronoun; *to* is only generally used when talking to close friends and relatives of the same generation or later, and to children and animals.

Ezāfé

This is a grammatical device which links a noun to a following word which describes or qualifies it in some way. It is equivalent to 'of' in English. The ezāfé takes the form of the suffix -*é* after nouns which end with a consonant or diphthong. If the noun ends with a vowel, the ezāfé is the suffix -*yé*. For example:

ketāb (book)	*ketāb-é Rezā* (Rezā's book)
tangé (strait)	*Tangé-yé Hormoz* (the Strait of Hormoz)
kheyābūn (street)	*Kheyābūn-é Zand* (Zand Street)
otāgh (room)	*otāgh-é arzūntar* (a cheaper room)

The ezāfé is not normally indicated in written Persian (except after ā, ō or ū), which is a problem for students of the language.

Plurals

Nouns remain in the singular when preceded by a numeral or qualified by a noun of quantity, so plural forms are less common than in English. In common usage, names of foods and drinks do not normally take the plural suffix.

Plural forms depend on whether the noun is for a rational being (ie a person), which takes the suffix -an, or an inanimate object or non-rational being, which takes the suffix -ha. There are also different plural forms if the noun ends in a vowel.

In everyday speech it is acceptable to use the suffix -hā as the plural for almost any noun, although a few animates ending in -é or -ā never take the inanimate plural. Where the plural -hā follows a word ending g, k, s or z, a hyphen has been inserted between the two for ease of pronunciation.

Useful Words & Phrases

Polite Forms of Address

When addressing a stranger, especially one older than you, it is polite to drop in one of the words for 'sir' or 'madam' at the beginning of the first sentence or after one of the standard greetings. The standard words for sir and madam are āghā and khānom respectively. Āghā-yé and Khānom-é are the equivalents of Mr, and Mrs/Miss/Ms. Āghā can be used before or after the first name as a title of respect, eg Mohammad Āghā or more likely Āghā Mohammad. For a list of some of the other common titles and forms of address (eg, hajjī, sayyed, and āyatollāh) see the Glossary.

Greetings & Civilities

The all-purpose greeting in Iran is salām aleikom, which does duty for good morning, good afternoon and good evening. The same expression is used throughout the Muslim world, so if you can learn only one phrase in Iran, this is the one. The Iranians are very courteous people and there are many polite or informal greetings and replies, but the following are some of the commonest:

welcome	khōsh āmadīd	خوش آمدید
thank you: you are very kind	motashakkeram, shomā kheilī mehrabūn hastīd	متشکرم ، شما خیلا مهربان هستید
hello	salām	سلام
peace be upon you	salām aleikom	سلام علیکم
good morning	sobh bekheir	صبح بخیر
good night, good evening	shab bekheir	شب بخیر
goodbye	khodāfez or more formally khodā hāfez	خدا حافظ
How do you do?	hāl-é shomā chetōr ast?	حال شما چطور است ؟
How are you?	hāl-é shomā khūb é?	حال شما خوب است ؟
How are you doing?	chetōr é?	چطور است
praise be to God! (ie I'm fine, thank you)	alhamdolellāh	الحمد لله
not bad, thanks	mersī, bad nīstam	مرسی، بد نیستم

What is your name?	esmetān chī st?	اسمتان چیست ؟
My name is...	esmam...é	اسمم ... است .
Bon voyage!	safar bekheir!	سفر بخیر !
yes	balé	بله
yes (answering a negative question)	cherā?	چرا؟
no	nakheir, na (less polite although not rude)	نخیر یا نه
No, you must be joking.	na bābā	نه بابا
God willing	enshāllāh or more correctly enshā'allāh	انشاءالله
please (requesting something, literally 'kindly')	lotfān	لطفاً
please (offering something)	befarmed or more correctly befarmā'īd	بفرمائید
thank you	mersī/tashakkor/motashakkeram	مرسی یا تشکر یا متشکرم
thank you very much	kheilī mamnūnam	خیلی ممنونم
Don't mention it.	ghābel nabūd	قابل نبود
It's nothing	chīzī nīst	چیزی نیست
excuse me/I'm sorry	bebakhshīd	ببخشید

Small Talk

Where do you come from?	shomā ahl-é kojā hastīd?	شمااهل کجا هستید ؟
I'm from...	man ahl-é...hastam	من...هستم .
America	Āmrīkā	آمریکا
Australia	Osterālyā	استرالیا
Canada	Kānādā	کانادا
Iran	Īrān	ایران
New Zealand	Zelānd-é Nō	زلاند نو
the UK (or England)	Engelestān	انگلستان
What's your occupation? (or What are you doing (here)?)	shoma chekār mīkonīd?	شما چکار میکنید؟
I'm a...	...hastam	...هستم
I'm not a...	...nīstam	...نیستم
businessman/businesswoman	ādam-é kāseb	آدم کاسب
diplomat	dīplomāt	دیپلمات
foreigner	khārejī	خارجی
friend of...	dūst-é...	دوست...
guest (of...)	mehmūn (-é...)	مهمان (...)
journalist	khabarnegār	خبرنگار
pilgrim	zovvār	زوار
spy	jāsūs	جاسوس
student	dāneshjū	دانشجو
tourist	jahāngard	جهانگرد
traveller/passenger	mosāfer	مسافر
Are you a Muslim?	shoma mosalmān hasfīd?	شما مسلمان هستید ؟
No, I'm a Christian/Jew/Zoroastrian	nakheir, masīhī/yahūdī/zartoshtī hastam	نخیر ، مسیحی / یهودی/ زرتشتی هستم

Useful Phrases

Do you know...?	*shomā...baladīd?*	شما...بلدید ؟
Persian	*Fārsī*	فارسی
English	*Engelīsī*	انگلیسی
French	*Ferānsé*	فرانسه
German	*Ālmānī*	آلمانی
a little/very little	*kamī/kheilī kam*	کمی/خیل کم
I'm sorry: I don't speak Persian.	*bebakhshīd: Fārsī balad nīstam*	
		ببخشید ، فارسی بلد نیستم .
What is this/that?	*īn/ān chīst?*	این/آن چیست ؟
Do(n't) you have...?	*shomā...(na)dārīd?*	شما...(ذ) دارید ؟
How many...?	*chand...?*	چند...؟
persons	*nafar*	نفر
How many? (of things)	*chand tā?*	چند تا
How much is it? (of money)	*chand é?*	چند است ؟
How much is this/that (one)? (of money)	*īn/ān (yekī) chand é?*	این/آن (یکی) چند است ؟
There is...	*...hast*	...هست
It is...	*...é*	...است
There/it isn't...	*...nīst*	...نیست
too much	*kheilī zeyād*	خیلی زیاد
too little	*kheilī kam*	خیلی کم
very/too...	*kheilī...*	خیلی
important	*mohemm*	مهم
cheap/expensive	*arzūn/gerūn*	ارزان/گران
big/small	*bozorg/kūchek*	بزرگ/کوچک
hot (*or* warm)/cold	*garm/sard*	گرم/ سرد
new	*jadīd* or *nō*	جدید یانو
old (of things)	*ghadīm*	قدیم
beautiful/ugly	*ghashang/zesht*	قشنگ/زشت
good/bad	*khūb/bad*	خوب /بد
far/near (from/to...)	*dūraz/nazdīk (-é...)*	دور (از...)/نزدیگ (...)
easy/difficult	*āsān/moshkel* (or *sakht*)	آسان/مشکل (یاسخت)
dangerous/safe	*khatarnāk/bī khatar*	خطرناک/بی خطر
open/closed	*bāz/taʕīl*	باز/تعطیل
OK	*dorost*	درست
Where?	*kojā?*	کجا ؟
Where is...?	*...kojāst?*	...کجاست ؟
Why?	*cherā?*	چرا؟
When?	*kei?*	کی؟
Who?	*kī?*	کی؟
What?	*chī?*	چه؟
Which...?	*kodām...?*	کدام...؟
and...	*va...* (in compound numerals and certain expressions pronounced *o*)	و...
but...	*valī...*	ولی...
in...	*dar/tū...*	در/تو...

restaurant	*restōrān* or *chelō kabābī* or *sālon-é ghezā*	رستوران یا چلو کبابی یِ سالن غذا
teahouse	*chāykhūné*	چایخانه
food	*ghezā*	غذا
drink	*nūshābé*	نوشابه
hotel	*hotel* or *mehmūnkhūné*	هتل یا مهمانخانه
cheap hotel, lodging-house	*mosāferkhūné*	مسافرخانه
lavatory	*dast shū ī*	دست شوئی

Accommodation

Do you have a...for tonight?	*emshab...dārīd?*	امشب ...دارید؟
room	*otāgh*	اطاق
single room	*otāgh-é ye nafarī*	اطاق یک نفری
double room	*otāgh-é do nafarī*	اطاق دو نفری
triple room	*otāgh-é sé nafarī*	اطاق سه نفری
suite	*sū īt*	سوئیت
better room	*otāgh-é behtar*	اطاق بهتر
cheaper room	*otāgh-é arzūntar*	اطاق ارزانتر
with bathroom	*bā hammūm*	باحمام
without bathroom	*bī hammūm*	بی حمام
for how many nights?	*chand shab?*	چند شب ؟
just for one night	*faghat yek shab*	فقط یک شب
How much is a room for one night?	*otāgh shabī chand é?*	اطاق شبی چند است؟

Getting Around

bus/train station	*termīnāl/īstgāh*	ترمینال/ایستگاه
Where is the...to Tabrīz?	*...betabrīz kojāst?*	...بتبریز کجاست ؟
The...has gone	*...raft*	...رفت
What time does the...leave?	*...chī vaght harakat mīkonad?*	...چه وقت حرکت میکند ؟
train	*ghetār*	قطار
bus	*otōbūs*	اتوبوس
first bus	*otōbūs-é avval*	اتوبوس اول
last bus	*otōbūs-é ākherīn*	اتوبوس آخرین
ship	*kashtī*	کشتی
motor-launch	*lenj*	لنج
boat, skiff, caïque	*ghāyegh*	قایق
taxi (any kind)	*tāksī*	تاکسی
minibus	*mīnībūs*	مینیبوس
savārī	*savārī*	سواری
aeroplane	*havāpeimā*	هواپیما
car (*or* taxi)	*māshīn*	ماشین
motorcycle	*mōtōrsīklet*	موتورسیکلت
airport	*forūdgāh*	فرودگاه
jetty, dock, harbour	*eskelé*	اسکله
ticket office	*daftar-é belīt forūshī*	دفتر بلیط فروشی

I would like to go to...	*mīkhāham bé...beravam*	میخواهم به...بروم .
Are you going to...?	*shomā bé...mīrīd?*	شما به...میروید ؟
It's full.	*jā nīst*	جا نیست
It's urgent.	*fōrī é*	فوری است
How many km is it to...?	*az īnjā be...chand kīlōmeter é?*	از اینجا به...چند کیلومتر است ؟
How many hours is the journey?	*safar chand sā'at é?*	سفر چند ساعت است ؟

I would like a..., please.	*lotfān...mīkhāham*	لطفاً ...میخواهم .
ticket	*belīt*	بلیط
...seat	*sandalī-yé...*	صندلی
good	*khūb*	خوب
1st class	*darajé-yé yek*	درجه ۱
2nd class	*darajé-yé do*	درجه ۲
3rd class	*darajé-yé sé*	درجه ۳
sleeper	*sandalī dar vāgon-é takht-é khāb dār*	صندلی در واگن تخت خواب دار

Around Town

Note that in Iran, at least outside Tehrān, street numbers are not used very much and addresses are often given as opposite, near, behind etc. Never ask 'Is it this way?', especially in rural areas, as the almost inevitable answer will be *mostaghīm* (straight ahead). Never take the directions given too seriously; Iranians do not like to appear unhelpful and would rather give you the temporary satisfaction of thinking you know where you're going.

Excuse me, where is the...?	*bebakhshīd,...kojāst?*	ببخشید ، ...کجاست ؟
house	*khūné* or *manzel*	خانه یا منزل
street, avenue	*kheyābūn*	خیابان
square	*meidūn*	میدان
lane, alley	*kūché*	کوچه
cul-de-sac, blind alley	*bombast*	بن بست
route, road	*rāh*	راه
road to...	*rāh-é...*	راه /...
town centre	*markaz-é shahr*	مرکز شهر
mosque	*masjed*	مسجد
church	*kelīsā*	کلیسا
embassy	*safārat*	سفارت
consulate	*konsūlgarī*	کنسولگری
museum	*mūzé*	موزه
post office	*postkhūné*	پستخانه
telegraph office	*telegrāfkhūné*	تلگرافخانه

here	*īnjā*	اینجا
there	*ānjā*	آنجا
this way	*īn taraf*	این طرف
that way	*ān taraf*	آن طرف
straight ahead	*mostaghīm*	مستقیم
left	*dast-é chap*	دست چپ
right	*dast-é rāst*	دست راست

Times & Dates

Time on the hour is given as *sā'at-é* (the hour of) followed by the number of hours. Time after the hour is given as the hour followed by *o* (and) followed by the number of minutes (or *yek rob'* for a quarter past, or *nīm* for half past). Time before the hour is given as the number of minutes (or *yek rob'* for a quarter to) followed by *bé* (to) followed by the hour. The 24 hour clock is widely used in written Persian.

2 pm	*sā'at-é do ba'd az zohr*	ساعت ۲ بعد از ظهر
2.10	*sā'at-é do o dah daghīghé*	۲/۱۰
8.30	*sā'at-é hasht o nīm*	۸/۳۰
10.45	*yek rob'bé sā'at-é dah*	۱۰/۴۵
11.23 Thursday evening	*panjshambé shab sā'at-é yāzdah o bīst o sé daghīghé*	پنجشنبه شب ساعت ۱۱/۲۳
What's the time?	*sā'at chand é?*	ساعت چند است ؟

today	*emrūz*	امروز
tomorrow	*fardā*	فردا
yesterday	*dīrūz*	دیروز
tonight	*emshab*	امشب
tomorrow night	*fardā shab*	فرداشب
last night	*dīshab*	دیشب
this morning	*emrūz sobh*	امروزصبح
morning, am	*sobh*	صبح
noon	*zohr*	ظهر
afternoon, pm	*ba'd az zohr*	بعد از ظهر
night, evening	*shab*	شب
minute	*daghīghé*	دقیقه
half an hour	*nīm sā'at*	نیم ساعت
quarter of an hour	*rob'sā'at*	ربع ساعت
hour	*sā'at*	ساعت
day	*rūz*	روز
week	*hafté*	هفته
month	*māh*	ماه
year	*sāl*	سال
this year	*emsāl*	امسال
next year	*sāl-é āyandé*	سال آینده
last year	*pārsāl*	پارسال
date	*tārīkh*	تاریخ
in 20 minutes' time	*bīst daghīghé-yé dīgar*	۲۰ دقیقه دیگر

Sunday	*yekshambé*	یکشنبه
Monday	*doshambé*	دوشنبه
Tuesday	*seshambé*	سه شنبه
Wednesday	*chahārshambé*	چهار شنبه
Thursday	*panjshambé*	پنجشنبه
Friday	*jom'é*	جمعه
Saturday	*shambé*	شنبه

Numbers

0	*sefr*	۰
1	*yek*	۱
2	*do*	۲
3	*sé*	۳
4	*chahār*	٤ or ۴
5	*panj*	٥ or ۵
6	*shesh*	٦ or ۶
7	*haft*	۷
8	*hasht*	۸
9	*noh*	۹
10	*dah*	۱۰
11	*yāzdah*	۱۱
12	*davāzdah*	۱۲
13	*sīzdah*	۱۳
14	*chahārdah*	۱٤
15	*pūnzdah*	۱۵
16	*shānzdah*	۱٦
17	*hefdah*	۱۷
18	*hejdah*	۱۸
19	*nūzdah*	۱۹
20	*bīst*	۲۰
21	*bīst o yek*	۲۱
22	*bīst o do*	۲۲
25	*bīst o panj*	۲۵
30	*sī*	۳۰
40	*chehel*	٤۰
50	*panjāh*	۵۰
60	*shast*	٦۰
70	*haftād*	۷۰
80	*hashtād*	۸۰
90	*navad*	۹۰
100	*sad*	۱۰۰
110	*sad o dah*	۱۱۰
169	*sad o shast o noh*	۱٦۹
200	*devīst*	۲۰۰
300	*sīsad*	۳۰۰
400	*chahārsad*	٤۰۰
500	*pūnsad*	۵۰۰
600	*sheshsad*	٦۰۰
700	*haftsad*	۷۰۰
800	*hashtsad*	۸۰۰
900	*nohsad*	۹۰۰
1000	*hezār*	۱۰۰۰
1371	*hezār o sīsad o haftād o yek*	۱۳۷۱
2000	*do hezār*	۲۰۰۰
10,000	*dah hezār*	۱۰,۰۰۰
100,000	*sad hezār*	۱۰۰,۰۰۰
(one) million	*(yek) mīleyūn*	میلیون (یگ)
1000 million	*(yek) mīleyārd*	میلیارد (یگ)

¼	*(yek) rob'*	١ / ٤
½	*nesf (nīm* with hours)	١ / ٢
¾	*sé rob'*	٣ / ٤

Colloquial Expressions

Here is a list of some common colloquial expressions in Persian, with their idiomatic equivalents in English. Because they are normally used only in speech, Persian script has not been used in this section. These phrases will lose their effect if pronounced with an atrocious accent.

It's OK; it's cool.	*bāsh é*
I'm fed up; I've had enough.	*kaf kardam*
Pigs might fly! (literally, the ceiling has cracked)	*saghf tarak khōrd*
None of your business!	*torā sannanā!*
Don't spill the beans.	*sé nakon*
You put me to shame. (ie with your generosity)	*chūb kārī nakon*
What's the damage? How many bucks does it cost?	*chand chūb é?*
Don't talk rubbish.	*chart o part nagū*

Persian Food & Menu Guide

The following menu translator is written with the optimist in mind. Few of these dishes are regular items on the menu, and many of them are far more often seen in cookery books than on the Iranian dinner table. However, if you make a point of asking for a menu at every restaurant you go to, and, if you can't read Persian, ask for all available dishes to be read out to you, you should get to appreciate that Iranian cooking is far more than *chelō kabāb*.

Breakfast

Breakfast is usually *lavāsh* bread with goat's milk cheese, yoghurt, jam or honey, sometimes a fried egg or two, and always washed down with tea. Cornflakes and the like are available, but very expensive and a luxury or an irrelevance for most Iranians. Many hotels serve breakfast, but this is not usually included in the room charge.

bread	*nūn* (in classical Persian, *nān*)	نان
cheese (many varieties, mostly of goats' milk, similar to Greek *feta*	*panīr*	پنیر
egg	*tokhm-é morgh*	تخم مرغ
honey	*angabīn*	انگبین
jam	*morabbā*	مربا
yoghurt	*māst*	ماست
dish of sheep's trotters	*gālé pāché*	گاله پاچه

Soups

soup	*sūp*	سوپ
soup or light stew	*āsh*	آش

lentil soup	sūp-é jō	سوپ جو
onion soup	sūp-é peyāz	سوپ پیاز
yoghurt soup	sūp-é māst	سوپ ماست
thick vermicelli and vegetable soup	āsh-é reshté	آش رشته
eggplant and meat soup	ābgūsht-é bādenjūn	آبگوشت بادنجان

Salads, Side-Dishes & Vegetables

salad	sālād	سالاد
yoghurt	māst	ماست
with chopped spinach	...va esfenāj	... و اسفناج
with diced cucumber	...va kheyār	... و خیار
with chopped mint	...va na'nā'	... و نعناع
pickle	torshī	ترشی
pickled dates	torshī-yé khormā	ترشی خرما
vegetables	sabzī	سبزی
onion	peyāz	پیاز
cucumber	kheyār	خیار
gherkins	kheyār-é torshī	خیار ترشی
olive	zeitūn	زیتون
tomato	gōjé-yé farangī	گوجه فرنگی
lettuce	kāhū	کاهو
spinach	esfenāj	اسفناج
eggplant	bādenjūn (in classical Persian, bādenjān)	بادنجان
green beans	lūbyā	لوبیا
beetroot	choghondar	چغندر
potato	sīb-é zamīnī	سیب زمینی
peas	nokhōd	نخود

Vegetable Dishes

rice cooked together with vegetables	sabzī polō	سبزی پلو
very thick omelette	kūkū	کوکو
vegetable kūkū	kūkū-yé sabzī	کوکوی سبزی
green bean kūkū	kūkū-yé lūbyā	کوکوی لوبیا
potato kūkū	kūkū-yé sīb-é zamīnī	کوکوی سیب زمینی
eggplant kūkū	kūkū-yé bādenjūn	کوکوی بادنجان
stuffed vine-leaf, or almost any stuffable vegetable or fruit	dolmé	دلمه

Fish & Seafood

fish	māhī	ماهی
Iranian whitefish	shīrmāhī	شیرماهی
whitefish, whiting	māhī-yé sefīd	ماهی سفید
sturgeon	sag māhī	سگ ماهی
salmon-trout	māhī-yé āzād	ماهی آزاد
trout	ghezel ālā	قزل آلا
perch	māhī-yé khārdār	ماهی خاردار
carp	māhī-yé gūl	ماهی گل

pike	*ordak māhī*	اردک ماهی
fish and vegetable stew	*ghormé-yé sabzī bā māhī*	قرمه سبزی با ماهی
fish kebab	*māhī kabāb*	ماهی کباب
fish with boiled rice	*chelō māhī*	چلو ماهی
prawns, shrimps	*meigū*	میگو
grilled prawns or shrimps with boiled rice	*chelō meigū*	چلو میگو
crab, lobster or crayfish	*kharachang*	خرچنگ
caviar	*khāveyār*	خاویار

Poultry & Game

(half a) chicken	*(nesf-é) jūjé*	(نصف) جوجه
hen, chicken	*morgh*	مرغ
duck	*ordak*	اردک
goose	*ghāz*	غاز
pigeon	*kabūtar*	کبوتر
pheasant	*gharghāvol*	قرقاول
quail	*belderchīn*	بلدرچین
turkey	*būghalamūn*	بوقلمون
duck, goose, chicken or quail in pomegranate and walnut sauce	*fesenjūn* (in classical Persian, *fesenjān*)	فسنجان
chicken with boiled rice	*chelō morgh*	چلو مرغ
chicken and tangerine stew	*khōresh-é nārangī*	خورش نارنگی
chicken kebabs	*jūjé kabāb*	جوجه کباب

Meat & Meat Dishes

meat	*gūsht*	گوشت
lamb	*gūsht-é barré*	گوشت بره
mutton	*gūsht-é gūsfand*	گوشت گوسفند
veal	*gūsht-é gūsālé*	گوشت گوساله
beef	*gūsht-é gāv*	گوشت گاو
goat meat	*gūsht-é boz*	گوشت بز
buffalo meat	*gūsht-é gāvmīsh*	گوشت گاومیش
camel meat	*gūsht-é shotor*	گوشت شتر
kebab, usually of lamb or mutton, with boiled rice	*chelō kabāb*	چلو کباب
made with inferior ground meat	*(chelō kabāb-é) kūbīdé*	(چلو کباب) کوبیده
made with thin, average quality meat	*(chelō kabāb-é) barg*	(چلو کباب) برگ
'special' *chelō kabāb*, thicker and of good quality meat	*(chelō kabāb-é) makhsūs*	(چلو کباب) مخصوص
lamb fillet kebab	*fīllé kabāb*	فیله کباب
small spicy meat kebabs like Turkish shish kebab, served with bread)	*shīshlīk* (or *shesh kabāb*)	شیشلیگ (یا شش کباب)
meat (or chicken) in thick sauce with vegetables and chopped nuts	*khōresh* (or *khōresht*)	خورش (یا خورشت)
with boiled rice	*chelō khōresh*	چلو خورش
meat and sour cherry stew	*khōresh-é ālūbālū*	خورش آلوبالو

meat and eggplant stew	*khōresh-é bādenjūn*	خورش بادنجان
meat and spinach stew with dried lime	*ghormé-yé sabzī*	قرمه سبزی
stew with thick chunks of potato, fatty meat and lentils	*ābgūsht (or dīzī)*	آبگوشت (یا دیزی)
meat and dried fruit stew	*ābgūsht-é mīvé*	آبگوشت میوه
meatballs	*kofté*	کفته
kofté à la Tabrīz – spicy meatballs stuffed with eggs and dried fruit in tomato sauce	*kofté-yé Tabrīzī*	کفته تبریزی
apple stuffed with rice and minced meat	*dolmé-yé sīb*	دلمه سیب
quince stuffed with rice and minced meat	*dolmé-yé beh*	دلمه به
stew of lamb, spinach, yoghurt and lentils	*būrānī-yé gūsht*	بورانی گوشت
steak	*esteik*	استیگ

Desserts & Sweets

ice-cream	*bastanī*	بستنی
pistachio ice-cream	*bastanī-yé pesté*	بستنی پسته
halva – sweet pastry with rosewater, saffron and chopped nuts	*halvā*	حلوا
vermicelli sorbet with rosewater, ground pistachios and sultanas	*pālūdé (or fālūdé)*	پالوده (یا فالوده)
flaky pastry filled with nuts and soaked in syrup	*bāghlavā*	باقلوا [*
rice-pudding with cinnamon and rosewater	*shīr berenj*	شیر برنج
finely-shredded pastry filled with nuts and soaked in syrup	*konāfé*	کنافه
compote or fruit salad	*khōshāb*	خوشاب
nougat (speciality of Esfahān)	*gaz*	گز
pistachio brittle	*sōhūn (in classical Persian sōhān)*	سوهان
sweets in general	*shīrīnī*	شیرینی

Fruit

fruit	*mīvé*	میوه
apple	*sīb*	سیب
apricot	*zardālū*	زردالو
banana/plantain	*mōz*	موز
cherries	*gīlās*	گیلاس
dates	*khormā*	خرما
figs	*anjīr*	انجیر
grapes	*angūr*	انگور
grapefruit	*gereipfrūt*	گریپفروت
(sour) lemon	*līmū*	لیمو
sweet lemon	*līmū-yé shīrīn*	لیموی شیرین
lime	*līmū-yé Ommānī (or līmū-yé sabz)*	لیموی عمانی (یا لیموی سبز)

melon	*kharbūzé*	خربوزه
orange	*portoghāl*	پرتقال
peach	*holū*	هلو
pear	*golābī*	گلابی
persimmon	*khormālū*	خرمالو
pineapple	*ānānās*	آناناس
plum	*ālū*	آلو
pomegranate	*anār*	انار
prune	*ālū-yé Bokhārā*	آلوی بخارا
quince	*beh*	به
raisins	*keshmesh*	کشمش
strawberries	*tūt-é farangī*	توت فرنگی
tangerine	*nārangī*	نارنگی
watermelon	*hendevāné*	هندوا

Nuts

almond	*bādām*	بادام
hazelnut	*fondogh*	فندق
walnut	*gerdū*	گردو
pistachio	*pesté*	پسته
salted pistachio	*pesté-yé namakīn*	پسته نمکین
unsalted pistachio	*pesté bī namak*	پسته بی نمک

Drinks

drink	*nūshābé*	نوشابه
tea	*chāy*	چای
coffee	*ghahvé*	قهوه
Turkish coffee	*ghahvé-yé Tork*	قهوه ترک
instant coffee (generic term)	*neskāfé*	نسکافه
water	*āb*	آب
boiled drinking water	*ābjūsh*	آبجوش
desalinated water	*āb-é shīrīn*	آب شیرین
fruit juice	*āb-é mīvé*	آب میوه
orange juice	*āb-é portoghāl*	آب پرتقال
cherry juice	*āb-é gīlās*	آب گیلاس
grape juice	*āb-é angūr*	آب انگور
pomegranate juice	*āb-é anār*	آب انار
cola	*kōkā*	کوکا
churned sour milk or yoghurt with salt, mint and other herbs	*dūgh*	دوغ
ice	*yakh*	یخ
lemonade	*līmōnād*	لیموناد
orangeade	*sharbat-é nāranj*	شربت نارنج
non-alcoholic beer ('Islamic beer' or 'Iranian beer')	*mā'-osh-sha'īr*	ماء الشعیر
hot chocolate	*shīr-é kākā'ō-yé garm*	شیر کاکانوی گرم
iced coffee	*kāfé gelāsé*	کافه گلاسه
with...	*bā...*	با ...

without...	*bī...*	بی...
lump sugar	*ghand*	قند
granulated sugar	*shekar*	شکر
bottle	*shīshé*	شیشه
milk	*shīr*	شیر
lemon	*līmū*	لیمو
salt	*namak*	نمگ
alcohol	*alkol*	الکل
beer	*ābjō*	آبجو
wine	*sharāb*	شراب
vodka	*vodkā*	ودکا

Condiments & Accompaniments

salt	*namak*	نمگ
pepper	*felfel*	فلفل
sumac – a reddish seasoning made from ground berries of the sumac tree (generally served only with chelō kabāb)	*somāgh*	سماق
rice	*berenj*	برنج
...of the day (as in 'soup of the day')	*...é/-yé rūz*	... روز
rice cooked together with...	*...polō*	... پلو
boiled rice with...	*chelō...*	چلو
garlic	*sīr*	سیر
sauce	*sōs*	سوس
omelette	*omlet*	املت
bread	*nūn* (in classical Persian *nān*)	نان
butter	*karé*	کره
sandwich (*or* snack-bar)	*sāndvīch*	ساندویچ
sausage	*sōsīs*	سوسیس
cream	*sarshīr*	سرشیر
cake	*keik*	کیک
vegetarian food	*ghezā-yé geyāh khār*	غذای گیاه خوار
lemon juice	*āblīmū*	آبلیمو

Miscellaneous

knife	*kārd*	کارد
fork	*changāl*	چنگال
spoon	*ghāshogh*	قاشق
paper tissue	*kelīnīks*	کلینیکس
breakfast	*sobhāné*	صبحانه
lunch	*nāhār*	ناهار
dinner	*shām*	شام
Do you have...?	*shomā...dārīd?*	شما...دارید
What's on the menu today?	*emrūz ghezā chī é?*	امروز غذا چیست ؟
I'd like the..., please	*lotfān...mīkhāham*	لطفاً...میخواهم
menu	*sūrat-é ghezā*	صورت غذا
bill	*sūrat-é hesāb*	صورت حساب
This is for you, waiter.	*āghā, īn māl-é shomāst*	آقا، این مال شماست

| Thank you, it was delicious. | *mersī, khōsh mazé būd* | مرسی ، خوش مزه بود |
| This isn't good. | *īn khūb nīst* | این خوب نیست |

Index

TEXT

Keep in touch!

We love hearing from you and think you'd like to hear from us.

The Lonely Planet Newsletter covers the when, where, how and what of travel. (AND it's free!)

When...is the right time to see reindeer in Finland?
Where...can you hear the best palm-wine music in Ghana?
How...do you get from Asunción to Areguá by steam train?
What...should you leave behind to avoid hassles with customs in Iran?

To join our mailing list just contact us at any of our offices. (details below)

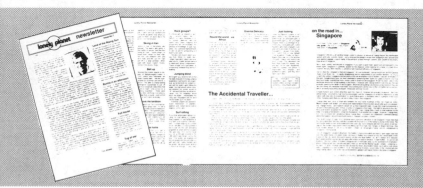

Every issue includes:

- *a letter from Lonely Planet founders Tony and Maureen Wheeler*
- *travel diary from a Lonely Planet author - find out what it's really like out on the road*
- *feature article on an important and topical travel issue*
- *a selection of recent letters from our readers*
- *the latest travel news from all over the world*
- *details on Lonely Planet's new and forthcoming releases*

Also available Lonely Planet T-shirts. 100% heavy weight cotton (S, M, L, XL)

LONELY PLANET PUBLICATIONS
Australia: PO Box 617, Hawthorn, 3122, Victoria (tel: 03-819 1877)
USA: Embarcadero West, 155 Filbert Street, Suite 251, Oakland, CA 94607 (tel: 510-893 8555)
UK: Devonshire House, 12 Barley Mow Passage, Chiswick, London W4 4PH (tel: 081-742 3161)

Guides to the Middle East

Egypt & the Sudan - a travel survival kit
This guide takes you into and beyond the spectacular pyramids, temples, tombs, monasteries and mosques, and the bustling main streets of these fascinating countries to discover their incredible beauty, unusual sights and friendly people.

Jordan & Syria - a travel survival kit
Two countries away from the usual travel routes, but with a wealth of natural and historical attractions for the adventurous traveller...12th century Crusader castles, ruined cities, the ancient Nabatean capital of Petra and haunting desert landscapes.

Turkey - a travel survival kit
This acclaimed guide takes you from Istanbul bazaars to Mediterranean beaches, from historic battlegrounds to the stamping grounds of St Paul, Alexander the Great, the Emperor Constantine, King Croesus and Omar Khayyam.

Trekking in Turkey
Explore beyond Turkey's coastline and you will be surprised to discover that Turkey has mountains with walks to rival those found in Nepal.

Yemen - a travel survival kit
The Yemen is one of the oldest inhabited regions in the world. This practical guide gives full details on a genuinely different travel experience.

West Asia on a shoestring
Want to cruise to Asia for 15 cents? Drink a great cup of tea while you view Mt Everest? Find the Garden of Eden? This guide has the complete story on the Asian overland trail from Bangladesh to Turkey, including Bhutan, India, Iran, the Maldives, Nepal, Pakistan, Sri Lanka and the Middle East.

Also available:
Arabic (Egyptian) phrasebook, **Arabic (Moroccan)** phrasebook and **Turkish** phrasebook.

Lonely Planet Guidebooks

Lonely Planet guidebooks cover every accessible part of Asia as well as Australia, the Pacific, South America, Africa, the Middle East, Europe and parts of North America. There are five series: *travel survival kits*, covering a country for a range of budgets; *shoestring guides* with compact information for low-budget travel in a major region; *walking guides*; *city guides* and *phrasebooks*.

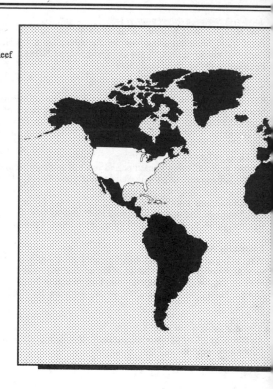

Mail Order

Lonely Planet guidebooks are distributed worldwide. They are also available by mail order from Lonely Planet, so if you have difficulty finding a title please write to us. US and Canadian residents should write to Embarcadero West, 155 Filbert St, Suite 251, Oakland CA 94607, USA; European residents should write to Devonshire House, 12 Barley Mow Passage, Chiswick, London W4 4PH; and residents of other countries to PO Box 617, Hawthorn, Victoria 3122, Australia.

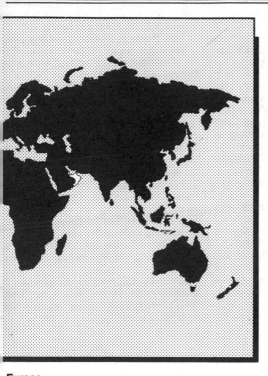

Indian Subcontinent
Bangladesh
India
Hindi/Urdu phrasebook
Trekking in the Indian Himalaya
Karakoram Highway
Kashmir, Ladakh & Zanskar
Nepal
Trekking in the Nepal Himalaya
Nepal phrasebook
Pakistan
Sri Lanka
Sri Lanka phrasebook

Africa
Africa on a shoestring
Central Africa
East Africa
Kenya
Swahili phrasebook
Morocco, Algeria & Tunisia
Moroccan Arabic phrasebook
South Africa, Lesotho & Swaziland
Zimbabwe, Botswana & Namibia
West Africa

Mexico
Baja California
Mexico

Central America
Central America on a shoestring
Costa Rica
La Ruta Maya

North America
Alaska
Canada
Hawaii

Europe
Eastern Europe on a shoestring
Eastern Europe phrasebook
Finland
Iceland, Greenland & the Faroe Islands
Mediterranean Europe on a shoestring
Mediterranean Europe phrasebook
Poland
Scandinavian & Baltic Europe on a shoestring
Scandinavian Europe phrasebook
Trekking in Spain
USSR
Russian phrasebook
Western Europe on a shoestring
Western Europe phrasebook

South America
Argentina, Uruguay & Paraguay
Bolivia
Brazil
Brazilian phrasebook
Chile & Easter Island
Colombia
Ecuador & the Galápagos Islands
Latin American Spanish phrasebook
Peru
Quechua phrasebook
South America on a shoestring
Trekking in the Patagonian Andes

The Lonely Planet Story

Lonely Planet published its first book in 1973 in response to the numerous 'How did you do it?' questions Maureen and Tony Wheeler were asked after driving, bussing, hitching, sailing and railing their way from England to Australia.

Written at a kitchen table and hand collated, trimmed and stapled, *Across Asia on the Cheap* became an instant local bestseller, inspiring thoughts of another book.

Eighteen months in South-East Asia resulted in their second guide, *South-East Asia on a shoestring*, which they put together in a backstreet Chinese hotel in Singapore in 1975. The 'yellow bible' as it quickly became known to backpackers around the world, soon became *the* guide to the region. It has sold well over half a million copies and is now in its 7th edition, still retaining its familiar yellow cover.

Today there are over 100 Lonely Planet titles – books that have that same adventurous approach to travel as those early guides; books that 'assume you know how to get your luggage off the carousel' as one reviewer put it.

Although Lonely Planet initially specialised in guides to Asia, they now cover most regions of the world, including the Pacific, South America, Africa, the Middle East and Europe. The list of *walking guides* and *phrasebooks* (for 'unusual' languages such as Quechua, Swahili, Nepalese and Egyptian Arabic) is also growing rapidly.

The emphasis continues to be on travel for independent travellers. Tony and Maureen still travel for several months of each year and play an active part in the writing, updating and quality control of Lonely Planet's guides.

They have been joined by over 50 authors, 48 staff – mainly editors, cartographers, & designers – at our office in Melbourne, Australia and another 10 at our US office in Oakland, California. In 1991 Lonely Planet opened a London office to handle sales for Britain, Europe and Africa. Travellers themselves also make a valuable contribution to the guides through the feedback we receive in thousands of letters each year.

The people at Lonely Planet strongly believe that travellers can make a positive contribution to the countries they visit, both through their appreciation of the countries' culture, wildlife and natural features, and through the money they spend. In addition, the company makes a direct contribution to the countries and regions it covers. Since 1986 a percentage of the income from each book has been donated to ventures such as famine relief in Africa; aid projects in India; agricultural projects in Central America; Greenpeace's efforts to halt French nuclear testing in the Pacific and Amnesty International. In 1991 $68,000 was donated to these causes.

Lonely Planet's basic travel philosophy is summed up in Tony Wheeler's comment, 'Don't worry about whether your trip will work out. Just go!'